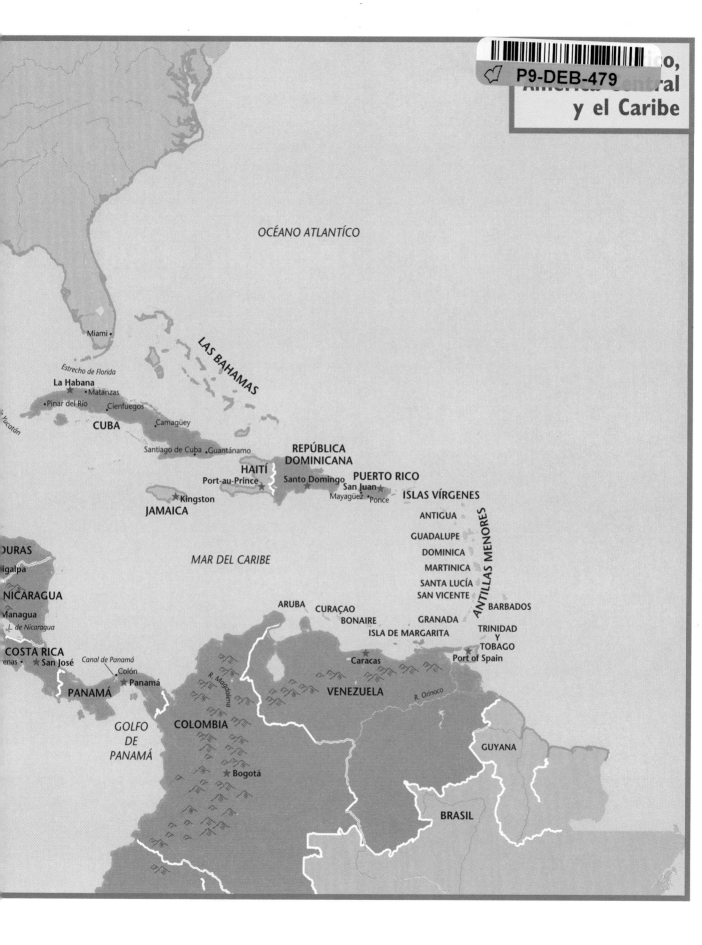

OCÉANO ATLANTÍCO

México,
América Central
y el Caribe

Miami •

Estrecho de Florida

LAS BAHAMAS

La Habana ★
• Matanzas
• Pinar del Río   • Cienfuegos
Yucatán   • Camagüey

CUBA

Santiago de Cuba • Guantánamo

REPÚBLICA
DOMINICANA

HAITÍ

Port-au-Prince   Santo Domingo   PUERTO RICO
                                     San Juan ★
★ Kingston   Mayagüez• •Ponce   ISLAS VÍRGENES

JAMAICA

ANTIGUA

GUADALUPE

DURAS   DOMINICA

igalpa   MARTINICA

MAR DEL CARIBE   SANTA LUCÍA

NICARAGUA   SAN VICENTE

Managua   BARBADOS
L. de Nicaragua   ARUBA   GRANADA
                     CURAÇAO   ISLA DE MARGARITA   TRINIDAD
COSTA RICA   BONAIRE   Y
enas • ★ San José   TOBAGO
Canal de Panamá   Caracas ★   Port of Spain
• Colón
• Panamá

PANAMÁ   R. Magdalena   VENEZUELA
                                              R. Orinoco

GOLFO
DE   COLOMBIA
PANAMÁ

                                              GUYANA

              ★ Bogotá

                                    BRASIL

ANTILLAS MENORES

SECOND EDITION

¡Tú dirás!

Introducción a la lengua y cultura hispánicas

John R. Gutiérrez-Candelaria
Penn State University

Harry L. Rosser
Boston College

Ana Martínez-Lage
Middlebury College

BOSTON–ALBANY–BONN–CINCINNATI–DETROIT–MADRID–MELBOURNE–MEXICO CITY
NEW YORK–PARIS–SAN FRANCISCO–SINGAPORE–TOKYO–TORONTO–WASHINGTON

HH Heinle & Heinle Publishers
Boston, Massachusetts 02116 U.S.A.

ITP® A division of International Thomson Publishing, Inc.
The ITP logo is a trademark under license.

INSTRUCTOR'S ANNOTATED EDITION

CONTENTS
INSTRUCTOR'S ANNOTATED EDITION

Preface

The authors of ¡Tú dirás! Second Edition are thankful for the enthusiastic and widespread support given to the first edition of this textbook, and to the many talented instructors who helped shape this new edition. ¡Tú dirás! Second Edition was designed to be more teacher- and student-friendly, with a new **task-directed** approach that ties every lesson directly to real-world of Spanish immediately that challenges students to do something with the language they are learning they've just learned.

As in the first edition, ¡Tú dirás! Second Edition has been designed to promote consistent interaction among students and their instructors, starting with the preliminary lesson and continuing throughout the entire program. Through this interaction ¡Tú dirás! Second Edition encourages students to:

▶ express themselves in a culturally acceptable and authentic way from the onset of their language study

▶ comprehend and produce oral and written Spanish in a gradually increasing number of real-life contexts

▶ acquire additional knowledge and information in areas of interest to them as they progress in their study of the language

▶ gain a better understanding of the cultures of the Spanish-speaking world that surrounds them

The fundamental premise of the program ¡Tú dirás! is that language becomes most immediately useful when it is based on a function or tied to a task that is carried out in a real-life context. These functions, common to all languages, include (but are not limited to)

▶ asking and answering questions on familiar topics

▶ narrating and describing in various time frames

▶ supporting an opinion

▶ hypothesizing

These functions have helped us establish a set of objectives and procedures for reaching or moving toward their fulfillment in ways that can be realistically expected of students who have little or no previous study of Spanish.

TASK-DIRECTED APPROACH

Definition of Tasks

Each chapter, and each etapa within a chapter, is driven by a series of tasks, or what Roger Shuy defines as "the things that get done with language." Some examples of these tasks are

◆ finding common likes and dislikes with peers

◆ making plans for the near future

Preface *(continued)*

◆ asking questions to gain important information and report on it

◆ giving short descriptions and directions

◆ telling about past or future events, etc.

Categorization of tasks

the organizational format of the ¡Tú dirás! program is as follows:

◆ the tasks in the first third of the textbook focus on asking and answering questions on familiar topics

◆ the tasks in the second third focus on narration and description

◆ the tasks in the last third focus move toward supporting opinion to various degrees, presenting structures that allow for doing this in different ways.

Open-ended, task-based activities, called ¡Tú dirás! and Intercambio in this textbook, are always linked to an array of tools, in the form of vocabulary and grammar, that allow the student to carry out the task. Furthermore, all tasks are preceded by a carefully sequenced set of activities, found in the Práctica sections of each etapa, that build upon each other, gradually increasing in difficulty.

The matter of control by the language-learner of the grammatical structures required to carry out designated tasks is tied to the perception that Accuracy is really a process that develops gradually (and on an individual basis) in the areas of vocabulary, grammar, pronunciation, fluency, sociolinguistic skills and culture. We recognize that accuracy advances along a continuum that begins with conceptual awareness, moves toward partial control, and eventually to a fuller control of these elements. Since language acquisition takes place in stages over time, ¡Tú dirás! is designed to expose students to the variety of factors in a short period of time that will allow them to move forward with confidence along the language-learning continuum for success in their language study.

Special consideration is also given to the way in which discourse is organized at the level of the word, phrase, sentence, and paragraph. Students are expected to comprehend and produce discourse that progresses along a range of levels, beginning with utterances of one to two words and moving toward phrases and sentences and, eventually strings of sentences and paragraphs.

WHAT'S NEW IN THE SECOND EDITION?

The major features of ¡Tú dirás! (2nd edition) are the following:

◆ **Multi-level classroom teaching tips and techniques recognizing the varying abilities of students enrolled in first-year Spanish courses.** Recognizing the trend towards mixed-level classrooms, ¡Tú dirás! Second Edition includes multi-level teaching tips to the instructor that provide suggestions for how to adapt material found in the textbook to the different needs of students. These multi-level teaching tips, identified by the balance icon, provide specific suggestions on how to motivate and challenge high-beginners while giving true-beginners the supportive and nurturing environment they need to perform successfully in the classroom. ¡Tú dirás! Instructor's Resource Manual provides additional mixed-level classroom teaching techniques.

◆ **Cuaderno para hispanohablantes.** The **Cuaderno para hispanohablantes** gives you added flexibility when heritage speakers of Spanish enroll in your introductory course. This group of students, who may have little or no formal training in the language but have some speaking ability, requires a specialized teaching tool, which is why the **Cuaderno para hispanohablantes** is available to users of ¡Tú dirás! Second edition.

◆ **A task-directed approach built into each etapa.** Each etapa builds towards an open-ended, task-based activitiy. To ensure that students are well-prepared to handle these tasks, exercises are clearly contextualized, and carefully sequenced in order to move consistently from mechanical, through meaningful, to open-ended activities.

◆ **Newly designed and improved task-based activities.** Each etapa ends with two open-ended, task-based activities that bring together the grammar and vocabulary that the students have been working with in the specific etapa. Each task is designed to be completed in either pairs or groups to facilitate in-class communication between students.

◆ **Extensive instructor annotations.** New annotations will provide tips on how to work with exercises and activities, preview upcoming material, and manage time. New Icons identify pair and group activities and provide cross references to other ancillaries including the **Instructor's Resource Manual.** The extensive annotations make this a user-friendly textbook for a variety of instructors.

◆ **A comprehensive multimedia package.** ¡Tú dirás! is enhanced by a wide array of text-related technology products that promote and enrich the learning experience of today's student. The ¡Tú dirás! multimedia CD-ROM packaged with every student textbook provides three unique options for additional skill development:

    a) **¡Tú dirás! Multimedia CD-ROM,** with full-motion video and related activities that correlate directly to the chapter themes, vocabulary and grammar of the textbook. All writing activities in the ¡Tú dirás! Activities Manual are correlated to the newest release of **Atajo: Writing Assistant for Spanish.**

    b) **¡Tú dirás! task-based Internet activities (http://tudiras.heinle.com)** that bring the Spanish-speaking world to your students while recycling the functions and tasks presented in the textbook

    c) **Misterio en Toluca,** an e-mail whodunit in which students must solve a mystery through extensive communication via e-mail and face to face interaction both in and out of the classroom.

P r e f a c e (continued) ....

◆ **New text-tied video.** Each chapter in the text is supported by a five to ten minute video segment featuring recurring characters. The language in each video segment is authentic and directly tied to the tasks presented in the textbook. Pre- and post-reading activities for the video are found in the **Integración** section at the end of each chapter of the student textbook.

◆ **Country-specific chapter focus.** Beautifully designed chapter openers highlight specific areas of the Spanish-speaking world, detailing geographic and demographic information about those regions and providing a cultural context for the functions provided within the chapter. Additional cultural commentaries about the highlighted Spanish-speaking region are presented within the **Comentarios culturales** of the chapter.

◆ **Cultural integration.** Through the new text-specific video program, a variety of readings including literary samples, and three brief texts per chapter called **Comentarios culturales,** students gain access to cultural knowledge of the Spanish-speaking world, including values, attitudes, behavior, and aesthetic expression. Each of the **Comentarios culturales** is accompanied by a variety of exercises to promote comprehension and critical-thinking skills.

◆ **Improved information-gap activities.** These activities have been streamlined and renamed as Intercambio activities found in the Integración section at the end of each chapter. These activites require students to exchange information and negotiate meaning as they carry out a specific task, promoting cooperative work and encouraging students to modify their output through the use of comprehension checks and requests for clarification, thereby creating optimal conditions for increased language acquisition.

◆ **Systematic recycling.** The **Repaso** exercises provide systematic recycling of the structures, vocabulary, and tasks presented in the previous two etapas. Throughout ¡Tú dirás!, vocabulary and grammar is recycled in activities and exercises along with newly presented material.

◆ **Integración.** This new section, formerly called the *Cuarta etapa*, appears at the end of each chapter and differs significantly from the etapas that precede it. The **Integración** section includes (a) an authentic reading along with reading strategies and exercises to develop reading skills; (b) pre- and post-viewing activities for the new text-tied video; (c) **Intercambio,** a culminating information-gap activity that links the tools with the tasks that have been presented and practiced throughout the entire chapter

Key to the ¡Tú dirás! Icon Program

TEACHER'S EDITION ONLY

 Transparency program correlation.

 Instructor's Resource Manual correlation.

 Accompanies teacher annotations that provide strategies for dealing with a mixed-level classroom

 Pair or group activity possibilities.

 Appears with teacher annotations that provide classroom time management tips.

Previews upcoming material.

STUDENT EDITION ONLY

 Textbook audio CD correlation

 Correlation to ¡Tú dirás! multimedia package.

 Correlation to ¡Tú dirás! task-based Internet activities.

 Correlation to new text-specific video.

An illustrated guide to

¡Tú dirás!

How can an introductory Spanish program help your students become more successful language learners?

We asked language educators this question, and this is what they told us…

> **"** Our students come to us with a wide range of abilities and backgrounds. A textbook should give **suggestions for dealing with these mixed-level classrooms.** **"**

> **"** We have lots of **native speakers,** and we don't have the resources to create a separate Spanish for Heritage Speakers course. How do I teach to both in one class? **"**

> **"** My students love **the Internet.** I want to take advantage of that enthusiasm. **"**

> **"** We run a lot of sections with less experienced TA's and instructors, so we need an excellent **Instructor's Annotated Edition** with teaching tips and strategies. A **separate instructor's manual** with even more detailed instructor support would be ideal. **"**

> **"** Too many textbooks today try to hide the grammar. Why? … Students get confused when they don't know the rules. You don't have to hit them over the head with it, but a **solid grammar foundation** is absolutely necessary for students to be more successful language learners. **"**

> **"** I want to give my student more **open-ended opportunities**. Information-gap activities, role-plays, surveys, and other pair and group work well for me. **"**

How does ¡Tú dirás! prepare students to learn Spanish?

¡Tú dirás! presents grammar and vocabulary, functionally, in context, with constant recycling.

PRIMERA ETAPA

PARA EMPEZAR: ¿De quién es?

Using the *Preparación* suggestions, brainstorm with students the vocabulary related to different possessions.

Preparación: As you begin this *etapa*, answer the following questions:

* Where do you live?
* What do you have in your dorm room, apartment, house, etc.?
* How do you get around town?

Transparency C-1: La casa, el transporte

Suggestion: Using the transparency of houses and possessions, begin each vocabulary group by talking about yourself. Yo vivo en una casa, ¿y tú? ¿Quién vive en un apartamento? En nuestra casa, hay un estéreo, pero no hay un televisor. ¿Y ...

¿Dónde vives?

Vivo en...

una casa   una residencia estudiantil   un apartamento

PARA EMPEZAR activities at the beginning of each etapa allow you to present and practice the language in a meaningful context, while giving your students a chance to warm up before more difficult tasks are attempted.

Carefully sequenced **PRÁCTICA** activities help prepare your students for the more challenging tasks at the end of the unit.

VOCABULARY EXPANSION: **Una billetera** is also used for wallet. **Un bolígrafo** is a ballpoint pen. **Una pluma** is a fountain pen.

Transparency C-2: En los cuartos

To aid vocabulary acquisition, encourage students to make Spanish name tags for the items in their room so that every time they see an item they will see its Spanish name.

In presenting the vocabulary, use intonation to highlight the verb tener when used since this verb will be presented in the *Enfoque estructural*.

Transparency D-2: ¿Qué llevas a la universidad?

Práctica

A. ¿Qué es? Identify the objects in the numbered photos.

■ **Modelo:** *Es un lápiz.*

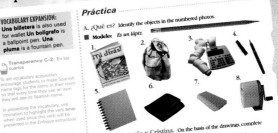

1.   2.   3.   4.

5.   6.   7.   8.

B. María, Antonio y Cristina. On the basis of the drawings, complete

How does ¡Tú dirás! present vocabulary?

5. comer o tomar un refresco

ENFOQUE LÉXICO   Expresiones con tener

The verb tener is used in many Spanish idiomatic expressions, or phrases. To ask someone's age in Spanish, use tener.

¿Cuántos años tienes?	How old are you?
Tengo veinte años.	I am twenty years old.
¿Cuántos años tiene tu hermana?	How old is your sister?
Tiene dieciocho.	She's eighteen.

Some other expressions that also use tener are tener hambre (to be hungry), tener sed (to be thirsty), tener sueño (to be sleepy), tener frío (to be cold), and tener calor (to be hot).

GRAMMAR NOTE: Mucha is used with sed because sed is feminine.

Tengo hambre. ¿Y tú?	I'm hungry. And you?
No, no tengo hambre, pero sí tengo mucha sed.	I'm not hungry, but I am very thirsty.

noventa y siete   **97**

Primera etapa

ENFOQUE LÉXICO boxes present new vocabulary and phrases in a functional context, facilitating faster acquisition.

VOCABULARY EXPANSION student annotations, on soft blue screens, encourage students to personalize vocabulary.

VOCABULARY EXPANSION: **Verdad** literally means *true* but in this context it means *isn't that so?*

How does ¡Tú dirás! present grammar?

◎ Easy-to-find **ENFOQUE ESTRUCTURAL** boxes, feature concise charts and clear explanations with sample sentences.

◎ Convenient **GRAMMAR ANNOTATIONS** remind your students, at appropriate times, of previously learned structures.

ENFOQUE ESTRUCTURAL   Gustar + cosas

El verbo gustar

In Chapter 1 you learned to use the verb **gustar** with other verbs to ta about the activities you like and don't like to do. **Gustar** can also be us to talk about things that you like and dislike.

Me gusta el disco compacto.	I like the CD.
Te gusta la cinta.	You like the tape.
Me gustan las cintas.	I like the tapes.
Te gustan los discos compactos.	You like the CDs.
A María le gusta el arte.	Maria likes art.
A Juan le gusta la música.	John likes music.
Nos gusta le ciencia.	We like science.
A ellos les gusta el cine.	They like the movies.

How does ¡Tú dirás! present culture?

◎ New to this edition, chapters 1 to 10 focus on different regions of the Spanish-speaking world. The chapter openers use graphs, charts and other visual devices to display background data specific to the featured geographic area. You can use these chapter openers for warm-up activities, conversation starters, or just to expand your students' knowledge base.

Chapters 11 to 14 focus on global cultural themes: the history of food and food customs; traditional and non-traditional forms of transportation; art and music; and literature.

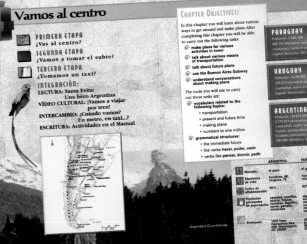

◎ Within every etapa, **COMENTARIOS CULTURALES** cover topics thematically related to the chapter's goals and objectives.

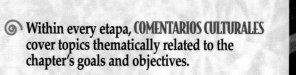

Comentarios culturales
Los taxis en la Ciudad de México

*L*a Ciudad de México es famosa por sus numerosos taxis, o libres como dicen los mexicanos. Hay taxis de varios colores y de varias marcas. Algunos, como los anaranjados, tienen el número de su **sitio** *(taxi stand)* pintado en la puerta y reciben llamadas telefónicas. Otros, como los amarillos y los verdes, van por las calles en busca de pasajeros. Los taxis son de varias marcas pero el tipo de automóvil que más se ve para los taxis es el pequeño y rápido Volkswagen.

Los taxistas a veces no usan **taxímetros** *(meters)* por el cambio en los precios que causa el problema de la inflación. Generalmente el pasajero tiene que preguntarle el precio y, a veces, llegar a un acuerdo con el chofer antes de tomar el taxi. La costumbre es siempre dar una buena propina después de llegar al destino. Por lo general, este tipo de **transporte** *(transportation)* es bastante económico para el pasajero que quiere conocer la ciudad en taxi.

How does ¡Tú dirás! teach listening?

Your students need input and lots of opportunities for meaningful practice. Input is provided through the textbook audio program, the laboratory audio program that accompanies the ACTIVITIES MANUAL, and through the text-specific video.

⟳ **PARA EMPEZAR** dialogues and readings are included on the textbook audio program to present new vocabulary AURALLY as well as VISUALLY. An audio icon in the margin of the Instructor's Annotated Edition notifies you when the textbook audio program can be used.

⟳ Within every etapa, **VAMOS A ESCUCHAR** sections help build students' listening skills through recorded dialogues and pre- and post-listening activities.

⟳ Within the **INTEGRACIÓN** section at the end of every chapter, pre-viewing and post-viewing exercises are provided to make it easier for you to use the new ¡Tú dirás! **VIDEO.**

> **"¡Tu dirás! provides language as it is needed to communicate or perform certain functions. (Other products) don't provide such rich input."**
>
> *Mariana Achugar,*
> *University of California*
> *at Davis*

VAMOS A ESCUCHAR: ¿QUIERES IR CONMIGO?

🎧 Play Textbook audio.

Laura and Juan run into each other on a street in Buenos Aires. One of them has to do an errand and invites the other to come along.

ANTES DE ESCUCHAR

Given what you've been working on in this *etapa*, what are some of the things they might say to each other?

Before listening to their short dialog, read the questions under the *Después de escuchar* section below.

DESPUÉS DE ESCUCHAR

J. Comprensión. As your instructor plays the tape, listen for the answers to the following questions.

1. Where does Laura have to go?

Answers, Ex. J
1. downtown 2. a new CD 3. an errand for Laura's dad 4. on foot 5.

ANTES DE LEER

A. Antes de leer el poema, mira el mapa que aparece al final del libro y localiza los países que se mencionan arriba.

B. ¿Qué significa el título del poema?

C. Lee el poema rápidamente y busca dos nombres. ¿A quién crees que se refieren?

GUÍA PARA LA LECTURA

D. Vocabulario. Identifica en el poema de Guillén las siguientes palabras. Después lee las definiciones de la columna de la derecha. Decide qué definición corresponde a cada palabra.

1.	Línea 1	sombra
2.	Línea 4	tambor
3.	Línea 7	armadura
4.	Línea 9	selva
5.	Línea 13	caimán
6.	Línea 14	coco
7.	Línea 28	mono

a. animal con cola larga que vive en los árboles
b. el comienzo del día
c. bosque de gran extensión
d. fruto de un tipo de palma
e. cuerda que se usa para golpear o castigar

How does ¡Tú dirás! teach reading?

Recent research indicates that students benefit from both literary and non-literary selections, authentic and author-generated.

⟳ Through **ANTES DE LEER** and **GUÍA PARA LA LECTURA** activities, students develop skills and strategies they need to read a variety of texts, including literary excerpts, poems, brochures, menus, travel guides and author generated readings.

INTEGRACIÓN

LECTURA: *Como agua para chocolate*—las cebollas y el nacimiento de Tita

Laura Esquivel (México, 1950-) es la autora de uno de los libros más vendidos, no sólo en su país sino en todo el mundo. Esta extraordinaria novela tiene el título completo de *Como agua para chocolate. Novela de entregas mensuales con recetas, amores y remedios caseros.* Es una obra sabrosa, romántica y dinámica, tanto por sus coloridas descripciones como por sus gráficas escenas de la tumultuosa vida de una familia mexicana a principios del siglo XX. La acción se desarrolla en Piedras Negras, lugar situado en la frontera con Texas.

La autora no sólo les enseña a sus lectores cómo se prepara la comida, sino que les abre el apetito para que sigan leyendo y leyendo sobre las aventuras tragicómicas de una serie de personajes inolvidables. La obra ha sido traducida a varias lenguas. La versión cinematográfica de la novela ha tenido... nal y con gran...

How does ¡Tú dirás! help students put it all together?

◉ Newly revised ¡Tú dirás! activities, two per etapa (6 total activities per chapter), present real world tasks that require students to use what they've learned in order to complete the task successfully.

¿Cuándo que el... sirve que... he has gotten everything he needs!

Tú dirás

O. ¿Cuánto cuesta todo esto? Unos amigos y tú están planeando una cena para cinco personas. No tienen mucho dinero, sólo 30 dólares, para las bebidas, el postre y el plato principal. Miren los precios de la lista siguiente y decidan cuánto pueden comprar de cada cosa sin gastar más de 30.00 dólares. Al terminar, compartan con la clase el menú que van a comprar y cuánto. Después de decidir, escriban que van a comprar y cuánto. Al terminar, compartan con la clase el menú para la cena.

■ **Modelo:**
—¿Qué vamos a servir?
—Bueno, para el plato principal, ¿por qué no preparamos pollo con papas fritas y vegetales?
—A ver El pollo cuesta...

Productos lácteos		Otros productos	
yogur	3 / $2	pan	$1
leche	1 litro / $1	galletas	$2
mantequilla	$1	arroz	$2
crema	2 / $1	pastas	$2
queso	$2	lechuga	$2
		tomates	$1
Conservas			1 kilo / $2
sopa	2 / $1	**Productos congelados**	
atún	2 / $2.50	pescado	1 kilo / $5
salsa de tomate	2 / $1.50	pizza	$5
aceitunas	2 / $1.50	papas fritas (fried)	$5
		pollo	$2
Bebidas		vegetales	$5
café	1 kilo / $5	helado	$2
refrescos	2 litros / $2	agua mineral	1 litro / $2
		limonada	2 litros / $3

doscientos veintidós

222

Capítulo 6

---

indicate what will be happening on each day shown and use future expressions to indicate what is going to happen. Today is May 10.

■ **Modelo:** *Esta noche, voy al cine en el centro. Mañana, quiero comer un restaurante con mis amigos. Mañana por la noche, quiero ir a bailar.*

D. Invitaciones. Invite a friend to go somewhere or to do something with you. When your friend accepts, suggest a way of getting there. Use the appropriate forms of **querer** and such expressions as **de acuerdo, claro que sí,** and **por supuesto** *(of course).*

El domingo por la mañana voy a la iglesia con mis padres. Por la tarde quiero jugar al tenis con mi amiga. El lunes por la tarde tengo que estudiar en la biblioteca. El martes por la mañana voy a clase. El miércoles deseo jugar al tenis por la mañana y cenar con mi familia por la noche. El jueves una amiga y yo vamos a la universidad. El viernes voy al estadio para ver un partido de fútbol.

- 10 de mayo viernes
- 11 de mayo sábado
- 12 de mayo domingo
- 13 de mayo lunes
- 14 de mayo martes
- 15 de mayo miércoles
- 16 de mayo jueves
- 17 de mayo viernes

ciento cuarenta y uno

141

Tercera etapa

◉ **REPASO** activities, two in the second etapa and two in the third etapa, ensure that your students are reviewing previously learned material in every class, not just the day before the quiz or test. Repaso activities keep material fresh in students' minds, improving their performance on tests and quizzes.

◉ The new **INTEGRACIÓN** section at the end of each chapter brings all chapter material integrated through applied four-skills practice.

◉INTEGRACIÓN

LECTURA: *Santa Evita: Una héroe argentina*

ANTES DE LEER

A. Look at the photo that accompanies this reading and answer the following questions:
1. Who is the reading about?
2. What do you know about this person?
3. What country do you associate her with?

GUÍA PARA LA LECTURA

B. Scan the first paragraph and answer the following questions:
1. When was she born?
2. Why did she go to Buenos Aires?

C. Scan the second paragraph and answer the following questions:
1. When did she meet Juan Perón?
2. What role did she play in his presidency?
3. Who did she stick up for during her husband's presidency?

D. Scan the third paragraph and answer the following questions:
1. What important right did women get as a result of Evita's efforts?
2. In what year did they get this right?
3. How old was she when she died?

E. ¿Qué opinas?
1. What do you think obras de teatro in paragraph 1 means?
2. What do you think ignorados hasta entonces in paragraph 2 means?
3. What do you think obras de caridad in paragraph 3 means?

SANTA EVITA: UNA HÉROE ARGENTINA

María Eva Duarte de Perón, popularmente conocida en todo el mundo como Evita, nació el 7 de mayo de 1919. A los 14 años se mudó a Buenos Aires para seguir su carrera como actriz. Vivió una vida miserable, siempre estaba enferma y no tenía mucho que comer. Después de un año de interpretar papeles secundarios en obras de teatro, su fortuna cambió...

How does ¡Tú dirás! meet the needs of students with different backgrounds?

⊚ MULTI-LEVEL CLASSROOMS

No introductory Spanish class is truly homogeneous. In fact, multi-level classrooms have become the norm more often than the exception. Recognizing this trend, the authors of ¡Tú dirás! have written multi-level classroom teacher annotations, printed in the margins of the Instructor's Annotated Edition and identified by the balance icon.

These unique annotations suggest varied ways in which activities can be tailored to meet the needs of all introductory Spanish students.

In addition, the **INSTRUCTOR'S RESOURCE MANUAL** discusses how to teach to multi-level classrooms.

⊚ HERITAGE SPEAKERS OF SPANISH

The **CUADERNO PARA HISPANOHABLANTES** addresses the needs of heritage speakers of Spanish. When heritage speakers enroll in an introductory Spanish course, for these students you may elect to order copies of the Cuaderno para hispanohablantes instead of the Activities Manual. Your heritage speakers of Spanish will gain extra confidence in skill areas where they may need the extra practice, such as spelling, writing, reading, and pronunciation.

The Cuaderno para hispanohablantes is thematically and functionally tied to the Student Textbook, and will help motivate students through hands-on projects, thought-provoking readings, and specific lessons tailored to their unique needs.

For you, the instructor, a section on WORKING WITH NATIVE SPEAKERS OF SPANISH is included in the INSTRUCTOR'S RESOURCE MANUAL.

How does the entire ¡Tú dirás! program fit together as a whole?

You may order the Student Textbook packaged with the textbook audio tape and ¡Tú dirás! CD-ROM, or packaged with the textbook audio compact disc and ¡Tú dirás! CD-ROM.

The ACTIVITIES MANUAL, with accompanying laboratory audio program is now easier to use, with an augmented grammar and vocabulary section, and more activities that require specific answers.

The INSTRUCTOR'S RESOURCE MANUAL, new to this edition, will help facilitate a smooth transition to ¡Tú dirás! SECOND EDITION. The INSTRUCTOR'S RESOURCE MANUAL combines the essentials of a methods course with specific teaching strategies, detailed lesson planning, grammar supplements, suggested syllabi, and assorted teacher ancillaries.

A COMPUTERIZED TEST BANK offers you two new exams per chapter, tests all four language skills plus culture, vocabulary and grammar, and offers specific guidance for evaluating oral proficiency.

The ¡Tú dirás! MULTIMEDIA SUPPORT PACKAGE delivers unmatched levels of sophistication, breadth and innovation in an introductory Spanish program. The new ¡Tú dirás! CD-ROM makes use of the latest digital technologies to deliver quality video, four-skills practice, a link to the ¡Tú dirás! TASK-BASED INTERNET ACTIVITIES on the WWW (featuring a new CyberJournal section), and access to the MISTÉRIO EN TOLUCA e-mail mystery game. Visit http://tudiras.heinle.com for more information.

The CUADERNO PARA HISPANOHABLANTES is an alternate workbook that students of Hispanic descent may choose to use.

What does this Instructor's Annotated Edition feature?

In addition to the orientation material provided in this guided tour, and the information available in the preface, this IAE has several features to help any instructor. Completely new instructor's annotations were written for this edition. The new annotations suggest tips for teaching to the multi-level classroom, variations on textbook activities, follow-up questions, time-management tips, how to implement ancillaries such as the Instructor's Resource Manual, transparency bank, and audio program, when to use group or pair work, ways to introduce cultural background, tips for presenting new material, and when to preview upcoming material.

An icon program has also been developed to help you locate specific information quickly. The following key is provided to help you recognize these icons when you see them in the margins. The blue icons are found only in the IAE, while black and white or full color icons are also found in the Student Textbook.

Multi-level classroom teacher annos help you balance the needs of your true beginners with false beginners enrolled in the same classroom.

Suggests when to use pair or group work to implement a specific activity.

Refers to the HEINLE & HEINLE TRANSPARENCY BANK, which includes over 100 color transparencies, identified by alpha-numeric code.

Directs the instructor to additional resources available in the ¡Tú dirás! INSTRUCTOR'S RESOURCE MANUAL, including reproducible activity or transparency masters.

Identifies structures that are presented for recognition only, or words and phrases that are being presented as lexical items rather than grammatical constructions. Also directs the instructor to where the grammar point is covered in depth.

Found in the PARA EMPEZAR and VAMOS A ESCUCHAR sections, this icon identifies where the textbook audio program should be used.

Found only in the INTEGRACIÓN section of the chapter, this icon directs the student or instructor to use the ¡Tú dirás! Vídeo cultural in conjunction with the activities found in the textbook.

Directs the student to the ¡Tú dirás! INTERNET HOME PAGE for task-based WWW activities, an on-line electronic study guide, and a CyberJournal activity.

Program Components

In addition to the student textbook, ¡Tú dirás!, provides a full array of ancillaries at your disposal. Contact your Heinle & Heinle/ITP representative for more information on the following program components, many of which are free to adopting institutions.

The **Activities Manual,** by Ana Martínez-Lage (Middlebury College) and Laura Arman (George Mason University) continues to offer out-of-class reading, writing, pronunciation, listening, grammar and vocabulary practice, the new edition continues to offer the rich variety of materials present in the first edition, and now has more activities with discrete answers so that assessment of student progress can be more readily recorded.

An **Answer Key to Activities Manual** is available free to adopting institutions, and may be bundled with the Activities Manual at the instructor's request.

The **Instructors's Annotated Edition,** with new annotations written by Jill Pellettieri (University of California at Davis), provides a wealth of ideas for activity expansion or variation, teaching tips for mixed-level classrooms, time-management tips, and correlations to teacher supplements.

The **Instructor's Resource Manual,** written by Charles Grove (Arizona State University), combines the essentials of teaching methods course (ideal for programs with large numbers of teaching assistants or less-experienced instructors), with sample syllabi, lesson plans for each chapter, tips for integrating multimedia and video components into the language curriculum, as well as, reproducible grammar sheets, and laboratory tapescripts

The new **Computerized Test Bank with Tape** by Edwin Lamboy (Penn State University) provides two new tests per chapter that reflect the revisions to the textbook. The testing program is truly compatible with the teaching goals of the textbook, and provides opportunity for testing all four skills, including tips on how to effectively test students' oral communication skills. The **Computerized Test Bank** also gives the instructor the flexibility to customize each test or quiz according to their own preferences.

Packaged with every text is the **Textbook Audio CD** or **Textbook Audio Cassettes** which contains the listening passages that are correlated to the *Para empezar* and *Vamos a escuchar* sections of the textbook.

Also packaged with every textbook is the **¡Tú dirás! CD-ROM** with full motion video and four-skills practice, the **Misterio en Toluca** email mystery game (writing, reading and communication skills), links to the ¡Tú dirás! home-page **http://tudiras.heinle.com,** with task-based www activities and process writing-activities Guide.

The new **¡Tú dirás! text specific video,** for purchase only, is supported by previewing and post-viewing activities found in the *Integración* section of the student textbook.

Teacher's Annotations include correlations to the **Heinle & Heinle Transparency Bank,** with over 100 full color transparencies.

The **Cuaderno para hispanohablantes,** which parallels the **Activities Manual,** but was written specifically for the heritage speaker of Spanish enrolled in the introductory Spanish course.

Photo-op gives you access to over 100 thematically organized photos from the Heinle & Heinle photo database. Use these photos to create texts, quizzes, handouts, or transparencies, or however you want to use them.

SECOND EDITION

¡Tú dirás!

Introducción a la lengua y cultura hispánicas

John R. Gutiérrez-Candelaria
Penn State University

Harry L. Rosser
Boston College

Ana Martínez-Lage
Middlebury College

BOSTON–ALBANY–BONN–CINCINNATI–DETROIT–MADRID–MELBOURNE–MEXICO CITY
NEW YORK–PARIS–SAN FRANCISCO–SINGAPORE–TOKYO–TORONTO–WASHINGTON

HH

Heinle & Heinle Publishers
Boston, Massachusetts 02116 U.S.A.

ITP® A division of International Thomson Publishing, Inc.
The ITP logo is a trademark under license.

The publication of *¡Tú dirás! Second Edition* was directed
by the members of the Heinle & Heinle College Foreign
Language Publishing Team:

Wendy Nelson, Editorial Director
Tracie Edwards, Market Development Director
Esther Marshall, Production Services Coordinator
Stephen Frail, Developmental Editor

Also participating in the publication of this program were:
Publisher: Vincent Duggan
Project Manager: Angela Castro
Photo/Video Specialist: Jonathan Stark
Associate Market Development Director: Rosie Romagnoli
Production Assistant: Lisa LaFortune
Manufacturing Coordinator: Wendy Kilborn
Photo Coordinator: Judy Mason
Illustrator, Second Edition:
Interior Designer: Monotype Composition
Cover: Monotype Composition
      M. Alicia Ziff, Art Director
      Ken Croghan, Photoshop Artist
Compositor: Monotype Composition

Library of Congress Cataloging-in Publication

Gutierrez, John R.
    ¡Tú dirás/John R. Gutíerrez, Harry L. Rosser, [y] Ana Martínez-Lage.
2nd ed.
      p.   cm.
    Spanish and English.
    Includes index.
    ISBN 0-8384-6133-6 (student edition). —ISBN 0-8384-6142-5
(instuctor's annotated edition)
    1. Spanish language–Conversation and phrase books–English.
2. Spanish language—Textbooks for foreign speakers–English.
I. Rosser. Harry L. II. Martínez-Lage, Ana. III. Title.
PC4121.G84 1998
468.3 421–dc21

Manufactured in the United States of America.

Student edition ISBN: 0-8384-6133-6
Instructor's Annotated Edition ISBN: 0-8384-6142-5
10 9 8 7 6 5 4 3 2 1

To the Student

Dear Student

We are living in an age when we can no longer afford to be ignorant of the languages and cultures of other peoples with whom we share this very small planet. Learning a new language is the first step toward increasing your awareness of our ever-shrinking world. This process will alter the way in which you view the world, for it will allow you to experience different ways of living, thinking, and seeing. In fact, there is an old Spanish proverb that underscores the importance of knowing another language. It states: *El que sabe dos lenguas vale por dos*— the person that speaks two languages is worth two people.

You are about to begin an exciting and valuable experience. Today the Spanish language is spoken all over the world by close to 400 million people. The North American Free Trade Agreement (NAFTA) has opened new markets for the United States in Mexico, and accords to be signed with Chile, Argentina and other Latin American countries will enhance business opportunities there as well. A recent issue of the Chronicle of Higher Education cited a study conducted among American businesses in which over 60% of those interviewed stated that after English, Spanish was the most important language of the business world.

Many of you will one day have the opportunity to visit a Spanish-speaking country. Your experiences will be all the richer if you can use your Spanish to enter into the cultures of those countries and interact with their people. However, even if you don't get to spend time in one of those countries, Spanish has become an important language in this country and is spoken every day by millions of people right here within our borders.

Once you begin to use the Spanish language in class, you will discover that you can interact with Spanish speakers or your classmates right away. Communication in a foreign language means receiving and sending messages (either oral or written) in ways that avoid misunderstandings. Therefore, the most important task ahead of you is NOT to accumulate a large quantity of knowledge ABOUT the grammatical rules that underlie the language, but USE the grammar and vocabulary you are taught to create messages as effectively and creatively as possible. As you learn to do this, you will make the kinds of errors that are necessary in language learning. DON'T BE AFRAID TO MAKE MISTAKES!! The errors you make are really positive steps toward effective communication. They don't hold you back; they actually advance your efforts. Learning a language is hard work, but the rewards that await you can also make it an enriching experience. *¡Tú dirás! or as you say in English, it's up to you!!*

Good Luck!

John

Harry

Ana

Acknowledgments

An extra word of thanks go to: Sheri Spaine Long and her faculty at University of Alabama at Birmingham for the detailed feedback they gathered while using the first edition; Mariana Achugar for her reading of the ¡Tú dirás! activities and suggestions for making them truly task-based; Judy Collier for her detailed reading of the second edition manuscript.

Finally, a very special work of acknowledgment goes to: Mia (age 14) and Steven (age 11) who are always on my mind and who I'm very proud of for the progress they are making in their study of Spanish.

John R. Gutiérrez

My parents, Edwin and Catherine, who raised me in Mexico.

Harry L. Rosser

Amalia and Manolo, my parents, for their support and encouragement.

Ana Martínez-Lage

Creating and revising a college-level language program is a long, complicated and difficult process. We express our gratitude to our Editorial Director, Wendy Nelson, whose foresight and encouragement inspired us to complete our work a year ahead of schedule; our Developmental Editor, Stephen Frail, who guided the project from its inception through its realization with skill necessary to coordinate the efforts of authors at three different venues; our Market Development Director, Tracie Edwards, whose creative marketing skills and keen suggestions have guided us throughout the revision process. We would also like to thank other dedicated people who played a key role in the production of the program, especially Esther Marshall, our Production Services Coordinator, who worked tirelessly with her production team to publish such a beautiful book on schedule.

Our thanks also go to others at Heinle and Heinle whose support helped make this project possible: Charles Heinle, Vince Duggan, Erek Smith. We also wish to express our appreciation to Edwin Lamboy for creating the Tests available with ¡Tú dirás! Second Edition, to Charles Grove for his creative work on the new Instructor's Resource Manual, to Laura Arman for the careful revisions she made to the Activities Manual, and to Jill Pellitieri for her terrific work on the Instructor's Annotated Edition.

The authors and the publisher thank the many instructor's at colleges and universities across the country who adopted the first edition of this textbook, especially those who contributed comments and suggestions on how to make the second edition even better.

Mariana Achugar, *University of California at Davis*

Judy Collier, *Goucher College*

Richard Curry, *Texas A&M*

Marisol Fernandez, *University of Michigan*

Juan Franco, *Tarrant County Junior College*

Frozina Gousack, *Colin County Community College*

Ana Hnat, *Houston Community College*

Evan Palomeque, *Texas A&M*

Jeffrey Reeder, *Baylor University*

Joy Renjilian-Burgy, *Wellesley College*

Victoria Rodrigo, *Lousiana State University*

Rafael Salaberry, *Penn State University*

Jonita Stepp, *Florida State University*

Carlos Villacis, *Houston Community College*

Nancy Whitman, *Porterville College*

How Does ¡Tú dirás! Work?

The primary focus of the main Textbook is to provide students with a variety of opportunities to develop the four skills and cultural knowledge in integrated, communicative ways in the classroom. The Textbook is divided into fourteen chapters, preceded by a Capítulo preliminar. ¡Tú dirás! contains a total of forty-two etapas (three per chapter), each of which presents new material, reviews the previous etapa, and utilizes carefully sequenced exercise progression that gives students the tools they need to communicate correctly and meaningfully, while carrying out useful, real-life tasks. Grammatical structures and vocabulary are presented according to their relevance to the completion of a task or communicative goal.

The final two chapters include more reading selections chosen explicitly for the substantial information they provide about the art, music, and literature of the cultures of the Spanish-speaking world.

Table of Contents

ix

SECOND EDITION

¡Tú dirás!

HH Heinle & Heinle Publishers
Boston, Massachusetts 02116 U.S.A.

ITP® A division of International Thomson Publishing, Inc.
The ITP logo is a trademark under license.

Capítulo preliminar

POINTER 1:
Sounds and letters

POINTER 2:
Cognates

POINTER 3:
Diacritical marks & punctuation

Saludos informales y despedidas

Saludos formales y presentaciones

Pronunciación

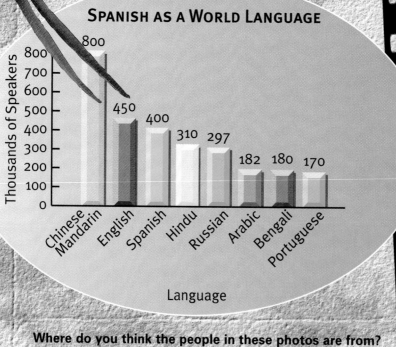

SPANISH AS A WORLD LANGUAGE

Thousands of Speakers

| 800 | | | | | | | |
| Chinese Mandarin | English 450 | Spanish 400 | Hindu 310 | Russian 297 | Arabic 182 | Bengali 180 | Portuguese 170 |

Language

Where do you think the people in these photos are from?

CHAPTER OBJECTIVES:

In this preliminary chapter, you will learn some interesting information about Spanish as a world language. You will also be given some pointers on the sound system of Spanish and the diacritical marks common to the language. In addition, you will learn what people say when they greet and/or take leave of each other.

After completing this chapter, you will be able to carry out the following tasks:

- ⊚ **meet and greet people**
- ⊚ **spell words using the Spanish alphabet**
- ⊚ **understand how the written accent and other diacritical marks work**

The tools you will use to carry out these tasks are:

- ⊚ **greetings**
- ⊚ **leave-takings**
- ⊚ **the Spanish alphabet**
- ⊚ **written accents and other diacritical marks**

San Juan, El Morro

Andes Range, Chile

Alcazar Castle, Segovia, built in the 13th century

SPANISH AS A WORLD LANGUAGE

As the Spanish language developed from Latin, it became known as *castellano* (Castillian) because of its association with the kingdom of Castilla, a part of Spain. The term is still used in Spain and parts of Latin America to refer to the Spanish language.

Students may be asked to read over pp. 0–0 outside of class.

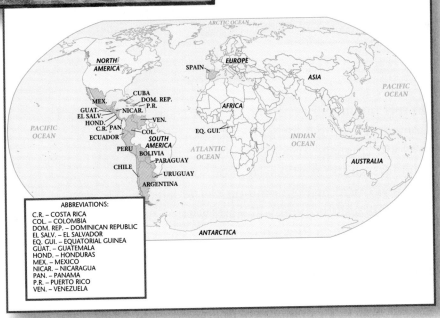

ABBREVIATIONS:
C.R. – COSTA RICA
COL. – COLOMBIA
DOM. REP. – DOMINICAN REPUBLIC
EL SALV. – EL SALVADOR
EQ. GUI. – EQUATORIAL GUINEA
GUAT. – GUATEMALA
HOND. – HONDURAS
MEX. – MEXICO
NICAR. – NICARAGUA
PAN. – PANAMA
P.R. – PUERTO RICO
VEN. – VENEZUELA

More than 400 million people speak Spanish as a native language in the world today. It is the official language of a number of countries and is one of the official languages of the United Nations. In terms of total number of speakers, after Chinese Mandarin, and English, it is the third most widely spoken language in the world.

As you can see in the map above, the primary areas where Spanish is spoken are Spain, South America, Central America, and the Carribean. Spanish is also an important language in the United States. There are now over 27 million Spanish speakers in this country. Spanish is spoken in parts of the Philippines, and it is also the official language of the tiny country of Equatorial Guinea in Western Africa.

Spanish evolved from Latin or what was known as *romanice* (the language of the Romans), and along with such languages as French, Portuguese, Galician, Catalan, Italian, and Rumanian, is part of the family of Romance languages.
As Rome was expanding the borders of its empire, it conquered the Iberian Peninsula (the peninsula in Western Europe where Portugal and Spain are located today) about 2001 B.C. With them they brought the Latin language. Over the course of several centuries, the Latin that was taken to that part of the world evolved into Portuguese, Galician, Catalan, and, of course, Spanish.

Because all languages undergo constant change, Spanish, too, has continued to evolve. The Spanish that is spoken in Spain is different from what is spoken in Argentina, Mexico, Bolivia, Puerto Rico, or other parts of the Spanish-speaking world. This is not unique to Spanish since differences exist in all languages, including English. You know that someone from Boston does not sound like someone from Georgia and that someone from California or Texas does not speak like someone from Nebraska or Indiana. Nevertheless, speakers of English from different areas are able to understand each other, just as people from different Spanish-speaking countries are able to understand each other. Through the audio and video components that accompany this textbook, you will be exposed to a wide variety of Spanish speakers. The Spanish you will be learning to speak in this text will allow you to be understood anywhere you go in the Spanish-speaking world.

Before you begin your study of Spanish, we would like to give you a few pointers about this language.

Pointer 1: Sounds and letters

There is generally a one-to-one correspondence between the spoken sounds and written letters of Spanish.

Pronounce the English words:

night   thorough   knave   knowledge   doubt

In each case, certain letters are not pronounced.

This situation occurs only occasionally in Spanish. For example, the letter "h" is never pronounced:
hambre   helado   hilo   hotel   humo

The letter "u" is never pronounced after "q":
que   queso   querer

The letter "u" is never pronounced after "g" before an "i" or an "e":
guitarra   Miguel   guerra

Except for these three examples, all Spanish letters are pronounced:
salsa   tomate   limonada   desayuno   mermelada

Suggestion: Have students repeat each word after you. You may want to review the pronunciation of each vowel.

Pointer 2: Cognates

There are many similarities between a number of words in the Spanish and English vocabularies.

Try to guess the English meaning of the following words:

imaginar   importante   marcar   católico   delicioso

dentista   farmacia   optimista   natural   profesión

You were undoubtedly able to guess the meanings of all of these words. These words are called cognates. Thanks to the large number of cognates shared by Spanish and English, you begin your study of Spanish with many known words.

Suggestion: Point out that the written accent indicates on which syllable the speaker puts the stress. **Preview:** Written accents and word stress are discussed in more detail on p. 9–10.

Pointer 3: Diacritical marks and punctuation

A Spanish word is not spelled correctly unless its diacritical marks are in place, nor is a sentence correct without proper punctuation.

The most frequently used diacritical marks are:

1. **el acento ortográfico** *(written accent)*	Used above the letter to signal that stress is placed on that letter or syllable
2. **la tilde** *(tilde)*	Used to distinguish between letters **n** and **ñ**
3. **la diéresis** *(dieresis)*	Used to distinguish between pronunciation of **gui** and **güi** and **gue** and **güe**
4. **¿ ? (puntos interrogativos)**	You will note in Spanish that every question must have an upside-down question mark at the beginning.
5. **¡ ! (puntos exclamativos)**	You will note in Spanish that every exclamation must have an upside-down exclamation mark at the beginning.

Note the spelling difference between these Spanish words.

hablo / habló	*I speak / he spoke*
de / dé	*of / give*
cana / caña	*gray hair / cane*
giro / güiro	*a turn / musical instrument*

Except for the letter **ñ** the letters of the Spanish alphabet are the same as those used in the English alphabet. Spanish uses diacritical marks, which have three basic purposes:

1. to distinguish between words that are spelled the same but have a different meaning when pronounced with the stress on a different syllable

    Example:

peso / pesó	*kind of money / it, he, she weighed*

2. to distinguish between words that are pronounced exactly the same but have different meanings

    Example:

se / sé	*reflexive pronoun / I know*
el / él	*the, he*
tu / tú	*you, yours*

3. to identify the pronunciation of **ue, ui** after the letter **g.** And to identify the letter **ñ** different from **n**

    Example:

    cigüeña *(stork)* is pronounced /gwe/

Now that you have these basic pointers in mind, it's time to begin learning some Spanish. *¡Tú dirás!*

PARA EMPEZAR: ¡Hola! ¿Qué tal?

—**Buenos días,** Raúl.
—**Buenos días,** Antonio.
  ¿Cómo estás?
—**Muy bien, gracias. ¿Y tú?**
—**Más o menos.**

🎧 Play Textbook audio.

¡Hola! ¿Qué tal?: Hello! How are you?

Good morning

How are you?
Very well, thank you. And you?
So-so.

Suggestions: A. Use the recordings on the tape to present these dialogs. As a short pre-listening exercise, ask students how they greet and introduce one another, then have them listen to each mini-dialog. Have students act out each mini-dialog by repeating or reading it. B. Then have them greet each other using the alternate expressions. Make sure students practice several introductions and leave-takings.

—¡Hola, Anita! ¿Qué tal?
—Muy bien, Laura. ¿Y tú?
—**Bien,** gracias. Anita, **te presento a** Juan. Juan, Anita.
—¡Hola!
—**Mucho gusto.**

Well/let me introduce you to

Nice to meet you.

—¡Hola! ¿Cómo te llamas?
—Me llamo Gabriel. ¿Y tú?
—Mi nombre es Patricia. Mucho gusto, Gabriel.
—Igualmente, Patricia

The expression **Me llamo...** is the most commonly used equivalent in Spanish of *My name is . . .* in English, but it actually reflects a different point of view because it communicates the idea of "I call myself . . ." Also used in Spanish is **Mi nombre es...**, which more literally fits with *My name is . . .* in English.

Preview: Reflexive verbs are presented formally in Chapter 10.

Me llamo Ana.

Mi nombre es Jorge.

Mi nombre es Claudia.

Me llamo Alberto.

Comentarios

culturales Saludos

*I*n Hispanic culture, the body language that accompanies greetings and good-byes is different from American customs. In both situations, it is customary for men to shake hands formally or, if they already know each other, even embrace and pat each other on the back. Among women, the custom is to shake hands and, if they know each other, kiss each other on both cheeks in Spain and on only one cheek in Latin America. When a man and woman who know each other meet, they generally kiss on one or both cheeks depending on where they are.

In addition, when Spanish speakers of any age greet each other or engage in conversation, they generally stand closer to each other than do speakers of English. This "closer" use of space is a normal, nonverbal behavior that Spanish speakers associate with greetings and leave-takings.

INTEGRACIÓN CULTURAL

1. What are some of the ways that Spanish speakers normally use to say hello? to say good-bye?
2. What do you do normally when you greet or say good-bye to people?
3. What main differences do you notice, if any, in the way greetings and leave-takings are conducted in Spanish compared to what is normal in other cultures? How do you react to these other ways and what effect do they have on you?

Saludos informales y despedidas

Saludos informales	Respuestas
Buenos días.	Buenos días.
Buenas tardes.	Buenas tardes.
Buenas noches.	Buenas noches.

¡Hola!	¡Hola!
Mucho gusto.	Igualmente.
¿Qué tal?	Bien gracias. ¿Y tú?
¿Cómo estás?	Muy bien, gracias. ¿Y tú?
¿Cómo te va?	Más o menos. ¿Y tú?
¿Cómo te llamas?	Me llamo... (o Mi nombre es...)
¿Qué hay?	Regular.

Despedidas

Adiós.	Adiós.
Hasta luego.	Chao.
Nos vemos.	Hasta luego.

Presentaciones

Te presento a...	Mucho gusto.

Informal greetings / Responses

Good afternoon.
Good evening.

Suggestion: Point out that some of these answers are interchangeable.

How's it going?

Saying good-bye

Presentations

Práctica

A. Saludos. Answer these greetings appropriately.

1. ¡Hola!
2. Buenos días.
3. ¿Cómo estás?
4. ¿Qué tal?
5. Buenas tardes.
6. ¿Cómo te va?
7. Buenas noches.
8. Hasta luego.

B. ¡Hola! ¿Qué tal? You are with a new student and you meet a friend in the hallway. You and your friend greet each other, and you introduce the new student. Divide into groups of three to act out the situation.

▪ **Modelo:**

Tú:	*¡Hola! ¿Qué tal?*
Amigo(a):	*Bien, gracias. ¿Y tú?*
Tú:	*Bien, gracias. Te presento a Marilú.*
Amigo(a):	*¡Hola!*
Marilú:	*Mucho gusto.*

C. ¿Cómo te llamas? Take a few minutes to walk around the classroom, greeting other people in the room and asking and telling each other your names. Follow the model.

▪ **Modelo:**
—*¡Hola! ¿Cómo te llamas?*
—*¿Qué tal? Me llamo... o Mi nombre es...*
—*¡Hola! Mi nombre es Martín. ¿Cómo te llamas?*
—*Carlos.*

Ex. A: Pairs
Encourage students to vary answers.

Suggestion: Do this exercise as a chain. The first student asks the student on his or her right a question; then the student who answers asks the person on his or her right, and so on. Have them include students' names: ¡Hola, Sara!

Ex. B: Group of 3
Encourage students to vary answers. For example:
¡Hola! ¿Cómo estás?
Más o menos. ¿Y tú?
Muy bien, gracias...
¡Buenos días!

Suggestion: Point out the use of the personal **a**. Explain that it is necessary after the verb **presentar** when a person is introduced.

Encourage students to vary answers.

Comentarios

culturales Saludos formales e informales

When greeting people and making introductions, there are expressions that denote different degrees of formality or informality. **¡Hola!, ¿Qué tal?, ¿Cómo estás?, ¿Cómo te va?, Te presento a...** are used informally with people you know well and with peers. **¿Cómo está usted?, ¿Cómo están ustedes?, Quisiera presentarle(les) a...** are more formal and are used with older people or people you do not know very well. It is not uncommon for older people or superiors to speak informally to a younger person who addresses them as **usted.**

INTEGRACIÓN CULTURAL

1. How do you normally greet people of your own age? people who are older than you? What are some of the expressions you use?
2. What does the use of **usted** vs. **tú** usually indicate in Spanish?
3. Do you notice any differences regarding formality among Spanish speakers and those of your own culture? What are they?

ENFOQUE LÉXICO | **Saludos formales y presentaciones**

Saludos formales	Respuestas
Buenos días.	Buenos días.
¿Cómo están ustedes?	Estamos bien, gracias.
¿Cómo está usted?	(Estoy) Bien, gracias. ¿Y Ud.?
¿Cómo se llama usted?	Me llamo... ¿Y Ud.?

Presentaciones	
Quisiera presentarle(les) a...	Encantado(a).

Práctica

D. ¿Qué respondes? *(What do you answer?)* Complete the dialog with an appropriate expression, and don't forget to address the person in parentheses by name.

■ **Modelo:** Buenos días, Alberto. (señor Pérez)
Buenos días, señor Pérez.

1. ¿Cómo estás, Adela? (señor Carrillo)
2. ¡Hola, Lourdes! (señor Ramírez)
3. Quisiera presentarle a mi amigo Pepe. (señora Ruiz)
4. ¿Cómo están ustedes, señores? (Margarita)
5. Mucho gusto, Raquel. (señorita Castillo)

E. Buenos días, señor (señora, señorita). Greet and shake hands with your instructor, introduce a classmate to him or her, and then say good-bye.

Pronunciación: El alfabeto

A good place to start your study of Spanish pronunciation is with the alphabet. Listed below are the letters of the Spanish alphabet along with their names. Repeat the letters after they have been modeled.

a	a	**j**	jota	**r**	ere
b	be	**k**	ka	**s**	ese
c	ce	**l**	ele	**t**	te
d	de	**m**	eme	**u**	u
e	e	**n**	ene	**v**	ve or uve
f	efe	**ñ**	eñe	**w**	doble ve, doble uve, doble u
g	ge	**o**	o	**x**	equis
h	hache	**p**	pe	**y**	i griega
i	i	**q**	cu	**z**	zeta

Práctica

F. Repeat the following words and then spell them using the Spanish alphabet.

1. pan
2. refresco
3. mantequilla
4. leche
5. aceitunas
6. bocadillo
7. naranja
8. limón
9. mermelada
10. calamares
11. sándwich
12. desayuno
13. jamón
14. pastel
15. tortilla

Now spell your first and last names.

Written accents

One way that Spanish spelling differs from English is that a written accent is sometimes used in addition to the letters of the alphabet. You can determine where the stress falls in a Spanish word by noticing if it has a written accent or not.

As a general rule, Spanish words are stressed on the next-to-last (penultimate) syllable, unless certain circumstances occur.

Encourage students to vary answers.

For advanced beginners: Encourage students to go beyond the initial greetings. If students feel comfortable, encourage them to have short conversations with classmates.

 Play Textbook audio.

Since b and v are usually pronounced similarly, people often say b de burro, v de vaca, to distinguish the different letters when spelling.

Suggestion: Emphasize the pronunciation of the vowels and the letters g and j. Remind students that the h is silent.

Suggestion: Explain that in Spain, uve and uve doble are used. In Mexico, doble u is used. In other Spanish-speaking countries, doble ve and doble u are used.

Suggestion: You might point out that when a letter is written with an accent on it but is being spelled out loud the phrase acento en la *(letter of alphabet)* may be used to be specific about where the accent goes.

Variation: To incorporate alphabet practice, ask students to write down the first and last names of 4 people they speak to. These people will spell their names in Spanish.

Suggestion: Read aloud each group of words and then have individual students repeat them. Be certain that students hear and understand where the stress belongs and that their pronunciation reflects their understanding.

1. If a word ends in a consonant, with the exception of the consonants "n" or "s," then it is stressed on the last syllable.

   verdad *(true)*   **feliz** *(happy)*   **azul** *(blue)*   **caminar** *(to walk)*

2. If a word ends in a vowel, or the consonants "n" or "s," then it is stressed on the penultimate syllable.

   cama *(bed)*   **libro** *(book)*   **cuaderno** *(notebook)*   **baile** *(dance)*
   lunes *(Monday)*

3. The only time words do not follow this pattern is when they have a written accent mark, in which case the syllable with the accent mark receives the stress.

   salió *(he/she left)*   **comí** *(I ate)*   **volveré** *(I will return)*
   avión *(airplane)*   **París** *(Paris)*   **fácil** *(easy)*
   cárcel *(jail)*   **mártir** *(martyr)*   **inútil** *(useless)*

By following these three simple guidelines, you will know how to pronounce all Spanish words.

The *Vocabulario* consists of all new words and expressions presented in the chapter. When reviewing or studying for a test, you can cover up the English and go through the list to see if you know the meaning of each item.

Para charlar   *Chatting*

Para saludar   *Greeting*
Buenos días.   *Good morning.*
Buenas tardes.   *Good afternoon.*
Buenas noches.   *Good evening.*
¿Cómo estás?   *How are you?*
¿Cómo te va?   *How's it going?*
¿Qué hay?   *What's new?*
¿Qué pasa?   *How are you? (informal)*
¿Qué tal?   *How are you?*
¡Hola!   *Hello!*
¿Cómo está Ud.?   *How are you? (formal)*
¿Cómo están Uds.?   *How are you? (formal plural)*

Para presentar   *Introducing*
Quisiera presentarle(les) a...   *I would like to introduce you to . . . (formal)*
Te presento a...   *This is . . . (introduction / informal)*

Para despedirse   *Saying good-bye*
Adiós.   *Good-bye.*
Chao.   *Good-bye.*
Hasta luego.   *See you later.*
Nos vemos.   *See you.*

Para contestar   *Answering*
Buenos días.   *Good morning.*
Buenas tardes.   *Good afternoon.*
Buenas noches.   *Good evening.*
Bien, gracias. ¿Y tú?   *Fine, thanks. And you? (informal)*
Encantado(a).   *Delighted.*
Igualmente.   *Likewise.*
Más o menos.   *So-so.*
Mucho gusto.   *Nice to meet you.*
Muy bien, gracias.   *Very well, thank you.*
Pues...   *Well . . .*
¡Hola!   *Hello!*
(Estoy) Bien, gracias. ¿Y Ud.?   *(I'm) Fine, thanks. And you? (formal)*

Vamos a tomar algo

PRIMERA ETAPA
Te invito a un café

SEGUNDA ETAPA
Vamos de tapas

TERCERA ETAPA
Antojitos mexicanos

INTEGRACIÓN:
LECTURA: El tapeo
VÍDEO CULTURAL: ¿Te gusta la comida mexicana?
INTERCAMBIO: ¿Quién es quién?
ESCRITURA: Actividades en el manual

Río Guadalquivir, Seville

Nautical Club, Barcelona

ESPAÑA

Población: 39.181.114

504.750 kilómetros cuadrados, más o menos dos veces el tamaño de Oregón

Capital: Madrid, 2.909.792

Ciudades principales
Barcelona, 1.623.542; Valencia 752.909; Sevilla 659.126; Zaragoza 586.219

CHAPTER OBJECTIVES:

In this chapter, you will learn about different kinds of foods and drinks. You will see that some of them are universal, while others are typical of specific areas in the Spanish-speaking world.

After completing this chapter, you will be able to carry out the following tasks:

- ⊚ **order something to eat and drink**
- ⊚ **discuss likes and dislikes**
- ⊚ **find out about other people**

The tools you will use to carry out these tasks are:

- ⊚ **vocabulary for:**
  - drinks, food, snacks
  - activities one enjoys doing
  - countries and nationalities
- ⊚ **grammatical structures:**
  - indefinite and definite articles
  - **gustar + acciones**
  - present tense **-ar, -er, -ir** verbs
  - present tense **ser**
  - **ser + adjetivos**

 Moneda: peseta

 **Esperanza de vida:
hombres, 75; mujéres, 82**

 Índice de alfabetización: 96%

 Televisores: 1 para cada 2,3 personas

 Radios: 1 para cada 3,3 personas

 Teléfonos: 1 para cada 3,1 personas

 **Lenguas: castellano, catalán,
gallego, vasco**

 **Productos principales de exportación:
coches, camiones, productos
manufacturados, productos agrícolas, aceite
de oliva, vino, productos químicos**

**Embajada:2375 Pennsylvania Avenue NW.
Washington, DC 20037**

PARA EMPEZAR: Te invito a un café

Using the Preparación questions, brainstorm with students the vocabulary related to different drinks, both hot and cold. Ask students to mention the things they drink during the day; use the transparency provided to point out the items. Do the same with the vocabulary for breakfast and snacks.

Preparación: As you begin this *etapa,* answer the following questions:

- **What are the different beverages you can order at a restaurant or a bar?**
- **What do you drink at different moments during the day?**
- **What do you normally have for breakfast?**
- **What, if anything, do you snack on?**

Suggestions: (1) First explain the scene; now look at the following exchange at an outdoor café and notice how people order something to drink. (2) Have students listen to the audio. Then have students act out the scene or you act as the waiter and have students get your attention to order a drink.

Transparency B-1: Bebidas calientes y frías. Introduce the vocabulary with transparencies, having students repeat the items. Ask students to point to specific beverages. Ask ¿Qué deseas tomar? randomly to elicit the names of the different beverages

Play Textbook audio.
waiter / Here you are.
what do you want to drink?
Thank you very much.
You're welcome.

—Pst, **camarero.**
—Sí señorita, **¿qué desea tomar?**
—Una limonada, por favor.
—¿Y usted?
—Un batido de fresa, por favor.

—**Aquí tienen.** Una limonada y un batido de fresa.
—**Muchas gracias.**
—**De nada.**

For advanced beginners, draw on board horizons with the sun at morning, noon, and night, and title each picture "la mañana", "la tarde", and "la noche". Point to pictures on board, then to transparency to refer to new vocabulary items in context. **Por la mañana, yo tomo café...**When finished, ask students: ¿Qué tomas tú por la mañana?...

VOCABULARY EXPANSION:
mesero = *waiter* in Mexico

▶ *Bebidas calientes y frías*

un café con leche

un café

un chocolate

café con leche: coffee with warm milk

granadina: grenadine, a nonalcoholic red syrup made from pomegranates, often mixed with mineral water and served with a wedge of lemon or lime

batido: a drink made by blending milk and fruit, such as peaches, strawberries, bananas

refresco: any soft drink

un jugo de naranja

una limonada

una botella de agua mineral

un vaso de agua con limón

una granadina con agua mineral

un batido de fresas

un refresco

una sangría

una cerveza

un vino tinto

un vino blanco

un té con leche

un té con limón

un té

▶ *El desayuno y la merienda*

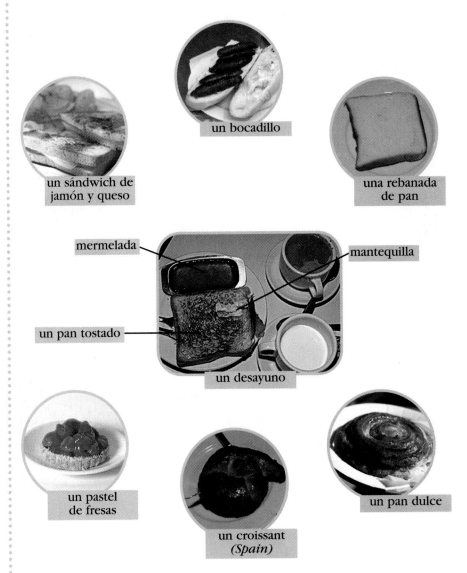

un bocadillo

un sándwich de jamón y queso

una rebanada de pan

mermelada

mantequilla

un pan tostado

un desayuno

un pastel de fresas

un croissant *(Spain)*

un pan dulce

un bocadillo: sandwich made with a hard-crust roll; may have different fillings, such as cheese, ham, sausage, an omelette, etc.; most common in Spain

un croissant: a word borrowed from French and used in Spain with the same meaning as in English; called a **medialuna** in other countries, such as Argentina, Uruguay, and Chile

un desayuno: breakfast; often a cup of coffee with warm milk and a piece of toast and marmalade or bread and butter

un pan dulce: any kind of sweet roll, cinnamon roll, danish, etc.; usually eaten with hot chocolate; this expression is commonly used in Mexico

un sándwich de jamón y queso: toasted sandwich made with white bread, ham, and cheese; common in Spain

►*Dos amigas°° en un café*

Two friends

Ana:	**Quisiera** tomar un café. ¿Y tú?	*I would like*
Clara:	Yo quisiera **comer algo.**	*to eat something*
Ana:	En **este** café **tienen** bocadillos, sándwiches y pasteles.	*this / they have*
Clara:	**Pues, voy a comer** un pastel, mm... con un café con leche.	*Then, I'm going to eat*
Ana:	Y **para mí** un sándwich de jamón y queso.	*for me*

Práctica

A. ¿Vas a comer algo? You and your friends are in a snack bar. Using the words suggested, decide what snack you will have.

■ **Modelo:** sándwich de queso / sándwich de jamón
—*¿Vas a comer algo?*
—*Yo quisiera un sándwich de queso. ¿Y tú?*
—*Mmm... voy a comer un sándwich de jamón.*

1. un bocadillo de jamón / un bocadillo de queso
2. un croissant / un pan dulce
3. un pan tostado / un sándwich de jamón y queso
4. un pastel de fresas / pan con mantequilla
5. pan con mermelada / una medialuna

B. En el café. You and your friend are in a café and want to order something to drink. Look at the menu to select your drinks. A classmate will play the role of the food server. When you order what you want, reverse roles.

■ **Modelo:** —*¿Qué desean tomar?*
—*Un café con leche, por favor.*
—*¿Y usted?*
—*Un té.*

Café Ibiza

Agua mineral	150 ptas
Refrescos	250 ptas
Zumo de naranja natural	350 ptas
Limonada	300 ptas
Batidos	250 ptas
Cerveza	250 ptas
Café solo o con leche	150 ptas
Té, tila, manzanilla	150 ptas
Chocolate	200 ptas

Comentarios

culturales   Los cafés

*I*n the Spanish-speaking world, young and old people enjoy meeting at a café for a drink and a snack at different times during the day. In every neighborhood of a town or city one can find cafés, each with its own particular clientele and atmosphere. In a café near a school or university, for example, it is possible to see groups of students sitting at tables discussing their studies and politics or just chatting with friends. Older people may prefer sitting in a quieter café where they can listen to music while they read the newspaper, play cards, or simply relax watching the passersby. In the summertime, tables are usually set outside for the enjoyment of the customers.

Las comidas

*I*n Spain it is very common to have a snack in the morning, between 11:00 and 2:00, and another snack between 6:00 and 9:00 in the evening because lunch and dinner are both served late. In Spain, lunch **(la comida)** is the major meal of the day and is eaten around 2:00 in the afternoon. Dinner **(la cena)** is usually a lighter meal and is served around 10:00 in the evening. On weekends it is very common to eat dinner, either at home or at a restaurant, as late as 11:00 and then go out for drinks and fun until 3:00, 4:00, or 5:00 A.M.

INTEGRACIÓN CULTURAL

Answer the following questions.
1. What are some of the similarities and differences between eating habits in Spain and in North America?
2. How do you think you would feel if you were living in Spain and you had to wait until 2:00 each day to eat lunch and until 10:00 to eat dinner?
3. How do you think Spaniards feel when they come to the USA and have to eat lunch at 12:00 and dinner at around 6:00? Try to find people from Spain in your school and ask them. Bring the information you find to the class.

El artículo indefinido

Notice that when people order drinks and food, they say:

> **Una** limonada, por favor.
> **Un** café con leche.
> Yo voy a comer **un** sándwich de jamón.

The English equivalent of **un, una** is *a* or *an*. The equivalent of **unos, unas** is *some*. In Spanish we distinguish between the masculine indefinite article **un** and the feminine indefinite article **una**.

	Masculino	Femenino
Singular	**un** refresco	**una** limonada
Plural	**unos** bocadillos	**unas** tostadas

For an English speaker it is not surprising that a waiter (**un camarero**) is masculine and a waitress (**una camarera**) is feminine. However, it is somehow startling to learn that **un refresco** is masculine and **una cerveza** is feminine. All nouns in Spanish have grammatical gender. The gender has nothing to do with what the word means.

If a word is masculine, it often ends with the vowel **-o** (**un refresco**). If a noun is feminine, it often ends with the vowel **-a** (**una granadina**). But not all words fall into these categories: **un café, un té** are both masculine although they don't end with an **-o. Leche** is a feminine noun not ending in **-a**. For this reason it is best to learn the noun with its corresponding article.

Preview: A more complete explanation of gender and agreement is presented in the *Tercera etapa*, and again in Chapter 2, page 74.

GRAMMAR NOTE:
There are some words in Spanish that do not follow the pattern **-o=masculine, -a=feminine.** Many words that end in **-ma, -pa, ta** are masculine: **problema, sistema, poema, programa, tema, mapa, planeta.** There is one word that ends in **-o** that is feminine: **mano** *(hand)*. Try to learn these with their corresponding article.

Práctica

C. ¿Un o una? In pairs, student A will read to student B the words in column A, and the person listening has to come up with the right indefinite article for each word. Then student B will read to student A the words in column B.

■ **Modelo:** Student A: *botella de agua mineral*
   Student B: *una botella de agua mineral*

A
1. jugo de naranja
2. limonada
3. té
4. chocolate
5. vaso de leche

B
6. café con leche
7. batido de fresa
8. té con leche
9. cerveza
10. vino tinto

Ex. C: Pairs

Answers, Ex C
1. un 2. una 3. un 4. un 5. un 6. un 7. un 8. un 9. una 10. un

D. Yo quisiera... ¿y tú? In groups of four, one student playing the role of the food server asks the other three students what they would like to eat or drink. Then, the food server writes down what the students order.

■ **Modelo:** —*¿Qué desean?*
   —*Yo quisiera una limonada...*

1. chocolate
2. té
3. croissant
4. jugo de naranja
5. cerveza
6. granadina
7. té con leche
8. refresco
9. batido de fresa
10. pan dulce

Ex. D: Groups

Answers, Ex. D
1. Yo quisiera un chocolate. ¿Y tú? 2. un té 3. un croissant 4. un jugo de naranja 5. una cerveza 6. una granadina 7. un té con leche 8. un refresco 9. un batido de fresa 10. un pan dulce

Preview: A more complete explanation of **gustar** will appear in Chapter 2, page 63. Other verbs like **gustar** are presented in Chapters 8 and 11.

Preview: Infinitives are presented here as vocabulary items to be used with **gustar.** For now, students only need to understand the meaning of the verbs. Details about their conjugation will be presented in the next two *etapas.*

Suggestion: Point out that a negative sentence is formed by adding **no.** Have students transform the affirmative sample sentences to negative ones.

GRAMMAR NOTE:

An infinitive is a verb that is not conjugated (does not show a different ending for each person). For example, in English *to introduce* is an infinitive, and *she introduces* is a conjugated verb.

ENFOQUE LÉXICO — Expresión de los gustos: **gustar** + acciones

When people go to a café together for a drink or a snack, they normally talk about themselves, their daily activities, the things they like to do, etc. These are also normal topics in a conversation when you are meeting people for the first time.

In order to express what activities you like or do not like to do, the following structure can be used:

Gustar + *infinitive*

Me gusta bailar.	*I like to dance.*
¿Te gusta cantar?	*Do you like to sing?*
No me gusta cantar. **Me gusta** escuchar música.	*I don't like to sing. I like to listen to music.*

Other activities: **hablar** *(to speak),* **estudiar** *(to study),* **escuchar** *(to listen),* **tomar** *(to take, to drink),* **viajar** *(to travel),* **beber** *(to drink),* **comer** *(to eat),* **leer** *(to read),* **escribir** *(to write)*

These are some words that can be used to express whether you like something very much or just a little.

mucho	*a lot*
muchísimo	*very much*
poco	*a little*
muy poco	*very little*
Me gusta **mucho** bailar.	*I like to dance **a lot.***
Me gusta **muy poco** escuchar música clásica.	*I like **very little** to listen to classical music.*

These words are called *adverbs* and in this structure they come after the verb **gustar.**

Práctica

Answers for E and F will vary.

Pair advanced beginners with true beginners. Encourage students to express other actions they enjoy doing. Allow students a few minutes to complete exercise, and when reviewing with them, ask what new verbs they learned from their partners. Write these verbs on the board.

E. ¿Qué *(What)* **te gusta?** Ask your classmate which of the following things he or she likes to do. Note the answers. Then tell her or him which ones you like or do not like to do.

■ **Modelo:** —*¿Te gusta cantar?*
—*Sí, me gusta.*
o
—*No, no me gusta.*

1. bailar	5. escuchar música
2. cantar	6. beber
3. viajar	7. leer
4. estudiar	8. escribir

F. ¿Muchísimo o muy poco? Say how much or how little you like to do these activities.

◼ **Modelo:** cantar

    Me gusta mucho cantar.

    o

    Me gusta muy poco cantar.

1. bailar
2. hablar en clase
3. hablar español
4. escuchar música rock
5. escuchar música clásica
6. estudiar
7. cantar
8. comer
9. leer
10. viajar

G. ¿Qué te gusta hacer? Imagine that you are one of the following people. According to the information provided, say one or two logical things that you like to do. The rest of the class has to guess who you are.

◼ **Modelo:** *Me gusta mucho escribir. Me llamo...*

1. Laura Esquivel (escritora)
2. Enrique Iglesias (cantante)
3. Gabriela Sabatini (tenista)
4. Jon Seda (actor)
5. María Hinojosa (periodista, corresponsal de televisión)

ENFOQUE ESTRUCTURAL   **Pronombres personales**

IRM Master 1: Pronombres y verbos -*ar* en el presente

Subject pronouns is the term used to refer to the following set of words: *I, you, he, she, it, we, they.*

Pronombres personales: *Spanish vs. English*		
yo	*I*	
tú	*you*	one person, used when you are on a first-name basis
usted (Ud.)	*you*	one person, used with people you do not know very well, your superiors, and older people in general
él	*he*	
ella	*she*	
nosotros(as)	*we*	**nosotras,** used when referring to a group of all women
vosotros(as)	*you*	used only in Spain with more than one person with whom you are on a first-name basis; **vosotras,** used when referring to a group of all women
ustedes (Uds.)	*you*	used with more than one person
ellos	*they*	two or more males or a group of males and females
ellas	*they*	two or more females

GRAMMAR NOTE:
When you answer a question in the negative form repeating the verb used in the question, you need to use the word **no** twice. **¿Bebes cerveza? No, no bebo cerveza.**

GRAMMAR NOTE:
Usted and **ustedes** are lowercased when spelled out, but are capitalized when abbreviated (**Ud., Uds.**).

Ustedes (*you*, plural) is used in Spain as the plural of **usted**; therefore, it is used with people you don't know very well, superiors, and older people. In the rest of the Spanish-speaking world, **ustedes** is also used with people with whom you are on a first-name basis.

Presente de los verbos regulares en -ar

1. Verbs consist of two parts: a *stem*, which carries the meaning, and an *ending*, which indicates the subject and the tense.

2. Although in English verb endings seldom change, in Spanish verb endings change for each person, and the endings let you know who the subject is in each case: **tomo un refresco** *(I)*, **tomamos cerveza** *(we)*. Look at the sentences below, and notice how the endings change in each case:

Tomo un refresco.	*I'm having a soft drink.*
¿Deseas un bocadillo?	*Do you want a sandwich?*
Ella **habla** con Juan.	*She is talking to Juan.*
Mis amigos y yo **cantamos.**	*My friends and I sing.*
Tus amigos y tú **bailáis.**	*You and your friends dance.*
Teresa y Paco **toman** una cerveza.	*Teresa and Paco are drinking a beer.*

3. To conjugate a regular **-ar** verb, drop the **-ar,** and add the appropriate endings to the stem:

Subject	Stem	Ending	Conjugated verb form
yo	**estudi-**	**-o**	estudio
tú		**-as**	estudias
Ud.			
él		**-a**	estudia
ella			
nosotros(as)		**-amos**	estudiamos
vosotros(as)		**-áis**	estudiáis
Uds.			
ellos		**-an**	estudian
ellas			

4. The present tense is used in Spanish as the equivalent of *I study, I am studying,* and *I do study.*

Some regular -*ar* verbs:

bailar *(to dance),* **cantar** *(to sing),* **desear** *(to want),* **escuchar** *(to listen),* **estudiar** *(to study),* **hablar** *(to speak, to talk),* **practicar** *(to practice),* **tomar** *(to take, to drink, to have),* **viajar** *(to travel)*

¿Cómo? ¿Cuándo?

The following words and phrases are used in Spanish to express how well or how often you do something.

bien	*well*
muy bien	*very well*
mal	*poorly*
todos los días	*every day*
siempre	*always*
a veces	*sometimes*

Practica el piano todos los días.

Práctica

H. ¿Cómo y cuándo? Here is a list of different activities along with another list of expressions. Match the activities and the expressions next to them to say how often or how well you do these things.

■ **Modelo:** *Canto muy mal.*

Actividades		Cómo/cuándo	
cantar	bailar	bien	mal
hablar en clase	trabajar	a veces	siempre
escuchar música	cantar	muy bien	muy mal
estudiar	viajar	todos los días	

I. Preguntas. Ask a classmate questions using the following verbs. Your classmate will answer, saying how often or how well she or he does the activities.

■ **Modelo:** hablar
　　　　　—Pablo, ¿hablas español?
　　　　　—Sí, todos los días.

1. bailar
2. trabajar
3. hablar
4. viajar
5. cantar
6. escuchar
7. estudiar

Answers for Exs. H and I will vary.

Suggestion, Ex. H: Allow students to do this activity in pairs, then review with the entire class, asking individual students if they do each activity. Personalize and vary the exercise by asking, **¿Te gusta cantar?** etc.

Review adverbs mucho, muchísimo, poco, muy poco. Practice these and new adverbs before doing Ex. H. ¿Trabajas mucho? ¿Estudias poco o mucho? ¿Bailas muchísimo?

Ana and her friends are having a snack at a café.

ANTES DE ESCUCHAR

Based on the information you have learned in this *etapa:*

1. What are some things you expect Ana and her friends will order?
2. What do you say to order something in Spanish?

Before you listen to the dialog, look at the exercises in the *Después de escuchar* section.

DESPUÉS DE ESCUCHAR

J. Comprensión. Which of the following things did Ana and her friends order?

limonada	_____	croissant	_____
té	_____	sándwich de jamón y queso	_____
refresco	_____	pan dulce	_____
agua mineral	_____	pastel	_____

K. ¿Cómo lo dicen? The instructor will play the tape again. Listen and see if you can determine the following:

1. What question does the waiter ask to get their order?
2. How does Francisco say that he would like something to eat?

Tú dirás

L. El menú. With a classmate, design a menu for a café in Spain. Include drinks and snacks as well as prices in **pesetas.** When you finish, pass your menu on to another pair of students in the class. They will use it to carry out the following exercise.

M. En el café. Use the menu you created above to complete the following task. One of you will play the role of the waiter or waitress.

- You meet a friend at a café after school. You greet each other and order something to eat and/or drink.
- Another friend of yours arrives. Introduce him or her to your first friend.

- The two people who just met try to get better acquainted by asking each other questions.
- Don't forget to have the third person order something, also.

Before you do this exercise, review the greetings presented in the Preliminary chapter, page 7.

Ex. M: Group
Do Ex. M in groups of four students. Allow students to write up their parts of the role play for practice, but encourage them to perform their parts for the class without notes.

SEGUNDA ETAPA

PARA EMPEZAR: Vamos de tapas

Preparación: **Tapas** are snacks served in many bars all over Spain (see *Comentarios culturales* on page 26 for more information). The pictures below show some typical **tapas**. As you begin to work with this *etapa*, answer the following questions:

- Look at the **tapas** in the pictures. Of the types of food included in these **tapas**, which ones are familiar to you? Which ones are new?
- Have you ever tried any of them? If so, where? when?

Suggestion, Ex. M:
Model the conversation with three students before dividing the class into groups.

Transparency B-3, B-4: Tapas. Introduce the vocabulary with the transparency, having students repeat the items. Ask students to point to specific tapas.

Suggestion: Begin with a mini-planning strategy, asking students what they eat after class if they are hungry. Then point out the tapas in the text or on the transparency.

pan con chorizo

calamares

aceitunas

queso

cacahuetes

patatas bravas

patatas bravas: cooked potatoes, diced and served in a spicy sauce

tortilla de patatas: an omelette made with eggs, potatoes, and onions; usually served in small bite-sized pieces

tortilla (de patatas)

VOCABULARY EXPANSION:
In Mexico a **tortilla** is a thin cornmeal pancake while in Spain and some parts of South America it is like an omelette.

VOCABULARY EXPANSION:
Another word for **patatas** is **papas**. **Papa** is a word of Quechua origin. It is used instead of **patatas** in most Latin American countries, in Southern Spain, and in the Canary Islands.

Práctica

A. De tapas. Imagine you have just arrived in a city in Spain. This is going to be your first **tapas** experience. Look at the photos on page 25 and decide which ones you want to try. Make your own list.

B. ¡Camarero, más..., por favor! Well, it seems that you like these **tapas** and want to order more. Ask a classmate, who will play the role of the food server, to bring you some **tapas.**

Repaso

Ex. C: Pairs

C. ¡Qué hambre! *(I'm famished!)* You are very hungry and those **tapas** were not enough. You want to eat something else. In groups of four, one student will play the role of the food server and the others will be customers. Using the vocabulary you learned in *Primera etapa*, order something to eat and drink.

VOCABULARY EXPANSION:
In Spain, there are other words for **tapas**. For instance, in northern Spain the word **pinchos** is used. You can also hear **banderillas**. In Andalucía, **pescado frito** is referred to as **pescaíto frito**.

Comentarios

culturales *Las tapas*

Spaniards commonly go to **bares de tapas** to see friends who frequent the same bar and to get a snack and something to drink. A visit to a **tapas** bar may take place at different times during the day, usually before lunch and before dinner.

To understand the original meaning of the word **tapas** you need to know that the verb **tapar** in Spanish means *to cover*. In the beginning, **tapas** consisted of a slice of bread with a slice of cured ham or chorizo put on the top of a glass of wine, and they were a complimentary offering of the bar. Tradition says that the **tapa** was used originally to protect the wine from getting dust.

Tapas include a wide variety of food items: olives, peanuts, cheese, potato chips, bite size pieces of tortilla with a slice of bread, small dishes of shrimp with garlic sauce, fried squid *(calamares)*, slices of cured ham *(jamón serrano)*, fried fish *(pescado frito)*, and many others.

The common theme is that they are served in small sizes.

Note: For more information on tapas in Spain, consult Penelope Casas's book, *Tapas: The Little Dishes of Spain.*

INTEGRACIÓN CULTURAL

1. Is there something similar to *tapas* in the United States?
2. Eating *tapas* is becoming more and more common in big cities all around the United States. Do a Web search and find out what cities in this country have tapas bars or restaurants that serve tapas. Then, share the information you find with the rest of the class.

INTERNET

http://tudiras.heinle.com

IRM Master 2: El artículo definido

Suggestion: Point out that the definite article agrees with its noun in gender and in number. For example, **queso** is masculine and singular and therefore takes the masculine, singular definite article **el,** while **patatas bravas,** feminine and plural, takes the feminine plural form **las.**

ENFOQUE ESTRUCTURAL — El artículo definido

In *Primera etapa* you learned about the use of indefinite articles in Spanish. As in English, Spanish has definite articles. See the sentences below:

> **Las** tapas son típicas de España.
> **El** bar La Chuleta sirve muchas tapas.

In Spanish, the definite article has two singular forms (feminine and masculine) and two plural forms (feminine and masculine). The English equivalent of these forms is *the.*

	Masculino	**Femenino**
Singular	**el** queso	**la** tortilla de patata
Plural	**los** cacahuetes	**las** patatas bravas

Uses of the definite article in Spanish

1. The definite article is used to designate a noun in a general or collective sense:

El café es una bebida popular.	***Coffee*** *is a popular drink.*
La leche tiene vitamina D.	***Milk*** *has vitamin D.*

2. The definite article is also used to designate a noun in a specific sense:

Me gustan **las** tapas del bar La Chuleta.	*I like tapas from La Chuleta bar.*
La tortilla de patata es mi tapa favorita.	*Tortilla de patata is my favorite tapa.*

3. The definite article is used in Spanish with such titles as **Sr., Sra., Srta., Dr., Dra.**

El Sr. Herrera come en un café.	*Mr. Herrera eats in a café.*
La Dra. Martínez habla español.	*Dr. Martínez speaks Spanish.*

GRAMMAR NOTE:

Use the definite article when you speak about someone who has a title.

The definite article is not used with titles when directly addressing the person in question: ¡Hola, Sr. Herrera!

Suggestion: Before presenting this section, review the present tense of -ar verbs.

Práctica

D. ¿Te gusta o no? Ask several of your classmates whether or not they like the following things:

■ **Modelo:** *¿Te gusta la leche?*
Sí, me gusta...,
o
No, no me gusta...

1. café
2. cerveza
3. queso
4. tortilla
5. vino tinto
6. agua mineral

E. ¿Qué vas a tomar? Offer one of the following items of food and drink to at least two of your classmates. They will either accept or ask for something else, depending on their personal preferences.

■ **Modelo:** *—¿Vas a tomar una cerveza?*
—¡Ah, sí! Me gusta mucho la cerveza.
—¿Y tú?
—No, gracias. Voy a tomar un vino.

1. un refresco
2. una cerveza
3. un café con leche
4. una limonada
5. un vino

ENFOQUE ESTRUCTURAL — **Presente de los verbos regulares en -er, -ir**

You learned in *Primera etapa* how verb endings change to indicate who is doing the action. You learned the specific ending for verbs like **hablar, cantar, viajar,** that is, verbs that have an **-ar** infinitive.

Now you are going to learn the endings for verbs that have an **-er** infinitive like **comer** *(to eat)*, **correr** *(to run)*, **leer** *(to read)*, **vender** *(to sell)*, and verbs that have an **-ir** infinitive like **vivir** *(to live)*, **escribir** *(to write)*.

Verbos en -er

Subject	Stem	Ending	Conjugated verb form
yo	corr	**-o**	corr**o**
tú		**-es**	corr**es**
Ud.			
él		**-e**	corr**e**
ella			
nosotros (as)		**-emos**	corr**emos**
vosotros (as)		**-éis**	corr**éis**
Uds.			
ellos		**-en**	corr**en**
ellas			

Verbos en -ir

Subject	Stem	Ending	Conjugated verb form
yo	viv	**-o**	viv**o**
tú		**-es**	viv**es**
Ud. } él } ella }		**-e**	viv**e**
nosotros (as)		**-imos**	viv**imos**
vosotros (as)		**-ís**	viv**ís**
Uds. } ellos } ellas }		**-en**	viv**en**

You will note that except for the **nosotros** and **vosotros** forms, the endings are exactly the same for both types of verbs.

Some regular -*er* verbs:

> **aprender** *(to learn)*   **beber** *(to drink)*
> **comer** *(to eat)*   **comprender** *(to understand)*
> **correr** *(to run)*   **leer** *(to read)*
> **vender** *(to sell)*

Some regular -*ir* verbs:

> **compartir** *(to share)*   **escribir** *(to write)*
> **recibir** *(to receive)*   **vivir** *(to live)*

Práctica

F. ¿Qué hacen? Look at the following drawings and match them with the appropriate description.

Answers, Ex. F
a. Miguel escribe una carta.
b. Rogelio y Lilia beben un batido.
c. Adela y Pepa corren en el parque.
d. Leo recibe una carta. e. Nosotros leemos revistas. f. Antonio come un bocadillo.

a.

b.

c.

d.

e.

f.

1. Adela y Pepa corren en el parque.
2. Nosotros leemos revistas.
3. Leo recibe una carta.
4. Antonio come un bocadillo.
5. Miguel escribe una carta.
6. Rogelio y Lilia beben un batido.

Play Textbook audio.

You may not understand everything in the dialog. Do not let yourself be distracted by words or expressions you do not understand. Instead, concentrate on capturing the overall meaning.

G. ¿Qué haces tú? Ask your classmate the following questions. Follow the model and then report to the class the information you have gathered.

■ **Modelo:** *¿Trabajas todos los días?*

Sí, trabajo todos los días.

o

No, no trabajo todos los días.

1. ¿Lees mucho?
2. ¿Vives en un apartamento?
3. ¿Recibes muchos mensajes electrónicos *(e-mail messages)*?
4. ¿Comprendes bien el español?
5. ¿Comes muchas tapas?

Linda, Cristina, and Beatriz are at the bar La Chuleta. It's 1:30 in the afternoon.

ANTES DE ESCUCHAR

Brainstorm the vocabulary you are about to hear by answering the following questions.

1. What do you think people eat as a midday snack in Spain?
2. What tapas would you order if you were in Madrid at a tapas bar?

Before you listen to the dialog, look at the exercises in the *Después de escuchar* section.

DESPUÉS DE ESCUCHAR

H. ¿Quién va a tomar qué? As you listen to the dialog, match the names on the left with the food items on the right.

Linda	cerveza
	tortilla
Beatriz	calamares
	chorizo con pan
Cristina	vino tinto

I. ¿Cómo lo dicen? Your instructor will play the tape again. As you listen, see if you can determine the following:

1. What does the food server say to get the order?
2. What is the filler that Beatriz and Linda use to express hesitation?

Tú dirás

J. Nuestro *(Our)* **bar de tapas.** You and your classmates are going to transform your class into a city square in Spain with several tapas bars that have tables and chairs outside. In groups of three, you are going to do the following:

1. Create a tapas menu, including prices in **pesetas.**
2. Set up your bar.

Then tell the rest of the class what two or three of your specialty items **(especialidades de la casa)** are.

K. Vamos a probar *(Let's taste)* **diferentes tapas.** While one of you stays at the bar "serving" **tapas**, the rest of the students should go around the classroom asking to try the different **tapas**. Be sure to ask for the **tapas** using the question forms you've learned in this chapter.

Ex. J:  Pairs

Suggestion, Ex. J: You may want to tell students to bring drawings or pictures of the different tapas they will offer or to bring the actual **tapas** to class.

Ex. K:  Group

Exercise K is a follow up of the previous one.

TERCERA ETAPA

PARA EMPEZAR: *Antojitos mexicanos*

Preparación: Before you start working on this *etapa,* take advantage of all the information you already know. Given the popularity of Mexican food in the USA, it is likely that you are already familiar with some of the dishes you are going to learn about in this *etapa.* Before moving on, answer the following questions:

- What Mexican dishes do you know? Which ones do you like?
- How would you describe Mexican food in general?

Group native speakers or students who have been to Mexico with those who don't have such experience. Ask them to discuss the Mexican food they are familiar with. Allow students 3 to 5 minutes, then ask them to share the foods they discussed. Write some of these dishes on the board. Preview new adjectives by commenting on each item you write (Frijoles, ¡qué sabrosos! ...)

Rafael y Pablo, dos estudiantes españoles, están en un restaurante en México.

Mesero:	Buenos días, señores. **¿Qué van a pedir?**
Rafael:	Yo quisiera comer un **taco de pollo** con **frijoles.**
Pablo:	Para mí, una **enchilada de carne** con **arroz.**
Mesero:	¿Y para tomar?
Rafael:	Un vaso de agua con limón.
Mesero:	¿Y para Ud., señor?
Pablo:	Una limonada, **muy** fría, por favor.
Mesero:	Muy bien.

Play Textbook audio.

are

What will you have?

chicken taco
beans
enchilada
meat / rice

very

(Sara y Carlos, dos turistas españoles, están de visita en México.)

Great food!	**Sara:** Mm… **¡Qué comida más rica!** ¿Qué es?
	Señora: Son enchiladas con **salsa.**
sauce	
How hot (spicy)!	**Carlos:** ¡Ay!… **¡Qué picantes!** No me gustan. Son muy picantes para mí.
Here is another	**Señora:** **Aquí hay otra** enchilada que no es picante.
	Carlos: Mm… ¡Sí! **Ésta me gusta. ¡Riquísima!**
This one I like. Delicious!	**Sara:** Carlos, el **flan** está delicioso también.
custard	
good	**Carlos:** Sí. ¡Qué **bueno!**
	Sara: Me gusta mucho la comida mexicana. Es muy diferente a la comida española.

enchilada: soft corn **tortilla** filled with cheese, meat, or chicken and served with hot sauce

frijoles: pinto or black beans cooked until tender; served mashed, most often as a side dish

taco: a corn **tortilla** filled with meat, chicken, or other fillings and topped with lettuce, tomato, grated cheese, and sauce

tortilla: made of cornmeal and shaped like a pancake; in Mexico, the **tortilla** is served with all meals and takes the place of bread

chile: a pepper ranging from mild to very hot; used to make sauces

flan: very common dessert in all Hispanic countries; baked custard topped with caramel sauce

Práctica

A. ¿Qué va a pedir? You are in a Mexican restaurant. Look at the pictures below and decide what you are going to order.

■ **Modelo:** enchilada de queso
— *¿Qué va a pedir?*
— *Yo quisiera comer una enchilada de queso.*
— *Muy bien.*

1. enchilada de carne 2. enchilada de queso 3. tacos de pollo

4. tacos de carne   5. arroz con frijoles   6. frijoles

B. ¿En España o en México? Are these people in Spain or in Mexico?
Decide according to the food they are eating.

1. A mí me gusta mucho comer tapas con un refresco.
2. Yo quisiera un bocadillo de jamón, por favor.
3. Para mí una enchilada de carne con salsa, por favor.
4. Yo voy a tomar un chocolate.
5. Voy a comer un sándwich de jamón y queso.
6. Yo deseo un taco de pollo con frijoles.

C. ¿Vamos a comer algo? When asked this question, the people pictured
below all answered **sí,** but each had a different place in mind. Match each statement with the appropriate person on the basis of the clues in the drawings.

a.

b.

c.

d.

1. Yo quisiera comer unas tapas y tomar algo bien frío.
2. A mí me gusta la comida mexicana… Mm, ¡tacos y frijoles con arroz!
3. Nosotros deseamos unos batidos de fresas con unos bocadillos.
4. Yo deseo un café con leche y un sándwich.

Transparency B-5: Comida mexicana. Use the transparency to introduce Mexican food items. Ask which students are familiar with Mexican food. You may have students visit a Mexican restaurant or bring in items (rice, beans, taco shells) used in Mexican food and make a presentation.

Ex. B: This information appears in the *Comentarios culturales* and throughout the unit. Possible answers: España 1, 2, 4, 5; México 3, 4, 6.

Suggestion: If you have access to menus from Spain and Mexico, bring them in and have students determine from the menu choices in which country the restaurant is located.

Ex. C, Answers: 1. a, 2. c, 3. d, 4. b

D. ¿Qué te gusta? ¿Qué no te gusta? Ask a classmate if he or she likes to eat or drink the following foods and beverages. Your classmate will indicate that he or she does not like to eat or drink items from one category, but that he or she likes to eat or drink items from the second category.

■ **Modelo:** batido / té

—*¿Te gusta beber batidos?*
—*No, no me gusta mucho beber batidos. Me gusta más beber té*
   calamares / pizza
—*¿Te gusta comer calamares?*
—*No, no me gusta mucho comer calamares. Me gusta más comer*
   pizza.

1. tacos / enchiladas
2. aceitunas / cacahuetes
3. cerveza / refrescos
4. café / té
5. patatas bravas / tortilla de patata

E. ¿Qué haces normalmente? With a classmate, take turns asking each other questions using the verbs below.

■ **Modelo:** —*¿Corres todos los días?*
              —*No, corro a veces.*

1. correr   5. comer
2. vivir   6. escribir
3. comprender   7. recibir
4. leer   8. beber

ENFOQUE ESTRUCTURAL | **El verbo ser + lugar de origen**

At the Mexican restaurant, the food server has the following exchange with a couple from Spain.

Mesera:	Perdón, ¿de dónde **son** ustedes?
Sara:	**Somos** españoles.
Carlos:	Estamos aquí de vacaciones, para visitar la ciudad.
Mesera:	Pues, ¡bienvenidos!

At a different table, several students:

Pablo:	¡Hola! **Soy** Pablo Hernández.
Ana:	¿De dónde **eres**, Pablo?
Pablo:	De Bogotá, Colombia. ¿Y tú?
Ana:	**Soy** peruano, de Lima. Luisa y Raquel **son** de Lima también.

Some Spanish verbs are called irregular verbs because their conjugations do not follow a fixed pattern, like those you learned in previous *etapas*. One of the most frequently used irregular verbs is **ser.**

ser			
yo	**soy**	nosotros(as)	**somos**
tú	**eres**	vosotros(as)	**sois**
Ud.		Uds.	
él	**es**	ellos	**son**
ella		ellas	

Ser + de followed by the name of a country or city is used to express place of origin.

> **Soy de** Lima pero mis padres **son de** Quito, Ecuador.

The expression **¿de dónde + verb ser?** is used to inquire where someone or something is from.

> **¿De dónde es** la tortilla de patata?
> De España.
> **¿De dónde eres,** John?
> De Nuevo México.

IRM Master 5: Adjetivos

Práctica

F. ¿De dónde son? There are many Spanish-speaking people who live in the United States. Some of them were born in the USA and some were not. For a few minutes you are going to adopt a new identity. Look at the maps of Central and South America that appear on the inside of the cover of this textbook, and pick a city and country to be your new home. Choose a new Hispanic first and last name for yourself. Walk around the class and find out your classmates' new names and countries. When you finish, introduce three of your classmates to the rest of the class using their new identities.

■ **Modelo:** —*¿Cómo te llamas?* —*María Castillo.*
              —*¿De dónde eres?* —*De San José, Costa Rica*

Suggestion: You may want to introduce adjectives that identify regional origin within a country and adjectives that indicate city of origin. In Spain some regional adjectives are andaluz (Andalucía), vasco (País vasco), and gallego (Galicia). Some city adjectives are madrileña (Madrid), sevillano (Sevilla), and bilbaíno (Bilbao). You may want to introduce other adjectives of origin such as bonaerense (Buenos Aires) and limeño (Lima).

Some countries, such as (la) Argentina, (el) Canadá, (la) China, (el) Ecuador, (los) Estados Unidos, (el) Japón, (el) Paraguay, (el) Perú and (el) Uruguay may or may not take an article.

Other adjectives of nationality: samoano, filipino, haitiano, camboyano, laosiano, coreano (all with 4 forms like cubano or peruano), tailandés (with 4 forms like francés or inglés), israelí, iraquí, iraní (all with only 2 forms like iraní, iraníes), vietnamita (with only 2 forms: vietnamita for masculine or feminine singular and vietnamitas for the plural)

GRAMMAR NOTE:

Agree in this context means that the adjective has to have the same gender and number the noun does. Carlos (masculine and singular) es peruano (also masculine and singular). Mirta (feminine and singular) es argentina (also feminine and singular).

Note that adjectives of nationality are spelled in Spanish with lower-case letters. Also, note the diacritic mark (diéresis) on top of the u of nicaragüense. Remember that the diéresis is used to indicate that the vowel u is pronounced. Other words with diéresis are: lingüística (linguistics) vergüenza (shame).

G. ¿De dónde eres? Now find out where five of your classmates are really from. Then report to the class.

■ **Modelo:** —¿De dónde eres, John?   —De New York.
—John es de New York.

ENFOQUE LÉXICO — Adjetivos de nacionalidad

Adjectives, that is, words that describe or qualify a noun, have to agree in gender (masculine/feminine) and number (singular/plural) with the person or thing they refer to.

1. Adjectives that end in **-o** are masculine, and they have a feminine form that ends in **-a**:

   Ángeles es argentina y Jorge es mexicano.

2. Adjectives that end in a consonant (**-l, -n, -s**) are, for the most part, masculine and form the feminine by adding an **-a**:

español	española
francés	francesa
alemán	alemana

   Juan, un amigo de Ángeles, es español. Jorge también (also) tiene (has) una amiga española, Anabel.

3. Some adjectives have identical masculine and feminine forms.

Él es **estadounidense**.	Ella es **estadounidense**.
Él es **canadiense**.	Ella es **canadiense**.

4. To form the plural of the adjectives that end in a vowel, simply add **-s** to the masculine or feminine singular forms. If the singular form ends in a consonant, add **-es** for masculine adjectives and **-as** for feminine adjectives.

Ellos son **mexicanos**.	Ellas son **mexicanas**.
Ellos son **españoles**.	Ellas son **españolas**.
Ellos son **canadienses**.	Ellas son **canadienses**.
Ellos son alemanes.	Ellas son alemanas.

Adjetivos de nacionalidad

País	Adjetivo
Argentina	argentino(a)
Bolivia	boliviano(a)
Brasil	brasileño(a)
Colombia	colombiano(a)
Costa Rica	costarricense
Cuba	cubano(a)
Chile	chileno(a)
Ecuador	ecuatoriano(a)
El Salvador	salvadoreño(a)
España	español(a)
Guatemala	guatemalteco(a)
Honduras	hondureño(a)
La República Dominicana	dominicano(a)

México	mexicano(a)
Nicaragua	nicaragüense
Panamá	panameño(a)
Paraguay	paraguayo(a)
Perú	peruano(a)
Puerto Rico	puertorriqueño(a)
Uruguay	uruguayo(a)
Venezuela	venezolano(a)

Más adjetivos de nacionalidad

País	Adjetivo
Alemania	alemán (alemana)
Canadá	canadiense
China	chino(a)
Egipto	egipcio(a)
Estados Unidos	estadounidense
Francia	francés (francesa)
Inglaterra	inglés (inglesa)
Italia	italiano(a)
Japón	japonés (japonesa)
Rusia	ruso(a)

Refer back to transparency map and discuss where different famous Hispanic figures are from. For example: **Esto es México, Selma Hayek es de México, es mexicana... Esto es Cuba, Gloria Estefan es de Cuba, es cubana.** etc.

Práctica

H. ¿De dónde son? Look at the names listed below. They are all famous Hispanic people in different disciplines: politics, art, music, etc. Then, look at the names of the countries listed and try to match each person with the country he or she is from. Once you have confirmed with the teacher the country of origin for each person, state the nationality of each one using the adjectives provided on page 36.

Isabel Allende	México
Gabriel García Márquez	Guatemala
Laura Esquivel	Argentina
Juan Carlos I	Colombia
Ernesto Ché Guevara	Chile
José Martí	España
Rigoberta Menchú	Cuba

Answers, Ex. H
Isabel Allende, Chile, chilena
Gabriel García Márquez, Colombia, colombiano
Laura Esquivel, México, mexicana
Juan Carlos I, España, español
Ernesto Ché Guevara, Argentina, argentino
José Martí, Cuba, cubano
Rigoberta Menchú, Guatemala, guatemalteca

I. Las nacionalidades. You are with a group of young people from all over the world. Find out their nationalities by making the assumptions indicated and then correcting your mistakes. Follow the model.

■ **Modelo:** Margarita / argentina / Nueva York
—*¿Margarita es argentina?*
—*No, ella es de Nueva York.*
—*Ah, ella es estadounidense entonces* (then).
—*Claro* (Of course).

1. Lin-Tao (m.) / japonés / Beijín
2. Sofía / mexicana / Roma
3. Jean-Pierre / francés / Québec
4. Jill / canadiense / Londres
5. Hilda y Helga / colombianas / Berlín
6. Olga y Nicolás / venezolanos / Moscú

Suggestion, Ex. I: 1. Have each student choose a new nationality and city of origin. Have other students try to guess them by asking: ¿Eres italiano? ¿Eres de Canadá? etc. 2. Use a world map and point to various countries while saying a name or names. For example, you point to Spain and say: María. Students respond: María es española.

Comentarios
culturales

Las lenguas de España

Spain is a country divided into seventeen autonomous communities **(comunidades autónomas):** Aragón, Andalucía, Castilla-La mancha, Cantabria, Castilla-León, Cataluña, Comunidad de Valencia, Comunidad de Madrid, Extremadura, Galicia, Islas Baleares, Islas Canarias, La Rioja, Navarra, País Vasco, Principado de Asturias, and Región de Murcia. This territorial division came into place after the restoration of democracy in Spain. The new Constitution, approved by referendum on December 6, 1978, establishes that along with the central government in the capital, Madrid, each community can have its own form of government.

As stated in the Spanish Constitution, the official language of the State is Castillian **(castellano)**. However, the constitution acknowledges that the Autonomous Communities have the right to their own languages. The languages that are officially recognized are **Euskera** in País Vasco and Navarra, **Gallego** in Galicia, **Catalán** in Cataluña and Islas Baleares, and **Valenciá** en la Comunidad Valenciana. All of these languages are taught in schools, and instruction in universities is offered both in Castilian and in the regional language.

If you go to a restaurant in Cataluña the menu may be either in Catalan or in Catalan and Spanish, as shown below.

Café Barcelona

Gambas al ajillo	Gambes a l'all
Tortilla de patatas	Truita de patates
Arroz al azafrán	Arros amb safrà
Pan con tomate	Pa amb tomàquet
Calamares	Calamars

INTEGRACIÓN CULTURAL

1. What are the names of the languages spoken in Spain?
2. What would you do if you go to a catalan restaurant and the menú is all in catalán?
3. Express your personal opinion of the information presented above. Compare the situation in Spain to the linguistic situation in the United States.

The verb **ser** plus an *adjective* is used to describe something or someone. In the conversation at the beginning of the *etapa*, we saw Carlos and Sara say the following:

| Carlos: | No me gusta. **Es muy picante.** |
| Sara: | El flan **es delicioso.** |

In Spanish, to ask what someone or something is like, you use **¿Cómo es... ?** or **¿Cómo son?**

¿Cómo es la tortilla?
Es muy rica y sabrosa.
Y **¿cómo es el pan con chorizo?**
Mmm... ¡exquisito!

Notice how **delicioso** ends in -o because it modifies **flan,** a masculine noun. Notice how **rica** ends in -a because it modifies **tortilla,** a feminine noun.

Remember that adjectives that end in **-e,** like **picante,** do not change the ending.

Suggestion, Ex. K: Pair students and have one describe a food from the vocabulary, using as many adjectives as possible (es delicioso, es sabroso...), while the other guesses what the food is.

GRAMMAR NOTE:
Remember, just like the adjectives of nationality that you saw on pages 36–37, adjectives in this exercise need to be in the plural to agree with the noun they modify. Notice how **picantes** ends in an -s to agree with **tacos.**

Preview: You will hear more about **ser + adjetivos** in chapter 2.

Práctica

J. ¿Cómo es? Complete the sentences according to your preferences in food.

■ **Modelo:** *El flan es delicioso.*

1. _____ riquísimo (a).
2. _____ rico (a).
3. _____ malo (a) *(bad)*.
4. _____ horrible.
5. _____ bueno (a).
6. _____ picante.

K. ¿Cómo son? Use the adjectives you have learned so far to describe the following foods.

■ **Modelo:** tacos con salsa

      Los tacos con salsa son muy picantes.

1. hamburguesas
2. pasteles
3. enchiladas de queso
4. batidos
5. croissants
6. cacahuetes
7. bocadillos de jamón
8. tacos de pollo

Play Textbook audio.

VAMOS A ESCUCHAR: EN UNA CANTINA MEXICANA

Carolina and her friends are at a Mexican restaurant.

ANTES DE ESCUCHAR

Brainstorm the vocabulary you might hear by answering the following questions.

1. What do people eat for lunch or dinner in Mexico?
2. What Mexican dishes would you order if you were in Guadalajara?

Before you listen to the dialog, look at the exercises in the *Después de escuchar* section.

DESPUÉS DE ESCUCHAR

L. Comprensión.

1. What time of the day does the conversation take place?
2. Does Verónica like beer?
3. Does Pepe order something to eat or drink?
4. Does Pepe like hot and spicy food?
5. What nationalities are mentioned?

M. ¿Cómo lo dicen? The instructor will play the tape again. Listen and see if you can determine the following.

1. How does Verónica say that she wants her lemonade very cold?
2. How does Pepe react to the food he tries?

Tú dirás ....

N. Una presentación. Question another student in order to introduce him or her to the class. Find out (1) his or her nationality, (2) where he or she is from, (3) what languages he or she speaks, (4) whether he or she likes to sing, dance, travel, etc., and (5) what kinds of food he or she eats. When you have finished, introduce the student to the class.

■ **Modelo:** *Quisiera presentarles a Clara. Ella es estadounidense. Es de El Paso, Texas, y habla inglés y un poco de español...*

Ñ. ¿Quién soy yo? Assume the identity of an international celebrity—actor or actress **(actor o actriz)**, political figure **(político[a])**, or author **(autor[a])**. Give a short description of yourself, your nationality, where you are from, and what you like to do, eat, etc. Your classmates will try to guess your identity. (Limit yourself as much as possible to words and structures you have studied in this first unit.)

Answers, Ex. L.
1. morning 2. no 3. no 4. yes 5. costarricense and español

Ask these questions in Spanish, using gestures, etc., to facilitate comprehension. Encourage students to answer in Spanish.

Answers, Ex. M
1. Bien fría. 2. ¡Qué picante!

Variation: Pair advanced with true beginners and have students reconstruct the role play they just listened to. Allow 6–7 minutes, then select a few groups to perform for the class.

Ex. N:  Pairs

Ex. Ñ:  Group
Variation, Ex. Ñ: Have students ask questions of the celebrities in an effort to guess their identities.

Have students write a description for homework. In class, place students in groups of 4. Allow 5–6 minutes for each to read descriptions and for others to guess. Have the group select the best one to be presented to the entire class for guessing. New adjectives that come up can be written on the board for vocabulary expansion.

⊚ INTEGRACIÓN

LECTURA: *El tapeo*

ANTES DE LEER

This text comments on the **tapas** that people eat in Sevilla during the **Feria**. This **Feria** takes place every year right after Holy Week. It was originally a market for livestock, and it is now a weeklong festivity during which people enjoy music and dance. There are many multicolored tents along the streets of the city, and you can see people dressed in Andalusian outfits and riding beautiful horses.

A. Before reading, do the following exercises.
1. Look at the map of Spain and locate Sevilla.
2. Look at the photos on page 42. What do they illustrate? (Remember the information you read in the *Comentarios culturales* on page 26.)
3. Look at the photos of different **tapas** on page 25 and read their names.
4. Look at the title, "**Tapeo**." What do you think this word refers to?
5. Here are a few cognates that appear in the first paragraph:
   origen   tabernas   preservar   insectos

When reading in a foreign language, it is very helpful to be able to anticipate the content of what you are about to read. You can anticipate the content of a text by following several steps before reading.

1. Look at the photos and illustrations that accompany a reading. What themes do the images suggest?
2. Read the titles and subtitles. What do the titles suggest the content of the reading will be?
3. Identify cognates.
4. Answer specific pre-reading questions.

The purpose of this reading is not for you to understand all the words that appear in the text. By focusing on the words you've learned in this chapter, and by recognizing cognates, you will be able to answer the questions below.

B. Read the whole paragraph and identify all the cognates you can find. Remember, some cognates are very clear **(origen),** but others may not be so at first glance **(sofisticando/**sophisticating). Now identify other cognates in the rest of the reading. Before reading the text, read the questions that appear in the *Guía para la lectura.*

GUÍA PARA LA LECTURA

C. According to the first paragraph, how has the meaning of **tapa** changed with the passing of time?

D. The last paragraph lists several **tapas** that people eat in Sevilla. Which one of the **tapas** included in this paragraph was mentioned in the chapter?

E. According to the text, which one of the **tapas** mentioned is the most representative of Sevilla?

▶ El tapeo

La "tapa" tiene su origen en un trozo de pan o embutido que antiguamente en las tabernas se colocaba sobre el jarro de vino para preservarlo de los insectos y el polvo de los caminos. Con el paso del tiempo esta "tapa" se fue sofisticando hasta convertirse en ingrediente esencial de cualquier reunión en torno a un vaso de vino o una caña de cerveza.

En toda Andalucía se practica el arte del buen tapeo y cada provincia, cada ciudad o pueblo han ido aportando lo mejor de su cocina hasta componer una variada lista de tapas que Sevilla ha sabido recoger y hacer suyas convirtiéndose en uno de los templos del tapeo andaluz por excelencia.

En la feria son tapas típicas entre otras la "tortilla de papas", los "pimientos fritos", las "gambas a la plancha" y por excelencia, el "pescaíto frito" que engloba una gran variedad de pescados rebozados en harina y luego fritos en aceite de oliva.

VÍDEO CULTURAL: ¿Te gusta la comida mexicana?

F. Anticipación. ¿Te gusta la comida mexicana? Check off all the items you think might be Mexican food ingredients.

1. el arroz
2. los tomates
3. las cebollas
4. la tortilla española
5. el cilantro
6. un refresco
7. un bocadillo
8. los aguacates
9. la carne
10. la salsa verde

G. Preparación. Match the Spanish words and phrases with their English equivalents.

1. variedad muy grande
2. la farolada
3. comida de paso
4. huele riquísimo
5. doble ración

a. he's rich
b. double serving
c. it smells delicious
d. a wide variety
e. beef/pork with melted cheese on a corn tortilla
f. fast food

H. Participación. Take notes as you watch the video. Write down words and phrases that you think may be useful during class discussion or that you'll use later in the **Personalización** exercise.

I. Comprensión. Based on what you saw in this video lesson, choose the best answer.

Answers, Ex. I: 1. a 2. b 3. a

1. ¿Cuándo va la gente a la taquería normalmente?
   a. durante la semana
   b. durante el fin de semana
2. ¿Qué clase de trabajo hace el hombre del vídeo?
   a. Lava los platos.
   b. Es cocinero y cajero.
3. ¿Cómo se llama un plato típico de esta taquería?
   a. las faroladas
   b. la sopa de hongos

J. Personalización. Write a short dialog in which you go out for fast food. Describe the place and the food. Work in groups of two or three. Later, share your activity with the class.

▶ Intercambio: ¿Quién es quién?

In this activity, as with all the *Intercambio* activities, one student will be A and another will be B. Neither of you should have access to the other person's information.

In order to fill out the chart below, you have to share the information you have with your partner. To keep track of everything your partner says, you will want to have a piece of paper next to you so you can write down some notes.

Look at the map on the inside of the cover as you complete this activity.

Estudiante A

Your partner will begin by reading the first sentence. Listen carefully. If you don't understand all of what your partner says, you can use the following expression: **No entiendo, ¿puedes repetir?**

Once you understand what your partner has said, you start reading your first statement.

1. La persona que es de San José se llama Belén.
2. La comida favorita de la costarricense es la tortilla.
3. Paco es mexicano.
4. El de Guadalajara viaja mucho.
5. La venezolana lee mucho.
6. A Carlos le gusta mucho escuchar música clásica.

Nombre	Ciudad	Gustos	Nacionalidad	Comi

Estudiante B

You will begin by reading the first statement. Make sure your partner understands what you say. To double check, you can ask the following: **¿Comprendes?**

1. A la costarricense le gusta bailar.
2. Al mexicano le gustan las enchiladas.
3. Cristina no es ecuatoriana, es de Caracas.
4. La comida favorita de la venezolana son los tacos.
5. El ecuatoriano no se llama Paco.
6. El de Quito come pan con chorizo todos los días.

Nombre	Ciudad	Gustos	Nacionalidad	Comida

The *Vocabulario* consists of all new words and expressions presented in the chapter. When reviewing or studying for a test, you can cover up the English and go through the list to see if you know the meaning of each item.

Para expresar gustos   *Expressing likes*
(No) Me gusta...   *I (don't) like . . .*
(No) Te gusta...   *You (don't) like . . .*

Para comentar sobre la comida   *Commenting about food*
¡Es riquísimo(a)!   *It's delicious!*
¡Es delicioso(a)!   *It's delicious!*
¡Qué bueno(a)!   *Great!*
¡Qué comida más rica!   *What delicious food!*
¡Qué picante!   *How spicy!*
Para hablar en un restaurante   *Talking in a restaurant*
Aquí tienen.   *Here you are.*
Para mí...   *For me . . .*
¿Qué desea(n) comer?   *What do you want to eat?*
¿Qué desea(n) tomar?   *What do you want to drink?*
¿Qué van a pedir?   *What are you going to order?*
¡Un refresco, por favor!   *A soft drink, please!*
Vamos al café.   *Let's go to the café.*
Vamos a tomar algo.   *Let's drink something.*
Voy a comer...   *I'm going to eat . . .*
Yo quisiera...   *I would like . . .*
¿Y Ud.?   *And you?*

Temas y contextos   *Themes and contexts*
Bebidas   *Drinks*
una botella de agua mineral   *bottle of mineral water*
un café   *coffee*
un café con leche   *coffee with milk*
un chocolate   *chocolate*
una cerveza   *beer*
una granadina (con agua mineral)   *grenadine (with mineral water)*
un jugo de naranja   *orange juice*
un batido de banana / fresa / melocotón   *banana / strawberry / peach milkshake*
una limonada   *lemonade*
un refresco   *soft drink*
una soda   *soda*
una sangría   *wine and fruit drink*

un té   *tea*
un té con leche   *tea with milk*
un té con limón   *tea with lemon*
un vaso de agua (con limón)   *glass of water (with lemon)*
un vino tinto   *red wine*
un vino blanco   *white wine*

Tapas españolas   *Spanish snacks*
unas aceitunas   *olives*
unos cacahuetes   *peanuts*
unos calamares   *squid*
el chorizo   *sausage*
el pan   *bread*
unas patatas bravas   *cooked potatoes diced and served in spicy sauce*
el queso   *cheese*
una tortilla de patatas   *potato omelette*

Comidas   *Foods*
un bocadillo   *sandwich (French roll)*
un croissant   *croissant*
el desayuno   *breakfast*
una hamburguesa   *hamburger*
la mantequilla   *butter*
una medialuna   *croissant*
la mermelada   *jelly*
un pan dulce   *sweet roll*
un pan tostado   *toast*
un pastel de fresas   *strawberry pie*
una rebanada de pan   *slice of bread*
un sándwich de jamón y queso   *ham and cheese sandwich*

La comida mexicana   *Mexican food*
el arroz   *rice*
la carne   *meat*
el chile   *hot pepper*
una enchilada   *soft corn tortilla filled with cheese, meat, or chicken*
el flan   *caramel custard*
unos frijoles   *beans*
el pollo   *chicken*
la salsa   *sauce*
un taco   *taco*
una tortilla   *cornmeal pancake*

Las nacionalidades *Nationalities*

alemán (alemana) *German*
argentino(a) *Argentinian*
australiano(a) *Australian*
brasileño(a) *Brasilian*
boliviano(a) *Bolivian*
canadiense *Canadian*
colombiano(a) *Colombian*
costarricense *Costa Rican*
cubano(a) *Cuban*
chileno(a) *Chilean*
chino(a) *Chinese*
dominicano(a) *Dominican*
ecuatoriano(a) *Ecuadoran*
egipcio(a) *Egyptian*
español(a) *Spanish*
estadounidense *American, from the United States*
francés (francesa) *French*
guatemalteco(a) *Guatemalan*
hondureño(a) *Honduran*
indio(a); hindú (pl. hindúes) *Indian (East)*
inglés (inglesa) *English*
italiano(a) *Italian*
japonés (japonesa) *Japanese*
keniata *Kenyan*
mexicano(a) *Mexican*
nicaragüense *Nicaraguan*
nigeriano(a) *Nigerian*
panameño(a) *Panamanian*
paraguayo(a) *Paraguayan*
peruano(a) *Peruvian*
puertorriqueño(a) *Puerto Rican*
ruso(a) *Russian*
salvadoreño(a) *Salvadoran*
surafricano(a) *South African*
uruguayo(a) *Uruguayan*
venezolano(a) *Venezuelan*

Los países *Countries*

Alemania *Germany*
Argentina *Argentina*
Australia *Australia*
Bolivia *Bolivia*
Canadá *Canada*
Colombia *Colombia*
Costa Rica *Costa Rica*
Cuba *Cuba*
Chile *Chile*
China *China*
Ecuador *Ecuador*
Egipto *Egypt*
El Salvador *El Salvador*
España *Spain*
Estados Unidos *United States*
Francia *France*
Guatemala *Guatemala*
Honduras *Honduras*
India *India*
Inglaterra *England*
Italia *Italy*
Japón *Japan*
Kenya *Kenya*
México *Mexico*
Nicaragua *Nicaragua*
Nigeria *Nigeria*
Panamá *Panama*
Paraguay *Paraguay*
Perú *Peru*
Puerto Rico *Puerto Rico*
La República Domicana *Dominican Republic*
Rusia *Russia*
Suráfrica *South Africa*
Uruguay *Uruguay*
Venezuela *Venezuela*

Vocabulario general   General vocabulary

Adverbios *Adverbs*

a veces *sometimes*
bien *well*
después *after*
mal *poorly*
muchísimo *very much*

mucho *a lot*
muy *very*
poco *a little*
siempre *always*
todos los días *every day*

Pronombres *Pronouns*

yo *I*
tú *you (familiar)*
él *he*
ella *she*
ellos *they*

ellas *they (f.)*
usted (Ud.) *you (formal)*
ustedes (Uds.) *you (formal plural)*
nosotros(as) *we*
vosotros(as) *you (familiar plural)*

Sustantivos *Nouns*
un(a) camarero(a) *waiter (waitress)*
una merienda *snack*
un señor *Mr., sir*
una señora *Mrs., ma'am*
una señorita *Miss*
la música *music*
la música clásica *classical music*

Verbos *Verbs*
aprender *to learn*
bailar *to dance*
beber *to drink*
cantar *to sing*
comer *to eat*
comprender *to understand*
compartir *to share*
correr *to run*
desear *to want*
escribir *to write*
escuchar *to listen to*
estudiar *to study*
hablar *to speak, talk*

ser *to be*
leer *to read*
mirar *to look at, watch*
necesitar *to need*
practicar *to practice*
recibir *to receive*
tocar *to touch, play an instrument*
tomar *to take, drink*
trabajar *to work*
vender *to sell*
viajar *to travel*
vivir *to live*

Otras palabras y expresiones *Other words and expressions*
algo *something*
Allí está... *There is . . .*
Aquí hay otro(a)... *Here is another . . .*
¿Cómo lo dicen? *How do they say it?*
¿De dónde es (eres)? *Where are you from?*
ésta *this one*
éste *this*
Gracias. *Thank you.*
¿Hablas español? *Do you speak Spanish?*
mi amigo(a) *my friend*
¡Mira! *Look!*
Muchas gracias. *Thank you very much.*
pues *then*
¿Qué es? *What is it?*
¿Qué hacen? *What are they doing?*
¿Qué haces tú? *What are you doing?*
¿Quién? *Who?*
quisiera *(I, you, he, she) would like*
también *also*
tampoco *neither*
ser de *to be from*
van a... *they are going . . .*
¿verdad? / ¿no? *right?*

Definite/indefinite articles
el *the (m.)*   la *the (f.)*   los *the (m. pl.)*   las *the (f. pl.)*
un *a (m.)*   una *a (f.)*   unos *some (m. pl.)*   unas *some (f. pl.)*

2 Vamos a conocernos

PRIMERA ETAPA
¿De quién es?

SEGUNDA ETAPA
¿Qué te gusta?

TERCERA ETAPA
Mi familia

INTEGRACIÓN:
LECTURA: Mini retratos
VÍDEO CULTURAL: ¿De quién es?
INTERCAMBIO: Juan Carlos y Álvaro
ESCRITURA: Actividades en el manual

Federico Peña

1996

10%
Hispanic
(272,300,000)

US Population
(Total: 27,230,000)

% of
Hispanic
Population
Living
in USA

64.2%

14.5%

10.5%

4.8%

6.0%

Mexico | Central & South America | Puerto Rico | Cuba | Other (Spain, Caribbean, etc.)

Country of Origin

California

Texas

FLORIDA

New York

Gloria Estefan

CHAPTER OBJECTIVES:

In this chapter you will continue learning to express biographical information about such topics as what you like and do not like, your family, and descriptions of family members. In addition, you will learn to get this type of information from others. After completing this first chapter you will be able to carry out the following tasks:

- 🌀 **talk about your possessions**
- 🌀 **continue talking about your likes and dislikes**
- 🌀 **describe your family**
- 🌀 **read short descriptive texts about people**
- 🌀 **understand people talking about themselves and their families**

The tools you will use to carry out these tasks are:

- 🌀 **vocabulary for:**
  - personal possessions
  - expressing more about likes and dislikes
  - talking about your family
  - describing people
  - professions
- 🌀 **grammatical structures:**
  - the verb tener
  - numbers to 100
  - hay
  - the verb gustar + nouns
  - possessive adjectives
  - possession with de
  - ser + adjectives
  - ser + nouns
  - yes/no and information questions

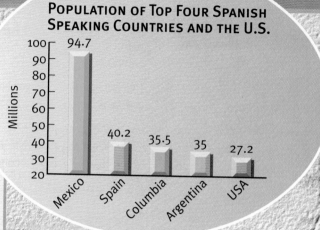

POPULATION OF TOP FOUR SPANISH SPEAKING COUNTRIES AND THE U.S.

Mexico 94.7, Spain 40.2, Columbia 35.5, Argentina 35, USA 27.2 (Millions)

Did you know?

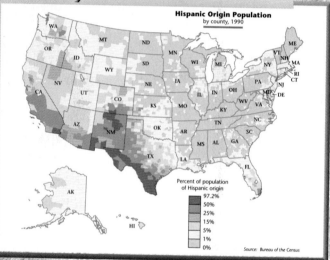

Hispanic Origin Population
by county, 1990

Percent of population
of Hispanic origin
97.2%
50%
25%
15%
5%
1%
0%

Source: Bureau of the Census

1528 Ponce de León explores Florida

1565 San Augustine, Florida founded by Pedro Menéndez Avilés

1598 San Gabriel, New Mexico founded by Juan de Oñate

1610 Sante Fe founded (oldest state capital)

PARA EMPEZAR: ¿De quién es?

Using the *Preparación* suggestions, brainstorm with students the vocabulary related to different possessions.

Preparación: As you begin this *etapa,* answer the following questions:

- Where do you live?
- What do you have in your dorm room, apartment, house, etc.?
- How do you get around town?

Transparency C-1: La casa, el transporte

Suggestion: Using the transparency of houses and possessions, begin each vocabulary group by talking about yourself. Yo vivo en una casa, ¿y tú? ¿Quién vive en un apartamento? En nuestra casa, hay un estéreo, pero no hay un televisor. ¿Y en tu casa?

¿Dónde vives?

Vivo en...

una casa   una residencia estudiantil   un apartamento

¿Qué hay en tu casa?

There   **Allí hay...**

un estéreo   un vídeo   un televisor

For false beginners: ask these questions in Spanish (¿Qué hay en tu habitación?...) and have students list as many items in Spanish as they can remember. After working with vocabulary in this section, have students mention those items that they remember but that aren't mentioned in the text. Write these words on the board for all students to share.

To help activate this vocabulary outside the classroom, encourage students to try to think of the Spanish name of these items whenever they see them.

¿Cómo vas al centro?

Para ir al centro voy...

a pie   en autobús   en coche   en bicicleta   en motocicleta

¿Qué hay en tu cuarto?

Me llamo Marta.
En mi cuarto hay...

In my room there is/are . . .

unos libros
una almohada
un estéreo
una cómoda
una lámpara
discos compactos
un ropero/clóset
una computadora
una ventana
un póster
una planta
una cama
una alfombra
un sillón
la pantalla
una silla
el teclado
el ratón
un escritorio

VOCABULARY EXPANSION:
In Spain, the word for a computer is **un ordenador.**

Suggestion: To present vocabulary items in a meaningful context, make up a humorous story using these terms. For example: Mi hermano es un estudiante en la universidad. Vive con sus amigos pero tiene su propio cuarto. Su cuarto es un desastre. Tiene muchas cosas, por ejemplo, tiene libros, tiene una grabadora y muchos discos compactos y tiene mucha ropa, y todas estas cosas siempre están en el suelo. Mi hermano tiene un ropero, pero la ropa siempre está en la alfombra... Use transparency to point out vocabulary items, or write key vocabulary words on the board as you use them. Ask yes/no or simple-answer questions throughout the story to check comprehension.

¿Qué llevas a la universidad?

un cuaderno
un borrador
unos libros
una mochila
un lápiz
un sacapuntas
un bolígrafo
una llave
una calculadora
una cartera
un portafolio

VOCABULARY EXPANSION:
Other words for poster are **afiche** and **cartel.** The word for drawer is **gaveta** or **cajón.**

Práctica

A. ¿Qué es? Identify the objects in the numbered photos.

◼ **Modelo:** *Es un lápiz.*

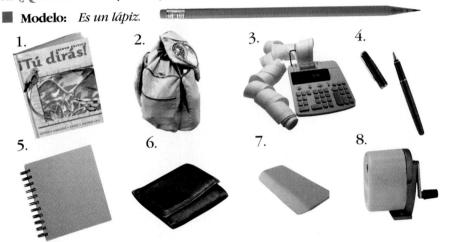

B. María, Antonio y Cristina. On the basis of the drawings, complete each person's description of where he or she lives.

1. Me llamo María González. Vivo en… Allí hay…, pero no hay… Para ir al centro voy en…

2. Me llamo Antonio Martínez. Vivo en… Allí hay… y… Para ir al centro voy en…

3. Me llamo Cristina Sánchez. Vivo en… Allí hay… pero no hay… Para ir al centro voy en…

C. Me llamo… vivo en… allí hay… pero no hay… Para ir al centro voy… Now, complete this exercise with your own information and share it with two of your classmates.

Ex. B: Pair higher level learners with lower level learners. With their books closed, have the lower level learners draw a sketch of their room and the higher level students label the items in the room. Allow about 10 minutes for this activity and then have pairs swap drawings to compare and to check accuracy of vocabulary. Finally, ask students to share new vocabulary they may have learned while working with their partners. This activity can also be done as a type of information gap activity, where while visually separated, one student can name, in Spanish, the items in his or her room or house. The other student sketches these items. When done, the pair can check for accuracy.

Possible answers, Ex. B
1. …una casa. …unas plantas, un televisor (a colores) y un sillón (una ventana) …un estéreo (un vídeo). …un coche.
2. …un apartamento (un condominio). … una lámpara, un vídeo, un estéreo. …una motocicleta.
3. …una casa. …una computadora y una grabadora. …un televisor (un vídeo, un estéreo). … una bicicleta.

Preview: Hay is presented here only lexically. It will be formally introduced on p. 56.

Variation, Ex. B: Have students ask each other questions.

IRM Master 6: El verbo *tener*

Suggestions, tener: A. Have students repeat conjugations while you write the following pronouns on the board: yo, tú, él, ella, Ud., nosotros, nosotras, ellos, ellas, Uds. B. Repeat, using the negative forms. C. Put written forms on the board. D. Go around the room asking if specific students have certain things. For example: ¿Tiene Robert un cuaderno? ¿Tiene Susan una calculadora?

Ex. D: Personalize this activity by following up each question with one directed toward students, i.e., ¿Tienes tú una motocicleta? ¿Quiénes tienen pósters en el cuarto? ¿De quiénes son? … ¿Madonna? ¿Michael Jordan? …

ENFOQUE ESTRUCTURAL | **El verbo tener**

In Spanish the verb **tener** can be used to talk about possessions.

Yo tengo dos hermanas.	*I have two sisters.*
¿Tienes tú un hermano?	*Do you have a brother?*
Nosotros tenemos dos gatos.	*We have two cats.*
Ellos no tienen un perro.	*They don't have a dog.*
Él tiene un abuelo en Miami.	*He has a grandfather in Miami.*

Here is how the verb **tener** (*to have*) is conjugated:

tener (ie)

yo	**tengo**	nosotros(as)	**tenemos**
tú	**tienes**	vosotros(as)	**tenéis**
Ud.		Uds.	
él	**tiene**	ellos	**tienen**
ella		ellas	

Práctica

D. No tengo…, pero tengo… Each time you ask about someone's possessions, you learn that he or she does not have the object you mention, but has something else instead.

■ **Modelo:** Felipe / computadora / calculadora
—*¿Tiene Felipe una computadora?*
—*No, no tiene una computadora pero tiene una calculadora.*

1. Natalia / motocicleta / bicicleta
2. tú / bolígrafo / lápiz
3. Mónica y Diego / casa / apartamento
4. Uds. / radio despertador / estéreo
5. tú / estéreo / televisor
6. Mía / discos compactos / cintas
7. Leonardo / portafolio / mochila

E. ¿Qué tienen? Look at the drawings below and tell what Ana and Esteban have and don't have. Follow the model.

◼ **Modelo:** *Ana tiene una cámara.*
Ana no tiene un portafolio.

◼ **Modelo:** *Esteban tiene un portafolio.*
Esteban no tiene una cámara.

F. ¿Qué tiene tu compañero(a)? Take some of the items you brought to class out of your backpack, briefcase, etc., and put them on your desk. Have a classmate say what you have on your desk. Then, reverse roles.

ENFOQUE LÉXICO

Los números de 0 a 100

The Spanish equivalent of number *one* agrees with the noun it introduces: **un libro, una limonada.** *Zero* and the numbers from *two* on always stay the same.

cero	0	siete	7	catorce	14
uno	1	ocho	8	quince	15
dos	2	nueve	9	dieciséis	16
tres	3	diez	10	diecisiete	17
cuatro	4	once	11	dieciocho	18
cinco	5	doce	12	diecinueve	19
seis	6	trece	13	veinte	20

The numbers 21–29 may be written as one word or three words. For example, 23 can be written as **veintitrés** or **veinte y tres.**

20	veinte	30	treinta
21	veintiuno	31	treinta y uno
22	veintidós	32	treinta y dos
23	veintitrés	40	cuarenta
24	veinticuatro	50	cincuenta
25	veinticinco	60	sesenta
26	veintiséis	70	setenta
27	veintisiete	80	ochenta
28	veintiocho	90	noventa
29	veintinueve	100	cien

Práctica

G. ¡Vamos a calcular! Do the following arithmetic problems.

■ **Modelo:** $2 + 2$

¿Cuántos son (How much is) dos y dos?
Dos y dos son cuatro.

1. $3 + 6$
2. $11 + 4$
3. $28 + 33$
4. $8 + 12$
5. $25 + 35$
6. $45 + 42$
7. $27 + 39$
8. $32 + 17$
9. $51 + 22$
10. $65 + 27$

■ **Modelo:** 3×20

¿Cuántos son tres por veinte?
Tres por veinte son 60.

11. 45×2
12. 32×3
13. 15×5
14. 33×3
15. 42×2
16. 22×4
17. 36×2
18. 27×3
19. 49×2

Suggestion, Ex. G.: To help students activate number vocabulary, play a few short games of bingo with the class.

Comentarios
culturales *El número de teléfono*

Many Latinos living in the USA still have relatives living in Spanish-speaking countries. In some of the larger cities of the Spanish-speaking world—such as Madrid and Mexico City—the telephone numbers have seven digits, for example, 2-12-16-46. This number would be read: **dos, doce, dieciséis, cuarenta y seis.** In other cities (e.g., Guadalajara, Mexico; Salamanca, Spain;

Suggestion, Comentarios: Point out that this system for reciting phone numbers can be heard on Spanish radio and television commercials in the USA; however, it is also possible to hear commercials reciting telephone numbers using the U.S. system. As a homework assignment ask students to listen to Spanish TV or radio commercials and note the phone numbers and the system used to recite them.

Dictate several phone numbers of six or seven digits to the students. Call on individual students to read them back to you.

Buenos Aires, Argentina) telephone numbers have only six digits, and a number like 22-28-70 would be read: **veintidós, veintiocho, setenta**. All of these countries also have an international code (**código internacional**) that must be dialed before the six- or seven-digit number.

Below are the Spanish-speaking countries with their codes:

Argentina	54	Honduras	50 + 4
Bolivia	59 + 1	México	52
Chile	56	Nicaragua	50 + 5
Colombia	57	Panamá	50 + 7
Costa Rica	50 + 6	Paraguay	59 + 5
Ecuador	59 + 3	Perú	51
El Salvador	50 + 3	Uruguay	59 + 8
España	34	Venezuela	58
Guatemala	50 + 2		

INTEGRACIÓN CULTURAL

1. What would your phone number be if we used the same system that is used in the Spanish-speaking world?
2. Work with a partner and ask each other what the codes are for the various countries.

■ **Modelo:** *¿Cuál es el código para México?*
Cincuenta y dos.
¿Cuál es el código para Nicaragua?
Cinco cero cinco.

Suggestions: A. Using some of the terms for school supplies learned in **Etapa 1**, ask students ¿Qué hay sobre la mesa? ¿Hay libros? ¿Hay un bolígrafo? B. Ask students to point out some objects around the room.

Note we are introducing hay here only lexically. There is no need to introduce hay as a form of the verb haber yet. Simply point out to the students that it means *there is* or *there are*.

ENFOQUE LÉXICO   **Hay + noun**

Hay un libro en mi cuarto.	***There is*** *a book in my room.*
Hay tres libros en mi cuarto.	***There are*** *three books in my room.*

You have already seen and used the word **hay** in this etapa. **Hay** means either *there is* or *there are*. It is used with nouns that are preceded by an indefinite article or by any number.

H. ¿Tienes el número de ... ?

Your friend from Chile is spending the semester here. He is organizing a party and wants to call several people. He doesn't have the numbers, but you do. Give them to him when he asks.

■ **Modelo:** Lizzy / 8-25-03-12
¿Tienes el número de Lizzy?
Sí, es el ocho, veinticinco, cero, tres, doce.

1. Julie / 2-33-94-47   4. Stephanie / 6-57-10-68
2. Jack / 5-38-25-62   5. Andy / 3-69-43-77
3. Sheri / 4-15-51-00   6. Suzi / 8-82-06-93

I. ¿Cuál es tu número de teléfono?

Ask several of your classmates what their telephone number is using the question: **¿Cuál es tu número de teléfono?** Have them answer with the phrase **Mi número de teléfono es...** and using the system common in Spanish-speaking countries.

Ex. I: Pairs

J. El cuarto de Mario.

First, indicate whether each item is or is not found in the room pictured below.

■ **Modelo:** unos discos compactos
Hay unos discos compactos.
una grabadora
No hay una grabadora.

1. unos pósters
2. unas sillas
3. unas cintas
4. una computadora
5. un televisor
6. un estéreo
7. unos libros
8. unos lápices
9. unos bolígrafos
10. un escritorio
11. unas plantas
12. una máquina de scribir
13. unos estantes
14. unos cuadernos

K. Hay… Now, point out to another student those items that are in the room on page 57.

■ **Modelo:** *Hay una cama allí* (there).

L. ¿Y tú? Indicate what you have and do not have in your room at home.

■ **Modelo:** *En mi cuarto, hay una cama y una cómoda, pero no hay un escritorio. También hay pósters en la pared* (on the wall).

🎧 Play Textbook audio.

Isabel and Miguel are providing information about themselves. Listen to their brief monologues and complete the following exercises.

ANTES DE ESCUCHAR

Based on what you've learned in this *etapa*, what information do you think Isabel and Miguel will give about:

1. where they live
2. what they have in their rooms at home
3. how they get to the university

Have students close their books and ask them to answer these questions in Spanish. Write student suggestions on the board to compare after they listen to the tape.

M. Comprensión. Before your instructor plays the tape, take a moment and look at the chart below. While you listen, write down who has what on a separate sheet of paper.

Answers, Ex. M
Miguel vive en una casa. Tiene un estéreo, un escritorio, una máquina de escribir, una cama y una silla. Isabel vive en un apartamento. Tiene unos pósters, una cómoda, una computadora, un televisor.

Suggestion, Ex. M
Ask students these questions in Spanish. **¿Cómo va Miguel a la universidad? ¿Por qué no tiene Isabel un estante?** Encourage students to answer in Spanish. You may also ask students if they are more similar to Miguel or to Isabel, and why.

	Miguel	Isabel
vive en		
una casa		
un apartamento		
tiene		
un escritorio		
un vídeo		
una cómoda		
unas plantas		
máquina de escribir		
unos pósters		
una calculadora		
una silla		

DESPUÉS DE ESCUCHAR

N. ¿Cómo lo dicen? Your instructor will play the tape again. Listen to try to determine the following.

1. How does Miguel say he gets to class?
2. How does Isabel say that she doesn't have bookshelves?

Answers, Ex. N
1. Para ir a clase voy en bicicleta.
2. No tengo estantes...

Tú dirás

Ñ. Mi vida ... Prepare your own personal picture strip story like the ones on pages 52 and 53 in which you describe your home, apartment, or dorm room, and what you have there (some of the things you don't have there) in some detail. Also indicate how you get to the university, downtown, etc.

Ex. Ñ:  Pairs

Now, work with a classmate and

1. each of you describe your own home, apartment, or dorm room, and how you get around town.
2. point out something your partner has that you don't have.
3. point out something your partner has that you have, too.

Now prepare a short report in which you share with the class what you and your partner have in common and some of the things you don't have in common.

O. ¿Tienes un ... en tu casa? Work with a partner and take turns asking each other specific questions about what you have in your room, apartment, or home. Take notes as you try to get as exhaustive a list as possible from each other. The instructor will then conduct a poll to determine which students have what. Begin by asking: **¿Tienes un estéreo?** and continue using the vocabulary presented at the beginning of the chapter.

Ex. O:  Pairs

SEGUNDA ETAPA

PARA EMPEZAR: ¿Qué te gusta?

Preparación: As you get ready to begin working on this *etapa*, answer the following questions:

- **What are some of the things you like and dislike?**
- **Do they include sports?**
- **What sports?**

Use Spanish to prepare students for the new vocabulary and forms in this *etapa*. Tell students: **Ahora vamos a hablar de los gustos personales.** Write the word **gustos** on the board. Continue: **A mí me gustan muchas cosas. Me gusta la música, especialmente la música rock.** Write key words on board and then pose comprehension check questions to students.

For advanced beginners, ask more open-ended comprehension check questions.

Play Textbook audio.

| **José:** | No me gusta la música. | **Mía:** | Me gustan los animales. |
| **Ana:** | Me gusta la música. | **Lucía:** | No me gustan los animales. |

Introduce the new vocabulary by using transparencies and the Audio Program with students' books closed. Read the text to them as they look at the transparencies. Ask questions such as: **¿A quién le gusta la música?** or: **¿A quién no le gusta la música?** Students answer by giving the name of the person who likes or does not like what you're asking. You could also read certain statements made by the various people in these drawings and ask students to identify who said it. For example, you read: **Me gusta la música** and you would expect the students to say: **Ana** or read: **No me gustan los deportes** and expect the students to say: **Olga.**

To engage students in the topic and present this structure and the vocabulary in context, make up a story about likes and dislikes. For example: **Mi familia es única porque cada persona en mi familia es totalmente diferente. A mi mamá le gusta el arte, pero a mi papá no. Mamá siempre va a los museos de arte, pero mi papá dice, No me gusta el arte, no voy al museo... A mí me gusta... pero a mi hermano no le gusta...** Ask comprehension questions throughout. Also, ask students if they also like some of the things you discuss.

Juan: Me gustan los deportes.
Olga: No me gustan los deportes.

Lucas: Me gusta la naturaleza.
María: No me gusta la naturaleza.

Jaime: No me gusta el arte.
Julia: Me gusta el arte.

Esteban: Me gustan las lenguas.
Roberto: No me gustan las lenguas.

chemistry

Enrique: No me gustan las ciencias… no me gusta la **química.**
Laura: Me gustan las ciencias… me gusta la química.

Marta: No me gusta la biología.
Anita: Me gusta la biología.

Suggestion: Read the statements about the people and then have students answer the questions. **¿Qué te gustan más, las películas de horror o las películas de aventuras?**

Note: Most new vocabulary words are not glossed because they are cognates.

Suggestion: You may explain that accents over capital vowels are optional, and that they will be used in class for reinforcement and practice.

Lourdes: Me gustan las películas.

Juan: ¿Qué películas te gustan más—las cómicas, las de horror, las de aventura o las de ciencia ficción?

Lourdes: Me gustan más las películas de horror.

Marta: Me gusta mucho la música.

Pablo: ¿Qué te gusta más —la música rock, el jazz o la música clásica?

Marta: Me gusta más la música rock.

Susana: Me gusta el arte.

Paco: ¿Qué te gusta más —la pintura o la escultura?

Susana: Me gusta más la escultura.

Point out the difference between American football and soccer.

Ángela: Me gustan los animales.

Raúl: ¿Qué animales te gustan más —los **perros,** los **gatos** o los **pájaros?**

Ángela: Me gustan más los pájaros.

Miguel: Me gustan los deportes.

Alán: ¿Qué te gusta más —el **fútbol,** el fútbol americano, el básquetbol, el béisbol o el vólibol?

Miguel: Me gusta más el béisbol.

dogs / cats / soccer
birds

Práctica

A. Me gustan los deportes, pero no me gusta la política.
You and your friends are talking about what you like and dislike. In each case, say that the person indicated likes the first activity or item but dislikes the second.

Modelo: me / deportes / política
Me gustan los deportes, pero no me gusta la política.

1. me / naturaleza / animales
2. te / música / arte
3. me / lenguas / literatura
4. me / lenguas / ciencias
5. te / política / matemáticas
6. te / música / deportes

B. ¿Qué te gusta más?
Of the following items, indicate which one you like more.

Modelo: el fútbol o el básquetbol
—¿Te gusta más el fútbol o el básquetbol?
—Me gusta más el básquetbol.

1. el fútbol americano o el béisbol
2. los perros o los gatos
3. la pintura o la escultura
4. las películas de ciencia ficción o las películas cómicas
5. la música clásica o la música rock
6. la biología o la química
7. las lenguas o las matemáticas
8. la historia o el español

C. Me gusta... no me gusta...
Using the vocabulary in this first part of the *etapa*, make a list of five things you like and five things you don't like. Compare it with two of your classmates' lists, and see if you have any likes and dislikes in common.

Repaso

D. Las posesiones de Julián.
Look at the drawing. Work with a partner to list as much information as you can about Julian's possessions.

Modelo: *En el cuarto de Julián hay..., pero no hay...*

E. Los delegados. At a reception being held as part of an international student congress, point out some of the delegates, indicate their nationalities, and tell what cities they are from.

■ **Modelo:** Justo Alarcón / Guadalajara, México
Allí está Justo. Él es mexicano.
Es de Guadalajara.

1. Michael Schnepf / Munich, Alemania
2. Pietro Canevalli y Gian Lanza / Roma, Italia
3. Sheryl Peet y Blanche Lowe / Manchester, Inglaterra
4. Salvador Oropesa y Nancy Landale / San Diego, California
5. Javier Herrera / Monterrey, México
6. Tashi Yokoshura (f.) / Tokio, Japón
7. Barbara Ashbrook y Elizabeth Welles / Ginebra, Suiza
8. Ivan Medchenko / Moscú, Rusia

Ex. E: Group of 3

Put students in groups of three. Have them take turns with one being the delegado, another being the presenter, and the third, the presentee. The presenter will introduce using the target structure. When doing the introduction the presenter will also tell the presentee something that the delegado likes or dislikes as a conversation starter. Presentee should respond appropriately and politely, also stating whether or not he/she likes or dislikes the same thing. Encourage students to carry on short conversations.

ENFOQUE ESTRUCTURAL · Gustar + cosas

El verbo gustar

In Chapter 1 you learned to use the verb **gustar** with other verbs to talk about the activities you like and don't like to do. **Gustar** can also be used to talk about things that you like and dislike.

Me gusta el disco compacto.	*I like the CD.*
Te gusta la cinta.	*You like the tape.*
Me gustan las cintas.	*I like the tapes.*
Te gustan los discos compactos.	*You like the CDs.*
A María le gusta el arte.	*Maria likes art.*
A Juan le gusta la música.	*John likes music.*
Nos gusta la ciencia.	*We like science.*
A ellos les gusta el cine.	*They like the movies.*

With **gustar** you use the pronouns **me, te, nos, le,** and **les,** and only the two forms of **gustar** are used: **gusta** and **gustan.** Use **gusta** if what is liked is singular and **gustan** if what is liked is plural.

Note that to clarify **le,** you use the preposition **a** plus the person, and to clarify **les** you use the preposition **a** plus the persons.

A Miguel le gustan los discos compactos.	*Michael likes CDs.*
A Juan y a María les gusta la clase.	*John and Maria like the class.*
A Uds. les gusta la música.	*You like music.*

IRM Master 7: El verbo *gustar*

Point out to students that while English doesn't have the verb "to gust," it has a similar construction with the verb "disgust," where we say "that food disgusts me" and "those foods disgust me."

Note: Literally, gustar means *to please* (or *to be pleasing*) and functions like that verb in English.

Práctica

Answers, Ex. F
1. (No) Me gusta el arte. 2. (No)
gusta la química. 3. (No) Me gusta la
naturaleza. 4. (No) Me gustan los
animales. 5. (No) Me gustan las
lenguas. 6. (No) Me gustan los
deportes.

Ex. F: Have students take notes as
each student gives his/her response.
Then follow up by asking true/false
questions.

F. ¡(No) Me gusta! Indicate how you feel about each activity pictured below.

■ **Modelo:** *Me gusta la música.*
o
No me gusta la música.

1.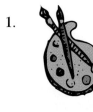

2.

3.

4.

5.

6.

Ex. G:  **Pairs**
Have students work in pairs and note
what their partner likes and dislikes.
Bring the class together and ask for
volunteers to report their findings.

Ex. G: Variation: Divide the class
into small groups. Have each
group create ten questions using **gustar.**
Use the questions for oral practice or
create a worksheet to be done as a
written exercise.

Ex. H:  **Pairs**
Encourage students to practice as
much Spanish as possible and to
extend the conversation as much as
possible.

Variation, Ex. H:
You may wish to have each student
ask a number of questions about the
likes and dislikes of the others.

G. ¿Te gusta… ? Ask a classmate whether he or she likes the activities in the
previous exercise and then report to the class.

■ **Modelo:**   —*¿Te gusta la música?*
—*No, no me gusta la música.*
Then report: *A Joe no le gusta la música.*

H. Me llamo… Imagine this is your first day at El Festival de las Américas in
Miami where the common language is Spanish. Go up to another student and
introduce yourself. Tell him or her where you are from. Then try to give the other
person an idea about what you like and dislike.

■ **Modelo:** *Me llamo Elizabeth. Soy de los Estados Unidos. Vivo en Rochester.
Me gusta comer, recibir cartas y correr. ¡Y me gusta muchísimo la
música rock!*

Comentarios

culturales

La presencia hispana en Norte América

*T*he Hispanic presence in what is now the USA dates back to 1528 when Ponce de León searched for the mythological Fountain of Youth in what is now Florida. Hernando de Soto explored much of what is today the states of Florida, Georgia, North and South Carolina, Alabama, Mississippi, Arkansas, and Louisiana (1539–43) and was among the first Europeans to see the Mississippi River. Francisco de Coronado explored what is now New Mexico, parts of Arizona, Oklahoma, Texas, and Kansas (1540–42), and his men were the first Europeans to see the Grand Canyon. Juan Rodríguez Cabrillo explored the Pacific Coast of what is today Baja California and California and discovered the San Diego and Mendocino bays in 1540. Pedro Menéndez Avilés founded the colony of San Agustín, near what is present-day Jacksonville, Florida, in 1565. Juan de Oñate founded the colony of San Gabriel, about 20 miles north of what is today Santa Fe, New Mexico, in 1598.

The imprint that was left by Spain's exploration and colonization can be seen in the names of some states (California, Montana, Nevada, New Mexico, Florida, Colorado), mountains (Sangre de Cristo, Sandía, Sierra Nevada), rivers (Río Grande, Río Nueces, Río Colorado), cities (Albuquerque, Amarillo, San Antonio, Boca Ratón, San Francisco, Durango), towns and villages (Velarde, Embudo, Truchas), streets (Alameda, Camino Encantado, Potrero, Rodeo), etc.

INTEGRACIÓN CULTURAL

1. When did the Pilgrims arrive at Plymouth Rock?
2. When did John Smith found Jamestown?
3. Compare these dates with those of the first colonies founded by the Spaniards in what is today the USA.
4. If Spanish has been spoken in parts of New Mexico since Oñate founded San Gabriel, how long has it been spoken there?

Answers, Integración:
1. The Pilgrims arrived at Plymouth Rock in 1620.
2. Jamestown was founded in 1607.
3. San Agustín was founded 55 years before the Pilgrims arrived and 42 years before Jamestown was founded.
   San Gabriel was founded 22 years before the Pilgrims arrived and 9 years before Jamestown was founded.
4. 400 years

ENFOQUE ESTRUCTURAL — Los posesivos

Think about how you use words such as my, your, his, her, our, their to express possession. Spanish uses similar words, which are called possessive adjectives. Look at the sentences below.

¿Necesitas **tu** libro?	*Do you need **your** book?*
Sí, necesito **mi** libro.	*Yes, I need **my** book.*
¿Dónde está **su** (Uds.) cuarto?	*Where is **your** room?*
Allí está **nuestro** cuarto.	*There is **our** room.*
¿Dónde están **mis** llaves?	*Where are **my** keys?*
Allí están **tus** llaves.	*There are **your** keys.*

Possessive adjectives must agree in number with the noun they modify. **Nuestro/a** and **vuestro/a** must also agree in gender with the noun they modify. Consequently, Spanish has two forms of *my* and *your* and four forms of *our* and *your* plural. The following chart summarizes the possessive adjectives:

SUJETO	MASC. SINGULAR	FEM. SINGULAR	MASC. PLURAL	FEM. PLURAL	INGLÉS
yo	**mi**	**mi**	**mis**	**mis**	*my*
tú	**tu**	**tu**	**tus**	**tus**	*your*
él, ella, usted	**su**	**su**	**sus**	**sus**	*his, her, your*
nosotros(as)	**nuestro**	**nuestra**	**nuestros**	**nuestras**	*our*
vosotros(as)	**vuestro**	**vuestra**	**vuestros**	**vuestras**	*your*
ellos, ellas, ustedes	**su**	**su**	**sus**	**sus**	*their, your*

The third-person singular possessive adjective is **su.** The plural form is **sus.** They have several equivalents in English.

> **su / sus** = *his, her, its, your (formal), and their*

¿Es la bicicleta de Vicente?	*Is it Vincent's bike?*
Sí, es **su** bicicleta.	*Yes, it's **his** bike.*
¿Son ellos los amigos de **tu** hermana?	*Are they **your** sister's friends?*
Sí, son **sus** amigos.	*Yes, they are **her** friends.*

In order to clarify meaning, sometimes the phrases **de él, de ella, de Ud., de Uds., de ellos,** and **de ellas** are used in place of the possessive adjective.

¿Es **su** coche?	*Is it **his** car?*
Sí, es el coche **de él.**	*Yes, it's **his** car.*

Práctica

I. ¡Qué confusión!
Your neighbors are confused about what belongs to them and what belongs to your family.

■ **Modelo:** —*¿Es nuestro coche?*
—*No, no es su coche. Es nuestro coche.*

1. ¿Es nuestro televisor a colores?
2. ¿Es nuestro radio despertador?
3. ¿Es nuestra cámara?
4. ¿Es nuestra computadora?

■ **Modelo:** —*¿Son nuestras plantas?*
—*No, no son sus plantas. Son nuestras plantas.*

5. ¿Son nuestros discos compactos?
6. ¿Son nuestras bicicletas?
7. ¿Son nuestras llaves?
8. ¿Son nuestras cintas?

J. No, no. No es mi libro.
Now you're confused! When you point out the following items and ask a classmate if they belong to him or her, your classmate responds negatively.

■ **Modelo:** —*¿Es tu cámara?*
—*No, no es mi cámara.*

—*¿Son tus plantas?*
—*No, no son mis plantas. Son tus plantas.*

1.

2.

3.

4.

5.

6.

7.

8.

9.

De y ser + de para expresar posesión

De *para expresar posesión*

While in English you use the apostrophe to express possession, you never use it in Spanish. Note the use of **de** in the sentences below.

el libro **de Juan**	**John's** book
los cuadernos **de Marta**	**Martha's** notebooks
la calculadora **de Ana**	**Ann's** calculator
las llaves de **Jorge**	**George's** keys

Spanish uses the preposition **de** to show possession. Notice that Spanish shows possession by changing the word order, not by using an apostrophe with the person's name, as in English.

Ser + de *para expresar posesión*

You can use the verb **ser** with **de** and a noun or a pronoun to show possession.

El libro es **de Juan.**	*The book is **John's.***
La calculadora es **de María.**	*The calculator is **Mary's.***
Los lápices son **de él.**	*The pencils are **his.***
Las mochilas son **de ellos.**	*The knapsacks are **theirs.***

To ask to whom something belongs, you would use **¿De quién es... ?** if there is one item and **¿De quién son... ?** if there is more than one item, as in the examples:

¿De quién es el libro?	***Whose** book **is it?***
¿De quién son los libros?	***Whose** books **are they?***

Práctica

K. El libro es de... Look at the drawings and indicate to whom the items belong. Follow the model.

■ **Modelo:** *El cuaderno es de José.*
    Los libros son de Bárbara.

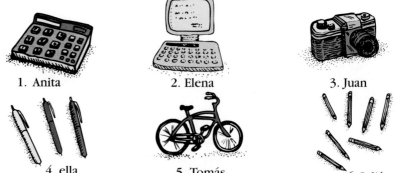

1. Anita 2. Elena 3. Juan

4. ella 5. Tomás 6. Julián

7. él   8. Carmen   9. Alicia y Susana   10. ellos

L. ¿De quién es? Indicate to whom each of the following items belongs, using **ser + de.**

■ **Modelo:**   —*¿De quién es la mochila?*
          —*La mochila es de María.*
          —*¿De quién son los cuadernos?*
          —*Los cuadernos son de José.*

      María   José

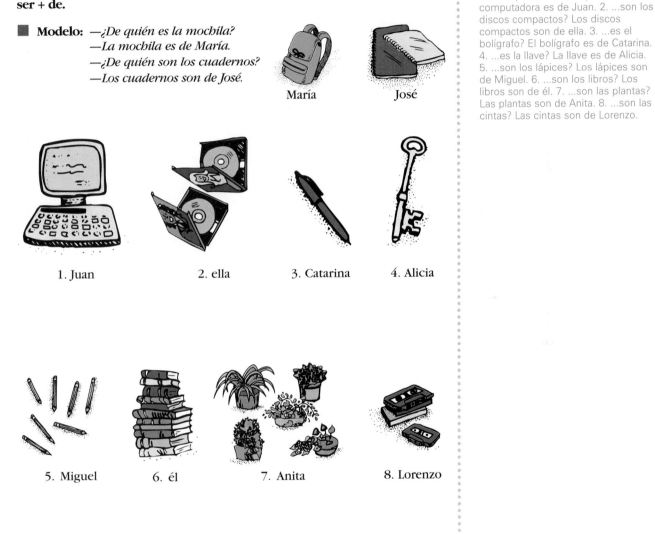

1. Juan   2. ella   3. Catarina   4. Alicia

5. Miguel   6. él   7. Anita   8. Lorenzo

M. ¿De quién es... ? Put an item you and other students brought to class on your desk. Take turns with your classmates asking: **¿De quién es el/la... ?** and answering with the name of the student to whom the item belongs.

■ **Modelo:**   —*¿De quién es la mochila?*
          —*Es de Joe.*

Have students pre-read the questions for *Después de escuchar* section.

Answers, Ex. N
A Miguel le gustan los deportes: el fútbol americano y el básquetbol. A Isabel le gustan las películas de horror y las de ciencia ficción.

Isabel and Miguel are now providing information about their likes and dislikes. Listen to their brief monologues and complete the following exercises.

ANTES DE ESCUCHAR

Based on what you've learned in this *etapa*, what are some of the likes and dislikes you expect Isabel and Miguel to talk about?

N. Comprensión. Before your instructor plays the tape, take a moment and look at the chart below. As you listen, write down who likes what on a separate piece of paper.

	Miguel	Isabel
animales		
la naturaleza		
películas		
de horror		
de aventura		
de ciencia ficción		
deportes		
tenis		
fútbol americano		
béisbol		
básquetbol		

DESPUÉS DE ESCUCHAR

Answers, Ex. Ñ
1. No mucho.
2. Las de ciencia ficción son mis favoritas.

Ñ. ¿Cómo lo dicen? Your instructor will play the tape again. Listen and try to determine the following:

1. How does Miguel say he doesn't especially like movies?
2. How does Isabel say that science fiction movies are her favorite?

Ex. O: Pairs

Suggestion, Ex. O:
You may wish to have each student ask a number of questions about the likes and dislikes of the others.

Variation Ex. O: Have each student prepare a brief introduction of a classmate based on the information gathered in these exercises. Provide students with the construction A [name] le gusta(n)...

Ex. P: Pairs

Tú dirás ....

O. Un(a) compañero(a) de cuarto *(My roommate)***...** Imagine you and your partner are looking for a couple of new roommates. As you know, it will be necessary to find someone with whom both of you have much in common. Make a list of what both of you like and don't like. Take notes as everyone presents their lists to the class. Then try to determine who is best suited to room with whom.

P. Un diálogo de contrarios *(A dialog of opposites)***.** Imagine that you and another student have a relationship similar to that of the people at the beginning of the following *etapa*. The two of you are friends, despite great differences in likes, dislikes, interests, and possessions. Invent the details of your two lives and present them to the class in the form of a dialog of opposites.

PARA EMPEZAR: Mi familia

Preparación: As you start working on this **etapa**, take a moment and think about the information you would include if you were going to talk about your family.

- What is your family like?
- Do you have step-parents?
- Do you have brothers and sisters?
- What about step-siblings?
- Do you have both sets of grandparents?

Bring pictures of different possible families. Discuss how these families resemble students' families. Discuss differences between families in the classroom and in the pictures. Discuss which of these differences are linked to culture.

Suggestions: A. Help students decipher the reading by using context clues (e.g., Tomás = nombre de pila; Torres = apellido), showing pictures that illustrate adjectives such as rizado, verde, corto, and drawing a family tree on the board. B. Point out cognates (personas, divorciados, maternos, paternos) and explain that largo and simpática are false cognates.

Additional family vocabulary:

padrastro	*stepfather*
madrastra	*stepmother*
hermanastro	*stepbrother*
hermanastra	*stepsister*

Assist pre-reading by having students scan for the gist of the reading. Have students generate a list of information they expect to get from the reading. After reading ask simple comprehension check questions. Then ask students in what way Tomás's and Juan's families are similar or different to theirs. Encourage students to discuss in Spanish.

Buenos días. Me llamo Tomás Torres Galindo. Tomás es mi nombre de pila y Torres es mi apellido. Tengo una familia pequeña. Hay cuatro personas en mi familia. Mi padre se llama Esteban y mi madre se llama Carmela. Mis padres están divorciados. No tengo hermanos pero tengo una hermana. Ella se llama Sofía. Ella es alta, delgada, morena y bonita. Tiene el pelo largo y rizado y los ojos verdes. Vivimos en una casa en Springfield, Massachusetts con mi madre, mi abuela Luisa y mi abuelo Fernando. Mi padre vive en Cabo Rojo, Puerto Rico. Los padres de mi padre también viven allí.

Hola, me llamo Juan Mejía Castillo. Vivo con mi padre y madre en San Antonio, Texas. Tengo una hermana. Se llama Elena. Es rubia, tiene los ojos azules y el pelo corto. Es divertida y simpática y tiene muchos amigos. Vive con su marido, Rafael, en Atlanta, Georgia. No tienen hijos. Cerca de nosotros vive mi tía Teresa, hermana de mi madre, y mi tío Felipe, su esposo. Mis abuelos maternos, es decir los padres de mi madre, también viven en San Antonio. No tengo abuelos paternos.

Práctica

A. Tú y tu familia.
First complete the following sentences with information about you and your family.

1. Mi nombre completo es...
2. Hay... personas en mi familia.
3. Mi padre se llama...
4. Mi madre se llama...
5. Tengo... hermanos. (o: No tengo hermanos.)
6. Ellos se llaman...
7. Tengo... hermanas. (o: No tengo hermanas.)
8. Ellas se llaman...

B. La familia de un(a) compañero(a) *(a classmate)*.
Now ask one of your classmates the following questions about himself or herself and his or her family.

1. ¿Cuál (What) es tu nombre completo?
2. ¿Cuántas (How many) personas hay en tu familia? (Hay...)
3. ¿Cómo se llama tu padre? ¿y tu madre?
4. ¿Cuántos hermanos tienes? ¿Cómo se llaman?
5. ¿Cuántas hermanas tienes? ¿Cómo se llaman?
6. ¿Cuántos abuelos tienes?
7. ¿Cuántas abuelas tienes?

Answers, Ex. B
Answers will vary.

Ex. B:  Pairs

Suggestion: After doing the exercise once, have students choose a different partner.

Variation, Ex. B: Have students ask you questions about your family.

Comentarios

culturales *Los apellidos*

Perhaps you have noticed that Latinos often use more than one last name. This is because many use their mother's maiden name along with their father's last name. For example, Leonardo Candelaria Márquez would use the last name of his father first (Candelaria), followed by his mother's (Márquez). Leonardo might also use the initial instead of the complete second name (Leonardo Candelaria M.). When addressing someone, you use the first of the two last names (Leonardo Candelaria). When looking up a name in a telephone book, you would always refer to the first of the two last names.

INTEGRACIÓN CULTURAL

1. What would be your complete name if we had this tradition here in the USA?
2. Ask several classmates, using the phrase: **¿Cómo te llamarías?** *(What would your name be?)* They answer using: **Me llamaría...** *My name would be...)*

Preview: Note that we are using a conditional form here lexically. There is no need to get into a complete explanation of the conditional tense. This will be covered thoroughly in Chapter 12.

Repaso

C. Me gusta más... Ask two of your classmates to choose from the following sets of items.

■ **Modelo:** la música clásica, el jazz, la música rock

—¿Qué te gusta más — la música clásica, el jazz o la música rock?

—Me gusta más la música clásica.

—¿Y a ti?

—Me gusta más la música rock.

1. el fútbol, el fútbol americano, el básquetbol
2. la pintura, la escultura, la arquitectura
3. las hamburguesas, los sándwiches de jamón, las hamburguesas con queso
4. las películas de horror, las películas de aventuras, las películas cómicas
5. la historia, las lenguas, las ciencias
6. la biología, la química, la física

D. ¿Qué tienes? ¿Qué no tienes? Work with a classmate to complete this exercise. Ask him/her what he/she has and doesn't have at home (dorm, apartment, house, etc.). Then have him/her ask you the same questions, and you respond.

■ **Modelo:** Tengo una bicicleta, unos libros y un estéreo. No tengo una calculadora, una cámara, y no tengo una computadora.

Ex. C: Set up activity by telling students they are to decide an appropriate activity to do in each case. They discuss their likes and dislikes and then discuss an appropriate activity to do based on their discussion. For example: Me gusta la música rock. Pues, vamos al concierto de Pearl Jam..

ENFOQUE ESTRUCTURAL — ser + sustantivo y ser + adjetivo

Think about how you would give information about someone, for example, about what they do for a living. In Spanish, **ser** can be used to give this type of information about people. You would always use **ser** + the noun that expresses this to provide this information. Note the following sentences.

Most nouns that refer to work or occupation follow the same patterns as adjectives of nationality.

1. If the masculine ends in **-o,** the feminine form changes **-o** to **-a.**

Masculine	Feminine
Él es **abogado** *(lawyer).*	Ella es **abogada.**
Él es **secretario** *(secretary).*	Ella es **secretaria.**
Él es **ingeniero** *(engineer).*	Ella es **ingeniera.**
Él es **enfermero** *(nurse).*	Ella es **enfermera.**
Él es **médico** *(doctor).*	Ella es **médica.**
Él es **mi esposo** *(husband).*	Ella es **mi esposa** *(wife).*

2. Nouns that end in the consonant **-r** form the feminine by adding **-a** to the end of the word.

Él es **profesor.**	Ella es **profesora.**
Él es **contador** *(accountant).*	Ella es **contadora.**

Remember in Chapter 1 you learned that adjectives must agree in number and gender with the noun they modify. Thus, an adjective like **alto** would have four forms, depending on the noun it is modifying:

Juan es alto.
María es alta.
Juan y Pablo son altos.
María y Paula son altas.

Mi papá es ingeniero y mi mamá es abogada.

Mi abuela es médica y mi hermana es estudiante.

Nouns that refer to work or occupation follow the same pattern as adjectives of nationality that you learned to express in Chapter 1 (i.e., if they end in **-o** they are masculine, and if they end in **-a** they are feminine).

3. Nouns that end in the vowel **-e**, as well as those that end in **-ista**, have the same masculine and feminine form.

Él es **estudiante.**	Ella es **estudiante.**
Él es **periodista** (*journalist*).	Ella es **periodista.**
Él es **dentista.**	Ella es **dentista.**

4. Nouns of profession form their plural in the same way as the adjectives of nationality. Add **-s** to the masculine or feminine singular form if the noun ends in a vowel. If the singular form ends in a consonant, add **-es** or **-as.**

Ellos son **abogados.**	Ellas son **abogadas.**
Ellos son **estudiantes.**	Ellas son **estudiantes.**
Ellos son **profesores.**	Ellas son **profesoras.**

In Chapter 1 you learned that **ser** can also be used with adjectives to describe someone or something. Here are some common adjectives that are used with **ser.**

aburrido (*boring*)	**guapo** (*handsome*)
alto (*tall*)	**malo** (*bad*)
antipático (*disagreeable*)	**moreno** (*dark haired, brunet*)
bajo (*short*)	**pelirrojo** (*red haired*)
bonito (*pretty*)	**pequeño** (*small*)
bueno (*good*)	**rubio** (*blond*)
delgado (*thin*)	**serio** (*serious*)
divertido (*fun, amusing*)	**simpático** (*nice*)
feo (*plain, ugly*)	**tonto** (*stupid, foolish*)
gordo (*fat*)	

Práctica

E. ¿El Sr. Santana? Él es… You and a friend are attending a function. Point out to your friend various acquaintances and state their professions.

■ **Modelo:** Sr. Santana / abogado
¿El Sr. Santana? Es abogado.
Sr. y Sra. Santana / ingeniero
¿El Sr. y la Sra. Santana? Son ingenieros.

1. Sr. y Sra. Herrera / médico
2. Sr. Pérez / dentista
3. Sr. y Sra. López / abogado
4. Sra. Dávila / ingeniero
5. Sr. y Sra. Valdés / profesor
6. Patricio / estudiante de universidad
7. Sra. González / contador
8. Sr. y Sra. Chávez / periodista

F. Yo quisiera ser abogado(a). From the following list, choose several careers or jobs that you would like and several that you would not like.

■ **Modelo:** *Yo quisiera ser médico(a), pero yo no quisiera ser abogado(a).*

periodista	hombre (mujer) de negocios
dentista	(businessman, businesswoman)
profesor(a)	abogado(a)
secretario(a)	camarero(a)
médico(a)	enfermero(a)
ingeniero(a)	contador(a)

G. No, no es..., es... Someone asks you about a trait of one of your friends and you respond with the opposite. Follow the model.

■ **Modelo:** alto / María
¿Es María alta?
No, no es alta. Es baja.

1. gordo / Juan
2. rubio / Anita
3. inteligente / David
4. divertido / Marina
5. simpático / Antonio
6. feo / Miguel y Luis
7. bajo / Ester y Marisa
8. aburrido / ellas
9. bueno / los niños
10. alto / Lourdes

H. Descripciones. Describe as many people as you can in this picture.

ENFOQUE ESTRUCTURAL **Las preguntas de tipo sí-no**

Think about how you ask questions in English. Some questions can be answered with a simple *yes* or *no*. Note the examples below.

¿Estudias mucho?	*Do you study a lot?*
Sí.	*Yes.*
¿Hablan ustedes francés?	*Do you speak French?*
No.	*No.*
Ella toca la guitarra, ¿verdad?	*She plays the guitar, doesn't she?*
Sí.	*Yes.*
Ellos trabajan mucho, ¿no?	*They work a lot, don't they?*
Sí.	*Yes.*

Expand practice and have students introduce each person to their partner, say what they do and where they are from.

Variation, Ex. F:
Have students ask each other: ¿Qué quisieras ser? Then ask them about others: ¿Quién quiere ser... ?

Ex. F: For advanced beginners: Have students say why they would like or not like to have that profession, i.e., Porque no me gusta trabajar mucho...

Answers, Ex. G
1. ¿Es Juan gordo? No, no es gordo. Es delgado.
2. ¿Es Anita rubia? No, no es rubia. Es morena (pelirroja).
3. ¿Es David inteligente? No, no es inteligente. Es tonto.
4. ¿Es Marina divertida? No, no es divertida. Es aburrida.
5. ¿Es Antonio simpático? No, no es simpático. Es antipático.
6. ¿Son Miguel y Luis feos? No, no son feos. Son guapos.
7. ¿Son Ester y Marisa bajas? No, no son bajas. Son altas.
8. ¿Son ellas aburridas? No, no son aburridas. Son divertidas.
9. ¿Son los niños buenos? No, no son buenos. Son malos.
10. ¿Es Lourdes alta? No, no es alta. Es baja.

Yes/no questions:
In spoken Spanish, the most frequently used interrogative marker is rising intonation. To reinforce this, do a short exercise where students indicate whether they hear a question or a statement. For example: **Tú estudias mucho. ¿Tú cantas bien? ¿Uds. trabajan? Ellos hablan español muy poco. ¿Desean tomar algo?**

Expand language practice by encouraging students to have conversations using structures they have learned to this point in addition to using the target structure.

CULTURE:
The tag question ¿no? is generally accompanied by a nod, since the speaker assumes it is an affirmative statement. **Ella canta bien, ¿no?** (nod)

There are three basic ways to ask such questions in Spanish.

1. Make your voice rise at the end of a group of words:

¿Usted mira mucho la TV?

2. Invert the order of the subject and the verb:

¿Practican ellas español en clase?
Verb   Subject

3. Add the words **¿verdad?** or **¿no?** after a statement:

Tú no ganas mucho, ¿verdad?
Clara canta bien, ¿no?

The questions **¿verdad?** or **¿no?** are the equivalent of *don't you?, isn't she?, isn't that right?,* etc., at the end of an English sentence.

To answer a yes/no question you can simply say **sí** or **no.** You can emphasize a negative response by saying **no** twice and repeating the verb used in the question.

¿Viajas mucho?	*Do you travel much?*
No, no viajo mucho.	***No, I don't*** *travel much.*

Práctica

I. Preguntas. Change each statement to a question by making your voice rise at the end of the sentence.

1. Usted desea café.
2. Tú miras mucho la TV.
3. Román trabaja poco.
4. Ustedes estudian mucho.
5. Ellos toman cerveza.
6. Reynaldo toca el violín.
7. Tú tienes una computadora.
8. Hay un estéreo en tu casa.
9. La calculadora es de Juan.
10. La mochila es de Marta.
11. Julia es alta.
12. Mario y Jaime son rubios.

Now repeat the exercise adding **no** or **verdad** and making your voice rise to change the statements to questions.

■ **Modelo:** *Usted desea café, ¿no?*

J. Hagan las preguntas *(Ask questions).* Laura is an exchange student from Ecuador and wants to know more about life and school in the USA. Work with a partner and play the role of Laura and ask him/her questions based on the cues below. Your partner will answer the questions. Begin by asking questions about what students do in general.

■ **Modelo:** ustedes / hablar / inglés
Ustedes hablan inglés, ¿verdad?
o
¿Hablan ustedes inglés?

1. ustedes / cantar / en clase
2. ustedes / viajar / mucho
3. ustedes / estudiar / poco
4. ustedes / trabajar / todos los días

5. ustedes / tomar / muchos refrescos
6. ustedes / trabajar / mucho

Now you will ask questions of individual students, following the model:

■ **Modelo:**   tú / escuchar / música rock
Tú escuchas música rock, ¿no?
o *¿Escuchas tú música rock?*

7. tú / hablar / inglés
8. tú / tocar / un instrumento
9. tú / estudiar / todos los días
10. tú / mirar la TV / mucho

ENFOQUE ESTRUCTURAL

Más preguntas con **quién, dónde, cómo, qué, cuántos(as), por qué, cuándo**

IRM Master 9:
Las preguntas

Other questions you may want to ask require answers with more specific information than a simple *yes* or *no*. In English, you may think of the basic *who, what, where, when, why*. The examples that follow show how you can ask this type of question in Spanish.

Suggestion: Make statements, then have students ask questions about them. Juan Roberto tiene un lápiz. ¿Qué tiene Juan Roberto? Write the question on the board. María vive en Pittsburgh. ¿Dónde vive María? José tiene seis hermanas. ¿Cuántas hermanas tiene José?

1. To find out *where* something is or where someone is located, use **¿dónde?**

¿Dónde vive tu hermano?	**Where** *does your brother live?*
En Pittsburgh.	*In Pittsburgh.*
¿Dónde está mi libro?	**Where** *is my book?*
En la mesa.	*On the table.*

2. To ask how many there are, you use **¿cuántos?** if what you are asking about is masculine and **¿cuántas?** if what you are asking about is feminine.

¿Cuántos hermanos tienes?	**How many** *brothers do you have?*
Dos.	*Two.*
¿Cuántas cintas tienes?	**How many** *tapes do you have?*
Tengo diez.	*I have ten.*

3. To find out who does something, use **¿quién?**

¿Quién come en la cafetería?	**Who** *eats in the cafeteria?*
Bárbara.	*Barbara.*
¿Quién estudia en la biblioteca?	**Who** *studies in the library?*
Roberto.	*Roberto.*

4. To find out what someone wants or is seeking, use **¿qué?**

¿Qué buscan ellos?	**What** *are they looking for?*
La casa de Marta.	*Martha's house.*
¿Qué compran ellos?	**What** *are they buying?*
Una mochila.	*A knapsack.*

5. To ask *why*, use **¿por qué?** The answer to a question with **¿por qué?** always includes **porque** *(because)*.

¿Por qué estudias?	**Why** *are you studying?*
Porque tengo un examen mañana.	**Because** *I have a test tomorrow.*
¿Por qué comes pizza?	**Why** *do you eat pizza?*
Porque me gusta.	**Because** *I like it.*

6. To find out what a person or thing is *like*, you would use **¿cómo?**

¿Cómo es María?	***What*** *is María like?*
María es inteligente y divertida.	*María is intelligent and fun.*
¿Cómo son Mario y Luis?	***What*** *are Mario and Luis like?*
Mario y Luis son altos y delgados.	*Mario and Luis are tall and thin.*
¿Cómo es la película?	***What*** *is the movie like?*
Es interesante.	*It is interesting.*

7. To find out when something is happening, **cuándo** is used:

¿Cuándo estudia José?	***When*** *does José study?*
¿Cuándo es el examin?	***When*** *is the exam?*

Práctica

K. ¡Vamos a conocernos! In order to know a student and her friends from Bogotá, Colombia a little better, you ask her questions about herself and her friends using e-mail. Use the suggested words to form your questions.

Modelo: hermanos / tener
      ¿Cuántos hermanos tienes?

1. vivir
2. gustar más / música / naturaleza
3. estudiar
4. alto(a) sus amigos(as)
5. programas de televisión / mirar
6. estar / ahora
7. trabajar
8. comes

L. Más detalles (*More details*). Conversation depends on the listener paying attention to the speaker's comments and reacting to them. You are talking with some of the Hispanic foreign students in your school. After a student makes a statement, ask a logical follow-up question.

Modelo: Esteban Candelaria:
      —*No vivo en Valencia.*
      —*¿Dónde vives?*

Esteban Candelaria:
1. Tengo hermanos, pero no tengo hermanas.
2. Mis hermanos no viven con mis padres.
3. Ellos no estudian ciencias.

Bárbara Martínez:
4. Mi padre y mi madre trabajan.
5. Mi hermana estudia muchas horas todos los días.
6. Mi hermano tiene muchos discos compactos.

Carlos López:
7. Tengo una clase.
8. Como en la cafetería.
9. No vivo aquí.

M. Intercambio. Strike up a conversation with a fellow student and ask him or her.

1. how many there are in his or her family
2. the number of brothers and sisters he/she has

3. what their names are
4. if he or she has grandparents
5. where they live
6. to describe the family members

VAMOS A ESCUCHAR: MI FAMILIA

Play Textbook audio.

Isabel and Miguel are now providing information about their families. Listen to their brief monologues and complete the following exercises.

ANTES DE ESCUCHAR

Based on what you've learned in this *etapa*, what information about their families do you expect Isabel and Miguel to include in their monologues?

N. Comprensión. Before your instructor plays the tape, take a moment to look at the chart below. As you listen, write down the information that pertains to each person on a separate piece of paper.

	Miguel	Isabel
familia		
grande		
pequeña		
padre		
contador		
profesor		
ingeniero		
mecánico		
madre		
enfermera		
abogada		
profesora		
periodista		
un hermano		
dos hermanos		
apellido		
García		
Vásquez		

DESPUÉS DE ESCUCHAR

Ñ. ¿Cómo lo dicen? Your instructor will play the tape again. As you listen, try to determine the following information.

1. How does Miguel say that he has a very big family?
2. How does Isabel say that her parents are not married to each other?

Pre-reading suggestion: Ask students how they determine one's identity. Have them look at the photos in the section and try to guess the identity of each person. Often students don't recognize cognates while reading because they are thinking in Spanish, or they are trying to pronounce the word according to Spanish phonology. If students can't recognize a particular cognate, have them pronounce it as if it were an English word. This often activates the recognition of the cognate.

Answers, Ex. Ñ
1. Tengo una familia muy grande.
2. Mis padres están divorciados.

Tercera etapa

setenta y nueve **79**

Tú dirás ....

Ex. O: Pairs

O. Tu familia. Find out as much as you can about another student's family. Begin by getting information about its size and composition. Then choose one member of the family (spouse, mother, father, brother, sister, grandparent, etc.) and ask more detailed questions to find out what that person is like. Share the information with the class.

Ex. P: Group of 3

P. Mi árbol genealógico. Construct a family tree as far back as your grandparents. Provide several bits of information for each living person: (1) where he or she lives and (2) what he or she does. You want to come up with a profile similar to the ones on pages 82 and 83. Using your family tree as a guide for your profile, tell two of your classmates about your family and see if they can draw your family tree correctly.

⊚ INTEGRACIÓN

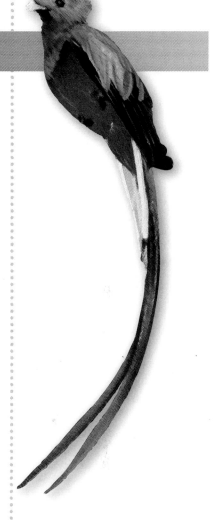

LECTURA: *Mini-retratos*

ANTES DE LEER

In this chapter you have been learning how to talk about possessions, likes and dislikes, and families and professions. As you get ready to read the mini-portraits of these Spanish speakers, what types of information do you think they will include?

A. Look at the pictures of the Spanish speakers on pages 82 and 83 that will be featured in each mini-portrait. What kind of information do you think each one will include?

B. Los cognados. The ability to read in Spanish develops more rapidly than the skills of speaking, listening, and writing. Remember, there is a large number of cognates shared by Spanish and English.

What do you think each of the following words means?

1. hospital
2. profesor
3. montañas
4. museo
5. arquitecto
6. universidad
7. divorciado
8. banco
9. ingeniero
10. presidente
11. compañía
12. garaje
13. condominio
14. privada
15. dentista
16. parque

Now scan the mini-portraits. Look for cognates to help you get the general idea of each paragraph.

GUÍA PARA LA LECTURA

C. ¿Cierto o falso? Reread the *Mini-retratos*, referring to the glosses in each reading. Then decide whether the statements made by each person are true or false. Support your answers by pointing out the relevant information in the *Lectura*.

Read the first paragraph and indicate whether the following statements are true or false.

1. La médica:
   a. Tengo cuatro hijas.
   b. Mi esposo trabaja todos los días en una oficina.
   c. Me gusta la naturaleza.
   d. Paso mucho tiempo con mis hijos.

Read the second paragraph and answer the following question.

2. La estudiante:
   a. Vivo con mi padre y mi madre en Albuquerque, Nuevo México.
   b. Hablo alemán y español.
   c. Tengo una familia grande.
   d. Paso el verano con mi mamá.

Read the third paragraph and answer the following question.

3. El presidente de la compañía:
   a. Soy materialista.
   b. Tengo una casa grande en Madrid.
   c. Soy rico.
   d. Paso mucho tiempo con mis hijos.

Read the fourth paragraph and answer the following question.

4. El hombre jubilado:
   a. Vivo con la familia de mi hijo en Nueva York.
   b. Camino a veces con mi esposa.
   c. Por la noche, yo como en un restaurante.
   d. Por la noche, me gusta mirar la televisión.

D. Más sobre cognados (*More about cognates*). Go back over each of the four readings and make a list of all of the cognates you can find.

MINI-RETRATOS

during / weekend
we spend time
Sometimes we go / game

wants

Yo soy médica y madre de familia. Trabajo en un hospital en Miami. Mi esposo es ingeniero. Él está mucho en casa con los niños. Tenemos un hijo y tres hijas. **Durante** el **fin de semana pasamos tiempo** con nuestros hijos. **A veces vamos** a acampar o a un **partido** de fútbol. A veces vamos a la playa. Me gusta el arte, y a veces mi esposo y yo vamos a los museos de arte. Llevamos a nuestros hijos con nosotros porque mi hijo **quiere** ser arquitecto, y una de mis hijas quiere estudiar pintura en la universidad.

Yo soy estudiante en la Escuela Secundaria de Albuquerque, Nuevo México. Estudio lenguas modernas — francés y español — porque me gusta mucho la literatura y también porque **quiero** viajar a Europa y a América Latina **algún día.** Mis padres están divorciados. Vivo con mi madre. Ella trabaja en un banco. Mi padre es profesor; vive en Pennsylvania. Tengo un hermano **menor** que se llama Esteban. No tengo hermanas. Tengo un perro y un gato. Pasamos el verano con nuestro papá.

I want
someday

younger

Yo soy presidente de una compañía. Vivo en Boston. Tengo una casa grande, tres televisores a color y dos coches en el garaje. Mi esposa y yo viajamos mucho. Tenemos un condominio en Puerto Rico y un apartamento en Madrid. Mis hijos no viven en casa y **asisten** a una escuela privada. Contribuimos con mucho dinero a diferentes instituciones **benéficas** cada año. Tenemos una **vida** muy **cómoda.**

attend

charitable
life / comfortable

Yo estoy **jubilado.** Mi esposa **murió** en 1985. Vivo con mi hijo en Nueva York. Él es dentista y está casado. Su esposa se llama Cecilia. Ellos tienen dos hijos. Yo no trabajo. Me gusta la naturaleza y me gusta mucho **caminar** en el parque. **Por la noche,** como con la familia y **después de** comer miro la televisión. Mi vida es muy tranquila y agradable.

retired/died

to walk
At night
after

VÍDEO CULTURAL: ¿De quién es?

E. Anticipación. **¿Qué cosas hay en una casa?** Check off all the vocabulary you think might be used to describe a home environment.

1. las escaleras
2. el techo
3. la bicicleta
4. el horno
5. la pizarra
6. la nevera
7. el dormitorio
8. me gusta
9. el baño
10. el armario

F. Preparación. Match the following Spanish words and phrases with their English equivalents.

1. ¿es tuyo?
2. el alquiler

a. is it yours?
b. the rent

G. Participación. Take notes as you watch the video. Write down words and phrases that you think may be useful during class discussion or that you'll use later in the *Personalización* exercise.

H. Comprensión. **¿Cuál es la respuesta correcta?** Based on what you saw in this video lesson, choose the best answer.

1. ¿De quién es el duplex?
   a. de Miguel
   b. de Eddy

2. ¿Quién trata de alquilar un piso?
   a. Marisol quiere alquilar su piso.
   b. Miguel quiere compartir su alquiler con un compañero.

3. ¿A quién le gustan los *comics?*
   a. A Miguel le gustan.
   b. A Miguel y a Francisco les gustan.

I. Personalización. Draw the house of your dreams, labeling the different rooms and the furniture/appliances in them. Later, share the **casa de tus sueños** with your classmates.

▶Intercambio: *Juan Carlos y Álvaro*

In this activity, as with all the *Intercambio* activities, one student will be **A** and another will be **B.** Neither of you has access to the other person's information. In order to get the information you need, you will ask *yes/no* questions. To keep track of everything your partner says, you want to have a piece of paper next to you so you can write down some notes. Your partner will need to get the information you have. Answer only **SÍ** or **NO** to his or her questions.

Estudiante A

Your partner will begin by asking the first question. Listen carefully. If you don't understand all or part of what your partner says, you can use the following expression: **No entiendo, ¿puedes repetir?** Once you understand what your partner has said, you answer. Then you ask your first question.

Ésta es la información que tienes sobre Álvaro:

Álvaro tiene 21 años y es estudiante. Vive en un apartamento con un amigo. Le gustan mucho los deportes, especialmente el tenis y el fútbol. No tiene coche pero tiene una bicicleta para ir a clase. En su cuarto hay una cama, una silla y una mesa. A Álvaro le gusta mucho la música y tiene un estéreo y muchos discos.

Ésta es la información que tienes que obtener sobre Juan Carlos:

1. place where he lives
2. things he likes to do
3. things he has in his room
4. his age

---

4. his age
3. things he has in his room
2. things he likes to do
1. place where he lives

Ésta es la información que tienes que obtener sobre Álvaro:

con libros.
su cuarto hay una cama, una silla y una mesa. Juan Carlos tiene muchos estantes coche para ir a trabajar y también tiene una bicicleta para los fines de semana. En casa. Le gusta mucho la naturaleza y tiene muchas plantas en su cuarto. Tiene un Juan Carlos tiene 23 años. No es estudiante. Trabaja en un restaurante. Vive en una

Ésta es la información que tienes sobre Juan Carlos:

will ask you the next question.
entiendo, **¿puedes repetir?** Once your partner answers your question, he or she stand all or part of what you say, you will hear the following expression: **No** You will begin by asking the first yes/no question. If your partner doesn't under-

Estudiante B

VOCABULARIO

Para charlar *Chatting*

Para preguntar *Asking*
¿Cuántas? *How many?*
¿Cuándo? *When?*
¿Cuántos? *How many?*
¿Dónde? *Where?*
¿Por qué? *Why?*
¿Qué? *What?*
¿Quién? *Who?*
¿Cómo es? / ¿Cómo son? *How is it? / How are they?*

Para expresar posesión *Expressing possession*
¿De quién es...? *Whose . . . is it?*
¿De quién son...? *Whose . . . are they?*
Es de... *It belongs to . . .*
Son de... *They belong to . . .*

Las viviendas *Housing*
apartamento *apartment*
casa *house*
cuarto *room*
una residencia estudiantil *dormitory*

Temas y contextos *Themes and contexts*

La familia *Family*
la abuela *grandmother*
el abuelo *grandfather*
la esposa *wife*
el esposo *husband*
la hermana *sister*
el hermano *brother*
la hija *daughter*
el hijo *son*
la madre *mother*
el padre *father*
la prima *cousin (f.)*
el primo *cousin (m.)*
la tía *aunt*
el tío *uncle*

Las profesiones *Professions*
abogado(a) *lawyer*
contador(a) *accountant*
dentista *dentist*
enfermero(a) *nurse*
estudiante *student*
hombre (mujer) de negocios *businessman (woman)*

ingeniero(a) *engineer*
médico(a) *doctor*
periodista *journalist*
profesor(a) *professor, teacher*
secretario(a) *secretary*

En la universidad *At the university*
el/la alumno(a) *student*
el bolígrafo *ballpoint pen*
el borrador *eraser*
la calculadora *calculator*
el compañero (la compañera) de cuarto *roommate*
el cuaderno *notebook*
el lápiz *pencil*
el libro *book*
la mochila *knapsack*
la pluma *fountain pen*
el portafolio *briefcase*
el sacapuntas *pencil sharpener*

Los medios de transporte *Means of transportation*
en autobús *bus*
en bicicleta *bicycle*
en coche *car*
en motocicleta *motorcycle*
a pie *on foot*

Las materias *Subjects*
la arquitectura *architecture*
el arte *art*
la biología *biology*
las ciencias *sciences*
la escultura *sculpture*
la historia *history*
las lenguas *languages*
las matemáticas *mathematics*
la naturaleza *nature*
la pintura *painting*
la química *chemistry*

En mi cuarto *In my room*
la alfombra *rug, carpet*
la almohada *pillow*
la cama *bed*
la cámara *camera*
la cartera *wallet*
la cinta *tape*

la cómoda *dresser*
la computadora/el ordenador *computer*
  la pantalla *screen*
  el teclado *keyboard*
  el ratón *mouse*
los cuadros *paintings*
el disco compacto *compact disc*
el escritorio *desk*
el estante *bookshelf*
el estéreo *stereo*
la llave *key*
la planta *plant*
el póster *poster*

el ropero *closet*
la silla *chair*
el sillón *armchair*
el televisor *television set*
el vídeo *video*

Los deportes *Sports*
el básquetbol *basketball*
el béisbol *baseball*
el fútbol americano *football*
el fútbol *soccer*
el vólibol *volleyball*

Vocabulario general   General vocabulary

Adjetivos *Adjectives*

aburrido(a) *boring*
alegre *happy*
alto(a) *tall*
antipático(a) *disagreeable*
bajo(a) *short*
bonito(a) *pretty*
bueno(a) *good*
cruel*
delgado(a) *thin*
dinámico(a)*
divertido(a) *fun, amusing*
egoísta *selfish*
feo(a) *plain, ugly*
frívolo(a)*
gordo(a) *fat*
grande *big, large*
guapo(a) *handsome*
honesto(a)*
imaginativo(a)*
indiscreto(a)*
ingenuo(a) *naïve*
inteligente *intelligent*

joven *young*
malo(a) *bad*
moreno(a) *dark-haired, brunet*
optimista*
paciente*
pelirrojo(a) *redheaded*
pequeño(a) *small*
perezoso(a) *lazy*
pesimista*
realista*
rubio(a) *blond*
serio(a) *serious*
simpático(a) *nice*
sincero(a)*
tonto(a) *stupid, foolish, silly*
valiente *brave*
viejo(a) *old*

Sustantivos *Nouns*
el animal doméstico *pet*
el apellido *last name*
la ciudad *city*
el gato cat
el nombre *name*

el pájaro *bird*
el perro *dog*
las personas *people*

Verbos *Verbs*
hay (haber) *there is/are*
gustar *to like*
llevar *to take, carry*
tener *to have*

Posesivos *Possessives*
mi(s) *my*
nuestro(s) *our*
nuestra(s) *our*
su(s) *his, her, your, their, its*
tu(s) *your*
vuestro(s) *your*
vuestra(s) *your*

Otras palabras y expresiones *Other words and expressions*

allí *there*
¿Cuántos hay? *How many are there?*
¿Dónde hay? *Where is/are there...?*
Está casado(a) con... *He/She is married to...*
Me llamo... *My name is...*
Para ir al centro, voy... *To go downtown, I go...*

¿Qué llevas tú a la universidad? *What do you take to the university?*
Se llama... *His/Her name is...*
Vivo en... *I live in...*

*These words are cognates in Spanish and English.

3 ¿Dónde y a qué hora?

PRIMERA ETAPA
¿Adónde vamos?

SEGUNDA ETAPA
¿Dónde está?

TERCERA ETAPA
La fiesta del pueblo

INTEGRACIÓN:
LECTURA: Las Mariposas Monarca de México
VÍDEO CULTURAL: ¡La fiesta del pueblo!
INTERCAMBIO: ¿Dónde está... ?
ESCRITURA: Actividades en el Manual

Avenida de la Reforma, México

Palacio de Bellas Artes, México

CHAPTER OBJECTIVES:

In this chapter you will learn about places like stores, buildings, and public areas that are common in the cities and towns of Spanish-speaking countries.

After completing this chapter you will be able to carry out the following tasks:

- **identify and locate places in a city or town**
- **express your wishes and preferences**
- **talk about how you or someone else feels**
- **tell time**
- **ask for directions and give directions**
- **tell others what/what not to do**

The linguistic tools that you will use to carry out these tasks are:

- **vocabulary for:**
  - places and locations in cities and towns
  - preferred activities
  - how you and others feel
  - the time, days of the week
- **grammatical structures:**
  - **tener, tener** + **que** + infinitive, **tener ganas de** + infinitive
  - present tense **ir**
  - present tense querer, preferir
  - present tense **estar, estar** + adjectives, **estar** + locations
  - prepositions of place or proximity
  - commands with **usted** and **ustedes**

MEXICO

Población: 95.772.462
1.958.201 kilómetros cuadrados (761.604 millas cuadradas)
Capital: Ciudad de México, 20.000.000
Ciudades principales: Guadalajara, 3.000.000; Monterrey, 2.700.000

 Moneda: el peso

Esperanza de vida:
hombres, 70; mujeres, 78

Índice de alfabetización: 90%

Televisores: 1 para cada 6,6 personas

Radios: 1 para cada 4,3 personas

Teléfonos: 1 para cada 11 personas

Principales productos de exportación: petróleo crudo, maquinarias y equipos de transporte, café, tomates, ganado vivo, productos químicos, derivados del petróleo, gas natural, algodón, cobre, camarones congelados

Embajada: 1911 Pennsylvania Ave. NW., Washington, DC 20006

PARA EMPEZAR: ¿Adónde vamos?

¿Adónde vamos?:
Where are we going?

Suggestion: Using the *Preparación* questions, brainstorm with students to review the vocabulary associated with places in cities and towns. As they mention a particular building or store, use the transparency provided to point out these places.

Preparación: Can you identify these places using the vocabulary that follows?

- What are some typical buildings to be found in any city or town?
- Think of different specialty stores or shops and what is sold there.
- Where do you normally go to shop?
- What kind of information do you need to give directions to someone?

Public places and business places

Suggestions: (1) Write on the board the names of the places (grouped by categories such as transportation, schools, public buildings). Have students ask you about the words they do not recognize: ¿Qué es una biblioteca? (2) Find large photos of the buildings or draw caricatures of the buildings on the board. Have students repeat: Es una catedral. Es una iglesia. Then ask: ¿Qué es? and/or say (pointing at the hospital): ¿Es una escuela? (No, es un hospital.)

▶ Los lugares públicos y los comercios

un
aeropuerto

una estación
de trenes

una terminal
de autobuses

una plaza

una escuela secundaria

un museo

un cine

una florería

una catedral

una iglesia

una universidad

un mercado

un parque

una panadería

una librería

una biblioteca

una oficina de correos

una estación de policía

un hospital

una farmacia

un estadio

una carnicería

un hotel

una discoteca

Especially with advanced beginners, present topic and vocabulary to students entirely in Spanish. Set up presentation by telling students: **Este verano voy a visitar la ciudad de México. Sólo voy a pasar una semana allí y quiero ver todo lo que tiene la ciudad. Tengo aquí un mapa que tiene todos los puntos de interés. La ciudad tiene museos, donde puedo ver arte de México...** Use gestures, intonation, and visuals to aid comprehension. Use comprehension checks throughout the presentation, for example: **Clase, ¿dónde puedo ver arte?...**

VOCABULARY EXPANSION:
In countries where bullfighting is popular, many towns have a **plaza de toros** *(bullring).*

Transparency F-1: Los lugares públicos y los comercios

Answers, Ex. A
1. Es una terminal de autobuses.
2. …una plaza
3. …una estación de policía
4. …un mercado
5. …un aeropuerto
6. …una estación de trenes
7. …una oficina de correos
8. …una iglesia

Variation: Have students describe a town or city they enjoy.

Note: Amecameca is a town 45 kms. southeast of Mexico City. Visitors enjoy the Parque Nacional nearby where the volcanoes Popocatépetl and Ixtaccíhuatl are located.

un café

un restaurante

Práctica

A. ¿Qué es? Identify each building or place.

■ **Modelo:** *Es un hospital.*

1.   2.   3.

4.   5.   6.

7.   8.

B. ¿Qué hay en Amecameca? Below are examples of public buildings that are found in many cities and towns. Using the map of Amecameca, indicate what there is and what there is not in this town.

■ **Modelo:** *En Amecameca hay un hotel pero no hay un aeropuerto.*

C. ¿Hay un(a)... en el barrio? Ask a passerby if the following places are in the area of downtown Cuernavaca. The passerby will answer affirmatively and will indicate where each place can be found. Act this out in pairs.

■ **Modelo:** restaurante / en la Calle Juárez
    —*Perdón, señor (señorita). ¿Hay un restaurante en el barrio?*
    —*Sí, hay un restaurante en la Calle Juárez.*

1. parque / en la Calle Salazar
2. discoteca / en la Calle Gutenberg
3. museo / en la Calle Leyva
4. cine / en la Avenida Morelos
5. una escuela de lenguas / en la Calle Isla Mujeres
6. oficina de correos / en la Calle Jardín de los Héroes
7. mercado / en la Avenida Madero
8. hotel / en la Calle Rayón

Ex. C: **Pairs**

Variation, Ex. C: Have students greet each other and ask, in Spanish, where each is from. Then have them ask if any of these particular buildings are in their hometown. The other student responds and tells the street where the building is located. Follow up by asking whose hometowns have each of these places.

Comentarios

culturales   *La plaza*

*E*n los pueblos y en las ciudades de los países del mundo hispano siempre hay una plaza. La plaza es su centro original. Una plaza siempre tiene la forma de un **cuadrado** *(square)* o de un rectángulo. Puede ser grande como el Zócalo en la Ciudad de México, la Plaza de Armas en Lima o la Plaza Mayor de Madrid. También puede ser pequeña como la plaza de muchos pueblos.

Los edificios públicos están **alrededor de** *(around)* la plaza: la iglesia, las oficinas del gobierno, la oficina de correos y el banco. También hay algunas tiendas, un hotel y un restaurante. La plaza tiene una larga tradición y todavía hoy es importante en la vida hispana. La gente va a la plaza para hablar con los amigos, para beber y comer, para comprar algo o para **divertirse** *(enjoy themselves)*. En la plaza siempre hay color, movimiento y mucha vida.

INTEGRACIÓN CULTURAL

1. Are you familiar with the word **plaza?** What does it mean to you and what do you associate with it?
2. What does a **plaza** refer to in Spanish?
3. Why do people like to go to a **plaza?**

True or False?
1. A plaza typically has a hospital and private homes.
2. There are large and small plazas.
3. A plaza is in the shape of a circle.
4. A plaza is a popular place in the Spanish-speaking world.

El verbo ir

IRM Master 10: El verbo *ir*

¿Adónde **vamos?**
Alicia **va** al centro.
Ellos **no van** al correo.

Where **are we going?**
Alicia **is going** downtown.
They **don't go** to the post office.

The present tense forms of the verb **ir** are:

ir			
yo	**voy**	nosotros(as)	**vamos**
tú	**vas**	vosotros(as)	**vais**
Ud. } él } ella	**va**	Uds. } ellos } ellas	**van**

Note that after the verb **ir** the preposition **a,** meaning **to,** is used to indicate destination, or where you are heading.

When followed by the article **el, a** combines with it and becomes **al.**

Suggestion, el verbo *ir*:
(1) Have students repeat the conjugation while you write pronouns on the board: yo / tú / él , ella, Ud. / nosotros / vosotros / ellos, ellas, Uds. (2) Repeat in the negative. (3) Add written forms to pronouns on the board.

Suggestion: If you prefer to present the verb ir inductively, you can combine the presentation of the verb with that of the adverbs frequently used with the idea of "going." Write rara vez, nunca, a menudo, de vez en cuando on the board. Illustrate the meanings with the verbs the students already know: estudiar, cantar, hablar español. Do this until the differences in meaning are clear. Then choose a city (one that is nearby or a famous one). Start by telling about yourself. Yo voy a Chicago de vez en cuando pero voy a Nueva York a menudo. Then ask a student: ¿Tú vas a Chicago a menudo? ¿Y a Nueva York? Continue until you have used most of the forms. Be careful to use **nunca** only at the beginning of the sentence. End the presentation by writing the forms of ir on the board.

Práctica

D. En la terminal de autobuses. Work with a partner. Take turns asking and answering questions at the bus station about a group of people who are traveling to different cities in Mexico. Each time one of you asks about who is going to a certain city, you find out that you are wrong. Follow the model.

■ **Modelo:** Carmen / Puebla / Morelia
—*¿Adónde va Carmen hoy? ¿Va a Puebla?*
—*No, Carmen no va a Puebla. Va a Morelia.*

1. Sergio / Monterrey / Tampico
2. María y Pedro / Guanajuato / Querétaro
3. Marco / Ensenada / Tijuana
4. Isabel / Zitácuaro / Tepic

5. Andrés y tú / Toluca / Taxco
6. Patricia / Guadalajara / Pachuca
7. Ana María / Mérida / Villahermosa
8. Gabriel, Tomás y Elena / San Miguel de Allende / San Luis Potosí

Ex. D: Pairs

E. Vamos al centro. You and a classmate are with a group of friends heading to downtown Mexico City to do some errands. Ask each other where different people are going. You each will choose a place from the possibilities listed, indicating where it is located.

■ **Modelo:** —*¿Adónde va Sara?*
—*Sara va al Banco de México que está en la Avenida 5 de Mayo.*

1. Jorge / Tienda El Palacio de Hierro / Avenida Venustiano Carranza
2. nosotros / Correo Mayor / Avenida Lázaro Cárdenas
3. tú / Banco de México / Avenida 5 de Mayo
4. María / Farmacia Sanborn's / Avenida Francisco Madero
5. Ana y Tomás / Pastelería Madrid / Calle 5 de Febrero
6. nosotros / Mercado de La Lagunilla / Calle Rayón

Ex. E: Pairs

Suggestion Ex. E:
Enhance activity and language practice after the exercise by asking students: ¿Qué hay en una pastelería? ... Pasteles, para comer, etc. Write new vocabulary on the board.

7. tus amigos / Librería Porrúa / Avenida República Argentina
8. Alejandro / Palacio de Bellas Artes / Avenida Juárez

IRM Master 11: Los verbos
querer y preferir

Suggestion, querer, preferir:
To introduce the verbs querer and
preferir inductively, use the
transparencies for buildings and say:
Hoy yo quiero ir al cine pero no voy
porque tengo que estudiar. ¿Adónde
quieres ir tú esta tarde? Have
students repeat: Yo quiero ir a...
Work through the different persons
in the same way. Then introduce
preferir. No me gusta ir a la
discoteca, prefiero ir a la piscina.
¿Tú prefieres ir a la piscina o a la
discoteca? ¿al museo o a la escuela?
¿al parque o al teatro? etc. Yo
también prefiero ir al parque.
Paul y yo preferimos ir al parque.

Ex. F:  **Pairs**

Suggestion Ex. F: Tell students
the verb ir requires the use of the
preposition a. When a follows the
verb, this will be obvious. But you
may need to point out its use at the
beginning of the activity with
interrogative adverb. Adónde, when
asking a question.

Suggestion, Exs. F and G: For
both of these exercises, place a
detailed city map on the overhead
and have pairs of students complete
the activity as the model indicates,
but then decide between the two of
them where they want to go and
indicate the street where the place is
located (Ex. F) and/or the name of the
establishment (Ex. G).

Los verbos **querer** y **preferir**

¿**Quieres** ir al cine?	*Do you want to go to the movies?*
No, **prefiero** ir al museo.	*I prefer to go to the museum.*
¿**Quieren** ir a la biblioteca?	*Do you want to go to the library.*

The verb **querer** (*to want, to love*) is used to express strong wishes or feelings. It is more commonly used than the verb **desear** (*to desire*).

Querer and **preferir** change the **e** in the stem to **ie** except in the **nosotros** and **vosotros** forms.

querer (ie)

yo	quiero	nosotros(as)	queremos
tú	quieres	vosotros(as)	queréis
Ud.		Uds.	
él	quiere	ellos	quieren
ella		ellas	

preferir (ie)

yo	prefiero	nosotros(as)	preferimos
tú	prefieres	vosotros(as)	preferís
Ud.		Uds.	
él	prefiere	ellos	prefieren
ella		ellas	

Querer and **preferir** may be followed by a noun or an infinitive.

¿**Quieres** un taco?	*¿Do you want a taco.*
Rosa **quiere comer** algo también.	*Rosa wants to eat something, too.*
Ellos **prefieren** el tren.	*They prefer the train.*
Prefiero viajar en autobús.	*I prefer to travel by bus.*

Práctica

F. ¿Adónde quieres ir? You and a friend are visiting a town in Mexico. Each of you wants to see something different. Find out what your friend wants to see by asking specific questions.

■ **Modelo:** la plaza / la iglesia

　　　　　—*¿Quieres ir a la plaza?*

　　　　　—*No, quiero ir a la iglesia.*

1. la biblioteca / la librería
2. la discoteca / el teatro
3. el museo / el cine
4. la plaza / el parque
5. la estación de trenes / la terminal de autobuses
6. el café / el mercado

Answers, Ex. F.
1. ¿Quieres ir a la biblioteca? No, quiero ir a la librería.
2. ...a la discoteca? ...al teatro.
3. ...al museo? ...al cine.
4. ...a la plaza? ...al parque.
5. ...a la estación de trenes? ...a la terminal de autobuses.
6. ...al café? ...al mercado

G. Preferencias. You and your friend are making plans for the afternoon. Your friend makes a suggestion. You don't agree and express your own preference.

Ex. G: Pairs

■ **Modelo:** ir al teatro

　　　　　—*¿Quieres ir al teatro?*

　　　　　—*No. Prefiero ir al cine.*

1. comer en un café
2. ir al estadio
3. bailar en la discoteca
4. visitar un museo
5. estudiar toda la mañana
6. correr por el parque
7. escuchar música
8. tomar algo

H. Decisiones. When presented with the following options, you and your friend need to decide what you want to do after class. In pairs decide what you want to do, and give your answer to the class.

Ex. H: Pairs

■ **Modelo:** ir en bicicleta o caminar

　　　　　—*¿Quieres ir en bicicleta o caminar?*

　　　　　—*Prefiero caminar.*

　　　　　—*Preferimos caminar.*

1. jugar *(to play)* al tenis o al vólibol
2. ir a mi casa o al café
3. visitar a nuestros amigos o estudiar
4. ir a la plaza o al parque
5. comer o tomar un refresco

ENFOQUE LÉXICO

Expresiones con tener

The verb **tener** is used in many Spanish idiomatic expressions, or phrases. To ask someone's age in Spanish, use **tener.**

¿Cuántos años tienes?	*How old are you?*
Tengo veinte años.	*I am twenty years old.*
¿Cuántos años tiene tu hermana?	*How old is your sister?*
Tiene dieciocho.	*She's eighteen.*

Some other expressions that also use **tener** are **tener hambre** *(to be hungry)*, **tener sed** *(to be thirsty)*, **tener sueño** *(to be sleepy)*, **tener frío** *(to be cold)*, and **tener calor** *(to be hot)*.

Tengo hambre. ¿Y tú?	*I'm hungry. And you?*
No, **no tengo hambre,** pero **sí tengo mucha sed.**	*I'm not hungry, but I am very thirsty.*

GRAMMAR NOTE:
Mucha is used with sed because sed is feminine.

VOCABULARY EXPANSION:
Una postal is a shortened version of una tarjeta postal.

VOCABULARY EXPANSION:
The word radio can be preceded by the masculine or feminine article. El radio refers to the apparatus or set, while la radio is used in reference to the system or network.

When you want to say that you have to do something, you do so by using the verb **tener** followed by **que**, followed by the *infinitive* form of the verb that expresses what you must do.

tener + que + *infinitive*

Tengo que comer.	*I have to eat.*
Tienes que estudiar.	*You have to study.*
Tiene que escribir una postal.	*He/She has to write a postcard.*

When you want to say that you feel like doing something, you do so with the expression **tener ganas de +** *infinitive*. Simply conjugate **tener** and use the infinitive form of the verb that expresses what you feel like doing.

tener ganas de + *infinitive*

¿Tienes ganas de comer una hamburguesa con queso?	*Do you feel like eating a cheeseburger?*
Tenemos ganas de bailar.	*We feel like dancing.*
Tiene ganas de escuchar la radio.	*He/She feels like listening to the radio.*

Práctica

I. ¿Cuántos años tienes? In the process of getting to know your friends, find out how old they are. Remember to use the verb **tener** and the word **años.**

■ **Modelo:** —¿Cuántos años tiene Felipe? (13)
—Felipe tiene trece años.

1. ¿Cuántos años tiene Carmelita? (17)
2. Y el señor Ramos, ¿cuántos años tiene? (64)
3. ¿Cuántos años tiene Ana María? (20)
4. ¿Cuántos años tiene Roberto? (12)
5. ¿Cuántos años tiene el señor García? (82)
6. Y la señora Méndez, ¿cuántos años tiene ella? (55)

J. ¿Tienen hambre? You are hosting a picnic and you want to know if your guests are hungry, hot or thirsty, and what they would like to have. Walk around the class asking five people what they want. Follow the model.

■ **Modelo:** —¿Tienes hambre? ¿Tienes sed?
—Sí, tengo mucha hambre. No tengo sed.
—¿Qué quieres comer?
—Un taco, por favor.

K. Sí..., pero primero tengo que... (*Yes . . . , but first I have to . . .*) A friend invites you to do something. You would like to accept, but you tell him or her that first you must do something else. Follow the model.

■ **Modelo:** ir al centro / estudiar
—¿Tienes ganas de ir al mercado?
—Sí, pero primero tengo que estudiar.

1. ir al cine / estudiar química
2. ir al centro / practicar el piano

3. ir a la discoteca / comer con mi familia
4. comer en el centro / ir a mi casa
5. visitar el museo / ir a la biblioteca

L. Tengo que... Now make a list of at least three things that you have to do by the end of the day. Compare your list with that of other students by asking them what they do and do not have to do today.

VAMOS A ESCUCHAR: ¿ADÓNDE VAN?

En el centro. Gloria and Marilú are going downtown to run some errands. Listen to their conversation and do the following exercises.

ANTES DE ESCUCHAR

Based on the information you have learned in this chapter:

1. What are some of the places you would expect Gloria and Marilú to go on a trip downtown?
2. How do you say in Spanish that you have to do something?

Before you listen to the dialog, read the questions in the *Después de escuchar* section.

M. Primero van a... Listen to the conversation between Gloria and Marilú and pay attention to the places where they plan to go. Make a list of as many places as you can.

DESPUÉS DE ESCUCHAR

N. Comprensión. Listen to the dialog again before answering the following questions in Spanish.

1. Where does Gloria want to go first?
2. Where does Gloria want to go next?
3. Where does her friend Marilú prefer to go?
4. What idea does Gloria have that Marilú likes?
5. What does Marilú want to eat?

Ex. L:  Pairs

Pair false with true beginners and have them note new vocabulary that comes out of this exercise.

Play Textbook audio.

To activate vocabulary they might hear, ask students, in Spanish, what they like to do with their friends when they go to town or downtown. Write vocabulary relevant to the listening exercise on the board as it comes up in this pre-listening activity, e.g., restaurante, comer, correo, farmacia.

Play audio recording 2 or 3 times for students. The first time encourage students to close their books and just listen to the conversation. The second and third time they can open their books and make notes as they listen.

Answers, Ex. N:
1. a la librería 2. a la farmacia y al correo 3. al cine 4. comer primero 5. ensalada de pasta

Answers, Ex. Ñ
1. ¡Un momento, un momento, Gloria! 2. ¡Ay, qué rico!

Ñ. ¿Cómo lo dicen? Listen to the tape again to determine the following:

1. How does Marilú tell Gloria "to hold on a minute"?
2. What expression does Marilú use that is the equivalent of "That's great"?

Tú dirás ....

Ex. O: **Pairs**

Ex. P: **Pairs**

Suggestion, Ex. P: Students choose destinations, then circulate, or you may give each student a piece of paper with a destination written on it. Give the same destination to three or four students. Ask them to find as many people as possible willing to go with them.

O. Una invitación. Your friend invites you to do something. Tell him or her that you are going somewhere else with another person. Your friend makes a polite remark and you finish the conversation.

P. En la calle. While heading for a place in town (your choice), you bump into a friend. Greet your friend, find out how he or she is, and ask where he or she is going. Your friend will ask you where you are going. If you are going to the same place, suggest that the two of you go there together (**¡Vamos juntos/juntas!**). If not, say good-bye and continue on your way.

⊚ SEGUNDA ETAPA

⊚ PARA EMPEZAR: ¿Dónde está?

🖳 **Transparency F–3: ¿Dónde está?**

Suggestion: Have students describe the location of one place in relation to another. List the expressions they use to indicate direction, distance, location, etc.

To present this vocabulary remind students of your **viaje a la Ciudad de México.** Tell them that you now have a good map of the city and are planning your visit. For example: **Clase, aquí hay un mapa y voy a ver dónde están los sitios importantes para mi viaje... Ahora, a ver, ¿dónde está el aeropuerto? Bien, está lejos de la ciudad, tengo que tomar el autobús al centro de la ciudad...** Use comprehension checks.

Suggestion: For homework, hand out the following list of stores found in the Spanish-speaking world: **peluquería, lavandería, ferretería, pescadería, zapatería, joyería, pastelería, dulcería, papelería, frutería.** Have students try to guess what product or service each store sells based on its name. As a check for their guesses, have them look them up in the dictionary.

Preparación

- **How do you find your way around a city when you have never been there before?**
- **When you ask for directions, what do you generally hope to find out?**
- **If someone asks you how to get to a particular place in town, what information do you give?**

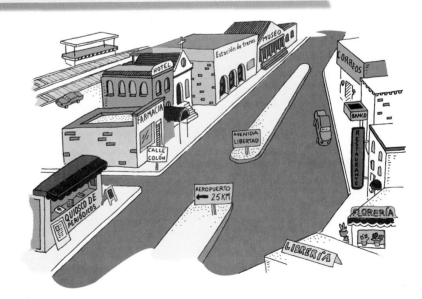

▶¿Está lejos de aquí?

¿Dónde está el aeropuerto?	**Está lejos de** la ciudad.	is (located) / far from
¿Dónde está la estación de trenes?	Está **cerca del** hotel.	near
¿Dónde está la oficina de correos?	Está **frente a** la estación.	across from (facing)
¿Dónde está la farmacia?	Está **al lado del** hotel.	next to
¿Dónde está el museo?	Está **al final de** la Avenida Libertad.	at the end of
¿Dónde está el **quiosco de periódicos?**	Está **en la esquina de** la Calle Colón y la Avenida Libertad.	newspaper kiosk / at the corner of
¿Dónde está el coche **verde**?	Está en un **estacionamiento detrás de** la iglesia.	green / parking lot behind
¿Dónde está el coche **azul**?	Está en la avenida **delante del** banco.	blue / in front of
¿Dónde está el banco?	Está **entre** el restaurante y la oficina de correos.	between
¿Dónde está el restaurante?	Está **a la derecha del** banco (**a la izquierda de** la florería).	to the right of to the left of

Comentarios
culturales Los taxis en la Ciudad de México

*L*a Ciudad de México es famosa por sus numerosos taxis, o libres como dicen los mexicanos. Hay taxis de varios colores y de varias marcas. Algunos, como los anaranjados, tienen el número de su **sitio** *(taxi stand)* pintado en la puerta y reciben llamadas telefónicas. Otros, como los amarillos y los verdes, van por las calles en busca de pasajeros. Los taxis son de varias marcas pero el tipo de automóvil que más se ve para los taxis es el pequeño y rápido Volkswagen.

Los taxistas a veces no usan **taxímetros** *(meters)* por el cambio en los precios que causa el problema de la inflación. Generalmente el pasajero tiene que preguntarle el precio y, a veces, llegar a un acuerdo con el chofer antes de tomar el taxi. La costumbre es siempre dar una buena propina después de llegar al destino. Por lo general, este tipo de **transporte** *(transportation)* es bastante económico para el pasajero que quiere conocer la ciudad en taxi.

INTEGRACIÓN CULTURAL

1. What other word is used in Mexico for "taxi"?
2. What colors are the taxis?
3. What kind of car is often used as a taxi?
4. What should a person sometimes do before getting into a taxi?
5. What other custom is important to remember when taking a taxi?

Answers, Intergración
1. un "libre"
2. verdes, amarillos, anaranjados
3. Volkswagens
4. preguntar el precio
5. dar una buena propina

Práctica

A. Mi ciudad. When someone asks you about the location of certain places in the town pictured on page 100, answer using the suggested expressions.

■ **Modelo:** —¿Dónde está la estación de trenes? (cerca del hotel)
—Está cerca del hotel.

1. ¿Dónde está el hotel? (al lado de la farmacia)
2. ¿Dónde está el banco? (frente a la iglesia)
3. ¿Dónde está el aeropuerto? (lejos de la ciudad)
4. ¿Dónde está la oficina de correos? (cerca del restaurante)
5. ¿Dónde está el museo? (al final de la Avenida Libertad)
6. ¿Dónde está la farmacia? (en la esquina de la Calle Colón y la Avenida Libertad)
7. ¿Dónde está la estación de trenes? (al lado del museo)
8. ¿Dónde está el restaurante? (entre la florería y el banco)

B. ¿Cierto o falso? Correct the false statements about the city pictured on page 100.

■ **Modelo:** —El aeropuerto está cerca de la ciudad, ¿no? (lejos de)
—No, está lejos de la ciudad.

1. El restaurante está al lado de la farmacia, ¿verdad?
2. La estación de trenes está lejos del museo, ¿no?
3. La florería está frente a la librería, ¿verdad?
4. El quiosco de periódicos está al final de la Avenida Libertad, ¿verdad?
5. El museo está al lado del banco, ¿no?
6. El coche está detrás de la iglesia, ¿verdad?
7. La florería está frente a la librería y el restaurante, ¿no?

Repaso

C. Grupo de estudio. You and your friends are studying together for a test. During a break you want to find out who is hungry or thirsty and what they want to eat or drink. One of you asks the question and the others answer. Work in groups of three and follow the model.

■ **Modelo:** —¿Tienes hambre o sed?
—Sí, tengo mucha hambre/sed.
—¿Qué quieres comer/beber?
—Quiero un sándwich de queso.

D. Un amigo nuevo. A Mexican exchange student whom you have just met is telling you about his family and his life in Mexico. Each time he makes a statement, you ask a follow-up question using **dónde, cuántos, cuántas, qué, por qué,** or **quién.**

■ **Modelo:** Tengo una familia grande. Tengo muchos hermanos.
—¿Cuántos hermanos tienes tú?

1. Somos de Guadalajara pero no vivimos ahí.
2. Vivimos en una ciudad pequeña en el norte.
3. Mi padre trabaja.
4. Soy estudiante en una escuela pequeña. No hay muchos estudiantes en mi escuela.
5. Estudio historia, inglés y español.
6. No estudio ciencias.
7. Me gustan mis profesores y mis compañeros de clase.
8. Tengo un profesor muy simpático.

Possible answers, Ex. D
1. ¿Dónde viven Uds.? 2. ¿Dónde está? 3. ¿Dónde trabaja?
4. ¿Cuántos estudiantes hay en tu escuela? 5. ¿Qué te gusta más?
6. ¿Por qué no estudias ciencias?
7. ¿Por qué te gustan tus profesores y tus compañeros de clase?
8. ¿Quién es?

IRM Master 12: El verbo estar

Sugestion, estar: To present structures in context, bring in pictures of people (your family, famous people, etc). Tell students: Ésta es una foto de mi hermano Juan. Juan está en Costa Rica ahora porque es estudiante internacional. Normalmente Juan está muy contento, pero en esta foto está muy triste porque quiere ver a su familia... Ask students comprehension questions.

ENFOQUE ESTRUCTURAL — El verbo estar

Estar + lugar

Estoy en el Hotel Alameda.	*I am in the Hotel Alameda.*
Toluca **está** en México.	*Toluca is in Mexico.*
Los coches **están** en el estacionamiento.	*The cars are in the parking lot.*

The present tense forms of the verb **estar** are:

estar

yo	**estoy**	nosotros(as)	**estamos**
tú	**estás**	vosotros(as)	**estáis**
Ud. él ella	**está**	Uds. ellos ellas	**están**

You will note that only the **yo** form (**estoy**) is irregular.

Estar + adjetivos

Estoy muy cansada.	*I am very tired.*
Estoy listo para continuar la lección.	*I am ready to continue with the lesson.*

1. **Estar** is used with adjectives to describe physical or emotional conditions:

aburrido	*bored*	enojado	*angry*
cansado	*tired*	listo	*ready*
contento	*happy*	triste	*sad*
enfermo	*sick*		

2. Remember, all adjectives agree in gender and number with the person they describe.

Ella está **cansada.**	**Ellas** están **cansadas.**
Él está **cansado.**	**Ellos** están **cansados.**

Possible answers, Ex. E
1. Está cansada. 2. Está contento.
3. Están tristes. 4. Está enferma.
5. Está contenta. 6. Están enojados.

 Preview: More uses of *estar*
+ *adjective* will appear in
Chapter 11.

Suggestion, Ex. E: Enhance
activity by asking follow-up questions
that push students to more
production. After each item, ask
students to make up a reason why
that person might be in that mood.
For example: **Está enojado porque
tiene que estudiar.**

Ex. F: **Pairs**

Suggestion, Ex. F: Have
students pretend they are different
famous people at a charity fund-
raiser. Students can approach and
greet each other, find out who they
are and how they are. Students
answer from the perspective of that
famous person. Encourage
spontaneous conversation in Spanish.

Suggestion, contracciones:
You can also present this structure by
putting drawings on the board or
writing the names of several places.
Group the places by gender.
Feminine: **biblioteca, estación,
catedral, piscina, discoteca, escuela,**
etc. Masculine: **cine, estadio, teatro,
museo,** etc. Ask students: **¿Adónde
van Uds.?** Have them respond:
Nosotros vamos… beginning with **a
la biblioteca, …a la estación…**
Continue through each list. Then have
students pick out three places to go:
**¿Adónde vas tú? Yo voy a la escuela,
luego voy a la iglesia y al cine.**
Encourage students to substitute
(from the vocabulary of this and the
previous *etapa*) other places they
actually go.

E. ¿Estás bien? Look at the pictures and describe how these people feel today.

1.　　　　2.　　　　3.

4.　　　　5.　　　　6.

F. ¿Cómo están Uds.? Ask five of your classmates how they are feeling
today. Then report to the class.

■ **Modelo:** —*¿Cómo estás?*
　　　　　　—*Estoy muy contento(a).*

ENFOQUE ESTRUCTURAL　　Las contracciones al y del

When the preposition **a** *(to)* is followed by the article **el**, they contract to
form one word, **al.**

a + el = al

José y yo vamos **al** museo.	*José and I go to the museum.*
Mi familia va **al** restaurante.	*My family goes to the restaurant.*

When the preposition **de** is followed by the definite article **el**, the two
words contract to form one word, **del.**

de + el = del

El coche blanco está delante **del** banco.	*The white car is in front of the bank.*
Es el portafolio **del** profesor.	*It is the professor's briefcase.*

Many of the prepositions of place presented at the beginning of this *etapa*
(on page 101) include **de:**

lejos de	al final de
cerca de	detrás de
al lado de	delante de

Remember to follow the same rules for contractions: **lejos del centro,
cerca del cine, al lado del restaurante.**

Práctica

G. ¿Adónde quiere ir… ?

You are talking to a friend about where your other friends want to go this weekend. Ask about each of the following people and your friend will answer using the places suggested.

■ **Modelo:** Alberto / el banco
  ¿Adónde quiere ir Alberto?
  Al banco.

1. Consuelo / el mercado
2. Isabel / el parque
3. Arturo / la discoteca
4. Mónica / el cine
5. Gabriel / el museo
6. Rosalba / el teatro
7. Sergio / el estadio
8. Ana María / el café

H. ¿Dónde esta?

Using the map, help Esteban describe precisely the location of the following places:

1. Mercado Libertad
2. Plaza de la Liberación
3. Antigua Universidad
4. Parque Morelos

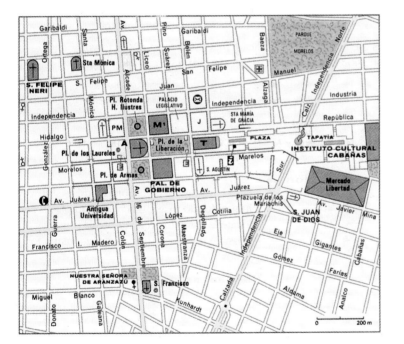

Variation, Vamos a escuchar:
To make the listening more challenging, put students in groups of 4. Send 2 students out of the room while playing the audio. After listening 2 times, the 2 remaining students discuss how to tell their 2 other groupmates what building the woman wanted to find and where it is located. Bring other students back into class and let their groupmates explain the audio content. Allow 3–4 minutes and then ask students who went out the comprehension questions. Allow all to listen a third time to answer the ¿Cómo lo dicen? questions.

Answers, Ex. I
1. a la biblioteca 2. el banco central

Answers, Ex. J
1. Perdón, señor. No soy de aquí.
2. Exacto.

Variation: Pair students and assign each one 2 or 3 locations that they must explain. Allow 3–4 minutes for completion, then ask each pair where their designated places are located. Interact with students questioning them on their answers. For example: ¿Está lejos del zócalo? ...bien, ¿en qué calle está?...

Ex. K: 👥 **Pairs**

ANTES DE ESCUCHAR

The woman in this dialog is lost and needs directions. Based on what you've learned in this *etapa*, what do you think she will ask the man she meets on the street?

Now look at the questions in the *Después de escuchar* section to anticipate what you will be listening for. Review the prepositions of place on page 101.

1. What is the opposite of **lejos de?**
2. What verb is used in Spanish to indicate location?

Now listen to the two people talk about the location of a building.

DESPUÉS DE ESCUCHAR

I. Comprensión. Listen to the dialog again before answering the following questions.

1. Where does the woman want to go?
2. What building is it close to?

J. ¿Cómo lo dicen? Listen to the tape again to determine the following:

1. What does the woman say to indicate that she is from out of town?
2. What expression does the man use to confirm where the building is?

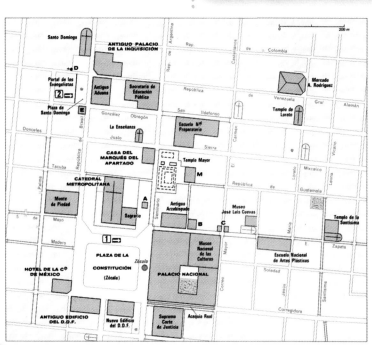

Tú dirás ....

K. ¿Por favor... ? Some tourists stop you in the Zócalo to ask where certain places are located. Using the map locate as precisely as possible the places that they are looking for. Follow the model.

■ **Modelo:** la Antigua Aduana
—*Perdón señor (a), ¿dónde está la Antigua Aduana, por favor?*
—*La Antigua Aduana está frente al Antiguo Palacio de la Inquisición.*

1. Casa del Marqués del Apartado
2. Monte de Piedad
3. Suprema Corte de Justicia
4. Secretaría de Educación Pública
5. Antiguo Arzobispado
6. Nuevo Edificio del D.D.F.

L. ¿Dónde están? Talk with a classmate about six different places or buildings on or near the campus, indicating specifically where they are located in relationship with other buildings or places on campus.

TERCERA ETAPA

PARA EMPEZAR: *La fiesta del pueblo*

Preparación: As you begin this *etapa*, think about the following questions.

- What are some of the holidays that are especially important to the people who live in your town or city?
- What kinds of events or activities take place where you live to celebrate a national holiday like the Fourth of July?

Suggestion: You may wish to treat the festival schedule as realia and have students work with it to answer questions from other tourists about the Día de la Independencia. Begin by playing the role of an American tourist, listening to their answers to the questions and eliciting further information when appropriate. The dialog will be in English at this point. What time is the Feria de la comida / the Bailes folklóricos / etc.? Where is the Misa / baile / etc.?

Ask students these questions in Spanish. Encourage them to answer in Spanish.

Note: Point out that for official time a 24-hour clock is used. Students can practice converting from the official time to conversational time.

Jorge Orozco vive en Querétaro, la capital del estado de Querétaro en México. Como en todas las ciudades y pueblos hispanos, la Ciudad de Querétaro tiene varias fiestas durante el año. Una de las más importantes es el Día de la Independencia que se celebra en todo México el 16 de septiembre. Jorge mira el póster que anuncia los programas para el festival en su ciudad.

Día de la Independencia, 16 de septiembre, Ciudad de Querétaro
Programa de actividades

8:30	**Misa** en la Catedral de San Francisco	Mass
10:00	Maratón en la Universidad Autónoma de Querétaro	
12:00	**Feria** de la comida en el Mesón Santa Rosa	Fair
13:30	Bailes folklóricos en la Plaza de la Independencia	
14:45	**Concurso** de poesía	Contest
	Premio al mejor poema	Prize

16:30	**Desfile** de las escuelas por las calles de la ciudad
19:00	Banquete en el Palacio Municipal
20:30	Concierto, Orquesta Filarmónica de Querétaro, en el Auditorio Josefa Ortíz de Domínguez
22:00	**Fuegos artificiales** en la Plaza Obregón
23:00	**Baile** popular en la Plaza de la Independencia

Fireworks

Dance

Práctica

A. El Día de la Independencia. Jorge is planning his activities for the day of the festival. Complete the paragraph according to the information on the poster on page 107.

Primero voy a la catedral para escuchar _____. Luego voy a comer en la casa de Adela. Después de comer, Adela y yo vamos a ver los bailes _____ en _____. Adela va a leer su poema en el _____ de _____ No vamos a ver el _____ de las escuelas porque va a ser muy largo. Tampoco vamos a ir al _____ en el _____ Municipal, porque es muy **caro**. Por la noche, vamos a ver los_____ _____ en _____ y luego vamos al _____ popular. **Va a ser** un día divertido.

B. ¿Qué quieren hacer (to do) Uds.? You and your friends are deciding what you want to do at the festival. Work in groups of three taking turns to ask and answer the questions.

■ **Modelo:** ver *(watch)* el desfile
—*¿Qué quieren hacer ustedes?*
—*Queremos ver el desfile.*

1. ver los bailes folklóricos
2. ir al baile popular
3. ver los fuegos artificiales
4. ir al banquete
5. comer las comidas regionales
6. ir al concurso de poesía

Repaso

C. Por favor, ¿dónde está... ? You are walking down the street in your town when a Spanish-speaking person stops you and asks where a certain place (movie theater, bank, train station, drug store, etc.) is located. You indicate the street or avenue and then try to describe the area (such as what it is near to, next to, across from, behind, between).

D. Quisiera..., pero tengo que... Make a list of five things you would like to do but can't because you have to do something else. Compare your list with a classmate's, and find out which activities you have in common.

■ **Modelo:** —*Quisiera mirar televisión pero tengo que estudiar.*

La hora y los días

¿Qué hora es?

1. To distinguish between A.M. and P.M., use the expressions **de la mañana** *(in the morning)*, **de la tarde** *(in the afternoon)*, or **de la noche** *(in the evening)*.

2. Notice that in Spanish **es la** is used for one o'clock and **son las** is used for all other hours.

Es la una

Son las dos

Son las dos y diez

Son las dos y cuarto

Son las dos y media

Son las tres menos veinte

Son las tres menos cuarto

Es medianoche

Es mediodia

3. To indicate that something happens **between** two times, use either
   ENTRE LAS... Y LAS... OR **DESDE LAS... HASTA LAS...**

Corro **entre las** 5:00 **y las** 6:00.	*I run **between** 5:00 **and** 6:00.*
Mi madre trabaja **desde las** 9:00 **hasta las** 5:00.	*My mother works **from** 9:00 **to** 5:00.*

4. To ask someone what time something happens, use **¿A qué hora... ?** The response to this question requires the preposition **a.**

¿A qué hora comes?	*What time do you eat?*
A las 6:15.	*At 6:15.*

Suggestion: Many cities and towns in Spain, Latin America, and the United States organize annual festivals celebrating some aspect of the area's culture. As a possible cultural activity, have students compare the activities at the festivals in Mexico with the activities at the festival held in their town or region.

Students may have problems with the **a las** and **son las** distinction. Point out to students that there is no difference here between Spanish and English. In English we say, "It *is* 4 o'clock" but "I will go *at* 4 o'clock."

To present the new structure, bring in a calender with different days marked with things to do at certain times. Put on overhead or display for class and tell them something like the following: **Estoy muy ocupada este mes** (point to the month), **tengo que hacer mucho. El 15 de** (month) **tengo que ir al médico a las 3 de la tarde...** Use comprehension checks.

CULTURE:
The calendar in the Spanish-speaking world starts on Monday, not Sunday.

5. To ask the time, use **¿Qué hora es?**

Los días de la semana

lunes   martes   miércoles   jueves   viernes   sábado   domingo

To express "on" with the days of the week, use the definite article and never the preposition **en: El viernes voy a Chicago; Los sábados voy al centro,** etc.

1. The definite article is used with the days of the week:

> **el lunes** = Monday, the upcoming Monday
> **los lunes** = on Mondays, indicates a customary action on a specific day of the week
> **El viernes** voy a una fiesta en casa de Jaime.
> **Los lunes** voy a la universidad.

2. Also note that the days ending in **s** do not change, whether they are singular or plural. For **sábado** and **domingo,** however, add an **s** when plural.

> **El domingo** voy a misa.
> **Los domingos** no voy a la universidad.
> **El lunes** voy a clase.
> **Los lunes** no voy a la playa.

Comentarios
culturales   *Los días de fiesta*

*E*n México, así como en los otros países de habla española, hay numerosas fiestas, de gran interés y color, que forman parte de la cultura. Estas fiestas del pueblo, casi siempre combinan tradiciones cristianas de España y las tradiciones de las antiguas culturas nativas de América.

El 6 de enero es el Día de los **Reyes Magos** *(Three Kings / Wise Men)* que dejan sus **regalos** *(gifts)* en los zapatos de los niños. Esta celebración tiene su origen en la visita de los Reyes Magos al niño Jesús. En español se llaman Melchor, Gaspar y Baltasar. En algunas ciudades de México, personas famosas se visten de Rey Mago y caminan por las calles.

Uno de los días de fiesta más importantes de México es el 12 de diciembre cuando se celebra la fiesta de la Virgen de Guadalupe. Cada año, miles y miles de personas van a la Basílica (o iglesia) de Guadalupe para ver el famoso cuadro milagroso de ella que hay allí. Después de una misa especial hay música y baile en las calles.

INTEGRACIÓN CULTURAL

1. What do a number of holiday celebrations in Latin America combine?
2. What happens on January 6?
3. What is the origin of **el Día de los Reyes Magos?**
4. When is **el Día de la Virgen de Guadalupe** celebrated?
5. What do many people in Mexico do on the holiday dedicated to her?

Answers, Integración cultural:
1. tradiciones cristianas de España y tradiciones nativas de América.
2. Es el Día de los Reyes Magos.
3. La visita de los Reyes al niño Jesús.
4. El 12 de diciembre.
5. Van a la iglesia, ven su cuadro, bailan en las calles.

Práctica

E. ¿Qué hora es? Find out the time from a classmate. Indicate whether it is morning **(de la mañana),** afternoon **(de la tarde),** or evening **(de la noche).** Alternate between who asks and who answers for every other question.

Ex. E: Pairs

For additional practice, tell students to find three people in class who can all meet for coffee outside of class time to practice Spanish. Students need to first consider their own schedule and when they would be available, then consult other students and find out if they are available at that time, also. When asked, students should say whether they can or can't, and if they can't, why. Students should advise you when they find three people who can meet with them. Encourage students to actually meet at that time.

■ **Modelo:**   2:20 A.M.
    —¿Qué hora es?
    —Son las dos y veinte de la mañana.

1. 8:20 A.M.
2. 1:00 P.M.
3. 1:30 A.M.
4. 3:10 P.M.
5. 10:55 A.M.

6. 11:45 P.M.
7. 4:15 P.M.
8. 5:35 A.M.
9. 7:45 A.M.
10. 10:25 P.M.

F. ¿A qué hora… ? Tell your friend at what times and on what days of the week you do the following activities.

Ex. F: Pairs

■ **Modelo:**   mirar la televisión
    —¿A qué hora miras la televisión?
    —Miro la televisión a las 9:00 de la noche los martes y los jueves.

1. preparar la lección (lesson) de español
2. usar el laboratorio de lenguas
3. correr
4. practicar el tenis
5. trabajar
6. leer
7. ir a la universidad
8. preferir salir

ENFOQUE ESTRUCTURAL — Mandatos con **usted y ustedes**

Tome la Calle Atocha.	*Take* Atocha Street.
¡Escuchen bien!	*Listen well!*

1. Command forms of a verb are used to tell someone to do something. Here you will learn how to give commands with **usted** and **ustedes.**

Mandatos formales

Verbos en **-ar:**	Verbos en **-er:**	Verbos en **-ir:**
cantar	**comer**	**escribir**
Cante Ud.	**Coma** Ud.	**Escriba** Ud.
Canten Uds.	**Coman** Uds.	**Escriban** Uds.

2. To form the **Ud.** and **Uds.** commands, drop the **o** from the **yo** form of the present tense and add **e/en** for **-ar** verbs and **a/an** for **-er** and **-ir** verbs:

yo **hablo** →	**habl-** →	**hable** Ud.	**hablen** Uds.
yo **bebo** →	**beb-** →	**beba** Ud.	**beban** Uds.
yo **escribo** →	**escrib-** →	**escriba** Ud.	**escriban** Uds.
yo **tengo** →	**teng-** →	**tenga** Ud.	**tengan** Uds.

3. The negative command is formed by placing **no** before the verb.

¡No baile!   **¡No canten!**

4. Verbs that end in **-car, -gar,** or **-zar,** such as **practicar** *(to practice),* **llegar** *(to arrive),* and **cruzar** *(to cross),* have a spelling change in the **Ud.** and **Uds.** command forms: **c → qu: practique, g → gu: llegue,** and **z → c: cruce.**

5. The verbs **ir** and **ser** have irregular command forms.

ir	**ser**
vaya Ud.	**sea** Ud.
vayan Uds.	**sean** Uds.

6. Commands are often used to give someone directions. Some common verbs for this are the following:

caminar *(to walk)*	Camine/Caminen a la Avenida Juárez.
cruzar *(to cross)*	Cruce/Crucen la Calle Hidalgo.
doblar *(to turn)*	Doble/Doblen (a la izquierda = *left;* a la derecha = *right).*
seguir *(to keep going)*	Siga/Sigan (directo, de frente = *straight/forward).*

Práctica

G. A mi profesor(a). Use the **Ud.** command with your teacher.

■ **Modelo:** no terminar la clase tarde
   —*No termine la clase tarde.*

1. ser paciente
2. no trabajar mucho
3. escribir las instrucciones
4. ir a la biblioteca
5. hablar despacio
6. buscar las llaves de la oficina
7. organizar una fiesta

H. Un grupo de estudiantes nuevos. You have been asked to speak to a group of incoming first-year students. Tell them six or eight things that they should or should not do in order to succeed at your school.

I. ¿Cómo llego a... ? *(How do I get to . . .)* Use the map on page 106 to work with a partner and give each other directions for getting from the Hotel de la Ciudad de México to the following places:

1. Museo José Luis Cuevas
2. Escuela Nacional Preparatoria
3. Plaza de Santo Domingo
4. Palacio Nacional

Answers, Ex. I
1. Cruce el zócalo y doble a la derecha en la Avenida 5 de Mayo. Vaya dos cuadras y doble a la izquierda. 2. Siga recto por la Avenida República de Brasil. Doble a la derecha en González Obregón. Vaya dos cuadras más. 3. Vaya por la Avenida República de Brasil. La Plaza de Santo Domingo está frente a la Antigua Aduana. 4. El Palacio Nacional está frente al zócalo en Seminario.

VAMOS A ESCUCHAR: ¿DÓNDE ESTÁ LA CALLE GONZÁLEZ OBREGÓN?

Have students read comprehension questions before listening. Play tape once, encouraging students to just listen with the book closed, without making notes, etc. Play a second time and ask them to note possible answers. Review answers, then play again and ask students to note any new language they notice. Discuss new vocabulary or other items they noted.

ANTES DE ESCUCHAR

In the following conversation a man asks a woman how to get to a certain place. What questions might you expect to hear? What might the woman respond?

Now look at the questions in the section *Después de escuchar.* Read the questions before listening to the conversation.

DESPUÉS DE ESCUCHAR

J. Comprensión. Listen to the dialog again before answering the following questions.

1. On what street is the building the man is looking for?
2. What building is he looking for?
3. What street are the man and woman on?

Answers, Ex. J
1. Calle González Obregón
2. Secretaría de Educación Pública
3. Calle Madero

K. ¿Cómo lo dicen?

1. How does the man excuse himself when he stops the woman to ask for directions?
2. What expression does the woman use to say "of course" or "certainly"?
3. After the man thanks her, what phrase does the woman use to say "You're welcome"?

Answers, Ex. K
1. Perdone, señorita. 2. Cómo no. 3. No hay de qué.

Tú dirás ....

L. Vamos a la universidad. Explain to an older person whom you have just met how to get from where he or she lives to your school. Give specific directions. Include in your explanation the verbs **ir, cruzar,** and **doblar.**

M. Direcciones. Working in groups of three, one person will give directions to the other two for getting to several different places in your town (e.g., bank, supermarket, post office, bookstore, movie theater). Take turns asking for and giving directions to each other.

Ex. L: Pairs

Ex. M: Groups

Variation, Ex. M: Put students in groups of four and then pair them in those groups. Each pair within a group will write directions to get to two different places in town. Each pair gives the directions to the other without saying the name of the actual place, and that pair must guess the place where the directions lead.

LECTURA: Las mariposas Monarca de México

ANTES DE LEER

A. Look at the title of the reading on page 115 and the photos that accompany it to guess what this reading may be about.

B. Find the Spanish word for this insect. What do you know about butterflies?

GUÍA PARA LA LECTURA

C. Read the first paragraph. Notice that **migración, anual, fantásticos,** and **volcanes** are similar to the English words *migration, annual, fantastic,* and *volcanoes.* These words are cognates. Now look quickly at the next two paragraphs and identify as many cognates as you can. Compare your list with another classmate's list.

D. This time skim the passage to determine in which paragraph you find the following information.

1. how butterflies are able to stay on course
2. the representation of the butterfly in pre-Hispanic art
3. when the butterflies arrive at their sanctuary and when they leave it

F. Now read the passage more carefully and find:

1. two or three ways that butterflies are assisted by nature in their migration.
2. the distance and speed involved in this migration.

Answers, Ex. D:
1. third paragraph
2. first paragraph
3. second paragraph

After completing the reading, ask students different comprehension questions. Use a map of the Americas and ask students to find and recite the route of the **mariposa Monarca.** Ask others about other animals with migratory patterns in the Americas. Ask them to point out and recite that animal's migratory pattern.

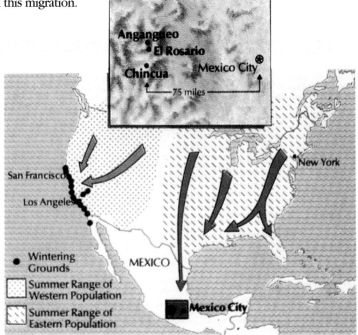

LAS MARIPOSAS MONARCA DE MEXICO

Uno de los fenómenos más fantásticos de la naturaleza es la migración anual de las mariposas Monarca. Durante el invierno, grandes grupos de estas mariposas van desde los Estados Unidos y Canadá hasta El Rosario, una región de enormes volcanes en el estado de Michoacán en México. Generalmente llegan en el mes de noviembre, después de viajar 3.000 millas a una velocidad de 9 a 27 millas por hora, y se van en el mes de abril.

Esta espectacular migración tiene una larga historia. En el arte de la gente nativa, cientos de años antes de la llegada de los españoles a México, hay representaciones de Xipe Totec, un dios tarasco, que tiene una mariposa Monarca en los labios. Estas mariposas existen desde hace millones de años y su migración, según los científicos, es única en el mundo de los insectos.

Las mariposas Monarca determinan la ruta de su largo viaje por la posición del sol y por la luz. Pero de mucha importancia es la alta intensidad del magnetismo en la zona de volcanes donde está el santuario. Cada mariposa tiene un sistema de antenas y una "cajita mágica", o un órgano especial, que reciben fuerzas magnéticas que ayudan en la orientación de la mariposa.

VÍDEO CULTURAL: ¡La fiesta del pueblo!

G. Anticipación. Una llamada telefónica. Check off all the vocabulary you think might be used in a phone conversation between two young Spanish-speaking people planning a party.

1. los toros
2. la música
3. una chava
4. pasarlo bien
5. el torero

6. la piñata
7. la bebida
8. los amigos
9. la comida
10. el banderillero

H. Preparación. Match the following Spanish words and phrases with their English equivalent.

1. estar de buen humor
2. Lo paso muy bien.
3. ¿Qué onda?
4. llevar el equipo
5. una chava

a. to be in a good mood
b. to take the equipment
c. a nice (cool) girl
d. What's up?
e. I have a good time.

I. Participación. Take notes as you watch the video. Write down words and phrases that you think may be useful during class discussion or that you'll use later in the *Personalización* exercise.

J. Comprensión. Based on what you saw in this video lesson, choose the best answer.

1. ¿Qué lleva Mauricio a la fiesta?
   a. la comida
   b. la música
2. ¿Quiénes van a la fiesta de Ricardo?
   a. los amigos de su equipo de fútbol
   b. los amigos de la clase
3. ¿Cómo es Irma?
   a. Muy preocupada y antipática
   b. muy simpática

K. Personalización. Write a short telephone dialog in which you and a friend plan a party. Work in groups of two or three. Later, share your activity with the class.

Estudiante A

Last year you met Anabel, an exchange student from Burgos, Spain. You became good freinds, and she invited you to visit her in the summer. You have just arrived in Burgos and now you need to find Anabel's house.

This is the information you have:

Anabel Gómez del Campo
Plaza de la Libertad 11
Burgos
Teléfono (947) 22 94 79

You just got off the bus at **la Estación de Autobuses** and you ask a passerby to give you directions. On a seperate piece of paper, write down the directions. When you finish, share the information you got with the rest of the *Estudiantes A* to see if all you obtained similar directions.

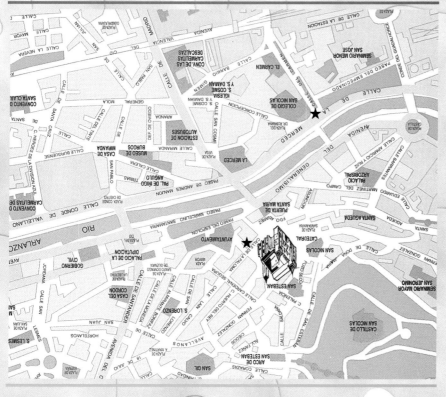

she needs to go.

Using the map of downtown Burgos, tell this person how to get to where he or

address.

Segovia. Someone approaches you asking for directions to get to a particular

You are a native from Burgos and happen to be at the bus station to buy a ticket to

Estudiante B

VOCABULARIO

Para charlar

Para preguntar la edad *Asking one's age*
¿Cuántos años tienes? *How old are you?*

Para preguntar y dar la hora *Asking for and giving the time*
A las cinco de la mañana. *At five in the morning.*
A la una de la tarde. *At one in the afternoon.*
A la medianoche. *At midnight.*
A las nueve de la noche. *At nine in the evening.*
¿A qué hora? *What time?*
Al mediodía. *At noon.*
¿Cuándo? *When?*
Es la una. *It's one o'clock.*
Es la una y media. *It's one thirty.*
¿Qué hora es? *What time is it?*
Son las tres menos veinte. *It's two forty.*
Son las dos. *It's two o'clock.*

Para dar direcciones *Giving directions*
Cruce la calle... *Cross... street.*
Doble a la derecha. *Turn right.*
Doble a la izquierda. *Turn left.*
Está al final de... *It's at the end of...*
    al lado de... *next to...*
    cerca de... *near...*
    delante de... *in front of...*
    detrás de... *behind...*
    entre... *between...*
    en la esquina de... *at the corner of...*
    frente a... *across from...*
    lejos de... *far from...*
Siga derecho por... *Go straight for...*

Para pedir direcciones *Asking for directions*
¿Cómo llego a...? *How do I get to...?*
¿Dónde está...? *Where is...?*
¿Está lejos/cerca de aquí? *Is it far from/near here?*

Temas y contextos

Los edificios y los lugares públicos *Buildings and public places*
el aeropuerto *airport*
el estacionamiento *parking lot*

la avenida *avenue*
el banco *bank*
la biblioteca *library*
la calle *street*
la catedral *cathedral*
el cine *movie theater*
la ciudad *city*
el colegio *school*
la discoteca *discotheque*
la escuela secundaria *high school*
la terminal de autobuses *bus terminal*
la estación de policía *police station*
la estación de trenes *railroad station*
el estadio *stadium*
el hospital *hospital*
el hotel *hotel*
la iglesia *church*
el museo *museum*
la oficina de correos *post office*
el parque *park*
la plaza *plaza, square*
el quiosco de periódicos *newspaper kiosk*
el teatro *theater*
la universidad *university*

Las tiendas *Stores*
la carnicería *butcher shop*
la farmacia *pharmacy, drugstore*
la florería *flower shop*
la librería *bookstore*
el mercado *market*
la panadería *bakery*

La fiesta del pueblo *A town's holiday celebration*
los bailes folklóricos *folk dances*
el baile popular *popular dance*
el concurso de poesía *poetry contest*
el desfile *parade*
el Día de la Independencia *Independence Day*
la feria *fair*
los fuegos artificiales *fireworks*
la misa *Mass*
el premio *prize*

Vocabulario general   General vocabulary

Adjetivos *Adjectives*

aburrido(a)   *bored*
cansado(a)   *tired*
contento(a)   *happy*
enfermo(a)   *sick*
enojado(a)   *angry*
hispano(a)   *Hispanic*
listo(a)   *ready*
triste   *sad*

Verbos *Verbs*

anunciar   *to announce*
celebrar   *to celebrate*
descansar   *to rest*
estar   *to be*
ir   *to go*
llegar   *to arrive*
querer (ie)   *to want, love*
preferir (ie)   *to prefer*
tener   *to have*
ver   *to see*

Imperativos *Imperatives*

¡Baile!   *Dance!*
¡No baile!   *Don't dance!*
¡Canten!   *Sing!*
¡No canten!   *Don't sing!*
Sea Ud....   *Be ...*
Sean Uds....   *Be ...*
Vaya Ud....   *Go ...*
Vayan Uds....   *Go ...*

Otras palabras y expresiones

¿Adónde vamos?   *Where are we going?*
ahora   *now*
a menudo   *frequently, often*
la conversación telefónica   *telephone conversation*
de acuerdo   *OK (Agreed)*
de vez en cuando   *from time to time*
del   *of the*
¿Dónde nos encontramos?   *Where should we meet?*
en otra oportunidad   *at some other time*
entonces   *then*
mejor   *better*
nunca   *never*
para   *for, in order to*
por supuesto   *of course*
rara vez   *rarely*
tener... años   *to be ... years old*
tener calor   *to be hot*
tener frío   *to be cold*
tener ganas de...   *to feel like ...*
tener hambre   *to be hungry*
tener que + *infinitive*   *to have to*
tener sed   *to be thirsty*
tener sueño   *to be sleepy*

4 Vamos al centro

CHAPTER OBJECTIVES:

In this chapter you will learn about various ways to get around and make plans. After completing this chapter you will be able to carry out the following tasks:

- ⦾ **make plans for various activities in town**
- ⦾ **talk about various means of transportation**
- ⦾ **talk about future plans**
- ⦾ **use the Buenos Aires Subway**
- ⦾ **understand conversations about making plans**

The tools you will use to carry out these tasks are:

- ⦾ **vocabulary related to the following topics:**
  - transportation
  - present and future time
  - making plans
  - numbers to one million
- ⦾ **grammatical structures:**
  - the immediate future
  - the verbs **hacer, poder, venir**
  - verbs like **pensar, dormir, pedir**

PARAGUAY

Población: 5.504.146
406.752 kilómetros cuadrados (157.047 millas cuadradas), como el tamaño de California
Capital: Asunción, 607.000

URUGUAY

Población: 3.238.952
176.215 kilómetros cuadrados (68.037 millas cuadradas), como el tamaño de Washington
Capital: Montevideo, 1.400.000

ARGENTINA

Población: 34.672.997
2.779.221 kilómetros cuadrados (1.073.518 millas cuadradas), cuatro veces el tamaño de Texas
Capital: Buenos Aires, 2.960.000
Ciudades principales: Córdoba, 1.100.000; Rosario, 750.000; Mendoza, 597.000; Tucumán, 497.000

Argentina Countryside

	ARGENTINA	PARAGUAY	URUGUAY
Moneda:	el peso	el guaraní	el peso
Esperanza de vida:	hombres, 68; mujeres, 75	hombres, 72; mujeres, 75	hombres, 72; mujeres, 78
Índice de alfabetización:	96%	92%	97%
Productos principales de exportación:	cereales, semillas, azúcar, frijoles, tomates, algodón, carne, ganado, minerales	algodón, soya, aceites vegetales, maderas, tabaco, cuero, café, yerba mate, frutas y vegetales	textiles, ganado, carne, cueros y pieles, productos vegetales, tabaco, plásticos y productos sintéticos, caucho, zapatos
Embajada:	1600 New Hampshire Ave. NW, Washington, DC 20009	2400 Massachusetts Ave. NW, Washington, DC 20008	1919 F St. NW, Washington, DC 20006

PRIMERA ETAPA

PARA EMPEZAR: ¿Vas al centro?

Preparación: As you begin this *etapa*, answer the following questions:
- How do you get around town?
- Do you use public transportation?
- Is there a public transportation system in your town?

🎧 Play Textbook audio.

🛒 Transparencies G-1 and G-2: Al centro #1 & #2

GRAMMAR NOTE:
Remember that in Spanish the preposition **en** is used in expressions **en coche, en autobús, en metro, en taxi, en bicicleta**, but **a** is used in **a pie.**

Suggestion: Point out the sentence from the dialog: **Voy a ver a unos amigos.** Explain that the personal **a** is used to introduce a direct object that represents a specific person or persons.

Present new vocabulary in context by telling students that you are in charge of creating a guide for exchange students new to your town. This guide will list how to get around in town. Tell them, in Spanish, and write on the board, some of the basic activities one does in town, i.e., **ir al cine, comer en un restaurante, hacer mandados como ir al correo,** etc. Use transparency to then point out the transportation someone would have to use to get to each of these places. Check for comprehension during presentation.

—¿Vas al centro esta tarde?
—Sí, voy a ver a unos amigos. Tenemos una cita a las 2:00.
—¿Vas en autobús?
—No, voy a tomar el metro.

—¿Tienes ganas de ir al cine esta noche?
—Sí, ¡qué buena idea! ¿Tomamos el metro?
—No, vamos en autobús.

—Tengo que ir al centro hoy para ir de compras. ¿Quieres ir conmigo?
—Sí, yo también tengo que comprar unas cosas. ¿Vamos a pie?
—No, vamos en el coche de mi hermana.

I should

—Tengo que ir al centro para hacer un mandado. **Debo** ir al correo.
—Voy contigo. Tengo que hacer un mandado.
—Perfecto. Vamos juntos y después damos un paseo.

Práctica

A. ¿Quieres ir al centro conmigo? You are going downtown and invite a friend to come along. When you explain your reason for going, he or she agrees and suggests a way of getting there. You have a different idea, which your friend accepts.

■ **Modelo:** ir al correo / metro / a pie
> —*¿Quieres ir al centro conmigo?*
> —*¿Para qué vas?*
> —*Debo ir al correo.*
> —*De acuerdo. ¿Vamos en metro?*
> —*No, no. Vamos a pie.*
> —*De acuerdo. Vamos a pie.*

1. ir de compras / autobús / coche
2. ver una película / coche / metro
3. ir al banco / bicicleta / a pie

Ex. A: Pairs

Answer, Ex. A
1. ¿Quieres ir al centro conmigo?
   ¿Para qué vas?
   Debo ir de compras.
   ¿Vamos en autobús?
   No, no. Vamos en coche.
   De acuerdo. Vamos en coche.

4. hacer un mandado / a pie / autobús
5. ver una exposición en un museo / metro / bicicleta
6. comer alguna cosita en un café / autobús / a pie
7. ver a unos amigos / a pie / autobús
8. comprar algo para mi hermano / metro / a pie

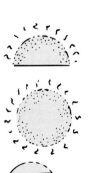
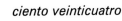
B. ¿Para qué, cómo y cuándo van al centro? Based on the drawings tell why, how, and when each student is going downtown.

■ **Modelo:** —*¿Para qué va Laura al centro?*
—*Para ver a una amiga.*
—*¿Cómo?*
—*En autobús.*
—*¿Cuándo?*
—*Por la tarde.*

Laura

1. Juan

2. Marta

3. Esteban

4. Elena

5. Pedro y Ana

6. Víctor y Raúl

C. ¿Quieres ir al centro conmigo? Make a list of things you want or need to do in town. Then interview your classmates to find someone who would like to go with you for some of the same reasons. When you find someone who wants to join you, arrange a means of transportation and a time that is convenient for both of you.

Comentarios

culturales

Argentina: Variación geográfica

Argentina, por su superficie geográfica, es el segundo país más grande de Sudamérica, después del Brasil. El país es tan grande que hay una gran variedad de climas dentro de sus fronteras. El norte y noreste son regiones tropicales, mientras que en las montañas y en el sur, que está muy cerca de la Antártida, hace mucho frío.

En el centro del país está la vasta zona de **llanuras** *(plains)* fértiles, La Pampa. Aquí, donde el clima es más seco pero con fuertes variaciones, cultivan **trigo** *(wheat)* y otros cereales. También crían **ganado** *(cattle)* para el consumo de carne por parte de los argentinos y para la exportación. La inmensa **cordillera** *(montain range)* de los Andes separa a Argentina de Chile. En la larga frontera que los dos países tienen en común están algunos de los picos más elevados del mundo, como el Aconcagua, que tiene 22.935 pies de altura.

INTEGRACIÓN CULTURAL

1. How does this country compare in size to other South American countries?
2. What is the climate like?
3. What is Argentina's most important export?
4. While the capital, Buenos Aires, is at sea level, what and where would the highest point in the country be?

1. What you have learned to say in Spanish so far refers mainly to the present tense. Note the following sentences and how they refer to future activities.

Voy a comer.	*I am going to eat.*
Vamos a estudiar.	*We are going to study.*
¿Qué vas a hacer esta tarde?	*What are you going to do this afternoon?*
Voy a dar un paseo.	*I am going to take a walk.*

2. The most common way to express future action in Spanish is to use the present tense form of ir + a + infinitive. Note from the examples that this structure is equivalent to the English use of going to + verb.

Voy a bailar.	*I'm going to dance.*
Vas a hablar español.	*You're going to speak Spanish.*
¿Va a comer Juan en el centro?	*Is John going to eat downtown?*
Vamos a escuchar la cinta.	*We're going to listen to the tape.*
Uds. van a estudiar.	*You're going to study.*
Ellos van a dar un paseo.	*They're going to take a walk.*
No voy a comer en el centro.	*I'm not going to eat downtown.*
Ellos no van a estudiar.	*They're not going to study.*

GRAMMAR NOTE:
Remember in Chapter 3, page 95, you learned the present tense of the verb **ir.** Here are the forms to refresh your memory:

voy	**vamos**
vas	**vais**
va	**van**

There is a separate future tense in Spanish. It appears in Chapter 12.

Práctica

D. Después de la clase. Use words from each column to form sentences to express what the people in Column A will do after class.

Column A	Column B	Column C
yo	ir a	dar un paseo
Susana		comer en un restaurante
Marcos		estudiar en la biblioteca
nosotros		comprar un disco compacto
Juan y su novia		mirar un programa de televisión
Uds.		hacer un mandado
tú		
vosotros		

E. ¿Qué vas a hacer el sábado por la tarde (*Saturday afternoon*)? You are trying to find out what your friends are going to do Saturday afternoon. A classmate will answer the questions using the expressions in parentheses.

■ **Modelo:** —Marcos, ¿qué vas a hacer el sábado por la tarde? (comer en un restaurante)
—*Voy a comer en un restaurante.*

1. ¿Qué va a hacer Carlos el sábado por la tarde? (estudiar en la biblioteca)
2. ¿Y qué va a hacer Juan? (ver a una amiga en el centro)
3. ¿Y Fernando y su amigo? (dar un paseo)
4. ¿Y Bárbara y Julián? (ir de compras)

Ex. E:  Pairs

Suggestion, Ex. E Have the partner who asks the first question ask a follow-up question about the transportation to be used, i.e., **¿Cómo vas? ¿A pie?**... The other partner will make up a response.

Answers, Ex. E
1. Va a estudiar... 2. Va a ver... 3. Van a dar... 4. Van a ir... 5. Va a comprar... 6. Voy a... 7. Vamos a...

Variation: Have students pretend they are famous people and tell them to make their list based on what they know about that person. When they share the list with their partners, the partner will try to guess who the famous person is.

IRM Master 14: El verbo *hacer*

Suggestion, the verb **hacer:** Ask several students, in English, what they are going to do later in the week. Point out that while a form of the verb *to do* is part of the question, it is not part of the answer. The response contains a form of the verb that expresses what they will do and not the verb *to do*.

Especially with advanced beginners, encourage students to use these questions as conversation starters, carrying out a conversation in Spanish if they can.

5. ¿Qué va a hacer Marcos? (comprar un disco compacto)
6. ¿Qué vas a hacer tú el sábado por la tarde?
7. ¿Qué van a hacer tú y tus amigos el sábado por la tarde?

F. Voy a ... Make a list of five things you will do in the next week. Tell two of your classmates what you will do and have them tell you what they're going to do.

ENFOQUE ESTRUCTURAL **El verbo hacer**

The verb **hacer** is conjugated as follows:

hacer			
yo	**hago**	nosotros	**hacemos**
tú	**haces**	vosotros	**hacéis**
Ud.		Uds.	
él	**hace**	ellos	**hacen**
ella		ellas	

Note that, except for the **yo** form **(hago)**, **hacer** is conjugated in the same way as the other regular **-er** verbs you have studied.

When asked a question that includes **hacer** or one of its forms, you normally answer with the verb that expresses what you do. For example:

¿Qué **haces** los lunes?	*What **do you do** on Mondays?*
Voy a la escuela.	*I **go** to school.*
¿Qué **vas a hacer** el viernes?	*What **are you going to do** on Friday?*
Voy a estudiar.	*I'm **going to study.***

Práctica

G. De costumbre, ¿qué haces los domingos por la tarde? With a classmate, take turns asking each other the following questions.

1. ¿Qué haces los sábados por la tarde?
2. ¿Qué hace tu amigo los lunes por la noche?
3. ¿Que hace tu compañero(a) de cuarto *(roommate)* los miércoles por la mañana?
4. ¿Qué hacen tú y tus amigos los fines de semana?
5. ¿Qué haces los viernes por la noche?
6. ¿Qué hace tu compañero(a) de cuarto los jueves por la tarde?

H. ¿Qué vas a hacer el domingo por la tarde? Now repeat the above exercise, changing each question to the future.

■ **Modelo:** —¿*Qué vas a hacer el sábado por la noche?*
—*Voy a visitar a un amigo.*

I. ¿Qué haces normalmente los viernes por la noche? ¿Qué vas a hacer el viernes por la noche? Ask a classmate what he or she does on a typical Friday night, then ask what he or she will do this Friday night. Have them ask you the same questions.

Ex. G  Pairs

Suggestion, Ex. G: Before doing exercise, brainstorm with students important days in the upcoming future. These might include New Year's Eve 1999, graduation day, etc. Have students mill about class and interview others about what they will do on those days. Have students note interesting answers to share with the class when done.

VAMOS A ESCUCHAR: ¿QUIERES IR CONMIGO?

🎧 Play Textbook audio.

Laura and Juan run into each other on a street in Buenos Aires. One of them has to do an errand and invites the other to come along.

ANTES DE ESCUCHAR

Given what you've been working on in this *etapa,* what are some of the things they might say to each other?

Before listening to their short dialog, read the questions under the *Después de escuchar* section below.

DESPUÉS DE ESCUCHAR

J. Comprensión. As your instructor plays the tape, listen for the answers to the following questions.

1. Where does Laura have to go?
2. What does Juan have to buy?
3. What will they do first?
4. How does Juan suggest they go?
5. How do they decide to go?

K. ¿Cómo lo dicen? Your instructor will play the tape again. Listen to try to determine the following:

1. How does Laura say she has to run an errand for her father?
2. What expression does Juan use when he agrees to accompany Laura?

Answers, Ex. J
1. downtown 2. a new CD 3. an errand for Laura's dad 4. on foot 5. on the metro

Suggestion, Ex. J After allowing students to listen to the tape two times, ask them these questions in Spanish. Encourage them to answer in Spanish.

Answers, Ex. K
1. Tengo que hacer un mandado para mi padre. 2. ¡Cómo no!

Tú dirás

L. ¿Quieres ir conmigo? Invite a classmate to do something with you. When you get an affirmative response, arrange a day and time, and agree on a means of transportation. Fill in the chart below, or use a separate piece of paper, and use the information to report back to the class.

■ **Modelo:** *Jennie y yo vamos a ver una película el viernes por la noche. Vamos en coche.*

¿Qué hacemos?	¿Cuándo?	¿Cómo vamos?
ver una película	el viernes por la noche	en coche

Ex. L:  Pairs

GRAMMAR NOTE:
To invite someone to do something, in Spanish you would use a conjugated form of the verb querer followed by the verb that expresses what you are inviting the person to do.

¿Quieres ir al cine?

¿Quieres cenar conmigo?

¿Quieres estudiar en la biblioteca esta noche?

M. ¿Para qué vas al centro? You want to conduct a survey to determine for what purposes and when your classmates go downtown. Ask several of your classmates when and for what purpose they go downtown and fill in the chart below or use a separate piece of paper to record the information you gather. Be ready to report the information back to the class.

Nombre	¿Cuándo?	¿Para qué?
Bill	sábado por la mañana	ir al correo

■ **Modelo:** *Bill va al centro el sábado por la mañana para ir al correo.*

⊚ SEGUNDA ETAPA

⊚ PARA EMPEZAR: ¿Vamos a tomar el subte?

VOCABULARY EXPANSION:
The technical name for the subway in Spanish is **metro,** but in Argentina it is known as **el subte,** which is a shortened form of the word **subterráneo.**

Transparency 6-3:
Buenos Aires Subway

Suggestion: On the transparency, show the places and routes mentioned in the dialog.

entrance

In Spanish remind students of the modes of transportation they have just learned about. Then talk about the metro, which allows rapid transportation in the city. Ask students about rapid transit in places they live or have visited. Encourage them to answer in Spanish.

Preparación: In this *etapa* you will become familiar with el subte, the Buenos Aires subway system. As you begin this *etapa,* answer the following questions:
- What cities in the USA have similar modes of public transportation?
- Have you heard of the "L" in Chicago? the "T" in Boston? MARTA in Atlanta? BART in San Francisco?

Elena y su prima Clara van a tomar el subte para ir al Museo de Arte Moderno. La casa de Elena está cerca de la estación del metro. Las dos jóvenes miran el mapa del subte que está a la **entrada** de la estación.

Elena:	Bueno. Estamos aquí, en la estación San Juan.
Clara:	¿Dónde está el museo?
Elena:	Está cerca de la Estación Callao. Allí.
Clara:	Entonces, ¿qué hacemos?
Elena:	Es fácil. Tomamos la línea C en dirección de Retiro.
Clara:	¿Tenemos que **cambiar** de tren?

Elena:	Sí, tenemos que cambiar de trenes. Cambiamos en 9 de julio. Allí tomamos la línea B en dirección de Federico Lacroz.	to change
Clara:	Y **bajamos** en Callao, ¿verdad?	
Elena:	Exacto, allí en Callao bajamos.	we get off

🎧 Play Textbook audio.

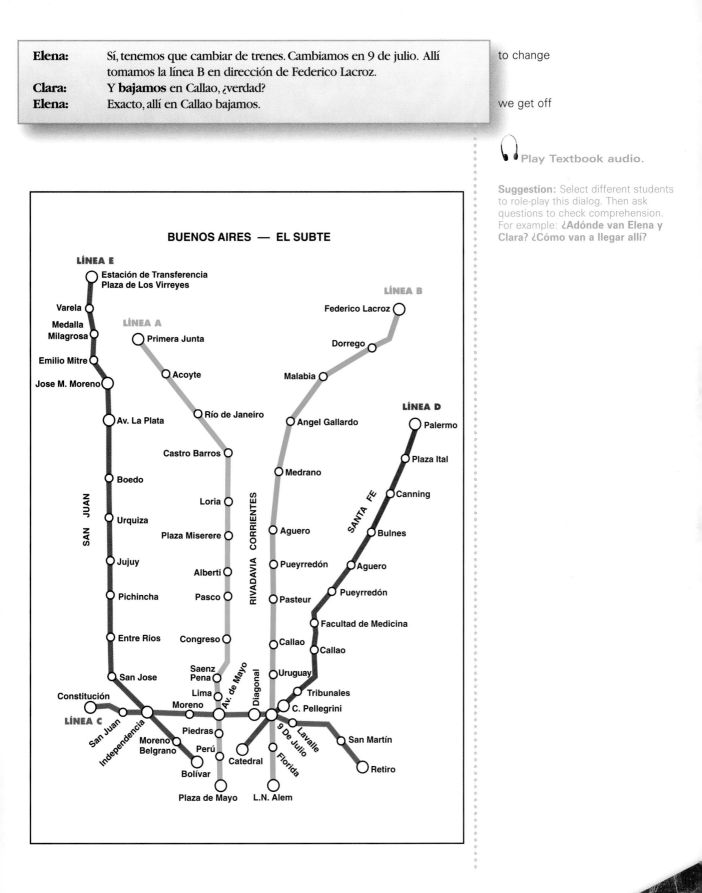

BUENOS AIRES — EL SUBTE

Comentarios

culturales El "subte" de Buenos Aires

El metro es uno de los **modos** *(means)* de transporte más populares en Buenos Aires, la capital de Argentina. Los porteños, otro nombre para los residentes de Buenos Aires, le llaman "el subte", la forma **apocopada** *(shortened)* de la palabra "subterráneo". Es la manera más fácil y eficaz de ir de un **sitio** *(place)* a otro en esta ciudad. El arte que está en las estaciones del subte tiene una historia interesante. Muchos de los **azulejos fueron hechos** *(tiles were made)* en España y Francia durante las primeras tres décadas de este **siglo** *(century).* Otras ciudades en el mundo hispano que tienen metros son Barcelona, Madrid, Caracas y la Ciudad de México.

INTEGRACIÓN CULTURAL

Vamos a conocer el subte. In order to familiarize yourself with the Buenos Aires subway, look at the map above and work with a partner to answer the following questions.

1. How many lines does the Buenos Aires subway have?
2. What are the names of the lines?
3. What are the names of the last stops on each line?
4. At which stations do two or more lines converge?
5. What other cities in the Spanish-speaking world have a subway?

Práctica

A. ¡Vamos a tomar el subte! Imagine you live in Buenos Aires. Following the model and using the **subte** map on page 131, tell your partner how you get from home to work every day. The subway line (shown in parentheses after the name of each station) will help you locate the stations.

■ **Modelo:** Alberti (A) / San Martín (C)
   Vivo cerca de Alberti. Tomo la línea A, dirección de Plaza de Mayo, cambio de trenes en Avenida de Mayo. Allí tomo la línea C, dirección de Retiro y bajo en San Martín.

Vivo cerca de...	Bajo en...
1. Avenida la Plata (E)	Diagonal (C)
2. Río de Janeiro (A)	San Juan (C)
3. Catedral (D)	Medrano (B)
4. Bulnes (D)	Moreno (C)
5. Jujuy (E)	Lavalle (C)

B. Now with a partner, determine how you would get from where you are to your destination. Note sometimes you will have to change trains twice.

Estoy en...   Voy a...
1. Boedo (E)   Canning (D)
2. Loria (A)   Pinchincha (E)
3. Dorrego (B)   Entre Ríos (E)
4. San Martín (C)   Castro Barros (A)
5. Medrano (B)   Medalla Milagrosa (E)

C. ¡En el subte! Explain to the people mentioned below how to take the subway. Consult the **subte** map on page 131. (Metro lines are given in parentheses.) Since all of the following people are strangers, use formal commands.

■ **Modelo:**   Vaya(n) a la estación Loria.
              Tome(n) la línea A, dirección de Plaza de Mayo.
              Cambie(n) de trenes en Avenida de Mayo.
              Baje(n) en Pasco.

1. A tourist from Italy is in Buenos Aires for a couple of days. Her hotel is near Avenida La Plata (E). She wants to see a church near Pasteur (B).
2. Sr. and Sra. Dávila are spending three weeks in Buenos Aires. Their hotel is near the Moreno Belgrano (E) station and they want to go to a museum near Callao (D).
3. Near the Boedo station (E), you meet a disoriented tourist who wants to get to the Casa Rosada near the Perú station (A).
4. Near the Acoyte station (A) you run into a person who wants to get to a store that is near Florida (B).
5. Near the Bolívar station (E) you meet a group of students who are meeting some friends for lunch at a restaurant near the Facultad de Medicina station (D).

Repaso

D. Visiten el museo. Using the verbs provided, give suggestions to each of the following people or groups about what to do in your town or city. Come up with your own suggestions using these verbs. Remember to use formal commands.

1. a group of Spanish-speaking visitors to your town or city
   a. ir   d. visitar
   b. mirar   e. beber
   c. comer
2. one Spanish-speaking visitor to your town or city
   a. hablar   d. comer
   b. visitar   e. ir
   c. cruzar

Suggestion, Ex. C
For additional practice and cultural awareness, have students look up subway maps for other major Spanish-speaking cities (in the library or on the Web). Have them decide two interesting things to do in that city and the subway lines that would take them there. They can then give a presentation to the class in Spanish.

E. ¿Qué van a hacer? Find out from several of your classmates what they're going to do at specific times tomorrow. Use the chart below to keep track of this information and report back to the class.

■ **Modelo:**   —*¿Qué vas a hacer, Wendy?*
              —*Voy a estudiar.*
              —*¿A qué hora?*
              —*A las 8.*

¿Quién?	¿Qué va a hacer?	¿A qué hora?
Wendy	estudiar	a las 8
Estudiante B		
Estudiante C		

Suggestion: Adverbs: (1) On board write today's date, dates for this week and next, the present year, and next year. (2) Review and introduce adverbs by using the dates. Begin with the present and move to the future.

Begin this presentation with a short personal anecdote about your plans for next week and next year. Then have students answer questions about plans, gradually familiarizing them with the notion of **próximo(a)**.

ENFOQUE LÉXICO   **Expresiones para indicar presente y futuro**

Note the expressions in the following sentences that indicate when the action takes place.

Mi compañera de cuarto trabaja **hoy**.	*My roommate is working **today**.*
Mañana no va a trabajar.	***Tomorrow** she's not going to work.*
¿Dónde están **ahora**?	*Where are they **now**?*

Adverbs to express present or future time:

hoy	esta mañana
esta tarde	esta noche
mañana	mañana por la mañana
mañana por la tarde	mañana por la noche

Some additional expressions:

ahora *(now)*	la semana próxima *(next week)*
esta semana *(this week)*	el mes próximo *(next month)*
este mes *(this month)*	el año próximo *(next year)*
este año *(this year)*	

In addition, the expressions **por la mañana, por la tarde, por la noche, and próximo(a)** can be combined with the days of the week: **el lunes por la mañana, el sábado por la tarde, el domingo por la noche, el lunes próximo,** etc. Time expressions are usually placed at the very beginning or end of a sentence.

Práctica

F. El horario (*schedule*) de los González. Answer the questions about the González family's activities during the month of February. Choose the appropriate time expressions, assuming that today is the morning of February 15.

Answers, Ex. F
1. El miércoles. 2. El lunes próximo.
3. Este viernes y el viernes próximo.
4. El martes próximo. 5. Mañana. 6.
El viernes. 7. Van al teatro. 8. Van a ir
a la iglesia. 9. Va a ir al curso de
francés. 10. Van a ir al restaurante.

FEBRERO						
lunes	martes	miércoles	jueves	viernes	sábado	domingo
1	2	3	4	5 *restaurante*	6	7 *iglesia*
8	9	10	11	12 *restaurante*	13	14 *iglesia*
15 *Sr y Sra teatro en el centro (noche)*	16 *Sr jugar al tenis*	17 *Sr trabajo (noche)*	18 *Sra museo*	19 *Sra trabajo (mañana) restaurante*	20 *Sra curso de francés (tarde)*	21 *iglesia*
22 *catedral*	23 *los Martínez*	24	25	26 *restaurante*	27	28 *iglesia*

■ **Modelo:** ¿Cuándo va a ir al museo la Sra. González?
    El jueves.

1. ¿Qué noche va a trabajar el Sr. González?
2. ¿Cuándo van a visitar los González la catedral?
3. ¿Cuándo van a comer en un restaurante?
4. ¿Cuándo van a llegar los Martínez?
5. ¿Cuándo va a jugar al tenis el Sr. González?
6. ¿Qué mañana va a trabajar la Sra. González?

■ **Modelo:** ¿Qué va a hacer el Sr. González el miércoles por la noche?
    Él va a trabajar.

7. ¿Qué van a hacer los González esta noche?
8. ¿Qué van a hacer el Sr. y la Sra. González el domingo?
9. ¿Qué va a hacer la Sra. González el sábado por la tarde?
10. ¿Qué van a hacer los González el viernes próximo?

G. Esta noche no… With a classmate, take turns asking each other the following questions indicating an alternative time in your answers.

Ex. G

Allow students 5–6 minutes to
complete. When done, ask
different students some of the
8 questions. Then follow up each
question with related spontaneous
questions. For example: **¿Qué van a
hacer en el centro?**

■ **Modelo:** ¿Van al cine tú y Luis esta noche?
    Esta noche no. Vamos al cine mañana por la noche.

1. ¿Van tú y tu amigo al centro el miércoles por la noche?
2. ¿Vas a hacer un mandado mañana por la mañana?
3. ¿Va a comer tu amigo en tu casa el viernes por la tarde?
4. ¿Vas a estudiar español el año próximo?
5. ¿Vas a ir al cine esta noche?
6. ¿Va a llevar el coche tu hermana mañana por la noche?
7. ¿Van a llegar tus padres el jueves próximo?
8. ¿Vas a estudiar esta noche?

Suggestion, Ex. H: Play biography bingo. Have students create 9 squares on a sheet of paper and in each square write an activity that people do on the weekends. Students then circulate and ask each other questions to find out who does each of the activities in the squares. The student who fills the card first wins.

Suggestion, esperar and **querer:** (1) Have students discuss in English the difference between *I want to go* and *I hope to go*. (2) Introduce **espero ir** and **quiero ir.** (3) Have students respond with one of the three expressions to **hacer mi tarea, ir al cine, tener un Mercedes,** e.g., **quiero hacer mi tarea, espero hacer mi tarea, voy a hacer mi tarea.**

H. ¿Qué haces los fines de semana? Circulate around the room and ask your classmates what they generally do on the weekends. Find students who go to a party, study in the library, go home for the weekend, play a sport, go to a concert, go to a movie, go to a restaurant.

ENFOQUE LÉXICO | **Expresiones para hacer planes**

Think about the expressions you use to make plans. The plans can be short-term or long-term. Note the following examples:

Quiero comprar un coche el año próximo.	*I want to buy a car next year.*
Quiero ir al cine el viernes próximo.	*I want to go to the movies next Friday.*

You have already learned two ways to talk about future actions: what you *want* to do **(querer),** what you *are going* to do **(ir).** You now have another expression for talking about your plans and what you *hope* to do **(esperar).** In all three expressions, the action of the verb is in the infinitive form.

Espero comprar un coche nuevo el año próximo.	*I hope to buy a new car next year.*
Esperamos ir al cine el viernes próximo.	*We hope to go to the movies next Friday.*

Note the meanings of these expressions in the following examples:

ir + a + *infinitive*

Voy a comprar un coche nuevo.	*I am going to buy a new car.*

querer + *infinitive*

Quiero comprar un coche nuevo.	*I want to buy a new car.*

esperar + *infinitive*

Espero comprar un coche nuevo.	*I hope to buy a new car.*

These expressions can also be used in the negative form:

No voy a comer en un restaurante.	*I am not going to eat in a restaurant.*

Práctica

I. Algún día. Indicate how definite each person feels about doing the following activities. Use the verbs **esperar, querer,** and **ir a.**

■ **Modelo:** ir a Argentina (tu padre / tus amigos / tú)
Mi padre no quiere ir a Argentina.
Mis amigos esperan ir a Argentina algún día.

1. ir a Buenos Aires (tu madre / tus hermanos [hermanas, amigos] / tú)
2. ser presidente (tú y tus amigos / tu padre / tu hermana [amigo])
3. tener un Rolls Royce (tu padre / tus amigos / tú)
4. vivir en Argentina (tu madre / tu hermana [hermano, amigo] / tú)

El verbo **poder**

When making plans, you often will invite someone to go with you. Note the sentences below:

¿Puedes ir al cine conmigo?	***Can you*** go to the movies with me?
Sí, **puedo.**	*Yes, **I can.***

To express in Spanish whether or not you are able to do something, use the irregular verb **poder.**

poder

yo	**puedo**	nosotros(as)	**podemos**
tú	**puedes**	vosotros(as)	**podéis**
Ud.		Uds.	
él	**puede**	ellos	**pueden**
ella		ellas	

To say that you cannot do something, place **no** before the conjugated form of **poder.**

¿Puede hablar Marcos francés?	***Can*** Mark speak French?
No, **no puede** hablar francés, **puede** hablar español.	*No, **he can't** speak French, but **he can** speak Spanish.*
¿Puedes ir al centro ahora?	***Can you*** go downtown now?
No, lo siento, pero **no puedo** ir.	*No, I'm sorry, but **I can't** go.*

Note in the above examples that the conjugated form of the verb **poder** can be followed directly by an infinitive.

■ **Modelo:**

Ana: ¿Quieres cenar conmigo esta noche?

Ernesto: Lo siento, pero no puedo cenar contigo esta noche porque tengo un compromiso. Puedo cenar contigo el viernes por la noche.

J. Intercambio. Ask the following questions of a classmate, who will then answer them.

1. ¿Qué quieres hacer esta noche?
2. ¿Qué vas a hacer el sábado por la tarde?
3. ¿Qué tienes ganas de hacer el sábado?
4. ¿Qué quieres hacer el domingo?
5. ¿Qué vas a hacer el año próximo?
6. ¿Qué esperas hacer algún día?

K. ¿Qué planes tienes? Work with a classmate to make a list of things you plan to do (**ir** + **a** + *infinitive*) within the next year. Add a sentence in which you indicate at least two of these activities that you hope to do (**esperar** + *infinitive* and want to do (**querer** + *infinitive*).

IRM Master 15: El verbo *poder* You will note that the **o** in the stem of the verb **poder** becomes **ue** in all forms except **nosotros** and **vosotros.** Later in this book you will learn other verbs that follow this pattern.

You can politely refuse an invitation in Spanish with the verb **poder** and by telling the person who is inviting you that you have another commitment (**compromiso**). **Lo siento, no puedo porque tengo un compromiso.**

Ex. J:  Pairs

Suggestion, Ex. J: On the overhead, project a picture of interesting-looking people for all students to see. Put students in small groups and have them write a paragraph about what these people will be doing or hope to do next week. Group advanced with true beginners to promote cooperative learning. Have groups share their paragraphs and select the one they like the best.

L. Hoy no puedo... A classmate invites you to do something. You cannot do it at the time he or she suggests, but you suggest another time when you can. Follow the model.

Modelo: ir al cine hoy / sábado por la noche
—¿Puedes ir al cine hoy?
—*No, hoy no puedo, pero puedo ir el sábado por la noche.*

1. ir al centro ahora / viernes por la tarde
2. ir a un restaurante esta noche / mañana por la noche
3. ir al museo esta tarde / domingo por la tarde
4. ir al concierto esta semana / la semana próxima
5. ir de compras esta mañana / sábado por la mañana
6. ir al partido esta tarde / sábado próximo

M. ¿Puedes ir... ? You ask a classmate if he or she can go somewhere with you. Your classmate responds negatively and tells you about his or her plans using an appropriate form of **querer, ir a,** or **esperar.** Follow the model.

Modelo: al centro, esta noche / estudiar en casa
—¿Puedes ir al centro esta noche?
—*Lo siento, pero no puedo ir esta noche. Voy a estudiar en casa.*

1. a la biblioteca, el domingo por la tarde / visitar a mi abuela
2. a un restaurante, el viernes por la noche / ver a un amigo
3. al baile, el sábado por la noche / estudiar español
4. al partido de fútbol, mañana / ir de compras con mi compañero(a) de cuarto
5. (Ask your partner whether he or she can do something with you. Your partner will respond affirmatively or negatively.)

N. ¿Puedes ir conmigo? Ask a classmate if he or she can do something with you. When you get an affirmative response, arrange a day, a time, and a place to meet. Then agree on a means of transportation.

Carmen and Ramón are making plans to go downtown. Listen to their brief conversation and complete the following exercises.

ANTES DE ESCUCHAR

Based on what you've learned in this *etapa,* what information do you expect Carmen and Ramón to give about:

1. why they have to go downtown
2. how they will get there

Before you listen to the brief dialog, take a moment to look over the questions in the *Después de escuchar* section below.

DESPUÉS DE ESCUCHAR

Ñ. Comprensión. Answer the questions after you listen to the tape.

1. Why does Carmen want to do downtown?
2. What does Ramón want to do?
3. Why don't they take the bus?
4. What metro line do they first take?
5. Where do they change trains?

O. ¿Cómo lo dicen? Your instructor will play the tape again. Listen to try to determine the following.

1. How does Carmen say they can stop by the bookstore first?
2. How does Carmen say the metro stop is very close?

Tú dirás

P. La semana próxima. Create a weekly calendar with information about what you have to do (**tener que**), want to do (**querer**), and hope to do (**esperar**) next week. Once you have filled in your own activities, ask several classmates what they have to do, want to do, and hope to do next week.

	domingo	lunes	martes	miércoles	jueves	viernes	sábado
mañana							
tarde							
noche							

Q. ¿Adónde vamos? Imagine you are in Buenos Aires and you and a friend want to do some sightseeing. Decide on three places you want to visit and, looking at the subway map on page 131, discuss how you will get there. You will start from your hotel, which is near the Emilio Mitre station on Line E. From there you will go to Destination 1, then to Destination 2, then to Destination 3, and back to the hotel. Pick three of the possible destinations listed below and plan your day.

1. La Casa Rosada near the Plaza de Mayo station
2. Teatro Colón near the Tribunales station
3. Centro Cultural near the Pasteur station
4. Congreso Nacional near the Congreso station
5. Correo Central near the L. N. Alem station

Once you have completed your plan, be ready to tell the class the places you will visit.

TERCERA ETAPA

PARA EMPEZAR: ¿Tomamos un taxi?

Preparación: As you begin this *etapa*, take a moment and answer the following questions:

- When you take a taxi, what information must you give the taxi driver?
- What information can you expect him or her to give you?
- What about payment?
- Are you expected to give a tip?

Play Textbook audio.

Linda y Julia van a almorzar en La Cabaña, un restaurante en Buenos Aires. Piensan tomar un taxi.

> **Linda:** ¡Taxi! ¡Taxi!
> **Chofer:** ¿Adónde van?

Ellas suben al taxi.

How long does it take?

> **Linda:** Al Restaurante La Cabaña, en la Calle Entre Ríos, por favor. **¿Cuánto tarda** en llegar?

at most

> **Chofer:** Diez minutos… quince **como máximo.**

to pay

Llegan al restaurante. Julia baja del taxi y Linda va a **pagar.**

> **Linda:** ¿Cuánto es, señor?
> **Chofer:** Ocho pesos.
> **Linda:** Tome, veinte pesos.
> **Chofer:** Aquí tiene Ud. **el cambio,** doce pesos.

change

Linda le **da** dos pesos de **propina** al chófer.

gives / tip

> **Linda:** Y **esto es para Ud.**
> **Chofer:** Muchas gracias. Hasta luego.

this is for you

Práctica

A. ¿Adónde van…? A taxi driver asks you where you and a friend are going. Tell him or her the name of the place and the address. Follow the model.

■ **Modelo:** Museo Histórico Nacional / Calle Defensa
   ¿Adónde van?
   Queremos ir al Museo Histórico Nacional en la Calle Defensa.

1. Hotel Phoenix / Calle San Martín
2. Restaurante Pedemonte / Avenida de Mayo
3. Hotel San Antonio / Calle Paraguay
4. Restaurante La Estancia / Calle Lavalle
5. Teatro Municipal / Calle Corrientes

B. ¿Cuánto tardas en ir?
As you make plans with your friends, you discuss how long it will take to get to your destination. The answer will depend on the means of transportation you choose. Follow the model.

■ **Modelo:** al parque / en autobús (10 minutos) / a pie (30 o 35 minutos)
—*¿Cuánto tardas en ir al parque?*
—*Para ir al parque en autobús, tardo diez minutos.*
—*¿Y para llegar a pie?*
—*¿A pie? Tardo treinta o treinta y cinco minutos.*

1. a la biblioteca / a pie (25 minutos) / en bicicleta (10 minutos)
2. al aeropuerto / en taxi (45 minutos) / en metro (30 o 35 minutos)
3. al centro / a pie (35 minutos) / en autobús (15 minutos)
4. a tu apartamento o dormitorio
5. al apartamento o dormitorio / de tu amigo(a)
6. a tu restaurante favorito

Repaso ···

C. ¡Soy muy activo!
You lead a very busy life. Based on your activity calendar, indicate what will be happening on each day shown and use future expressions to indicate what is going to happen. Today is May 10.

■ **Modelo:** *Esta noche, voy al cine en el centro. Mañana, quiero comer en un restaurante con mis amigos. Mañana por la noche, quiero ir a bailar.*

Suggestion, Ex. C
Allow students to complete these activities in small groups. Circulate around the classroom to check for accuracy.

Remind students that in Spanish the preposition **en** is used in expressions **en coche, en autobús, en metro, en taxi, en bicicleta,** but **a** is used in **a pie.**

Possible Answers Ex. C:

El domingo por la mañana voy a la iglesia con mis padres. Por la tarde quiero jugar al tenis con mi amiga. El lunes por la tarde tengo que estudiar en la biblioteca. El martes por la mañana voy a clase. El miércoles deseo jugar al tenis por la mañana y cenar con mi familia por la noche. El jueves una amiga y yo vamos a la universidad. El viernes voy al estadio para ver un partido de fútbol.

10 de mayo
viernes

11 de mayo
sábado

12 de mayo
domingo

13 de mayo
lunes

14 de mayo
martes

15 de mayo
miércoles

16 de mayo
jueves

17 de mayo
viernes

D. Invitaciones.
Invite a friend to go somewhere or to do something with you. When your friend accepts, suggest a way of getting there. Use the appropriate forms of **querer** and such expressions as **de acuerdo, claro que sí,** and **por supuesto** (*of course*).

■ **Modelo:** ir al centro / en autobús
—*¿Quieres ir al centro?*
—*Claro que sí.*
—*Vamos en autobús.*
—*De acuerdo. Está bien.*

1. ir al cine / en metro
2. comer en un restaurante / en taxi
3. visitar la catedral / a pie
4. hacer un mandado / en nuestras bicicletas
5. ir al museo / en mi coche

Now invite a group of friends to do something or to go somewhere. When they accept, suggest a day.

■ **Modelo:** ir al centro / sábado
—*¿Quieren ir al centro?*
—*Claro que sí.*
—*Vamos el sábado.*
—*De acuerdo. Está bien.*

6. ir al concierto conmigo / jueves
7. cenar con nosotros en un restaurante / martes
8. dar un paseo / domingo
9. visitar la catedral con nosotros / sábado
10. ir al museo conmigo / lunes

IRM Master 16:
El verbo *venir*

ENFOQUE ESTRUCTURAL El verbo **venir**

In Spanish you use the verb **venir** the same way you would in English. Note the examples below:

Nosotros **venimos** a este café todos los días después de las clases.	We **come** to this café every day after classes.
¿Quién **viene** a la fiesta?	Who **is coming** to the party?
Suzy **viene.**	Suzy **is coming.**
¿A qué hora?	At what time?
A las 7:30.	At 7:30.

You will note that the verb **venir** follows a pattern similar to the verb **tener.** The present tense forms of the verb **venir** are:

°**venir (ie)**

yo	**vengo**	nosotros(as)	**venimos**
tú	**vienes**	vosotros(as)	**venís**
Ud.		Uds.	
él	**viene**	ellos	**vienen**
ella		ellas	

Práctica

E. ¿Quién viene al baile con nosotros? You and your date are going to the dance for el **Día de la Independencia.** You want to know who else is coming with you.

■ **Modelo:** Ana / sí
Ana viene al baile.

1. Elena y su hermano / no
2. Elvira / no
3. tú / sí
4. mis amigos / sí
5. David y Juliana / sí
6. Uds. / no

F. ¿Quieres venir a mi fiesta esta noche? You are doing something tonight and you are asking people in your class if they want to come along. Ask five people. If they cannot come, they must give you an excuse. Possible destinations: **la cena, el baile, la reunión, el partido, la biblioteca, el concierto, el cine,** etc.

■ **Modelo:** —Rob, ¿quieres venir a mi fiesta esta noche?
—Sí, ¡cómo no!
o
—No, lo siento, no puedo. Tengo que estudiar.

Especially with advanced beginners, encourage students to engage in short conversations, asking and answering other relevant questions about the invitation.

The verb **jugar** is one in which the **u** of the stem changes to **ue** in all forms except **nosotros** and **vosotros.**

IRM Master 17: Verbos irregulares en el presente

ENFOQUE ESTRUCTURAL **Verbos como pensar, dormir, pedir**

As you have already learned, with **querer, preferir, poder,** and **venir** some verbs change their stems in the present tense. Stem-changing verbs are verbs that have a change in the vowels of the stem. All the endings, however, remain regular.

Yo siempre **juego** al fútbol por la tarde. ¿Y tú?	*I always **play** soccer in the afternoon. What about you?*
Yo también. **¿Juegas** mañana?	*I do, too. **Are you playing** tomorrow?*
¿Mañana? Sí. Y Juan **piensa** jugar también.	*Tomorrow? Yes. And Juan is **thinking about** playing also.*
Bueno, **podemos** jugar juntos.	*Good, **we can** play together.*

There are three types of stem-changing verbs in the present:

1. Stem vowel changes to **ie: pensar, empezar, comenzar, empezar, querer, preferir, sentir**

pienso	pensamos
piensas	pensáis
piensa	piensan

---

2. Stem vowel changes to **ue: dormir, jugar, poder, volver**

duermo	dormimos
duermes	dormís
duerme	duermen

3. Stem vowel changes to **i: pedir, servir, seguir**

pido	pedimos
pides	pedís
pide	piden

The verb **decir** follows the same pattern (**e>i**) except in the **yo** form

digo	decimos
dices	decís
dice	dicen

The expression **decir que** is used to report something someone says:

¿Qué **dice** Juan que va a hacer mañana por la noche?	*What does John **say** he's going to do tomorrow night?*
Dice que va a cine	*He **says** he's going to the movies*

The expression **decir que sí, decir que no** is used to report whether someone is going to do something or not:

¿Va Juan al cine con nosotros mañana?	*Is Juan going to the movies with us tomorrow?*
Dice que sí. / Dice que no.	*He says no / He says yes.*

As you can see, in all stem-changing verbs the vowel changes in all persons except for **nosotros** and **vosotros**.

Práctica

G. Preguntas. Use each of the cues to ask questions of other students in your group.

■ **Modelo:** jugar mucho al fútbol
Katie, ¿juegas mucho al fútbol?
Sí, juego todos los sábados.

1. jugar a veces al fútbol *(soccer)*
2. pedir ayuda con la tarea
3. querer viajar mucho
4. poder tocar la guitarra
5. pensar ir al cine mañana
6. dormir mucho

H. ¿Qué piensas hacer después de las clases? You've just seen a new person who has moved into the neighborhood. After saying hello, tell each other what you do on a typical day and what you plan to do today. Invite him or her along. Use the verbs **jugar** and **volver** and other verbs you know.

Modelo: —*Buenos días. ¿Cómo estás?*
—*Muy bien. ¿Y tú?*
—*Bien, gracias. Oye, ¿qué piensas hacer después de las clases?*
—*No sé. Hoy no tengo planes. Generalmente vuelvo a la casa a las 3:30 y empiezo a hacer la tarea. A veces juego al béisbol.*
—*Ah, ¿sí? Pues, hoy yo voy al café para tomar un refresco y después voy al centro. ¿Quieres ir conmigo?*

I. ¿Qué dicen que van a hacer?

Ask a classmate what he or she is going to do tonight, then report to the class using **decir** + **que** + what they're going to do.

Ex. I: Group of 3

Modelo: —*¿Qué dice Joe?*
—*Dice que va a estudiar.*
—*¿Y qué dice Jenny?*
—*Dice que va a dormir.*

Comentarios

culturales

Paraguay: Un país bilingüe

*L*a población paraguaya desciende en su totalidad del **mestizaje** *(mixture)* entre los indígenas guaraníes y los conquistadores españoles. Por lo tanto, la Constitución del país reconoce oficialmente como lenguas nacionales el guaraní y el español. La característica más **destacada** *(outstanding)* de la cultura paraguaya es la persistencia de la tradición guaraní **enlazada** *(woven together)* con la hispánica.

La gran **mayoría** *(majority)* de la población paraguaya habla los dos **idiomas** *(languages)*. El guaraní se habla normalmente en la casa **mientras** *(while)* que el español se habla en la vida comercial y pública. Los periódicos se publican tanto en español como en guaraní. En guaraní la palabra "paraguay" significa "río de las palmas", nombre que hace referencia a los grandes **bosques de palmeras** *(palm groves)* que bordean el curso del Río Paraguay.

INTEGRACIÓN CULTURAL

1. What is special about the linguistic situation of Paraguay?
2. Where is Guaraní spoken?
3. Where is Spanish spoken?
4. What does the word "paraguay" mean in Guaraní?

Answers, Integración:
1. Both Spanish and Guaraní are recognized as official languages by the Constitution.
2. Guaraní is spoken at home.
3. Spanish is spoken in the more public arenas: stores, businesses, etc.
4. A river lined with palm trees.

Suggesstions, Los números:
Remind students that the number "one" must agree in gender with the noun it modifies, e.g., **treinta y un hombres, treinta y una mujeres.** Write **nací en** and **nació en** on the board. Have students write out in Spanish the year in which they were born: **Nací en** + the year. Then have them do the same for one of their parents or siblings with **Mi papá (mamá, hermano, hermana,** etc.) **nació en** + year.
Present this material in context by telling students that you have a millionaire friend who always buys her friends extravagant gifts. Tell them some of the gifts and the cost. After doing a few, have students try to guess the cost of other items.

CULTURE:

In most of the Hispanic world, the decimal point is expressed as a comma: English 1,452.5 = Spanish 1.452,5. A square mile is about 5/8 of a square kilometer, i.e., if something measures 80 square kilometers, it is the equivalent of 50 square miles. For example, a small state like Rhode Island measures 3,140 square kilometers and 1,962.5 square miles, while a larger state like Texas measures 691,030 square kilometers and 431,893 square miles. To convert the number of square kilometers into square miles, simply multiply square kilometers by .625.

ENFOQUE LÉXICO — # Los números de cien a un millón

100	ciento/cien	800	ochocientos(as)
101	ciento uno	900	novecientos(as)
102	ciento dos	1.000	mil
120	ciento veinte	2.000	dos mil
130	ciento treinta	4.576	cuatro mil quinientos
200	doscientos(as)		setenta y seis
300	trescientos(as)	25.489	veinticinco mil
400	cuatrocientos(as)		cuatrocientos ochenta
500	quinientos(as)		y nueve
600	seiscientos(as)	1.000.000	un millón
700	setecientos(as)	2.000.000	dos millones

1. The word **cien** is used before a noun: **cien discos.**
2. **Ciento** is used with numbers from 101–199. There is no **y** following the word **ciento:** 120 = **ciento veinte.**
3. **Cientos** changes to **cientas** before a feminine noun: **doscientos hombres, doscientas mujeres.**
4. Notice that Spanish uses a period where English uses a comma: 3.400 = 3,400 (three thousand four hundred).
5. **millón/millones** is followed by **de** when it accompanies a noun: **un millón de dólares, tres millones de habitantes.**

Práctica

J. ¿Cuántos kilómetros cuadrados ocupa (How many square kilometers does it measure)? In the chart below and on page 147 is a list of the 23 Argentinian provinces and the square kilometers they measure. With a classmate, ask each other about the size of specific provinces.

■ **Modelo:** —¿Cuántos kilómetros cuadrados ocupa San Juan?
—San Juan ocupa 89.651 kilómetros cuadrados.

División Territorial
Area Km²
Distrito Federal
Buenos Aires 200

Provincias
Buenos Aires 307.571
Catamarca 102.602
Córdoba..165.321
Las Corrientes 88.199
Chaco..99.633
Chubut 224.686
Entre Ríos 78.781

Formosa	72.066
Jujuy	53.219
La Rampa	143.440
La Rioja	89.680
Mendoza	148.827
Misiones	29.801
Neuquén	94.078
Rio Negro	203.013
Salta	155.488
San Juan	89.651
San Luis	76.748
Santa Cruz	243.943
Santa Fe	133.007
Santiago del Estero	136.351
Tierra del Fuego	20.392
Tucumán	22.524
Total	2.779.221 Km²

Source: *World Almanac*

K. ¿Adónde quieren ir? When the taxi driver asks you where you want to go in Buenos Aires, give the name of the place, the street name, and the number.

■ **Modelo:** Museo Histórico Nacional / Calle Defensa 1600
—*¿Adónde quieren ir?*
—*Queremos ir al Museo Histórico Nacional, Calle Defensa 1600.*

1. Hotel Phoenix / Calle San Martín 780
2. Restaurante Pedemonte / Avenida de Mayo 676
3. Hotel San Antonio / Calle Paraguay 372
4. Restaurante La Estancia / Calle Lavalle 941
5. Teatro Municipal General San Martín/ Calle Corrientes 1532
6. Restaurante Don Pipón / Avenida de Mayo 1249
7. Librería El Ateneo / Calle Florida 340
8. Café Filo / Calle San Martin 974
9. Los Patios de San Telmo / Calle San Lorenzo 319
10. Museo de Bellas Artes / Calle Pedro de Mendoza 1835

L. ¿Cuál es tu dirección? Ask several classmates to give their addresses, then report to the class where some of them live.

■ **Modelo:** —*¿Cuál es tu dirección?*
—*Calle Smith 345 (trescientos cuarenta y cinco) Apartamento Número 26.*

VAMOS A ESCUCHAR: VAMOS A CENAR

Play Textbook audio.

Pedro and Lydia are making plans to go downtown and get a bite to eat.

ANTES DE ESCUCHAR

Based on what you've learned in this *etapa*, what information do you expect Pedro and Lydia to give about:

1. where they will go eat
2. how they will get there

Before you listen to their brief dialog, take a moment to look at the questions in the *Después de escuchar* section below.

M. Comprensión. Before your instructor plays the tape, take a moment to think about the questions below. Answer the questions after listening to the tape.

1. What does Pedro suggest they do?
2. Where does Lydia suggest they go?
3. Why do they decide to take a taxi?
4. How long does the taxi driver say it will take?
5. How much does the taxi ride cost?

DESPUÉS DE ESCUCHAR

N. ¿Cómo lo dicen? Listen to the conversation again and try to determine the following:

1. How does the taxi driver say "about" when he says how long the trip will take?
2. How does the taxi driver say "here's your change"?

Tú dirás ....

Ñ. ¿Qué piensas hacer el sábado próximo? When the instructor gives the signal, circulate around the room and ask several of your classmates what they plan to do on Saturday. Ask about their plans for different segments of the day using **por la mañana, por la tarde,** and **por la noche.** Report to the class what different things people plan to do, hope to do.

O. ¡Taxi! ¡Taxi! Imagine you are in Buenos Aires and you are going to meet one of your friends at a restaurant. You're running late so you decide to take a taxi. Working with a classmate, one of you plays the role of the taxi driver and the other, the role of the passenger. Here are some possible restaurants along with their addresses: Restaurante Fellini at 1209 Avenida Paraná; Restaurante Filo at 975 Calle San Martín; Restaurante El Gato Dumas at 1745 Avenida Junín; Restaurante Chiquilín at 1599 Calle Sarmiento.

Passenger

1. Hail the taxi.

2. Tell the driver the name and address of the restaurant and ask how long it will take to get there.

3. Once you arrive, ask the driver how much you owe him/her.

4. Give the driver 20 pesos.

5. Offer the driver a tip.

Taxi driver

1. Greet the passenger and ask where he/she is going.

2. Tell the passenger about how long it will take to get there.

3. Tell the passenger it costs 7 pesos.

4. Give the passenger his/her change.

5. Accept the tip, say thanks and goodbye.

INTEGRACIÓN

LECTURA: Santa Evita: Una héroe argentina

ANTES DE LEER

A. Look at the photo that accompanies this reading and answer the following questions:
1. Who is the reading about?
2. What do you know about this person?
3. What country do you associate her with?

GUÍA PARA LA LECTURA

B. Scan the first paragraph and answer the following questions:
1. When was she born?
2. Why did she go to Buenos Aires?

C. Scan the second paragraph and answer the following questions:
3. When did she meet Juan Perón?
4. What role did she play in his presidency?
5. Who did she stick up for during her husband's presidency?

D. Scan the third paragraph and answer the following questions:
6. What important right did women get as a result of Evita's efforts?
7. In what year did they get this right?
8. How old was she when she died?

E. ¿Qué opinas?
1. What do you think **obras de teatro** in paragraph 1 means?
2. What do you think **ignorados hasta entonces** in paragraph 2 means?
3. What do you think **obras de caridad** in paragraph 3 means?

SANTA EVITA: UNA HÉROE ARGENTINA

María Eva Duarte de Perón, popularmente conocida en todo el mundo como Evita, nació el 7 de mayo de 1919. A los 14 años se mudó a Buenos Aires para seguir su carrera como actriz. Vivió una vida miserable, siempre estaba enferma y no tenía mucho que comer. Después de un año de interpretar **papeles** secundarios en obras de teatro, su fortuna cambió. **Consiguió** su **propio** programa de radio y sus programas, transmitidos por las **ondas** de Radio Argentina y Radio El Mundo, llegaron a ser muy populares y su voz llegó a ser conocida en todo el país.

roles
got/her own
waves

En 1944 **conoció** a Juan Perón y se casaron en 1945. Perón era entonces un coronel en el ejército argentino. En 1946 Perón fue candidato para la presidencia y Evita

met

tuvo un papel muy importante en la campaña electoral de su esposo. Ella convenció a su esposo de que su poder estaba en manos de las masas de trabajadores, ignorados hasta entonces por el gobierno argentino. Evita representó en su país la **esperanza** de los más pobres, de las clases sociales más bajas, a los que ella llamaba "**descamisados**". Como presidente, Perón inició una gran reforma social y durante su presidencia el nivel económico de los trabajadores y empleados públicos aumentó muchísimo.

Desde 1945 Evita fue un ejemplo de participación de la mujer en la realidad nacional. Formó el primer partido político de mujeres en Argentina, el Partido Peronista Femenino. **En gran medida** representó la irrupción femenina en el poder. Varias intelectuales habían intentado hacerse escuchar, pero sus propuestas siempre quedaban en promesas. Evita impulsó el voto de la mujer. Este **acontecimiento** profundizó la democracia y perfeccionó la representatividad. Hasta 1951 solamente la mitad de los habitantes de Argentina **elegían** a sus gobernantes y sólo los hombres ocupaban espacios de poder. En ese año por fin todas las mujeres pudieron votar y muchas **lograron** ocupar una importante cantidad de **escaños** en el Congreso y Senado. Esta gran mujer también se dedicó a obras de caridad que resultaron en la construcción de hospitales y escuelas. Víctima del cáncer, murió a una edad muy joven el 26 de julio de 1952. Evita **tuvo** un impacto enorme en la vida política argentina que continúa hoy casi medio **siglo** después de su muerte.

VÍDEO CULTURAL: *¡Vamos a viajar por tren!*

F. Anticipación. Check off all the vocabulary you think a person might use when organizing a trip by train in Spain.
1. el jueves
2. viajar
3. salir
4. fumar
5. un taxi
6. llegar
7. regresar
8. México
9. ida y vuelta
10. tacos

G. Preparación. Complete the following words or phrases, which appear in the *Vocabulario esencial* section of the video, by filling in the blanks.
1. _l _rec_o
2. n_ f_mad_re_
3. _uisi_ra
4. _ia_an
5. _las_ _uris_a

H. Participación. Take notes as you watch the video. Write down words and phrases that you think may be useful during class discussion or that you'll use later in the **¡A escribir!** exercise.

I. Comprensión. Based on what you saw in this video lesson, choose the best answer.
1. ¿Por cuántos días más o menos va Carmen a Madrid?
   a. un fin de semana largo   b. una semana entera
2. ¿A quién visita en Madrid?
   a. a su tía   b. a su sobrino
3. ¿Quiere viajar en fumadores o no fumadores?
   a. no fumadores   b. fumadores

J. Personalización. You are planning a trip to visit a relative. Write a dialog in which you plan the trip at a travel agent's office. Later, share your activity with the class.

Intercambio: ¿Cuándo vamos?

You want to plan a series of activities with your friend for the coming week. You are a very busy person and so is your friend, so you need to plan ahead with the calendar in front of you

Estudiante A

Below you have a calendar with the things you already know you will be doing during the coming week.

MARZO

6 lunes	7 martes	8 miércoles	9 jueves	10 viernes	11 sábado	12 domingo
Clase Clase Clase Clase	Clase Clase Clase Clase		Clase Clase Clase Clase			
		Teatro Alicia				

Now you and your friend need to find the time to do the following:

1. Go to the movies. You want to go Thursday night.
2. Get together to play tennis. You can do it on Saturday morning.
3. Go out to lunch together and then go to the library to prepare for a test.

Estudiante B

Looking at your calendar, try to agree on a day and a time to do what your friend proposes, provided you want to do so, too.

If he or she suggests a day or a time that you are not free, propose a different one.

Here is what your calendar looks like for next week.

MARZO

6 lunes	7 martes	8 miércoles	9 jueves	10 viernes	11 sábado	12 domingo
Estudiar Estudiar		Estudiar Estudiar	Estudiar	Estudiar		Dentista
Clase Clase Clase Clase		Clase Clase Clase Clase				

When your friend finishes, suggest that you want to do the following:

1. go shopping on a weekday
2. play a soccer game on Sunday

Vocabulario

Para charlar

Para hablar de planes *Talking about plans*
Debo + *infinitive* *I should*
esperar + *infinitive* *to hope to*
ir + a + *infinitive* *to be going to*
pensar *to think of*
poder + *infinitive* *to be able to*
preferir + *infinitive* *to prefer to*
querer + *infinitive* *to want to*

Para decir para qué vas *Saying why you are going*
Voy a dar un paseo. *I'm going to take a walk.*
hacer un mandado *do an errand*
ir de compras *go shopping*
ver a un amigo *see a friend*

Para ir al centro *Going downtown*
¿Cuánto tardas en llegar a...? *How long does it take you to get to . . . ?*
Esto es para Ud., señor (señora, señorita). *This is for you, sir (ma'am, miss).*
Muchas gracias. *Thank you very much.*
Tardo diez minutos, como máximo. *It takes me ten minutes, at the most.*
Voy en autobús. *I'm going by bus.*
  a pie *on foot*
  en bicicleta *by bicycle*
  en coche *by car*
  en metro *by subway*
  en taxi *by taxi*

Para decir cuándo *Saying when*
Vamos esta mañana. *Let's go this morning.*
  esta tarde *this afternoon*
  hoy *today*
  mañana *tomorrow*
  mañana por la mañana *tomorrow morning*
  mañana por la tarde *tomorrow afternoon*
  mañana por la noche *tomorrow night*

Para decir sí o no *Saying yes or no*
¡Claro que sí! *Of course!*
Es imposible. *It's impossible.*
No, no puedo. *No, I can't.*

Lo siento *I'm sorry.*
Sí, puedo. *Yes, I can.*
Sí, tengo ganas de... *Yes, I feel like . . .*
Tengo un compromiso... *I have another commitment . . .*

Para tomar el metro *Taking the subway*
Bajamos en... *We get off at . . .*
bajar *to get off*
Cambiamos en... *We change at . . .*
cambiar *to change*
¿En qué dirección? *In which direction?*

Para hablar del futuro *Talking about the future*
el año próximo *next year*
el mes (el año, la semana) entero(a) *the whole month (year, week)*
el mes próximo *next month*
esta semana *this week*
este año *this year*
este mes *this month*
la semana próxima *next week*
mañana (el sábado, el domingo, etc.) *tomorrow (Saturday, Sunday, etc.)*
  por la mañana *in the morning*
  por la tarde *in the afternoon*
  por la noche *in the evening*

Otros números *Other numbers*
cien *one hundred*
ciento *a hundred*
doscientos(as) *two hundred*
trescientos(as) *three hundred*
cuatrocientos(as) *four hundred*
quinientos(as) *five hundred*
seiscientos(as) *six hundred*
setecientos(as) *seven hundred*
ochocientos(as) *eight hundred*
novecientos(as) *nine hundred*
mil *thousand*
millón *million*

Vocabulario general   General vocabulary

Verbos

comenzar   *to begin*
decir   *to say, to tell*
dormir   *to sleep*
empezar   *to begin*
hacer   *to do, make*
pagar   *to pay*

pedir   *to ask for*
poder   *to be able to*
seguir   *to follow*
sentir   *to feel*
servir   *to serve*
venir   *to come*

Adjetivos

famoso(a)   *famous*
hermoso(a)   *beautiful*
nuevo(a)   *new*

Otras palabras y expresiones

ahora   *now*
algún día   *someday*
barato(a)   *cheap*
el cambio   *change, alteration*
cita   *date, appointment*
como de costumbre   *as usual*
conmigo   *with me*
decir + que   *to say that*
decir que no   *to say no*
decir que sí   *to say yes*
especial   *special*
frecuentemente   *frequently*
el horario   *schedule*
jugar (al tenis)   *to play (tennis)*
otra cosa   *another thing*
Pregúntales a los otros.   *Ask the others.*
propina   *tip*
próximo(a)   *next*
si   *if*
sin límite   *unlimited*
usualmente   *usually*

5 Pasatiempos y diversiones

PRIMERA ETAPA
¿Qué te gusta hacer?

SEGUNDA ETAPA
¿Adónde fuiste?

TERCERA ETAPA
¿Qué deportes practicaste ayer?

INTEGRACIÓN:

LECTURA: Roberto Clemente: Un héroe nacional de Puerto Rico
VÍDEO CULTURAL: Lo que me gusta es...
INTERCAMBIO: Vacaciones en la República Dominicana
ESCRITURA: Actividades en el manual

Roberto Clemente

REPÚBLICA DOMINICANA

Población: 8.088.881
48.308 kilómetros cuadrados (18.704 millas cuadradas), como el tamaño de New Hampshire y Vermont juntos
Capital: Santo Domingo, 2.100.000
Ciudades principales: Santiago de los Caballeros, 690.000

PUERTO RICO

Población:3,622,063
8.897 kilómetros cuadrados (3.427 millas cuadradas) Capital: San Juan, 443.372
Ciudades principales: Bayamón, 225.338; Ponce, 189.734; Carolina, 185.732; Caguas, 139.228; Mayagüez, 102.390; Arecibo, 94.513; Aguadilla, 64.176

CUBA

Población: 10.319.000
110.922 kilómetros cuadrados (44.804 millas cuadradas), casi como el tamaño de Pennsylvania
Capital: La Havana, 2.200.000
Ciudades principales:Santiago de Cuba, 440.000; Camagüey, 294.000

Gabriela Sabatini

CHAPTER OBJECTIVES:

In this chapter you will learn to provide and obtain information about activities associated with leisure time: places to go, hobbies, games, sports, etc.

After completing this first chapter you will be able to carry out the following tasks:

- ⟳ **talk more about likes and dislikes**

- ⟳ **express dates and the seasons of the year**

- ⟳ **talk about events in the past**

- ⟳ **link activities and events with specific moments or periods of time in the past**

The tools you will use to carry out these tasks are:

- ⟳ **vocabulary for:**
  - days, months, and seasons of the year
  - expressing how long an activity has been going on with **hace** and **hace que**
  - what you do and where you go in your free time
  - a variety of individual and team sports

- ⟳ **grammatical structures:**
  - preterite of **-ar, -er,** and **-ir** verbs
  - preterite of **ir** and **hacer**
  - preterite of verbs like **buscar** and **llegar**
  - preterite of irregular verbs: **andar, estar, tener**

	PUERTO RICO	CUBA	REPÚBLICA DOMINICANA
Moneda:	el dólar	el peso	el peso
Esperanza de vida:	hombres, 76; mujeres, 78	hombres, 73; mujeres, 78	hombres, 67; mujeres, 71
Índice de alfabetización:	89%	96%	82%
Productos principales de exportación:	productos químicos, derivados del petróleo, productos de metal y maquinarias, vegetales, textiles	azúcar, derivados del petróleo, níquel, cítricos, pescado, tabaco	azúcar, café, cacao, tabaco, miel
Embajada:	No hay embajada porque Puerto Rico desde 1952 es Estado Libre Asociado con Estados Unidos	No hay embajada en este país porque los Estados Unidos suspendió las relaciones diplomáticas con Cuba en 1959	1715 22nd St. NW, Washington DC 20008

⊚ *PARA EMPEZAR: ¿Qué te gusta hacer?*

⊥ Introduce new topic by pairing advanced students with beginning students and asking them to think about the kinds of things they both like to do regularly. Ask them to make a short list of their likes and dislikes in music, art, movies, sports, etc. Have them place a star by the likes and dislikes they have in common. Allow 5 minutes for activity and then ask pairs to share their ideas. Write new vocabulary items on the board.

Suggestion: Present new vocabulary here in context. Think of, or make up, a funny story about your family, circle of friends, etc., and how hard it is for all of you to agree on something to do in your free time because you all have different likes and dislikes. Pantomime the activities as you mention them to increase understanding. Use comprehension check questions throughout your story to check students' understanding.

Students should remember the **me gusta/te gusta** + *infinitive* construction from Chapter 1, and will become familiar with **nos gusta** in this etapa. Use the illustrations and gestures to ensure students understand the meaning of **nos**.

VOCABULARY EXPANSION: Note that **vídeo** is the term for "VCR" or for "videotape." **Bicicleta** is often shortened to **bici.**

Preparación: As you get ready to begin this *etapa*, think about your free time. Make a mental note of what you like to do and what you don't like to do on a regular basis. Think about your personal preferences regarding such activities as music, nature, art, sports, shopping, ways to exercise, etc., during your leisure time.

Le gusta ir de compras.

Le gusta alquilar vídeos.

Les gusta montar en bicicleta.

Le gusta levantar pesas.

Le gusta patinar.

Le gusta patinar en ruedas.

Le gusta hacer surfing (o velear).

Le gusta practicar la vela.

Les gusta ir de camping.

Transparency G-5, G-6, G-7

Le gusta la natación/ nadar.

Le gusta practicar alpinismo.

Les gusta la pesca/ir de pesca.

Le gusta el buceo/bucear.

Le gusta caminar en la playa.

Les gusta ir al cine.

Le gusta hacer ejercicio aeróbico.

Nos gusta correr.

Nos gusta bailar.

Práctica

A. Me gusta... Imagina que eres la persona en los siguientes dibujos. Tu compañero(a) de clase va a preguntarte si te gusta hacer cada actividad. Contesta según el modelo.

■ **Modelo:** —¿Te gusta nadar?
　　　　　　—Sí, me gusta nadar.
　　　　　　　o
　　　　　　—No, no me gusta nadar.

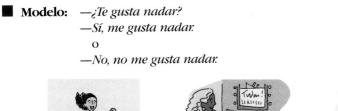

1.　　　　　　2.　　　　　　3.

4. 5. 6.

7. 8.

B. ¿Qué deportes te gustan más?

1. De los varios deportes que ahora puedes expresar en español, haz una lista de tres deportes que te gustan más.

2. Ahora circula por la clase y busca a las personas a quienes también les gustan esos deportes.

3. Habla con una persona a quien le gustan los mismos deportes que te gustan a ti y arreglen una hora para practicar ese deporte juntos.

■ **Modelo:**

Estudiante 1:	*¿Qué deporte te gusta, Juana?*
Estudiante 2:	*Me gusta nadar. ¿Y a ti?*
Estudiante 1:	*¡Claro que sí! ¿Quieres ir a la piscina juntos?*
Estudiante 2:	*¿Cuándo?*
Estudiante 1:	*El sábado por la tarde. ¿Está bien?*
Estudiante 2:	*¡Qué buena idea!* (o: *No, no puedo ir el sábado. ¿Podemos ir el domingo?*)
Estudiante 1:	*Sí, cómo no.*

ENFOQUE ESTRUCTURAL · Más sobre el verbo **gustar**

You are already familiar with the verb **gustar.** Here is a review of what you have leqrned in Chapter 1 (**gustar** + actions) and Chapter 2 (**gustar** + nouns):

Me gusta bailar.	*I like to dance.*
Te gusta la música rock.	*You like rock music.*
Le gusta Jon Secada.	*You (formal) / He / She likes Jon Secada.*
Nos gusta la música latina.	*We like Latin music.*
Les gusta el concierto.	*You (plural) / They like the concert.*

Remember that **gusta** (singular) and **gustan** (plural) agree in number with the words that follow them (the subject).

| Me / te / le / nos / les | GUSTA | el español |
| Me / te / le / nos / les | GUSTAN | las lenguas |

Notice that **le** can refer to he, she, and you (formal) and that **les** can refer to they and you (plural, formal). In order to clarify or to emphasize who likes something, the preposition **a** must be placed before the noun or the pronoun that identifies the person.

A Luis le gusta el jazz.	**A mí me gusta** el rock.
A Ana y a Javier les gusta la música clásica.	**¿A tí te gusta** bailar?
A Lucy y a mí nos gusta bailar.	**A nosotros nos gusta** ir al cine.
A Uds. les gusta las fiestas.	**A Ud. le gusta** cantar.

The following chart summarizes all the possibilities.

	mí	**me**		
A +	**ti** +	**te**	**+GUSTA/N**	**+(sujeto)**
	Ud.	**le**		
	él/ella	**le**		
A +	**nosotros/as**	**nos**	**+GUSTA/N**	**+(sujeto)**
	Ustedes	**les**		
	ellos/ellas	**les**		

Práctica

C. Gustos. Combina un elemento de la lista I, de la lista II y de la lista III en una oración completa.

■ **Modelo:** *Me gusta hablar por teléfono.*

I	II	III
me	gusta	los deportes
le	gustan	bailar
nos		levantar pesas
te		ir de camping
les		los discos de rock
		el arte
		hablar por teléfono
		alquilar un vídeo
		las películas francesas
		ir de compras
		patinar en ruedas
		las tapas
		hacer surfing

D. Preferencias. Trabaja con otro(a) estudiante para indicar lo que les gusta hacer y lo que no les gusta hacer. Cuando una persona pregunta si a la otra persona le gusta hacer algo, si la otra contesta que sí le gusta, debe hacer la misma pregunta a la primera persona. Si no le gusta algo, debe indicar lo que prefiere hacer y después debe hacer otra pregunta a la otra persona sobre la misma actividad. Sigan el modelo.

■ **Modelo:**   —*¿Te gusta nadar?*
   —*Sí, me gusta nadar. ¿Te gusta nadar?*
      o
   —*No, no me gusta nadar. Prefiero correr.*
   ¿Te gusta correr?
   Etc.

Comentarios

culturales   *Puertorriqueños y norteamericanos*

Puerto Rico es un ejemplo de cómo sigue **viva** *(alive)* la cultura hispánica en un país que originalmente fue territorio español pero que ahora se considera un Estado Libre Asociado o *Commonwealth* **bajo** *(under)* los Estados Unidos. La incorporación de Puerto Rico a la esfera política norteamericana fue uno de los resultados de la **guerra** *(war)* entre España y los Estados Unidos en el año 1898 cuando los norteamericanos incondicionalmente tomaron posesión de **la isla** *(island)*.

Desde 1917 los puertorriqueños tienen los **derechos** *(rights)* de **ciudadanía** *(citizenship)* norteamericana pero **todavía** *(still)* mantienen su personalidad hispanoamericana. **Viven,** *(They live)* en gran parte, en Puerto Rico pero las ciudades de Nueva York, Filadelfia, Boston y Providence entre otras, tienen barrios donde viven personas de origen puertorriqueño.

Todavía hay mucho debate en Puerto Rico y en los Estados Unidos sobre (1) la continuación del Estado Libre Asociado, (2) la transformación del país en un nuevo estado norteamericano o (3) la eventual independencia completa de Puerto Rico. En todo caso, son los puertorriqueños quienes deben decidir. Su decisión depende de sus preferencias y también de las **ventajas** *(advantages)* y desventajas de cada uno de los tres sistemas políticos.

INTEGRACIÓN CULTURAL

1. ¿Cuál es la nacionalidad original de los puertorriqueños?
2. ¿Qué importancia tiene el año 1898 en la historia de Puerto Rico?
3. ¿Por qué es importante el año 1917?
4. ¿En qué ciudades norteamericanas hay barrios puertorriqueños?
5. ¿Cuál es la problemática cultural del puertorriqueño?
6. ¿Qué debate político hay todavía entre Puerto Rico y los Estados Unidos?

Answers:
1. española
2. Los EE.UU. tomaron posesión de Puerto Rico.
3. Los puertorriqueños ganaron los derechos de ciudadania.
4. Nueva York, Filadelfia, Boston, Providence.
5. Cómo ser norteamericano y mantener la cultura hispánica.
6. Ser Estado Libre Asóciado, un nuevo estado norteamericano o un país independiente.

Variation: Put students in groups of 3 and do the reading as a jigsaw activity. Pre-read and assign certain comprehension questions to different groups. After reading, have each group present their information.

When presenting this new tense, emphasize the importance of the accents on the meaning of the verb: hablo vs. habló etc. Do some pronunciation/conjugation drills with class to model the paradigm. As students produce the new forms in subsequent exercises, monitor pronunciation.

IRM Master 18: El pretérito de los verbos en *-ar.*

Preview: Expressions of time are presented on page 164.

Bring in some audio/video of a news broadcast. After presenting the new tense and pronunciation to students, have them listen to a minute or so of the broadcast. Have them note as many preterite tense verb forms as they can hear. Write these on the board, along with their infinitive.

For additional practice with these new forms, do some dictation exercises in which the present and preterite tense forms both appear. Tell students they will have to pay attention to context and vocalic stress to hear the sentences properly.

Use a round-robin series of questions to introduce the verbs here. Ask student A: ¿Bailaste mucho anoche? Student A answers and then asks student B a question in the preterite using the next verb.

ENFOQUE ESTRUCTURAL — El pretérito de los verbos en -ar

Hablé con Juan ayer.	*I **talked** with Juan yesterday.*
Bailó mucho anoche.	*He **danced** a lot last night.*
Nosotros estudiamos ayer por la tarde.	*We **studied** yesterday afternoon.*
María y Luis no miraron televisión el lunes por la noche.	*María and Luis **did not watch** television on Monday night.*
¿**Compraste tú** un disco el fin de semana pasado?	***Did you buy** a CD last weekend?*

In Spanish, to talk about actions that happened in the past, you use a past tense called the *preterite*. To conjugate -**ar** verbs in this tense, drop the -**ar** and add the following endings:

cantar

yo	cant-	é	**canté**
tú	cant-	aste	**cantaste**
Ud. él ella	cant-	ó	**cantó**
nosotros(as)	cant-	amos	**cantamos**
vosotros(as)	cant-	asteis	**cantasteis**
Uds. ellos ellas	cant-	aron	**cantaron**

Notice that the **yo** and the **él, ella, Ud.** forms have a written accent.

Some common -**ar** verbs:

alquilar	cantar	charlar	escuchar	mirar	trabajar	volar
bailar	celebrar	comprar	estudiar	pasar	viajar	
caminar	cenar	descansar	ganar	tomar	visitar	

Ex. E: **Pairs**

Answers, Ex. E
1. ...hablé... 2. ...cené...
3. ...estudié... 4. ...miré...
5. ...escuché... 6. ...compré...
7. ...visité... 8. ...alquilé...

Suggestion EX. E: Do this exercise in pairs. Circulate to check for accurate use and pronunciation.

Ex. F: **Pairs**

Answers, Ex. F
1. ¿Caminaste... ? ...caminé...
2. ¿Cenaste... ? ...cené...
3. ¿Desayunaste... ? ...desayuné...
4. ¿Escuchaste... ? ... escuché mi estéreo.
5. ¿Pasaste... ? ...pasé... con mi familia.
6. ¿Visitaste... ? ...visité...
7. ¿Alquilaste... ? ..alquilé...

Ex. G: **Pairs**

IRM Master 19: *Hacer* en el pretérito

You may be wondering why hacer is introduced here before the students have seen -er and -ir verbs in the preterite. The reason is that the overwhelming majority of verbs in Spanish are of the -ar type. By presenting hacer here, they can learn to ask questions using hacer (¿Qué hiciste anoche? ¿Qué hizo María ayer? etc.) and practice using the many regular -ar verbs they know to answer these questions with information that is both "real" and meaningful to them.

Práctica

E. Intercambio... Tus compañeros de cuarto regresaron de un viaje y ahora te preguntan lo qué hiciste durante su ausencia. Contesta sus preguntas en la forma afirmativa.

■ **Modelo:** ¿Terminaste tu tarea?
 Sí, por supuesto. Terminé la tarea.

1. ¿Hablaste por teléfono con tu amigo?
2. ¿Cenaste aquí?
3. ¿Estudiaste para el examen de español?
4. ¿Miraste un programa de televisión?
5. ¿Escuchaste música?
6. ¿Compraste alguna cosa ayer?
7. ¿Visitaste a alguien anoche?
8. ¿Alquilaste un vídeo?

F. El sábado pasado *(Last Saturday)*. Pregúntales *(Ask)* a tus amigos lo que hicieron el sábado pasado. Usa preguntas *(questions)* de tipo sí/no. Sigue el modelo.

■ **Modelo:** —¿Estudiaste el sábado pasado?
 —*No, no estudié el sábado pasado.*
  o
 —*Sí, estudié. Preparé mi examen de matemáticas.*

1. caminar al centro
2. cenar con un(a) amigo(a)
3. desayunar en un restaurante
4. escuchar tu estéreo
5. pasar tiempo con tu familia
6. visitar a un(a) amigo(a)
7. alquilar un vídeo

G. El fin de semana pasado... Trabaja con otro(a) estudiante. Dile lo que hiciste durante el fin de semana pasado usando seis verbos distintos. Después escucha lo que él o ella hizo.

ENFOQUE ESTRUCTURAL **El pretérito del verbo hacer**

The verb **hacer** is used in the preterite to talk about what was done in the past. Notice that when you are asked a question about the past with the verb **hacer,** you respond with a different verb that expresses what was done. Use **hacer** in your response only if you want to say that nothing was done, in which case you would say **no hice nada, no hicimos nada,** etc.

¿Qué **hizo** Tomás ayer?	*What **did** Tomás **do** yesterday?*
Tomás **habló** con el profesor.	*Tomás **talked** to the professor.*
¿Qué **hicieron** ellos anoche?	*What **did** they **do** last night?*
Pedro y Raúl **estudiaron** mucho.	*Pedro and Raúl **studied** a lot.*
¿Qué **hiciste** tú anoche?	*What **did** you **do** last night?*
No hice nada.	*I **didn't do** anything.*

In the preterite, the verb **hacer** is conjugated as follows:

hacer			
yo	**hice**	nosotros(as)	**hicimos**
tú	**hiciste**	vosotros(as)	**hicisteis**
Ud. él ella	**hizo**	Uds. ellos ellas	**hicieron**

Here are some expressions with **hacer:**

hacer un viaje	*to take a triip*
hacer la cama	*to make the bed*
hacer las maletas	*to pack*

Eduardo y María **hicieron un viaje** a Puerto Rico el año pasado.	*Eduardo y María **took a trip** to Puerto Rico, last year.*
Ernesto **hizo la cama** ayer.	*Ernesto **made the bed** yesterday.*
¿Hiciste **las maletas** para tu viaje a Santiago de Cuba?	*Did you **pack your bags** for your trip to Santiago de Cuba?*

Práctica

H. ¿Qué hicieron anoche? Un(a) amigo(a) quiere saber lo que tú y tus amigos hicieron anoche. Trabaja con otro(a) estudiante y contesta las preguntas según el modelo.

■ **Modelo:**   Roberto / hablar con María
   —*¿Qué hizo Roberto anoche?*
   —*Roberto habló con María.*

1. José / cenar en un restaurante
2. Marta y Ana / escuchar una cinta
3. tú / mirar un programa de televisión
4. Luis / visitar a un amigo
5. Esteban / hacer las maletas para su viaje
6. ustedes / no hacer nada

I. ¿Qué hiciste en casa de tus amigos? Un compañero de clase quiere saber lo que hiciste ayer. Trabaja con otro(a) estudiante, siguiendo el modelo.

■ **Modelo:**   hablar por teléfono con María (no / Natalia)
   —*¿Qué hiciste ayer? ¿Hablaste con María?*
   —*No, no hablé con María, pero hablé con Natalia.*

1. preparar tapas con Julián y Alicia (sí)
2. estudiar por dos horas (sí)
3. hablar con los padres de Miguel (no / su hermana)
4. tomar café (no / jugo de naranja)
5. escuchar la radio (no / una cinta de Gloria Estefan)

Ex. H: Pairs

Answers, Ex. H
Students substitute the cues, using these forms of the verbs: 1. hizo / cenó 2. hicieron / escucharon 3. hiciste / miré 4. hizo / visitó 5. hizo / hizo 6. (hicieron) hicimos / no hicimos

Suggestion: As a follow-up activity, assign as homework for students to turn into "spies." Have them make a list of 6 or 7 things their roommate, friend, boyfriend, girlfriend, etc., did that night and the times at which they did them. The next day have students report to the class their findings, using the preterite tense.

Ex. I: Pairs

Answers, Ex. I
Students substitute the cues, using these forms of the verbs:
1. preparaste / preparé 2. estudiaste / estudié 3. hablaste / hablé 4. tomaste / tomé 5. escuchaste / escuché 6. miraron / Miramos... 7. estudiaron / Estudiamos... 8. visitaron / Visitamos... 9. bailaron / Bailamos... 10. compraron / Compramos... 11. caminaron / Caminamos...

Suggestion, Ex. I: Encourage students to make this activity more communicative by continuing short conversation lines after each number. For example: ¿Hablaste con Natalia? No, hablé con María... ¿Quién es María?...

Ahora tú quieres saber lo que hicieron tus amigos ayer. Usa los verbos siguientes para hacerles preguntas.

■ **Modelo:** escuchar

—*¿Qué hicieron Uds. ayer?*

—*Escuchamos unas cintas nuevas de música latina.*

6. mirar 8. visitar 10. comprar

7. estudiar 9. bailar 11. caminar

ENFOQUE LÉXICO

Expresiones para indicar el tiempo pasado

La semana pasada compré un disco compacto.	*Last week I bought a CD.*
El viernes pasado comimos en un restaurante.	*Last Friday we ate at a restaurant.*

The following time expressions are used to talk about an action in the past:

ayer	*yesterday*
ayer por la mañana	*yesterday morning*
ayer por la tarde	*yesterday afternoon*
anoche	*last night*
anteayer	*the day before yesterday*
el jueves (sábado, etc.) pasado	*last Thursday (Saturday, etc.)*
la semana pasada	*last week*
el fin de semana pasado	*last weekend*
el mes pasado	*last month*
el año pasado	*last year*

The preposition **por** will enable you to express how long you did something.

Estudié **por** dos horas.	*I studied **for** two hours.*
Trabajó **por** veinte minutos.	*She worked **for** twenty minutes.*
por una hora (un día, tres años, cuatro meses, quince minutos, etc.)	***for one hour (one day, three years, four months, fifteen minutes,** etc.)*

Suggestion: To present this vocabulary in context, have students write the following phrases on a sheet of paper: ayer, anteayer, la semana pasada, el fin de semana pasado... Then ask the class when the last time they did various activities was: ¿Cuándo fue la última vez que... ? They will mark their sheets accordingly. Compare answers at the end of the activity.

Suggestion: Write on the board today's date plus dates for last week and for previous years.

Práctica

J. ¿Estudiaste tú anoche? Un(a) amigo(a) te pregunta lo que hiciste a cierta hora. Contesta lo que hiciste e indica cuánto tiempo tomó esa actividad. Trabaja con otro(a) estudiante siguiendo el modelo.

■ **Modelo:** estudiar anoche / 3 horas

—*¿Estudiaste anoche?*

—*Sí, estudié por tres horas.*

1. escuchar un disco compacto ayer / 30 minutos
2. hablar por teléfono con tu amigo ayer / 1 hora
3. hacer ejercicio anteayer / 20 minutos
4. caminar ayer por la tarde / 45 minutos
5. estudiar alemán el año pasado / 8 meses

Ex. J: Pairs

Answers, Ex. J
1. escuchaste / escuché 2. hablaste / hablé 3. hiciste / hice 4. caminaste / caminé 5. estudiaste / estudié

K. ¿Cuándo? Usa los verbos para hacer preguntas y la información entre paréntesis para contestarlas con una oración completa.

■ **Modelo:** hablar (ayer por la mañana)
—¿*Cuándo hablaste con María?*
—*Hablé con María ayer por la mañana.*

1. estudiar (el año pasado)
2. alquilar (ayer por la tarde)
3. llamar (el viernes pasado)
4. comprar (el mes pasado)
5. hacer ejercicio (el sábado por la mañana)
6. viajar (el domingo pasado)

L. La semana pasada (*Last week*). Trabaja con otro(a) estudiante para discutir lo que hicieron ciertos días de la semana pasada por la mañana, la tarde y la noche.

Elena y Rafael, dos amigos, hablan por teléfono de un viaje que acaba de hacer Elena.

ANTES DE ESCUCHAR

¿De qué piensas que van a hablar? ¿Qué haces tú para pasar el tiempo en un viaje largo? Ahora lee las preguntas en la sección *Después de escuchar* para tener una idea del contenido del diálogo que vas a escuchar.

DESPUÉS DE ESCUCHAR

M. Comprensión

1. ¿Quién llamó a quién anoche?
2. ¿Cuándo regresó Elena de su viaje a Los Ángeles?
3. ¿Cómo viajó Elena a Los Ángeles?
4. ¿Cuáles son algunas de las cosas que Elena hizo durante el viaje?

N. ¿Cómo lo dicen? Escucha el diálogo otra vez para determinar lo siguiente:

1. ¿Cómo dice Rafael "at 7:30"?
2. ¿Cómo dice Elena "pretty good"?
3. ¿Qué expresión usan los dos para decir "See you later"?

Tú dirás ....

Ñ. ¿Qué tenemos en común? Imagina que estás buscando una persona para viajar contigo durante los meses del verano. Habla con otro(a) estudiante para descubrir si ustedes son compatibles, siempre usando el verbo **gustar** en las preguntas y respuestas. Preparen una lista de cinco cosas/actividades que le gustan a cada individuo y otra lista de cinco cosas/actividades que no le gustan. Cada persona debe hacer una lista de dos columnas para después decidir si deben vivir viajar o no. Prepárense para compartir sus conclusiones con la clase.

Ex. K: 👤👤 Pairs

Answers
1. estudiaste / estudié 2. alquilaste / alquilé 3. llamaste / llamé
4. compraste / compré 5. hiciste / hice 6. viajaste / viajé

Ex. L: 👤👤 Pairs

Suggestion: Have students role-play their answers, and the others can guess the activity being portrayed and describe it using the preterite tense appropriately.

🎧 Play Textbook audio.

Answers, Ex. M
1. Rafael llamó a Elena.
2. Esta mañana.
3. Voló.
4. Escuchó música, vio una película, jugó naipes, habió, tomó refrescos.

Suggestion: Before listening to the tape, dictate a few phrases from the dialog. Have students work in pairs to try to reconstruct the sentences as they hear them.

Answers, Ex. N
1. a las 7:30 2. Bastante bien.
3. Hasta luego.

Suggestion, Ex.Ñ: Before doing the activity write some communication phrases on the board and encourage students to use them during their interaction. Some suggestions for this type of activity might be: ¿Qué crees tú? ¿Qué opinas tú? or Te gusta limpiar, ¿no?/¿verdad? Also encourage students to request clarification when they don't understand something: No entiendo, por favor, una vez más...

Ex.Ñ: 👤👤 Pairs

Suggestion: After working with a partner, students may report to the rest of the class what they found out about their partner's activities.

O. ¿Qué hiciste durante el fin de semana? Es lunes por la mañana y tus amigos hablan de lo que hicieron y no hicieron durante el fin de semana. Trabaja con otro(a) estudiante. Escojan verbos de la lista. Usen el pretérito durante toda la conversación. Hagan preguntas específicas sobre cada día del fin de semana, usando el verbo **hacer** con expresiones como **por la mañana, por la tarde, por la noche.** (Por ejemplo: ¿Qué hiciste tú el viernes por la tarde?)

alquilar un vídeo	escuchar	hacer ejercicio	tomar una siesta
bailar	estudiar	mirar	trabajar
caminar	hablar	nadar	visitar

SEGUNDA ETAPA

PARA EMPEZAR: ¿Adónde fuiste?

Preparación: As you get ready to begin this *etapa*, once again think about your free time. Make a mental note of the places you like to go and the events you attend in your free time.

Play Textbook audio.

Suggestion: Prepare students for this *etapa* by asking them these questions in Spanish.

—¿Adónde fuiste anoche?
—A un partido de fútbol. ¿Y tú?
—Fui a un concierto.

Es el lunes por la mañana, antes de clase. Carlos y su amiga Cristina hablan de adónde fueron ellos y algunos de sus amigos el sábado por la tarde.

Carlos:	Hola, Cristina, ¿cómo estás?
Cristina:	Bien, y tú, ¿qué tal?
Carlos:	Muy bien. ¿Qué hiciste el sábado pasado? ¿Fuiste al cine?
Cristina:	No, no. No fui al cine. Roberto y yo fuimos al concierto. ¿Y tú?
Carlos:	Yo fui a la biblioteca.
Cristina:	¿Fuiste con tu **novia**?
Carlos:	No, ella fue al gimnasio.
Cristina:	Y tu hermano, ¿qué hizo? ¿Fue al gimnasio, también?
Carlos:	No, mi hermano y su novia fueron al partido de fútbol.

girlfriend

▶ *¿Adónde fuiste tú?*

(Yo) fui a la biblioteca.

Fui a un restaurante.

Fui a la piscina.

Fui al cine.

▶ *¿Adónde fueron Uds.?*

(Nosotros) Fuimos de compras.

Fuimos a una fiesta.

Fuimos a la playa.

Fuimos a un museo.

¿Adónde fueron ellos?

(Ellos) fueron al parque.

Fueron al parque zoológico.

Fueron al gimnasio.

Fueron a casa de un(a) amigo(a).

¿Adónde fue tu amigo(a)?

Ella fue al centro.

Él fue al médico.

IRM Master 21: *ir* en el pretérito

You may want to review regular -ar verb endings before presenting this new verb.

ENFOQUE ESTRUCTURAL El pretérito del verbo **ir**

Fui al cine anoche.	*I **went** to the movies last night.*
Ellos **fueron** a un concierto el sábado pasado.	*They **went** to a concert last Saturday.*
Fuimos al centro ayer.	*We **went** downtown yesterday.*
¿**Fuiste** tú a la fiesta de Julia el viernes pasado?	*Did you **go** to Julia's party last Friday?*
No, no **fui**.	*No, I **did** not **go**.*

In the preterite, the verb **ir** has exactly the same form as **ser** and is therefore conjugated as follows:

ir			
yo	**fui**	nosotros(as)	**fuimos**
tú	**fuiste**	vosotros(as)	**fuisteis**
Ud.		Uds.	
él	**fue**	ellos	**fueron**
ella		ellas	

Práctica

A. ¿Adónde fue... ? Un(a) amigo(a) te pregunta adónde fueron todos por la tarde. Contesta con las palabras indicadas. Trabaja con otro(a) estudiante.

■ **Modelo:** David / cine
—¿Adónde fue David?
—Fue al cine.

1. Carmen / concierto
2. tu hermana / museo
3. tú / centro
4. Jorge y Hernando / banco
5. Victoria y Claudia / restaurante mexicano
6. la profesora / médico
7. tus padres / mercado
8. el profesor de francés / biblioteca

B. ¿Adónde fuiste? Ahora pregúntale a un(a) compañero(a) adónde fue ayer. Sigue el modelo.

■ **Modelo:** biblioteca / cine
—¿Adónde fuiste ayer? ¿A la biblioteca?
—No, fui al cine.

1. a la playa / a la piscina
2. a un restaurante / a casa de un(a) amigo(a)
3. al parque / al gimnasio
4. al partido de básquetbol / al concierto
5. a la biblioteca / de compras
6. a la piscina / a una fiesta

C. ¿Adónde fuiste y qué hiciste el año pasado? Pregúntales a tus compañeros de clase adónde fueron y qué hicieron el año pasado. Haz una lista y después informa a la clase de estas actividades.

Repaso

D. ¡Preguntas y más preguntas! Túrnate con otro(a) estudiante para hacer y contestar las preguntas siguientes.

Ex. A: Pairs

Answers, Ex. A
Students substitute the cues, using these verbs and articles: 1. fue / fue al 2. fue / fue al 3. fuiste / fui al 4. fueron / fueron al 5. fueron / fueron al 6. fue / fue al 7. fueron / fueron al 8. fue / fue a la

Ex. C: Pairs

Variation:
As a follow-up to the spy activity from the last *etapa*, you may wish to have students give another report about their roommate, friend, etc., and tell what this person did and where he/she went this weekend. To review time telling, have them include the hour at which the person did these things.

Ex. D: Pairs

Answers, Ex. D
Students' answers will vary, but the verb forms used should be these:
1. hice 2. miré 3. hablé 4. hice (or any other verb in the past) 5. estudié

Circulate through class to check for accuracy. While circulating ask follow-up questions of individual students, e.g., ¿Qué programa miraste? ¿Te gustó?...

1. ¿Hiciste un viaje el año pasado?
2. ¿Miraste un programa de televisión el domingo por la noche?
3. ¿Hablaste por teléfono con alguien anoche?
4. ¿Hiciste algo el domingo pasado?
5. ¿Estudiaste anteayer?

E. Susana quiere saber. Tu familia tiene una visitante de habla española durante el fin de semana. Esta visitante tiene interés en las actividades de la familia. Contesta sus preguntas.

1. ¿A qué hora piensan Uds. ir de compras?
2. ¿Dónde duermo este fin de semana?
3. ¿Quién juega al golf?
4. ¿Cuándo empiezan las clases de los niños?
5. ¿A qué hora sirven la comida?
6. ¿A qué hora empieza el desayuno?

📖 **Transparency H-1:** Las estaciones

Present vocabulary in context. Tell students that your best friend has a very large family and everyone has a birthday in a different month. Show pictures of different people. Give them names and write their birthdays on the board. Tell the class what activity each person likes to do on his or her birthday. For example: Juan cumple años en enero. A él no le gusta el invierno así que siempre va al Caribe para celebrar su cumpleaños. En el Caribe, en enero, le gusta nadar y...

Suggestions:
(1) Write today's date on the board.
(2) Ask several students to give their birthdays.

ENFOQUE LÉXICO — **Los meses, la fecha y las estaciones del año**

Los meses del año

enero	abril	julio	octubre
febrero	mayo	agosto	noviembre
marzo	junio	septiembre	diciembre

All the months of the year are masculine. They are used without articles and they are not capitalized. To express the idea of *in* a month, use **en** or **en el mes de.**

En enero, es verano en Argentina.	***In January,*** *it is summer in Argentina.*
En el mes de agosto nadamos mucho.	***In the month of August*** *we swim a lot.*

La fecha

¿Cuál es la fecha de hoy?	
¿Qué fecha es hoy?	*What is today's date?*
¿A cuánto estamos?	
Hoy es el 5 de octubre.	*Today is October 5.*
¿Cuál es la fecha de tu cumpleaños?	***What is the date*** *of your birthday?*
Yo nací **el primero de febrero de mil novecientos setenta y cinco.**	*I was born **on the first of February** 1975.*
Mi hermana nació **el once de junio de mil novecientos setenta y seis.**	*My sister was born **on June 11,** 1976.*

To express the date in Spanish, use the definite article **el,** a cardinal number (**treinta, diez, cinco**), **de,** and the name of the month. The one exception is the first of the month, expressed by **el primero.** The day, the month, and the year of any date are connected by **de.**

Las estaciones del año

la primavera

el verano

el otoño

el invierno

All the nouns for the seasons are masculine except **la primavera.** To express the idea of *in* a particular season, use **en** and the appropriate definite article.

En el otoño jugamos al fútbol.	*In the fall we play soccer.*
En el invierno tengo frío.	*In the winter I am cold.*
Corro mucho **en la primavera.**	*I run a lot in the spring.*
Todos van a la playa **en el verano.**	*Everybody goes to the beach in the summer.*

Suggestions: (1) Have students repeat the seasons as they look at the drawings. (2) Have them complete: Los meses de otoño son... etc. (3) Ask: ¿En qué estación naciste?

Práctica

F. ¿Qué estación es en... ? Para cada mes, menciona la estación que le corresponde al lugar donde vives tú.

■ **Modelo:** septiembre

   En septiembre, es otoño.

1. enero
2. julio
3. marzo
4. noviembre
5. mayo
6. agosto
7. diciembre
8. junio

G. ¿Cuándo practicas deportes? ¿Cuál es la estación del año en que generalmente participas en las actividades que siguen?

■ **Modelo:** jugar al fútbol
Juego al fútbol en el otoño.

1. jugar al tenis
2. jugar al básquetbol
3. jugar al béisbol
4. nadar
5. jugar al golf
6. jugar al jai alai
7. practicar el alpinismo
8. patinar
9. pescar
10. montar en bicicleta

H. Preguntas sobre las estaciones. Trabajas con unos niños hispanos en los Estados Unidos que te hacen muchas preguntas sobre las estaciones. Contéstalas.

1. ¿Cuántas estaciones hay en un año?
2. ¿Cuáles son los meses de verano aquí?
3. ¿En qué estación es posible esquiar?
4. ¿En qué estación vamos a la playa?
5. ¿En qué estaciones jugamos al fútbol? ¿al básquetbol?
6. ¿En qué estación celebramos el día de la Independencia de los Estados Unidos?

I. ¿En qué año? ¿Cuál es la fecha, en español, de los hechos históricos que siguen?

1. October 12, 1492—el descubrimiento de América por Colón
2. November 20, 1910—la revolución mexicana
3. April 23, 1616—la muerte (*death*) de Cervantes y Shakespeare
4. July 16, 1789—la revolución francesa
5. September 16, 1821—la independencia de México
6. November 22, 1963—el asesinato del Presidente Kennedy
7. July 21, 1969—el primer hombre en la luna (*moon*)
8. November 9, 1989—la caída (*fall*) del muro (*wall*) de Berlín
9. January 17, 1994—el terremoto (*earthquake*) de Los Ángeles, California
10. tu cumpleaños (*your birthday*)

ENFOQUE ESTRUCTURAL El pretérito de los verbos en -er, -ir

Comí en un restaurante anoche.	*I **ate** in a restaurant last night.*
Escribimos una carta ayer.	*We **wrote** a letter yesterday.*
Susana **no comprendió** la lección.	*Susana **did not understand** the lesson.*
¿Recibieron Uds. una invitación para la fiesta?	***Did** you **receive** an invitation to the party?*
Ella **salió de** casa temprano ayer.	*She **left** home early yesterday.*

To conjugate -**er** and -**ir** verbs in the preterite, drop the -**er** or -**ir** and add the following endings:

comer			
yo	com-	í	comí
tú	com-	iste	comiste
Ud.			
él	com-	ió	comió
ella			
nosotros(as)	com-	imos	comimos
vosotros(as)	com-	isteis	comisteis
Uds.			
ellos	com-	ieron	comieron
ellas			

vivir			
yo	viv-	í	viví
tú	viv-	iste	viviste
Ud.			
él	viv-	ió	vivió
ella			
nosotros(as)	viv-	imos	vivimos
vosotros(as)	viv-	isteis	vivisteis
Uds.			
ellos	viv-	ieron	vivieron
ellas			

Notice that the preterite endings for both -**er** and -**ir** verbs are identical and that the **yo** and the **él, ella, Ud.** forms have a written accent.

Common -*er* verbs		**Common -*ir* verbs**	
aprender	correr	asistir (a)	recibir
beber	perder	compartir	salir (de), salir (con)
comer	vender	discutir	vivir
comprender		volver	escribir

Práctica

J. Ayer después de la escuela. Di lo que hicieron tú y tus amigos ayer después de la escuela.

A	B	C	D
yo	(no)	comer	pizza
Miguel		escribir	dos cartas
tú		recibir	los ejercicios del libro
Pedro y yo		salir con	un(a) amigo(a)
Linda y Fernando		asistir a	un partido
Ud.		correr	un libro
		perder	dos millas

K. El fin de semana. Compara con otro estudiante las actividades que cada uno hizo durante el fin de semana. Usa las siguientes expresiones en tus preguntas. Nota las actividades que tienen ustedes en común.

■ **Modelo:** comer en un restaurante

—*¿Comiste en un restaurante?*
—*Sí, comí en un restaurante.*
    o
—*No, no comí en un restaurante.*

1. aprender información interesante
2. asistir a un concierto
3. perder la cartera
4. escribir una carta a tu amigo(a)
5. discutir algún problema
   con un(a) amigo(a)
6. recibir un regalo (*gift*)
7. correr un poco
8. comer en un restaurante
9. salir con un(a) amigo(a)
10. volver a casa tarde

Ex. J: Pairs

Answers, Ex. J
1. aprendiste / aprendí
2. asististe / asistí
3. perdiste / perdí
4. escribiste / escribí
5. discutiste / discutí
6. recibiste / recibí
7. corriste / corrí
8. comiste / comí
9. saliste / salí
10. volviste / volví

Suggestion, Ex. K: Continue to ask questions with interrogative words to practice listening comprehension. Ask follow-up questions in the third person to practice all of the forms. Start out with **tú** questions and then practice **Uds.** questions. For example: ¿Qué hiciste anoche, Juan? (Yo estudié.) ¿Qué hizo Juan? ¿Miró la televisión?, etc. ¿Qué hicieron tú y tus amigos/amigas el sábado pasado? (Asistimos a un partido de básquetbol.) ¿Qué hicieron ellos? ¿Estudiaron para un examen?, etc.

L. Una tarde típica. Usa los dibujos y los verbos para ayudarte a explicar cómo pasaron el fin de semana estas personas.

■ **Modelo:** salir

Salimos de la universidad.

1. tomar

2. estudiar

3. comprar

4. escuchar

5. entrar

6. comer

7. mirar

8. escribir

9. beber

🎧 Play Textbook audio.

ANTES DE ESCUCHAR

Antes de escuchar una conversación en que Olga y Juan hablan de las vacaciones de Juan y de lo que él hizo, piensa en tus vacaciones, en adónde fuiste y en qué hiciste. Ahora contesta las siguientes preguntas.

1. ¿Adónde crees que fue Juan, posiblemente?
2. ¿Cuáles son algunas de las actividades que crees que Juan va a mencionar?

Repasa las preguntas en la sección *Después de escuchar* para tener una mejor idea del contenido del diálogo.

DESPUÉS DE ESCUCHAR

M. Comprensión. Ahora escucha la cinta y contesta las preguntas.

1. ¿Adónde fue Juan de vacaciones y con quién?
2. ¿Qué hicieron Juan y sus hermanos cada día por la mañana?
3. ¿Qué hicieron por la tarde?
4. ¿Fue difícil para Juan aprender un nuevo deporte acuático? ¿Quién le ayudó a aprender a hacerlo?
5. ¿A quién no le gustó esta actividad?
6. ¿Cuál fue la reacción de Olga a la experiencia de Juan?

N. ¿Cómo lo dicen?

Escucha el diálogo otra vez para determinar lo siguiente.

1. ¿Cómo dice Olga "How was your vacation?"
2. ¿Cómo dice Juan "We had a great time"?
3. ¿Cómo dice Olga "Great idea!"?

Comentarios

culturales La Pequeña Habana

*L*a Pequeña Habana es un barrio de la ciudad de Miami. Aquí se reúnen muchos de los cubanos que vienen de Cuba porque no quieren vivir bajo el sistema político establecido en la isla por Fidel Castro en 1959. Hoy en día, este sector de la ciudad es un centro social y comercial importante, no sólo para los cubanos sino también para las numerosas personas de otros países de habla española, como El Salvador, Panamá y Colombia. Para esta gente, La Pequeña Habana es como un segundo **hogar** *(home)*.

Para los norteamericanos, europeos y turistas de otras nacionalidades que visitan La Pequeña Habana el área es uno de los sectores más atractivos del sur de la Florida. La gente **disfruta** *(enjoy)* enormemente de la cultura cubana—su comida, sus fiestas y su **artesanía** *(crafts)*. **Por dondequiera** *(Wherever)* que se camina en La Pequeña Habana, los **cafetines,** *(small cafes),* el dominó, el sonido de la música y de los radios son evidencia de que en el **corazón** *(heart)* de Miami el español sigue vivo, igual que la imagen romántica de Cuba.

INTEGRACIÓN CULTURAL

1. ¿Dónde está La Pequeña Habana?
2. ¿De dónde es la mayoría de las personas que viven allí?
3. ¿Por qué fueron tantas personas a vivir en La Pequeña Habana?
4. ¿De qué otras nacionalidades son algunos de los otros habitantes de La Pequeña Habana?
5. ¿Cuáles son algunas de las atracciones para los turistas que visitan La Pequeña Habana?
6. ¿Cómo describes tú el ambiente de La Pequeña Habana después de leer la información anterior sobre ella?

Tú dirás ....

Ñ. ¿Adónde fuiste y qué hiciste el verano pasado? Habla con cinco de tus compañeros(as) de clase para preguntar adónde fueron y qué hicieron el verano pasado. Haz una lista de sus respuestas. Prepárense para hablar de esta información con el resto de la clase.

O. Un viaje interesante. Habla con otro(a) estudiante de un viaje interesante que cada uno hizo en alguna ocasión. Usando verbos en el pretérito, indiquen (1) adónde fueron, (2) cuándo, (3) con quién, (4) por cuánto tiempo, (5) cuatro o cinco cosas que hicieron y (6) la actividad que más les gustó. Prepárense para hablar de esta información con el resto de la clase.

To review and to present vocabulary in context, tell students some of the sports you like to do. Use transparency to refer to each sport. Ask different students if they also like that sport and when was the last time they did that sport. To vary conjugations used, tell them sports that your friends like, ask if their friends like them also, and ask when was the last time they all did that particular sport together.

Ex. Ñ: Group

Ex. O: Pairs

PARA EMPEZAR: ¿Qué deportes practicaste ayer?

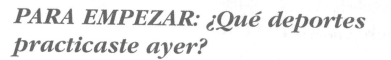

Preparación: As you get ready to begin this *etapa*, think about the sports you play.

- Do you play them just for fun? for the exercise?
- Are you on a team?
- Which sports did you play last summer? last winter? other seasons?

To prepare students for new topic, ask them these questions in Spanish.

Select students to role-play this dialog. Ask comprehension questions.

Play Textbook audio.

Esteban:	¡Hola! ¿Cómo estás?
Alberto:	Bien, gracias, ¿y tú?
Esteban:	Pues, estoy un poco cansado hoy porque jugué al fútbol ayer.
Alberto:	¿Estás en algún **equipo**?
Esteban:	Sí, estoy en el equipo de nuestra escuela.
Alberto:	¿Vas a practicar?
Esteban:	Sí, tengo que practicar los lunes, martes, miércoles y jueves.
Alberto:	¿Cuándo son los partidos?
Esteban:	Los partidos son los viernes por la noche. Y tú, ¿estás en algún equipo?
Alberto:	No. Me gusta mucho jugar al baloncesto, pero no estoy en un equipo. Sólo juego para hacer ejercicio.

team

¿Qué deportes jugaste el año pasado?

Jugué al béisbol.

Jugué al baloncesto.

Jugué al fútbol americano.

Jugué al fútbol.

Jugué al tenis.

Jugué al golf.

Jugué al hockey.

Jugué al hockey sobre hierba.

Jugué al vólibol.

Practiqué el esquí acuático.

Practiqué el windsurf.

Práctica

Ex. A:  Pairs

A. ¿Qué deporte practicaste? Pregúntale a un(a) amigo(a) acerca de las actividades y deportes que practicó ayer. Sigue el modelo.

■ **Modelo:**   montar en bicicleta / jugar al vólibol
        —*¿Montaste en bicicleta ayer?*
        —*No, no monté en bicicleta. Jugué al vólibol.*

1. correr / levantar pesas
2. patinar / jugar al vólibol
3. jugar al golf / jugar al tenis
4. nadar / hacer ejercicio aeróbico
5. jugar al balconcesto / jugar al béisbol
6. jugar al fútbol americano / jugar al fútbol
7. jugar al hockey / jugar al hockey sobre hierba
8. montar en bicicleta / patinar en ruedas
9. ir de pesca / nadar
10. practicar la vela / practicar el windsurf
11. hacer surfing / caminar en la playa
12. practicar alpinismo / ir de camping
13. hacer ciclismo / tomar el sol
14. practicar el esquí acuático / bucear

B. ¿Qué hicieron? Basándote en los dibujos, di lo que hizo cada persona.

■ **Modelo:**   Julián
        Julián practicó el esquí acuático.

Julián

1. Isabel

2. Juana

3. Mario

4. Elena

5. Pedro y Félix

6. Tomás, Laura y Julio

IRM Master 23: El pretérito de los verbos en -car, -gar

Drill pronunciation/conjugation patterns with students. You may wish to do a dictation exercise of sentences with these verbs in both the present and the past. Encourage students to listen for stressed vowels and contextual clues to hear the verb tense.

Point out to students why the c of verbs ending in -car must change to qu before e and i.

Point out that tocar also means to knock.

Supplementary vocabulary for tocar: trompeta, violín, órgano, flauta, clarinete, guitarra, piano, tambores

Point out to students why the g of verbs ending in -gar must change to gu before e and i.

ENFOQUE ESTRUCTURAL

El pretérito de los verbos que terminan en -car o -gar

¿Buscaste el libro?	*Did you **look for** the book?*
Sí, lo **busqué** pero no lo encontré.	*Yes, I **looked for** it, but I didn't find it.*
¿Tocó Julián la guitarra en la fiesta anoche?	*Did Julián **play** the guitar at the party last night?*
No, yo **toqué** la guitarra anoche.	*No, I **played** the guitar last night.*

Verbs that end in **-car** are conjugated in the preterite as follows:

buscar

yo	**busqué**	nosotros(as)	**buscamos**
tú	**buscaste**	vosotros(as)	**buscasteis**
Ud. él ella	**buscó**	Uds. ellos ellas	**buscaron**

You will note that in the **yo** form of these verbs, the **c** of the stem changes to **qu** before you add the **é**. The other forms of the verb are conjugated exactly like those you studied in the Primera etapa. Some common verbs that end in **-car** are:

tocar	*to play (a musical instrument); to touch*
sacar	*to take out*
practicar	*to practice*

¿A qué hora **llegaste** a la escuela ayer?	*What time **did** you **arrive** at school yesterday?*
Llegué a las 8:00 de la mañana.	*I **arrived** at 8:00 a.m.*
¿**Jugaron** al tenis tú y Julián el domingo pasado?	***Did** you and Julián **play** tennis last Sunday?*
Yo **jugué**, pero Julián no **jugó.**	*I **played,** but Julián did not **play.***
¿Cuánto **pagaste** tú por la bicicleta?	*How much **did** you **pay** for the bicycle?*
Pagué 150 dólares.	*I **paid** 150 dollars.*

In the preterite, verbs that end in **-gar** are conjugated as follows:

llegar

yo	**llegué**	nosotros(as)	**llegamos**
tú	**llegaste**	vosotros(as)	**llegasteis**
Ud.		Uds.	
él	**llegó**	ellos	**llegaron**
ella		ellas	

Notice that in the **yo** form of these verbs, the **g** of the stem changes to gu before you add the **é**. The other forms of the verb are just like those you studied in the Primera etapa. Two common verbs that end in **-gar** are:

pagar	*to pay*
jugar	*to play (a game)*

Práctica

C. ¿Qué deporte practicaste el verano pasado? Un(a) amigo(a) quiere saber algo de *(wants to know something about)* los deportes que practicaste el verano pasado. Contesta según el modelo.

■ **Modelo:** el windsurf
—*¿Practicaste el windsurf el verano pasado?*
—*No, no practiqué el windsurf, practiqué el buceo.*

1. el buceo
2. el surfing
3. el esquí acuático
4. la vela
5. el alpinismo
6. el ciclismo

Ex. D: Pairs

Ex. E: Pairs

Ex. F: Pairs

D. ¿Qué... ? Con un(a) compañero(a), túrnense para hacer y contestar las siguientes preguntas.

1. ¿Qué deporte practicaste el sábado pasado?
2. ¿Buscaste el libro que perdiste?
3. ¿Quién tocó la guitarra en la fiesta?
4. ¿Tocaste un instrumento musical el año pasado?
5. ¿Sacaste la basura *(the trash)* ayer?
6. ¿Dónde practicaron Uds. anoche?

E. Preguntas. Trabaja con otro(a) estudiante para hacer y contestar preguntas sobre la siguiente información:

1. qué cosa él (ella) compró recientemente, y cuánto dinero pagó por esa cosa. (Sugerencias: una mochila, un disco compacto, una pizza, etc.)
2. cuándo llegó a la universidad esta mañana
3. qué deporte jugó recientemente y en qué días jugó el deporte

Prepárense para hablar de esta información con el resto de la clase.

Repaso

F. ¡Qué curioso! Para cada cosa que dice tu compañero(a), hazle tres preguntas para obtener más información. Tu compañero(a) tiene que inventar algunos detalles para contestar a tus preguntas. Sigue el modelo.

Modelo: —*El verano pasado fui a la República Dominicana.*
—*¿Cuándo saliste para la República Dominicana?*
—*El 2 de julio.*
—*¿Qué hiciste?*
—*Fui a la playa y visité a un amigo en Santo Domingo.*
—*¿Cuánto tiempo pasaste en la República Dominicana?*
—*Pasé dos semanas.*

1. Este verano acampamos.
2. El año pasado mi hermano y yo fuimos a La Habana.
3. Anoche mis amigos y yo comimos en un restaurante.
4. El fin de semana pasado me quedé en casa.
5. Nuestro profesor pasó el verano en Puerto Rico.
6. Mis padres acaban de comprar un coche.
7. El sábado pasado fui al centro.

Ex. G: Pairs

G. ¡Son muy activos! Esteban Candelaria, su hermana Catarina y sus padres (el Sr. y la Sra. Candelaria) son muy activos. Basándote en el calendario de sus actividades, indica lo que pasó cada día. Contesta desde el punto de vista de Esteban (es decir, Esteban-*yo*) y usa el pasado para indicar lo que hicieron. Hoy es el 18 de mayo.

Modelo: *Anoche mis amigos cenaron en un restaurante.*
Ayer yo comí en un restaurante con mi primo.
El sábado pasado fui a bailar.

10 de
mayo
viernes

11 de
mayo
sábado

12 de
mayo
domingo

13 de
mayo
lunes

14 de
mayo
martes

15 de
mayo
miércoles

16 de
mayo
jueves

17 de
mayo
viernes

Comentarios

Las tenistas hispanas

Mary Joe Fernández

El tenis requiere agilidad y control del cuerpo, pero no necesariamente gran fuerza. Por eso es un deporte que pueden jugar personas de diversas edades y condiciones físicas. Al nivel profesional, se necesita una combinación de habilidad, buena técnica y una excelente condición física.

Gabriela Sabatini

Entre las mejores tenistas del mundo, hay un grupo de hispanas: Mary Joe Fernández de Puerto Rico, Gabriela Sabatini de Argentina, Arantxa Sánchez Vicario y Conchita Martínez de España. Todas han participado en los grandes torneos que se juegan en Inglaterra, en Francia, en los Estados Unidos y en Australia. En 1994, Conchita ganó el prestigioso torneo en Wimbledon y Arantxa ganó el U.S. Open y el French Open, y también ganó el French Open en 1998. Arantxa, aunque es española, vive en Andorra, un pequeño país entre Francia y España.

Conchita Martínez

Arantxa Sánchez Vicario

INTEGRACIÓN CULTURAL

1. ¿De dónde son las tenistas hispanas?
2. ¿Qué hizo Conchita en 1994?
3. ¿Dónde vive Arantxa?
4. ¿Te gusta el tenis? ¿Te gusta jugarlo o mirarlo?
5. ¿Quién es tu tenista favorita?

ENFOQUE ESTRUCTURAL   Pretérito de los verbos **andar, estar, tener**

Estuve en casa de Antonio anteayer.	*I **was** at Antonio's house the day before yesterday.*
¿Anduviste por el parque ayer?	***Did** you **walk** in the park yesterday?*
Sí, **anduve** con mi amiga Paula.	*Yes, I **walked** with my friend Paula.*
No **tuvimos** que estudiar anoche.	*We **did** not **have to** study last night.*

Many common Spanish verbs are irregular in the preterite tense. However, some can be grouped together because they follow a similar pattern when conjugated. Note the similarities among the following three verbs when they are conjugated in the preterite.

andar, estar, tener

yo	anduve estuve tuve	nosotros(as)	anduvimos estuvimos tuvimos	
tú	anduviste estuviste tuviste	vosotros(as)	anduvisteis estuvisteis tuvisteis	
Ud. él ella	anduvo estuvo tuvo	Uds. ellos ellas	anduvieron estuvieron tuvieron	

Práctica

H. ¿Qué hicieron ayer? Di lo que hicieron tú y tus amigos ayer.

A	B	C	D
yo Ana tú Silvia y yo Anita y Francisco Ud.	(no)	andar estar tener	a mi casa que estudiar al centro al parque en la fiesta de María que trabajar

I. Preguntas y respuestas. Con un(a) compañero(a), túrnense para hacer y contestar las siguientes preguntas.

1. ¿Qué tuviste que estudiar anoche?
2. ¿Dónde estuviste el sábado pasado?
3. ¿Anduviste mucho el fin de semana pasado?
4. ¿Dónde estuviste el verano pasado?
5. ¿Qué tuviste que hacer ayer por la tarde?
6. ¿Anduviste anteayer por la mañana?

J. ¡Un crimen! Hace tres horas alguien robó un banco en tu ciudad. Cuando llegas al centro a pie, un policía te hace algunas preguntas. Tu compañero(a) de clase debe tomar el papel del policía. Contesta sus preguntas según el modelo.

■ **Modelo:**
1. ¿Dónde estuviste a las diez de la mañana?
   Estuve en la piscina de mi hotel.
2. ¿Adónde anduviste cuando saliste de la piscina?
   Anduve al parque para leer.
3. ¿Qué tuviste que hacer en el centro hoy?
   Tuve que mandar unas cartas.

Circulate through the class to check for accuracy on these irregular forms.

Ex. I:  Pairs

Answers, Ex. I
1. tuve que 2. estuve 3. anduve
4. estuve 5. tuve que 6. anduve
Variation Ex. I: Assign 1 or 2 questions to each student. Students then ask their classmates if they did these things last evening. Students record the number who say yes and the number who say no and report to the class. Some possible activities include: mirar la televisión, estudiar, mirar un vídeo, hablar con mis amigos, estudiar para un examen, trabajar, hablar por teléfono con..., escuchar música, comer pizza, chocolate, etc., ir de compras, bailar, correr, salir de casa, etc.

Point out to students that Spanish has no equivalent for the English word *ago*. To express this concept in Spanish, they must use one of the two structures presented here.

Have students generate sentences in English in which they would use the word *ago* (e.g., I lived in Indiana 5 years *ago*; I talked to my parents 2 days *ago*; I went to Spain 3 months *ago*; I ate breakfast 15 minutes *ago*). Put some of these sentences on the board and have students substitute different lengths of time, subjects, and verbs.

 Preview: More information on **hace/hace...que** is presented on chapter 7, page 245.

ENFOQUE LÉXICO   **Hace y hace que para expresar tiempo transcurrido**

> **Hace dos semanas** que Raúl compró el disco compacto.   *Two weeks ago, Raúl bought the CD.*

To express how long ago something happened, you use **hace** + *length of time* + **que** + *subject* + *verb in the preterite* as in the following:

    Hace + **dos horas** + **que** + **Miguel** + **comió.**

Or you may use *subject* + *verb in the preterite* + **hace** + *length of time* as in the following:

    Miguel + **comió** + **hace** + **dos horas.**

Notice that when **hace** is placed at the beginning of the sentence, you must insert **que** before the subject.

> **¿Cuánto hace que hablaste** con tu amigo?   *How long ago did you talk to your friend?*
>
> **Hace una semana que hablé** con él.   *I spoke to him a week ago.*

To ask a question with this time expression, use the following model:

    ¿Cuánto + **hace** + **que** + *verb in the preterite?*

Some expressions you have already learned for expressing length of time are:

    un minuto, dos minutos, tres minutos, etc.
    una hora, dos horas, tres horas, etc.
    un día, dos días, tres días, etc.
    una semana, dos semanas, tres semanas, etc.
    un mes, dos meses, tres meses, etc.
    un año, dos años, tres años, etc.

Práctica

K. Hablé con ella hace... Un(a) amigo(a) quiere saber cuánto tiempo hace que tú y otra persona hicieron algo. Trabaja con un(a) compañero(a) y contesta las preguntas según el modelo.

◼ **Modelo:**   hablar con ella /horas
          —*¿Cuánto hace que hablaron con ella?*
          —*Hablamos con ella hace dos horas.*

1. vivir en Indiana / años
2. estudiar francés / años
3. comprar la bicicleta /meses
4. recibir la carta de Ana / días
5. comer en un restaurante / semanas
6. ir al cine / semanas

L. Hace... Ahora hazle a tu compañero(a) las preguntas del ejercicio K. Él/Ella las contesta usando una de dos posibilidades. Sigan el modelo.

◼ **Modelo:**   hablar con ella / horas
          —*¿Cuánto hace que hablaste con ella?*
          —*Hace dos horas que hablé con ella.*
             o
          —*Hablé con ella hace dos horas.*

 Ex. K: Pairs

Answers, Ex. K
Students substitute the cues following the models, using these verb forms: 1. vivieron / vivimos 2. estudiaron / estudiamos 3. compraron / compramos 4. recibieron / recibimos 5. comieron / comimos 6. fueron / fuimos

 Ex. L: Pairs

Answers, Ex. L
Students substitute the cues following the models, using these verb forms: 1. viviste / viví 2. estudiaste / estudié 3. compraste / compré 4. recibiste / recibí 5. comiste / comí 6. fuiste / fui

M. ¿Cuánto hace que... ?Túrnate con otro(a) estudiante para hacer y contestar preguntas basadas en los dibujos siguientes.

■ **Modelo:**

1.   2.

—¿Cuánto hace que comiste pizza?
—Comí pizza hace una semana.

3.   4.   5.

7.   8.

Possible answers, Ex. M

All of the questions will begin with ¿Cuánto hace que... ?
1. ...fuiste al cine? / Fui al cine hace...
2. ...fuiste al correo? / Fui al correo hace...
3. ...corriste? / Corrí hace...
4. ...visitaste a tus abuelos? / Visité a mis abuelos hace...
5. ...compraste una mochila? / Compré una mochila hace...
6. ...miraste la televisión? / Miré la televisión hace...
7. ...cantaste? Canté hace...

VAMOS A ESCUCHAR: UN PARTIDO IMPORTANTE

🎧 **Play Textbook audio.**

Reminder: Students will be able to use these monologues as models when they speak about their own activities.

ANTES DE ESCUCHAR

N. Piensa en los deportes que juegan tú y tus amigos. Vas a escuchar una conversación breve entre Sonia y Mari sobre un deporte que juega Sonia y un partido importante. ¿De qué tipo de información crees que hablan en el diálogo?

Ahora repasa las preguntas en la sección *Después de escuchar.*

DESPUÉS DE ESCUCHAR

Ñ. Comprensión. Ahora escucha el diálogo y contesta las preguntas.

1. ¿En qué equipo está Sonia?
2. ¿Por qué está cansada?
3. ¿Qué día y a qué hora tiene el partido importante?
4. ¿Contra qué equipo juega Sonia?
5. ¿Qué pasó el año pasado cuando el equipo de Sonia jugó contra este equipo?
6. ¿Qué piensa Sonia sobre las posibilidades de ganar el partido?
7. ¿Qué dice Mari que ella quiere hacer?

O. ¿Cómo lo dicen? Escucha el diálogo otra vez para determinar lo siguiente.

1. ¿Cómo dice Sonia "we have to win"?
2. ¿Cómo dice Mari "Good luck" al final?

Tú dirás ···

P. El verano pasado. Tu compañero(a) de clase y tú estuvieron muy ocupados el verano pasado porque participaron en muchos deportes y actividades. Para hacer un informe de sus actividades, organicen las que hicieron en el orden en que las hicieron. (Usen expresiones apropiadas de tiempo al preparar su lista de actividades.) Incluyan por lo menos tres actividades en que los dos de ustedes participaron.

Q. Un partido inolvidable *(memorable).* Habla con otro(a) estudiante sobre un deporte en que les gusta participar como jugador o ver como espectador. Cada uno(a) debe usar verbos en el pretérito para hablar de un partido inolvidable, indicando lo siguiente:

1. el deporte y los equipos
2. la fecha y el lugar
3. qué equipo ganó/perdió
4. quién o quiénes fueron los mejores jugadores
5. por qué gustó tanto el partido.

LECTURA: Roberto Clemente: Un héroe nacional de Puerto Rico

ANTES DE LEER

A. Mira la foto. ¿Quién crees que está en la foto? ¿Qué deporte juega?

B. Ahora mira el título. ¿De dónde es el atleta?

GUÍA PARA LA LECTURA

A. Lee la primera oración de cada párrafo de la lectura y resume el contenido en tus propias palabras.

B. Ahora, lee el primer párrafo y contesta las preguntas siguientes:

1. ¿Qué hizo Roberto Clemente en 1955?
2. ¿Qué pasó en 1971?

C. Ahora, lee el segundo párrafo e indica si las frases siguientes son verdaderas o falsas.

1. Cada invierno, Roberto Clemente volvió a Puerto Rico.
2. En diciembre de 1992, hubo un terremoto en Nicaragua.
3. Clemente organizó una campaña para las víctimas del terremoto.

D. Finalmente, lee el último párrafo e identifica dos acontecimientos que se le ocurrió a este hombre.

ROBERTO CLEMENTE

Roberto Clemente nació en Carolina, Puerto Rico, en 1934. A los 20 años firmó su primer contrato para jugar al béisbol profesional con los Brooklyn Dodgers. Un año más tarde, en 1955, firmó un contrato para jugar con los Pittsburgh Pirates. En

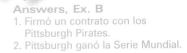

Answers, Ex. B
1. Firmó un contrato con los Pittsburgh Pirates.
2. Pittsburgh ganó la Serie Mundial.

Answers, Ex. C
1. verdadera
2. verdadera
3. verdadera

Answers, Ex. D
Murió en un accidente de avión; Fue elegido para la Sala de la Fama.

Have students discuss the positive and negative impact of sports on American culture, and how influential sports are in their lives. As a lead-in to the Roberto Clemente reading, have students discuss whether or not they think of sports figures as heroes, and keep that discussion in mind as they read about Clemente.

Roberto con su familia

Pittsburgh tuvo una carrera brillante y todavía se considera como uno de los mejores jugadores de la historia del béisbol. En octubre de 1971 Clemente fue la razón principal por la cual Pittsburgh ganó la Serie Mundial. Clemente fue nombrado el jugador más valioso (MVP) para esa serie. En 1972 bateó su hit número 3000—número que muy pocos jugadores alcanzan.

Ese año después de terminar la temporada de béisbol, como siempre Clemente volvió a Puerto Rico para pasar el invierno. A fines de diciembre hubo un terremoto desastroso en Nicaragua. Muchas personas se quedaron sin casa y sin comida. Clemente organizó una campaña para llevar comida y provisiones médicas a las víctimas del terremoto.

El 31 de diciembre de 1972, Clemente murió en un accidente de avión—el mismo avión en que llevaba provisiones a las víctimas del terremoto. Fue un acontecimiento muy trágico para todos los aficionados del béisbol y, por supuesto, para todo Puerto Rico donde él era un héroe. Después de su muerte fue el primer jugador hispano en ser elegido para la Sala de la Fama en Cooperstown, Nueva York. Recordamos a Clemente no sólo por su habilidad atlética sino también por sus actos humanitarios.

VÍDEO CULTURAL

VÍDEO CULTURAL: Lo que me gusta es...

E. Anticipación. Check off all the vocabulary you think might be used when talking about hobbies and leisure time.

1. el parque
2. las gambas
3. el cine
4. las películas
5. un taxi

6. ir
7. el periódico
8. México
9. la televisión
10. leer

F. Preparación. Match the following Spanish words and phrases with their English equivalent.

1. cumplió tres años
2. el fin de semana pasado
3. ¿qué hiciste tú?
4. estuvimos en...
5. nos sentamos

a. what did you do?
b. we sat down
c. we were in
d. turned three years old
e. completed three years
f. last weekend

Answers, Ex. F
1. d   2. f   3. a   4. c   5. b

G. Participación. Take notes as you watch the video. Write down words and phrases that you think may be useful during class discussion or that you'll use later in the **Personalización** exercise.

H. Comprensión. Based on what you saw in this video lesson, choose the best answer.

1. ¿Qué hizo Juan Carlos el fin de semana pasado?
   a. Comió una hambuguesa.   b. Hizo su tarea y fue al parque.

2. ¿Qué hizo Luis Antonio el fin de semana pasado?
   a. Jugó al baloncesto en el gimnasio.   b. Fue a una reunión infantil.

3. ¿Qué hizo Lizette el fin de semana pasado?
   a. No salió.   b. Salió a divertirse con unos amigos.

I. Personalización. Create a list of all of the hobbies or leisure activities that you and your friends enjoy. If you can't think of how to say it in Spanish, use the dictionary or ask your teacher for help. Later, ask your classmates if they did any of the activities yesterday, last night, last weekend, or last year.

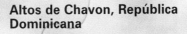

Altos de Chavon, República Dominicana

▶ *Intercambio: Vacaciones en la República Dominicana*

Estudiante A

Tus amigos y tú están planeando unas vacaciones en el Caribe. Ayer fuiste a una agencia de viajes y te dieron la siguiente información sobre la República Dominicana.

Uno(a) de tus amigos(as) que piensa ir de viaje contigo te llama por teléfono. Comparte con él/ella la información que tienes en el folleto *(brochure)*.

Debes preguntarle a tu amigo(a) información sobre la ropa necesaria, la comida, las compras y los deportes que se pueden practicar.

REPÚBLICA DOMINICANA: GUÍA PRÁCTICA

Documentación. Pasaporte en vigor. A la entrada al país se cumplimenta la "tarjeta de turista" que debe guardarse hasta el día de salida.

Equipaje. Máximo 20 Kg., por persona (el exceso de equipaje tiene tarifa suplementaria). Sólo se permite un bulto de mano.

Moneda. La unidad monetaria es el Peso Dominicano, dividido en 100 centavos. Los pagos deben hacerse en moneda local que puede cambiar en hoteles y bancos.

Propinas e impuestos. Todos los productos tienen un 8% de impuestos de venta. Los hoteles añaden un 15% de impuestos y los restaurantes cobran un 10% por servicio. Los clientes normalmente dan un 5% o un 10% de propina.

Información turística. La Secretaria de Estado de Turismo ofrece información sobre las agencias que operan en el país. Está localizada en las Oficinas Gubernamentales, Bloque D, Avenida México / 30 de Marzo, Santo Domingo, D.R. Tel. 809.221.4666 y Fax 809.682.3806.

Ecoturismo. La República Dominicana tiene 22 parques nacionales y reservas naturales, como el Parque Nacional Armando Bermúdez y el parque de Los Haitises. La Ruta de las Gaviotas pasa por Santo Domingo y atraviesa la costa sur. La Ruta Verde de Quisqueya ofrece un tour ecológico completo de todo el país.

Estudiante B

Estás pensando ir de vacaciones a la República Dominicana. Ayer fuiste a una agencia de viajes y te dieron la siguiente información sobre la República Dominicana. Llamas a tu amigo(a) para compartir la información con él/ella.

Debes preguntarle a tu amigo(a) información sobre la documentación necesaria, la moneda del país, el máximo de equipaje que puedes llevar, las propinas y actividades turísticas en la isla.

REPÚBLICA DOMINICANA: GUÍA PRÁCTICA

Ropa. Utilice ropa ligera de tejidos naturales e informal. Se requiere vestido de cocktail para ocasiones especiales. Caballeros: Pantalón largo en la mayoría de los hoteles.

Comida. Mariscos, carnes, deliciosos postres a base de frutas tropicales (cocos, guayabas, piñas, etc.). Las bebidas nacionales son la cerveza y el ron, con el que se elaboran bebidas como ron sour y piña colada.

Compras. Artesanía nativa, sombreros de paja, pinturas, ron de caña, etc. y joyas de ámbar. Las tiendas abren normalmente de las 8 de la mañana hasta las 12:00 de mediodía y desde las 2:00 de la tarde hasta las 7:00.

Deportes. En la República Dominicana el deporte nacional es el béisbol. La liga profesional se juega de octubre a final de enero. Los partidos son en el Estadio Quisqueya en Santo Domingo y en los estadios de Santiago, San Pedro de Macorís y La Romana. Además de béisbol, se puede jugar al golf en Santo Domingo, Punta Cana, Puerto Plata y Juan Dolio. Si te gusta correr, en Santo Domingo hay muchas zonas verdes como el Paseo de los Indios o el Malecón. Finalmente, todos los deportes de agua son muy populares en la isla. El Club Náutico de Santo Domingo y muchos hoteles ofrecen información sobre estos deportes.

Vocabulario

Para charlar

Para preguntar y dar la fecha   *Asking and giving the date*

¿A cuánto estamos?   *What is the date?*

¿Cuál es la fecha de hoy (de tu cumpleaños, etc.)?   *What is the date today (of your birthday, etc.)?*

¿Qué fecha es hoy?   *What is today's date?*

Hoy es el 5 de abril.   *Today is April 5.*

En (el mes de) enero (febrero, marzo, etc.)...   *In (the month of) January (February, March, etc.) . . .*

Él (Ella) nació   *He (She) was born*

Para hablar de pasatiempos y diversiones   *Talking about hobbies and amusements*

alquilar vídeos   *to rent videos*

caminar en la playa   *to walk on the beach*

hacer ejercicio (aeróbico)   *to do (aerobic) exercise*

ir de camping   *to go camping*

ir de pesca   *to go fishing*

montar en bicicleta   *to ride a bicycle*

tomar el sol   *to sunbathe*

Para hablar de deportes   *Talking about sports*

jugar...   *to play . . .*

   al baloncesto   *basketball*

   al béisbol   *baseball*

   al fúbol   *football*

   al fútbol ameriano   *football*

   al golf   *golf*

   al hockey   *hockey*

   al hockey sobre hierba   *field hockey*

   al jai-alai   *jai-alai*

   al tenis   *tennis*

   al vólibol   *volleyball*

practicar...   *to practice . . .*

   el alpinismo   *mountain climbing*

   el ciclismo   *cycling*

   el esquí acuático   *waterskiing*

   el surfing   *surfing*

   la vela (o velear)   *sailing*

   el windsurf   *windsurfing*

   el buceo   *diving*

levantar pesas   *to lift weights*

la natación   *swimming*

el partido   *game*

patinar   *to iceskate*

patinar en ruedas   *to roller skate*

la pesca   *fishing*

Para hablar del tiempo
Talking about time

el año   *year*

el día (m.)   *day*

la hora   *hour*

el mes   *month*

el minuto   *minute*

la semana   *week*

Para hablar de una acción en el pasado
Talking about a past action

el fin de semana pasado   *last weekend*

anoche   *last night*

el jueves (sábado, etc.) pasado   *last Thursday (Saturday, etc.)*

anteayer   *the day before yesterday*

el año pasado   *last year*

el mes pasado   *last month*

ayer   *yesterday*

por una hora (un día, tres años, cuatro meses)   *for an hour (a day, three years, four months)*

ayer por la mañana   *yesterday morning*

ayer por la tarde   *yesterday afternoon*

la semana pasada   *last week*

por un año   *for a year*

por un día   *for one day*

por un mes   *for a month*

por unos minutos   *for a few minutes*

Temas y contextos

Los meses del año   *Months of the year*

enero   *January*

febrero   *February*

marzo   *March*

abril   *April*

mayo   *May*

junio   *June*

julio   *July*

agosto   *August*

septiembre   *September*

octubre   *October*

noviembre   *November*

diciembre   *December*

Las estaciones del año   *Seasons of the year*

la primavera   *spring*

el verano   *summer*

el otoño   *fall*

el invierno   *winter*

Vocabulario general   General vocabulary

Sustantivos

la guitarra *guitar*
el mar *sea*
la montaña *mountain*

Verbos

andar *to walk*
asistir a *to attend*
buscar *to look for*
caminar *to walk*
cantar *to sing*
cenar *to eat dinner*
comprar *to buy*
depender de *to depend on*
escribir *to write*
hablar *to talk*
hacer *to do, make (with time reference = "ago, since")*
jugar *to play*
llegar *to arrive*
pagar *to pay*
pasar tiempo *to spend time*
perder *to lose*
saber *to know*
sacar *to take out something, obtain*
salir de *to leave*
tocar *to play an instrument*
visitar *to visit*
volar *to fly*
volver *to return*

Otras palabras y expresiones

demasiado *too (much)*
echar/tomar/dormir una siesta *to take a nap*
estar de mal humor *to be in a bad mood*
por lo menos *at least*
hacer las maletas *to pack*
hacer un viaje *to take a trip*
una milla *a mile*
nada *nothing*
no hacer nada *to do nothing*

6 Vamos de compras

Machu Picchu

mercado Chincheros
cerca de Cuzco
Cajamarca,

Chapter Objectives:

In this chapter you will learn about shopping in different environments and for different purposes. You will also learn some basic information about Ecuador, Bolivia, and Perú, three Andean countries.

After completing this chapter you should be able to carry out the following tasks:

- make purchases at different locations
- indicate quantities
- ask for prices
- make comparisons
- point out places, objects, people
- give orders and express influence
- talk about shopping experiences

The tools you will use to help you carry out these tasks are:

- vocabulary for:
  - shopping at a mall and at various stores: music, sports, clothing, grocery stores, open-air markets
- grammatical structures:
  - familiar affirmative and negative commands
  - subjunctive with expressions of influence
  - preterite of irregular verbs
  - comparatives
  - demonstrative adjectives and pronouns

PERÚ

Población: 24.500.000   1.285.220 kilómetros cuadrados, un poco más pequeño que Alaska
Capital: Lima, 5.700.000
Ciudades principales: Arequipa, 619.150; Callao, 615.046; Trujillo, 509.300.

BOLIVIA

Población: 7.165.257   1.098.580 kilómetros cuadrados, más o menos tres veces Montana
Capital: La Paz, 711.036
Ciudades principales: Santa Cruz, 694.616; El Alto, 404.367; Cochabamba, 404.102

ECUADOR

Población: 11.466.29   1283.560 kilómetros cuadrados, más o menos como Nevada
Capital: Quito, 1.100.847
Ciudades principales; Guayaquil, 1.508.844; Cuenca, 194.981

	PERÚ	BOLIVIA	ECUADOR
Moneda:	nuevo sol	boliviano	sucre
Esperanza de vida:	hombres, 62; mujeres, 66	hombres, 60; mujeres, 63	hombres, 67; mujeres, 73
Índice de alfabetización:	87,2%	83,1%	90,1%
Productos principales de exportación:	cobre, petróleo crudo y derivados, plomo, plata refinada, café, algodón, pescado	metales, gas natural, joyas, madera	petróleo, bananas, gambas, cacao, café
Embajada:	1700 Massachusetts Avenue NW, Washington, DC 20036	3014 Massachusetts Avenue NW, Washington, DC 20008	2535 15th Street NW, Washington, DC 20009

PARA EMPEZAR: En el centro comercial

🎧 **Play Textbook audio.**

Suggestion: Start discussion of the topic by asking students these questions in Spanish.

Present vocabulary to students in context of a short story. Tell students about your shopping experiences. For example: A mí me gusta ir de compras, y mi amigo Nacho se vuelve loco cuando va de compras. Siempre que tiene dinero corre a las tiendas para comprar de todo. Compra música y no le importan los precios... Ask questions to check for comprehension.

After telling story, go over each dialog. Then have students work in small groups to "personalize" it. They might choose to change the characters, the items mentioned, or the prices. Remind them to make any necessary changes in agreement that their new dialogs require.

Preparación

- **Do you enjoy going shopping?**
- **Where do you usually go to buy the things you need?**
- **What questions do you nornally ask when you are in a store?**
- **What questions does the sales person usually ask the customer?**

▶ En una tienda de discos

Anoche, Beatriz y Mónica fueron a un concierto en el Centro Cultural de la Universidad Católica de Lima a escuchar a Patricia Saravia, una cantante peruana. A las dos les gustó mucho la música de Patricia y por eso hoy van a comprar uno de sus discos, "De Inga y de Mandinga".

look / What a shame!
enough

Beatriz: **Mira,** aquí están los discos compactos de Patricia. **¡Qué pena!** No tengo **suficiente** dinero para comprarlos todos.

Mónica: ¿Cuáles quieres comprar?

Beatriz: Bueno, sólo tengo dinero para uno, así que voy a comprar el último, "De Inga y de Mandinga".

tapes / cheap

Mónica: ¿Quieres ir a mirar las **cintas?** Normalmente son más **baratas.**

Beatriz: ¿Dónde están?

there

Mónica: **Allí,** al lado de los vídeos.

Beatriz: Bien, vamos.

Suggestions: Use the teacher tape to introduce the dialog. Then ask ¿Qué compró la muchacha en la tienda de deportes? ¿Está en oferta la raqueta del escaparate?

▶ En una tienda de deportes

Elsa y Norma viven en La Paz. A las dos les gusta jugar al tenis y lo hacen con frecuencia. Hoy las dos amigas van a una tienda de deportes que está en Shopping Norte, uno de los centros comerciales de la ciudad. Elsa necesita comprar una raqueta nueva.

how much the raquet costs /
display window
Good eye.

Dependiente: Sí, señoritas, ¿qué necesitan?

Elsa: Quisiera saber **cuánto cuesta la raqueta** del **escaparate.**

Dependiente: ¡Ah! **Buen ojo.** Es una raqueta muy buena y cuesta 300 bolivianos.

Elsa:	¿Cómo? ¿No está **en oferta**?	on sale
Dependiente:	No, lo siento. La oferta terminó ayer.	
Elsa:	¡Qué pena! Bueno. Y las **pelotas de tenis, ¿qué precio tienen?**	tennis balls / what price are they?
Dependiente:	Mmm… nueve bolivianos la **lata.**	can
Elsa:	Bueno, **voy a llevar** tres.	I'll take
Dependiente:	Aquí tiene. ¿Algo más?	
Elsa:	Sí. Quiero ver unos **zapatos de tenis** también, por favor.	tennis shoes
Dependiente:	Sí, ahora mismo. ¿Qué **número** tiene?	size
Elsa:	El 36.	
Dependiente:	A ver **éstos.**	these ones
Elsa:	Sí, éstos están bien. Son muy cómodos. ¿Cuánto cuestan?	
Dependiente:	260	
Elsa:	Perfecto. Entonces, **¿cuánto cuesta todo?**	how much is everything
Dependiente:	A ver, tres latas de pelotas, 27, más las zapatillas, 260, total, 287. **¿Cómo va a pagar?**	How are you going to pay?
Elsa:	**Con tarjeta.** Aquí tiene.	with a card

▶ *En la Tienda Moda Joven, en el centro comercial en Quito*

Hoy sábado Mercedes y Sara van de compras al centro comercial en Quito, Ecuador. Necesitan comprar un **regalo** para el cumpleaños de Rosa. A las dos les gusta **mirar escaparates.**	gift go window shopping
Mercedes: Aquí tienen **ropa bonita.**	nice clothes
Sara: ¡Mira esta **falda azul!** ¡Qué linda!	blue skirt
Mercedes: A Rosa le va a gustar ese color. Con este **cinturón negro queda muy bien.** Creo que le va a gustar.	black belt looks really good
Sara: Sí, tienes razón. Perfecto. Ahora quiero ver un **vestido** para mí.	dress
Mercedes: Aquí en frente hay una boutique muy elegante.	
Sara: Mmm… entonces, **seguro** que es cara.	surely
Mercedes: No sé. ¿Vamos a ver el escaparate?	
Sara: Sí, ¿por qué no?	

VOCABULARY EXPANSION:

To indicate what size of shoes you wear, the word **número** is used. For clothes, the word for size is **talla.**

To indicate the way you want to pay for something, besides **con tarjeta,** you can say **en efectivo** *(in cash)* or **con cheque** *(by check).*

Una oferta is a special; una liquidación is a clearance sale. Shops announcing a sale often post signs saying **grandes rebajas.**

ENFOQUE LÉXICO | **Los colores y la ropa**

una blusa amarilla

un vestido marrón

una chaqueta verde

s pantalones negros

un abrigo rojo

na falda azul

n impermeable marrón

una camisa rosada

una camiseta azul

un suéter morado

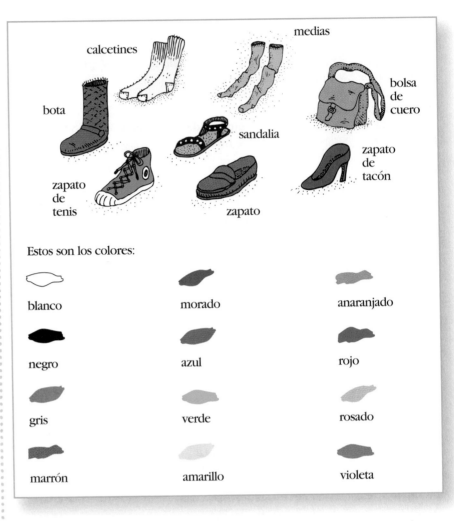

Práctica

A. ¿Qué llevas hoy? Eres el encargado de la sección de moda en el periódico de la universidad. Necesitas saber qué ropa llevan los estudiantes y profesores. Describe lo que lleva cada una de las siguientes personas. Sigue el modelo.

■ **Modelo:** *Luis lleva una camisa roja con unos pantalones blancos.*

1. Roberta   2. Nadia   3. Alfonso   4. Arturo   5. Olga   6. Esteban

B. ¿Cuánto cuesta... ? Estás en una tienda de deportes. Quieres saber los precios de varios artículos. Tu compañero(a) va a ser el dependiente *(clerk).* Habla con él o ella y pregunta cuánto cuesta cada una de las cosas siguientes:

Modelo: pelotas de tenis *(tennis balls)*
—*Buenos días. ¿Cuánto cuestan las pelotas de tenis del escaparate?*
—*Tres por tres dólares.*
—*Mmm... bien. Voy a llevar seis. Aquí tiene, seis dólares.*

After exercise have students share any new vocabulary that their partners may have used.

VOCABULARY EXPANSION:
The word for jeans in Spain is **vaqueros,** in other parts of the Spanish speaking world, **blue jeans,** or **jeans** is used.

1   2   3   4

5   6

C. El regalo perfecto. Imagina que vas a comprar regalos para diferentes miembros de tu familia. Sólo tienes 250 dólares para los regalos. Compra algo adecuado para cada persona de tu familia, elige un color en caso que sea necesario y recuerda cuánto dinero gastas en cada regalo.

Voy a comprar...	para...	por
		Total

Ahora, pregúntale a un(a) compañero(a) de clase qué compró para su familia. Sigue el modelo.

Modelo: —*¿Qué compraste?*
—*Compré unas pelotas de tenis para mi hermano porque le gusta jugar al tenis. Compré los pantalones verdes para mi padre porque necesita pantalones nuevos. También, compré una camisa amarilla para mi madre porque es su color favorito. Y tú, ¿qué compraste?*
—*Yo compré...*

ENFOQUE ESTRUCTURAL — Mandatos con **tú**: afirmativos y negativos

In the opening dialogs, we have seen how friends tried to get each other's attention.

> En la tienda de discos:
>   **Mira,** encontré la cinta de Gloria Estefan.
> En la tienda de ropa:
>   ¡**Mira** esa falda azul!

Friends can also give advice to one another.

> En la tienda de ropa:
>   Rosa, **no compres** esa falda, no me gusta.
> En la tienda de deportes:
>   Mira, **ven,** ¿te gustan estas camisetas?
>   Sí, **compra** dos, son muy baratas.

1. In Chapter 3, you learned to give orders, directions, and suggestions using the command form with **Ud.** and **Uds.** Here you will learn the command form for **tú,** used to make requests of family members, peers, or younger people.

Regular tú affirmative commands

Verbs ending in -ar: bailar	Verbs ending in -er: beber	Verbs ending in -ir: escribir
baila	bebe	escribe

2. The regular affirmative **tú** command has the same ending as the third-person singular (**él, ella**) of the present tense.

3. The verbs **decir, hacer, ir, poner, salir, ser, tener,** and **venir** have irregular affirmative command forms.

Irregular tú affirmative commands

decir	**di**	salir	**sal**
hacer	**haz**	ser	**sé**
ir	**ve**	tener	**ten**
poner	**pon**	venir	**ven**

Regular tú negative commands

Verbs ending in -ar: bailar	Verbs ending in -er: beber	Verbs ending in -ir: escribir
no bailes	no bebas	no escribas

1. To form the negative **tú** command, drop the **o** from the **yo** form of the present tense and add **-es** for **-ar** verbs and **-as** for **-er** and **-ir** verbs:

yo **bailo**	→bail-	→no **bailes**
yo **bebo**	→beb-	→no **bebas**
yo **escribo**	→escrib-	→no **escribas**
yo **digo**	→dig-	→no **digas**
yo **quiero**	→quier-	→no **quieras**
yo **vengo**	→veng-	→no **vengas**
yo **hago**	→hag-	→no **hagas**

2. Verbs that end in **-car, -gar,** or **-zar** such as **practicar, llegar,** and **cruzar** change the spelling in the negative **tú** command: **c → qu–no practiques, g → gu–no llegues,** and **z → c–no cruces.**

3. In chapter 3 you learned that the verbs **ir** and **ser** have irregular **usted** and **ustedes** command forms:

ir: **vaya,   vayan**
ser: **sea,   sean**

To form the negative **tú** command of these verbs add an **-s** to the **usted** command form:

no **vayas**
no **seas**

Práctica

D. Consejos. Uno(a) de tus amigos(as) tiene los siguientes problemas en la universidad. Intenta ayudarle, dándole *(giving him/her)* consejos para mejorar su situación. Puedes usar los siguientes verbos: **estudiar, trabajar, hablar, hacer, practicar, escribir, ir.**

Problemas:

1. Mis notas en las clases no son muy buenas.
2. No tengo mucho dinero.
3. Mi compañero(a) de cuarto pone la música muy alta.
4. Tengo problemas con mi clase de matemáticas.
5. No sé qué hacer para divertirme.
6. Necesito muchos libros para mis clases, pero no tengo dinero.
7. Mi compañero(a) de cuarto es muy desordenado(a). Deja su ropa por todos lados.
8. Mi camisa favorita tiene una mancha *(stain)* de salsa.
9. Es el cumpleaños de mi mejor amigo(a). No sé qué regalarle.
10. Mi compañero(a) usa mi ropa.

E. ¿Quién va a hacer qué? Tú y tus amigos van a tener una fiesta en un apartamento. Con un(a) compañero(a) de clase, haz una lista de tres mandatos afirmativos y tres negativos que indiquen qué va a hacer cada persona para tener todo listo. Usa los siguientes verbos: **limpiar, decorar, comprar, hacer, ir, llamar, olvidar, comer.**

■ **Modelo:** *Marco, pon tus zapatillas de tenis en tu cuarto.*

Comentarios

culturales · El Imperio Inca

AMÉRICA CENTRAL

Mar Caribe

OCÉANO ATLÁNTICO

R. Orinoco

R. Negro

R. Amazon

R. Madeira

OCÉANO PACÍFCO

AMÉRICA DEL SUR

R. São Francisco

CORDILLERA

Lago Titicaca

IMPERIO DE LAS INCAS

Lago Poopó

R. Paraguay

R. Paraná

DE LOS ANDES

R. Salado

OCÉANO ATLÁNTICO

N

| 0 | 500 | 1,000 mi |
| 0 | 500 | 1,000 km |

*E*l Imperio Inca, uno de los mayores imperios en América del sur, comenzó a extenderse desde el Cuzco, su capital, a finales del siglo XIV. Antes de la llegada de los españoles, en 1532, bajo el mando de Franciso Pizarro, el imperio incluía unos 12 millones de personas repartidas por lo que es hoy Perú, Ecuador, partes de Chile, Bolivia y Argentina. El nombre que los Incas le dieron a su tierra es *Tahuantinsuyu* que en quechua, la lengua de los incas, quiere decir "cuatro partes". Estas cuatro partes se refieren a las diferentes zonas geográficas del Imperio: el desierto a lo largo de la costa, los altos picos de los Andes, los valles y la región de la selva tropical en el este.

La arquitectura funcional y las técnicas de ingeniería desarrolladas por los incas son algunos de los aspectos más notables de su civilización. Sus ciudades se caracterizaban por la presencia de anchas avenidas, atravesadas por calles más pequeñas, que llegaban a una plaza abierta. En la plaza estaban los edificios públicos y los templos.

Macchu Picchu es un ejemplo de la superioridad de la arquitectura inca y una muestra de la gran habilidad de los incas para construir edificios adaptándose al terreno.

INTEGRACIÓN CULTURAL

1. ¿Qué países actuales fueron parte del Imperio Inca?
2. ¿Qué quiere decir *Tahuantinsuyu*? ¿Qué otra palabra de origen quechua conoces?
3. ¿Cuándo y cómo terminó el Imperio Inca?

ENFOQUE ESTRUCTURAL

El subjuntivo de verbos regulares con expresiones de voluntad

You learned that the command forms are used to give orders or instructions.

No gastes mucho dinero.	**Don't spend** a lot of money.
No vuelvas tarde a casa.	**Don't come** home late.
Vengan al concierto con nosotros.	**Come** to the concert with us.
Por favor, **compren** el regalo de Rosa.	Please, **buy** Rosa's present.

Use of the subjunctive with expressions of necessity and desire

In Spanish there is another way to express necessity with regard to someone's actions, or to express that you want/don't want people to do something. Here, we are going to focus on the *subjunctive mood* and on the structure of a type of sentence in which it is used. The *subjunctive mood* is used in sentences that have more than one clause and where the subjects in the two clauses are different. The first part of the sentence expresses necessity or a desire regarding the person or subject in the second part of the sentence. Look at the following sentences:

> No quiero que **gastes** mucho dinero.
> No quiero que **vuelvas** tarde a clase.
> Quiero que (ellos) **vengan** al concierto con nosotros.
> Quiero que (ustedes) **compren** el regalo de Rosa.

Notice that the two parts of the sentence are connected by the word **que.** The verb following **que** is in the present subjunctive.

In the following sentence, there are two clauses: a main (independent) clause and a dependent (subordinate) clause. The main clause in the first part of the sentence expresses a desire regarding the subject of the dependent clause in the second part of the sentence, also called the **que** clause because it follows the word **que.** Because the subjects of the main clause (**mi compañero de clase**) and the **que** clause (**yo**) are different, the *subjunctive* is used.

Mi compañero de cuarto no quiere que (main clause)	**ponga** la música muy alta. (dependent clause)

Occasionally, a main clause will not have a subject but an impersonal generalization of influence or desire, such as the following expressions:

Es necesario que…	It is necessary that . . .
Es importante que…	It is important that . . .
Es mejor que…	It is better that . . .
Es aconsejable que…	It is advisable that . . .

Because these expressions express influence regarding the subject of the **que** clause, the subjunctive is used.

> Es necesario que **compren** el regalo de Rosa.

For most regular verbs you have already learned, the present subjunctive is formed by removing the **o** of the **yo** form of the present indicative tense and adding the following endings:

VERBOS EN -AR: Hablar

Present Indicative, **Yo** form	Subjunctive	
hablo	hable	hablemos
	hables	habléis
	hable	hablen

VERBOS EN -ER: Comer °

Present Indicative, **Yo** form	Subjunctive	
como	coma	comamos
	comas	comáis
	coma	coman

VERBOS EN -IR: Escribir

Present Indicative, **Yo** form	Subjunctive	
escribo	escriba	escribamos
	escribas	escribáis
	escriba	escriban

Práctica

F. ¡Tantos mandatos! Indica lo que quiere Esteban que haga cada persona. Sigue el modelo.

Modelo: No gastes todo tu dinero, Ernesto.
Esteban no quiere que Ernesto gaste todo su dinero.

1. Rosa y Elisa, por favor, inviten a Juan a la fiesta.
2. No comas demasiado, Juana.
3. Pedro, manda estas cartas cuando vayas al centro.
4. Señora, hable más despacio, por favor.
5. María y Teresa, no olviden comprar una tarjeta de cumpleaños para papá.
6. Lleva una chaqueta, Laura, porque hace frío *(it's cool)*.

G. Consejos. Indica ahora si es necesario o no que tu amigo(a) haga las siguientes cosas. Puedes usar cualquiera de las expresiones en la columna izquierda para completar la frase.

(No) Es necesario que...   escribir cartas a sus padres a menudo
(No) Es aconsejable que...   comer bananas verdes
(No) Es importante que...   añadir *(add)* mucha sal a la comida
Es mejor que...   llevar las botas sin calcetines
                                tomar un vaso de leche cada día
                                comprar una tarjeta de cumpleaños para
                                    su mejor amigo(a)
                                pasar tiempo con su familia
                                hablar demasiado por teléfono

El subjuntivo de verbos irregulares con expresiones de voluntad

1. For verbs that undergo the spelling change **e > ie** when conjugated in the present indicative, the **e** changes to **ie** in the present subjunctive in all forms except **nosotros(as)** and **vosotros(as).**

Pensar (ie)

yo	piense		nosotros	pensemos
tú	pienses		vosotros	penséis
Ud.			Uds.	
él	piense		ellos	piensen
ella			ellas	

2. For verbs that undergo the spelling change **o > ue** when conjugated in the present indicative, the **o** changes to **ue** in the present subjunctive in all forms except **nosotros(as)** and **vosotros(as).**

Volver (ue)

yo	vuelva		nosotros	volvamos
tú	vuelvas		vosotros	volváis
Ud.			Uds.	
él	vuelva		ellos	vuelvan
ella			ellas	

3. For verbs that undergo the spelling change **e > i** when conjugated in the present indicative, the **e** changes to an **i** *even* in the **nosotros(as)** and **vosotros(as)** forms.

Pedir (i)

yo	pida		nosotros	pidamos
tú	pidas		vosotros	pidáis
Ud.			Uds.	
él	pida		ellos	pidan
ella			ellas	

4. To form the present subjunctive for verbs that have a **-go** ending in the **yo** form of the present indicative, drop the **-o** off the **yo** form and add the same endings you would for any **-ar, -er,** or **-ir** verb.

	Present Indicative *yo*	Present Subjunctive
decir	**digo**	diga, digas, diga, digamos, digáis, digan
hacer	**hago**	haga, hagas, haga, hagamos, hagáis, hagan
oír	**oigo**	oiga, oigas, oiga, oigamos, oigáis, oigan
poner	**pongo**	ponga, pongas, ponga, pongamos, pongáis, pongan
salir	**salgo**	salga, salgas, salga, salgamos, salgáis, salgan
tener	**tengo**	tenga, tengas, tenga, tengamos, tengáis, tengan
venir	**vengo**	venga, vengas, venga, vengamos, vengáis, vengan

The change from **z** to **c** before **e** or **i** is simply a spelling change dictated by the Real Academia Española in 1726 to avoid any comination of **z** + **e** or **z** + **i**. It was an arificial rule since a word spelled with a **c** + **e** or a **z** + **e** would be prounounced the same way by a speaker of peninsular Spanish or of the Spanish of the Americas. The rule was also applied to words Spanish borrowed from other launguages and that were spelled with the "ze" or "zi" combination, e.g., **cero** (zero), **cebra** (zebra), **cénit** (zenith), **circón** (zercon), **citara** (zither).

The change from **c** to **qu** is not artificial, however. It conserves the sound of /k/ when **-e** is added to the stem of the infinitive. Reveiw with students the sounds of:

a	*café*
c + o	*comer*
u	*cubano*

and have them compare these sounds to:

e	*cena*
c + i	*cine*

On a transparency or the board you may want to write the word **practicar**; take off the **ar** and all the **-e** so you have "practice" and have students prounce the word. Point out that changing the **c** to **qu** conserves the /k/ sound of the infinitive.

The change from **g** to **gu** is not artificial, either. It conserves the sound of /g/ when **-e** is added to the stem of the inifinitive. Review with students the sounds of:

a	*gato*
g + o	*gordo*
u	*gustar*

and have them compare these sounds to:

e	*general*
g + i	*gimnasio*

Again you may want to write the word **pagar**; take off the **ar** and the **-e** so you have "page" and have students pronounce the word. Point out that changing the **g** to **gu** conserves the /g/ sound of the infinitive.

5. The subjunctive forms of **ser** and **ir** are the following:

ser			
yo	sea	nosotros	seamos
tú	seas	vosotros	seáis
Ud.		Uds.	
él	sea	ellos	sean
ella		ellas	

ir			
yo	vaya	nosotros	vayamos
tú	vayas	vosotros	vayáis
Ud.		Uds.	
él	vaya	ellos	vayan
ella		ellas	

6. For verbs that end in **-zar, -car,** and **-gar,** the present subjunctive is formed as follows:

cruzar:	cruce	crucemos
	cruces	crucéis
	cruce	crucen
practicar:	practique	practiquemos
	practiques	practiquéis
	practique	practiquen
llegar:	llegue	lleguemos
	llegues	lleguéis
	llegue	lleguen

Práctica

H. Sara quiere que... Indica lo que Sara quiere que hagan las siguientes personas. Sigue el modelo.

Modelo: nosotros / comer más
Sara quiere que nosotros comamos más.

1. Rosa / organizar una fiesta de cumpleaños
2. Juan / ir a la fiesta de Rosa
3. Beatriz y Mónica / traer el disco de Patricia Saravia
4. Norma / invitar a Elsa
5. Mercedes / poner buena música en la fiesta
6. Isabel / volver pronto
7. Norma y Mercedes / no decir cosas inconvenientes
8. Juan / no pedir más cerveza
9. Los invitados / no beber mucho

I. No es necesario que...
Indica ahora lo que no es necesario que hagan las siguientes personas. Sigue el modelo.

■ **Modelo:** Uds. / comprar muchas bebidas
No es necesario que Uds. compren muchas bebidas.

1. Rosa / preparar mucha comida para la fiesta
2. Juan / venir antes de las cuatro de la tarde
3. Beatriz y Mónica / cantar las canciones de Patricia
4. Norma y Elsa / regresar temprano a casa
5. Mercedes / cambiar la música cada cinco minutos
6. Los invitados / limpiar la sala
7. Mercedes / poner la música muy alta
8. Carolina / hablar con Juan
9. Los invitados / salir antes de las 12:00
10. Rosa / pasar mucho tiempo en la cocina

J. ¿Qué quieres tú?
Ahora imagina que estás preparando una fiesta para la clase de español. Trabaja con un(a) compañero(a) y haz una lista de las cosas que tú quieres que hagan varias personas de tu clase.

VAMOS A ESCUCHAR: EN EL CENTRO COMERCIAL

Imagina que estás en un centro comercial. Mientras paseas y miras escaparates, escuchas varias conversaciones en diferentes tiendas.

ANTES DE ESCUCHAR

Antes de escuchar las conversaciones, contesta las siguientes preguntas.

1. ¿Qué tipos de tiendas hay en un centro comercial?
2. ¿Qué preguntas hacen los clientes y los dependientes en una tienda?

Ahora mira los ejercicios que aparecen en la sección *Después de escuchar.*

DESPUÉS DE ESCUCHAR

K. Comprensión. ¿Dónde están?
Para cada una de las conversaciones que vas a oír, di en qué tienda están las personas que hablan.
1. _____
2. _____
3. _____

L. ¿Cómo lo dicen?
Escucha los diálogos otra vez y contesta las preguntas.

1. En la primera conversación, ¿cómo dice el vendedor "can I help you"?
2. ¿Cómo dice el cliente que "he wants to see the items he is inquiring about"?
3. En la segunda conversación, ¿cómo pregunta el cliente el precio?
4. En la tercera conversación, ¿qué dice un cliente para llamar la atención del otro?

Tú dirás ....

M. Las compras de ropa.

Imagínate que vas a pasar un año entero estudiando en la Universidad Católica de Lima. Antes de salir de viaje necesitas comprar ropa. Con un(a) compañero(a) prepara la siguiente escena.

Estudiante A: cliente en la tienda de ropa

1. Haz una lista de las cosas que necesitas comprar (tipo de ropa, colores).
2. Ve a la tienda y saluda al dependiente.
3. Pide las cosas que necesitas.
4. Pregunta los precios de las cosas que quieres comprar.
5. Decide qué vas a comprar.
6. Paga tus compras.
7. Despídete del dependiente.

Estudiante B: dependiente en una tienda de ropa

1. Trabajas en una tienda de ropa. Piensa en los precios de las cosas que hay en tu tienda.
2. Saluda al cliente que viene a comprar.
3. Contesta sus preguntas sobre precios.
4. Haz las sugerencias necesarias.
5. Indica el total de la compra.
6. Despídete del cliente.

N. Un regalo de cumpleaños.

Imagina que la semana que viene es el cumpleaños de un(a) amigo(a) y quieres comprar un regalo para esta persona.

Antes de preparar el diálogo piensa: ¿Qué cosas le gustan a tu amigo(a)? Haz una lista de posibles regalos.

A continuación tienes el bosquejo *(outline)* de un diálogo en el que la persona decide comprar un disco compacto como regalo para su amigo(a).

Si vas a comprar una cosa diferente, debes adaptar el diálogo a tu propia situación.

Estudiante A: Cliente en la tienda de discos

1. Saluda al dependiente.
2. Explica qué tipo de música le gusta a tu amigo(a).
3. Decide qué disco vas a comprar.
4. Paga tu compra
5. Despídete.

Estudiante B: Dependiente en la tienda de discos

1. Saluda al cliente.
2. Contesta sus preguntas.
3. Haz las sugerencias necesarias.
4. Indica el total de la compra.
5. Despídete.

PARA EMPEZAR: ¿Cuánto cuesta?

Preparación

- Have you ever been to an open-air market? If so, where? when?
- What kinds of products can one buy in an open-air market?
- How is the shopping experience in a place like this different from a regular supermarket?
- What products can you find at a supermarket that you could not get at an open-air market?

▶ En el mercado

Ayer domingo fue **día de feria** en Chincheros, un pueblo cerca de Cuzco. La señora Fernández, como siempre que hay feria, caminó al mercado para hacer las compras de frutas y **verduras.** En el mercado de Chinchero siempre encuentra productos **frescos,** baratos y de excelente calidad.

Play Textbook audio.

market day

vegetables
fresh

CULTURE:

Chincheros, near Cuzco, is a well-known place for its Sunday market. Cuzco is probably one of the most beautiful towns in Perú. The Chincheros market is one of the best markets in the region. It is a produce market, but it also has handicrafts.

¿Qué se puede comprar?

Las verduras	Las frutas
cebollas	aguacates
champiñones	bananas
espárragos	fresas
guisantes	limones
lechuga	mangos
maíz	manzanas
papas	melocotones
pepinos	melón
tomates	naranjas
zanahorias	peras
	uvas

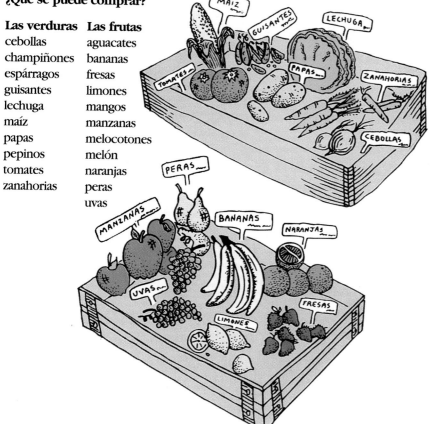

En el supermercado

Once
food
together / dairy products

packaged goods / cans of soup
can of tuna / oil / cookies

Then they pass by / frozen
fish / ice cream

flour / salt / pepper
shopping cart / full

Una vez por semana Ricardo hace las compras para su casa en el supermercado. Hoy Rosa también tiene que ir al supermercado para comprar **alimentos** para su familia y los dos amigos van **juntos**. Primero, van a la sección de **productos lácteos** porque Ricardo tiene que comprar mantequilla, leche, yogur, crema y queso. Después van a la sección de **conservas** porque necesitan tres **latas de sopa, una lata de atún,** una botella de **aceite** y un paquete de **galletas**.

Luego pasan por la sección de productos **congelados** porque Rosa tiene que comprar **pescado**, una pizza, un pollo y también ¡**helado** de chocolate! A Rosa le encanta el helado.

Para terminar, compran pastas, **harina,** azúcar, **sal, pimienta,** arroz y mayonesa. El **carrito** de Rosa está muy **lleno**.

Práctica

A. ¿Qué son? Identifica las frutas y verduras a continuación.

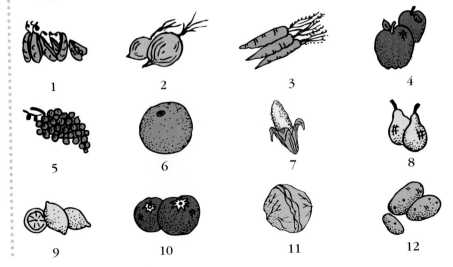

B. Preparando una ensalada de verduras.
Tienes que preparar una ensalada. Un(a) amigo(a) te quiere ayudar, pero no sabe qué hace falta poner en la ensalada. Dile si sus sugerencias son buenas o no.

■ **Modelo:** *¿Fresas?*
No, una ensalada de verduras no tiene fresas.

Ex. B: Pairs

Answers, Ex. B
1. peras 2. cebollas 3. lechuga
4. manzanas 5. uvas 6. guisantes/
chícharos 7 . tomates/jitomates
8. naranjas 9. zanahorias 10. maíz

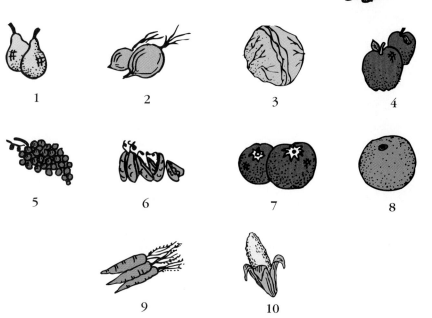

1 2 3 4

5 6 7 8

9 10

C. Se me olvidó *(I forgot)* la lista.
Hoy vas a comprar comida al super-mercado pero olvidaste tu lista de compra en casa. La persona que trabaja en el supermercado te ayuda a recordar lo que necesitas mencionando algunos artículos *(items)*. Tu compañero(a) va a hacer el papel de dependiente.

■ **Modelo:** **Dependiente:** *¿Necesita arroz?*
    Tú: *No, pero necesito pasta.*

Ex. C: Pairs

Answers, Ex. C
Students follow the model,
substituting the following cues:
1. pizza 2. sal 3. pescado 4. helado
5. leche 6. atún

Pasta

¿Necesita harina? ¿Necesita pimienta? ¿Necesita pollo?

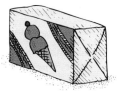

¿Necesita galletas? ¿Necesita yogur? ¿Necesita mayonesa?

Comentarios

culturales **Los mercados al aire libre**

*L*os mercados al aire libre están presentes en todos los países del mundo hispanohablante, tanto en las ciudades como en los pueblos. Algunos de estos mercados son permanentes y están

abiertos al público todos los días de la semana, pero hay otros mercados que sólo se abren un día a la semana. El día que hay mercado se llama día de feria. Estos mercados son especialmente importantes en las zonas rurales porque ofrecen un lugar de encuentro para la gente que vive en los pueblos cercanos.

Normalmente, una vez a la semana, vendedores y compradores se reúnen en el lugar designado para el mercado que generalmente es la plaza principal del pueblo. Los **agricultores** *(farmers)*, granjeros y **ganaderos** *(stock farmers)* de la localidad traen sus productos frescos al mercado: frutas, verduras, huevos, productos lácteos, etc.

Además de productos alimenticios, en estos mercados también se pueden comprar otras cosas necesarias para la casa como utensilios de cocina, platos, muebles, etc. Con frecuencia, la mayoría de estos mercados ofrecen también una gran variedad de objetos propios de la artesanía local: cestas, vasijas, instrumentos musicales, telas, ropa, etc. En algunos casos, también se pueden comprar productos manufacturados como **electrodomésticos** (appliances), radios y televisores.

INTEGRACIÓN CULTURAL

1. ¿Qué importancia tienen los mercados al aire libre en las zonas rurales?
2. ¿Cuáles son las semejanzas y diferencias que ves entre estos mercados del mundo hispanohablante y los *farmers' markets* que hay en muchos pueblos de los EE.UU.?

Repaso

D. Los favores. Hoy estás en casa muy enfermo. Tienes dolor de garganta *(sore throat)*. Necesitas que tus compañeros te hagan algunos favores. Como no puedes hablar, decides escribirles varios mensajes. Utiliza las siguientes frases y escribe varios mandatos para tus compañeros.

1. comprar jugos de fruta / Juan
2. ir a la farmacia / Pablo
3. no hacer ruido / María
4. llamar a mis padres y decir que estoy enfermo / Juan
5. traer unas cintas de vídeo / María
6. preparar la cena / Juan

E. ¿Qué hicieron el fin de semana?

E. ¿Qué hicieron el fin de semana? Hazles preguntas a tus compañeros de clase para averiguar *(find out)* quién hizo las siguientes actividades durante el fin de semana. Después comparte la información con el resto de la clase.

■ **Modelo:**   Salir el sábado por la noche. ¿Con quién?
¿Saliste el sábado por la noche?
¿Con quién saliste?

1. Cocinar. ¿Qué? ¿Para quién?
2. Ir a un restaurante. ¿A cuál? ¿Con quién?
3. Ir de compras. ¿Adónde?
4. Comer. ¿Qué? ¿Dónde?
5. ¿Recibir un regalo? ¿Qué? ¿Por qué?
6. Comprar un regalo. ¿Qué? ¿Para quién?

ENFOQUE LÉXICO   Expresiones de cantidad

At the market Sra. Fernández says the following:

Bueno, deme dos **kilos.**

This is a common expression in the Spanish-speaking world to indicate quantity for vegetables. Note the following examples:

¿Cuánto cuesta un **litro** de leche?	*How much is a **liter** of milk?*
Quisiera **medio kilo** de uvas.	*I would like a **half kilo** of grapes.*

The following expressions are used to indicate quantities.

un kilo de	*a kilogram of*
medio kilo de	*a half kilogram of*
un cuarto de kilo de	*a quarter of a kilogram of*
una libra de	*a pound of*
50 gramos de	*50 grams of*
un litro de	*a liter of*
medio litro de	*a half liter of*
una botella de	*a bottle of*
un galón de	*a gallon of*
una docena de	*a dozen of*
un pedazo de	*a piece of*
un paquete de	*a package of*

Práctica

F. ¿Cuánto compraron? Mira los dibujos y di cuánto compró cada cliente.

Modelo: ¿Qué compró Juanita?
Cincuenta gramos de queso.

1. ¿Qué compró Mercedes?

2. ¿Qué compró el señor González?

3. ¿Qué compró Antonio?

4. ¿Qué compró Maribel?

5. ¿Qué compró la señora Ruiz?

6. ¿Qué compró Francisco?

G. En el mercado. Estás comprando en un mercado al aire libre. Pregunta el precio de cada cosa y di cuánto necesitas. Tu compañero(a) va a hacer el papel de vendedor. Sigue el modelo.

Modelo: zanahorias: 2 dólares el kilo / 2 kilos
—*¿Cuánto cuestan estas zanahorias?*
—*Dos dólares el kilo.*
—*Quiero dos kilos, por favor.*
—*Aquí tiene. Cuatro dólares.*

1. leche: 2 dólares la botella / 3 botellas
2. naranjas: 3 dólares la docena / media docena
3. papas: 2 dólares el kilo / 500 gramos
4. cebollas: 1.50 dólares el kilo / medio kilo
5. mantequilla: 2.50 dólares el paquete / 2 paquetes
6. pastel: 1 dólar el pedazo / 2 pedazos

Expresiones para comparar

Suggestion: Expressions of comparison. Give students different numbers of objects (pencils, pens, etc.) to illustrate the comparative. (Julia tiene más lápices que Felipe. Felipe tiene menos lápices que Julia.) To make the meaning clear, first count the number of objects each student has. Ask personalized questions: ¿Eres menor/mayor que tu hermano(a)? ¿Juegas al tenis (béisbol, básquetbol, fútbol, etc.) muy bien? ¿Juegas al tenis mejor/peor que tu amigo? etc.

Contextualize presentation by bringing in pictures of people (perhaps your family) and describing them and their differences for the class. After describing a few people, check for comprehension, e.g., Clase, ¿quién es más alto, mi hermano o mi hermana?

Más / menos... que

1. To establish a comparison in Spanish, use these phrases:

más... que	*more . . . than*
menos... que	*less . . . than*
Hoy hay **menos** clientes **que** ayer.	*Today there are **fewer** customers **than** yesterday.*
Estos tomates son **más** caros **que** ésos. ¿Por qué?	*These tomatoes are **more** expensive **than** those. Why?*

2. There are a few adjectives that have an irregular comparative form and do not make comparisons using **más** or **menos**.

bueno(s)/buen	*good*	→	**mejor(es)**	*better*
malo(s)/mal	*bad/sick*	→	**peor(es)**	*worse*
joven/jóvenes	*young*	→	**menor(es)**	*younger*
viejo(s)	*old*	→	**mayor(es)**	*older*

Estos vestidos **son mejores que** esas blusas.	*These dresses **are better than** those blouses.*
Yo soy **menor que** mi hermano.	*I am **younger than** my brother.*

Tan... como / Tanto... como

1. To express equality in Spanish, use the phrase **tan** + *adjective/ adverb* + **como** = *as . . . as.*

El carrito de Rosa está **tan** lleno **como** el de Ricardo.	*Rosa's shopping cart is **as** full **as** Richard's.*
Margarita compra **tan** frecuentemente **como** Linda.	*Margarita shops **as** frequently **as** Linda.*

2. Another way to express equality in Spanish is with the words **tanto** and **como. Tanto** and **como** are used with nouns, as in the examples below.

tanto(a) + noun + **como** = *as much* + noun + *as*
tantos(as) + noun + **como** = *as many* + noun + *as*

Este señor compró **tanta** mercadería **como** esa señora.	*This man bought **as much** merchandise **as** that woman.*
Laura compró **tantos** huevos **como** Sonia.	*Laura bought **as many** eggs **as** Sonia.*

The words **tanto(a)/tantos(as)** agree in gender and number with the nouns that follow.

Práctica

H. La ropa de María y Marta. Utiliza la información del cuadro siguiente para hacer comparaciones entre la ropa de María y Marta.

■ **Modelo:** *María tiene menos camisetas que Marta.*

	MARÍA	**MARTA**
CAMISETAS	5	6
FALDAS	2 faldas cortas	1 falda azul
	1 falda larga	1 falda amarilla
		2 faldas negras
VESTIDOS	1 vestido de fiesta	1 vestido de fiesta
	1 vestido rojo	4 vestidos rojos
	1 vestido verde	1 vestido verde
SUÉTERES	5	4
CINTURONES	1	3
PANTALONES	4	2

I. Comparaciones. Compara las posesiones de las siguientes personas.

	vídeos	cintas	discos compactos
Ángeles	3	15	32
Pancho	10	27	32
José	10	34	35
Delia	12	27	38

Answers, Ex. I
1. Pancho tiene tantos vídeos como José.
2. José tiene menos discos compactos que Delia.
3. Delia tiene más cintas que Ángeles.
4. Ángeles tiene tantos discos compactos como Pancho.
5. José tiene menos vídeos que Delia.
6. Pancho tiene tantas cintas como Delia.

■ **Modelo:** discos compactos / Ángeles y José
Ángeles tiene menos discos compactos que José.

1. vídeos / Pancho y José
2. discos compactos / José y Delia
3. cintas / Delia y Ángeles
4. discos compactos / Ángeles y Pancho
5. vídeos / José y Delia
6. cintas / Pancho y Delia

J. Mis amigos y yo. Utiliza las palabras siguientes para hacer comparaciones entre tú y tus amigos. Primero pregunta a tu compañero(a) cuántos(as) tiene. Después utiliza las expresiones **más... que, menos... que.**

■ **Modelo:** —*¿Cuántos primos* (cousins) *tienes?*
—*Cuatro.*
—*Tienes menos primos que mi amiga Teresa.*

1. hermanos(as)   3. camisetas   5. dinero
2. tíos(as)   4. cintas   6. vídeo-juegos

K. ¿Son iguales o no? Compara a las siguientes personas utilizando los adjetivos que aparecen en la lista. Tus comparaciones pueden ser afirmativas o negativas.

■ **Modelo:** *Gabriela Sabatini es tan buena tenista como Conchita Martínez.*

Adjetivos: famoso(a) joven viejo(a) inteligente deportista buen(a)

1. Isabel Allende (escritora)
2. Gabriel García Márquez (escritor)
3. Laura Esquivel (escritora)
4. Jon Secada (cantante)
5. Gloria Estefan (cantante)
6. Antonio Banderas (actor)
7. Edward James Olmos (actor)
8. Rosie Pérez (actriz)
9. Pablo Picasso (pintor)
10. Salvador Dalí (pintor)
11. Frida Kahlo (pintora)
12. Conchita Martínez (deportista)
13. Juan González (deportista)

Los demostrativos

Suggestion: To introduce the demonstrative adjectives inductively, place different objects (or fruits and vegetables) around the classroom. Point to them while you say: **Estas manzanas son ricas pero esas peras no.** Or: **Este cuaderno es de Antonia. Aquel lápiz es de Marta. ¿De quién es este papel?** Tell the students that the difference between **este, ese,** and **aquel** is usually clarified by using **aquí, ahí,** and **allá: éste de aquí, ése de ahí, aquél de allá.**

There are many instances when we need to point out objects, places, and people. If you go shopping at an open-air market, you will have to talk to the **vendedor(a)** and point to the products you want to buy. Look at the exchange below:

Vendedor:	¿Quiere **estos** pimientos o **aquéllos?**
Cliente:	Pues, a ver, **aquéllos** de allí, los rojos.

Adjetivos demostrativos

Demonstrative adjectives are used to point out specific people or things. They agree in number and gender with the nouns that follow them. There are three sets of demonstrative adjectives:

Singular		Plural	
este...	*this...*	**estos...**	*these...*
ese...	*that...*	**esos...**	*those...*
aquel...	*that over there...*	**aquellos...**	*those over there...*

To point out people or things . . .

	near the speaker	near the listener	far from both speaker and listener
Sing. masc.	**este** limón	**ese** limón	**aquel** limón
Sing. fem.	**esta** manzana	**esa** manzana	**aquella** manzana
Plural masc.	**estos** limones	**esos** limones	**aquellos** limones
Plural fem.	**estas** uvas	**esas** uvas	**aquellas** uvas

Pronombres demostrativos

1. Demonstrative pronouns are used to indicate a person, object, or place when the noun itself is not mentioned.

Ese yogur no es muy bueno.	*That yogurt is not very good.*
Éste de **aquí** es mejor.	*This one here is better.*

2. Demonstrative pronouns have the same form as demonstrative adjectives, but they add an accent mark to show that they have different uses and meanings.

éste / ésta	*this one*	éstos / éstas	*these*
ése / ésa	*that one*	ésos / ésas	*those*
aquél / aquélla	*that one (over there)*	aquéllos / aquéllas	*those (over there)*

IRM Master 26: Los demostrativos

For homework the night before presenting this grammatical point in class, ask students to read over this section. In class, present the structure in context by placing three groups of CDs or cassettes at varying distances from yourself. Tell students to pretend that you are in a music store and are trying to decide what music to buy to bring to a business party. Pick up one CD and tell students: **Este CD es muy bueno, pero es música rock y no sé si es apropiada para la fiesta... Ese CD** (point to next set) **es música clásica... Aquel CD...** Check comprehension using demonstratives in the questions, e.g.: **¿Cuál es mejor, este CD o ese CD?**

3. Demonstrative pronouns agree in gender and number with the nouns they replace.

Esta manzana es roja, **ésa** es amarilla y **aquélla** es verde.	*This apple is red, **that one** is yellow, and **that one over there** is green.*
Me gusta más esta naranja que **ésa** o **aquélla.**	*I like this orange better than **that one** or **that one over there.***

4. When using demonstrative pronouns, it is helpful to use adverbs of location to indicate how close to you an object is. The location helps you decide whether you should refer to the object using **éste(a), ése(a), aquél(la),** or the plural forms.

5. You have already learned **aquí** (*here*). Here are two other adverbs you can use to talk about location: **ahí** (*there*) **allí** (*over there*)

¿Quieres **esta** lechuga de aquí, **ésa** de ahí o **aquélla** de allí?	*Do you want **this** lettuce here, **that** one there, or **that one over there?***

Pronombres demostrativos neutros: esto, eso, aquello

The neuter demonstrative pronouns in Spanish are used to refer to an abstract concept, an idea, an action, or an indefinite object. They never take an accent mark.

¿Cuánto cuesta todo **esto?**	How much does **this** cost?
Son 3.340 pesos.	3,340 pesos.
¿Cómo se llama **aquello?**	What do you call **that**
Son guayabas.	They're guayabas.

Práctica

L. ¿Estas manzanas o esos tomates? Mira el dibujo. Después completa los mini-diálogos con el pronombre o adjetivo correspondiente según la distancia de los objetos en relación al hablante (*speaker*) y al oyente (*listener*).

1. ¡Qué buenos están _____ plátanos!
   Sí, y _____ patatas parecen muy ricas

2. ¿Quiere usted _____ lechuga?
   Sí, deme _____.

3. ¿Quiere usted _____ melón?
   No, gracias, prefiero _____ nara

M. ¿Cuál? Estás de compras con un(a) amigo(a). Hay tantas cosas para elegir que tienes que explicar exactamente a cuál te refieres. Utiliza **éste(a), ése(a)** o **aquél(la)** en tus respuestas de acuerdo con la información entre paréntesis. Sigue el modelo.

■ **Modelo:** ¿Qué libros vas a comprar? (those)
Voy a comprar ésos. Son más baratos.

1. ¿Qué frutas vas a comprar? (those over there)
2. ¿Qué galletas quieres? (those)
3. ¿Qué paquete de arroz quieres? (this one)
4. ¿Qué pescado vas a comprar? (that one)
5. ¿Qué jamón quieres? (that one over there)

🎧 Play Textbook audio.

El Sr. Estévez está de compras en el mercado. Vas a escuchar la conversación entre él y la dependienta.

ANTES DE ESCUCHAR

Antes de escuchar el diálogo, contesta las siguientes preguntas.

1. ¿Qué tipo de productos se compran en un mercado al aire libre?
2. ¿Cómo crees que va a ser la conversación entre el Sr. Estévez y la dependienta?

Antes de escuchar el diálogo, mira los ejercicios que aparecen en la sección *Después de escuchar.*

DESPUÉS DE ESCUCHAR

N. Comprensión: ¿Qué compró? Mira la lista de palabras que hay a continuación. Pon una marca al lado de cada cosa que compró el Sr. Estévez.

☐ cebollas   ☐ plátanos
☐ guisantes   ☐ mangos
☐ tomates   ☐ aguacates
☐ papas   ☐ fresas
☐ maíz   ☐ uvas
☐ zanahorias   ☐ manzanas
☐ lechuga   ☐ melón

Ñ. ¿Cómo lo dicen? Escucha la conversación una vez más y contesta las preguntas.

1. ¿Cómo dice la dependienta que "they are out of avocados and that she is sorry"?
2. ¿Cómo reacciona el Sr. Estévez?
3. Varias veces durante la conversación la dependienta le pregunta al Sr. Estévez "if he needs something else." ¿Cómo lo dice?
4. ¿Cómo dice el Sr. Estévez que "he has gotten everything he needs"?

Answers, Ex. M
1. Voy a comprar aquéllas. 2. Quiero ésas. 3. Quiero éste. 4. Ése. 5. Aquél.

Pair students together and ask them to listen to the tape once without taking any notes and with their text closed. Have students then discuss what they heard and try to answer the comprehension questions. Listen a second time, this time allowing them to have the text open. Review comprehension questions and answers. Finally, have students listen a third time, this time trying to answer the **"cómo lo dicen"** questions.

Answers, Ex. N .
papas, cebollas, mangos, lechuga, tomate

Answers, Ex. Ñ
1. Se acabaron ya. Lo siento. 2. No importa. 3. ¿Algo más? 4. Eso es todo.

O. ¿Cuánto cuesta todo esto? Unos amigos y tú están planeando una cena para cinco personas. No tienen mucho dinero, sólo 30 dólares, para las bebidas, el postre y el plato principal. Miren los precios de la lista siguiente y decidan cuánto pueden comprar de cada cosa sin gastar más de 30.00 dólares. Después de decidir, escriban qué van a comprar y cuánto. Al terminar, compartan con la clase el menú para la cena.

■ **Modelo:**   —¿Qué vamos a servir?
—*Bueno, para el plato principal, ¿por qué no preparamos pollo con papas fritas y vegetales?*
—*A ver. El pollo cuesta...*

Productos lácteos		Otros productos	
yogur	3 / $2	pan	$1
leche	1 litro / $1	galletas	$2
mantequilla	$1	arroz	$2
crema	2 / $1	pastas	$2
queso	$2	lechuga	$1
		tomates	1 kilo / $2
Conservas		**Productos congelados**	
sopa	2 / $1	pescado	1 kilo / $5
atún	2 / $2.50	pizza	$5
salsa de tomate	2 / $1.50	papas fritas (fried)	$2
aceitunas	2 / $1.50	pollo	$5
		vegetales	$2
		helado	$4
Bebidas			
café	1 kilo / $5	agua mineral	1 litro / $2
refrescos	2 litros / $2	limonada	2 litros / $3

P. En un mercado al aire libre. Entre todos, conviertan la clase en un mercado al aire libre. Decidan en qué parte del mundo hispano están.

Estudiante A: vendedor

1. Decide qué productos vas a tener en tu puesto.
2. Indica los precios de los productos.
3. Saluda a los compradores.
4. Contesta sus preguntas.

Estudiante B: comprador

1. Visita los puestos de mercado.
2. Haz preguntas sobre los productos y los precios.
3. Compara los precios de los productos en los diferentes puestos.
4. Compra los productos que necesites.

PARA EMPEZAR: ¿Qué compraste?

Preparación

- Look at the title of the *etapa* and at the drawing below. What do you think the women are talking about?
- Skim the last part of the dialog. What have these two friends agreed on?

In preparation for the activity, tell students the day before to prepare the materials they will need to set up the **puestos**. All students should participate in the preparation.

You may also have small groups set this up and take turns role-playing in front of class

Review the vocabulary for clothes in the first *etapa,* the vocabulary for fruits and vegetables in this *etapa,* as well as the use of **expresiones de cantidad, expresiones para comparar,** and **los demostrativos.**

🎧 Play Textbook audio.

VOCABULARY EXPANSION:

There are several expressions for answering the phone in the Spanish-speaking world. Here are several you can use: **¿Diga?** or **¿Dígame?** (common in Spain); **¿Bueno?** (common in Mexico); **¿Aló?** (common in the Caribbean countries and in some countries in South America).

¡RING RING!

Teresa: ¿Aló?

Patricia: ¿Está Teresa?

Teresa: Sí, soy yo. ¿Quién es?

Patricia: ¿Teresa? Hola, soy Patricia. ¿Qué tal?

Teresa: Hola, Patricia. Oye, te llamé ayer pero no te encontré en casa.

Patricia: **Estuve fuera** toda la tarde.

Teresa: ¿Qué hiciste?

Patricia: **Pues** fui con mi prima Clara al centro comercial. Pasamos la tarde mirando escaparates y también compramos algunas cosas.

Teresa: ¡Ah!

Patricia: Sí, la semana pasada Clara **leyó** en el periódico un anuncio sobre ofertas especiales para este fin de semana y **decidimos** ir a ver. Al llegar al centro comercial fuimos **lo primero de todo** a la tienda de discos. Allí **oímos** el último disco compacto de Rubén Blades y también **vimos** algunos vídeos.

Teresa: ¿Compraron algo?

Patricia: Bueno vimos muchas cosas pero al final lo único que compramos fue un par de **cintas vírgenes** para **grabar** en casa.

Teresa: ¿**Vieron** algo más?

Patricia: Sí, después de ver los discos, yo me fui a ver los escaparates de las tiendas de ropa. Vi unos vestidos increíbles pero sólo compré una camiseta para mí y otra para Jorge.

I was out

Well . . .

read
we decided
first of all
listened / watched

blank tapes / record
Did you see
Ask students these questions in Spanish. Have several students perform this dialog, each time asking different comprehension check questions.

stationary store / birthday card
envelopes / paper
computer

I'm exhausted
a while ago

After

Teresa:	¿Y Clara?
Patricia:	Creo que vio unas zapatillas de tenis en oferta y decidió comprarlas. Después fuimos juntas a la **papelería.** Allí Clara compró una **tarjeta de cumpleaños** para un amigo y unos **sobres.** Yo compré **papel** para la **computadora.**
Teresa:	¿Oye? ¿Qué vas a hacer esta tarde?
Patricia:	No sé, creo que me voy a quedar en casa a descansar. **Estoy muerta.**
Teresa:	Bueno, es que Martín llamó **hace un rato** para invitarnos a una fiesta en su apartamento.
Patricia:	¿A qué hora?
Teresa:	**A partir** de las ocho. ¿Te apetece ir?
Patricia:	Sí, sí, ¿nos vemos a las 7:30 en tu casa?
Teresa:	Bien, entonces hasta las 7:30. Hasta luego.
Patricia:	Adiós.

Práctica

A. Las compras de Teresa y su prima. Contesta las siguientes preguntas de acuerdo con la información de las conversaciones anteriores.

1. ¿Qué compraron en la tienda de discos?
2. ¿A qué tiendas fueron después?
3. ¿Qué van a hacer esta tarde?

B. ¿Dónde lo compraste? Haz una lista de las diferentes tiendas que uno puede encontrar en un centro comercial. Después haz una lista de las cosas que puedes comprar en cada una de esas tiendas. Con un(a) compañero(a) de clase, menciona una serie de cosas que compraste en una de esas tiendas. Tu compañero(a) tiene que adivinar (guess) a qué tienda fuiste. Cuando adivine, cambien los papeles.

▪ **Modelo:** **Tú:** *Ayer por la tarde compré...*
Tu compañero(a): *Fuiste a...*

Repaso

C. Las comparaciones. Un(a) compañero(a) de clase y tú están discutiendo las distintas tiendas y centros comerciales de la zona *(in the area).* Cada uno tiene sus preferencias sobre cuál es la mejor tienda de discos, de comida, el mejor centro comercial…. Comparen las diferencias en relación a los precios, el servicio y la calidad.

▪ **Modelo:** *La ropa en la tienda X es más bonita que la ropa en la tienda Y.*

D. ¿Qué es necesario que haga una persona cuando va de compras? Con un(a) compañero(a) de clase, haz una lista de tres cosas que son necesarias y tres cosas que no son necesarias que haga una persona cuando va de compras y quiere comprar buenos productos y no gastar mucho dinero. Al terminar, comparte tu información con la clase.

▪ **Modelo:** *Es necesario que tenga una lista de lo que va a comprar.*
No es necesario que vaya a tiendas caras

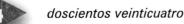

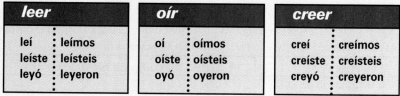

IRM Master 27: Verbos irregulares en el pretérito

In the phone conversation between Teresa and Patricia, Teresa said:

> Mi prima Clara **leyó** un anuncio en el periódico.
> ...**Oímos** el disco compacto de Rubén Blades y vimos unos vídeos.

Here you have the complete conjugation for the highlighted verbs and two more that are conjugated similarly.

leer	
leí	leímos
leíste	leísteis
leyó	leyeron

oír	
oí	oímos
oíste	oísteis
oyó	oyeron

creer	
creí	creímos
creíste	creísteis
creyó	creyeron

Assign this section and Ex. E as homework. In class, pair students together to review their answers.

Suggestion: Mention to students that caer and caerse, a reflexive verb, follow the same pattern as leer, oír, and creer in the preterite.

Los verbos *poder y poner*

Poder and **poner** are conjugated in a similar way. Note that the vowel in the stem of each verb changes to **u**.

> Sara, ¿dónde **pusiste** los compactos?
> En la mesa de la cocina.
> Oye, Rosa, ¿terminaste el trabajo?
> Mira, lo siento. Traté de hacerlo, pero **no pude.**

did you put

I couldn't

IRM Master 25: Poder y poner en el pretérito

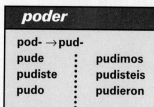

poder	
pod- → pud-	
pude	pudimos
pudiste	pudisteis
pudo	pudieron

poner	
pon- → pus-	
puse	pusimos
pusiste	pusisteis
puso	pusieron

GRAMMAR NOTE:
Note that the preterite forms of poder and poner are also different in that the stress in the yo and él forms falls on the first syllable, not on the last.

When the verb **poner** is used with a reflexive pronoun (**ponerse**), it has two very different meanings:

1. to put on (an article of clothing)

Me puse el abrigo.	*I put on my coat.*

Reflexive verbs and pronouns are fully explained in Ch. 10.

2. to get or become (an emotion, a state)

Jorge **se puso** furioso cuando perdió el partido de tenis.	*Jorge **became** furious when he lost the tennis match.*
Mis amigos siempre **se ponen** nerviosos cuando viajan en avión.	*My friends always **get** nervous when they travel by plane.*

Ex. F: Pairs

Allow 5 minutes for activity and circulate through class to check for accuracy.

Ex. G: Pairs

Práctica

E. ¿Qué hicieron? Completa las siguientes frases con el verbo indicado para expresar lo que hicieron las siguientes personas.

1. Los estudiantes de la clase de español avanzado / leer...
2. Mis compañeros y yo / oír...
3. Mi profesor(a) de español / poder...
4. Mi compañero(a) de cuarto / ponerse furioso(a)...
5. La semana pasada (yo) / no leer...
6. Mis profesores nunca / creer...

F. ¿Qué pasó? De acuerdo con la información que tienes a continuación, dile a un(a) compañero(a) de clase lo que pasó el fin de semana pasado.

El viernes (yo):	El sábado mi compañero(a) de cuarto
oír un anuncio de radio	ir a casa de Isabel
llamar a un amigo	oír música
ir al centro comercial	poner la tele
ver ofertas interesantes	ver vídeos musicales
no poder comprar nada	
ponerme muy furioso(a)	

G. ¿Qué hiciste? Utiliza los siguientes verbos para hacerle preguntas a tu compañero(a) sobre su fin de semana. Tu compañero(a) contestará tus preguntas.

■ **Modelo:** ver

¿Viste una película? / Sí, vi una película el viernes.

1. oír
2. leer
3. poder
4. ir
5. poner

Comentarios

culturales *Las nuevas repúblicas andinas*

*L*a declaración de la Independencia en los EE.UU. en 1776 y la Revolución francesa en 1789 fueron dos acontecimientos históricos que tuvieron un gran impacto en las personas que luchaban por la independencia de los virreinatos andinos: Simón Bolívar y José de San Martín.

Las guerras de independencia en la región andina se iniciaron en 1808 y terminaron hacia 1824 con la derrota de los españoles. Tras la victoria se establecieron siete repúblicas: Venezuela, Colombia, Ecuador, Perú, Bolivia, Chile y Argentina. En cada república se estableció una constitución, se eligió a un presidente y se impuso un sistema legislativo con dos cámaras.

Ecuador declaró su independencia el 10 de agosto de 1822. La Jura de la Independencia en Perú fue el 9 de enero de 1825, en la Plaza de Armas del Cuzco. A la ceremonia asistieron los altos mandos del ejército patriota y el general Simón Bolívar. En Bolivia se declaró la independencia el 5 de agosto de 1825 en Chuquisaca (Sucre). El general Antonio José de Sucre, que dirigió las tropas colombianas, tuvo un papel muy importante en la derrota de los españoles y fue elegido el primer presidente de Bolivia.

INTEGRACIÓN CULTURAL

Answers Integración:
1. líderes de la lucha por la independencia en América Latina
2. la república 3. Ecuador

1. ¿Quiénes fueron Simón Bolívar y José de San Martín?
2. ¿Qué sistema político se estableció en los países andinos tras las guerras de independencia?
3. De los países mencionados en el último párrafo, ¿cuál fue el primero en declarar su independencia?

ENFOQUE ESTRUCTURAL

Verbos irregulares en el pretérito: conducir, traer, decir

IRM Transparency Master 28: *Conducir, traer, decir* en el pretérito
to drive / to bring / to say

You are learning how to conjugate most Spanish verbs in the preterite form. This section presents three more verbs that do not follow completely the regular conjugation you learned in Chapters 5 and 6. Look at the examples in the dialog below:

> **Patricia:** ¿Cómo fuiste al centro comercial, en autobús?
> **Teresa:** No, en coche.
> **Patricia:** ¿Y quién **condujo,** tu prima o tú?
> **Teresa:** A la ida **conduje** yo, y a la vuelta **trajo el coche** Clara.

The following verbs change their stems in the preterite, but actually have a clear pattern of their own. Note that they all have **j** in the stem. In addition, the **yo** form does not have an accent on the last syllable, and the **él/ella/Ud.** form ends in **-o.** Also note that the **ellos/ellas/Uds.** form uses **-eron** (and not **-ieron**) after the **j.**

drove
I drove / brought the car back

Suggestion, pretéritos irregulares: Assign this section as homework. In class, you might spend 3–5 minutes drilling these verbs and throw in previously learned verbs in the preterite. Pay attention to stressed vowels and the appropriate personal endings. Students often interchange the first and the third person preterite endings.

conducir

yo	conduje	nosotros(as)	condujimos
tú	condujiste	vosotros(as)	condujisteis
Ud.		Uds.	
él	condujo	ellos	condujeron
ella		ellas	

GRAMMAR NOTE:
The verb **ver** (to see) follows the same pattern as any other -er verb: **vi, viste, vio, vimos, visteis, vieron.** The only difference is that none of the forms carries a written accent.

traer

yo	traje	nosotros(as)	trajimos
tú	trajiste	vosotros(as)	trajisteis
Ud.		Uds.	
él	trajo	ellos	trajeron
ella		ellas	

decir			
yo	**dije**	nosotros(as)	**dijimos**
tú	**dijiste**	vosotros(as)	**dijisteis**
Ud.		Uds.	
él	**dijo**	ellos	**dijeron**
ella		ellas	

Note that the stem of the verb **decir** has the same vowel change in the preterite, **e** becoming **i,** as in the present tense (except for the nosotros(as) and vosotros(as) forms in the present).

Práctica

Ex. H:  Pairs

Suggestion: Bring an interesting photo and ask students to recount the events of the last 5 minutes before the photo was taken.

H. La fiesta de Juan. Ayer estuviste en la fiesta de Juan. Cuéntale a un(a) compañero(a) cómo fue:

Ayer por la noche:
1. Juan *tener* una fiesta en su apartamento
2. Julián y José *conducir* el coche de sus padres
3. Todos *traer* discos compactos
4. Isabel *decir* que la fiesta fue aburrida

Ex. I  Pairs

I. ¿Qué pasó? Con un(a) compañero(a) de clase entabla *(carry out)* la siguiente conversación. Ask when was the last time he/she went to a store, if he/she drove his/her car to get there, what he/she told the salesperson, what he/she bought, and how much he/she paid for it.

ENFOQUE ESTRUCTURAL

Verbos irregulares en el pretérito: **dar, pedir, querer y venir**

Ayer **dimos** una vuelta por el mercado.	*Yesterday **we took** a walk through the market.*
Mi amiga **pidió** un kilo de papas en uno de los puestos.	*My friend **asked** for a kilo of potatoes at one of the stands.*
Un señor **quiso** hablar con nosotras.	*A man **tried** to talk with us.*
Cuando **vino** el autobús nos fuimos.	*When the bus **came** we left.*

These four verbs also have irregular preterite forms.

dar			
yo	**di**	nosotros(as)	**dimos**
tú	**diste**	vosotros(as)	**disteis**
Ud.		Uds.	
él	**dio**	ellos	**dieron**
ella		ellas	

pedir

yo	**pedí**	nosotros(as)	**pedimos**	
tú	**pediste**	vosotros(as)	**pedisteis**	
Ud.		Uds.		
él	**pidió**	ellos	**pidieron**	
ella		ellas		

Notice that the **e** in the stem of the verb **pedir** changes to **i** in the third person singular and plural of the preterite. Remember that **pedir** means *to ask for something* as opposed to **preguntar**, which means *to ask questions*.

Other verbs like **pedir** are: **servir** *(to serve)*, **medir** *(to measure)*, **reírse** *(to laugh)*, **sonreír** *(to smile)*, **repetir** *(to repeat)*, and **elegir** *(to choose)*.

querer

yo	**quise**	nosotros(as)	**quisimos**	
tú	**quisiste**	vosotros(as)	**quisisteis**	
Ud.		Uds.		
él	**quiso**	ellos	**quisieron**	
ella		ellas		

venir

yo	**vine**	nosotros(as)	**vinimos**	
tú	**viniste**	vosotros(as)	**vinisteis**	
Ud.		Uds.		
él	**vino**	ellos	**vinieron**	
ella		ellas		

Notice that the stress in the first and third persons singular of the preterite of **querer** and **venir** falls on the first syllable. All the other persons have the stress on the second-to-last syllable. Both verbs change the **e** of the infinitive to an **i** in all persons of the preterite.

Práctica

J. ¿Qué hizo quién? Completa las siguientes frases con los verbos indicados.

1. Mis amigos ayer / dar / una fiesta
2. Mi mejor amigo(a) / venir / conmigo
3. Los dos / pedir / lo mismo para beber
4. Casi al final de la fiesta / venir / más personas
5. Después de comer y beber mucho, nadie / querer / bailar

K. De compras en el mercado. A continuación tienes una pequeña narración sobre algo que pasó ayer en el mercado al aire libre de Chinchero, cerca de Cuzco, en Perú. Completa la narración con los verbos en la forma correspondiente.

Ayer mi hermana y yo _____ (dar) una vuelta por el mercado. _____ (llegar) temprano para tener tiempo de ver muchos puestos. Primero _____ (ir) a un puesto de verduras. Mi hermana _____ (pedir) un kilo de tomates, dos lechugas y dos kilos de papas. Después de pagar, yo _____ (ver) que mi hermana _____ (olvidar) comprar cebollas. Por eso _____ (volver) al puesto y le _____ (pedir) al vendedor dos kilos. _____ (pagar) las cebollas y el vendedor me _____ (dar) el cambio.

Play Textbook audio.

ANTES DE ESCUCHAR

Silvia tiene un problema y llama a su amiga Laura por teléfono para pedirle ayuda.

1. ¿Qué te sugiere el título de la actividad sobre el contenido de la conversación entre Laura y Silvia?
2. ¿Te gusta comprar regalos?
3. ¿Cuánto dinero gastas normalmente en un regalo para alguien especial?
4. ¿Qué haces cuando no tienes el dinero que necesitas para comprar algo?

Antes de escuchar la conversación, mira los ejercicios que aparecen en la sección de *Después de escuchar.*

DESPUÉS DE ESCUCHAR

L. Comprensión. Escucha la conversación y contesta las siguientes preguntas.

1. ¿Adónde fue Silvia ayer?
2. ¿Qué compró?
3. ¿Compró algo para Alberto?
4. ¿Cuánto dinero le pide a su amiga?
5. ¿Para qué es el dinero?

M. ¿Cómo lo dicen? Escucha otra vez la conversación y contesta las preguntas.

1. ¿Cómo reacciona Laura cuando Silvia le dice qué compró?
2. ¿Cómo le dice Laura a Silvia:"to forget about the shoes"?

Tú dirás ....

N. Las compras del fin de semana.
Este fin de semana fuiste a tu centro comercial favorito y compraste varias cosas. Al volver, llamas por teléfono a un(a) amigo(a) y le cuentas lo que hiciste en el centro comercial.

Estudiante A: llama por teléfono

1. Say you want to talk to . . .
2. Say who you are, ask how he/she is doing.
3. Tell your friend that you went to the mall.
4. Explain what stores you went to.
5. Tell your friend what you bought and what you didn't buy.
6. End the conversation in a natural way.

Estudiante B: contesta el teléfono

1. Answer the phone.
2. Say it is you.
3. Ask what is going on.
4. React to what your friend tells you with appropiate questions and comments.
5. End the conversation in a natural way.

Ñ. En el supermercado.
Estás en el supermercado comprando comida para preparar una cena para unos amigos. Utiliza diferentes expresiones para explicar lo que quieres. Pregunta el precio de las cosas. Utiliza las expresiones necesarias para saludar, dar las gracias y despedirte.

Ex. N:  Pairs
Have several pairs perform their role play after practicing. After role play is complete, comment on language usage.

Ex. Ñ:  Pairs

LECTURA: Cajamarca: Tumba de un imperio

ANTES DE LEER

A. El texto que vas a leer presenta información sobre un departamento de Perú, Cajamarca, y en especial sobre su capital que tiene el mismo nombre. La lectura está dividida en tres secciones: Introducción, Historia y Actualidad.

Antes de leer el texto, contesta las siguientes preguntas:

1. Mira el mapa de Perú. ¿En qué parte del país está Cajamarca? De las ciudades importantes que se mencionan al principio de este capítulo, ¿cuál está cerca de Cajamarca?
2. Mira la foto de la región. ¿Cómo es la geografía de esta parte del país?
3. Lee el título, "Cajamarca: Tumba de un imperio". ¿A qué imperio se refiere? Explica con tus palabras el significado de este título.

Ex. A: 👥👥
Group of 2-3

Have students work in pairs or groups of three to negotiate reading and discussing answers.

Answers, Ex. A
1. En el noreste. Trujillo. 2. Hay montañas. 3. Al Imperio Inca. Significa el fin del imperio.

Answers, Ex. B
1. The Inca Empire ended in Cajamarca. 2. Pizarro arrived in the town square and waited for Atahualpa. 3. He threw the Bible on the ground. 4. 300 years 5. green 6. coffee 7. gold

GUÍA PARA LA LECTURA

Sigue las instrucciones que aparecen a continuación y contesta las preguntas en inglés.

B. Introducción.

1. Lee el primer párrafo y explica el significado de la primera frase: "Cajamarca es uno de los departamentos más significativos en la historia del Perú."

Historia

2. Lee ahora el primer párrafo. ¿Qué pasó el 15 de noviembre de 1532?
3. Lee el segundo párrafo. ¿Qué hizo Atahualpa que provocó el ataque de los españoles?
4. Lee el tercer párrafo. ¿Cuánto tiempo duró la dominación española?

Actualidad

5. De acuerdo con la información que aparece en el segundo párrafo de esta sección, ¿cuál es el color que domina en esta región?
6. De acuerdo con la información que aparece en el tercer párrafo, ¿por qué motivo se conoce Jaén?
7. Lee el último párrafo. ¿Por qué es importante Yanacocha?

Suggestion: As a follow-up for this reading, you may want to ask students the following questions for discussion in class:

1. If you were traveling in Perú, would you like to visit this area? Why?
2. Can you think of others incidents in the history of the world that were caused by religious intolerance?

CAJAMARCA: TUMBA DE UN IMPERIO

Introducción

Cajamarca es uno de los departamentos más significativos en la historia del Perú.

Se puede afirmar con toda seguridad que en la ciudad capital del mismo nombre se puso punto final al esplendoroso Imperio de los Incas a la vez que empezó la era del colonialismo español. La capital del mismo nombre es una ciudad "grande y hermosa" como decían ya los cronistas en el siglo XVIII.

Historia

Quienes visiten Cajamarca no podrán dejar de revivir una escena que marcó sombríamente el destino del Tahuantinsuyo. El 15 de noviembre de 1532, el conquistador Francisco Pizarro llegó hasta la actual plaza de armas que, por entonces, era triangular. Allí esperó a Atahualpa, el último monarca de la dinastía inca, quien **estaba** reposando en los ahora llamados Baños del Inca.

Al día siguiente, Atahualpa hizo su ingreso a la plaza en medio de una multitud y un aparato ceremonial esplendoroso. Lo recibió el padre Vicente Valverde, quien le mostró una Biblia. Atahualpa arrojó el libro sagrado al suelo porque **no entendía** de qué **se trataba** y, entonces, los soldados españoles entraron en la plaza y derrotaron al ejército imperial.

Atahualpa fue juzgado como hereje y condenado a morir ahorcado, aunque esa pena le fue conmutada por la del garrote. Al siguiente día empezó una nueva historia: la del colonialismo español que duró 300 años.

Remember that you don't need to understand all the words that appear in this reading. In order to successfully complete the tasks included under the *Guía para la lectura* section, you need to do the activities in the *Antes de leer* section and follow the instructions.

was

did not understand
was about

Actualidad

La ciudad de Cajamarca es un lugar privilegiado para el turismo; está situada en las faldas del cerro Santa Apolonia y goza de un clima primaveral, la gente tiene fama de ser muy acogedora. Quienes llegan a visitarla regresan alabando el afecto inge- nuo de la gente de la ciudad y de los campesinos.

En Cajamarca se respira aire puro. La vista se recrea en el verde de la campiña que la cerca por todos los costados y en todas las tonalidades. Hay verde-esmeralda, verde-oscuro, el "verde que te quiero verde" de García Lorca y hasta el verde-espe- ranza que alienta a los hombres de todas las latitudes de la tierra.

Cajamarca es un departamento histórico y de geografía muy diversa. Sus campos de cultivo producen papa, trigo, yuca, coca y café. El café de Jaén es muy conocido en el mundo. La cría de ganado tiene suma importancia. En la actualidad el departa- mento cuenta con más de 600 mil cabezas de ganado vacuno.

Cajamarca constituye uno de los lugares más codiciados en el mundo de la minería. Yanacocha es actualmente uno de los yacimientos más importantes en producción de oro en el país.

VÍDEO CULTURAL:
¿Qué quieres comprar?

C. Anticipación. Lee la lista de palabras y expresiones que aparece a contin- uación. Selecciona todas aquellas que, en tu opinión, se pueden utilizar cuando uno va a comprar ropa.

1. ____ el kilo
2. ____ el vestido
3. ____ la cuenta
4. ____ probar
5. ____ quedar bien

6. ____ me cobra, por favor
7. ____ el chaleco
8. ____ el cambio
9. ____ precioso
10. ____ la tela

D. Preparación. Lee la lista de las palabras y expresiones en español que aparece en la columna de la izquierda y después identifica su equivalente en inglés.

1. combina
2. el vestidor
3. traje sastre
4. probar
5. mostrar
6. la tela
7. vestidos

a. dressing room
b. to show
c. to try on
d. goes well/matches
e. the material
f. dresses
g. tailored suit
h. vest
i. chalet

E. Participación. Toma notas mientras ves el vídeo. Escribe todas las palabras y expresiones que, en tu opinión, te pueden servir para hablar sobre el vídeo con tus compañeros de clase y para hacer el ejercicio *Personalización* que aparece más adelante.

F. Comprensión. De acuerdo con lo que has visto en este vídeo, indica cuál es la respuesta adecuada para las siguientes preguntas.

Answers, Ex. F: 1. a 2. a

1. ¿Qué artículos de ropa compra Laura en la tienda de ropa?
   a. una falda y dos camisetas   b. un traje sastre y dos blusas
2. ¿Cuesta mucho dinero su ropa?
   a. bastante   b. no, no tanto

G. Personalización. Traigan a clase diferentes tipos de ropa y organicen un desfile de modas (fashion show). Varios estudiantes harán el papel (role) de modelos y otros serán los presentadores del desfile. Mientras los modelos se pasean por la clase, los presentadores deben hacer lo siguiente: a) describir el tipo de ropa que lleva cada persona; b) indicar el precio de cada prenda (item of clothing); y c) decir dónde se puede comprar esa ropa.

Intercambio: Compras por catálogo

Estudiante A

Este verano estás trabajando en la sección de pedidos por catálogo de la librería "*El mundo del libro*". Esta mañana llama un cliente para hacer un pedido. Escucha atentamente y completa la hoja que tienes a continuación. Haz las preguntas necesarias para obtener toda la información que necesitas.

PEDIDO HECHO POR:

C/o DATEL Special Products
12901 Coral Tree Place
Los Angeles, CA 90066

EL MUNDO DEL LIBRO

| Nombre | Inicial | Apellido |

| Número de la calle | Departamento |

| Ciudad | Estado | Zona Postal |

| Número de teléfono de la casa | Número de teléfono del trabajo |

	No. de Catálogo	Título del Libro	Editorial	Cuántos de C/U	Precio de C/U	Total
1						
2						
3						

Cómo calcular el costo de manejo y envío.
El cargo mínimo es $4 por los dos primeros libros y $1 por cada libro adicional. Si los libros tienen uno o mas asteriscos (*), entonces aplique el cargo especial de $5 a los marcados con*, $6 a los marcados con ** y $7 a los marcados con***.

Suggestion, Intercambio: Before doing activity, review with students telephone etiquette. Brainstorm with students some of the phrases of courtesy that might be associated with this type of telephone transaction and write them on the board. Encourage students to utilize these phrases in their interaction. After the activity, discuss with students any questions of vocabulary or grammar that may have come up.

Estudiante B

Quieres comprar libros para varias personas, pero no tienes mucho tiempo libre para ir a la librería. ¡No importa! La librería "*El mundo del libro*" te ofrece la posibilidad de comprar libros por correo o por teléfono por medio de un catálogo. Antes de decidir qué libros vas a comprar, mira el catálogo a continuación atentamente y selecciona un libro para las siguientes personas:

a. Tu tía—le gusta leer biografías: _____

b. Una persona muy consciente de su salud: _____

c. Una persona a quien le gusta la naturaleza: _____

Catálogo Septiembre - Octubre '90
Lo mejor en Español al alcance de sus manos
*Promociones del bimestre ***** Excelentes ideas para regalos*

GUIA DE PLANTAS Y FLORES   GRIJALBO
Francesco Bianchini y Azurra Carrara Pantano

Excelente guía, fácil de usar, a todo color catalogando 522 plantas y flores diferentes, cada una con su ficha descriptiva. Cada ficha descriptiva contiene los siguientes datos: familia, lugar de origen, descripción, utilización, multipicación, ambiente y exposición a la luz solar, época de floración, tipo de terreno, humedad. Incluye tanto a plantas de exterior, como de interior. Además las fichas vienen organizadas por familias ofreciendo así, su localización inmediata.

No. 0156MCJ $ 39.95

EL GENERAL EN SU LABERINTO   DIANA
Gabriel García Márquez (Premio Nobel 1982)

¡Continúa como gran éxito de ventas desde 1989 la última novela del gran escritor latinoamericano! La obra presenta a un Bolívar más humano, atormentado por la enfermedad, la proscripción política y el abandono de sus amigos durante sus últimos días. Haciendo uso de un fantástico despliegue verbal, de un lenguaje genial, caribeño, puro; García Márquez se posesiona de su personaje para brindarnos una gran obra literaria.

No. 0174BCT $ 18.50

CONFIESO QUE HE VIVIDO. Memorias
Pablo Neruda   SEIX BARRAL

"El poeta, ha escrito Neruda, debe ser, parcialmente, el **cronista** de su época", y el se muestra aquí como un auténtico cronista y testigo de nuestro tiempo. Con la inigualable potencia verbal que caracteriza a sus mejores escritos nos ofrece una verdadera joya literaria. En ella nos expone tanto su concepción del arte y de la poesía como sus posiciones políticas. A este respecto, resulta particularmente emotiva la evocación del presidente Allende a los tres días de su trágica muerte.

No. 0061BCT $ 15.95

TODO SOBRE LAS VITAMINAS
Earl Mindell   EDICIONES CEAC

¡La auténtica biblia de las vitaminas! Descubra este maravilloso mundo. Conozca, de verdad, lo que son las proteínas. ¿Y los sorprendentes aminoácidos, cómo le afectan? Tome las vitaminas juntas…en el momento justo. Cuándo deben tomarse y cuando no deben tomarse. ¿Poca azúcar? ¿Poca sal? Vitaminas y medicamentos ¡no los confunda! ¿Cómo conservarse joven y enérgico? ¡El libro definitivo para conocer cuáles son las vitaminas que usted precisa!

No. 0043MSF $ 15.95

PEREGRINOS DE AZTLAN
Miguel Méndez   EDICIONES ERA

Aquella tradición oral, voces del pueblo que se escuchan en las plazas pueblerinas, y que migran por todo México y el sur de Estados Unidos en busca de esperanza, narran esta obra ya clásica de la literatura chicana. Su aventura espiritual y dramática, el desierto que une y separa a dos países, Tijuana, Tucson, la vida peculiar en la frontera, Valle Imperial encuentra un terreno encantado para expresarse, que en su autor es tan hondo como libre. ¡He aquí todo un México que ignorábamos!

No. 0216BCT $ 16.95

CUENTOS DE HADAS
Raymond E. Feist   GRIJALBO

Cuentos de hadas nos descubre un mundo excepcional donde la percepción de la realidad se desdibuja magistralmente en los contornos de la fantasía y el terror. Su lectura encierra, sin duda alguna, una experiencia escalofriante e inolvidable, un aviso de que el mundo apacible y natural que vemos desenvolverse en nuestro entorno bien puede convertirse en cualquier momento en una trampa escapatoria.

No. 0038CCT $ 15.95

Para charlar

Expresiones para comprar *Expressions for buying*
¿Algo más? *Something else?*
Aquí tiene(n). *Here you are.*
¿En qué puedo servirle(s)? *How can I help you?*
Es todo por hoy. *That's all for today.*
No hay más. *There aren't any more.*
¿Qué necesita(n)? *What do you need?*
Voy a llevar... *I'll take . . .*

Para preguntar el precio *Asking the price*
¿Cuánto cuesta(n)? *How much is it (are they)?*
¿Qué precio tiene(n)? *How much is it (are they)?*
¿No está(n) en oferta? *It's not on sale?*
¿Cuánto cuesta todo? *How much does everything cost?*

Temas y contextos

Lugares para comprar *Places for buying*
la papelería *stationery store*
la tienda de deportes *sporting goods store*
la tienda de discos *record shop*
la tienda de ropa *clothing store*

Una tienda de discos *Record shop*
la cinta *tape*
la cinta virgen *blank tape*
el disco *record album*
el disco compacto *compact disc*
el vídeo *video*

Una tienda de deportes *Sporting goods store*
los esquíes *skis*
la pelota de tenis *tennis ball*
la raqueta *racquet*
los zapatos de tenis *tennis shoes*

Expresiones para pagar *Expressions for paying*
con tarjeta *with a credit card*
con cheque *by check*
en efectivo *in cash*

Para preguntar sobre preferencias *Asking about preferences*
¿Cuál prefieres...? *Which do you prefer?*
¿Cuál quieres...? *Which one do you want?*

Para hacer comparaciones *Making comparisons*
mayor *older*
más...que *more . . . than*
mejor *better*
menor *younger*
menos...que *less . . . than*
peor *worse*

Para establecer igualdad *Establishing equality*
tan/tanto...como *as/as much . . . as*

Para hablar por teléfono *Talking by telephone*
¿Aló?
¿Bueno? } *Hello.*
¿Diga?
¿Está...? *Is . . . there?*
Sí, soy yo. *Yes. It's me speaking.*
Sí, un momento. *Yes, just a moment.*

Una papelería *Stationery store*
la hoja *piece of paper*
el papel *paper*
el sobre *envelope*
la tarjeta de cumpleaños *birthday card*

Una tienda de ropa *Clothing store*
el abrigo *coat*
la blusa *blouse*
la camisa *shirt*
la camiseta *t-shirt*
la chaqueta *jacket*
el cinturón *belt*
la falda *skirt*
el impermeable *raincoat*
los pantalones *trousers*
el suéter *sweater*
el vestido *dress*

Una zapatería   *Shoe store*
la bolsa de cuero   *leather handbag*
la bota   *boot*
los calcetines   *socks*
las medias   *stockings*
las sandalias   *sandals*
el zapato   *shoe*
el zapato de tacón   *high-heeled shoe*
el zapato de tenis   *tennis shoe*

Cantidades   *Quantities*
un kilo de   *a kilogram of*
medio kilo de   *a half kilogram of*
un cuarto de kilo de   *a quarter of a kilogram of*
una libra de   *a pound of*
50 gramos de   *50 grams of*
un litro de   *a liter of*
medio litro de   *a half liter of*
una botella de   *a bottle of*
un galón de   *a gallon of*
una docena de   *a dozen of*
un pedazo de   *a piece of*
un paquete de   *a package of*

Carne y pescado   *Meat and fish*
el bistec   *steak*
el pescado   *fish*
el pollo   *chicken*

Productos congelados   *Frozen products*
el helado   *ice cream*

Productos lácteos   *Dairy products*
la crema   *cream*
la mantequilla   *butter*
el queso   *cheese*
el yogur   *yogurt*

Productos varios   *Varied products*
el aceite   *oil*
el azúcar   *sugar*
la galleta   *biscuit, cookie*
la harina   *flour*
la mayonesa   *mayonnaise*
el pan   *bread*
la pasta   *pasta*
la pimienta   *pepper*

la sal   *salt*

Las verduras   *Vegetables*
las cebollas   *onions*
los champiñones   *mushrooms*
los espárragos   *asparagus*
los guisantes   *peas*
la lechuga   *lettuce*
el maíz   *corn*
las papas   *potatoes*
los pepinos   *cucumbers*
los tomates   *tomatoes*
las zanahorias   *carrots*

Las frutas   *Fruits*
los aguacates   *avocados*
las bananas   *bananas*
las fresas   *strawberries*
los limones   *lemons*
los mangos   *mangoes*
las manzanas   *apples*
los melocotones   *peaches*
el melón   *melon*
las naranjas   *oranges*
las peras   *pears*
las uvas   *grapes*

Expresiones de persuasión   *Expresions that convey influence*
querer que...   *to want that . . .*
necesitar que...   *to need that . . .*
Es necesario que...   *It is necessary that . . .*
Es mejor que...   *It is better that . . .*
Es aconsejable que...   *It is advisable that . . .*

Vocabulario general   General vocabulary

Sustantivos
los alimentos   *food*
el carrito   *shopping cart*
el centro comercial   *shopping center*
el/la cliente   *customer*
el/la dependiente   *salesperson*
el escaparate   *shop window*
el mercado al aire libre   *open-air market*
la moda   *style*
el precio   *price*
el/la vendedor(a)   *salesman (woman)*

Adjetivos
amarillo(a)   *yellow*
aquel(la)   *that*
azul   *blue*
barato(a)   *cheap*
blanco(a)   *white*
bonito(a)   *pretty*
caro(a)   *expensive*
ese(a)   *that*
este(a)   *this*
favorito(a)   *favorite*
fresco(a)   *cool*
lleno(a)   *full*
marrón   *brown*
moderno(a)   *modern*
morado(a)   *purple*
negro(a)   *black*
rojo(a)   *red*
rosa/rosado(a)   *pink*
seguro(a)   *sure*
suficiente   *enough*
verde   *green*

Verbos
conducir   *to drive*
creer   *to believe*
decir   *to say*
elegir   *to choose*
dar   *to give*
leer   *to read*
llevar   *to take, carry*
medir   *to measure*
ofrecer   *to offer*
oír   *to listen*
pasar   *to pass*
pedir   *to ask for*
poder   *to be able to*
poner   *to put*
reír   *to laugh*
repetir   *to repeat*
servir   *to serve*
sonreír   *to smile*
traer   *to bring*

Otras palabras y expresiones
A ver.   *Let's see.*
Buen ojo.   *Good eye.*
por eso   *that is why*
¡Qué pena!   *What a pity!*
¡Super!   *Super!*
además   *besides*
ahí   *there*
allí   *over there*
aquél(la)/aquéllos(as)   *that one/those*

cada   *each, every*
ése(a)/ésos(as)   *that one/those*
éste(a)/éstos(as)   *this one/these*
hasta   *until*
juntos   *together*
luego   *then, afterwards*
para   *for; in order to*
una vez   *once*

Descripciones

Los edificios de Santiago perfilados contra el horizonte

Santiago, Chile

Monolitos de la Isla de Pascua

CHAPTER OBJECTIVES:

In this chapter you will learn about the weather and weather reports. You will also describe objects, places, and people.

After completing this chapter you should be able to carry out the following tasks:

- **describe weather conditions in different locations**
- **indicate centigrade temperatures**
- **describe places and things**
- **describe people's physical features and personality traits**
- **convey emotional reactions**

The tools you will use to carry out these tasks are:

- **vocabulary for:**
  - the weather in different regions
  - expressions to indicate duration
  - colors and sizes
  - people's physical and personality characteristics

- **grammatical structures:**
  - the verb **saber** in present and preterite tenses
  - descriptive adjectives
  - agreement, position, and shortening of adjectives
  - the subjunctive with expressions of emotion
  - the verb **conocer** and the personal **a**
  - direct object pronouns

CHILE Población: 14.333.258

736.902.9 kilómetros cuadrados
292.135 millas cuadradas), un poco más grande que Texas
Capital: Santiago, 5.236.000
Ciudades principales: Concepción, Viña del Mar,
Valparaíso, Temuco, Antofagasta

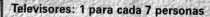

 Moneda: el peso

 Esperanza de vida: hombres, 71; mujeres, 78

 Índice de alfabetización: 95%

 Televisores: 1 para cada 7 personas

 Radios: 1 para cada 3,2 personas

 Teléfonos: 1 para cada 9 personas

Principales productos de exportación: cobre, frutas y vegetales, harina de pescado, nitrato de sodio, hierro, productos químicos, papel y derivados, productos derivados del petróleo

Embajada: 1732 Massachusetts Ave. NW, Washington, DC 20036

PARA EMPEZAR: ¿Qué tiempo hace?

Start discussion of the topic by asking students these questions in Spanish.

Transparency 20: El tiempo
Show students the transparency with the captions. You say ¿Qué tiempo hace? (Give a translation of the question, if necessary.) Then point to the first symbol and say: Hace sol. Hace calor. Está despejado. You may need to use some gestures to reinforce meaning. Have students repeat after each statement you make. After practicing with the captions, cover them and have students make the statement according to the symbol you point out. Throughout this procedure, keep asking the question ¿Qué tiempo hace? Finally, have the students ask and answer the question as you continue to point to the symbols in random order.

Present vocabulary by using a transparency and describing the weather conditions in various places where you are considering vacationing during the next break. Point to the different weather conditions and name the place where these conditions will prevail. For comprehension checks, ask students: Clase, si quiero ir a un lugar donde hace mucho calor, ¿adónde puedo ir? You can incorporate sports vocabulary from Chapter 5 and talk about the different activities you might do under each weather condition.

Preparación

- What kinds of questions do you normally ask when talking about the weather?
- What are some of the expressions used frequently in English to describe weather conditions?
- What temperature system is used in the United States? What system is more commonly used in other parts of the world?

▶ **¡Hace frío hoy!**

Hace sol.
Hace calor.
Está despejado.

Hace mal tiempo.
Truena. Hay tormenta.

Llueve.
Llovizna.

Hace buen tiempo.
No hace mucho frío.
No hace mucho calor.

Nieva.
Hace frío.

Está nublado.
Hay nubes.

Hace viento.
Hace fresco.

Hay niebla.
Hay neblina.

Hay hielo.
Está resbaloso.

GRAMMAR NOTE:

Tronar (ue), llover (ue), and **nevar (ie)** are stem-changing verbs.

Possible Answers, Ex. A
1. Está nublado. Nieva. Hace frío. 2. Hay nubes. Está nublado. 3. Hace fresco. Hace viento. 4. Truena. Hace mal tiempo. Hay tormenta. 5. Hay hielo. Hace frío. Está resbaloso.

Práctica

A. ¿Qué tiempo hace? Comenta sobre el tiempo que representa cada dibujo. Utiliza todas las expresiones posibles.

■ **Modelo:** *Hace sol. Hace mucho calor. Está despejado.*

1.　　　　　2.　　　　　3.　　　　　4.　　　　　5.

B. ¿Qué tiempo va a hacer?
Mira las temperaturas de las ciudades en el mapa. Según las temperaturas, indica el tiempo que va a hacer en mayo.

■ **Modelo:** Lima

Va a hacer fresco.

1. México, D.F.
2. Caracas
3. Santiago
4. San José
5. Buenos Aires
6. La Habana
7. Asunción
8. Bogotá
9. La Paz
10. Montevideo

C. ¿Hace buen tiempo hoy?
Trabaja con otro(a) estudiante. Imagina que llamas por teléfono a un(a) amigo(a) en Chile que quiere saber qué tiempo hace en los Estados Unidos. Contesta negativamente sus preguntas e indica cómo es el tiempo con información contraria a la que contiene la pregunta. Sigue el modelo.

■ **Modelo:** ¿Hace buen tiempo hoy?

No, no hace buen tiempo hoy. Hace mal tiempo.

1. ¿Hace calor hoy?
2. ¿Llueve hoy?
3. ¿Está nublado?
4. ¿Hay tormenta?
5. ¿Hace fresco?
6. ¿Nieva?
7. ¿Hace sol?
8. ¿Hace frío?
9. ¿Está despejado?
10. ¿Truena?

Comentarios

culturales *El clima*

El clima de Chile, así como el de todos los países de América Latina, es muy diverso. Hay más variedad de climas dentro de pocas distancias que en cualquier otra parte del mundo. En los países que quedan al sur de la línea ecuatorial (como Chile, Argentina y Uruguay), es invierno en los meses de junio, julio y agosto y hace bastante frío. La temperatura media en enero sube a 27 grados C (80 grados F), mientras que en julio hay nieve.

En los países que están al norte de la línea ecuatorial (como Venezuela, Costa Rica o México), hay una temporada calurosa de lluvias entre mayo y octubre y una temporada templada y seca el resto del año. En julio, por ejemplo, la temperatura sube a más de 27 grados C (80 grados F), mientras que en enero la temperatura media es de 16 grados C (60 grados F).

Chile produce vinos de alta calidad. Su sistema de irrigación y la temperatura ideal de sus fértiles valles contribuyen al cultivo de uvas de gran variedad y excelente sabor.

INTEGRACIÓN CULTURAL

1. En general, ¿cómo es el clima de los países de América Latina?
2. ¿Cuáles son algunos países que están al sur de la línea ecuatorial? ¿al norte?
3. ¿En qué meses llueve frecuentemente en los países al norte de la línea ecuatorial?
4. ¿Cúando es invierno en Chile? ¿Hay nieve?

Expresiones para indicar tiempo transcurrido— desde cuándo, desde (que), cuánto tiempo hace que, hace (...que)

Contextualize presentation of this vocabulary by telling students about a phone conversation you had with a friend in Argentina. Tell them what the prevailing weather conditions are and how long it's been that way. Talk about how long it's been since you've seen this friend, how long he/she has been in Argentina, etc.

Enfoque: (1) To accustom students to these time expressions, make some personal statements. **Yo soy profesor(a) desde hace... años. Estamos en la clase desde hace... minutos.** Then lead students to answer **¿Desde cuándo vives en... ? ¿Desde cuándo sabes nadar?** (2) Write some of the answers on the board, using a time line with statements such as **Tú comenzaste a estudiar español en septiembre de 19—. La clase comenzó a las...** Show two different ways to express these ideas: desde cuándo / cuánto tiempo hace. You will probably want to use their English equivalents.

1. These time expressions can be used to ask and answer questions about something that started in the past and is continuing in the present.

Question:	Answer:
¿Desde cuándo + present tense. . . ?	**Desde** + specific point in time
¿Desde cuándo estudias español? *How long have you been studying Spanish?*	**Desde** el año pasado. *Since last year.*
¿Desde cuándo + present tense?	**Desde que** + past tense
¿Desde cuándo esquias? How long have you been skiing?	**Desde que** tenía 15 años. *Since I was 15.*
¿Cuánto tiempo hace que + present tense?	**Hace** + length of time
¿Cuánto tiempo hace que vives aquí? *For how long have you lived here?*	**Hace** dos años. *For two years.*

GRAMMAR NOTE:
In Chapter 5, page 187, you learned the expression **hace** and **hace... que** + preterite tense.

2. When you want to indicate *for how long* something has been going on, you use the time expressions as follows:

hace + length of time + **que** + present tense

Hace dos semanas **que** no llueve aquí.	*It has not rained here for two weeks.*

3. When you want to indicate *how long ago* something happened, you use the same structure but with the verb in the past tense:

hace + length of time + **que** + past tense

Hace siete años **que** salí de Chile.	*I left Chile seven years ago.*

Práctica

Answers, Ex. D
1. Hace sol desde el jueves.
2. Hace un día que hace viento.
3. Hace cinco días que hubo tormenta.
4. Hace cuatro días que no hace fresco.
5. Hace cuatro días que llovió.

D. Hoy es sábado. Contesta las siguientes preguntas según la información.

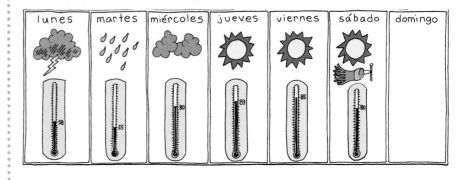

1. ¿Desde cuándo hace sol?
2. ¿Cuánto tiempo hace que hace viento?
3. ¿Hace cuántos días que tronó?
4. ¿Cuánto tiempo hace que no hace fresco?
5. ¿Cuánto tiempo hace que llovió?

Possible Answers, Ex. E
1. No, no llueve. Hace... días que no llueve. o: Sí, hace dos días que llueve. (Llueve desde el...)
2. Hace dos semanas que llovió aquí.
3. Hace... aquí desde...
4. Hace... que nevó aquí.
5. Hace... que vivo aquí.
6. Llevamos ropa de... aquí desde...

E. Una visitante. Imagina que una amiga de Chile viene a los Estados Unidos por primera vez. Te hace preguntas por teléfono sobre el tiempo para saber qué ropa debe traer. Contesta sus preguntas, y dile desde cuándo hace tal tiempo.

■ **Modelo:**   ¿Hace sol hoy?
  Sí, hace sol desde el lunes.
  o
  No, no hace sol. Hace dos días que no hace sol.

1. ¿Llueve allá?
2. ¿Cuánto tiempo hace que llovió *(it rained)* donde vives?
3. ¿Hace calor o hace frío donde vives?
4. ¿Cuánto tiempo hace que nevó allá?
5. ¿Cuánto tiempo hace que vives allá?
6. ¿Cuánto tiempo hace que llevan ropa de invierno o ropa de verano allá?

F. ¿Cuánto hace que... ? Pregúntales a varios compañeros de clase cuánto tiempo hace que hacen o no las siguientes actividades.

 Ex. F   Pairs

■ **Modelo:**   ir al cine
    —¿Cuánto tiempo hace que no vas al cine?
    —Hace dos semanas.

1. jugar al (tenis...)
2. trabajar en...
3. estudiar...
4. vivir aquí
5. conocer a...
6. ir a un concierto, al teatro...

El verbo **saber**

Assign this section as homework.

IRM Master 29:
Saber en el presente y el pretérito

¿**Sabes** qué tiempo va a hacer mañana? No, **no sé.**	***Do you know** what the weather will be like tomorrow?* *No, **I don't know.***

Here is the way to form the present tense of the verb **saber:**

saber

yo	**sé**	nosotros(as)	**sabemos**
tú	**sabes**	vosotros(as)	**sabéis**
Ud.		Uds.	
él	**sabe**	ellos	**saben**
ella		ellas	

Saber is used to talk about knowledge of facts or something that has been learned thoroughly, as well as to say that you know how to do something. In this last instance, **saber** is used before an infinitive form of another verb.

Rita **sabe bailar** bien. Tú **sabes hablar** tres idiomas, ¿verdad?	*Rita **knows how to dance** well.* *You **know how to speak** three languages, right?*

Note that in the preterite the vowel in the stem of the verb changes to **u.** The following chart shows the forms in the preterite.

saber

sab-	→**sup-**		
yo	**supe**	nosotros(as)	**supimos**
tú	**supiste**	vosotros(as)	**supisteis**
Ud.		Uds.	
él	**supo**	ellos	**supieron**
ella		ellas	

The verb **saber** in the preterite means to know something in the sense of the English expressions "to find out" or "to discover." See the following examples:

Cuando llamó José, **supimos** lo que pasó. Los niños **supieron** las buenas noticias.	*When José called, **we found out** what happened.* *The children **found out** the good news.*

Ex. G: Pairs

Ex. H: Pairs

Variation: Have students combine the preterite of **saber** with the time expressions by asking questions about themselves or current events, e.g., ¿Cuánto tiempo hace que supiste que tu amigo ganó la lotería?

Play Textbook audio.

Suggestion: Begin by summarizing the dialog. La familia Valenzuela está de vacaciones en Portillo. Hace mal tiempo y los hijos no están contentos. Pero por lo menos esquiaron un poco, todos comen bien y están de vacaciones en familia.

Pair students together for this activity. Ask them to listen to the tape once without taking any notes. Then have students discuss what they heard and try to answer the comprehension questions. Have students listen a second time, this time allowing them to take notes if they wish. Review comprehension questions and answers. Finally, have students listen a third time, this time trying to answer the **cómo lo dicen** questions.

Answers, Ex. I
1. Porque hace mal tiempo. 2. Buen tiempo con mucho sol. 3. Esquiaron un poco. 4. No, no hay música en el hotel. 5. Por lo menos estamos de vacaciones en familia y eso es bueno.

Ex. J: Pairs
Answers, Ex. J
1. ¡Qué aburrido estoy! 2. ¿Por qué están de mal humor? 3. por lo menos

---

Práctica

G. ¿Qué sabes hacer? Pregúntale a tu compañero(a) si sabe hacer las siguientes cosas: *to sing, to play an instrument, to play a sport (choose the ones you want), to cook,* etc. Después informa a la clase.

■ **Modelo:** *¿Sabes hablar otro idioma?*

H. ¿Cuándo lo supiste? Estos son algunos comentarios sobre el tiempo. Tu compañero(a) quiere saber cuándo supiste esta información.

■ **Modelo:** —*Mañana va a nevar.*
—*¿Cuándo lo supiste?*
—*Lo supe ayer.* (*o esta mañana o anoche,* etc.)

1. No va a llover por dos o tres meses.
2. Va a hacer mucho calor el domingo.
3. Va a empezar a nevar mucho en diciembre.
4. Este fin de semana va a hacer mucho viento.
5. Va a haber tormentas en abril.
6. Este viernes empieza a hacer calor.

Diálogo 1
En la primera conversación sobre el tiempo, la familia Valenzuela está de vacaciones en Portillo, Chile, pero hace mal tiempo y los hijos no están contentos.

ANTES DE ESCUCHAR

Basándote en lo que has aprendido en esta etapa, ¿cuáles son algunas expresiones que esperas escuchar?

Antes de escuchar el diálogo, lee las preguntas en la sección *Después de escuchar.*

DESPUÉS DE ESCUCHAR

I. Comprensión. Ahora escucha el diálogo y contesta las siguientes preguntas.
1. ¿Por qué no están contentos los hijos?
2. ¿Qué tiempo hace en Acapulco, probablemente?
3. ¿Qué hizo la familia ayer?
4. ¿Hay música en el hotel?
5. ¿Qué cosa positiva dice el padre?

J. ¿Cómo lo dicen? Escucha el diálogo una vez más y contesta las preguntas.
1. A Marcelo no le gusta el tiempo que hace. ¿Qué dice?
2. El padre quiere saber cómo están sus hijos. ¿Qué les pregunta?
3. ¿Cómo se dice "at least" en español?

Diálogo 2
En la segunda conversación Patricia y sus amigos hablan de sus planes para el fin de semana, pero sus planes dependen del tiempo que va a hacer.

ANTES DE ESCUCHAR

Basándote en lo que has aprendido en esta etapa, ¿qué tipo de información esperas escuchar?

Antes de escuchar el diálogo, lee las preguntas en la sección *Después de escuchar*.

DESPUÉS DE ESCUCHAR

K. Comprensión. Ahora escucha el diálogo y contesta las siguientes preguntas.

1. ¿Qué tiempo va a hacer mañana por la mañana? ¿y por la tarde?
2. ¿Cómo saben esto?
3. ¿Adónde quiere ir Patricia?
4. ¿Qué van a hacer por la mañana?
5. ¿Adónde van a ir por la tarde?

L. ¿Cómo lo dicen? Escucha el segundo diálogo una vez más y contesta las preguntas.

1. ¿Cómo se dice "weather forecast" en español?
2. ¿Cómo dice Elena "it will rain a lot"?
3. ¿Cómo dicen Elena y Patricia que les gusta la misma idea?

Tú dirás

M. Habla con tres compañeras(os) de clase sobre la estación que más les gusta y que menos les gusta. Investiga lo que les gusta hacer en cada estación. Despúes, preséntale la información a la clase.

En julio nieva mucho en Portillo, Chile.

Las estaciones	¿A cuántas personas les gusta esta estación?	¿A cuántas personas no les gusta esta estación?	¿Qué les gusta hacer durante esta estación?
la primavera			
el verano			
el otoño			
el invierno			

N. Datos biográficos. Habla con otro(a) estudiante sobre la siguiente información, notando lo que tienen en común. Prepárense para presentar a la clase los datos qué supieron.

- where he or she is from, and how long they've lived where they live
- if he or she likes where they live
- what the weather is like where they live
- whether he or she lives near the beach, the mountains, the plains
- when he or she was born
- what his or her parents do
- whether he or she has any siblings
- what his or her favorite pastimes are

SEGUNDA ETAPA

PARA EMPEZAR: ¿Cómo es?

Preparación

- When you describe an object, what details do you normally take into account?
- When you are planning to go to a movie or a play, what information do you usually like to have?
- What is important to know when choosing a restaurant?
- What kind of information is found in a horoscope?

easy / difficult
short / long

Describe...

Este coche es pequeño.
Este coche es bonito.
Este coche es moderno.
Este coche es bueno.

Ese coche es grande.
Ese coche es feo.
Ese coche es viejo.
Ese coche es barato.

Este libro es interesante.
Este libro es **fácil.**
Este libro es **breve.**

Ese libro es aburrido.
Ese libro es **difícil.**
Ese libro es **largo.**

NACIO USTED EN ESTE DÍA

Es inventivo, nervioso y
un poco sensible. Usual-
mente es talentoso en las
líneas creativas. Para lograr sus habilidades tie-
ne que aprender a con-
trolar su temperamento. Tendrá éxito en
cualquier carrera que mida sus ideales.
Necesita autodisciplina. Tiene buena in-
tuición en la cual debería aprender a con-
fiar. Deje a un lado el escepticismo y la
tendencia a ser muy sensible.

¿Es un horóscopo muy positivo
o demasiado pesimista?

¿Es un programa teatral variado?
¿Completo?
¿Es un buen programa?
¿Es un programa norteamericano?

¿Es una película interesante?
¿Sensacional?
¿Aburrida?

¿Es un buen restaurante?
¿Nuevo?
¿Chino?
¿Elegante?
¿Caro?

¿Es un libro difícil?
¿Histórico?
¿Infantil?
¿Bonito?

¿Es un lugar serio y formal
o alegre y divertido?

Práctica

Answers, Ex. A
1. El examen es fácil (difícil). 2. El
auto es grande. 3. La iglesia es vieja.
4. El libro es aburrido. 5. La playa es
bonita. 6. La película es mala. 7. La
maleta es pesada. 8. El pueblo es
bonito.

GRAMMAR NOTE:
Remember that all
adjectives have to agree in
gender and number with
the noun they describe.

A. ¿Cómo es? ¿Qué adjetivo describe mejor el dibujo?

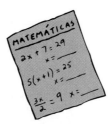

1. ¿Es fácil o difícil el examen?

2. ¿Es grande o pequeño el auto?

3. ¿Es vieja o moderna la iglesia?

4. ¿Es aburrido o interesante el libro?

5. ¿Es bonita o fea la playa?

6. ¿Es buena o mala la película?

7. ¿Es ligera o pesada la maleta?

8. ¿Es bonito o feo el pueblo?

B. ¿Qué piensas? Usa tres adjetivos para describir cada objeto o para dar tu opinión.

■ **Modelo:** *Es una novela buena, interesante y sensacional.*

1. una novela

2. un periódico

3. una obra teatral

4. un programa

5. un cuadro

6. un vídeo

Ex. B:  Pairs
Do the model and a few items before dividing the class into small groups. As a follow-up, have each group say which adjectives they used for each item.

Variation: Have students prepare short descriptions of people or objects commonly found on campus and others guess what they are based on the description.

Possible answers, Ex. B
1. Es una novela vieja (clásica, larga, aburrida, etc.). 2. Es un periódico chileno (viejo, interesante, etc.). 3. Es una obra teatral clásica (vieja, romántica, etc.). 4. Es un programa divertido (bueno, interesante, etc.). 5. Es un cuadro interesante (extraño, caro, moderno, etc.). 6. Es un vídeo formidable (largo, divertido, etc.).

Do as a class and encourage students to think of as many adjectives as possible. Where possible try to point out synonyms.

C. ¿Qué tienen en común? Explica qué tienen en común los objetos siguientes.

■ **Modelo:** un elefante y las nubes de tormentas
     Son grises. Son grandes.

1. el cielo de día y el mar
2. el sol y el girasol *(sunflower)*
3. el cielo de noche y las letras en estas frases
4. la nieve y el algodón *(cotton)*
5. una naranja y una pelota de básquetbol

Answers, Ex. C
1. Son azules. Son bonitos. Son grandes, etc. 2. Son amarillos, circulares, etc. 3. Son negros. 4. Son blancos, suaves, etc. 5. Son anaranjadas, redondas, duras, etc.

Repaso ....

D. ¿Hace cuánto tiempo? Túrnate con un(a) compañero(a) para hacer preguntas según la información y para contestarlas con la información entre paréntesis.

■ **Modelo:** Mi hermana estudia francés. (5 años)
     —*¿De veras? ¿Hace cuánto tiempo que estudia francés?*
     —*Hace cinco años.*

1. Tengo un disc-man. (2 meses)
2. Nosotros vivimos aquí por mucho tiempo. (1984)

VOCABULARY EXPANSION:
Remember that **programa** is a masculine noun even though it ends in **-a.**

Ex. D:  Group

3. Mi hermana Gloria mira la televisión. (1:30)
4. Mi compañero(a) tiene un coche nuevo. (4 días)
5. Mis vecinos tocan el piano. (2 semanas)
6. Mi novio está de vuelta (*back home*). (8 días)

Ex. E:  **Pairs**
Suggestion: Encourage students to use this activity as a springboard for conversation and follow up each question with appropriate questions, e.g., ¿Cuál es tu canción favorita? Ask them to make up two questions in addition to those provided by the exercise. Review answers with class and also personalize each question with follow-up questions.

E. ¿Cuánto tiempo hace que... ? Pregúntale a un(a) compañero(a) de clase cuánto tiempo hace que hizo las siguientes cosas.

■ **Modelo:** leer una novela interesante
—*¿Cuánto tiempo hace que leíste una novela interesante?*
—*Hace dos meses que leí una novela interesante.*

1. oír su canción favorita en la radio
2. ver una película sensacional
3. caerse y lastimarse
4. leer el horóscopo en el periódico

Comentarios

culturales La temperatura

Cuando se habla de la temperatura en España y América Latina, se usa el sistema que se llama Celsius (centígrados) en lugar del sistema Fahrenheit.

C:	30	25	20	15	10	5	0	−5
F:	86	77	68	59	50	41	32	23

Para convertir de Celsius a Fahrenheit, divide la temperatura por 5, multiplica por 9 y **añade** 32.

Para convertir de Fahrenheit a Celsius, **substrae** 32, multiplica por 5 y divide por 9.

Atención: Para hablar de la temperatura, se dice "Estamos a cinco grados" o "La temperatura es de cinco grados." "Bajo cero" quiere decir "below zero".

add

subtract

°C / °F

35 — 95
30 — 86
25 — 77
20 — 68
15 — 59
10 — 50
5 — 41
0 — 32
-5 — 23
-10 — 14

INTEGRACIÓN CULTURAL

1. Convierte las siguientes temperaturas del sistema Celsius al sistema Fahrenheit.
   Celsius 28 13 8 20 33
2. Convierte las siguientes temperaturas del sistema Fahrenheit al sistema Celsius.
   Fahrenheit 70 46 65 90 10
3. ¿Qué temperatura hace ahora donde vives? Conviértela al sistema Celsius.

Answers, Integración
1. (Fahrenheit) 82.4; 55.4; 46.4; 68; 91.4
2. (Celsius) 21; 7.7; 18.3; 32.2; −12.2

Los adjetivos

Concordancia de los adjetivos

1. As you have already learned, many adjectives end in **-o** if they are masculine and in **-a** if they are feminine. If the masculine form of an adjective ends in **-e**, the feminine form also ends in **-e**. To make these adjectives plural, you simply add **-s**.

El muchacho es **alto.**	La muchacha es **alta.**
El libro es **interesante.**	La pregunta es **interesante.**
Los hombres son **inteligentes.**	Las mujeres son **inteligentes.**

2. An adjective ending in **-sta** has the same ending for both the masculine and feminine forms. To make these adjectives plural, simply add an **-s**.

El abogado es **pesimista.**	Las abogadas son **pesimistas.**

3. If the masculine form of an adjective ends in **-l, -r, -n, -s,** or **-z,** the ending for the feminine form is also **-l, -r, -n, -s,** and **-z**. To make these plural, you add **-es**. Note that in the plural form, **z** changes to **c**.

El examen es **difícil.**	Las preguntas son **difíciles.**
El vestido es **gris.**	Las faldas son **grises.**
El niño es **feliz.**	Las niñas son **felices.**

Remember: The exception to this is that when an adjective of nationality ends in **-s** in the masculine form, the feminine form then ends in **-sa**.

El profesor es **francés.**	La profesora es **francesa.**

Preppy

"Un estilo diferente en el vestir
con toque tradicional práctico,
elegante, sencillo,
que distingue..."

Calle Igualdad a 50 m de la Av. Santiago Mariño.
Telfs.: (095) 61.33.68 · 61.17.79. Porlamar

Posición de los adjetivos

1. In Spanish an adjective is almost always placed *after* the noun it describes:

una película **japonesa**
una lección **fácil**
los libros **interesantes**

Acabo de comprar una
motocicleta **nueva.**

*I just bought a **new** motorcycle.*

Es una motocicleta **estupenda.**

*It's a **great** motorcycle.*

2. Adjectives indicating nationality always *follow* the noun.

Los automóviles **japoneses**
son buenos.

__Japanese__ cars are good.

3. When two adjectives modify the same noun, they are placed after
the noun and are connected to each other with **y.**

una universidad **buena y grande**

a large and good university

unos muchachos **inteligentes
y responsables**

*some intelligent and
responsible boys*

Adjetivos apocopados—buen, mal, gran

When the adjectives **bueno, malo,** and **grande** are used before a
masculine singular noun, they are shortened to **buen, mal,** and **gran.**
The meaning of **grande** is radically different when it precedes the
noun, for then it means *great* instead of *large.*

Ramón es un **buen** muchacho.

*Ramón is a **good** boy.*
(no emphasis on how good)

Ramón es un muchacho **bueno.**

*Ramón is a **good** boy.*
(emphasis on how good)

Éste es un **mal** día para esquiar.

*This is a **bad** day for skiing.*
(no emphasis on how bad)

Éste es un día **malo** para esquiar.

*This is a **bad** day for skiing.*
(emphasis on how bad)

Plácido Domingo es un **gran**
hombre.

*Plácido Domingo is a **great** man.*

Plácido Domingo es un hombre
grande.

*Plácido Domingo is a **big** man.*

Práctica

F. ¿Cómo son? Usa los adjetivos sugeridos de dos maneras para describir los
siguientes sustantivos *(nouns).* Cambia las formas si es necesario.

■ **Modelo:** Es un museo. (grande)
   Es un gran museo.
   Es un museo grande.

1. Es un libro. (bueno)
2. Son unos niños. (malo)
3. Es un hombre. (grande)

4. Son unos amigos. (bueno)
5. Son unas ideas. (bueno)
6. Es una situación. (malo)
7. Es un perro. (grande)
8. Es un cuadro *(painting)*. (grande)
9. Es una característica. (bueno)
10. Son unos futbolistas. (malo)

G. Mi casa es...
Usa un adjetivo para hacer un comentario sobre cada objeto. Después hazle una pregunta a otro(a) estudiante. Sigue el modelo.

■ **Modelo:** mi casa
—*Mi casa es grande. ¿Y tu casa?*
—*Mi casa es grande también.*
   o
—*Mi casa no es grande. Es pequeña.*

1. mi apartamento
2. mi cuarto
3. mis libros
4. mi coche
5. mis compactos
6. mi computadora
7. mi ciudad
8. mi clase de...

H. ¿Qué tipo *(kind)* de... tienes?
Trabaja con un(a) compañero(a) y escojan uno o dos adjetivos de la lista para contestar cada pregunta.

alemán	chino	feo	inteligente	largo	rojo
azul	difícil	francés	italiano	moderno	simpático
bonito	español	grande	japonés	nuevo	verde
blanco	fácil	gris	joven	pequeño	viejo

■ **Modelo:** ¿Qué tipo de casa tienes?
Tenemos una casa pequeña y amarilla.

1. ¿Qué tipo de apartamento tienes?
2. ¿Qué tipo de coche tiene tu familia?
3. ¿Qué tipo de restaurante prefieres?
4. ¿Qué tipos de amigos tienes?
5. ¿Qué tipo de tarea tienes para la clase de español?
6. ¿Qué tipo de viaje haces cuando vas de vacaciones?
7. ¿Qué tipo de exámenes tienes en la clase de español?

I. Acabo de comprar...
Descríbele a otro(a) estudiante algo que acabas de comprar. Dile lo que es y usa diferentes adjetivos para describir su color, tamaño *(size)* y otras características. **Sugerencias: una bicicleta, un vídeo, una mochila, un coche, un televisor, un disco compacto, una camisa, una computadora, un libro.**

■ **Modelo:** *Acabo de comprar una bicicleta. Es francesa. Es azul y gris. Es muy ligera. ¡Es muy rápida también!* etc.

Ex. G:  **Pairs**

Do the model and a few items before dividing the class into pairs.

Ex. H: **Pairs**

Suggestion, Ex. I: Have each student think of 2 items they own and would like to sell. Have them write a description of these items, embellishing as much as possible. To practice expressions of time, tell students to incorporate a phrase about how long it has been since they have been used, etc. Put students in groups of 4 to share their descriptions and then have all vote on the most valuable item.

El subjuntivo con expresiones de emoción

In sentences where the main clause has a verb or an expression that conveys emotion regarding the person, situation, or event in the second part of the sentence, the form of the verb used after the word **que** is in the subjunctive. Note the following examples:

Me alegro de que **puedas** ir a la fiesta.	***I'm glad*** *that* ***you can*** *go to the party.*
¡Qué lástima que **llueva!**	***Too bad*** *that* ***it's*** *raining!*
Carlos **siente** mucho que Marilú **esté** descontenta.	*Carlos* ***is*** *very* ***sorry*** *that Marilú* ***is*** *unhappy.*

Here are some verbs and expressions that convey emotion and trigger the use of the subjunctive in the **que** clause.

alegrarse (de) que…	*to be glad that* …
sentir que…	*to feel sorry that* …
¡Qué bueno que… !	*How great/It's great that* … *!*
¡Qué lástima que… !	*Too bad that* … *!*
¡Qué pena que… !	*What a shame that* … *!*

Práctica

Answers, Ex. J
1. …que haga mal tiempo. 2. …que no haga mucho frío. 3. …que nieve mucho. 4. …que haga calor. 5. …que llueva. 6. …que esté nublado.

Variation: Remind your students of your two friends who are so different. Tell students that you received a postcard from them during their ski trip to Argentina. It seems that Jaime won a ski competition, but Rafa broke his leg. Use a blank transparency and write out a short letter to them. For example: Hola…, me alegro de que Uds. estén en Argentina por fin. Hace mucho tiempo que Uds. han querido ir a Argentina. Qué bueno que Jaime… Es una lástima que Rafa… Check comprehension. When done comment on the use of the subjunctive.

You may want to review the subjunctive forms presented in Chapter 6.

Answers, Ex. K
1. esté 2. quieran 3. tenga 4. vengan 5. beba 6. podamos 7. cuesten 8. juegue

J. ¿Qué bueno o qué pena? Indica cuál es tu reacción al tiempo que hace.

■ **Modelo:** Hace sol.
¡Qué bueno que haga sol!

1. Hace mal tiempo.
2. No hace mucho frío.
3. Nieva mucho.
4. Hacer calor.
5. Llueve.
6. Está nublado.

K. Me alegro de… o ¡Qué lástima… ! Trabaja con un(a) compañero(a) de clase para indicar su reacción a lo que hacen las siguientes personas o a la situación que se presenta. Sigue el modelo.

■ **Modelo:** Sergio no puede ir al concierto esta noche.
¡Qué lástima que Sergio no pueda ir!

1. El/La profesor(a) está de vacaciones.
2. Esos estudiantes no quieren bailar.
3. Mi amigo José tiene que trabajar mañana.
4. Susana y Vicente no vienen a visitarnos este fin de semana.
5. Ese señor bebe demasiado.
6. No podemos usar la computadora hoy.
7. Esos suéteres cuestan demasiado.
8. Julia no juega al tenis.

L. Reacciones… Trabaja con otro(a) estudiante y hablen de lo que hacen ciertas personas así como de ciertas situaciones, usando las expresiones en la página 258 a para indicar su reacción a esas acciones o situaciones. Traten de usar por lo menos seis verbos distintos en el subjuntivo en sus respuestas.

■ **Modelo:** Estudiante A: Alicia no quiere ir a la playa.
Estudiante B: *¡Qué pena que no quiera ir!*

VAMOS A ESCUCHAR: ¡QUÉ FEO ES ESTE AUTO!

Play Textbook audio.

Have students work in pairs. Play recording once and ask students to listen with their texts closed. After listening once ask students to open their texts and answer the questions. Play again so students can check their answers.

Felipe ahorró su dinero y por fin compró un coche. Sus amigos inspeccionan el coche, pero sus reacciones no son muy positivas.

ANTES DE ESCUCHAR

Basándote en lo que has aprendido en esta etapa, piensa en algunos de los adjetivos que pueden describir un automóvil. ¿Qué información crees que vas a escuchar? Ahora lee las preguntas en la sección *Después de escuchar.*

DESPUÉS DE ESCUCHAR

M. Comprensión. Escucha el diálogo y contesta las siguientes preguntas.

1. ¿Le gusta a la muchacha el coche?
2. ¿De qué color es el coche?
3. ¿Qué dice Felipe de su coche?
4. ¿Qué quiere hacer la muchacha?

N. ¿Cómo lo dicen?

1. ¿Cómo dice Felipe "What do you mean"?
2. ¿Qué verbo usa Pablo para preguntar si el coche "works"?
3. ¿Cómo se dice en español "to go for a ride"?

Answers, Ex. M
1. no 2. violeta 3. No es caro, es muy práctico. Es pequeño, es económico y funciona muy bien. 4. dar una vuelta

Answers, Ex. N
1. ¡Cómo que feo! 2. funciona 3. dar una vuelta

Incorporate already learned structures by asking students to also make recommendations for how this student can best get along here on campus.

Tú dirás ....

Ñ. Un(a) amigo(a).

Un(a) estudiante de Valparaíso, Chile acaba de llegar a los Estados Unidos y quiere saber cómo es tu universidad. Usa todos los adjetivos necesarios para ser preciso(a) en tus descripciones. Incluye la librería, la cafetería, la biblioteca, la piscina, el estadio, la clase de inglés (de matemáticas), etc. Tu nuevo(a) amigo(a) te va a hacer preguntas para obtener más información.

Ex. Ñ: Pairs

O. El automovil de la familia. Habla con otro(a) estudiante sobre cómo es el automovil que tiene la familia de cada uno de ustedes. Incluyen detalles sobre su tamaño, color, precio, edad, cómo funciona y alguna otra característica. Si uno o los dos de ustedes tienen su propio coche, pueden hablar de cómo es ese coche también, comparándolo con el coche de la familia.

Ex. O: Pairs

⊚ PARA EMPEZAR: La gente que conoces

Ask students these questions in Spanish.

Contextualize the presentation of the theme and vocabulary. Use pictures provided or others and tell students that you like to play matchmaker for your friends. Describe a female friend, including physical and personality traits, and then describe 2 male friends. Write key descriptive words on the board. Check comprehension of terms by asking students to explain them in Spanish using paraphrase or explanation. For example: Hector también es honesto. Clase, ¿qué significa honesto? Ask students which male friend would be better suited for your female friend. Have them explain their choice.

Preparación

- **When you make a physical description of a person, what kind of information is useful to include?**
- **What are some of the personality traits that are taken into account when you talk about what someone is like?**
- **How would you describe yourself over the telephone to someone who has never seen you or talked with you before?**

▶ *Nuestros vecinos y nuestros amigos*

neighbor

thin
eyes
hair / a little long
nose
beard
mustache

Aquí está nuestro **vecino,** el señor Salazar.
Tiene 82 años.
No es muy **delgado.**
Tiene los **ojos** azules.
Tiene el **pelo** un **poco largo.**
Tiene la **nariz** grande.
No tiene **barba.**
Tiene **bigote.**

granddaughter

strong
hazel

Aquí está su **nieta,** Susana.
Es joven; tiene veinte años.
Es alta y **fuerte.**
Tiene los ojos **castaños.**
Tiene el pelo rubio y largo.

Aquí está mi amigo Eduardo.

☐ No es pesimista.   ☐ Es serio.

☐ Es trabajador.   ☐ No es **perezoso.**

☐ Es idealista.   ☐ Es generoso.

☐ Es honesto.   ☐ Es independiente.

☐ Es paciente.   ☐ Es responsable.

☐ Es intelectual.   ☐ No es triste.

Aquí está mi amiga Cecilia.

☐ Es optimista.   ☐ Es **cómica.**

☐ Es valiente.   ☐ Es activa y enérgica.

☐ Es realista.   ☐ Es generosa también.

☐ Es honesta.   ☐ Es independiente.

☐ Es impaciente.   ☐ Es inteligente.

☐ Es atlética.   ☐ Es alegre.

☐ Es simpática.

PREVIEW: Point out that ni is used instead of y in a negative sentence. More on negative words will appear in Chapter 11,

lazy

Transparency J-4: El carácter

Suggestion: Introduce the new vocabulary through personalized questions. Begin with cognates. ¿Eres optimista? ¿Eres idealista? etc.

funny

Práctica

A. José Manuel y la señora Velázquez: retratos *(portraits)* físicos. Contesta las preguntas según lo que representan los dibujos.

1. Aquí está José Manuel. Tiene
veinticinco años. ¿Es viejo? ¿Es
grande? ¿Es fuerte? ¿Tiene los
ojos negros? ¿Tiene bigote?
¿Tiene la nariz pequeña?

2. Aquí está la señora Velázquez.
¿Es gorda? ¿Es delgada? ¿Tiene
el pelo rubio? ¿Es joven?
¿Es alta?

B. José Manuel y la señora Velázquez: retratos psicológicos.
Contesta las preguntas sobre la personalidad de José Manuel y de la Sra. Velázquez.

1. A José Manuel le gustan mucho los coches rápidos y las actividades peligrosas
(dangerous). ¿Es valiente o tímido?
2. La señora Velázquez les da dinero a los amigos que no son ricos. ¿Es generosa o
tacaña *(stingy)*?
3. A José Manuel le gusta arreglar automóviles y leer novelas de detectives. ¿Es trabajador o perezoso?
4. La señora Velázquez encontró 50.000 pesos. Llamó por teléfono a la policía. ¿Es
honesta o deshonesta?
5. A José Manuel no le gusta tocar el piano, pero le encanta jugar al béisbol y le
gusta esquiar. ¿Es atlético o musical?
6. La señora Velázquez siempre escucha la radio. Le gustan la música clásica y las
discusiones políticas. ¿Es seria o cómica?
7. A José Manuel le gusta disfrutar de la vida y tiene muchos amigos. ¿Es triste
o alegre?
8. La señora Velázquez trabaja mucho. Va al teatro, al museo y al cine. ¿Es activa o
perezosa?

C. Escoge adjetivos de la lista para describir a las personas indicadas.

activo	dinámico	honesto	joven	serio
alegre	egoísta	idealista	malo	simpático
antipático	enérgico	imaginativo	optimista	sincero
bonito	frívolo	impaciente	paciente	tímido
bueno	fuerte	independiente	pequeño	trabajador
cómico	guapo	indiscreto	perezoso	triste
cruel	generoso	ingenuo	pesimista	valiente
delgado	grande	inteligente	realista	viejo
discreto				

1. tú
2. un amigo
3. una amiga
4. un(a) profesor(a)
5. uno de tus parientes

D. Retrato de un(a) compañero(a) de clase. Usa los adjetivos en el ejercicio **C** para describir a uno(a) de tus compañeros(as) de clase. No menciones su nombre. La clase va a tratar de adivinar *(guess)* quién es.

Repaso

E. ¡Vamos a visitar el museo y el parque en Santiago! Descríbeles a tus amigos el museo y el parque en la ciudad de Santiago. Usa la información dada a continuación para hacer tus descripciones. Puedes usar más detalles si quieres.

■ **Modelo:** parque / bello / popular
Es un parque bello y popular.

El Parque Metropolitano
1. árboles / grande / bonito
2. turistas / norteamericano
3. monumentos / histórico / popular
4. lugar / tranquilo / romántico
5. restaurante / típico / popular

El Museo de Arte Colonial de San Francisco
6. museo / chileno / grande
7. patios / elegante / tranquilo
8. vistas / espectacular / bello
9. cuadros / viejo / famoso
10. terraza / alto / blanco

Variation: Before beginning exercise have students think of 3 things they did in the past week. Then have students circulate around the classroom to find 1 or 2 other people who did the same 3 things.

El Parque Metropolitano, en Santiago, es un lugar agradable que incluye el cerro San Cristóbal y el cerro Chacarillas. Es un lugar popular para dar un paseo, especialmente los fines de semana.

F. Hice lo siguiente... Trabaja con otro(a) estudiante para hablar de varias cosas (ordinarias o interesantes) que hicieron la semana pasada. Traten de incluir los siguientes verbos en el pretérito: leer, conducir, traer, decir, oír, pedir, dar, venir, poner.

Ex. F:  Pairs

El verbo **conocer** y la **a** personal

¿Quieres **conocer** a Raúl, ese muchacho guapo?	*Do you want to* ***meet*** *Raúl, that good-looking boy?*
¡Cómo no! ¿Tú lo **conoces?**	*Of course!* ***Do you know*** *him?*
¡Claro que sí! Es mi hermano.	*Of course! He's my brother.*

conocer

yo	**conozco**	nosotros (as)	**conocemos**
tú	**conoces**	vosotros (as)	**conocéis**
Ud.		Uds.	
él	**conoce**	ellos	**conocen**
ella		ellas	

This verb is used to indicate an acquaintance or familiarity with someone, something, or some place. It can also be used to talk about the act of meeting someone or visiting a place for the first time.

¿Conoces **a** Catalina?	*Do you* ***know*** *Catalina?*
¿Conocen **la** ciudad?	*Do you* ***know*** *the city?*

The object of a verb is a person, a thing, or an idea that receives the action of that verb. When the direct object is a specific *human being or an animal that is personalized,* it is preceded by **a.** When the definite article in the masculine singular form follows the personal **a,** the contraction **al** is used.

¿Admiras **al** presidente?	*Do you admire the president?*
¿Ves **a** la mujer alta?	*Do you see the tall woman?*
¿Llevo **a** mi perro?	*Shall I take my dog?*
¿Ves el edificio grande?	*Do you see the big building?*
¿Admiras la inteligencia de Carlos?	*Do you admire Carlos's intelligence?*

Práctica

G. ¿Con "a" o sin "a"? Usa el modelo para completar las oraciones, usando más palabras si es necesario.

■ **Modelo:** Miro… (la televisión / los estudiantes).
    Miro la televisión. Miro a los estudiantes.

1. Buscamos… (el parque / los turistas / Roberto / el restaurante nuevo / mi perro).
2. Voy a visitar… (el estadio / la señora Mendoza / mis amigos / Buenos Aires).

3. El presidente no comprende… (la gente / los jóvenes / la situación / la lengua japonesa).

4. Josefina piensa visitar… (el museo / Chile / su familia / los tíos).

H. Preguntas.
Hazles preguntas a los estudiantes en tu grupo sobre cada tema a continuación.

■ **Modelo:** Chile

¿Conoces Chile?

¿Qué conoces de Chile?

1. Santiago, Chile
2. la comida mexicana
3. a Gloria Estefan
4. el Parque Metropolitano
5. las mejores tiendas de esta ciudad (pueblo)
6. a algún estudiante extranjero

I. ¿Conoces a... ?
Pregúntale a otro(a) estudiante si conoce a gente que tú conoces. Si ya (*already*) conoce a las personas que conoces, pregúntale cuando las conoció. Si no conoce a las personas que conoces, pregúntale si quiere conocerlas.

Ex. I:  Pairs

■ **Modelo:** —*¿Conoces a mi amigo Ken?*

—*Sí, conozco a Ken.*

—*¿Cúando conociste a Ken?*

—*Conocí a Ken hace dos semanas.*

Comentarios

culturales *La Isla de Pascua*

*L*a Isla de Pascua es uno de los lugares más **aislados** *(isolated)* del mundo. Situada en el Océano Pacífico, está a más de 3.000 kilómetros del lugar habitado más cercano (Tahiti al oeste y Chile al este). Su nombre original era "Te Pito O Te Hénua", que significa "el **ombligo** *(navel)* del mundo". En 1722 el almirante holandés Roggeveen, al llegar allí el día de Pascua, la nombró Isla de Pascua. A mediados del siglo XIX los marineros de Tahiti la llamaron Rapa Nui ("Gran Rapa"), por **parecerse** *(to look like)* a otra isla de la Polinesia llamada Rapa.

La población es de origen polinésico, y hay aproximadamente 2.100 habitantes. El clima es subtropical, con una temperatura media de 24 grados centígrados. La isla es de forma triangular y su origen geológico es volcánico. Su superficie total es de 179 kilómetros cuadrados. Tiene dos playas de espectacular belleza: Anakena y Ovahe.

Expand activity by asking students to incorporate as much descriptive vocabulary and grammatical structures as possible in their answers. Before beginning exercise, remind students of the comparatives learned in Chapter 6. Allow 5 minutes to complete exercise and then review answers and select students to share their descriptions.

En esta isla **se encuentran** *(are located)* los moais, uno de los mayores misterios arqueológicos del mundo. Son más de 300 estatuas de piedra, gigantescas y monolíticas, que están situadas alrededor del volcán Ranu Raraku. Estos monumentos, tan colosales y legendarios como las antiguas pirámides, son el testimonio de una civilización completa y misteriosa. Todavía hoy no han revelado sus secretos y siguen siendo un enigma para la ciencia.

La compañía chilena LAN (Líneas Aéreas Nacionales) tiene un vuelo semanal que tarda cinco horas en **recorrer** *(to run over)* los 3.700 kilómetros que hay entre Santiago y la Isla de Pascua.

INTEGRACIÓN CULTURAL

1. ¿A qué distancia de Chile continental está la Isla de Pascua?
2. ¿Cuántas horas dura un viaje en avión desde Santiago a la isla?
3. ¿Cuántos habitantes tiene?
4. ¿Cuántos kilómetros cuadrados ocupa la isla?
5. ¿Qué son los moais? ¿Cuántos hay en este lugar misterioso?

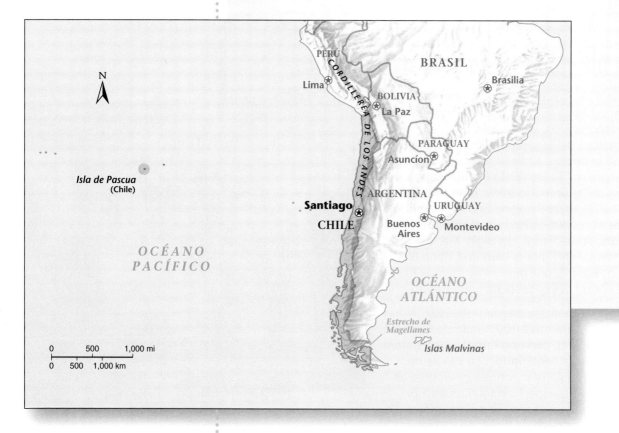

Los pronombres de complemento directo

Direct object pronouns

me	me	**nos**	us
te	you (*fam. Sing.*)	**os**	you (*fam. Pl.*)
lo	you (*form. Sing.*), him, it (m.)	**los**	you (*form. Pl.*), them (m., m. + f.)
la	you (*form. Sing.*), her, it (*f.*)	**las**	you (*form. Pl.*), them (*f.*)

1. As you saw in the previous *Enfoque estructural*, a direct object is the person or thing that is directly affected by a verb. The direct object tells who or what receives the action. In the first column of the sentences below, **mi coche** and **los muchachos** are direct objects.

¿El policía mira **mi coche**?	*Is the police officer looking at my car?*
Sí, **lo** mira.	*Yes, he's looking at it.*
¿Ven a **los muchachos**?	*Do they see the children?*
No, no **los** ven.	*No, they don't see them.*

2. Whenever possible, speakers tend to take shortcuts by using pronouns, and to replace direct objects with direct object pronouns. The pronouns agree with the direct object they stand for in both number (singular and plural) and gender (masculine and feminine).

To refer to things:

¿Ves **mi cuaderno**?	*Do you see my notebook?*
No, no **lo** veo.	*No, I don't see it.*
Escucho **música clásica.**	*I listen to classical music.*
La escucho también.	*I listen to it, too.*
¿Despertaste a **tus hermanos**?	*Did you wake your brothers?*
Sí, **los** desperté.	*Yes, I woke them.*

To refer to people:

Gracias por invitar**me** a tu casa.	*Thank you for inviting me to your house.*
Mi hermano **nos** acompaño a la tienda.	*My brother accompanies us to the store.*

Position of direct object pronouns

1. The direct object pronoun is placed immediately *in front of* the conjugated verb, and immediately *after* an infinitive, attached to it.

¿El edificio? **Lo** conozco.	*The building? I'm familiar with **it.***
¿El número? Es importante saber**lo.**	*The number? It's important to know **it.***
Nosotros vamos a la tienda. ¿Quieres acompañar**nos?**	*We are going to the store. Would you like to accompany **us?***
¿Los libros? **Los** quiero comprar ahora.	*The books? I want to buy **them** now.*
Leo **la revista.**	*I read **the magazine.***
La leo.	*I read **it.***
Es posible vender **el coche.**	*It's possible to sell **the car.***
Es posible vender**lo.**	*It's possible to sell **it.***

2. When a conjugated verb and an infinitive are used together, the direct object pronoun can be placed *either* in front of the conjugated verb or attached to the end of the infinitive. Attaching the pronoun to the infinitive is usually the more common practice.

Quiero comprar **la cámara.**	*I want to buy **the camera.***
La quiero comprar.	*I want to buy **it.***
Quiero comprar**la.**	

Práctica

J. En pocas palabras. Abrevia *(shorten)* cada oración, reemplazando el complemento directo con el pronombre que le corresponde. Sigue el modelo.

■ **Modelo:** Ruth llama a Francisco por teléfono.
Ruth lo llama por teléfono.

1. Hago la tarea ahora.
2. Los estudiantes no leen el libro.
3. No como carne.
4. Compramos los cuadernos en la librería.
5. Invitan a las muchachas.
6. Dan una película después de la clase.
7. No conozco al profesor Valdéz.
8. Mis padres prefieren la música clásica.

K. Es decir... Escribe una oración breve con el pronombre apropiado en lugar de los sustantivos en la lista, utilizando los verbos **buscar, ver, necesitar,** o **llevar.**

These can be assigned for homework. In class students can be paired together to discuss their answers before reviewing answers with the entire class.

Modelo: un libro de matemáticas

     Lo necesito.

1. otro coche
2. cincuenta dólares
3. unos vídeos
4. la profesora Herrera
5. unos discos compactos nuevos

6. dos raquetas de tenis
7. un amigo
8. el número de teléfono
9. clases de química
10. un horario fácil

L. ¿Sí o no? Trabaja con otro(a) estudiante para hacer y contestar las siguientes preguntas. Usen el pronombre apropiado para los sustantivos que aparecen en las preguntas.

Ex. L: Pairs

Modelo: ¿Hablas alemán?

     Sí, lo hablo.

     o

     No, no lo hablo.

1. ¿Miras la televisión por la noche?
2. ¿Tomas el autobús a la universidad?
3. ¿Tus profesores dan mucha tarea?
4. ¿Tienes tiempo para practicar deportes?
5. ¿Quién prepara la comida en tu casa?
6. ¿Lees el periódico cuando desayunas?
7. ¿Haces tus tareas por la tarde o por la noche?
8. ¿Lavas los platos después de la cena?

M. ¡Ya lo hice! Cuando tu amigo(a) te dice que hagas algo, indica que ya lo hiciste. Sigue el modelo.

Ex. M: Pairs
Pair students together and allow 5 minutes for these activities. Circulate around class to check for accuracy.

Modelo: ¡Lava los platos!

     ¡Ya los lavé!

1. ¡Compra el pan!
2. ¡Prepara el desayuno!
3. ¡Recoge la mesa!
4. ¡Lava los platos!

5. ¡Termina tu tarea!
6. ¡Escucha el nuevo disco!
7. ¡Busca mis llaves!

N. No quiero hacerlo... no voy a hacerlo... Estás de muy mal humor esta noche. Cuando te preguntan si vas a hacer lo que haces normalmente, contestas que no lo quieres hacer y más específicamente que no lo vas a hacer. Sigue el modelo.

Ex. N: Pairs

Play Textbook audio.

Modelo: preparar la cena

     —*¿Vas a preparar la cena esta noche?*

     —*No, no quiero prepararla esta noche.*

     —*Pero, vas a prepararla de todas maneras* (anyway), *¿no?*

     —*No, no quiero prepararla y no voy a prepararla.*

1. lavar la ropa
2. ayudar a tu hermano
3. quitar la mesa
4. leer el libro

5. terminar tu tarea
6. mirar la televisión
7. comprar comida
8. lavar los platos

ANTES DE ESCUCHAR

Diálogo 1

Roberto va a visitar a su hermana Silvia el próximo fin de semana. Su amigo Raúl quiere saber cómo es Silvia y Roberto la describe.

Describe la personalidad de alguien que tú conoces bien. Haz una lista de posibles adjetivos.

Basándote en lo que has aprendido en esta etapa, ¿cómo crees que Roberto va a describir a su hermana?

Ahora lee las preguntas en la sección *Después de escuchar* para anticipar el contenido de la conversación.

DESPUÉS DE ESCUCHAR

Ñ. Comprensión. Escucha el diálogo 1 y contesta las siguientes preguntas.
1. ¿Cuál es la profesión de la hermana de Roberto?
2. ¿Dónde vive ella?
3. ¿Cuántos años tiene ella?
4. ¿Le gustan los deportes?
5. ¿Cómo la describe su hermano?
6. ¿Qué piensa Raúl cuando oye hablar de la hermana de su amigo?

O. ¿Cómo lo dicen?
1. Raúl quiere saber la edad de la hermana de su amigo. ¿Qué le pregunta?
2. ¿Cómo se dice "hardworking" en español?
3. ¿Cómo dice Roberto "Of course"?
4. ¿Cómo se dice "Be careful" en español?

Diálogo 2

Cecilia va a visitar a Manuel, su hermano mayor, el próximo fin de semana. Ahora, ella le describe a su amiga Claudia cómo es su hermano.

ANTES DE ESCUCHAR

Basándote en lo que has aprendido en esta *etapa*, ¿cómo crees que Cecilia va a describir a su hermano?

Ahora lee las preguntas en la sección *Después de escuchar.*

DESPUÉS DE ESCUCHAR

P. Comprensión. Escucha el diálogo 2 y contesta las siguientes preguntas.
1. ¿Qué hace el hermano de Cecilia?
2. ¿De qué color tiene Manuel el pelo?
3. ¿Cómo reacciona Claudia?
4. ¿Cuál es el problema que menciona Cecilia?

Q. ¿Cómo lo dicen?

1. ¿Cómo dice Cecilia que su hermano es "likeable" y "good-looking"?
2. ¿Cómo se dice "mustache" en español?
3. ¿Cómo se dice "girlfriend" en español?

Tú dirás

R. ¿Quién es? Descríbeles a los otros estudiantes una persona famosa, sin decirles su nombre. Ellos van a tratar de adivinar (*guess*) quién es. Antes de hacer la descripción, di lo que la persona hace (es cantante, es actor/actriz, es profesor(a), etc.). Junto con la descripción física, dales otros detalles (e.g., dónde vive, su nacionalidad, cómo es su personalidad, sus preferencias, etc.).

Ex. R: Group

S. Mi retrato. Usa diferentes adjetivos para dar una descripción de ti mismo(a) a otro(a) estudiante en tu clase. Si es posible da algunos ejemplos para explicar las características. Por ejemplo, si eres atlético(a), indica los deportes en que participas.

Ex. S: Pairs

⊚ INTEGRACIÓN

LECTURA: *El tiempo es relativo*

ANTES DE LEER

A. ¿Qué significa la palabra "tiempo" en español? ¿Tiene más de un significado? ¿Qué significado crees que tiene en esta lectura?

B. Si el tiempo se presenta como un tema cuando hablas con alguien en inglés, ¿en qué momento de la conversación pasa esto normalmente?

C. ¿Qué palabras o expresiones contiene normalmente un artículo sobre el tiempo? Prepara una lista de algunas de estas palabras.

D. ¿Tienes algunas de estas palabras en tu lista? ¿Qué significan?

condiciones atmosféricas   está lloviendo
hace buen/mal tiempo   boletín meteorológico
hace calor/frío

GUÍA PARA LA LECTURA

A. Lee la lectura rápidamente para encontrar las expresiones de la pregunta **D** en la sección *Antes de leer.*

B. Ahora lee cada párrafo con más atención para indicar si los siguientes comentarios son verdaderos o falsos. Si uno es falso, da la información correcta de acuerdo con la lectura.

1. El tiempo es de igual importancia en todas las culturas.
2. Cada cultura determina los usos y los significados de una palabra.
3. La palabra *tiempo* tiene varios significados en español.
4. Cuando hace buen tiempo en los países de habla española casi no se habla del clima.
5. Es una costumbre entre hispanohablantes iniciar una conversación sobre el clima.
6. Hay muchas expresiones para preguntar sobre la salud de una persona.

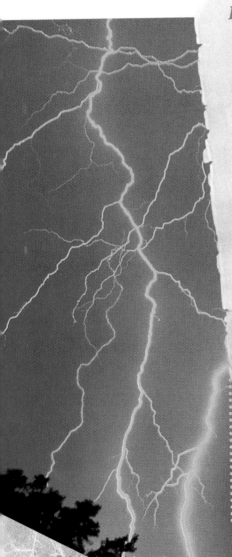

EL TIEMPO ES RELATIVO

José Juan Arrom

Para muchas personas que viven la mayor parte de su vida en Nueva Inglaterra, uno de los primeros temas de una conversación es el tiempo. Esta palabra tiene usos muy variados que dependen de su contexto cultural. Es decir, los significados y la importancia que tiene el tiempo en los países de habla española no siempre corresponden a los que tiene en los países de habla inglesa.

Es evidente que la palabra *tiempo,* tal como se acaba de usar, equivale a *condiciones atmosféricas.* También, como en inglés, es la idea que usamos para hablar de la duración de algo que pasa, calculándolo por segundos, minutos, horas, días, meses, años y hasta siglos. Pero aquí vamos a limitar la discusión del tiempo, por ahora, a lo que también se llama *el clima.*

En este sentido de la palabra, en España y en América Latina de vez en cuando se dice que hace buen tiempo o que hace mal tiempo. Pero con más frecuencia, si el tiempo es bueno, se acepta como una realidad y no se dice más. Y si es malo, la gente puede decir que "hace un calor horroroso", que "está lloviendo a cántaros" o que "hace un frío de los mil diablos".

Aun así, hablar del tiempo es una manera poco usada para comenzar una conversación en español. Generalmente, el boletín meteorológico le interesa mucho menos a la persona de habla española que la salud de la persona con quien habla y la de su familia. Por eso el idioma español es tan rico en frases como: "¿Qué tal? ¿Cómo te va? ¿Cómo estás? ¿Qué cuentas? ¿Qué me dices? ¿Qué pasó? ¿Qué onda? ¿Qué hubo? ¿Cómo andan por tu casa? ¿Qué me dices de la familia?" etc. Y la persona que recibe la pregunta sabe que no es de mal gusto contestar con detalles. Al contrario, es importante dar esos detalles.

VÍDEO CULTURAL: ¿Cómo es?

A. Anticipación. ¿Cómo te identificas? Marca con un círculo las frases que puedes utilizar para describirte. Compara tus respuestas con las de otro(a) estudiante y da las razones de tus preferiencias.

tu grado escolar

las materias que estudias

dónde naciste

las lenguas que hablas

dónde viven tus parientes

dónde vives tú

lo que comes

tu religión

la música que te gusta

Ex. A: Pairs

B. Preparación. Completa las frases siguientes. Si hay dificultades, ve de nuevo la sección *Vocabulario esencial* del vídeo. Compara tus respuestas con las de otro(a) estudiante.

1. __angre his__a__a

2. m__s r__íce__

3. qui__ro __ucho __ m__pa__s

4. ma__rile__a

5. __emos __acide__

Answers, Ex. B
1. sangre hisfana
2. mis raíces
3. quiero mucho a mi paí
4. madrileña
5. homos nacido

C. Participación. Mientras escuchas a las personas a que entrevistan, toma apuntes de lo que cada uno(a) dice para describir a si mismo(a).

Patricio _____

D. Comprensión. Lee las frases siguientes y escoge la mejor respuesta.

1. Somos muy patrióticos. Es decir,
   a. hemos nacido en los Estados Unidos.
   b. queremos a nuestro país

2. Mis padres son de Chile. Mi hermana y yo
   a. tenemos sangre hispana.
   b. vivimos dentro del país.

3. Me gusta hablar con mis abuelos porque
   a. son madrileños.
   b. mis raíces son importantes para mí.

Ex. D: Pairs

Answers, Ex. D
1. b 2. a, 3. b

E. Personalización. Escribe una descripción de ti. Explica si te sientes orgulloso, indiferente, etc. Usa seis adjetivos a lo menos.

ATAJO

Writing activities for this chapter are presented in the Activities Manual. For specific references to tasks supported by Atajo, please consult the Activities Manual.

Intercambio: ¿Sabes quién es?

Estudiante A

Aquí tienes varias fotos de gente famosa. Describe la primera. Tu compañero(a) tiene que adivinar quién es. Al terminar con la primera foto, tu compañero(a) va a describir una de sus fotos y tú tienes que adivinar quién es.

Gabriel García Márquez

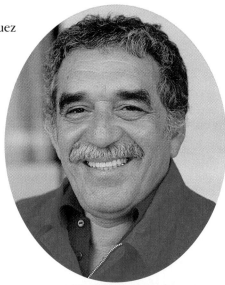

Pablo Picasso

Gabriela Sabatini

Estudiante B

Tu compañero(a) va a describir a una persona. Escucha atentamente, porque tienes que adivinar quién es. Al terminar, tú vas a describir a una persona y tu compañero(a) tiene que adivinar quién es.

Gloria Estefan

Salvador Dalí frente al Museo Dalí, Figueiras, España

Cristóbal Colón

Vocabulario

Para charlar

Para hablar del tiempo *Talking about the weather*

¿Qué tiempo hace? *What's the weather like?*
Está despejado. *It's clear.*
Está nublado. *It's cloudy.*
Está resbaloso. *It's slippery.*
Hace buen tiempo. *It's nice.*
Hace (mucho) calor. *It's (very) hot.*
Hace fresco. *It's cool.*
Hace frío. *It's cold.*
Hace mal tiempo. *It's bad.*
Hace sol. *It's sunny.*
Hace viento. *It's windy.*
Hay hielo. *It's icy.*
Hay neblina. *It's foggy.*
Hay niebla. *It's foggy.*
Hay nubes. *It's cloudy.*
Hay tormenta. *It's stormy.*
Llovizna. *It's drizzling.*
Llueve. *It's raining.*
Nieva. *It's snowing.*
Truena. *It's thundering.*

Para hacer una descripción física *Making a physical description*

alto(a)/bajo(a) *tall/short*
feo(a)/bonito(a) *ugly/pretty*
joven/viejo(a) *young/old*
largo(a)/corto(a)/breve *long/short*
ligero(a)/pesado(a) *light/heavy*
moderno(a)/viejo(a) *modern/old*
pequeño(a)/grande *small/big*
rubio(a)/moreno(a) *blond/brown-haired*

Para dar una opinión *Giving an opinion*

aburrido(a)/interesante *boring/interesting*
alegre/triste *happy/sad*
bueno(a)/malo(a) *good/bad*
caro(a) *expensive*
clásico(a) *classic(al)*
completo(a) *complete*
divertido(a)/serio(a) *fun/serious*
económico(a) *economical*
elegante *elegant*

extraño(a) *strange*
formal *formal*
formidable *formidable*
histórico(a) *historical*
infantil *infantile, childish*
optimista/pesimista *optimistic/pessimistic*
positivo *positive*
práctico(a) *practical*
regular *okay, regular*
romántico(a) *romantic*
sensacional *sensational*
teatral *theatrical*
variado(a) *varied*

Para dar una descripción física de una persona *Giving a physical description of a person*

Tiene... *He/she has . . .*
  los ojos azules/verdes/castaños/negros *blue/green/hazel/black eyes*
  el pelo corto/largo *short/long hair*
  la nariz grande/pequeña *a big/small nose*
  bigote/barba *a mustache/beard*
Es... *He/she is . . .*
  débil/fuerte *weak/strong*
  pálido(a)/bronceado(a) *pale/tan*

Para describir el carácter *Describing someone's personality*

Él (Ella) es... *He (She) is . . .*
  activo(a)/perezoso(a) *active/lazy*
  ambicioso(a) *ambitious*
  atlético(a) *athletic*
  cómico(a) *funny*
  deshonesto(a)/honesto(a) *dishonest/honest*
  discreto(a)/indiscreto(a) *discreet/indiscreet*
  generoso(a)/tacaño(a) *generous/costly*
  idealista/realista *idealistic/realistic*
  impaciente/paciente *impatient/patient*
  independiente *independent*
  intelectual *intellectual*
  perfecto(a) *perfect*
  responsable *responsible*
  serio(a) *serious*
  tímido(a)/valiente *timid/brave*
  trabajador(a) *hard-working*

Para expresar emoción *Expressing emotion*
Me alegro de que... *I'm glad that . . .*
Siento que... *I am sorry that . . .*
¡Qué lástima que...! *Too bad that . . . !*
¡Qué bueno que...! *How great that . . . !*
¡Qué pena que...! *What a shame that . . . !*

Vocabulario general   General vocabulary

Sustantivos
el cuadro *painting*
el estilo *style*
el horóscopo *horoscope*
el mar *sea*
la montaña *mountain*
la niebla *fog*
nieto(a) *grandson(daughter)*
la nieve *snow*
novio(a) *boy(girl)friend, fiancé(e)*
el período *period (of time)*
pintor(a) *painter*
el pronóstico *forecast*
la reacción *reaction*
la temperatura *temperature*
la tormenta *storm*
vecino(a) *neighbor*

Otras palabras y expresiones
¡Cuidado! *Careful! Watch out!*
dar una vuelta *to go for a walk*
¿De qué color es...? *What color is . . . ?*
Descríbeme... *Describe . . . for me.*
estar de mal humor *to be in a bad mood*
las estrellas *stars*

llover a cántaros *to rain cats and dogs*
por lo menos *at least*

Verbos
ahorrar *to save*
conocer *to know (person, place)*
funcionar *to function, work*
llover (ie) *to rain*
nevar (ie) *to snow*
parece *it appears*
saber *to know (fact)*
supe... *I found out . . .*
tronar (ue) *to thunder*
volver *to return*

Adjetivos
alegre *happy*
antipático(a) *disagreeable*
bueno(a) *good*
cruel *cruel*
delgado(a) *thin*
dinámico(a) *energetic*
egoísta *selfish*
enérgico(a) *energetic*
frívolo(a) *frivolous*
fuerte *strong*
guapo(a) *good-looking*
imaginativo(a) *imaginative*
ingenuo(a) *naive*

inteligente *intelligent*
malo(a) *bad*
perezoso(a) *lazy*
pesimista *pessimistic*
realista *realistic*
simpático(a) *agreeable*
sincero(a) *sincere*
triste *sad*
valiente *brave*

8 La salud

Bogotá/Candelaria

CHAPTER OBJECTIVES:

This chapter deals with topics relating to health, nutrition, and physical fitness.

After completing this first chapter you will be able to carry out the following tasks:

- ◉ talk about your own and other people's health and physical fitness
- ◉ refer to habitual actions in the past
- ◉ understand conversations about health and physical fitness
- ◉ recommend, react, and advise

The tools you will use to carry out these tasks are:

- ◉ **vocabulary for:**
  - parts of the body
  - symptoms of common illnesses
  - habitual actions
  - the basic food groups
- ◉ **grammatical structures:**
  - indirect object pronouns and the verb **doler**
  - reflexive verbs
  - the imperfect tense
  - indirect object pronouns with **dar** and **pedir**
  - subjunctive for influence and emotion

VENEZUELA
Población: 21.983.188   916.445 kilómetros cuadrados, más que dos veces el tamaño de California
Capital: Caracas, 1.800.000
Ciudades principales: Maracaibo, 1.300.000; Valencia, 903.600; Barquisimeto, 625.500

COLOMBIA
Población: 36.813.161   1.141.748 kilómetros cuadrados, como el tamaño de Nuevo México y Texas juntos
Capital: Bogotá, 5.000.000
Ciudades principales: Medellín, 1.664.000; Cali, 1.637.000; Barranquilla, 1.000.000

PANAMÁ
Población: 2.655.094
75.517 kilómetros cuadrados, un poco más grande que West Virginia
Capital: Ciudad de Panamá, 450.700

	VENEZUELA	COLOMBIA	PANAMÁ
Moneda:	el bolívar	el peso	el balboa
Esperanza de vida:	hombres, 69; mujeres, 75	hombres, 56; mujeres, 61	hombres, 71; mujeres, 77
Índice de alfabetización:	91%	91%	91%
Productos principales de exportación:	petróleo y lubricantes, productos derivados del petróleo, tabaco, animales vivos, productos químicos, equipo de transporte y maquinarias	café, fruta, bananas, flores, algodón, textiles, carne, caña de azúcar, esmeraldas	bananas, camarones, azúcar, café, derivados del petróleo
Embajada:	1099 30th St. NW, Washington, DC 20007	2118 Leroy Place NW, Washington, DC 20008	2862 McGill Tererace NW, Washington, DC 20008

PARA EMPEZAR: *Un accidente*

To set the theme for this chapter ask students, in Spanish, to recall any time they may have had an accident or an injury. Ask them what happened, what kind of injury, etc. You may model the vocabulary by first describing for them an accident you have had.

Transparency K-1: El cuerpo. Use students or the transparency to demonstrate parts of the body.

Suggestion: Body parts are an excellent topic to present using TPR (Total Physical Response). First have students repeat the various parts of the body as you say them. Then ask them to point to the parts of the body you name. If you wish, you can divide the vocabulary into sections—the head, the upper body, the lower body—thus reducing the amount of vocabulary to be presented each time.

Preparación: As you get ready to start this *etapa,* think about how you express such things as a hurt knee, a stomachache, a headache, a sprained ankle, or other aches and pains you may have or have had.

El cuerpo:

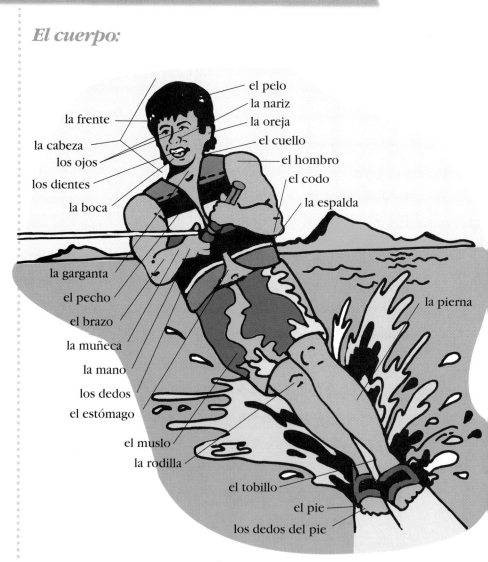

el pelo
la nariz
la oreja
el cuello
el hombro
el codo
la espalda
la frente
la cabeza
los ojos
los dientes
la boca
la garganta
el pecho
el brazo
la muñeca
la mano
los dedos
el estómago
el muslo
la rodilla
la pierna
el tobillo
el pie
los dedos del pie

Al leer el siguiente artículo sobre un accidente de un estudiante y un taxi, presta *(pay)* atención a las partes del cuerpo que se mencionan.

Estudiante choca con taxi

Amarilis Carrero, una estudiante de 22 años, **montaba** su bicicleta y chocó con un taxi ayer a las 9:30 de la mañana en la calle Bolívar. La estudiante iba a la universidad y chocó con el coche cuando **cruzaba** la calle. El conductor del taxi se lastimó una pierna. El pasajero no se lastimó. La Srta. Carrero se rompió un brazo, se torció un tobillo y se cortó la frente. La llevaron al Hospital Santa Cruz en una ambulancia de la Cruz Roja.

was crossing

was riding

Práctica

A. Estudio de palabras. Busca en el artículo de arriba las palabras que significan lo siguiente.

1. collided
2. broke
3. sprained
4. cut
5. hurt
6. was not hurt

B. Un accidente. En español frecuentemente se usan los verbos **lastimarse** *(to hurt oneself)*, **torcerse** *(to sprain)*, **romperse** *(to break)* y **cortarse** *(to cut oneself)* con las partes del cuerpo para expresar los resultados de un accidente. Emplea las expresiones sugeridas a continuación para indicar lo que te pasó. Sigue el modelo.

■ **Modelo:** (Yo) Me lastimé…
(Yo) *Me lastimé la mano.*

1. (Yo) Me lastimé…

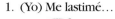

2. (Yo) Me torcí…

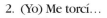

3. (Yo) Me rompí…

4. (Yo) Me corté…

C. Las partes del cuerpo. Identifica las partes del cuerpo que asocias con las siguientes actividades.

■ **Modelo:** Para *jugar al futbol* tienes que usar *los pies.*

1. tocar el piano
2. correr
3. nadar
4. saludar a alguien
5. mirar televisión
6. comprar perfume
7. comer
8. cantar
9. bailar
10. escribir

ENFOQUE ESTRUCTURAL   ## Los verbos reflexivos

Me levanto temprano.	*I get up early.*
Mi amigo **se levanta** temprano también.	*My friend gets up early, too.*
Me duermo a las 11:00.	*I go to sleep at 11:00.*
¿Te afeitas cada mañana?	*Do you shave every morning?*

Reflexive verbs are used when the doer of the action (subject) and the receiver of that action are the same.

Marta **lava** el coche.	*Marta washes the car.*
Marta **se lava.**	*Marta washes herself.*

In the first sentence Marta is the one performing the action and the car is the receiver of that action. In the second sentence, Marta both performs the action and is the receiver of that action.

These verbs must be conjugated along with the accompanying reflexive pronoun.

bañarse

yo	**me** baño	nosotros(as)	**nos** bañanos
tú	**te** bañas	vosotros(as)	**os** bañáis
Ud.		Uds.	
él	**se** baña	ellos	**se** bañan
ella		ellas	

The reflexive verb must agree with the subject of the verb with which it is used (i.e., **me** with **yo**, **te** with **tú**, **nos** with **nosotros**, etc.). When the verb is conjugated, the pronoun precedes it; with an infinitive, the pronoun is attached to it.

> **Me levanto** a las 6:30 todas las mañanas.
> Quiero **levantarme** a las 6:30 mañana.

Here is a list of some frequently used reflexive verbs. The pronoun **se**, attached to the end of the infinitive, distinguishes these reflexive verbs from nonreflexive verbs.

acostarse	*to go to bed*
afeitarse	*to shave*
cepillarse (el pelo, los dientes)	*to brush (one's hair, teeth)*
cortarse (el dedo)	*to cut (one's finger)*
desayunarse	*to eat breakfast*
despertarse (ie)	*to wake up*
divertirse (ie, i)	*to have a good time*
dormirse (ue, u)	*to fall asleep*
ducharse	*to take a shower*
lastimarse	*to hurt oneself*
lavarse (las manos, el pelo)	*to wash (one's hands, hair)*
lavarse (los dientes)	*to brush (one's teeth)*
levantarse	*to get up*
maquillarse	*to put on make-up*
peinarse	*to comb one's hair*
ponerse	*to put on (clothes)*
quedarse	*to stay, remain*
romperse	*to break*
sentarse (ie)	*to sit down*
torcerse	*to twist, sprain*
vestirse (i)	*to get dressed*

GRAMMAR NOTE:
Note that the verb **domir** is followed by (ue, u). You are already familiar with the notation (ue) indicating that this is a stem-changing verb in the present. The notation (u) indicates that this verb also undergoes a stem change in the preterire. This is explained in Chapter 9.

Práctica

D. Miguel o Marta y yo. Compara tus actividades con las de Miguel si eres hombre o con las de Marta si eres mujer.

Los hombres:

■ **Modelo:** Miguel se despierta a las siete.
Yo me despierto a las siete menos cuarto.

1. Miguel se levanta a las seis y media.
2. Miguel no se baña por la mañana.
3. Miguel se lava los dientes una vez al día.
4. Miguel se afeita todos los días.
5. Miguel no se desayuna por la mañana.

Suggestion, Ex. D
Have each student prepare a list according to their own schedules. Allow 3–4 minutes, then share lists and comment on how students differ. Personalize activity by asking students questions such as: **¿A qué hora te levantas?**

Las mujeres

■ **Modelo:** Marta se despierta a las siete.
Yo me despierto a las seis y media.

1. Marta se levanta a las seis.
2. Marta se baña todas las mañanas.
3. Marta se cepilla el pelo.
4. Marta se maquilla todas las mañanas.
5. Marta se desayuna todas las mañanas.

E. ¿Qué haces primero? Pon las siguientes actividades en orden cronológico según tu rutina diaria.

1. vestirme
2. levantarme
3. desayunarme
4. peinarme
5. ducharme
6. despertarme
7. afeitarme
8. maquillarme

○ IRM Master 33: Pronombres
de complemento indirecto

Ask students to read over this section for homework before presenting it in class.

○ IRM Master 34: El
verbo *doler*

Contextualize the presentation of these verbs. Tell students about how difficult your daily routine is. Use gestures as you explain your routine. Check for comprehension frequently, e.g., **Yo me acuesto muy tarde, como a las 11 de la noche. ¿A qué hora te acuestas tú?**

GRAMMAR NOTE:

As you learned with direct object pronouns, indirect object pronouns are placed before the conjugated verb, and can be placed before or after the infinitive.

ENFOQUE ESTRUCTURAL **Pronombres de complemento indirecto y el verbo *doler***

Indirect object pronouns are used to indicate what person or thing receives the direct object. Note the following examples:

Él **me** escribió una carta.	*He wrote a letter **to me**.*
Ella **te** compró un disco.	*She bought a record **for you**.*
Tú **nos** vendiste el coche.	*You sold the car **to us**.*
¿**Le** escribió ella una carta **a Juan?**	*Did she write a letter **to Juan?***
No, ella **les** escribió una carta **a sus amigas.**	*No, she wrote a letter **to her friends**.*

Indirect object pronouns

me	to (for) me	**nos**	to (for) us
te	to (for) you	**os**	to (for) you
le	to (for) him, her, you	**les**	to (for) them, you

El verbo *doler*

¿Cómo estás?	*How are you?*
No muy bien. **Me duele** la garganta.	*Not too well. My throat **hurts**.*
¿**Te duele** la cabeza?	***Does** your head **ache?***
Sí, y **me duelen** la espalda y las piernas también.	*Yes, and my back and legs **hurt** also.*

The verb **doler** is just like the verb **gustar** in that it is used with the indirect object pronouns **me, te, le, nos, os,** and **les.** Like **gustar,** the third-person singular and plural forms are usually used, depending on whether what hurts is singular or plural. Also notice that in the above examples, Spanish uses definite articles for body parts where English uses possessives.

Práctica

F. ¿Te duele... ? Pregúntales a varios compañeros de clase si les duele algo. Emplea las sugerencias y sigue el modelo.

■ **Modelo:** la muñeca / la espalda
—*¿Te duele la muñeca?*
—*No, no me duele la muñeca, pero me duele la espalda.*

1. el tobillo / los pies
2. los ojos / la cabeza
3. la espalda / las piernas
4. las orejas / el brazo
5. el hombro / las piernas
6. la rodilla / la garganta

Ahora con varios compañeros, repite el ejercicio y diles *(tell them)* que contesten verdaderamente *(truthfully)*.

■ **Modelo:** —*¿Te duele la muñeca?*
—*No, me duele la cabeza.*
o
—*No, no me duele nada* (nothing hurts).

Comentarios

culturales *La medicina*

*L*a medicina en algunas partes del mundo hispano es una rara combinación de prácticas indígenas, africanas y europeas. Al lado de estas influencias también existen programas de medicina que son tan modernos como los que tenemos en este país.

En algunas regiones rurales donde no hay muchos médicos ni grandes hospitales modernos, a veces la gente va a ver al curandero o curandera local. Ésta es una persona que tiene gran conocimiento de las hierbas y otros ingredientes naturales y sabe cómo usarlas para hacer remedios que curan a la gente. Éstas son medicinas que tienen mucha tradición entre la gente rural. El proceso parece poco científico, pero muchas de las medicinas naturales tienen los mismos ingredientes que las medicinas que recomiendan los médicos en los grandes hospitales modernos.

INTEGRACIÓN CULTURAL

1. ¿Qué solución hay para un(a) enfermo(a) si no hay médico?
2. ¿Qué usa esta persona para curar a la gente?
3. ¿Qué tienen en común las medicinas naturales y las medicinas producidas por compañías farmacéuticas?
4. En este país, ¿existen métodos alternativos para curar las enfermedades? ¿Cuáles son algunos?

VAMOS A ESCUCHAR: EL ACCIDENTE DE FELIPE

Carlos y Felipe hablan por teléfono sobre *(about)* un accidente que tuvo Felipe ayer.

ANTES DE ESCUCHAR

Basándote en lo que has aprendido en esta *etapa*, ¿qué información esperas que incluyan Carlos y Felipe en su conversación sobre el accidente que tuvo Felipe? Antes de escuchar la conversación, repasa las preguntas que aparecen en la sección *Después de escuchar.*

DESPUÉS DE ESCUCHAR

G. Comprensión. Contesta las siguientes preguntas después de escuchar la conversación entre Felipe y Carlos.

1. ¿Qué parte del cuerpo se lastimó Felipe?
2. ¿Cómo pasó el accidente?
3. ¿Se lastimó otra persona también?
4. ¿Qué le pasó?

H. ¿Cómo lo dicen? Escucha la conversación otra vez y contesta las siguientes preguntas.

1. ¿Cómo se describe Felipe?
2. ¿Cómo dice Felipe que "they weren't paying attention"?

Tú dirás ....

I. Tuve un accidente. Piensa en un accidente que tuviste en el pasado. Imagina que ocurrió recientemente. Cuando un(a) compañero(a) de clase te llama por teléfono, dile lo que pasó *(what happened)*. ¿Cuándo ocurrió? ¿Dónde? ¿Qué te pasó?

J. La rutina diaria. Haz una lista de las actividades que caracterizan tu rutina de cada mañana (i.e., desde el momento en que te despiertas hasta el momento en que sales a trabajar o a la universidad). Compara tu rutina con la rutina de un(a) compañero(a). ¿En qué son semejantes *(alike)* las rutinas? ¿En qué son diferentes?

	yo	mi compañero(a)
1.	_____	_____
2.	_____	_____
3.	_____	_____
etc.		

Luego comparte *(share)* la información con el resto de la clase.

Answers, Ex. G
1. la pierna 2. cruzó un perro grande y se cayeron. 3. sí, Catarina 4. (Catarina) Se torció un tobillo y se cortó el brazo.

Answers, Ex. H
1. Soy verdaderamente torpe 2. No prestábamos atención

Ex. I:  **Pairs**
Have students practice in small groups. Then "call" several students on the phone to hear about their accidents.

Ex. J:  **Pairs**

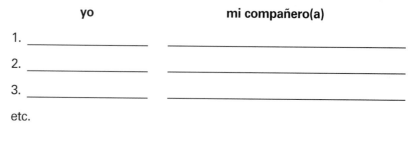

PARA EMPEZAR: *Las enfermedades y los remedios*

Preparación: Think about the various common illnesses we tend to get in the winter.

- What are some of them?
- What are the symptoms?
- What are some of the medicines we take for these illnesses?
- Are these over-the-counter medicines?
- Do you need a prescription?

Ask students these questions in Spanish. Utilize transparency and talk about the ailments pictured.

🔍 **IRM K-2: Las enfermedades**

Al leer la siguiente información sobre una enfermedad común, presta atención a las expresiones para síntomas y remedios.

Cada invierno los microbios cruzan **las fronteras.** Llegan de todas partes del mundo. Es la temporada de **la gripe.** Esta epidemia **alcanza** su **punto** más alto en diciembre, enero y febrero. Estas personas tienen la gripe. Nota los síntomas que tienen.

border
flu / reaches / point

Estornuda.

Tiene fiebre.

Tiene dolor de estómago.

Tiene escalofríos.

Tiene dolor de garganta.

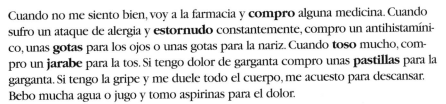
Tiene dolor de cabeza.   Tose.

Cuando no me siento bien, voy a la farmacia y **compro** alguna medicina. Cuando sufro un ataque de alergia y **estornudo** constantemente, compro un antihistamínico, unas **gotas** para los ojos o unas gotas para la nariz. Cuando **toso** mucho, compro un **jarabe** para la tos. Si tengo dolor de garganta compro unas **pastillas** para la garganta. Si tengo la gripe y me duele todo el cuerpo, me acuesto para descansar. Bebo mucha agua o jugo y tomo aspirinas para el dolor.

I buy
I sneeze
drops / I cough
syrup / lozenges

Cuando estoy muy enfermo, tengo que ir a la doctora. Ella me examina y me toma la temperatura. Si tengo una infección y si tengo fiebre, ella me da una **receta.** Con la receta voy a la farmacia y compro un antibiótico. Descanso y **me cuido** muy bien cuando estoy enfermo.

▶*En la farmacia*

Práctica

A. ¿Qué tienen? Describe los síntomas de las personas en los dibujos.

■ **Modelo:** *El Sr. González tiene dolor de estómago.*

Sr. González

1. Sr. López 2. Cristina 3. Beatriz 4. Sra. Torres 5. Srta. Martín 6. Isabel

Suggestion, Ex. A:
If you are doing this unit during the flu season, ask students about their symptoms and those of family members and/or friends.

Answers, Ex. A
1. El Sr. López estornuda. 2. Cristina tiene fiebre. 3. Beatriz tiene escalofríos. 4. La Sra. Torres tiene dolor de garganta. 5. La Srta. Martín tiene dolor de cabeza. 6. Isabel tose.

B. ¿Qué necesitan? Estás de vacaciones con tu familia en Venezuela. Cuando alguien no se siente bien, te pide ayuda. Vas a la farmacia y hablas con el (la) farmacéutico(a). Sigue el modelo.

■ **Modelo:** your father has a headache
  Estudiante A: *Mi papá tiene dolor de cabeza.*
  Estudiante B: *Necesita unas aspirinas.*

1. Your sister has a very bad cough.
2. Your father has a backache.
3. Your brother's allergies are acting up and he can't stop sneezing.
4. You have a fever and ache all over.
5. Your mother has a sore throat.

Ex. B: Pairs

Possible answers, Ex. B
1. Necesita un jarabe. 2. Necesita acostarse para descansar y tomar aspirina para el dolor. 3. Necesita un antihistamínico. 4. Ud. necesita esta receta para un antibiótico y también necesita descansar y tomar aspirina para el dolor. 5. Necesita unas pastillas para la garganta.

Before beginning activity, brainstorm with students the type of information a pharmacist would need to recommend a treatment. Write some key words on the board. Then have students work in pairs and role-play the interchanges between patient and pharmacist.

Use this reading to promote conversation about trips students have taken where they, or a companion, have become ill. Have them share what happened, how they handled it, etc.

pharmacist

cold

Comentarios
culturales · La farmacia de turno

*E*n muchos países del mundo hispano, cuando alguien se enferma o no se siente bien, puede consultar al **farmacéutico** o a la **farmacéutica**. Si el (la) farmacéutico(a) considera que la enfermedad es seria, le aconseja a la persona que vaya a ver a un médico o a una médica. Si simplemente es un **catarro,** la gripe, una alergia o un accidente que no es muy serio, el (la) farmacéutico(a) le puede recomendar algunas medicinas. Para algunas enfermedades no es necesario ir al médico o a la médica—el (la) farmacéutico(a) puede recomendarle ciertas medicinas sin receta.

Cada ciudad y pueblo tiene una farmacia que está abierta toda la noche y se conoce como la farmacia de turno. Las otras farmacias en ese pueblo o esa ciudad indican en la puerta cuál es la farmacia de turno para esa noche o semana. El periódico también tiene esta información.

INTEGRACIÓN CULTURAL

1. ¿Qué haces si te enfermas a las 3:00 de la mañana?
2. ¿Existe la farmacia de turno en este país?
3. ¿En qué son las farmacias de este país diferentes de las farmacias de los países hispanos?

Repaso

C. En casa de Victoria y Miguel. Miguel y Victoria tienen rutinas muy diferentes. Mira los dibujos que hay a continuación y describe la rutina de Miguel y la de Victoria. Puedes utilizar los siguientes verbos: despertarse, levantarse, quedarse en la cama, ducharse, lavarse, cepillarse, afeitarse, maquillarse, vestirse, peinarse, desayunarse, irse.

D. Mi mejor amigo(a). Trabaja con otro(a) estudiante. Cada persona va a hablar de un(a) amigo(a). Hagan una descripción física y luego describan el carácter de la persona. Repasen los adjetivos en el capítulo 7.

IRM Master 31: El imperfecto

ENFOQUE ESTRUCTURAL · **El imperfecto**

You have already learned to express actions in the past by using the *preterite*. Now you will learn a second past tense, the *imperfect*, which will allow you to express what you *used to do*. Note the following examples:

¿Dónde **vivías** cuando tenías 10 años?	Where **did you use to live** when you were 10 years old?
Vivía en Indiana.	**I used to live** in Indiana.
¿Qué **hacías** durante el verano?	What **did you use to do** during the summer?
Nadaba y **jugaba** al tenis todos los días.	**I used to swim** and **play** tennis every day.

To form the imperfect, note the following:

hablar	**comer**	**vivir**
habl-	**com-**	**viv-**
yo	habl**aba**	com**ía**	viv**ía**
tú	habl**abas**	com**ías**	viv**ías**
Ud., él, ella	habl**aba**	com**ía**	viv**ía**
nosotros(as)	habl**ábamos**	com**íamos**	viv**íamos**
vosotros(as)	habl**abais**	com**íais**	viv**íais**
Uds., ellos, ellas	habl**aban**	com**ían**	viv**ían**

The imperfect tense can have three equivalents in English:

Ella vivía en Colombia. {
She lived in Colombia.
She used to live in Colombia.
She was living in Colombia.

The imperfect is discussed in three different sections. In this initial presentation, we concentrate on the forms of the imperfect. Later in this *etapa* and also in the next *etapa*, exercises are aimed at demonstrating the most frequent uses of this tense. The use of the imperfect here is limited to what you used to do. Additional uses will be discussed later in this chapter.

Introduce this structure in context. Tell students about your childhood and the things you used to do, how you used to be, etc. Try to incorporate previously studied adjectives of personality and physical description.

Suggestions: (1) Ask students what fruits and vegetables they like now. Then ask them if they liked those fruits and vegetables when they were 4 or 5 years old (**cuando tenías 4 o 5 años).** (2) Contrast the imperfect forms with those of the present, then with those of the preterite. (3) Write out the verb forms.

El imperfecto de *ver, ser* e *ir*

The verbs **ver, ser,** and **ir** do not follow the pattern presented above. Instead they form the imperfect in the following way:

	ver	*ser*	*ir*
yo	**veía**	**era**	**iba**
tú	**veías**	**eras**	**ibas**
Ud., él, ella	**veía**	**era**	**iba**
nosotros(as)	**veíamos**	**éramos**	**íbamos**
vosotros(as)	**veíais**	**erais**	**ibais**
Uds., ellos, ellas	**veían**	**eran**	**iban**

Práctica

E. La juventud *(youth)* del padre de Diana. El padre de Diana recuerda lo que hacía cuando era niño en Colombia. En la descripción de su vida, cambia los verbos del presente al imperfecto.

■ **Modelo:** Vivimos en Valencia.
Vivíamos en Valencia.

1. Mi padre trabaja en un banco.
2. Mi mamá se queda en casa.
3. Yo asisto a la escuela primaria de nuestro barrio.
4. Mi hermana estudia en la universidad.
5. Nosotros pasamos los veranos en el Caribe.
6. Mis padres alquilan una casa cerca del mar.
7. A mi hermana le gusta nadar.
8. Yo juego al vólibol en la playa.
9. Mi padre y yo vamos de pesca.
10. Nosotros nos divertimos mucho durante nuestras vacaciones en el Caribe.

F. El año pasado... cada jueves por la tarde. Cuenta lo que hacían las personas en los dibujos cada jueves por la tarde.

■ **Modelo:** *Carmen el año pasado, Carmen corría cada jueves por la tarde.*

Carmen

1. Carlos

2. Dina y su novio

3. Jaime

4. Mónica

5. Olga y Lucía

6. Alberto

7. Miguel y Patricia

8. Isabel

9. Luisa y Daniel

10. Paula y Marcos

G. El año pasado, mi amigo y yo… cada sábado por la tarde.

Ahora imagina que cada sábado por la tarde tú y un(a) amigo(a) hacían lo mismo que las personas en los dibujos del Ejercicio F.

Imperfect—habitual actions. Ask students questions about a typical day and/or week during summer vacation when they were younger. **¿A qué hora te levantabas? ¿A qué hora te acostabas?** etc.

ENFOQUE LÉXICO

Expresiones para hablar de acciones habituales

The imperfect tense is used to express something that happened over and over again in the past.

Todos los veranos íbamos a la playa.	***Every summer*** *we used to go to the beach.*
Cada tarde mi hermana nadaba en el mar.	***Every afternoon*** *my sister used to swim in the sea.*
Cada noche escribíamos postales y mis padres leían revistas.	***Every evening*** *we used to write postcards and my parents used to read magazines.*

Certain adverbs and expressions that convey the idea of a routine often accompany the imperfect tense and are listed below:

a menudo	*often*
a veces	*sometimes*
cada día (viernes, sábado, tarde, mañana, noche, semana, mes, etc.)	*every day (Friday, Saturday, afternoon, morning, night, week, month, etc.)*
con frecuencia	*frequently*
con regularidad	*regularly*
de vez en cuando	*from time to time*
frecuentemente	*frequently*
muchas veces	*many times*
normalmente	*normally*
por lo general	*in general*
siempre	*always*
todos los días (lunes, martes, etc.)	*every day (Monday, Tuesday, etc.)*
una vez al día (a la semana, al mes, al año, etc.)	*once a day (week, month, year, etc.)*

Práctica

Answers, Ex. H
1. nosotras nos despertábamos
2. yo me quedaba 3. Elisabeth se levantaba 4. nosotras nos duchábamo 5. nosotras nos desayunábamos 6. Elisabeth arreglaba 7. yo leía 8. nosotras nadábamos 9. yo hablaba
10. nosotras comíamos 11. nosotras íbamos 12. nosotras nos acostábamos

H. El verano pasado. Silvia pasó el verano pasado con su amiga Elisabeth. Emplea las sugerencias y el imperfecto para contar lo que hacían Silvia y su amiga.

■ **Modelo:**   cada sábado por la noche / nosotras / salir con nuestros amigos
Cada sábado por la noche salíamos con nuestros amigos.

1. cada día / nosotras / despertarse temprano
2. muchas veces / yo / quedarse en cama una hora o dos
3. con frecuencia / Elisabeth / levantarse enseguida
4. todos los días / nosotras / ducharse
5. normalmente / nosotras / desayunarse juntas
6. cada mañana / Elisabeth / arreglar la casa
7. a veces / yo / leer revistas en cama
8. cada tarde / nosotras / nadar en la piscina con nuestros amigos
9. cada noche / yo / hablar por teléfono con mis amigas

10. cada día / nosotras / comer pizza

11. de vez en cuando / nosotras / ir al cine

12. por lo general / nosotras / acostarse a las 11:00 o 12:00

I. Cuando tú tenías siete años...

Emplea las sugerencias y pregúntale a un(a) compañero(a) sobre su vida cuando tenía siete años. Escribe las respuestas en una hoja de papel para que puedas informarle a la clase.

■ **Modelo:** ir a la escuela

—¿*Dónde ibas a la escuela?*

—*Cerca de casa.*

1. vivir aquí
2. tener muchos amigos
3. ir a la playa
4. dormir una siesta
5. comer mucho

6. ser travieso(a) (*mischievous*)
7. jugar con los compañeros
8. levantarse temprano
9. acostarse tarde
10. beber mucha leche

ENFOQUE ESTRUCTURAL

El imperfecto—usos adicionales

In addition to indicating habitual past actions, the imperfect tense is used to talk about several other kinds of situations in the past:

1. To indicate actions that *were going on* at the time about which you are speaking.

| **Mientras hablábamos ella leía una revista.** | *While **we were talking**, she **was reading** a magazine.* |

2. To describe the physical attributes of people you are remembering.

| **Ella tenía los ojos azules.** | *She **had** blue eyes.* |

3. To express attitudes and beliefs that were held at that time in the past, using verbs such as **creer, pensar,** etc.

| **Yo creía que era bonita.** | *I **thought** she was pretty.* |

4. To express how old someone was in the past.

| **Él tenía cincuenta años.** | *He **was** fifty years old.* |

5. To describe past states of health.

| **Yo no me sentía bien.** | *I **didn't feel** well.* |

6. To set the background or context for a story that takes place in the past.

Eran las nueve de la noche.	*It **was** 9:00 at night.*
Yo **estaba de visita** en Phoenix.	*I **was visiting** Phoenix.*
Era invierno, pero **hacía** muchísimo calor allí. **Estábamos** en un pequeño restaurante.	*It **was** winter, but **it was** very hot there. **We were** in a tiny restaurant.*

Práctica

J. La fiesta de Cecilia. Daniel llegó tarde a la fiesta de Cecilia. De acuerdo con el dibujo, emplea el imperfecto para indicar lo que hacían sus amigos cuando él llegó.

■ **Modelo:** Olga

Olga escuchaba discos compactos.

K. ¿Qué pasó? Cuéntale a un(a) compañero(a) de clase algo que te pasó en los momentos que se mencionan a continuación. En cada caso indica: ¿dónde estabas? ¿qué hacías? ¿cómo te sentías? ¿estabas solo(a) *(alone)* o con otras personas? ¿qué hacían ellos(as)?

1. ayer por la noche a las 8:00
2. esta mañana a las 7:30
3. el sábado pasado a las 10:00 de la noche
4. el viernes pasado por la noche
5. un momento importante de tu vida

Un cliente va la farmacia y discute sus síntomas con la farmacéutica.

ANTES DE ESCUCHAR

Basándote en lo que has aprendido en esta *etapa*, qué información esperas escuchar con respecto a *(with regard to):*

1. los síntomas
2. las medicinas
3. las sugerencias de la farmacéutica

Antes de escuchar la conversación, repasa las preguntas que aparecen en la sección *Después de escuchar.*

DESPUÉS DE ESCUCHAR

L. Comprensión. Contesta las siguientes preguntas después de escuchar la conversación entre el cliente y la farmacéutica.

1. ¿Cuáles son los síntomas del cliente?
2. ¿Qué le da la farmacéutica?
3. ¿Para qué síntomas?
4. ¿Qué más le pide el cliente a la farmacéutica?
5. ¿Qué consejos le da la farmacéutica al cliente?

M. ¿Cómo lo dicen? Escucha la conversación otra vez y contesta las siguientes preguntas.

1. ¿Cómo dice la farmacéutica "may I help you"?
2. ¿Cómo dice la farmacéutica "of course"?

Tú dirás ....

N. ¿Qué hacías en el verano cuando eras niño(a)? Quieres llegar a conocer a alguien un poquito mejor, así que van a comparar lo que hacían en el verano cuando eran niños. Pregúntale lo que le gustaba hacer y lo que no le gustaba hacer. Pregúntale adónde iba y qué hacía durante los veranos. Identifica tres actividades que tienen en común y tres actividades que no tienen en común y compártelas con la clase.

Ñ. En la farmacia. Trabaja con varios(as) compañeros(as) de clase. Uno(a) va a jugar el papel *(play the role)* de farmacéutico(a) y los otros el papel de clientes. Túrnense explicándole al / a la farmacéutico(a) sus síntomas. El (La) farmacéutico(a) va a recomendarles algún remedio o medicina.

PARA EMPEZAR: *La salud: mejor que la riqueza*

Discuss food and eating habits with students in Spanish. Use the transparency to point out needed vocabulary

Transparency K-3: La nutrición.

Using the transparency, have students identify the foods in each group. Then, as a class, read the outline of functions summarizing the roles of each food group.

Preparación: As you get ready to begin this *etapa,* think about the food craze this country has gone through in the past few years. Think about your own eating habits. Do you eat health foods? Do you eat junk foods? What about meat?

Los cinco grupos alimenticios

1		**Leche y productos lácteos**	calcio, proteína, grasa, vitamina B, vitamina A
2		**Carne, pescado, huevos**	proteína, grasa, hierro, vitamina A, vitamina B
3		**Frutas y vegetales**	vitamina C, fibra, minerales
4		**Pan, cereales, papas, vegetales secos**	almidón, proteína, vitamina B
5		**Grasa**	lípidos, vitamina A en la mantequilla y la crema

Funciones de los cinco grupos alimenticios

Grupos 1 y 2: **Desarrollan,** mantienen y **renuevan** los **tejidos** del cuerpo. Forman los **huesos** y los dientes; mantienen **sanos** los nervios y los músculos; regulan el tono muscular y el ritmo cardíaco.

Grupo 3: Facilitan la digestión; mejoran la visión nocturna; ayudan al movimiento muscular.

Grupos 4 y 5: Le dan energía al cuerpo (calorías).

Práctica

A. Debes comer los alimentos del grupo...
La dieta tiene una influencia muy importante en nuestra condición física. De acuerdo con la información al principio de esta *etapa*, recomienda lo que deben comer las siguientes personas.

■ **Modelo:** Paula Lerma tiene problemas cuando maneja *(drives)* el coche de noche; ella no puede ver muy bien.
Debe comer los alimentos del grupo 3, frutas y vegetales.

1. Mateo Torres se prepara para una competencia deportiva.
2. Virginia Estrada siempre está cansada.
3. Adela López empieza a echar los dientes *(to teethe)*.
4. Pablo Chávez tiene problemas después de comer: le duele el estómago.
5. Juan José Cisneros se rompió el brazo tres veces.
6. A Genoveva Candelaria le late *(beats)* el corazón irregularmente.

B. ¿Comes bien?
Comenta sobre lo que comiste ayer en términos de los cinco grupos básicos. Tu compañero(a) va a decirte si comiste bien o comiste mal.

■ **Modelo:** —*Del primer grupo comí queso para el almuerzo y bebí leche para la cena. Del segundo grupo... etc.*
—*Comiste muy bien.*
o
—*Comiste muy mal.*

C. ¿Qué comías?
Con un(a) compañero(a), compara lo que comes hoy con lo que comías cuando eras más joven.

■ **Modelo:** *Cuando era más joven, comía mucho helado, ahora como yogur.*

Repaso

D. Cuando tenías diecisiete años.
Haz una lista de las cosas que hacías habitualmente cuando tenías diecisiete años. Después habla con un(a) compañero(a) y pregúntale si hacía o no las mismas cosas que tú.

E. La rutina de tu compañero(a) de cuarto.
Tú y tu amigo(a) están discutiendo la rutina de tu compañero(a) de cuarto. Sigue el modelo.

■ **Modelo:** despertarse
¿A qué hora se despierta tu compañero(a) de cuarto?
Se despierta a las 7:30.

Develop / renew / tissues
bones / healthy

GRAMMAR NOTE:
As you begin this *etapa*, you may want to review the vocabulary for fruits, vegetables, and other foods at the end of Chapter 6.

Ex. A: Use the transparency of the five food groups.

Possible answers, Ex. A
1. Debe comer alimentos de los grupos 1 y 2 y también alimentos de los grupos 3, 4 y 5. 2. Debe comer alimentos de los grupos 4 y 5. 3. Debe comer alimentos de los grupos 1 y 2. 4. Debe comer alimentos del grupo 3. 5. Debe comer alimentos de los grupos 1 y 2. 6. Debe comer alimentos de los grupos 1 y 2.

Ex. B:  **Pairs**
Suggestion, Ex. B: Assign as homework for students to make a list of everything they ate the day before. Bring the list to class and share with a partner. The partner will play the part of the nutritionist and will make recommendations for their partner's diet based on this list. Before doing this activity review the subjunctive in phrases of recommendation.

Suggestion, Ex. C: To increase interest have students discuss nostalgia, such as the breakfast cereals they used to eat, lunches at school, or their favorite deserts. Encourage students whose families had different eating traditions to share their memories with the class.

Ex. D: **Pairs**
Suggestion, Ex. D: Contextualize activity by suggesting that the roommate in question is a disaster. Students discuss this person's routine as if they are complaining about his or her bad habits. Expand into a writing activity by telling students to, when done, jointly compose and edit a short note to that roommate in which they complain about his/her bad habits and ask him/her to move.

---

1. acostarse
2. levantarse
3. cepillarse los dientes dos veces cada día
4. ducharse todas las mañanas
5. afeitarse todos los días
6. maquillarse todos los días
7. vestirse
8. desayunarse

ENFOQUE ESTRUCTURAL

Pronombres de complemento indirecto y los verbos *dar* y *pedir*

El médico me **dio** una receta.	*The doctor **gave** me a prescription.*
Yo le **pedí** un jarabe a la farmacéutica.	*I **asked** the pharmacist for cough syrup.*
Yo les **di** la medicina.	*I **gave** them the medicine.*

Both of these verbs are often used with indirect object pronouns. The verb **dar** is often used with indirect object pronouns to indicate to whom something is being given. The verb **pedir** is used with indirect object pronouns to indicate the person who is being asked for something.

Dar

Le **doy** el libro a mi compañero.	*I **give** the book to my classmate.*
La profesora nos **da** la tarea.	*The instructor **gives** the homework to us.*
¿Le **diste** la carta a tu novia?	***Did you give** the letter to your girlfriend?*
Sí, le **di** la carta a ella.	*Yes, **I gave** the letter to her.*

Except for the **yo** form, the verb **dar** is conjugated in the present tense in the same way as other **-ar** verbs.

Present of the verb *dar*

yo	**doy**	nosotros(as)	**damos**
tú	**das**	vosotros(as)	**dais**
Ud.		Uds.	
él	**da**	ellos	**dan**
ella		ellas	

Preterite of the verb *dar*

yo	**di**	nosotros(as)	**dimos**
tú	**diste**	vosotros(as)	**disteis**
Ud.		Uds.	
él	**dio**	ellos	**dieron**
ella		ellas	

Although **dar** is an **-ar** verb, it is conjugated in the preterite with the endings that you use for **-er** and **-ir** verbs. Also notice that the forms **di** and **dio** do not take an accent mark.

The verb **dar** is often used with indirect object pronouns that indicate to whom something is being given. Other verbs commonly used with indirect object pronouns are **hablar, decir, mandar** *(to send)*, and **escribir.**

Pedir

¿Le **pides** permiso a alguien cuando quieres salir?	***Do you ask*** *anyone for permission when you want to go out?*
No, no le **pido** permiso a nadie.	*No, I don't **ask** anyone for permission.*
¿Le **pediste** dinero a Juan para ir al concierto?	***Did you ask*** *Juan for money to go to the concert?*
Sí, le **pedí** 50 dólares.	*Yes, **I asked** him for 50 dollars.*

Pedir means *to ask for something* as opposed to **preguntar,** which means *to ask questions.* Here are the conjugations of **pedir.**

Notice that the **e** in the stem of **pedir** changes to **i** in all forms of the present except **nosotros** and **vosotros.**

Present tense of *pedir*

yo	**pido**	nosotros(as)	**pedimos**
tú	**pides**	vosotros(as)	**pedís**
Ud.		Uds.	
él	**pide**	ellos	**piden**
ella		ellas	

Preterite tense of *pedir*

yo	**pedí**	nosotros(as)	**pedimos**
tú	**pediste**	vosotros(as)	**pedisteis**
Ud.		Uds.	
él	**pidió**	ellos	**pidieron**
ella		ellas	

Notice that the **e** in the stem of **pedir** changes to **i** in the third person singular and plural of the preterite. Other verbs conjugated like this are:

servir
medir *(to measure)*
reírse *(to laugh)*

repetir *(to repeat)*
sonreír *(to smile)*

Práctica

F. El médico le dio la medicina a... Indica a quién le dio el médico cada medicina. Emplea las sugerencias y sigue el modelo.

■ **Modelo:** el jarabe / Mario
         Le dio el jarabe a Mario.

1. la medicina / Laura
2. el jarabe / mis hermanos
3. el antihistamínico / Ud.
4. el antibiótico / yo
5. el jarabe / tú

6. la receta / la profesora
7. la aspirina / mi esposo(a)
8. las gotas para los ojos / tú
9. la medicina / mi novio(a)
10. las aspirinas / mi amigo(a)

G. ¿Qué pides? Tu amigo(a) te pregunta si en la cafetería de la universidad te dan ciertas comidas. Tú le contestas que les pides ciertas comidas y te dan otras. Sigue el modelo.

■ **Modelo:** dulces / fruta
         —*¿Les pides dulces?*
         —*Sí, pero me dan fruta.*

1. pasteles / yogur
2. papas fritas / zanahorias
3. dulces / pasas *(raisins)*
4. helado / manzanas o peras
5. galletas / bananas
6. torta / fruta y queso

H. Tu cumpleaños *(Your birthday).* Pregúntales a varios compañeros de clase lo que les pidieron a sus padres, amigos, etc. para su cumpleaños. Tienen que contestar con lo que verdaderamente recibieron.

■ **Modelo:** ¿Qué les pediste a tus padres para tu cumpleaños?
         Les pedí una bicleta nueva, pero me dieron un estéreo.

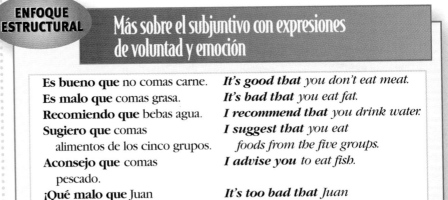

ENFOQUE ESTRUCTURAL

Más sobre el subjuntivo con expresiones de voluntad y emoción

Es bueno que no comas carne.	***It's good that*** *you don't eat meat.*
Es malo que comas grasa.	***It's bad that*** *you eat fat.*
Recomiendo que bebas agua.	***I recommend that*** *you drink water.*
Sugiero que comas alimentos de los cinco grupos.	***I suggest that*** *you eat foods from the five groups.*
Aconsejo que comas pescado.	***I advise you*** *to eat fish.*
¡Qué malo que Juan esté enfermo!	***It's too bad that*** *Juan is sick!*

In Chapters 6 and 7 you were introduced the use of the subjunctive with expressions that convey a feeling of necessity, desire, and emotion. Remember that when these expressions are part of the main clause of the sentence, the subjunctive is required in the second part, that is the part of the sentence introduced by **que**.

Here are a few more expressions that convey these feelings of necessity, desire, and emotion.

es bueno que...	*it's good that* …
es malo que...	*it's bad that* …
¡qué malo que...!	*too bad that* …!

GRAMMAR NOTE:
Other expressions requiring the subjunctive that you saw in Chapters 6 and 7 are:

querer que...
necesitar que...
sentir (ie) que...
alegrarse (de) que...
¡qué bueno que...!
¡qué lástima que...!
¡qué pena que...!
es necesario que...

Práctica

I. Recomiendo... Dales consejos *(Give advice)* a las personas indicadas. Sigue el modelo.

◼ **Modelo:**   Marta / beber agua
  Recomiendo que Marta beba agua.

1. Juan / tomar una aspirina
2. tú / ir a médico
3. nosotros / no comer carne
4. ellos / dormir 8 horas
5. Marta / descansar más
6. tú / beber jugo
7. Felipe / hacer ejercicio
8. ellas / comer pescado
9. Ud. / ir a la farmacia
10. tú / comprar unas pastillas

J. Aconsejo... Ordena las siguientes actividades cronológicamente. Usa las expresiones **primero, después** y **finalmente** para establecer el orden. Sigue el modelo.

◼ **Modelo:**   tú / desayunarse / lavarse los dientes / ducharse
  Primero aconsejo que te duches.
  Después aconsejo que te desayunes.
  Finalmente aconsejo que te laves los dientes.

1. Juan / acostarse / dormirse / bañarse
2. tú / desayunarse / lavarse los dientes / levantarse
3. ella / maquillarse / peinarse / vestirse
4. Ud. / quitarse la ropa / acostarse / ducharse
5. ellos / afeitarse / ducharse / peinarse
6. nosotros / despertarse / levantarse / ducharse

K. Es malo... es bueno... es aconsejable. Quieres preparar una dieta ideal para un grupo de atletas. Repasa las comidas de los cinco grupos en la página 298. Con un(a) compañero(a) haz una lista de recomendaciones sobre lo que es malo, es bueno y es aconsejable que coman.

Answers, Ex. I:
1. Recomiendo que Juan tome una aspirina. 2. Recomiendo que tú vayas al médico. 3. Recomiendo que nosotros no comamos carne. 4. Recomiendo que ellos duerman 8 horas. 5. Recomiendo que Marta descanse más. 6. Recomiendo que tú bebas jugo. 7. Recomiendo que Felipe haga ejercicio. 8. Recomiendo que ellas coman pescado. 9. Recomiendo que Ud. vaya a la farmacia. 10. Recomiendo que tú compres unas pastillas.

Answers, Ex. J:
1. Aconsejo que Juan se bañe, se acueste, se duerme. 2. que te levantes, te desayunes, te laves los dientes. 3. que ella se peine, se maquille, se vista 4. que Ud. se quite la ropa, se duche, se acueste. 5. que ellos se duchen, se afeiten, se peinen. 6. que nosotros nos despertamos, nos duchemos.

Ex. K:  Pairs

Comentarios

culturales *Metros y kilos*

*E*n el mundo hispano para expresar **lo que uno mide** *(how tall one is)* y **pesa** *(how much one weighs)* se usa el sistema métrico, o sea se expresa en metros y kilos.

Un metro es igual a 3,28 **pies** *(feet)*, más o menos 39 **pulgadas** *(inches)*. Una pulgada equivale a 2,5 centímetros. Para convertir lo que mides al sistema métrico, multiplica lo que mides en pulgadas por 2,5. Por ejemplo, si mides 5 pies y 8 pulgadas, multiplica 68 pulgadas por 2,5. El resultado es 170 centímetros. Cien centímetros equivalen a un metro y la manera más común para expresar esto es un metro y setenta centímetros. Así que para expresar cuánto mides, dices: mido un metro setenta.

Un kilogramo es igual a 2,2 **libras** *(pounds)*. Para convertir libras en kilos, divide **tu peso** *(your weight)* en libras por 2,2. Por ejemplo, si pesas 145 libras, divides 145 por 2,2. El resultado es 65,9

INTEGRACIÓN CULTURAL

1. ¿Cuánto mides usando el sistema métrico?
2. ¿Cuánto pesas usando el sistema métrico?
3. ¿Cuánto miden algunos baloncelistas famosos?
4. ¿Cuánto pesan algunos futbolistas famosos?

Héctor y Felipe están conversando sobre lo que comen y cómo se mantienen en forma.

ANTES DE ESCUCHAR

Basándote en lo que has aprendido en esta *etapa*, qué información esperas escuchar en su conversación en cuanto a *(with regard to)*:

1. ¿cuánto miden?
2. ¿cuánto pesan?
3. ¿qué comen?
4. ¿qué no comen?

Antes de escuchar la conversación, repasa las preguntas que aparecen en la sección *Después de escuchar.*

DESPUÉS DE ESCUCHAR

L. Comprensión. Contesta las siguientes preguntas después de escuchar la conversación entre Felipe y Carlos.

1. ¿Cuánto mide Felipe?
2. ¿Cuánto pesa?
3. ¿Cómo guarda la línea?
4. ¿Qué tipo de comidas preparan?

Answers, Ex. L
1. un metro setenta y ocho 2. setenta y dos kilos 3. hace gimnasia y come bien 4. comidas estupendas, balanceadas

M. ¿Cómo lo dicen? Escucha la conversación otra vez y contesta las siguientes preguntas.

1. ¿Cómo expresa Felipe "how tall he is" en español?
2. ¿Cómo dice "he exercises" en español?

Answers, Ex. M
1. mido un metro setenta y ocho.
2. Hago gimnasia

Tú dirás ....

N. Costumbres alimenticias. Tú estás llevando a cabo una encuesta *(questionnaire)* sobre las costumbres alimenticias y la salud en general de tus compañeros de clase. Primero, pregúntales acerca de *(about)* sus costumbres alimenticias y cómo se sienten en general. Luego, pregúntales sobre qué tipos de ejercicio hacen. Finalmente, recomiéndales una dieta nueva y un régimen de ejercicio.

Ex. N:  Group of 3
Expand this exercise into a discussion of the "typical college student" diet.

Ñ. La dieta ideal. En grupos de cuatro, diseñen un folleto *(brochure)* sobre la salud. Incluyan consejos sobre las comidas que hay que comer para cada día de la semana: desayuno, almuerzo y cena. Den sugerencias sobre un programa de ejercicio y sobre cómo mantener la buena salud.

Ex. Ñ: Group of 4

Lectura: Balada de los dos abuelos

Nicolás Guillén

En Cuba, la República Dominicana, Puerto Rico y las costas caribeñas de Panamá, Venezuela y Colombia existe una fuerte influencia africana. Nicolás Guillén, un poeta cubano, es famoso por la musicalidad de sus versos así como por la protesta que expresa contra la opresión y la desigualdad. Los versos de su poema la "Balada de los dos abuelos" demuestran que Guillén es muy consciente de la presencia africana en América. El poema que sigue representa el espíritu africano en la formación de la multiplicidad étnica de América.

ANTES DE LEER

A. Antes de leer el poema, mira el mapa que aparece al final del libro y localiza los países que se mencionan arriba.

B. ¿Qué crees que significa el título del poema?

C. Lee el poema rápidamente y busca dos nombres propios. ¿A quién crees que se refieren?

GUÍA PARA LA LECTURA

D. Vocabulario. Identifica en el poema de Guillén las siguientes palabras. Después lee las definiciones de la columna de la derecha. Decide qué definición corresponde a cada palabra.

1.	Línea 1	sombra	a. animal con cola larga que vive en los árboles
2.	Línea 4	tambor	b. el comienzo del día
3.	Línea 7	armadura	c. bosque de gran extensión
4.	Línea 9	selva	d. fruto de un tipo de palma
5.	Línea 13	caimán	e. cuerda que se usa para golpear o castigar
6.	Línea 14	coco	f. proyección oscura de un cuerpo
7.	Línea 28	mono	g. reptil parecido al cocodrilo
8.	Línea 32	látigo	h. instrumento musical de percusión
9.	Línea 33	llanto	i. pieza protectora hecha de acero
10.	Línea 35	madrugada	j. efusión de lágrimas

E. Ahora lee el poema varias veces (en voz alta si quieres). Luego contesta las siguientes preguntas.

1. En las líneas 1–2 y 41–42, ¿quiénes acompañan al poeta siempre?
2. En las líneas 1–2 y 41–42, ¿con qué compara el poeta a las dos personas?
3. En las líneas 3 a 8, ¿cuál es la diferencia entre los dos hombres?
4. En las líneas 10 a 29, ¿qué repite cada hombre varias veces?
5. En las líneas 40 a 50, ¿qué nombres les da el poeta a los dos hombres?
6. En las líneas 45 a 55, ¿qué hacen los dos hombres?
7. En las líneas 50 a 60, ¿por qué crees que dice el poeta que los dos hombres son del mismo tamaño?

F. La forma y el estilo.

Escoge la respuesta más apropiada sobre la forma y el estilo del poema.

1. La rima general de los versos depende más que nada de los sonidos de _____.
   a. las vocales **i** y **e**
   b. las vocales **a** y **o**
   c. las vocales **e** y **u**

2. Los signos de exclamación en varios de los versos sirven para expresar _____.
   a. cierta paz interior
   b. una actitud imparcial
   c. la fuerte pasión

3. La repetición es una técnica que Guillén usa para _____.
   a. enfatizar imágenes y sonidos
   b. complicar el poema
   c. enseñar vocabulario

4. Según el tono general del poema, la actitud del narrador es _____.
   a. nerviosa y contradictoria
   b. apasionada y orgullosa
   c. intelectual y contemplativa

5. Por lo general, el vocabulario que el poeta usa es _____.
   a. concreto y descriptivo
   b. refinado y abstracto
   c. objetivo y filosófico

BALADA DE LOS DOS ABUELOS

POR NICOLÁS GUILLÉN

Left-margin glosses:

- shadows
- escort, accompany
- bone
- drum
- throat piece of
- suit of armor
- jungles
- thick, muted gongs
- dark water / alligators
- coconuts
- sails / bitter
- burning
- glass beads
- embossed
- hoop, ring
- monkeys
- How many . . .

Right-margin glosses:

- shining
- whip / slavedriver
- weeping
- half open
- dawns
- dusks / sugar mill
- shattering
- father or grandfather (colloquial)
- combine, mix, bring together
- sigh
- lift up, raise
- size
- stars
- intense desire

Sombras que sólo yo veo,
me **escoltan** mis dos abuelos.
Lanza con punta de **hueso,**
tambor de cuero y madera:
5 mi abuelo negro.
Gorguera en el cuello ancho,
gris **armadura** guerrera:
mi abuelo blanco.
África de **selvas** húmedas
10 y de **gordos gongos sordos...**
—¡Me muero!
(Dice mi abuelo negro.)
Aguaprieta de **caimanes,**
verdes mañanas de **cocos...**
15 —¡Me canso!
(Dice mi abuelo blanco.)
Oh **velas** de **amargo** viento,
galeón **ardiendo** en oro...
—¡Me muero!
20 (Dice mi abuelo negro.)
Oh costas de cuello virgen
engañadas de **abalorios...**
—¡Me canso!
(Dice mi abuelo blanco.)
25 ¡Oh puro sol **repujado,**
preso en **el aro** del trópico;
oh luna redonda y limpia
sobre el sueño de los **monos!**
¡Qué de barcos, qué de barcos!
30 ¡Qué de negros, qué de negros!

¡Qué largo **fulgor** de cañas!
¡Qué **látigo** el del **negrero!**
Piedra de **llanto** y de sangre,
venas y ojos **entreabiertos,**
35 y **madrugadas** vacías,
y **atardeceres** de **ingenio,**
y una gran voz, fuerte voz
despedazando el silencio.
¡Qué de barcos, qué de barcos,
40 qué de negros!
Sombras que sólo yo veo,
me escoltan mis dos abuelos.
Don Federico me grita,
y **Taita** Facundo calla;
45 los dos en la noche sueñan,
y andan, andan.
Yo los **junto.**
—¡Federico!
¡Facundo! Los dos se abrazan.
50 Los dos **suspiran.** Los dos
las fuertes cabezas **alzan;**
los dos del mismo **tamaño,**
bajo las **estrellas** altas;
los dos del mismo tamaño,
55 **ansia** negra y ansia blanca,
los dos del mismo tamaño
gritan, sueñan, lloran, cantan.
Sueñan, lloran, cantan.
Lloran, cantan.
60 ¡Cantan!

VÍDEO CULTURAL: ¿Cómo te sientes?

A. Anticipación. Marca si es probable oír esta información en un segmento sobre la salud. Si es probable, márcala con una **X**; si no es probable, márcala con una **O**. Después de terminar, compara tus respuestas con las de un(a) compañero(a) de clase.

1. _____ Que Pati tomó pastillas en la escuela.
2. _____ Que la temperatura bajó a 30° anoche.
3. _____ Que estudió mucho para el examen de español.
4. _____ Que mira mucha televisión.
5. _____ Que fue de compras con su madre.
6. _____ Que Pati comió algo malo en la cafetería.
7. _____ Que la familia tiene alergias.
8. _____ Que no le gusta la directora de la escuela.

B. Preparación. Ahora, usa las palabras o frases siguientes que vienen de la sección *Vocabulario esencial* del video. Después de terminar, compara tus frases con las de un(a) compañero(a) de clase. Luego, practiquen juntos la pronunciación de las palabras y frases.

1. pediatra
2. duérmete
3. el consultorio
4. abre grande
5. fiebre
6. 39 grados de temperatura
7. respira hondo
8. recoger

C. Participación. Toma notas mientras miras el vídeo. Más tarde, organiza la información en orden secuencial.

La directora dice:
Laura le dice al médico:
El médico les dice a Laura y a Pati:

D. Comprensión. Acabas de ver el segmento acerca de la salud. Ahora, contesta las preguntas siguientes.

1. ¿Qué le pasó a Patricia?
   a. No se siente bien y tiene fiebre.
   b. Se rompió los dedos.

2. ¿Cuáles son los síntomas?
   a. Le duelen el pecho y la garganta.
   b. Le duelen el estómago y la cabeza.

3. ¿Qué otros síntomas tiene la niña?
   a. Tiene 39° de temperatura.
   b. Tiene un problema respiratorio.

E. Personalización. Describe qué pasó en alguna ocasión en que no te sentías bien. Incluye los detalles en orden secuencial: los primeros síntomas, cómo te sentías, si fuiste o no al médico, los medicamentos que tomaste para curarte, etc.

Writing activities for this chapter are presented in the Activities Manual. For specific references to tasks supported by *Atajo*, please consult the Activities Manual.

Answers, EX. D
1. a   2. b   3. a

▷*Intercambio: Partes del cuerpo*

Con un(a) compañero(a), completa el crucigrama en esta página y en la página 311 usando palabras para las diferentes partes del cuerpo humano.

Van a necesitar las siguientes expresiones:

> **Es la parte que está…**
>
> **Sirve para…**
>
> **Tiene…**

Estudiante A

En este crucigrama tienes la parte horizontal pero faltan las respuestas para la parte vertical.

Tu compañero(a) va a describir, sin mencionar la palabra, las partes del cuerpo que aparecen en su crucigrama y tú tienes que escuchar atentamente y adivinar la parte del cuerpo que está describiendo.

Tu compañero(a) va a empezar describiendo el número 1 vertical. Cuando descubras la respuesta, tú sigues describiendo el número 1 horizontal.

Estudiante B

En este crucigrama tienes la parte vertical pero faltan las respuestas para la parte horizontal.

Tu compañero(a) va a describir, sin mencionar la palabra, las partes del cuerpo que aparecen en su crucigrama y tú tienes que escuchar atentamente y adivinar la parte del cuerpo que está describiendo.

Tú vas a empezar describiendo el número 1 vertical. Cuando tu compañero(a) descubra la respuesta, le toca a él (ella) describir el número 1 horizontal.

Vocabulario

Para charlar *Talking about your physical state*

bajar de peso *to lose weight*

caerse *to fall*

cortarse *to cut*

guardar la línea *to watch one's weight*

lastimarse *to hurt*

mantenerse en condiciones óptimas *to stay in top condition*

ponerse en forma *to get in shape*

romperse *to break*

(no)sentirse bien (mal) *(not) to feel good (bad)*

tener dolor de... *to have a ... ache*

tener un accidente *to have an accident*

torcerse *to sprain*

Para hablar del estado físico de otra persona *Talking about the physical state of another person*

¿Cómo te sientes? *How do you feel?*

¿Te sientes bien (mal)? *Do you feel good (bad)?*

No te ves muy bien. *You don't look very well.*

¿Estás en forma? *Are you in shape?*

¿Qué te pasa? *What's the matter with you?*

¿Qué te pasó? *What happened to you?*

¿Te lastimaste? *Did you hurt yourself?*

¿Tuviste algún accidente? *Did you have an accident?*

Para describir los síntomas *Describing symptoms*

Estornudo. *I sneeze.*

No puedo dormir. *I can't sleep.*

Me duele(n). *It hurts.*

Tengo una alergia. *I have an allergy.*

  un catarro *a cold*

  un dolor de cabeza *a headache*

         espalda *a backache*

         estómago *a stomachache*

Tengo escalofríos. *I have chills.*

    fiebre *a fever*

    la gripe *the flu*

    una infección *an infection*

    tos *a cough*

    un virus *a virus*

Toso. *I cough.*

Para comprar medicina en la farmacia *Buying medicine at the drugstore*

Necesito... (remedio) *I need ... (remedy)*

Necesito algo para... (parte del cuerpo) *I need something for ... (part of body)*

Necesito alguna cosa para... (parte del cuerpo) *I need something for ... (part of body)*

Para hablar de actividades habituales *Talking about habitual activities*

a menudo *often*

a veces *sometimes*

cada día (viernes, sábado, tarde, mañana, noche, semana, mes, etc.) *every day (Friday, Saturday, afternoon, morning, night, week, month, etc.)*

con frecuencia *frequently*

con regularidad *regularly*

de repente *suddenly*

de vez en cuando *from time to time*

muchas veces *many times*

todos los días *siempre*

Temas y contextos

El cuerpo *The body*

la boca *mouth*

el brazo *arm*

la cabeza *head*

la cara *face*

el codo *elbow*

el corazón *heart*

el cuello *neck*

el dedo (de la mano) *finger*

el dedo del pie *toe*

el diente *tooth*

la espalda *back*

el estómago *stomach*

la frente *forehead*

la garganta *throat*

el hombro *shoulder*

la mano *hand*

la muñeca *wrist*

el muslo *thigh*

la nariz *nose*

el ojo *eye*
la oreja *ear*
el pecho *chest*
el pelo *hair*
el pie *foot*
la pierna *leg*
el pulmón *lung*
la rodilla *knee*
el tobillo *ankle*

Los remedios *Remedies*
un antibiótico *antibiotic*
un antihistamínico *antihistamine*
una aspirina *aspirin*
unas gotas para los ojos *eye drops*
un jarabe *syrup*
unas pastillas *pills*

Los alimentos *Foods*

el almidón *starch*
el calcio *calcium*
el cereal *cereal*
la fibra *fiber*
la fruta *fruit*
la grasa *fat*
el hierro *iron*
la leche *milk*
los lípidos *lipids*
los minerales *minerals*
el pan *bread*
las papas *potatoes*
los productos lácteos *dairy products*
la proteína *protein*
los vegetales *vegetables*
las vitaminas *vitamins*

Vocabulario general   General vocabulary

Adverbios
normalmente *normally*
verdaderamente *truly*
constantemente *constantly*
aparentemente *apparently*
exactamente *exactly*

Verbos reflexivos
acostarse *to go to bed*
afeitarse *to shave*
cepillarse (el pelo, los dientes) *to brush (one's hair, teeth)*
cortarse *to cut*
desayunarse *to eat breakfast*
despertarse (ie) *to wake up*
divertirse (ie, i) *to have a good time*
dormirse (ue, u) *to fall asleep*
ducharse *to take a shower*
lastimarse *to hurt*
lavarse (las manos, el pelo) *to wash (one's hands, hair)*
los dientes *to brush (one's teeth)*
levantarse *to get up*
maquillarse *to put on make-up*
peinarse *to comb one's hair*
ponerse *to put on (clothes)*
quedarse *to stay, remain*
romperse *to break*

sentarse (ie) *to sit down*
torcerse *to twist, sprain*
vestirse (i) *to get dressed*

Expresiones que requieren el subjuntivo
es bueno *it's good*
es malo *it's bad*
es mejor *it's better*
es necesario *it's necessary*
es aconsejable *it's advisable*
¡qué malo! *too bad!*

Sustantivos
un artículo *article*
un(a) bebé *baby*
unas calorías *calories*
una causa *cause*
una dificultad *difficulty*
la digestión *digestion*
una duda *doubt*
la energía *energy*
una epidemia *epidemic*
una frontera *border*
un hueso *bone*
una indicación *indication*
un microbio *microbe*
un movimiento muscular *muscle movement*

un músculo *muscle*
un nervio *nerve*
un punto *point*
un resultado *result*
el ritmo cardíaco *heart rate*
la salud *health*
una señal *signal, sign*
el tono muscular *muscle tone*
la visión nocturna *night vision*

Adjetivos
adicional *additional*
anual *annual*
balanceado(a) *balanced*
preocupado(a) *worried, preoccupied*

Verbos
admitir *to admit*
desarrollar *to develop*
facilitar *to facilitate*
formar *to form*
mejorar *to improve*
presentar *to present, introduce*
recuperar *to recuperate*
regular *to regulate*
renovar *to renew*
tratar de *to try to*

9 los estudios en el extranjero

PRIMERA ETAPA
Un programa de intercambio

SEGUNDA ETAPA
Un par de días
en un hotel

TERCERA ETAPA
¿Buscas apartamento?

INTEGRACIÓN:
LECTURA: Las pintorescas
carretas de Sarchí
VÍDEO CULTURAL: Buscamos un hotel
INTERCAMBIO: ¿Tienen habitaciones?
ESCRITURA: Actividades en el manual

Costa
Rica
carreta

Entrada al
Teatro Nacional
en Costa Rica

Estudiantes de la Universidad de Costa Rica en San José

COSTA RICA

Población: 3.463.083

51.000 kilómetros cuadrados (19.730 millas cuadradas), un poco más pequeño que West Virginia

Capital: San José, 922.000

Ciudades principales: Cartago, Heredia, Limón, Alajuela, Puntarenas, Guanacaste

CHAPTER OBJECTIVES:

In this chapter you will learn about study- abroad programs and how to make short- and long-term living arrangements in a Spanish-speaking country.

After completing this chapter you should be able to carry out the following tasks:

- ⊚ **determine which aspects of a study-abroad program are most interesting to you**

- ⊚ **make short- and long-term living arrangements**

- ⊚ **request and provide information that is necessary when you live and study in a different country**

- ⊚ **communicate with others about past activities and events**

The tools you will use to carry out these tasks are:

- ⊚ **vocabulary for:**
    - study-abroad programs: classes, activities, etc.
    - the 24-hour clock: official schedules
    - finding a room in a hotel
    - renting an apartment

- ⊚ **grammatical structures:**
    - the preterite of **dormir, salir, llegar**
    - imperfect tense: describing the past (review)
    - integrating past tenses: preterite and imperfect

 Moneda: colón

 **Esperanza de vida:
hombres, 73; mujeres, 78**

 Índice de alfabetización: 95%

Televisores: 1 para cada 9,6 personas

 Radios: 1 para cada 4,3 personas

 Teléfonos: 1 para cada 8,8 personas

 Principales productos de exportación: café, bananas, ganado y carne, caña de azúcar

Embajada: 1825 Connecticut Ave. NW, Washington, DC 20009

PARA EMPEZAR: Un programa de intercambio

Preparación

- Do you want to study abroad? In what country? What do you plan to study there?
- Do you know some student who is studying in another country? Do you think it's important to live outside your own country for a while?
- Does your college or university have study-abroad programs? In what countries? What types of programs?

Práctica

A. La Universidad de Costa Rica

1. Mira el folleto sobre la Universidad de Costa Rica. ¿Qué tipo de información crees que contiene?
2. ¿Puedes anticipar el contenido de la sección "De interés académico"?
3. ¿Qué información crees que hay en la sección "De interés extra-académico"?
4. Después de leer el folleto, ¿pudiste anticipar el contenido? Resume brevemente la información.

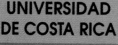

La Universidad de Costa Rica

De interés académico

Los antecedentes históricos de la Universidad de Costa Rica remontan al año 1843 cuando se abrió la Universidad de Santo Tomás, convertida en 1940 en la actual institución autónoma situada en la ciudad capital de San José. Dedicada a la formación espiritual y profesional de los ciudadanos, la universidad también ofrece un programa de intercambio internacional. Grupos numerosos de estudiantes norteamericanos y europeos se integran por unos meses a la universidad, como estudiantes visitantes. Hay una amplia diversidad de cursos y de opciones perso-

nalizadas que cada estudiante puede elegir para iniciarse o progresar en el aprendizaje del español y en el desarrollo de su conocimiento de las sociedades iberoamericanas. El número reducido de estudiantes por aula en las clases de lengua permite la participación activa del alumno en español.

De interés extra-académico

Fuera del ámbito estrictamente académico, la universidad sirve de base también al desarrollo continuo de extensas y atractivas actividades culturales que incluyen teatro, danza, conciertos, programación de películas y otros espectáculos. Hay actividades deportivas programadas en nuestros tres gimnasios de multiuso, un área de natación con dos piscinas y áreas de tenis, fútbol, baloncesto y atletismo al aire libre. Los estudiantes pueden, por lo demás, participar en excursiones a montañas y selvas de extraordinaria belleza para conocer los diferentes sistemas ecológicos de Costa Rica.

B. Una escuela de lengua española

1. ¿Te interesa la idea de estudiar español todos los días? ¿Por qué sí o por qué no?
2. ¿Para quiénes crees que son los cursos de español que ofrece esta escuela?
3. Mira el folleto del Centro Lingüístico Conversa. ¿Qué tipo de información crees que contiene?
4. Después de leer, ¿coincide el contenido con lo que anticipaste? Indica qué partes.

El idioma:

EL ESPAÑOL

El país:

COSTA RICA

La escuela:

CONVERSA

El programa de español
más intensivo de Costa Rica

Desde su fundación en San José, Costa Rica, en 1974, en el Centro Lingüístico Conversa nos hemos dedicado a la enseñanza del español y del inglés, ambos como lenguas extranjeras. Ofrecemos una amplia gama de cursos de español para estudiantes provenientes de universidades norteamericanas. Recomendamos que el estudiante participe en una jornada de estudio de cuatro semanas con cuatro horas diarias de clase, pero es posible elegir programas más breves o más largos. En Conversa se forman grupos homogéneos que no superan los cuatro miembros. Éstos cuentan cada semana con un nuevo instructor que es experto en combinar la conversación con la gramática para ajustarse a las necesidades individuales de los miembros del grupo.

En 1980 adquirimos un campus de seis acres cerca de la ciudad de San José para nuestro programa de español de alta intensidad. Rodeado de montañas y árboles frutales, este campus en Santa Ana cuenta con

veinte aulas, un comedor, un albergue, muchas hamacas e instalaciones deportivas con una piscina de catorce metros de largo, una cancha de vóli-bol, una de baloncesto y una cancha de tenis con muro para practicar pre-botes individualmente. También es posible vivir en el pueblo con una familia anfitriona.

A medida que el estudiante se adentra en una jornada de estudio en Conversa, el español cobra una nueva dimensión: ya no es sólo un ejercicio académico, sino más bien un instrumento que le facilita la comunicación con los demás.

C. ¿Quieres estudiar en la Universidad de Costa Rica? Después de leer los folletos otra vez, ya tienes suficiente información sobre el programa. Menciona una serie de razones por las que un estudiante como tú puede elegir la Universidad de Costa Rica para estudiar allí. Incluye información relacionada con los cursos, el número de estudiantes en las clases, las actividades extra-académicas, la situación geográfica, el ambiente, etc.

D. De interés especial. Pregúntale a otro(a) estudiante de tu clase qué ventajas *(advantages)* ofrece el programa del Centro Lingüístico Conversa. Comparen estas ventajas con las de la universidad. Después, dile qué programa prefieres tú, indicando qué aspectos son de interés especial para ti.

■ **Modelo:** *De interés especial para mí son las excursiones, las fiestas,* etc.
Prefiero el programa de... porque... etc.

ENFOQUE LÉXICO — La hora oficial

You have already learned the conversational method of telling time in Spanish. The basic differences between the two methods are:

Conversational time	Official time
• Is based on a 12-hour clock	• Is based on the 24-hour clock (0 = midnight, 12 = noon)
• Divides the hour into two 30 minute segments (after and before the hour)	• Treats the hour as a 60-minute whole (that is, only moves forward)
• Uses **y cuarto, y media, menos cuarto, media, noche, mediodía**	• Uses only cardinal numbers: **y quince, y treinta, y cuarenta y cinco, veinte y cuatro horas, doce horas**

The easiest way to switch from official time to conversational time is to *subtract* twelve from the hour of official time unless the hour is already less than twelve.

Conversational time		Official time	
9:45 A.M.	las diez menos cuarto	9:45	nueve horas y cuarenta y cinco
12:30 P.M.	las doce y media	12:30	doce horas y treinta
2:50 P.M.	las tres menos diez	14:50	catorce horas y cincuenta
11:15 P.M.	las once y cuarto	23:15	veintitrés horas y quince

Práctica ·········

E. ¿A qué hora?

Eres un estudiante de intercambio durante un semestre en Costa Rica. Tienes un periódico con el calendario para los programas de la temporada en el Teatro Nacional en San José y quieres planear varias actividades con un(a) amigo(a). Selecciona al menos cuatro actividades posibles y apunta la fecha y la hora para cada una.

Calendario de actividades
Teatro Nacional

Fecha	Actividad	Hora
1–10 de agosto	Festival Internacional de Música Clásica	20:00
21, 22 y 24 de agosto	Concierto Paquito de Rivera Jazz con la Orquesta Sinfónica Nacional	21:00
11 de septiembre	Espectáculo Compañía Nacional de Danza y Orquesta Sinfónica Nacional	16:00
18–21 de septiembre	Danza Universitaria de la Universidad de Costa Rica	19:30
23 y 24 de septiembre	Mercedes Sosa Concierto	20:30
25 de septiembre	Espectáculo "Carnaval de los Animales" del mimo israelí Eno Rossen	17:00
18 de octubre	Espectáculo Els Comedians, Barcelona, España	17:00
24 y 26 de octubre	Concierto Orquesta Sinfónica Nacional	20:00
13, 14 y 16 de noviembre	Espectáculo "Amor Brujo", de Manuel de Falla, con la Orquesta Sinfónica Nacional	21:00
15 de noviembre	Concierto de Piano, Scarlett Brebion	14:00
19, 20 de noviembre	Escuela de Ballet Clásico Ruso	20:30

Answers, Ex. F
1. F 2. V 3. F 4. V 5. F 6. V)

F. Horarios de avión. En clase, conociste a José Luis Méndez, un estudiante de intercambio de Costa Rica. Estás considerando la posibilidad de pasar una semana en Costa Rica durante las vacaciones de Semana Santa *(Easter)*. Cada semana Lacsa, (Líneas Aereas Costarricenses) y Continental Airlines tienen varios vuelos de Miami a San José, Costa Rica. Mira los horarios a continuación e indica si las siguientes afirmaciones son verdaderas o falsas.

San José–Miami–Salidas del Aeropuerto Internacional Juan Santamaría

Día	Vuelo	Salida	Llegada
martes	Lacsa 831	8:15	1:15
jueves	Continental 29	18:30	23:30
sábado	Continental 37	10:45	15:45
domingo	Lacsa 867	16:00	21:00

Miami–San José–Llegadas al Aeropuerto Internacional Juan Santamaría

lunes	Lacsa 868	13:30	18:30
miércoles	Lacsa 832	6:15	11:15
viernes	Continental 30	12:40	17:55
domingo	Continental 38	17:15	22:30

¿Verdadero o Falso?

1. Los lunes el avión de Lacsa llega a San José a las cinco menos cinco.
2. Los martes el vuelo de Lacsa sale de San José a las ocho y cuarto.
3. Los domingos el avión de Continental sale de Miami a las cinco de la tarde.
4. Los jueves el vuelo de Continental sale de San José a las seis y media de la tarde.
5. Los miércoles el avión de Lacsa llega a San José a las diez.
6. El vuelo generalmente es de cinco horas.

Answers, Ex. G
1. el de las 18:00 2. a las 13:00
3. no 4. sí 5. a las 20:30 ó antes

G. Una pequeña prueba. Para practicar cómo se usa el tiempo oficial, Jorge Luis te hace las siguientes preguntas.

1. El avión de Atlanta a Miami tarda una hora en llegar. Quieres estar en Miami a las 8:00 de la noche. ¿Vas a tomar el avión de las 18:00 o el de las 20:00?
2. Quieres ir al cine pero tienes que volver a casa antes de las 6:00 de la tarde. La película dura dos horas y comienza a las 13:00, 16:00, 19:00 y 22:00. ¿A qué hora vas a poder ir al cine?
3. Hay un programa de televisión a las 22:30. Normalmente te acuestas a las 10:00 de la noche y te levantas a las 6:00 de la mañana. ¿Vas a poder mirar el programa?
4. Vas a la estación de trenes para recoger *(to pick up)* a tus padres. El tren llega de Nueva York a las 17:30. Llegas a la estación a las 4:30 de la tarde. ¿Llegaste a tiempo?
5. Invitaste a un(a) amigo(a) a un concierto. El concierto comienza a las 21:00. Se tarda media hora en ir de tu apartamento al concierto. ¿A qué hora tiene que llegar tu amigo a tu apartamento?

Comentarios
culturales

Parque Nacional Volcán Poás

$\mathcal{E}$l Servicio de Parques Nacionales de Costa Rica administra veintinueve áreas silvestres entre parques nacionales y otras reservas. Estas áreas cubren 425.329 hectáreas, *(1 hectárea = 2,5 acers)* lo que equivale a ocho por ciento del territorio nacional. El principal objetivo del Servicio de Parques Nacionales es preservar áreas naturales para beneficio y disfrute de las generaciones futuras.

En el Parque Nacional Volcán Poás está uno de los volcanes más espectaculares del país. Es de extraordinaria belleza escénica. Posee varios tipos de hábitats y en algunos abundan las plantas tropicales como helechos, bromelias y orquídeas. También es una región de gran interés geológico y es importante porque en este volcán nacen varios ríos que alimentan a otros que dan origen a las cuencas del río Grande Tárcoles y el río Sarapiquí.

INTEGRACIÓN CULTURAL

1. ¿Cuántas áreas silvestres administra el Servicio de Parques Nacionales?
2. ¿Por qué preservan las áreas naturales?
3. ¿Qué tipos de plantas abundan en los hábitats de este volcán?

ENFOQUE LÉXICO

Salir, llegar y dormir

In the context of this *etapa* you will talk about studying abroad. At this point it is useful to review the use of the past tense that allows you to talk about the time you left, arrived somewhere, how things went during your trip, and what you did. Studying abroad, meeting new friends, living with a family, and so on, will provide you with situations in which you may want to talk about how you spent your weekend, what you saw, who you met, when you left home and came back, etc.

Al llegar al aeropuerto de Costa Rica

¿Qué tal el viaje?
Ah, muy bien, sin problemas.
¿A qué hora **salió** el avión? Llega con **un poco de retraso,** (*a little late*) ¿no?
Bueno, sí, **salimos** de Miami a las once y cuarto.
¿Dormiste algo en el avión?
No, unos minutos.

Notice that during the exchange both friends are using the preterite to refer to past actions.

Preguntas y comentarios que puedes oír de la gente

¿A qué hora **saliste** de clase ayer?
Eh, no sé, creo que **salí** a las 4:00. Pero no **llegué** a casa hasta las 5:30.
¿A qué hora dices que **llegaste?**
A las 5:30.

Here are all the past tense forms of the verbs used in the preceding exchanges:

dormir			
yo	dormí	nosotros	dormimos
tú	dormiste	vosotros	dormisteis
Ud.		Uds.	
él	**durmió**	ellos	**durmieron**
ella		ellas	

The verb *dormir* in the preterite is irregular only in the third person singular and plural. Notice that in these forms, only the **o** of the stem changes to **u.**

A common expression with **dormir** is **dormir la siesta** (*to take a nap*).

Expresiones con **salir**

salir			
salí	salimos	**salir para**	*to leave for* (a place)
saliste	salisteis	**salir de**	*to leave from* (a place)
salió	salieron	**salir cono**	*go out with* (someone)
		salir bien/mal	*to turn out fine/badly*

Expresiones con **llegar**

llegar			
llegué	llegamos	**llegar a**	*to arrive at* (a place)
llegaste	llegasteis	**llegar de**	*to arrive from* (a place)
llegó	llegaron	**llegar tarde**	*to be late*
		llegar a tiempo	*to be on time*
		llegar con retraso	*to be delayed*

Práctica

H. Preguntas. Ya conoces a la familia de José Luis Méndez, tu amigo de Costa Rica. Después de dos días en su casa, ya te atreves a *(you dare to)* iniciar una conversación en español. Utilizando un elemento de cada columna, crea cinco posibles preguntas que les puedes hacer a José Luis o a otros miembros de su familia.

Quién	Qué	Cuándo
la madre de José Luis	salir	ayer
la hermana	llegar	el viernes
su padre	volver	el domingo
José Luis	dormir	esta tarde
los amigos de José Luis	ir	el fin de semana pasado

I. En el aeropuerto. Circula entre tus compañeros de clase, imaginando que todos están en el aeropuerto. Selecciona a cinco estudiantes y hazles preguntas similares a las del ejercicio H.

Patrick McGill es un estudiante norteamericano en su tercer año de universidad. Después de consultar los folletos de diferentes programas y universidades, decide ir a la Universidad de Costa Rica. Viaja a San José donde una familia costarricense lo recoge en el aeropuerto.

ANTES DE ESCUCHAR

Basándote en lo que has aprendido en esta *etapa*, contesta las siguientes preguntas.

1. ¿Cómo crees que la familia va a recibir a Patrick?
2. ¿Qué tipo de preguntas le pueden hacer?
3. ¿Adónde crees que va a ir primero?

Ahora lee las preguntas en la sección *Después de escuchar.*

DESPUÉS DE ESCUCHAR

J. Comprensión
1. ¿Cómo estaba Patrick al llegar?
2. ¿A qué hora salió de Nueva York?
3. ¿Qué sugirió la señora Álvarez que podía hacer Patrick al llegar a casa?
4. ¿Qué había en la habitación?

K. ¿Cómo lo dicen? Escucha la cinta otra vez para determinar lo siguiente.
1. ¿Cómo preguntó Pedro sobre el viaje?
2. ¿Cómo reaccionó Patrick cuando vió la habitación?

Suggestion, Ex. H: Expand activity into a role play where pairs of students role-play a conversation that might be typical in each of the situations.

Suggestion: Remind students that mechanical exercises to practice all forms of these verbs are included in the corresponding section of the workbook.

Ex. H: Pairs

Suggestion, Ex. H: Have students share what they find out about their classmates.

 Play Textbook audio.

Suggestion: Before listening to the tape, have students review vocabulary for furniture on Chapter 2. Pair students for this activity. Ask them to listen to the tape once without taking any notes. Then have students discuss what they heard and try to answer the comprehension questions. Have students listen a second time, this time allowing them to take notes if they wish. Review comprehension questions and answers. Finally, have students listen a third time, this time trying to answer the cómo lo dicen questions.

Suggestion: On a separate sheet of paper have students write the words and phrases below. Play the tape and have them put a checkmark next to the word each time they hear it: **Llegamos, dormir una siesta, dormí, es muy bonita, todos los sábados.**

Answers, Ex. J
1. un poco cansado 2. A las 6:00
3. dormir una siesta 4. cama, sillón, escritorio, estantes, lámpara

Answers, Ex. K
1. ¿Qué tal el viaje? 2. Oh, es muy bonita.

Ex. L: Pairs

Suggestion: Encourage students to bring in photos of an enjoyable trip they took. Put students in groups of 4 and have each group select the most evocative picture. The owner of the picture does not offer any information, but rather waits for students to ask him/her questions about the trip. After asking the owner 10 questions, the others construct a short paragraph describing the trip. At this time the owners change groups to work on the construction of stories about other pictures. Share stories and pictures with the class.

Tú dirás ....

L. Un viaje interesante. Habla con otro estudiante sobre un viaje interesante en el pasado. Incluye detalles desde que saliste de casa hasta que te levantaste por primera vez en otro país o estado. Incluye la siguiente información:

- time you left for the airport
- who took you there
- what happened on the plane
- time you arrived at your destination
- how you felt when meeting your host family/friends, relatives
- how you slept that first night in an unfamiliar room

M. Estudiantes de intercambio y familias anfitrionas *(host)*.
Trabajen en grupos de tres estudiantes para hacer el papel *(play the role)* de un estudiante y una pareja de anfitriones *(hosts)* en un programa de intercambio. Imaginen que se están conociendo por primera vez y hablen

- del viaje que acabas de hacer a su país,
- de tu familia y de la familia de los anfitriones,
- de la casa o el apartamento en que vas a vivir con ellos,
- y de algunos intereses personales (i.e., actividades, preferencias, hábitos), notando los que tienen en común.

Estos estudiantes se escriben en la Universidad de Costa Rica.

SEGUNDA ETAPA

PARA EMPEZAR: Un par de días en un hotel

Preparación: Antes de empezar a trabajar con esta *etapa*, contesta las siguientes preguntas.

- Do you like to travel?
- What types of trips interest you?
- When you travel, where do you prefer to stay?
- Do you like organized tours or do you prefer to travel on your own?
- What information do you need to prepare for your trip?
- What do you need to do to make a hotel reservation?

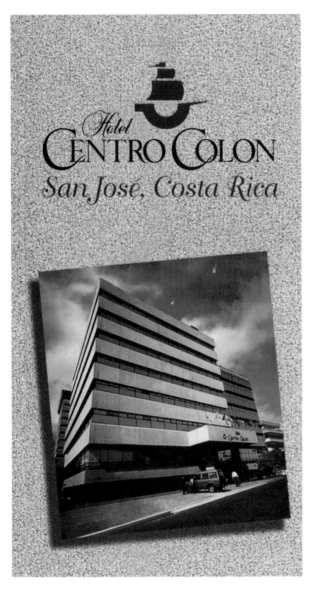

Hotel Centro Colón

En el corazón de la ciudad capital de San José, el Hotel Centro Colón es el lugar ideal para el viajero de negocios así como para quien busca el descanso y entretenimiento. A sólo quince minutos del aeropuerto, se encuentra estratégicamente ubicado como punto de partida para parques nacionales y playas. Nuestro mayor deseo es hacerlo sentir como en su casa. Estamos orgullosos de contar con un grupo de profesionales muy unidos para servirle.

Ficha técnica

- 124 habitaciones, incluyendo 42 suites (6 Junior suites y 1 Suite Presidencial)
- Todas las habitaciones están equipadas con aire acondicionado, teléfono directo, TV por cable, baño privado, **ducha/tina** *(shower / tub)*
- Habitaciones disponibles para no fumadores
- Salas para reuniones hasta para 65 personas, todas equipadas con modernos equipos audiovisuales
- Bar y casino
- Servicio de parqueo para nuestros huéspedes
- Vista a las montañas y la ciudad
- **Alquiler** *(rent)* de fax, computadoras y teléfonos portátiles
- Caja de seguridad

- Servicio despertador
- Servicio disponible para copiado y transmisiones vía fax
- Cambio de moneda en la recepción
- **Secadora** *(Dryer)* de pelo, **plancha** *(iron)* y planchados
- Tienda de regalos
- Disponibilidad de alquiler de carros y tours
- Servicio de Taxi
- Lavandería y **lavado en seco** *(dry cleaning)*

Hotel Centro Colón:
Phone: (506) 257-2580
Fax: (506) 257-2582
Sales fax: (506) 257-9650

Consult your travel agency

Práctica

A. Para servirle. Para familiarizarte con la información sobre los hoteles, mira el contenido del folleto y contesta las siguientes preguntas.

1. ¿Dónde está este hotel?
2. ¿Con qué están equipadas todas las habitaciones?
3. ¿Hay habitaciones disponibles para no fumadores?
4. ¿Qué vista tienen las habitaciones?
5. ¿Qué servicios le ofrecen al viajero de negocios?
6. ¿Hay bar y casino?
7. ¿Hay piscina?
8. Busca dos servicios más en la lista que no has mencionado.

B. Los hoteles de Costa Rica. Unos amigos españoles que conoces quieren ir de viaje a Costa Rica. Como saben que tienes una guía de hoteles, te llaman para pedirte información sobre unos hoteles allí. Contesta sus preguntas de acuerdo con la información que aparece en la guía abajo y en las páginas 325 y 327.

San José, Costa Rica

Hotel Kekoldi

Hotel Kekoldi, Barrio Amón, Avenida 9, calle 3 Bis, frente al INVU, a 200 metros norte del Parque Morazán. Reservaciones: Tel: (506) 223-3244, Fax: (506) 257-5476. Administración alemana, hablamos español, alemán e inglés. Histórico edificio renovado, atmósfera llena de color de las soleadas islas caribeñas. 20 habitaciones grandes con camas "King size", baño privado, teléfono y cajas de seguridad, también desayunos y servicio de lavandería. Le damos asistencia completa en servicio de tours.

PUERTO VIEJO
Magia entre mar y selva... El Caribe
Magic between sea and jungle... The Caribbean

PUERTO VIEJO , LIMON
COSTA RICA

Hotel Maritza, Puerto Viejo, Limón. Reservaciones: Tel./Fax (506) 750-0003. Es un hotel de familia con una larga tradición en la Costa Caribeña. Contamos con modernas habitaciones frente al mar, localizados en el centro de Puerto Viejo. A sólo 3 horas de San José. 14 habitaciones, baño privado con agua caliente, refrigeradora, **abanico** *(fan)* de techo, parqueo privado, buzón de correo, se aceptan tarjetas de crédito. Servicio de fax. Se habla inglés. Actividades: buceo en arrecife de coral, pesca en bote con motor, alquiler de bicicleta, paseo a caballo, paseo a la selva, Tour al Parque Nacional Cahuita, Reserva indígena de Talamanca, Aviarios del Caribe. No olvide que ofrecemos precios moderados.

> **VOCABULARY EXPANSION:**
> Besides **abanico** there is another word for "fan" in Spanish: **ventilador.**

1. ¿Qué hotel tiene más habitaciones?
2. ¿Qué hotel está cerca de la playa?
3. ¿En qué hotel se hablan tres idiomas?
4. ¿Qué hotel tiene habitaciones con refrigerador y abanico de techo?
5. ¿Qué hotel ofrece más variedad de actividades interesantes? ¿Cuáles son algunas de estas actividades?
6. ¿Qué hotel ofrece desayunos?
7. ¿En qué hotel hay parqueo privado?
8. ¿Qué hotel parece tener los precios más bajos?

Answers, Ex. B
1. Kekoldi, 20 habitaciones
2. Maritza 3. Kikoldi 4. Maritza
5. Maritza. Actividades: buceo en arrecife de coral, pesca en bote con motor, alquiler de bicicleta, paseo a caballo, paseo a la selva, Tour al Parque Nacional Cahuita, Reserva indígena de Talamanca, Aviarios del Caribe. 6. Kekoldi 7. Maritza
8. Maritza

Comentarios

culturales · Los albergues juveniles

Youth Hostels

Si viajas por el mundo hispano, una forma conveniente y económica de alojamiento son los albergues juveniles. Estos albergues están diseñados para acomodar a gente joven, sobre todo estudiantes, menores de 26 años. Las habitaciones son realmente baratas y también se puede comer por poco dinero. Como todos los lugares baratos, los albergues presentan algunos inconvenientes. En la mayoría de ellos se cierra la puerta a partir de una hora determinada (normalmente entre las 23:00 y las 24:00 horas). Por lo general, las personas que se alojan en estos lugares tienen que compartir la habitación con otros viajeros. Sin embargo, junto a los precios económicos, los albergues ofrecen al turista la posibilidad de conocer a personas de todas partes del mundo. Una de las mayores ventajas es, sin duda, la oportunidad de hacer nuevas amistades que pueden durar toda la vida.

La Red Costarricense de Albergues Juveniles dirige los hospedajes para jóvenes en todo el país. La central se encuentra en el Hospedaje Toruma en San José (Avenida Central, Calles 29/31).

Algunos albergues populares son:

Toruma, San José, tel. 224-4085, fax 224-4085, 95 camas

El Plástico, Sarapiquí, tel. 253-0844, fax 253-0844, 29 camas

Cabinas San Isidro, Puntarenas, tel. 221-1225, fax 221-6822, 260 camas.

Mar Paraíso, Jacó, tel. 221-6544, fax 221-6601, 70 camas

INTEGRACIÓN CULTURAL

1. ¿Cuál es la edad máxima que aceptan los albergues?
2. ¿Cuáles son algunos de los inconvenientes que presentan los albergues?
3. ¿En qué ciudades se encuentran los albergues más populares de Costa Rica?
4. ¿Cuál es el más grande? ¿Cuántas camas tiene?
5. ¿Cuál es el más pequeño? ¿Cuántas camas tiene?

Repaso

C. ¿Dormiste bien? Estás en San José con tus amigos. Por la mañana, durante el desayuno, ustedes tienen la siguiente conversación.

Estudiante A

Greet your friend.
Find out how he or she slept last night.
Say you went out last night and didn't get back until late.

Estudiante B

Respond to the greeting.
Answer the question.

Say you didn't leave the hotel and ask where your friend went.

Ex. C Allow students 4–5 minutes to practice, then select pairs to perform the role play for the class. Encourage students to be as creative as possible.

Encourage students to improvise, adding more details to the conversation.

D. La farmacéutica le dio la medicina... Hace seis meses que vives en Costa Rica como estudiante de intercambio. Durante los primeros meses después de llegar al país tú y tus amigos tuvieron que ir a la farmacia. Indica a quién le dio la farmacéutica cada remedio. Sigue el modelo.

▪ **Modelo:** el jarabe / Mario
  Le dio el jarabe a Mario.

1. la medicina / Laura
2. el jarabe / mis hermanos
3. el antihistamínico / Ud.
4. el antibiótico / yo
5. el jarabe / tú

6. la receta / la profesora
7. la aspirina / mi padre
8. las gotas para los ojos / tú
9. la medicina / mis padres
10. las pastillas / mis primos

ENFOQUE ESTRUCTURAL | **Más sobre el imperfecto**

IRM Master 38: El imperfecto—las descripciones

Al volver de San José

¿Qué tal el viaje?
Bien, muy bien.
¿Y el hotel?
Bueno, no **estaba** mal. **Era** un hotel barato pero bastante cómodo. **Tenía** piscina, teléfono y televisión en la habitación y ¡**costaba** sólo 8.000 colones la noche!
¡Oye! no está nada mal. **¿Había** mucha gente? Supongo que sí.
Sí, **estaba** lleno. ¡No **quedaba** ni una habitación libre!

Notice that during the exchange both friends are using the imperfect (**-aba, -ía,** and **era**) to describe the hotel.

To review, the imperfect is generally used in Spanish in four types of descriptions in the past:

1. **physical**   El hotel **era** cómodo.
2. **feelings**   Juan y yo **estábamos** contentos con la habitación.
3. **attitudes and beliefs** Yo **creía** que el hotel no **tenía** piscina.
4. **state of health**   Juan siempre **estaba** cansado.

GRAMMAR NOTE:
In Chapter 2 you learned the verb **hay** to express "there is," "there are." **Había,** imperfect of **haber,** means "there was," "there were."

Práctica

E. ¿Cómo era? Los folletos en la *Primera etapa* contienen información sobre una universidad y una escuela de lengua española. Trabaja con otro(a) estudiante y vuelvan a leer los textos en las páginas 316 y 317 para repasar su contenido, especialmente los verbos que se utilizan. Ahora uno(a) de ustedes describe cómo era el programa de la Universidad de Costa Rica y la otra persona describe cómo era él del Instituto Lingüístico Conversa, usando el tiempo imperfecto.

F. ¿Cómo era tu universidad hace unos años? Probablemente la universidad a la que asistes es diferente ahora de cómo era hace unos años. Posiblemente los estudiantes también son distintos. Utilizando los siguientes verbos describe cómo era **antes** tu universidad y cómo es ahora. Algunos verbos útiles son **ser, tener, estar, haber, llevar.**

La universidad	
antes	ahora

Los estudiantes	
antes	ahora

G. ¿Cómo era el hotel? Habla con otro estudiante de un hotel al que fuiste durante unas vacaciones. Describe dónde estaba, cómo era el hotel y cuáles eran algunos de los servicios que ofrecían en ese hotel. (Si es necesario, repasa el vocabulario sobre los hoteles en la página 325 de esta *etapa*.)

ENFOQUE ESTRUCTURAL Pretérito e imperfecto–acciones en el pasado

Patrick habla de las vacaciones con su amiga Berta.

> **Patrick:** Antes, yo **iba todos los años** a Florida de vacaciones. Pero **el año pasado fui** a Texas con mi novia porque **queríamos** conocer esa parte del país.
>
> **Berta:** ¿A qué parte de Texas **fueron**?
>
> **Patrick:** Bueno, primero **estuvimos** en San Antonio y después en El Paso. Y tú, ¿qué **hiciste**?
>
> **Berta:** Pues antes **siempre pasaba** las vacaciones de verano en México, pero **el verano pasado me quedé** aquí en San José porque no **tenía** suficiente dinero.

Note that the preceding exchange contains verbs in both the preterite and the imperfect. In previous chapters you learned two past tenses: the preterite **(fui, fuimos, me quedé)** and the imperfect **(iba, íbamos, pasaba).** Although both tenses are used to report past actions, each tense is used in different contexts.

The main distinction between the use of the preterite and the imperfect in this context has to do with certain aspects of actions in the past.

1. If an action is viewed as having been either begun or completed within any definite time period, occurs only once, or is repeated a specific number of times, the verb will be in the preterite.

> **Fui** a Texas **tres veces.** *(specific number of times)*

2. If a past action is habitual, repeated an unspecified number of times, the verb will be in the imperfect.

> **Siempre pasaba** las vacaciones de verano en México. *(habitual occurrence)*

3. To justify the reason someone did or did not do something, or to explain why something did or did not get done, the verb will be in the imperfect.

> El verano pasado me quedé aquí en San José **porque no tenía suficiente dinero.**

Preview: A summary of the uses of preterite and imperfect is presented in Chapter 10.

Práctica

H. ¿Siempre? ¿Una vez? Un día, mientras están en San José, tú y tus amigos hablan de lo que hacían normalmente hace unos años y de lo que hicieron sólo una vez. Completa las frases siguientes con las expresiones de tiempo correspondientes.

1. Mi familia y yo íbamos a los parques nacionales...
2. Mis amigos fueron a México...
3. No iba de vacaciones; me quedaba en casa para trabajar...
4. Mis padres nos llevaban a ver los museos de la ciudad...
5. Alquilamos un coche y fuimos a Nuevo México...
6. Fui a esquiar a Colorado...

el verano pasado
todos los veranos
todos los inviernos
siempre
normalmente
una vez

Ex. H
There are several possible correct answers for most of these examples.

I. ¿Por qué no lo hiciste? Una tarde, mientras Patrick está en casa con la familia costarricense, escucha a la Sra. Álvarez hacerles las siguientes preguntas a sus hijos. ¿Qué contestó cada hijo como una explicación?

■ **Modelo:** ¿Hiciste la tarea? (no tener los libros)
No, porque no tenía los libros.

Sra Álvarez	Sus hijos
1. ¿Te duchaste?	(no haber agua caliente)
2. ¿Comiste?	(no tener hambre)
3. ¿Hiciste los mandados?	(ser muy tarde)
4. ¿Acompañaste a tu hermana?	(querer ir sola)
5. ¿Compraste el pan?	(estar muy ocupado)
6. ¿Llamaste a tus amigos?	(no saber el número de teléfono)

Answers, Ex. I
1. No, porque no había agua caliente. 2. No, porque no tenía hambre. 3. No, porque era muy tarde. 4. No, porque (ella) quería ir sola. 5. No, porque (yo) estaba muy ocupado. 6. No, porque (yo) no sabía el número de teléfono.

Linda y su amiga Kelly estudian durante el año con Patrick en un programa universitario en San José. Un fin de semana Linda y Kelly decidieron viajar un poco por su cuenta en vez de participar en la excursión organizada por la universidad. Fueron al Parque Nacional Volcán Irazú. Al llegar al Hotel Irazú fueron a la recepción donde Linda habló con el empleado.

ANTES DE ESCUCHAR

Basándote en lo que has aprendido en esta *etapa*, ¿qué esperas escuchar en la conversación de Linda y el recepcionista sobre la habitación que Linda y su amiga quieren?

Lee las preguntas en la sección *Después de escuchar.*

DESPUÉS DE ESCUCHAR

J. Comprensión

1. ¿Tenían Linda y Kelly una habitación reservada?
2. ¿Cuánto costó la habitación?
3. ¿Dónde desayunaron?
4. ¿Qué número de habitación tenían?
5. ¿En qué piso estaban?

K. ¿Cómo lo dicen? Escucha otra vez la conversación e identifica las siguientes expresiones.

1. ¿Cómo pregunta el recepcionista si "he can help them"?
2. ¿Cómo dice Linda "we have a reservation"?
3. ¿Cómo pregunta Linda "is breakfast included"?

Tú dirás ···

Ex. L: 👤👤 Pairs

L. La reservación. Con un(a) compañero(a) de clase haz la siguiente actividad.

Estudiante A

Imagina de nuevo que eres un estudiante de intercambio en San José. Estás planeando una excursión a otra ciudad. A ti y a tus amigos no quieren alojarse en un albergue juvenil; prefieren ir a un hotel. Llama por teléfono para hacer la reservación.

1. Greet the clerk and say that you would like two rooms with a bath.
2. The rooms are for four persons for three nights.
3. Find out the price of the room. Have your credit card number ready to guarantee the reservation.
4. Ask if breakfast is included. If not, ask how much it costs.
5. Ask about transportation from the hotel to downtown.
6. Thank the hotel clerk and say good-bye.

Estudiante B

Imagina que trabajas en la recepción de un hotel en San José. Contesta el teléfono y habla con un cliente.

1. Greet the customer.
2. Ask for how many people the rooms are.
3. Tell how much the rooms cost.
4. Ask the customer if he or she wants to guarantee the room with a credit card.
5. Say whether breakfast is included in the price of the room.
6. Mention what transportation is available from the hotel to downtown.
7. Ask if the customer needs any other information. Say good-bye.

M. Mi habitación. Habla con otro(a) estudiante sobre el hotel en que está tu habitación. Dale la siguiente información en español:

(1) the name of the hotel,
(2) what floor your room is on,
(3) whether there is a private bathroom,
(4) how the room is furnished,
(5) whether breakfast is included in the price, and
(6) whether you like the hotel and the room and why.

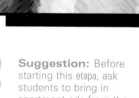

TERCERA ETAPA

PARA EMPEZAR: ¿Buscas un apartamento?

Preparación: Think about what you generally would like about an apartment for rent. What sort of information do you expect to find about an apartment in a newspaper? Before reading the ads that follow, make a mental list of four or five things you are likely to find in such a small space.

Suggestion: Before starting this etapa, ask students to bring in apartment ads from the campus or local paper. Discuss, in Spanish, which ads are good deals and why.

Allow students to work in pairs or small groups to try to answer these questions. When done, have students compare the ads they brought in with these. Comment on any differences found.

Mira el texto por encima. ¿Cuántos anuncios hay? ¿Qué crees que significa la primera palabra de cada anuncio? ¿Qué anuncio contiene la información más completa?

Paseo Colón. Vacío. Dos dormitorios. 60 m². Cocina amueblada. Comedor. Baño. Teléfono. Terraza. 5° piso. Ascensor. Tel. 2 43 94 54

Escazú. Completamente amueblado. 225 m². Aire acondicionado. Piscina. Tres dormitorios. Garaje. Dos baños. Dos terrazas. 4° piso. Ascensor. Llamar después de las 20hs. Tel. 4 20 28 87

Sabana Norte. Un dormitorio. Baño. Teléfono. Cocina amueblada. Piscina. Jardín. Tenis. Llamar después de las 16hs. Tel. 5 31 67 06

San Francisco 2 Ríos. Vacío. 185 m². Cuatro dormitorios. Dos baños. Dos terrazas. Cocina grande. Estacionamiento. Comedor. 7° piso. Dos ascensores. Tel 5 73 34 30

Santa Ana. Completamente amueblado. Sala de estar grande. Dos dormitorios. 125 m². Cocina grande. Baño. 3er piso. Llamar mañanas. Tel. 2 45 85 42

Los Yoses. Tres dormitorios. Cocina amueblada. Garaje. Piscina. Jardín. Tel. 4 52 58 24 noche

Práctica

A. Palabras claves. Lee los anuncios con cuidado. ¿Qué crees que significan las siguientes palabras?

1. aire acondicionado
2. amueblado
3. dormitorio
4. terraza
5. estacionamiento
6. vacío
7. garaje

B. Anuncios por palabras (Classified ads). Estás revisando los anuncios de apartamentos que hay en el periódico hoy. Llama a un(a) amigo(a) por teléfono y descríbele uno de los apartamentos. Basa tu descripción en uno de los anuncios de la página 333.

■ **Modelo:** *El apartamento está cerca al Paseo Colón. Está vacío y tiene dos dormitorios. Tiene 60 metros cuadrados (square meters) y la cocina está amueblada. También tiene un comedor, baño, teléfono y terraza. Está en el quinto piso y hay un ascensor en el edificio.*

Repaso

C. Una tarde en el parque. Mira el dibujo que aparece a continuación y describe lo que la gente hacía en el parque el domingo pasado por la tarde.

■ **Modelo:** *Dos niños jugaban al fútbol.*

D. Nuestras vacaciones en Costa Rica. Cambia los verbos subrayados *(underlined)* al pretérito.

El año pasado nosotros <u>pasamos</u> una semana de vacaciones en Costa Rica. Nuestro viaje <u>comienza</u> en San José, donde mi padre <u>hace</u> reservaciones en el famoso Hotel Cariari. El primer día, <u>damos</u> un paseo por el mercado, donde <u>compramos</u> mucho café para nuestros amigos en los Estados Unidos. También <u>visitamos</u> el Museo de Arte Costarricense y el Monumento a la Guerra de 1856. El segundo día <u>salimos</u> para Puntarenas. <u>Conducimos</u> a la costa en un coche que mi papá <u>alquila</u> para el viaje. En camino *(On the way)*, <u>conocemos</u> varios pueblos interesantes. Por fin, <u>llegamos</u> a una hermosa playa de arenas *(sands)* blancas en el Pacífico. Después de pasar unos días en la playa, toda la familia <u>va</u> a visitar el Parque Nacional Volcán Poás. Aunque <u>empieza</u> a llover, <u>podemos</u> subir al enorme cráter de este volcán activo. Por suerte *(Luckily)* <u>vemos</u> una pequeña erupción de vapores y gases. Después <u>volvemos</u> a San José donde <u>vamos</u> a un concierto en el famoso Teatro Nacional. Finalmente, <u>salimos</u> para los EE.UU. Todos <u>estamos</u> de acuerdo que el viaje a Costa Rica <u>es</u> muy interesante y que <u>aprendemos</u> mucho.

GRAMMAR NOTE:
The preterite of **ser** is presented in Chapter 5, on page 168.

ENFOQUE ESTRUCTURAL — Preterite e imperfecto—Resumen

IRM Master 40: Pretérito e imperfecto—Resumen

To review the contrast, display a piece of text in the past tense on an overhead. Select different students to read each sentence and determine the meaning based on the aspect of the verb. Where applicable, discuss how the meaning would change if the aspect were changed.

This activity can be assigned as homework. In class, pair students to compare answers. Allow 3–4 minutes, then discuss answers as a class.

Preterite	Imperfect
Actions that are begun or completed as single events:	*Actions repeated habitually:*
Ella **corrió** hacia el parque.	Ella **comía** conmigo todos los días.
Ellos **llegaron** a las 7:00.	Siempre **salíamos** a bailar.
Actions that are repeated a specified number of times or that have a time limit:	*Actions that occur simultaneously over an indefinite period of time:*
Fui a la tienda tres veces.	Mientras **corría** por el parque **pensaba** en sus planes para la noche.
Vi la televisión toda la tarde.	
Sudden changes in mental states or conditions seen as completed (moods, feelings, opinions, illnesses, or other physical complaints):	*General mental states:*
En ese momento, **tuve** miedo de subir al avión.	En esos días, **tenía** miedo de subir al avión.
Hasta ese día, **creí** que podía hacerlo.	En aquellos días **creía** que podía hacerlo.
Estuve preparado para subir hasta que **me puse** tan nervioso que **fue** imposible seguir.	**Estaba** tan preparado para subir que me **sentía** valiente.
	Descriptions of characteristics of people, things, or physical conditions: **Era** un muchacho sano y fuerte.
	Telling time and age: **Eran** las 5:00 de la tarde. El actor **tenía** 38 años.

Práctica

Answers, Ex. E
1. Catalina se despertó a las 7:00; se quedó en la cama 15 minutos.
2. Catalina se levantó; estaba cansada; se vistió; no estaba bien vestida.
3. Catalina salió de casa; llovía; se dio prisa para llegar a la escuela.
4. Catalina esperó el autobús; subió al autobús; no pudo sentarse.
5. Catalina entró en la clase a las 9:10; llegó tarde; no sabía las respuestas; recibió una mala nota; no estaba contenta.
6. Regresó a su casa; se acostó.

E. Un mal día. Basándote en los dibujos, cuenta cómo le fue a Catalina ayer. Usa el pretérito o el imperfecto según el contexto.

■ **Modelo:** despertarse
Catalina se despertó a las 7:00.

1.

despertarse a las 7:00
quedarse en la cama quince minutos

2.

levantarse
estar cansada
vestirse, / no estar bien vestida

3.

salir de casa
llover
darse prisa para llegar a la escuela

4.

esperar
subir
no poder sentarse

5.

entrar en
llegar tarde
no saber las respuestas
recibir una mala nota
no estar contenta

6.

regresar a su casa
acostarse

F. Ayer. Con otro(a) estudiante, habla de cómo te fue ayer. Puedes usar los verbos de la lista u otros que necesites. Usa el pretérito o el imperfecto según el contexto.

Ex. F: Pairs

levantarse	estar contento(a)	llegar tarde
lavarse	estar de mal humor	estar cansado(a)
tener hambre	tener mucho trabajo	comer
llegar	salir	dormir la siesta
ir	tener sed	acostarse
hacer sol, etc.	hablar con	pasear
vestirse	jugar deporte	tener mucho trabajo

G. Cuando yo era niño(a)… Habla con otro(a) estudiante sobre tu niñez. ¿Dónde vivías? ¿Qué tiempo hacía en esa región? ¿A qué escuela asistías? ¿Qué hacías durante las vacaciones? ¿Qué hacías durante los fines de semana? Menciona algo extraordinario que te ocurrió durante una de tus vacaciones (una aventura, un accidente, un viaje especial, etc.). Usa el pretérito o el imperfecto según el contexto.

Ex. G: Pairs

Comentarios

culturales *El café*

$\mathcal{E}$l café es el principal producto de exportación de Costa Rica. La tierra volcánica del país es ideal para el cultivo del café porque la ceniza en la tierra le da al café un sabor muy especial. Los cafetaleros cosechan los granos de las plantas del café a mano, casi uno por uno. Luego secan los granos bajo el sol antes de lavarlos, tostarlos y empacarlos.

En general, la vida del campesino es bastante buena porque muchos son propietarios de tierra. El cafetalero costarricense típico tiene casi una hectárea (cerca de dos acres y medio) de terreno para cultivar su exquisito café. Este sistema contribuye al relativamente alto nivel de vida en general en Costa Rica en comparación con el de los otros países de Centroamérica.

INTEGRACIÓN CULTURAL

Answers Integración:
1. V 2. F 3. F 4. V

¿Verdadero o falso?

1. El proceso de cosechar el café requiere tiempo y paciencia.
2. La ceniza de los volcanes causa problemas para el cafetalero.
3. Es necesario lavar los granos antes de secarlos.
4. Los campesinos generalmente son propietarios de la tierra que cultivan.

VAMOS A ESCUCHAR BUSCAMOS UN APARTAMENTO

Patrick está revisando los anuncios del periódico con un amigo.

ANTES DE ESCUCHAR

Basándote en lo que has aprendido en esta *etapa*, contesta las siguientes preguntas.

1. ¿Qué es lo más importante para ti cuando buscas un apartamento?
2. ¿Qué crees que van a comentar los dos amigos mientras revisan los anuncios?

Ahora lee las preguntas en la sección *Después de escuchar.*

DESPUÉS DE ESCUCHAR

H. Comprensión.
1. ¿Qué encuentra Patrick?
2. ¿Dónde está?
3. ¿Cuánto cuesta?
4. ¿Qué piensa Richard del apartamento?
5. ¿Cómo es el apartamento que encuentra Richard?
6. Según Patrick, ¿cuál es el problema con ese apartamento?
7. ¿Dónde compraron muebles Cristina y Berta?
8. ¿Cómo es el apartamento que deciden ir a ver?

I. ¿Cómo lo dicen?
1. ¿Qué expresión usó Patrick para agarrar la atención de Richard?
2. ¿Cómo dice Richard que el apartamento "is very expensive"?
3. ¿Cómo dice Richard que el apartamento "is exactly what they need"?

Tú dirás ....

J. Buscamos un apartamento. Hace un mes que tú y otro estudiante viven con una familia en un programa de intercambio de su universidad. Ahora deciden que van a vivir en un apartamento. Miren los anuncios en la página 339 para hacer lo siguiente:

- describan los apartamentos según la información en los anuncios
- decidan qué apartamentos son demasiado caros para ustedes
- escojan el apartamento que van a alquilar
- digan por qué les gusta el apartamento que han escogido

K. Quisiéramos alquilar este apartamento. Trabaja con otros dos estudiantes para alquilar un apartamento. Uno de ustedes va a hacer el papel de la persona que ofrece el apartamento y los otros dos van a ser las personas que quieren alquilar el apartamento. Incluyan la siguiente información en su conversación:

- saludos y presentaciones
- una descripción de lo que ustedes desean en cuanto al lugar, servicios, precio, etc.
- información sobre tres o cuatro apartamentos que el agente tiene
- preguntas sobre estos apartamentos
- arreglos para ver el apartamento que más les interesa de los tres
- despedidas.

San Antonio. Amueblado. Cuatro dormitorios. Dos baños. Comedor. Dos terrazas. Piscina. 80.000 colones.
Tel. 4 12 54 40

Paseo Colón. Tres dormitorios. Cocina grande. Comedor. Todo amueblado excepto salón. 60.000 colones.
Tel. 6 10 90 87

Alajuela. Amueblado. Comedor. Un dormitorio. Teléfono. Terraza. Piscina. Tenis. 40.000 colones.
Tel. 8 14 23 85

Sabanilla. Un dormitorio grande. Cocina amueblada. Aire acondicionado. Jardín. 45.000 colones.
Tel. 7 21 40 89 noche.

Escazú. Vacío. Dos dormitorios. Comedor. Baño. Cocina. 70.000 colones.
Tel. 4 50 17 76

Pinares. Amueblado. Dos dormitorios. Comedor. Cocina. Baño. Terraza. 55.000 colones. Tel. 3 15 41 55

LECTURA: *Las pintorescas carretas de Sarchí*

ANTES DE LEER

A. Mira el título de esta lectura y las fotos que aparecen en esta página y en la página 341.
1. ¿Qué objetos aparecen en las fotos?
2. ¿Hay alguna palabra en el título de la lectura que corresponde a estos objetos?
3. ¿Qué hace el señor en una de las fotos?

GUÍA PARA LA LECTURA

B. Lee el artículo rápidamente y busca el párrafo en que se menciona(n)
1. una descripción de Sarchí
2. la fecha de una celebración nacional
3. datos históricos sobre Costa Rica

C. Lee el primer párrafo rápidamente y contesta las siguientes preguntas.
1. ¿Cómo recibió su nombre Costa Rica?
2. ¿En qué año?
3. ¿Por qué llegó a ser la carreta el medio de transporte ideal en Costa Rica?

D. Lee el segundo párrafo y contesta las siguientes preguntas.
1. ¿Dónde está situado Sarchí?
2. ¿Por qué son especiales las carretas de Sarchí?
3. ¿Qué colores y diseños usa la gente para pintar las carretas?

E. Lee el último párrafo y contesta la siguiente pregunta: ¿Por qué es el año 1985 tan importante para la gente de Sarchí?

LAS PINTORESCAS CARRETAS DE SARCHÍ

Las carretas de Costa Rica, policromas como las **mariposas,** van pasando a la historia como símbolo de la nación y parte integral de su folklore. Costa Rica es un país singular de playas tropicales y grandes montañas. Colón descubrió la costa oriental de Costa Rica en 1502 y el nombre que le dio fue muy apropiado, pues esa tierra resultó ser sumamente "rica", no de la manera que pensaban

butterflies

Suggestion: Put students in groups of 3 and do this activity as a jigsaw reading. Assign each student a different paragraph to read. Then allow 4–5 minutes for students to share information from their sections. Then have students close their books and together construct a brief summary of the reading.

Un artesano pinta carretas en Sarchí, Costa Rica. Los colores que se usan para pintar las carretas son intensos.

los conquistadores qué buscaban oro, sino porque atrajo a muchos colonizadores. Los colonizadores trajeron caballos y **vacas.** Eran personas trabajadoras que construyeron viviendas y **labraron** la tierra. La carreta de **bueyes** pronto llegó a ser el medio más práctico de transporte en esa tierra, donde llueve torrencialmente de mayo a octubre y donde la variación del terreno va desde la **arena** de las playas de ambas costas hasta las **llanuras** extensas, los valles amplios y los precipicios de la escarpada Cordillera Central.

cows

worked / cultivated
oxen

sand
plains

Sarchí, que hoy día tiene casi 10.000 habitantes, está situado en un valle **hondo** y elevado entre montañas, por donde millares de **arroyuelos** bajan por **cauces pedregosos.** Allí prosperó la fabricación de carretas, porque había gran diversidad de **maderas duras** para hacerlas fuertes y hombres que combinan la habilidad para la pintura y un espíritu creador. A principios de este siglo empezaron a pintar carretas con motivos geométricos en tres colores fundamentales: anaranjado rojizo, azul celeste y blanco.

deep
little streams / rocky river beds
hardwoods

Cada año cuando termina la temporada de lluvias, sale el sol y se aclara el cielo. Florecen los **bosques** de orquídeas y **relucen** las carretas pintadas, verdaderas obras de arte popular. El 22 de septiembre de 1985 tuvo lugar la primera celebración nacional que honra a Sarchí como centro costarricense de artesanías, evento que se va a efectuar todos los años. Ese día **hubo** desfiles, fiestas y **se bendijeron** las carretas pintadas en los colores de siempre: anaranjado rojizo, azul celeste y blanco.

forests / shine

there were / they blessed

VÍDEO CULTURAL

VÍDEO CULTURAL: *Buscamos un hotel*

A. Anticipación. ¿Qué información necesitas para poder reservar una habitación en un hotes? ¿Y para registrarte en un hotel? Mira los temas que aparecen a continuación. Indica cuáles son importantes cuando una persona tiene que decidir en qué hotel quedarse y por cuánto tiempo. Al terminar tu selección, compara tus respuestas con las de otros(as) compañeros(as) de clase.

1. _____ las fechas del viaje

2. _____ cómo pagar

3. _____ qué tipo de ropa se vende

4. _____ cuántos baños tiene la habitación

5. _____ si tiene un bidé

6. _____ la comida en el hotel

7. _____ carnet de identidad

8. _____ dónde viven los recepcionistas

B. Preparación. Lee las siguientes expresiones en español tomadas de la sección *Vocabulario esencial* del vídeo. Para cada expresión indica cuál es su equivalente en inglés. Al terminar, compara tus respuestas con las de otros(as) compañeros(as) de clase.

1. documento de identidad	a. three-star hotel
2. no fumadores	b. tourist class
3. (hotel de) tres estrellas	c. seventh floor
4. reserva/reservación	d. round trip
5. los ascensores	e. no smoking section
6. ida y vuelta	f. I. D. card
7. clase turista	g. sixth floor
8. sexta planta	h. one way
	i. smoking section
	j. the elevators
	k. reservation

C. Participación. Toma notas sobre lo que pasa en el vídeo.

D. Comprensión. Elige la respuesta adecuada para cada una de las siguientes preguntas.
a. por dos días
b. por dos semanas
2. ¿Qué información pide el recepcionista?
    a. su nombre y su tarjeta de crédito
    b. su nombre y su carnet de identidad
3. ¿Cuánto cuesta un viaje de ida y vuelta en clase club?
    a. 16.500 pesetas
    b. 9.100 pesetas

E. Personalización. Escribe un párrafo de cinco a siete oraciones en lo que describas lo que acabas de ver en el vídeo. Utiliza el vocabulario nuevo.

Intercambio: ¿Tienen habitaciones?

Estudiante A

El hermano de Patrick va a venir este fin de semana y quiere pasar tres días en Sarchí. Ayer, al llegar a casa, tenías este mensaje en tu contestador automático.

> ¡Hola! Como sabes, pienso llegar el viernes a las 3:00. ¿Puedes llamar al hotel para hacer la reservación? Necesito una habitación individual para tres días. Puedo gastar 5.000 colones por noche. ¡Ah! Quiero una habitación con baño privado. Gracias y nos vemos el viernes.

Llama al hotel, explica lo que necesitas y haz la reservación para el hermano de Patrick.

Estudiante B

Imagina que trabajas en el hotel Lisboa. Suena el teléfono. Alguien quiere hacer una reservación para el fin de semana próximo.

Hay un problema...

Como el fin de semana es la celebración nacional de artesanías de Sarchí, todas las habitaciones están ocupadas, menos dos: una individual, sin baño, 4.500 colones. La otra, doble, con baño privado, 7.000 colones.

Intenta llegar a un acuerdo con la persona que llama para hacer una reservación.

ATAJO

Writing activities for this chapter are presented in the Activities Manual. For specific references to tasks supported by Atajo, please consult the Activities Manual.

Vocabulario

Para charlar

Para hablar del pasado *Talking about the past*
¿Qué tal el viaje? *How was the trip?*
¿A qué hora salió el avión? *What time did the plane leave?*
¿A qué hora saliste? *What time did you leave?*
¿Dormiste algo? *Did you sleep at all?*
¿Dormiste la siesta? *Did you take a nap?*

Para hablar de una habitación en un hotel
  Talking about a hotel room
Yo quisiera... *I would like . . .*
  una habitación *a room*
Nosotros quisiéramos... *We would like . . .*
Necesitamos... *We need . . .*
Buscamos... *We are looking for . . .*
Tenemos una reserva... *We have a reservation . . .*
  para dos personas. *for two people.*
  por tres noches. *for three nights.*
  con camas sencillas. *with single beds.*
  con baño. *with bath.*
  sin baño. *without bath.*
  en el primer piso. *on the first floor.*
  con televisor. *with a television set.*
  con teléfono. *with a telephone.*
Se aceptan tarjetas de crédito. *Credit cards are accepted.*

Para hablar del horario *Talking about a schedule*
llegar con retraso *to arrive late*
llegar de *to arrive from*
llegar a *to arrive at*
llegar a tiempo *to arrive on time*
llegar tarde *to arrive late*
llegar temprano *to arrive early*
en (veinte, treinta minutos, etc.) *in (twenty, thirty minutes, etc.)*
por (una hora, etc.) *for (an hour, etc.)*
un cuarto de hora *quarter of an hour*
media hora *half hour*
tres cuartos de hora *three quarters of an hour*
(cinco, diez, etc.) minutos *(five, ten, etc.) minutes*

Temas y contextos

En el hotel *At the hotel*
aire acondicionado *air conditioned*
un ascensor *elevator*
un baño (una sala de baño) *bath (bathroom)*
baño privado *private bath*
caja de seguridad *safe, security deposit box*
cambio de moneda *money exchange*
el desayuno (incluido en el precio o no incluido en el precio) *breakfast (included in the price or not included in the price)*
una ducha *shower*
el (la) empleado(a) *employee*
una habitación *room*
habitación para no fumadores *nonsmoking room*
lavado en seco *dry cleaning*
lavandería *laundry*
el (primer, segundo, tercer, cuarto, quinto) piso *(first, second, third, fourth, fifth) floor*
la recepción *reception desk*
la reservación / reserva *reservation*
secadora de pelo *hair dryer*
servicio despertador *wake-up service*
teléfono directo *direct phone*
TV por cable *cable TV*

Los anuncios del periódico para una casa o un apartamento *Newspaper ads for a house or an apartment*
aire acondicionado *air-conditioned*
(completamente) amueblado *(fully) furnished*
la cocina *kitchen*
el comedor *dining room*
el dormitorio *bedroom*
el estacionamiento *parking*
el garaje (para dos coches) *(two-car) garage*
el jardín *garden*
la piscina *pool*
la sala de estar *living room*
la terraza *terrace, porch*
vacío(a) *vacant, empty*

Vocabulario general   General vocabulary

Sustantivos

el alquiler   *rent*
anfitrión / anfitriona   *host, hostess*
ciudadanos   *citizens*
estudiantes visitantes provenientes   *visiting students*
una jornada de estudio   *a study, journey*
semanalmente de alta intensidad   *high intensity proceeding weekly*
el periódico   *newspaper*
el plan   *floor plan*
un programa de intercambio   *exchange program*
una salida   *exit*
la ventana   *window*
un albergue   *lodge*
una cancha (de tenis, básquetbol, etc.)   *(tennis, basketball, etc.) court*
un folleto   *brochure*
una ventaja   *advantage*
una excursión   *excursion*
un curso   *course*
un volcán   *volcano*

Otras palabras y expresiones

al fondo   *at the end*
al menos   *at least*

Adjetivos

amable   *friendly*
cómodo(a)   *comfortable*
confortable   *comfortable*
extra-académico   *extra-curricular*
incluido(a)   *included*
increíble   *incredible*
portátil   *portable*
simple   *simple*
útil   *useful*

Verbos

arreglar   *to arrange, fix*
cocinar   *to cook*
decir   *to say, tell*
dormir (ue, u) (la siesta)   *to sleep (take a nap)*
lavar   *to wash*
llegar de (a)   *to arrive from (at)*
poner   *to put*
salir con   *to go out with*
   de   *to leave from*
   para   *to leave for*
subir   *to go up, climb, rise*

10 Hoy, ayer y mañana

PRIMERA ETAPA
¿Qué haces normalmente?

SEGUNDA ETAPA
¿Qué hiciste el verano pasado?

TERCERA ETAPA
¿Qué vas a hacer?

INTEGRACIÓN:

LECTURA: "El eclipse",
de Augusto Monterroso
VÍDEO CULTURAL: ¿Qué vas a hacer
este fin de semana?
INTERCAMBIO: Rigoberta Menchú,
Premio Nóbel de la Paz
ESCRITURA: Actividades en el manual

Rigoberta
Menchú

CHAPTER OBJECTIVES:

In this chapter you are going to expand the knowledge you have already acquired to talk about your daily routine, to narrate and describe past events, and to make future plans. After completing this chapter you should be able to carry out the following tasks:

- ☺ **communicate with others about your daily activities and those of your friends**

- ☺ **narrate and describe different past events and activities**

- ☺ **make plans for the near future and discuss them with others**

The tools you will use to carry out these tasks are:

- ☺ **vocabulary for:**
  - daily routine
  - past activities
  - future events

- ☺ **grammatical structures:**
  - reflexive verbs vs. nonreflexive verbs
  - specific time expressions
  - discourse organizers

GUATEMALA
Población: 11.277.614
108.890 kilómetros cuadrados, un poco más pequeño que Tennessee
Capital: Ciudad de Guatemala, 1.167.495
Ciudades principales: Mixco, 436.668; Villa Nueva, 165.567; Chinautla, 61.335; Anatitlán, 40.229

HONDURAS
Población: 5.770.000
112.088 kilómetros cuadrados, un poco más grande que Tennessee
Capital: Tegucigalpa, 738.500
Ciudades principales: San Pedro Sula, 353.800; La Ceiba, 82.900; El Progreso, 77.300; Choluteca, 69.400

NICARAGUA
Población: 4.300.000
129.500 kilómetros cuadrados, un poco más grande que Nueva York
Capital: Managua, 937.759; Ciudades principales: León, 172.042; Masaya, 101.878; Chinandega, 101.605; Matagalpa, 92.268; Granada, 91.929

EL SALVADOR
Población: 5.828.900
21.040 kilómetros cuadrados, un poco más pequeño que Massachusetts
Capital: San Salvador, 1.522.126
Ciudades principales: Soyapango, 251.811; Santa Ana, 202.337; San Miguel, 182.817; Mejicanos, 145.000

	GUATEMALA	HONDURAS	NICARAGUA	EL SALVADOR
Moneda:	quetzal	lempira	córdoba oro	colón salvadoreño
Esperanza de vida:	hombres, 62; mujeres, 68	hombres, 66; mujeres, 71	hombres, 63; mujeres, 68	hombres, 65; mujeres, 72
Índice de alfabetización:	55,6%	72,7%	65,7%	71,5%
Productos principales de exportación:	café, azúcar, bananas	bananas, café, mariscos, minerales	carne, café, algodón, azúcar, mariscos, oro, bananas	café, caña de azúcar, mariscos
Embajada:	2220 R Street NW, Washington, DC 20008	3007 Tilden Street NW, Washington, DC 20008	1627 New Hampshire Avenue NW, Washington, DC 20009	2308 California Street NW, Washington, DC 20008

⊚ PARA EMPEZAR: ¿Qué haces normalmente?

Preparación: Before you move ahead, answer the following questions:

- What do you usually do during the week? What does a typical day look like for you?
- What do you like to do on weekends? Where do you go? Who do you go out with?
- When and with whom do you talk about your daily activities?
- How is an unusual day different from a normal one?

Remind students of reading strategies, i.e., looking at pictures, scanning the first phrases of each paragraph, searching for cognates, etc.

You may want to ask students to prepare the questions in the *Antes de leer* sections as homework. Also, you can have students read the text on pages 348–349 before they come to class, so you can spend class time doing the exercises under *Práctica* page 350. You can begin the class by having students respond to the questions in the *Preparación* section.

INTERNET

For whole language practice, before beginning this chapter ask several students to visit Web pages or to log on to Internet newsgroups or chat lines for these countries. Students can give a brief presentation to the class on events of importance that happened recently or issues of importance that people have been discussing. This will also offer practice of past tense usage.

VOCABULARY EXPANSION:
Notice that **quedarse en** means *to stay somewhere,* but **quedar con** means *to arrange to meet (with).*

it takes me 20 minutes to get there

⟩ stay / to chat

ANTES DE LEER

1. En el siguiente texto, Cristina Gallegos, una profesora hondureña que da clases de español, nos cuenta lo que hace normalmente. Antes de leer, haz una lista de las actividades que en tu opinión pueden aparecer en el texto.
2. Ahora lee la primera frase de cada párrafo. ¿Qué te indica esta frase sobre el contenido global del texto?

▶ *Cristina Gallegos nos habla de sus actividades diarias*

Me llamo Cristina, soy de Tegucigalpa pero vivo en La Ceiba, un pueblo en la costa norte de Honduras. Trabajo aquí como profesora de español en una escuela que se llama Eco-Honduras. Durante la semana me levanto temprano, a las 6:30. Después de ducharme y vestirme, desayuno tranquilamente y me voy a dar mis clases. Salgo de casa a las 7:30 y voy a la escuela a pie pues está bastante cerca de mi casa. Generalmente **tardo 20 minutos en llegar.** Empiezo a dar mi primera clase a las 8:00 y tengo clases toda la mañana. Enseño español a estudiantes extranjeros y doy clases de diferentes niveles.

Al terminar la última clase, me gusta **quedarme** en la escuela a **charlar** con los otros profesores que trabajan allí. Después me voy a casa a comer. Por las tardes suelo quedarme en casa a trabajar. Cada día tengo cosas que preparar para las clases del día siguiente y siempre tengo tareas para corregir. Los fines de semana no hay clases pero muy a menudo la escuela organiza **excursiones** para los estudiantes y algunas veces voy con ellos. Cuando no voy de excursión con los alumnos, me gusta levantarme tarde y quedar con mis amigos para ir a la playa. A veces **nos reunimos** en casa de alguien para cenar. Después, nos gusta salir a tomar **un trago** en uno de los bares del pueblo. Algunos fines de semana voy a Tegucigalpa a visitar a mi familia que vive allí.

short trips

we get together
a drink

ANTES DE LEER

1. En el siguiente texto, Jim, un estudiante matriculado en un curso de español en la escuela de La Ceiba, nos cuenta lo que hace normalmente. Antes de leer el texto, haz una lista de las actividades que piensas que va a mencionar Jim.
2. Ahora lee la primera frase de cada párrafo. ¿Qué te indica esta frase sobre el contenido global del texto?
3. ¿Qué día de la semana te gusta más? ¿Y el que menos? Explica por qué.

▶*Jim nos habla de sus actividades como estudiante de español en La Ceiba*

Me llamo Jim. Este semestre estoy estudiando español en Eco-Honduras, una escuela de español en La Ceiba. Vivo con una familia hondureña en una casa muy cerca de la escuela. Durante la semana me levanto temprano, a las 6:00, y voy a correr por la playa durante media hora. Después, vuelvo a casa, me ducho y desayuno. A las ocho menos cuarto salgo de casa para ir a clase.

Estoy en el nivel avanzado y tengo clases todos los días, desde las 8:00 de la mañana hasta las 12:00. Cada mañana las clases empiezan con un **repaso** de gramática. Después practicamos vocabulario y tenemos discusiones sobre diferentes lecturas. La parte que más me gusta son las prácticas de conversación.

review

Al terminar las clases **me reúno con** otros estudiantes y nos vamos a **dar un paseo** por el pueblo. A la una vuelvo a casa para comer con mi familia. Durante la comida charlo con ellos y les cuento anécdotas de las clases. Por las tardes me quedo en casa para estudiar durante dos o tres horas. Después, casi todos los días, quedo con mis amigos antes de cenar para dar una vuelta o para ir a la playa. Algunas noches, vamos a bailar a una de las discotecas del pueblo.

I get together with / take a walk

Los fines de semana son los días que más me gustan. La escuela organiza muchas actividades y viajes para visitar diferentes lugares. A veces son excursiones de un día pero otras son escursiones más largas y estamos fuera todo el fin de semana. Los domingos me gusta acostarme temprano para poder levantarme a las 6:00 al día siguiente.

Práctica

A. Cierto o falso. De acuerdo con la información que nos ofrece Cristina, di si las siguientes afirmaciones son verdaderas o falsas. Si alguna de las afirmaciones es falsa, explica por qué.

1. Cristina nació en el mismo lugar en el que trabaja.
2. Cristina se levanta temprano todos los días.
3. Cristina necesita normalmente una hora desde que se levanta hasta que sale de casa.
4. Después de las clases, Cristina se va directamente a casa.
5. Algunos fines de semana, Cristina va de excursión con los estudiantes de la escuela.

B. Jim y tú. Completa las siguientes frases indicando lo que hace Jim normalmente. Después di lo que haces tú.

1. Durante la semana, a las seis de la mañana, Jim...Yo...
2. A las ocho menos cuarto, Jim...Yo...
3. Al terminar las clases, Jim...Yo...
4. Por las tardes, Jim...Yo...
5. Algunas noches, Jim...Yo...
6. Los domingos, a Jim...A mí...

Answers, Ex. A
1. F. Cristina nació en Tegucigalpa, pero trabaja en La Ceiba 2. F. Los fines de semana le gusta levantarse tarde 3. C. 4. F. A Cristina le gusta quedarse a charlar con otros profesores. 5. C.

Suggestion: After completing these questions, ask how similar or different Cristina's daily routine is from that of people in the USA.

Answers, Ex. B
1. Se levanta y va a correr. 2. Sale de casa. 3. Se reúne con otros estudiantes. 4. Se queda en casa y estudia. 5. Va a bailar. 6. Le gusta acostarse temprano.

After completing these questions, ask students how similar or different Jim's daily routine is from that of people in the USA.

IRM Master 41:
Expresiones para hablar del presente

Ask students to look over this section and the following *Enfoque estructural* as homework. In class combine the presentation of both sections by telling students a story about yourself, whom you depict as very exciting, and another person, whom you depict as boring. Use as many of the adverbial phrases and reflexive verbs as possible. While telling the story, check comprehension by asking students if they act the same or differently. For example: **¿Tú también te levantas siempre a las 11 de la mañana los sábados?**

Suggestion: Point out the use of **al** + *infinitive* to express time. For example: **al salir de casa** can be used to express *when I leave home*.

ENFOQUE LÉXICO

Expresiones para hablar de una secuencia de acciones en el presente

When you talk about your daily routine you can use the following expressions to organize your discourse. Below, you have a summary of the different expressions available in Spanish that answer the following questions: **¿Cuándo? ¿En qué momento del día? ¿Con qué frecuencia?**

1. ¿Cuándo?

durante el día	por la mañana	*in the morning*
	por la tarde	*in the afternoon*
	por la noche	*in the evening/at night*
	todos los días	*every day*
durante la semana	los lunes (martes, miércoles...)	*on Mondays (Tuesdays, Wednesdays ...)*
durante el fin de semana	los sábados	*on Saturdays*
	los domingos	*on Sundays*

2. ¿En qué momento del día?

los lunes	por la mañana	*Monday mornings*
	por la tarde	*Monday afternoons*
	por la noche	*Mon. evening/nights*
	al despertarme	*when I get up*
	al salir de casa	*when I leave home*

después de comer	*after lunch*
antes de clase	*before class*
a la hora de cenar	*at dinner time*

3. ¿Con qué frecuencia?

siempre	*always*
normalmente	*usually*
por lo general	*in general*
generalmente	*generally*
a menudo	*often*
con frecuencia	*frequently*
casi siempre	*almost always*
de vez en cuando	*once in a while*
a veces	*sometimes*
algunas veces	*sometimes*
casi nunca	*almost never*
nunca	*never*

Suggestion: This Enfoque and the one on page 366 elaborate on information presented in Chapter 4, pages 134, 136.

ENFOQUE ESTRUCTURAL — ## Verbos reflexivos y no reflexivos

1. Many Spanish verbs have both a reflexive and a nonreflexive form. In some cases, the meanings of the verbs change when they are used with reflexive pronouns:

Siempre **duermo** ocho horas.	*I always **sleep** eight hours.*
Casi siempre **me duermo** cuando estudio en la biblioteca.	*I almost always **fall asleep** when I study in the library.*
Me pongo los zapatos.	*I **put on** my shoes.*
Pongo los zapatos afuera.	*I **put** the shoes outside.*

2. In other cases, the meaning of the verbs is the same, but the meaning of the sentence changes. The nonreflexive verb expresses an action that goes from the subject to the object. The reflexive verb expresses a reciprocal action (the idea of *each other*):

Llamo a Claudia por teléfono a menudo.	*I **call** Claudia on the telephone often.*
Claudia y yo **nos llamamos** por teléfono a menudo.	*Claudia and I **call each other** on the telephone often.*

3. In most cases, however, the nonreflexive verb indicates an action that the subject does to someone else and the reflexive verb expresses an action that the subject does to itself.

Yo **lavo** el coche.	*I **wash** the car.*
Yo **me lavo.**	*I **wash** myself.*
Yo **me lavo** las manos.	*I **wash my** hands.*

Reflexive versus nonreflexive verbs: This section is designed to help students grasp the difference between reflexive and nonreflexive forms of the same verb. You may wish to present the idea by using corresponding expressions such as **lavar, lavarse, levantar, levantarse.** You may use Ex. E to underscore the differences.

Práctica

C. ¿Cuándo lo haces tú? Utiliza las siguientes actividades para hacerle preguntas a tu compañero(a) sobre su rutina diaria. Tu compañero(a) debe contestar tus preguntas utilizando las expresiones que aparecen en las páginas 350–351. Al terminar, diles al resto de la clase cuándo y con qué frecuencia hace tu compañero(a) las actividades que se mencionan.

1. levantarse temprano
2. ir a clase
3. desayunar tranquilamente
4. charlar con los compañeros de clase
5. comer a las 2:30
6. estudiar en la biblioteca
7. tomar un café con los amigos
8. ver la tele
9. lavar los platos
10. preparar la cena

D. ¿Qué haces primero? ¿Qué después? Pon las siguientes actividades en orden utilizando las expresiones de las páginas 350 y 351.
1. vestirme
2. salir de casa
3. desayunar
4. ducharme
5. recoger la ropa
6. despertarme

E. Se lava la cara. Utiliza los verbos indicados para describir las actividades de las personas que aparecen en los dibujos. Para cada caso tienes que decidir si necesitas un verbo reflexivo o no.

Miguel

La Sra. Perez

Miguel se lava la cara.　　　*La Sra. Pérez lava el coche.*

Jorge

Octavio

Jaime

1. despertar

Luisa / Alberto

2. mirar

Olga / Marisol

3. hablar

El Sr. González / La Sra. Sierra

4. acostar

Comentarios

culturales

La civilización maya: pasado y presente

*L*a civilización maya se originó hacia el año 2.600 a.C. en la península de Yucatán y alcanzó su máximo esplendor hacia el año 250 d.C. El territorio maya, conocido como Mesoamérica, ocupaba el sur de México, Guatemala, el norte de Belice y la parte oeste de Honduras.

Durante el período clásico (desde el año 200 hasta el 900 d.C.), el mundo maya estaba perfectamente estructurado en distintos **reinos** *(kingdoms)* gobernados por nobles y reyes. Eran estados independientes que tenían una comunidad rural y grandes centros urbanos construidos alrededor de templos y pirámides. El corazón de la civilización maya incluía ciudades como Copán en Honduras, Yaxchilán y Tikal en Guatemala y Palenque en México.

La mayoría de la ciudades mayas estaban formadas por una serie de plataformas dispuestas alrededor de una amplia plaza, **encima de las cuales** *(on top of which)* se elevaban grandes templos piramidales y extraordinarios palacios hechos de piedra.

Los mayas se pueden considerar como los más grandes astrónomos y matemáticos de la América precolombina. Entre sus grandes logros está el desarrollo de un sistema de escritura jeroglífica así como el establecimiento de un sistema de calendario altamente sofisticado. Los mayas eran también una sociedad agrícola que cultivaba entre otros productos maíz, frijoles y tabaco.

En la actualidad hay en Centroamérica unos 6 millones de mayas divididos en 31 grupos diferentes. Cada uno de estos grupos conserva su identidad, su lengua y costumbres mayas. Los grupos más numerosos son los Yucatecos en la Península de Yucatán, los Tzotzil y Tzeltal en Chiapas y los Quiché y Cakchiquel en Guatemala.

INTEGRACIÓN CULTURAL

1. Explica la importancia de las siguientes fechas para la civilización maya:

   2.600 a.C.   250 d.C.   900 d.C.

2. ¿Cuáles son algunas de las contribuciones más importantes de la civilización maya?

3. En la actualidad, ¿dónde se encuentran las mayores concentraciones de grupos mayas?

VAMOS A ESCUCHAR: VIERNES POR LA MAÑANA EN CASA DE LA FAMILIA DE CRISTINA GALLEGOS

Play Textbook audio.

Esta semana Cristina no tiene clases el viernes. Tampoco tiene que ir a la excursión organizada por la escuela y ha ido a visitar a sus padres en Tegucigalpa. Hoy es viernes y, aunque Cristina no tiene clases, sus hermanas María y Belén sí tienen que ir a la escuela.

ANTES DE ESCUCHAR

Antes de escuchar la conversación, contesta las siguientes preguntas.

1. Es un día de clase por la mañana. ¿Qué esperas que ocurra en esta conversación?
2. Cuándo eras estudiante en la escuela secundaria, ¿cómo era tu rutina por las mañanas antes de salir para clase?

Ahora mira los ejercicios que aparecen en la sección *Después de escuchar.*

DESPUÉS DE ESCUCHAR

F. Comprensión. Escucha la conversación y contesta las siguientes preguntas.

1. ¿Cuál de las dos hermanas se levanta antes, María o Belén?
2. ¿Qué hace Belén después de levantarse?
3. ¿Por qué no tiene María tiempo para nada?
4. ¿Desayuna Belén antes de ir a clase?

G. ¿Cómo lo dicen? Escucha otra vez la conversación y determina lo siguiente.

1. ¿Cómo les dice la señora Gallegos a sus hijas "to hurry up"?
2. ¿Qué dice Belén para mostrar su desacuerdo con María?
3. ¿Cómo dice María "we will see you this afternoon"?

Tú dirás ....

H. Una mañana típica. Un(a) compañero(a) de clase va a pasar el fin de semana contigo en la casa de tu familia. Es la primera vez que va a tu casa y quiere saber cuáles son las costumbres de la familia y la rutina diaria.

Estudiante A:

1. Invita a un(a) compañero(a) a casa de tu familia.
2. Contesta sus preguntas.

Estudiante B:

1. Acepta la invitación.
2. Haz preguntas a tu compañero(a) relacionadas con la rutina de la familia. Tu compañero(a) te tiene que dar toda la información posible sobre las cosas que hace su familia por las mañanas.

Ex. F: **Pairs**
Do as a pair activity. Ask students to listen twice with their books closed. Then have them open their books and try to answer the comprehension questions. Play a third time so students can check answers and complete the *Cómo lo dicen* section.

Answers, Ex. F
1. Belén. 2. Va al baño, se ducha, se lava el pelo. 3. Porque se levanta tarde. 4. No.

Answers, Ex. G
1. Dénse prisa. 2. No es verdad. 3. Nos vemos esta tarde.

Suggestion, Ex. H: Before doing this activity have students, in Spanish, review the kinds of questions the classmate might ask. Do not allow students to use notes while performing their role play.

As a follow-up, once students have finished the phone conversation, ask the students who are gathering information about schools whether or not they like the students' routine as it was described by their friends.

I. La rutina de los estudiantes en tu universidad. Imagina que conoces a un(a) estudiante que está en su último año de la escuela secundaria. Este(a) estudiante está considerando varias universidades a las que le gustaría asistir el año que viene.

Estudiante A: estudiante de la escuela secundaria

1. Llama por teléfono a tu amigo(a) que asiste a una universidad que te interesa.
2. Haz las preguntas necesarias para descubrir *(to find out)* todo lo que puedas sobre cómo es la rutina de los estudiantes en ese campus.
3. Termina la conversación en una forma adecuada.

Estudiante B: estudiante de la universidad

1. Contesta el teléfono en una forma adecuada.
2. Contesta las preguntas de tu amigo(a) dándole toda la información necesaria.
3. Termina la conversación en una forma adecuada.

⊚ SEGUNDA ETAPA

PARA EMPEZAR: ¿Qué hiciste el verano pasado?

Suggestion: You may want to ask students to prepare the questions in the *Antes de leer* sections as homework. Also, you can have them read the text on page 357 before they come to class, so you can spend class time doing the exercises under *Práctica* on pages 357–358. You can begin the class by having students respond to the questions in the *Preparación* section.

Preparación

- **What did you do last summer?**
- **Did you go somewhere on vacation?**
- **Where did you go on the last trip you took? What memories do you keep of that last trip?**

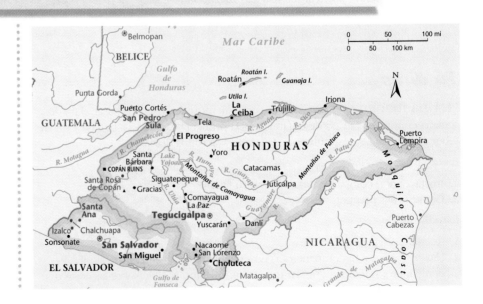

1. El siguiente texto es una narración sobre un viaje a través de El Salvador y Honduras. ¿Cuáles son las capitales de estos dos países?
2. Mira el mapa de El Salvador y Honduras. Localiza los siguientes lugares.
   a. En El Salvador: San Salvador, Santa Ana, Chalchuapa, Izalco
   b. En Honduras: Tegucigalpa, San Pedro Sula, Copán

▶ *Esteban Beltrán narra sus recuerdos de un viaje por El Salvador y Honduras*

Nuestro viaje comenzó en la capital de El Salvador, San Salvador. Allí pasamos una tarde y una noche y a la mañana siguiente fuimos a visitar las ruinas de la Joya de Cerén, media hora al norte de la capital. Estas ruinas se descubrieron en 1989 y **muestran** los restos de la civilización maya existente en el país desde el año 1.500 a.C. De allí partimos hacia el oeste para visitar varias ciudades que conservan importantes muestras del pasado precolombino y colonial.

show

Primero visitamos Santa Ana donde pasamos un día. Cuando los españoles llegaron a Santa Ana en 1525, la ciudad se llamaba Sihuatehuacán (de sihuat, "mujer", tehua, "brujo", y can, "ciudad", es decir, "ciudad de las hechiceras"). Allí pudimos ver la Catedral, el Teatro Nacional y paseamos por las calles del pueblo. Al día siguiente visitamos Chalchuapa, muy cerca de Santa Ana, para ver las ruinas del Tazumal, otro ejemplo del pasado maya de El Salvador.

Después de visitar estos lugares, decidimos pasar dos días **disfrutando** de los increíbles **parajes** naturales que ofrece esta zona del país. Reservamos una habitación en el Hotel de Montaña que está en Cerro Verde, una de las reservas naturales de El Salvador. Desde allí pudimos contemplar el volcán de Izalco, de 1.870 metros de altura.

enjoying
area, spot

Regresamos a San Salvador y de allí seguimos nuestro viaje hacia Honduras. La primera **parada** fue en Tegucigalpa, la capital. Llegamos allí a media tarde y después de dejar las cosas en el hotel, salimos a pasear por la parte antigua de la ciudad. Entre otras muchas cosas visitamos la Basílica de Nuestra Señora de Suyapa, la patrona de Honduras. Las **vidrieras** de la Basílica son realmente bellas.

stop

stained glass

No tuvimos mucho tiempo para ver más en Tegucigalpa pues al día siguiente salimos para San Pedro Sula, ciudad fundada en 1536 por Pedro de Alvarado. Una de las cosas que más nos gustó allí fue la visita al mercado de Guamilito donde compramos algunos objetos de artesanía local. También fue muy interesante la visita al Museo de Antropología e Historia donde aprendimos muchas cosas sobre los indios Payas que habitaban esta región del país antes de la llegada de los españoles.

Al día siguiente comenzamos a explorar el valle de Copán. Allí está la ciudad del mismo nombre, una de las ciudades mayas más avanzadas y **desarrolladas.** Pasamos **dos días enteros** visitando las ruinas de la civilización maya que todavía se conservan allí. ¡Fue una experiencia increíble!

developed
two full days

Práctica

A. ¿Honduras o El Salvador? Di a cuál de los dos países pertenece cada uno de estos lugares.

1. Cerro Verde
2. Chalchuapa
3. Copán
4. La Joya de Cerén
5. San Pedro Sula
6. Santa Anaa
7. Tegucigalpa

B. Identifica. Indica los elementos de la columna de la derecha que corresponden a los elementos de la columna de la izquierda.

1. _____   Cerro Verde   a. ruinas mayas en El Salvador
2. _____   Chalchuapa   b. reserva natural
3. _____   Copán   c. Basílica de Nuestra Señora de Suyapa
4. _____   Tegucigalpa   d. ruinas mayas Honduras
5. _____   Santa Ana   e. Pedro de Alvarado
6. _____   San Pedro Sula   f. Sihuatehuacán

C. Mis vacaciones. Tomando como modelo la narración de Esteban en la página 357, usa los siguientes verbos y expresiones para hablar de tus vacaciones más recientes. Usa el pretérito, según el modelo, para indicar qué hiciste. Si en realidad no fuiste de vacaciones, inventa los detalles *(details)*. Sigue el modelo.

> ■ **Modelo:**   el verano pasado / ir
>   *El verano pasado nosotros fuimos a Guatemala.*

1. el verano pasado / ir
2. el primer día / desayunar
3. primero / visitar
4. después / ver
5. esa noche / ir
6. el día siguiente / comprar
7. más tarde / comer
8. después de unos días / salir
9. por fin / regresar

Repaso

D. ¿Y tú? Habla con un(a) compañero(a) sobre tus actividades durante el día. Puedes hablar sobre un día de clase normal, o sobre un día del fin de semana.

E. Una experiencia del pasado. Piensa en un lugar muy especial para ti cuando eras niño(a) (por ejemplo, tu habitación, algún lugar en tu escuela, algún lugar cerca de tu casa, etc.). Háblale de este sitio a un(a) compañero(a) de clase. Primero haz una descripción del lugar (usa el imperfecto) y después cuéntale algo que pasó en ese lugar (usa el pretérito).

ENFOQUE LÉXICO

Expresiones para hablar de secuencia de acciones puntuales en el pasado

You have already learned the verb structure necessary to talk about past events. When you talk about the things you did yesterday, or the day before, or last week, weekend, month, summer, and so on, you will use the preterite tense as in the example below.

> Ayer, después de levantarme, primero de todo **me tomé** un café.
> Luego, **me duché** rápidamente, **limpié** un poco el apartamento y, por fin, **salí** de casa a eso de las 10:00 para ir a clase.

A continuación tienes algunas expresiones de tiempo para hablar de una secuencia de acciones puntuales en el pasado.

Expresiones para organizar el discurso en el pasado

When you talk about what you did in the past, you can refer either to a particular day (**un día determinado**) or to a period of time (**un período de tiempo**). In Spanish you can use the following expressions to organize your discourse:

Un día determinado en el pasado

1. To refer to a particular day you can begin with:

ayer	*yesterday*
anteayer	*the day before yesterday*
el lunes (martes...) pasado	*last Monday (Tuesday...)*

2. To indicate exactly when in the day, you can use **por la mañana, por la tarde, por la noche...**

3. Then, you can use the following expressions to indicate what you did first, second, or last.

primero		*first*
primero de todo		*first of all*
después		*then*
luego		
más tarde		*later on*
por fin		*finally*
finalmente		
por último		*at the end*
al final...	**del día**	*at the end . . . of the day*
	de la tarde	*of the afternoon*
	de la noche	*of the evening/night*

Un período de tiempo en el pasado

1. To refer to a period of time in the past you can begin with:

el fin de semana pasado	*last weekend*
la semana pasada	*last week*
el mes pasado	*last month*
el verano pasado	*last summer*
las vacaciones pasadas	*last vacation*

2. After you indicate what you did, you can continue your narration by using first expressions from column A, and then expressions from column B:

Ejemplo:

> **El fin de semana pasado** fuimos a visitar a unos amigos en San José. **Al llegar** descansamos un rato. Después, **ese mismo día** salimos a dar una vuelta por el centro.

A		B	
el primer día	*the first day*	**ese mismo día**	*that same day*
los primeros días	*the first days*	**al día siguiente**	*the next day*
al llegar	*upon arriving*	**el último día**	*the last day*
el día que llegamos	*the day we arrived*		

**Expresiones para hablar de secuencia de acciones
habituales en el pasado**

You have already learned the verb structure necessary to talk about past
events. When you talk about the things you used to do X years ago **(hace
X años),** or when you were X years old **(cuando tenía X años)** or
when you lived somewhere else **(cuando vivía en),** you will use the
imperfect tense, as in the example below.

> Hace cinco años **vivía** en un apartamento de estudiantes. Durante la
> semana **tenía** clase todos los días a las 8:00, así que normalmente **me
> levantaba** temprano y casi siempre de mal humor. No **me gustaba**
> madrugar *(get up early).* Después de la primera taza de café, **me sentía**
> un poco mejor y entonces **era** capaz *(be able to)* de hablar con mi
> compañera de apartamento.

To organize your discourse when you refer to habitual past actions, you
can use the same expressions presented on pages 350–351 to talk about
daily routine.

Práctica

Ex. F: Pair
Suggestion: To offer guided
practice with these past structures,
do this activity with the entire class.
Write the first sentence of the story
on the board and then ask students,
one by one, to add another sentence
that fits in with the previous one.
After each sentence, comment on the
accuracy of the usage of the preterite
and imperfect. When completed,
comment on any questions students
may have.

Ex. G: Pairs

F. Una llamada de teléfono inesperada. Imagina que estás en tu casa
o en tu residencia. Son como *(It's around)* las 8:00 de la noche y estás mirando la
televisión. De repente suena el teléfono y ¡sorpresa! es un(a) amigo(a) tuyo(a) con
el (la) que *(with whom)* hace mucho tiempo no hablas. Tu amigo(a) quiere que le
cuentes *(tell him/her)* todo lo que hiciste desde la última vez que te vio *(he/she
saw you).*

Con un(a) compañero(a) de clase imagina esta conversación telefónica. Antes de
empezar, cada uno, individualmente, preparará su papel.

G. Cuando vivía en... con... Hace ya varias semanas que compartes con
tus compañeros varias horas de clase a la semana. Seguramente, ya sabes muchas
cosas sobre ellos y ellos saben muchas cosas sobre ti. Sin embargo, es posible que
todavía no hayan *(you haven't yet)* hablado mucho sobre cómo eran sus vidas
hace unos años. Utiliza las siguientes preguntas como guía para hablar con un(a)
compañero(a) de clase sobre esos años pasados antes de llegar aquí.

1. ¿Cómo era tu vida hace unos años?
2. ¿Dónde vivías? ¿Con quién?
3. ¿Qué hacías normalmente durante la semana, los fines de semana, los
   veranos?
4. ¿Quiénes eran tus amigos(as)?

Comentarios

culturales

Conquista e independencia en Centro América

Nicaragua: Cristobal Colón llegó a la costa este de Nicaragua en 1502. Hacia 1520, el explorador Hernández de Córdoba estableció las ciudades de Granada y León, ciudades rivales durante muchos años. Los españoles dominaron a los indios de Nicaragua (Sumo, Miskito, Rama) tras la conversión al cristianismo de una de las tribus principales.

Honduras: Al igual que Nicaragua, Colón pisó la costa de Honduras en el año 1502. Los primeros **asentamientos** *(settlements)* españoles se establecieron en 1522. En 1537 un ejército indígena de unos 30.000 soldados dirigidos por el jefe Lempira se enfrentó a los españoles. En 1539 la muerte de Lempira condujo a la victoria final de los españoles contra los indios.

Guatemala: La conquista de Guatemala comenzó en 1523. Tras un año de enfrentamientos, los españoles dirigidos por Pedro de Alvarado **derrotaron** *(defeated)* a los indios Maya-Quiché de Guatemala en 1524. Establecieron la capital en Antigua, pero en 1773 fue destruida por un **terremoto** y *(earthquake)* trasladada a la Ciudad de Guatemala.

El Salvador: Cuando los españoles llegaron a El Salvador en 1524 encontraron el reino de Cuzcatlán donde vivían los indios Pipil. Dirigidos por Pedro de Alvarado, los españoles dominaron a los indios y conquistaron sus tierras en 1539.

La independencia

El primer movimiento hacia la independencia en Centro América tuvo lugar en El Salvador en 1811. En 1821 se declaró la Independencia de todas las colonias de Centro América en la Ciudad de Guatemala.

INTEGRACIÓN CULTURAL

1. ¿Cuáles son los dos países a los que primero llegó Colón?
2. ¿Qué ocurrió entre 1537 y 1539 en Honduras?
3. ¿Por qué se trasladó la capital de Antigua a la Ciudad de Guatemala en Guatemala?
4. ¿Quién fue el responsable de la conquista en Guatemala y El Salvador?
5. Indica la importancia del año 1821 para los países de América Central.

VAMOS A ESCUCHAR: EL ENCUENTRO DE ESTEBAN Y PATRICIA DESPUÉS DEL VIAJE POR CENTRO AMÉRICA

Play Textbook audio.

Suggestion: Do as a pair activity. Ask students to listen twice with their books closed. Then have them open their books and try to answer the comprehension questions. Play a third time so students can check answers and complete the *Cómo lo dicen* section.

Acaba de empezar el semestre y Esteban Beltrán, al salir de clase, se encuentra con Patricia, una de sus compañeras del año pasado.

ANTES DE ESCUCHAR

Antes de escuchar la conversación, contesta estas preguntas.

Imagina que acabas de empezar el semestre y te encuentras con un(a) amigo(a) que no has visto durante el verano,

1. ¿Cómo reaccionas al ver a tu amigo(a)?
2. ¿De qué hablas con él (ella)?
3. ¿Qué preguntas le haces?

Ahora mira los ejercicios que aparecen en la sección *Después de escuchar.*

Answers, Ex. H
1. V 2. V 3. F 4. V 5. F 6. V

DESPUÉS DE ESCUCHAR

H. Comprensión. Escucha la conversación entre Esteban y Patricia y decide si las siguientes afirmaciones son verdaderas o falsas.

1. Esteban no sabe todavía qué clases va a tener.
2. Patricia quiere saber adónde fue Esteban de vacaciones.
3. Esteban pasó las primeras semanas del verano con su familia.
4. Esteban estuvo de viaje con unos amigos.
5. Patricia le cuenta a Esteban lo que hizo durante las vacaciones.
6. Al final, Patricia y Esteban discuten la posibilidad de reunirse un día para comer o tomar un café.

Ex. I: Pairs

Answers, Ex. I
1. ¿Acabas de llegar? 2. la primera semana, después, otra semana, luego

I. ¿Cómo lo dicen? Escucha otra vez la conversación para determinar lo siguiente.

1. ¿Cómo dice Patricia "you just came back"?
2. ¿Cuáles son algunas expresiones de tiempo que usa Esteban en su narración?

Ex. J: Group of 3

Suggestion, Ex. J: The purpose of this activity is to let students use their imagination and creativity. You may want to brainstorm with them before they begin working on the story. You can suggest the following:
• la resistencia del héroe Lempira y el ataque de los españoles
• la conquista de El Salvador
• la independencia de los países de Centroamérica

Tú dirás ....

J. Una historia. En grupos de tres personas elaboren una historia en el pasado. Va a empezar una persona del grupo y después cada uno va a añadir una frase. Una persona se va a encargar de escribir la historia y, al terminar, van a leerla al resto de la clase. Usen los tiempos del pasado y las expresiones temporales que han aprendido en esta *etapa*.

362 *trescientos sesenta y dos*

Capítulo 10

K. Un viaje. Habla con un(a) compañero(a) sobre un viaje que hiciste. Incluye la siguiente información:

1. el lugar al que fuiste
2. las personas con las que viajaste
3. el tiempo que estuviste allí
4. las cosas que viste
5. las actividades que hiciste
6. las cosas que compraste
7. cualquier otra cosa que quieras añadir

Al terminar, tu compañero(a) va a hablar de su viaje.

Ex. K: Pairs

TERCERA ETAPA

PARA EMPEZAR: ¿Qué vas a hacer?

Preparación: Antes de seguir adelante, contesta las siguientes preguntas:

- **What plans do you have for the weekend?**
- **When you are visiting a city you don't know, how do you get information about what there is to do in that city?**

You may want to ask students to prepare the questions in the *Antes de leer* section as homework. Also, you can have them read the text on pages 364–365 before they come to class, so you can spend class time doing the exercises under *Práctica* on page 365. You can begin the class by having students respond to the questions in the *Preparación* section.

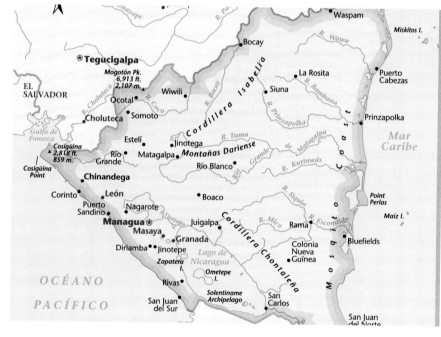

Suggestion: To encourage cultural and geographic learning, put students in groups of 3 or 4 and have them research a 7-day trip to a Latin American country. Encourage them to use the Internet for information, maps, pictures, etc. They then prepare a report for the class on that trip, as if they had taken it.

ANTES DE LEER

Enrique y Mónica están pasando una semana en Nicaragua. Ahora están en Managua, la capital. Hoy es jueves y están haciendo planes para el fin de semana. Para organizar su tiempo libre tienen a su disposición una guía de Nicaragua que ofrece información sobre diferentes lugares de interés turístico.

1. Mónica y Enrique quieren pasar el viernes, sábado y parte del domingo fuera de Managua. A Enrique le interesa mucho la naturaleza, y quiere ver algunos de los volcanes y lagos que hay en la región. A Mónica también le gusta la naturaleza, pero le interesa más la historia y el pasado colonial. Mónica tiene especial interés en visitar el museo del poeta Rubén Darío.
2. Mira el mapa y localiza los siguientes lugares: Managua, Masaya, Granada, León.
3. El domingo por la noche, al volver a Managua, quieren ir a un bar para tomar un trago y escuchar música. Mónica quiere ir a escuchar rock pero Enrique prefiere ir a un lugar donde pueda oír música de Nicaragua.
4. Lee la información que aparece en la guía y después contesta las preguntas de la *Práctica*.

GUÍA DE NICARAGUA

LUGARES PARA VISITAR

MASAYA Situada a 29 kilómetros de Managua, es el centro del folklore y la artesanía de Nicaragua. En el pintoresco mercado de Masaya y en su barrio indígena Monimbó siempre hay **hamacas tejidas a mano,** sombreros, alfombras, blusas **bordadas** y otras artesanías.

Muy cerca de la ciudad está el Volcán Masaya, el único de Nicaragua al que se puede llegar por carretera **pavimentada** hasta su borde mismo, desde el que se observa el magma **hirviendo** en el centro de su cráter, en una de las más espectaculares vistas del mundo volcánico.

GRANADA Sobria y elegante con sus construcciones coloniales. Fundada a la orilla del Lago Cocibolca y a la sombra del Volcán Mombacho. La Plaza Central, rodeada por la Catedral, el Ayuntamiento y la Casa de los Tres Mundos, es uno de los principales lugares de interés.

Las 300 isletas de su lago cubiertas de diversa vegetación y de la alegría de los **pájaros** tropicales, ofrecen un espectáculo ecológico. La isla más grande del mundo inmersa en un lago es Ometepe, formada por dos volcanes, Concepción y Maderas; y muy cerca de ella, está el Parque Nacional Isla Zapatera. Ambas islas fueron centros funerarios religiosos de pobladores precolombinos.

LEÓN Capital de Nicaragua durante 200 años, típicamente colonial. Muchos la consideran el centro intelectual del país, porque allí está el núcleo central de la Universidad Nacional Autónoma de Nicaragua.

Su Catedral Metropolitana guarda en su interior verdaderas obras maestras de la pintura y las tumbas de destacados nicaragüenses, entre ellos Rubén Darío. Una visita al Museo Rubén Darío sólo puede conducir a la poesía.

Hacia el noroeste de León, en las faldas del Volcán Momotombo, se encuentran las ruinas de León Viejo, donde se fundó la primera ciudad de León y que fue **arrasada** por el volcán.

BARES EN MANAGUA

LA BUENA NOTA. Km 3½ Carretera Sur. Abierto de 12:00 A.M. 12:00 P.M. Cerrado domingo. Barra, sala de espectáculos y show en vivo de artistas nacionales.

CORO DE ÁNGELES. Km. 5½ Carretera a Masaya. Abierto de 2:00 P.M. hasta el amanecer. Tardes de librería, noches culturales y cinema cultural.

Marginal glosses:

handmade hammocks
broided

paved
boiling

birds

Rubén Darío is a poet from Nicaragua. You will learn more about him in the *Comentarios culturales* on page 368.

devastated

CHAMAN. Carretera a Masaya. Conciertos de rock en vivo los jueves, ambiente abierto a todas las opciones. Mesas de billar.

LUZ Y SOMBRA. Del Banco Popular Monseñor Lezcano 1c. al lago, ½ c. abajo. Jueves a sábado Noches Culturales con artistas nacionales. Abierto desde las 11:00 AM hasta el amanecer.

RUTA MAYA. De Montoya 150 vrs. arriba. En la semana presentaciones musicales en directo. Noches de humor y videoteca. Hora Feliz de 5:00 a 8:00 P.M.

EL PARNASO. Rotonda Metrocentro 1c. al sur. Comidas y bebidas nacionales e internacionales. Lugar de reunión de escritores y cantautores nicaragüenses.

LIGHT CITY. Contiguo a los cinemas. Jueves: Rock en vivo de los años 60 y 70. Viernes a sábado: Música europea, salsa y merengue hasta el amanecer.

Práctica

A. Los planes de Enrique y Mónica. Junto con un(a) compañero(a) de clase y de acuerdo con la información sobre Enrique y Mónica que aparece en la página 364, contesta las siguientes preguntas.

1. ¿Qué volcanes puede ver Enrique? ¿Dónde están?
2. ¿Adónde va a ir Mónica para ver el museo de Rubén Darío?
3. Si quieren comprar cosas de artesanía, ¿adónde pueden ir?
4. ¿Crees que Mónica va a poder escuchar rock en vivo el domingo?
5. ¿A qué bares crees que puede ir Enrique?

B. Tus planes y los de tus amigos. Imagina que estás en Nicaragua con unos amigos. De acuerdo con la información que aparece en la guía, decide qué vas a hacer tú el fin de semana. Después pregunta a tus amigos qué quieren hacer ellos. Entre todos, elaboren un plan para las actividades que van a hacer el fin de semana.

Repaso

C. La rutina de tu profesor(a). Con un(a) compañero(a) de clase imagina la rutina diaria de tu profesor(a). Escriban cinco frases en las que indiquen qué hace normalmente durante un día de clase y cinco frases en las que indiquen qué hace normalmente los fines de semana. Después, compartan su información con el (la) profesor(a) y vean si lo que han escrito es cierto o no.

Ex. A: Pairs

Answers, Ex. A
1. El volcán Masaya, en Masaya. El volcán Mombacho, en Granada. Los volcanes Concepción y Maderas en Ometepe, cerca de Granada. El volcán Momotombo, en León. 2. A León. 3. Al mercado de Masaya. 4. No, en los bares de la guía no hay rock en vivo los domingos. 5. La Buena Nota; Luz y Sombra, El Parnaso.

Ex. C: Pairs

Suggestion, Ex. C: For a more challenging review, incorporate the past tense into their descriptions. Put students in groups of 3 and ask each group to describe what you used to do at different ages of your life. Ask one group to describe your current routine.

D. Un mal día. Claudia y Juan Pablo tuvieron ayer un mal día. Utiliza los siguientes dibujos para comentar lo que ocurrió. Emplea los verbos indicados y no olvides conectar las acciones con las expresiones aprendidas en la *Segunda etapa*.

■ **Modelo:** *Ayer Juan Pablo se despertó a las 8:00 muy contento. Después...*

despertarse

levantarse

ducharse

salir

vestirse

cepillarse los dientes

reunirse

separarse

pelearse

pasear

IRM Master 45: Expresiones para hablar del futuro #1

Combine your presentation of this vocabulary with the epxressions to talk about the future. Present an overhead transparency of a calendar page with dates filled with appointments. Tell students that you have been invited to visit a friend in México and you need to figure out if you will have time to make the trip in the next month. Go over your calendar and comment on things you will be doing that month to see if you have time.

ENFOQUE LÉXICO

Expresiones para hablar de una secuencia de acciones en el futuro

To organize your discourse when you refer to future actions you can use the following expressions:

hoy por la noche	la tarde	*this evening*	*afternoon*
esta	tarde noche		
esta semana			*this week*
este mes			*this month*
este año			*this year*
mañana por	la mañana la tarde la noche	*tomorrow*	*morning* *afternoon* *evening/night*

pasado mañana por...	la mañana la tarde la noche	the day after tomorrow in the ...	morning afternoon evening
el lunes 　(martes...) el fin de 　semana la semana el mes el año el curso	que viene	next	Monday ... weekend week month year academic year

IRM Master 46:
Expresiones para hablar del futuro #2

Preview: The future tense and its special uses are presented in Chapter 12.

ENFOQUE ESTRUCTURAL Expresiones verbales para hablar del futuro

The previous *Enfoque léxico* provided you with a number of time expressions you will find useful when you talk about your plans for the future. The following are verb structures you will need to use along with the previous expressions when you refer to events to come.

To make your speech more fluent and varied, it is better to avoid using only one expression by making use of several of them.

ir a + otro verbo en infinitivo

Este fin de semana Cristina y Enrique **van a tener** mucho tiempo libre.	*This weekend Cristina and Enrique **are going to have** a lot of free time.*

querer + otro verbo en infinitivo

Está claro que Enrique y Cristina quieren pasarlo bien estos días.	*It's obvious that Enrique and Cristina want to have a good time over the next few days.*

pensar + otro verbo en infinitivo

El sábado por la tarde **piensan** ir a un bar.	*Saturday afternoon **they plan to** go to a bar.*

tener (muchas) ganas de + otro verbo en infinitivo

Enrique **tiene muchas ganas de ver** volcanes.	*Enrique **would like to see** volcanoes.*

Remember that you will use reflexive verbs (**levantarse, vestirse, lavarse...**) as you do any other verb. Don't forget the reflexive pronouns (**me, te, se...**) that always accompany the verbs. Although the pronoun can be placed immediately before **ir, querer, pensar, tener ganas de,** we recommend that you keep it attached to the infinitive, as in the examples that follow, on the next page.

Creo que Cristina **va a levantarse** más tarde que de costumbre este fin de semana.	*I think that Cristina **is going to get up** later than usual this weekend.*
El sábado próximo no **pienso despertarme** antes de las 11:00.	*Next Saturday I **don't plan to wake up** until 11:00.*
¿A qué hora **vas a levantarte** tú?	*What time **do you plan to get up**?*

Práctica

E. El sábado que viene. El sábado que viene es un día especial. Por lo tanto *(Consequently)* no vas a seguir tu rutina habitual. Dile a tu compañero(a) las cosas que haces normalmente los sábados. Después, explica qué vas a hacer este sábado.

■ **Modelo:** *Normalmente los sábados por la mañana me quedo en casa. Pero el sábado que viene pienso salir de compras con unos amigos.*

F. El lunes que viene. Por otra parte *(On the other hand)*, el lunes que viene es un día completamente normal para ti y tu familia (o tus compañeros de apartamento o cuarto). Cuéntale a tu compañero(a) de clase qué vas a hacer el lunes. Intenta incluir todos los detalles que puedas. No te olvides de usar las expresiones aprendidas hasta ahora para conectar y organizar el discurso.

Ex. E:  Pairs

Ex. F: Pairs

Comentarios

culturales **Algunos escritores de Centroamérica de fama universal**

*R*ubén Darío, poeta nicaragüense, nació en 1867 en Metapa, hoy conocida como Ciudad Darío. En 1879, a los doce años de edad, escribió su primer poema, el soneto "La Fe". Después de la publicación de su libro *Azul* en 1888 en Valparaíso, Chile, se convirtió en el escritor de habla castellana más universalmente conocido de fines del siglo XIX y comienzos del XX. Rubén Darío fue el centro en torno al cual se desarrolló el modernismo hispano-americano. Murió en febrero de 1916 a causa de una enfermedad.

Rubén Darío, Nicaragua

Unos versos muy conocidos de Rubén Darío son:

> ¡Juventud, divino tesoro,
> ya te vas para no volver!
> Cuando quiero llorar, no lloro...
> y a veces lloro sin querer...

Miguel Ángel Asturias, Guatemala

Nació en 1899 en Ciudad de Guatemala. Estudió primero medicina y después derecho en la Universidad de San Carlos de Guatemala. Fue uno de los fundadores de la Universidad Popular de Guatemala (1922) y en ella dio clases de gramática y enseñó a leer a los **obreros** *(workers)*.

Viajó a Europa para seguir sus estudios en Londres y en París. Allí conoció a numerosos escritores importantes del momento. En 1926 publicó la traducción del maya al español del libro *Popol Vuh* con el título de *Los dioses, los héroes y los hombres de Guatemala Antigua o El libro del Consejo, Popol Vuh de los indios quichés.* En 1967 recibió el premio Nobel de Literatura.

Miguel Ángel Asturias murió en Madrid en 1974 y, de acuerdo con su voluntad, fue **enterrado** *(buried)* en París. Asturias mostró siempre una gran preocupación por la situación de la población indígena en Guatemala. Protestó contra la injusticia de las compañías bananeras norteamericanas y contra la intervención de los EE.UU. en su país. Entre sus numerosas obras, destacan *El Señor Presidente, Leyendas de Guatemala* y *Los hombres del maíz.*

INTEGRACIÓN CULTURAL

1. ¿A partir de qué momento se hace universalmente famoso Rubén Darío?
2. Indica qué aspectos de la vida de Miguel Ángel Asturias te parecen más interesantes. Explica por qué.

VAMOS A ESCUCHAR: ¿QUÉ HACEMOS MAÑANA POR LA NOCHE?

Enrique y Mónica están hablando sobre lo que quieren hacer mañana por la noche.

ANTES DE ESCUCHAR

Contesta las siguientes preguntas.

1. ¿Te gusta ir a bailar? ¿Vas a discotecas?
2. ¿Qué música te gusta más para bailar?
3. ¿Hay buenas discotecas donde vives?

Ahora, mira los ejercicios que aparecen en la sección *Después de escuchar.*

Ex. I: Pairs

Ex. J: Pairs

DESPUÉS DE ESCUCHAR

G. Comprensión. Escucha el diálogo y contesta las preguntas.

1. ¿Qué quiere hacer Mónica mañana por la noche?
2. ¿Cómo reacciona Enrique?
3. ¿Acepta Enrique el plan de Mónica?
4. ¿Qué plan propone Enrique?

H. ¿Cómo lo dicen? Escucha otra vez el diálogo entre Enrique y Mónica y contesta las preguntas.

1. ¿Cómo empieza Mónica la conversación?
2. ¿Cómo dice Mónica que "the atmosphere in Stratos is great"?
3. ¿Cómo dice Enrique: "let's see, let me see the guide"?

Tú dirás

I. ¿Qué hacemos esta noche? Quieres hacer algo este fin de semana con un(a) compañero(a) de tu clase. Para decidir qué van a hacer, le llamas por teléfono.

Estudiante A: Llama por teléfono.

1. Call your friend.
2. Tell him/her that you want to get together this weekend.
3. Suggest something to do.
4. React to his/her responses.
5. End the conversation appropriately.

Estudiante B: Contesta la llamada.

1. Answer the phone.
2. Tell your friend you will be happy to do something with him/her this weekend.
3. Say that you don't really like what your friends suggests.
4. Suggest a different idea.
5. Agree on how, where, and when you are going to meet.
6. End the conversation appropriately.

J. Las vacaciones de la familia. Con otro(a) estudiante de la clase discute los planes de tu familia (o tus amigos) para las próximas vacaciones. Puedes incluir la información siguiente:

1. where everyone is going
2. when you are leaving
3. what you are going to do

Al terminar, pregúntale a tu compañero(a) qué van a hacer él (ella) y su familia (o sus amigos) para las vacaciones.

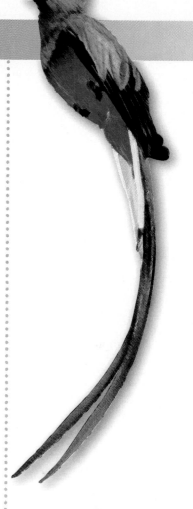

⊚ INTEGRACIÓN

LECTURA: "El eclipse"

ANTES DE LEER

Augusto Monterroso es un escritor guatemalteco. Escribe cuentos cortos en los que domina la sátira y la ironía. "El eclipse" pertenece a su libro *Obras completas y otros cuentos.*

A. Antes de leer el texto contesta las siguientes preguntas.

1. ¿Cómo crees que se siente una persona que está perdida *(lost)* en medio de la selva *(jungle)*?
2. ¿Cómo piensas que era en Guatemala la relación entre los indígenas y los frailes *(priests)* españoles?
3. ¿Qué opinión crees que tenían los españoles de la cultura indígena? ¿Piensas que los españoles creían que su cultura era superior a la de los mayas? ¿En qué sentido?

B. Exploración del título.

1. ¿Qué significa la palabra "eclipse"?
2. De acuerdo con la información que has leído sobre la civilización maya, ¿crees que los mayas sabían determinar las fechas de los eclipses?

C. Vocabulario útil.

rostro: sinónimo de "cara"
lecho: sinónimo de "cama"
conferir: sinónimo de "dar"
florecer en él una idea: pensar en algo, tener una idea
valerse de: sinónimo de "utilizar"
oscurecerse: no tener luz, es lo que le ocurre al sol cuando hay un eclipse.
sangre: *blood*

GUÍA PARA LA LECTURA

D. Lee el primer párrafo. ¿Dónde está fray Bartolomé? ¿Qué actitud tiene frente a la situación en que se encuentra?

E. Lee el segundo párrafo. ¿Qué vio fray Bartolomé al despertar? ¿Está su vida en peligro *(danger)*? Explica tu respuesta.

F. Lee el resto del cuento. Al leer piensa en las siguientes preguntas:

1. ¿Qué sabía Bartolomé?
2. ¿Cómo usó su conocimiento?
3. ¿En qué sentido fueron los mayas más sabios *(knowledgeable)* que el español?

Answers, Ex. D
Está en la selva de Guatemala. Decide esperar la muerte con tranquilidad.
Answers, Ex. E
Vio un grupo de indígenas. Sí, los indígenas lo van a sacrificar.
Answers, Ex. F
1. He knew there was going to be an eclipse. 2. to threaten the indians 3. They knew the dates of all solar and lunar eclipses.

EL ECLIPSE

Cuando fray Bartolomé Arrazola se sintió perdido aceptó que ya nada podría salvarlo. La selva poderosa de Guatemala lo había apresado, implacable y definitiva. Ante su ignorancia topográfica se sentó con tranquilidad a esperar la muerte. Quiso morir allí, sin ninguna esperanza, aislado con el pensamiento fijo en la España distante.

Al despertar se encontró rodeado por un grupo de indígenas de rostro impasible que se disponían a sacrificarlo ante un altar, un altar que a Bartolomé le pareció como el lecho en que descansaría, al fin, de sus temores, de su destino, de sí mismo.

Tres años en el país le habían conferido un mediano dominio de las lenguas nativas. Intentó algo. Dijo algunas palabras que fueron comprendidas.

Entonces floreció en él una idea que tuvo por digna de su talento y de su cultura universal y de su arduo conocimiento de Aristóteles. Recordó que para ese día se esperaba un eclipse total de sol. Y dispuso, en lo más íntimo, valerse de ese conocimiento para engañar a sus opresores y salvar la vida.

—Si me matáis —les dijo— puedo hacer que el sol se oscurezca en su altura.

Los indígenas lo miraron fijamente y Bartolomé sorprendió la incredulidad en sus ojos. Vio que se produjo un pequeño consejo y esperó confiado, no sin cierto desdén.

Dos horas después el corazón de fray Bartolomé Arrazola chorreaba su sangre vehemente sobre la piedra de los sacrificios (brillante bajo la opaca luz de un sol eclipsado), mientras uno de los indígenas recitaba sin ninguna inflexión de voz, sin prisa, una por una, las infinitas fechas en que se producirían eclipses solares y lunares, que los astrónomos de la comunidad maya habían previsto y anotado en sus códices sin la valiosa ayuda de Aristóteles.

DESPUÉS DE LEER

G. Ahora que sabes lo que le ocurrió a fray Bartolomé, contesta las siguientes preguntas.

1. ¿Qué información te da este cuento sobre la actitud de los españoles hacia los indígenas?
2. ¿Qué opinas de lo que hicieron los mayas con el fraile?
3. ¿Qué has aprendido tú con este cuento?

VÍDEO CULTURAL: ¿Cuándo son las vacaciones?

ATAJO

Writing activities for this chapter are presented in the Activities Manual. For specific references to tasks supported by Atajo, please consult the Activities Manual.

A. Anticipación. En el espacio, marca si es probable oír esta información en un segmento sobre el cine. Si es probable, márcala con una **X.** Después de terminar, compara tus respuestas con las de un(a) compañero(a) de clase.

1. _____ Lo que van a comer en el cine.
2. _____ El tiempo que hace.
3. _____ Lo que van a hacer después de la película.
4. _____ Lo que dicen tus amigos de la película.
5. _____ Quién va a ir a la fiesta.
6. _____ La novela de la cual hicieron la película.
7. _____ Quiénes son los actores.
8. _____ Si tiene subtítulos en inglés o en español.
9. _____ Las horas que dan la película.

B. Preparación. Completa las palabras y frases siguientes que aparecen en la sección *Vocabulario esencial* del vídeo. Después de terminar, compara tus respuestas con las de un(a) compañero(a) de clase. Luego, practiquen la pronunciación de las palabras y frases.

1. __a casa de l__s espír__tus
2. Cl__r__s
3. el __ire__tor
4. __o tie__e di__uj__tos

Answers, Ex. B:
1. La casa de los espíritus
2. clerks
3. el director
4. no tiene dibujitos

C. Participación. Toma notas acerca de las películas.

Las películas que se mencionan: _____

La hora de la sesión: _____

La hora ahora: _____

Van a ver la película _____ porque _____

D. Comprensión. Acabas de ver el segmento sobre el cine. Ahora, contesta las preguntas siguientes.

1. ¿Qué película deciden ver?
   a. *Salto al vacío.*
   b. *Clerks.*
2. ¿Por qué considera la película *Salto al vacío* una película buena?
   a. Porque los actores son maravillosos.
   b. Porque el director es maravilloso.
3. ¿Por qué no pueden ir a ver *Clerks*?
   a. Porque no hay entradas para la sesión.
   b. Porque llegan tarde para la sesión.

Answers, Ex. D:
1. b   2. b   3. b

E. Personalización. Ahora describe una película que hayas visto recientemente. Incluye toda la información pertinente: la sesión, cuánto costó la entrada *(ticket),* con quién(es) fuiste, quiénes fueron los actores y el/la director(a). Si necesitas más espacio, escribe al otro lado de esta hoja.

▶ *Intercambio: Rigoberta Menchú, Premio Nóbel de la Paz*

Cada uno de ustedes tiene información incompleta sobre Rigoberta Menchú. Lean la información que tienen y contesten las preguntas de su compañero(a).

Estudiante A

1. Lee la información que tienes sobre Rigoberta Menchú. Después contesta las preguntas que te va a hacer tu compañero(a).

Rigoberta Menchú es de origen maya quiché. Nació en 1956 en Chimel, un pueblo en el norte de Guatemala. Creció en una familia indígena muy humilde. Con ellos aprendió la lengua quiché y las costumbres de su gente. Cuando era muy niña tuvo que trabajar en el campo recogiendo algodón y café. Después trabajó en la ciudad como empleada doméstica. Rigoberta hablaba sólo quiché y cuando tenía 20 años decidió aprender español para poder informar a la gente de la represión que sufría su pueblo.

Las fuerzas de seguridad de Guatemala asesinaron a su hermano cuando tenía 16 años. En 1980 murieron sus padres, también víctimas de la violencia existente en el país.

2. Tu compañero(a) tiene información que tú no tienes. Haz las preguntas siguientes para obtener la información que necesitas.
   a. When did Rigoberta start working actively in defense of the Mayan people?
   b What happened in 1981?
   c. Is there anything I can read to learn more about her?
   d. What year did she receive the Nobel Peace Prize?

Desde 1980 Rigoberta empezó a participar activamente en numerosas organizaciones en contra de la opresión y la discriminación sufrida por el pueblo maya. Su trabajo en defensa de los pueblos indígenas y en la promoción de sus valores puso su vida en peligro. Por esta razón, en 1981 tuvo que salir de Guatemala. Fue a México y allí organizó un movimiento de resistencia campesina.

En 1983 se publicó su libro testimonial *Me llamo Rigoberta Menchú y así me nació la conciencia.*

En 1992 recibió el Premio Nóbel de la Paz por su labor en defensa de los derechos de los seis millones de indios mayas que viven en Guatemala. Rigoberta aceptó el premio en nombre de todo el pueblo indígena.

2. Lee la información que tienes sobre Rigoberta Menchú. Después contesta las preguntas que te va a hacer tu compañero(a).

   d. What happened in 1980 to her family?
   c. When and why did she learn Spanish?
   b. What language did she speak with her family?
   a. Where and when was Rigoberta Menchú born?

   siguientes para obtener la información que necesitas.
1. Tu compañero(a) tiene información que tú no tienes. Haz las preguntas

Estudiante B

Vocabulario

Verbos reflexivos y no reflexivos

dormir *to sleep* / dormirse *to fall asleep*
levantar *to lift* / levantarse *to get up*
poner *to put* / ponerse *to put on*

Verbos recíprocos

abrazarse *to hug each other*
besarse *to kiss each other*
despedirse *to say good by to each other*
encontrarse *to meet each other*
escribirse *to write to each other*
hablarse *to talk to each other*
llamarse *to call each other*
mandarse *to send to each other*
mirarse *to look at each other*
saludarse *to great each other*
verse *to see each other*

Expresiones para hablar de una secuencia de acciones en el presente y acciones habituales en el pasado:

por la mañana *in the morning*
por la tarde *in the afternoon*
por la noche *in the evening/at night*
todos los días *everyday*
los lunes (martes...) *Mondays, Tuesdays ...*
al despertarme *when I get up*
al salir de casa *when I leave home*
después de comer *after lunch*
antes de clase *before class*
a la hora de comer/cenar *at lunch/dinner time*
siempre *always*
normalmente *ususally*
por lo genera *in general*
a menudo *often*
con frecuencia *frequently*
casi siempre *almost always*
de vez en cuando *once in a while*
a veces/algunas veces *sometimes*
casi nunca *almost never*
nunca *never*

Expresiones para hablar de una secuencia de acciones puntuales en el pasado

ayer *yesterday*
anteayer *the day before yesterday*
el lunes (martes...) pasado *last Monday (Tuesday...)*

primero *first*
lo primero de todo *first of all*
después *then*
por fin *finally*
luego *then*
por último *at the end*
más tarde *later on*
finalmente *at the end*
al final del día *at the end of the day*
  de la tarde *of the afternoon*
  de la noche *of the evening/night*
el fin de semana pasado *last weekend*
la semana pasada *last week*
el mes pasado *last month*
el verano pasado *last summer*
las vacaciones pasadas *last vacation*
el primer día *the first day*
los primerros días *the first days*
al llegar *upon arriving*
el día que llegamos *the day we arrived*
ese mismo día *that same day*
al día siguiente *the next day*
el último día *the last day*

Expresiones para hablar de una secuencia de acciones en el futuro

hoy por la tarde/por la noche *this afternoon, this evening*
esta tarde/esta noche *this afternoon, this evening*
esta semana, este mes, este año *this week, this month, this year*
mañana por la mañana, tarde, noche *tomorrow morning, afternoon, evening*
pasado mañana *the day after tomorrow*
el lunes (martes...) que viene *next Monday, Tuesday...*
el fin de semana *next weekend*
la semana *next week*
el mes que viene *next month*
el año *next year*
el curso *next academic year*

Expresiones verbales para hablar del futuro

pienso ir a... *I intend to go to*
Quiero visitar... *I want to visit*
Tengo ganas de... *I feel like*
Voy a... *I am going to go*

11 la comida en el mundo hispano

PRIMERA ETAPA
Un restaurante español

SEGUNDA ETAPA
La Guía del ocio

TERCERA ETAPA
La comida Tex-Mex

INTEGRACIÓN:

LECTURA: Como agua para chocolate
VÍDEO CULTURAL: Ricos sabores
INTERCAMBIO: Para poner la mesa
ESCRITURA: Actividades en el manual

AMÉRICA DEL NORTE

maíz

maíz   maíz
maíz   chile
con
carne
maíz

Cacao (chocolate), Chiles, Maíz, Patata, Tomate

A España, 1500s

Naranjas, Arroz

Bananas
Caña de azúcar

De España, 1500s

EUROPA

maíz
CHILES
MAÍZ   TOMATE
cacao   maíz

Mar Caribe

De África, 1500s

ÁFRICA

patata
maíz
cacao
patata
CACAO   chiles
chiles
maíz
cacao
PATATA
MAÍZ
patata chiles
maíz

AMÉRICA DEL SUR

OCÉANO ATLÁNTICO

OCÉANO PACÍFICO

N

patata

cacao
PATATA

Inicio del desarrollo agrícola

Expansión temprana agrícola

Expansión subsiguiente agrícola

Chapter Objectives:

After completing this chapter you should be able to carry out the following tasks:

- ꩜ **read a menu**
- ꩜ **order a meal in a restaurant**
- ꩜ **understand conversations about food**
- ꩜ **understand cultural aspects related to food in the Spanish-speaking world**

The tools you will use to carry out these tasks are:

- ꩜ **Vocabulary for:**
  - food
  - restaurants
  - affirmative and negative expressions
- ꩜ **Grammatical structures:**
  - verbs like **gustar: apetecer, encantar, tocar, faltar**
  - **estar** + adjectives
  - present progressive
  - double object pronouns
  - impersonal **se**

⊚ *PARA EMPEZAR:* *Un restaurante español*

▢ **Transparency**
Menú Restaurante La Barraca
N-1: Start discussion by asking students these questions in Spanish.

Preparación: As you begin this *etapa,* answer the following questions:

- What do you know about the food in Spain?
- Are you familiar with the food from some other Spanish-speaking country?
- Are you familiar with the food of the Caribbean?
- What dishes are you familiar with?

Restaurante La Barraca

Aperitivos

Espárragos a la parmesana	Chorizo
Tortilla española	**Jamón serrano**
Calamares **fritos**	**Gambas al ajillo**

appetizers
asparagus
Spanish ham, similar to prosciutto / fried / shrimp in garlic

Sopas

Gazpacho andaluz	Sopa de pescado
Sopa de **ajo**	Sopa del día
Sopa de **mariscos**	

cold soup with tomatoes, garlic, onion (from Andalucía) / garlic
seafood

Segundo plato

Pescado frito	Filete de **ternera**
Paella valenciana	**Chuletas de cordero**
Pollo al chilindrón	Bistec

entrees
veal
Spanish dish with rice, shellfish, and chicken / lamb chops / Spanish dish with chicken in a spicy tomato sauce

Ensaladas

Ensalada mixta (lechuga, cebolla, tomate)

Postres

Flan	**Queso manchego**
Fruta	Helados **variados**

cheese from La Mancha region in Spain / assorted

Bebidas

Agua mineral con gas	Sangría
sin gas	Vino tinto
Café	Vino blanco
Té	Cerveza
Refrescos **surtidos**	

assorted

el azúcar
la pimienta
la mantequilla
la copa
la taza
la sal
el platillo
el plato hondo
el tenedor
el cuchillo
la cuchara
la cucharita
la servilleta
el plato

◢ **Transparency N-3: Para poner la mesa**

Present vocabulary in context. Bring in place setting props and use a transparency to display a menu. Tell students that the menu is from one of your favorite restaurants. You want to tell them all about the experience of eating in this restaurant. Talk about how the table is set, pointing out items as you use their names. Then discuss what you would like to eat from the menu. During your presentation check comprehension by asking students questions, e.g.; **¿Te gustan los aperitivos?**

ENFOQUE LÉXICO — Expresiones que se usan en un restaurante

Expresiones para pedir una mesa en un restaurante

Quisiera	una mesa para...	***I would like***	*a table for ...*
Quisiéramos	personas, por favor.	***We would like***	*people, please.*

Expresiones para pedir la comida

¿Qué quisiera pedir	***What would you*** *(sing.)* ***like***
como aperitivo?	***as*** *an appetizer?*
¿...sopa?	*...a soup?*
¿Qué quisieran pedir	***What would you*** *(pl.)* ***like***
como segundo plato?	***as*** *an entree?*
¿...postre?	*...a dessert?*
¿Qué quisiera para beber?	*What would you like to drink?*

Para beber quisiera	agua mineral un vino blanco una cerveza	*To drink I would like*	*mineral water white wine a beer*

Como	aperitivo sopa segundo plato postre	**quisiera...**	*As*	*an appetizer soup an entree a dessert*	***I would like ...***

Expresiones para pedir la cuenta

La cuenta, por favor.	*The check, please.*
¿Podría traernos la cuenta, por favor?	*Could you bring us the check, please?*
Quisiera la cuenta, por favor.	*I would like the check, please.*
Quisiéramos la cuenta, por favor.	*We would like the check, please.*

Práctica

A. ¿Qué vas a comer? Estás en el Restaurante La Barraca con unos amigos. Ellos te dicen lo que tienen ganas de comer y te piden recomendaciones.

1. Tengo ganas de comer vegetales. ¿Qué puedo comer como aperitivo?
2. Tengo ganas de comer carne. ¿Qué puedo comer como aperitivo?
3. Tengo ganas de comer mariscos. ¿Qué puedo comer como aperitivo? ¿Qué puedo comer como segundo plato?
4. No quiero comer pescado. ¿Qué platos debo evitar *(avoid)*?
5. ¿Qué tipos de carne sirven como segundo plato?

B. ¿Qué le recomiendas? Consulta el menú del Restaurante La Barraca y pide una comida que incluya aperitivo, sopa, segundo plato y postre para cada una de las siguientes personas.

1. una persona que quiere pescado
2. una persona que quiere mariscos
3. una persona que es vegetariana
4. una persona que come mucho
5. una persona que quiere comer comida norteamericana tradicional

ENFOQUE ESTRUCTURAL — **Verbos como gustar**

As you have seen previously, **gustar** and verbs like it are used in the third person singular (**gusta**) or plural (**gustan**) forms along with the indirect object pronouns: **me, te, le, nos, os,** and **les.** Note the following:

¿Te gusta la comida italiana?	***Do you like*** *Italian food?*
No, pero **me gusta** la comida china.	*No, but **I like** Chinese food.*
¿Te gusta comer?	***Do you like*** *to eat?*
Sí.	*Yes, I do.*
¿A quién **le toca** pagar?	***Whose turn is it*** *to pay?*
Te toca pagar a ti.	***It is your turn*** *to pay.*
¿Qué **te falta?**	*What do **you need?***
Me falta una servilleta.	***I need*** *a napkin.*

Ex. A **Group**
Encourage students to role-play a restaurant situation to carry out these activities. Use props to simulate a restaurant atmosphere.

Answers, Ex. A
1. Puedes comer espárragos a la parmesana como aperitivo.
2. Puedes comer chorizo o jamón serrano como aperitivo. 3. Puedes comer gambas al ajillo como aperitivo y paella valenciana como segundo plato. 4. Debes evitar la sopa de pescado y el pescado frito. 5. Sirven pollo al chilindrón, filete de ternera, chuletas de cordero y bistec.

Possible answers, Ex. B
1. Le recomiendo los calamares fritos, la sopa de pescado, el pescado frito y el flan. 2. Le recomiendo las gambas al ajillo, la sopa del día, la paella valenciana y helados variados. 3. Le recomiendo los espárragos a la parmesana, la sopa de ajo, la ensalada mixta y la fruta. 4. Le recomiendo la tortilla española, la sopa de pescado, el bistec, la ensalada mixta y el queso manchego. 5. Le recomiendo el jamón serrano, la sopa de pescado, el bistec y los helados variados.

IRM Master 47: Verbos como *gustar*

Note that when verbs like **gustar** are followed by an infinitive, regardless of how many, the third person singular is always used.

¿Qué **te gusta** hacer en tu tiempo libre?	What **do you like** to do in your free time?
Me gusta comer, estudiar y dormir.	**I like** to eat, study, and sleep.

Here are some other verbs that can be used in the same way as **gustar.**

encantar	*to like very much*	tocar	*to be one's turn*
faltar	*to need, lack*	apetecer	*to appeal*

GRAMMAR NOTE:

Remember that when you use **gustar** with **le** or **les,** you may want to clarify it:

A Juan le gusta la paella.
A Marta le gustan las gambas.
A Juan y a Marta les gusta el pescado.
The same would hold for the other verbs presented here.

A ellos les toca pagar la cuenta.
A Sara le apetecen unas gambas.

Práctica

C. ¿A quién le gusta… ? Tú y varios amigos están en un restaurante. Haz preguntas y contéstalas refiriéndote a las personas indicadas según el modelo.

■ **Modelo:**   gustar / sopa de ajo (Juan)
¿A quién le gusta la sopa de ajo?
A Juan.

1. encantar / calamares (nosotros)
2. tocar / pagar la cuenta (Jaime)
3. faltar / tenedor (Linda)
4. tocar / comprar las bebidas (ellas)
5. faltar / dinero (Julieta)
6. encantar / paella (José)
7. faltar / servilleta (ella)
8. apetecer / una ensalada mixta (ellos)

D. ¿Qué le falta a… ? Tú y tus amigos llegan a su mesa en un restaurante y notan que les faltan algunas cosas. Sigan el modelo.

■ **Modelo:**   *¿Qué le falta a Luisa?*
A Luisa le falta una servilleta.

1. Mónica   2. Jaime   3. Sara   4. Tomás   5. Carmen

Answers, Ex. C
1. ¿A quién le encantan los calamares? A nosotros nos encantan los calamares. 2. ¿A quién le toca pagar la cuenta? A Jaime le toca pagar la cuenta. 3. ¿A quién le falta un tenedor? A Linda le falta un tenedor. 4. ¿A quién le toca comprar las bebidas? A ellas les toca comprar las bebidas. 5. ¿A quién le falta dinero? A Julieta le falta dinero. 6. ¿A quién le encanta la paella? A José le encanta la paella. 7. ¿A quién le falta una servilleta? A ella le falta una servilleta. 8. ¿A quién le apetece una ensalada mixta? A ellos les apetece una ensalada mixta.

Answers, Ex. D
1. ¿Qué le falta a Mónica? A Mónica le faltan dos cucharas/cucharitas. 2. A Jaime le falta una copa. 3. A Sara le falta un plato. 4. A Tomás le faltan dos tenedores. 5. A Carmen le falta un cuchillo.

E. Una encuesta. Pregúntales a varios de tus compañeros lo que piensan de las siguientes comidas o bebidas. Después comparte con la clase lo que piensan tus compañeros.

■ **Modelo:** *A Mary le apetece la ensalada, no le gustan los espárragos y le encantan los mariscos.*

(no) apetecer   (no) gustar   (no) encantar

1. los mariscos
2. los espárragos
3. los calamares
4. las gambas
5. el pollo
6. la ensalada
7. el café
8. el té
9. el vino
10. la cerveza
11. ???

ENFOQUE ESTRUCTURAL — Estar + adjetivos para expresar estado o condición

The verb **estar** is used with certain adjectives to express conditions that are true at a given moment, but not necessarily permanent. Note the following examples:

¿Qué tal **está** la sopa?	*How's the soup?*
¡**Está** muy **rica**! (¡**Está riquísima**!)	*It's very good!*
¿Qué tal **están** los tacos?	*How are the tacos?*
Están muy **ricos**. (¡**Están riquísimos**!)	*They're very good!*
¡Qué **rica está** la hamburguesa!	*This hamburger is delicious!*
¡Qué **ricos están** los tacos!	*These tacos are great!*
Camarero, este plato **está sucio**. Tráigame otro, por favor.	*Waiter, this plate is dirty. Please bring me another one.*
Yo **estoy nervioso** hoy porque tengo un examen.	*I am nervous today because I have an exam.*
Marta **está triste** hoy porque no hace sol.	*Marta is sad today because it is not sunny.*

Remember that these, like all adjectives in Spanish, must agree with the nouns they modify.

La sopa está fría.
El vaso está limpio.
Las gambas están saladas.
Los espárragos están ricos.
María está alegre hoy.
Ellos están tristes hoy.

Some common adjectives that are used with **estar** to express these types of conditions are:

abierto(a)	*open*	lleno(a)	*full*
aburrido(a)	*bored*	limpio(a)	*clean*
alegre	*happy*	mojado(a)	*wet*
avergonzado(a)	*embarrassed*	nervioso(a)	*nervous*
caliente	*hot*	ocupado(a)	*busy*
cansado(a)	*tired*	picante	*spicy*
cerrado(a)	*closed*	preocupado	*worried*
contento(a)	*happy*	sabroso(a)	*tasty*
dulce	*sweet*	salado(a)	*salty*
enfermo(a)	*sick*	seco(a)	*dry*
enojado(a)	*angry*	sucio(a)	*dirty*
frío(a)	*cold*	tranquilo(a)	*calm*
furioso(a)	*furious*	triste	*sad*
		vacío(a)	*empty*

Adding emphasis to a description

¿Cómo está Alberto hoy?	*How is Alberto today?*
Está **un poco** cansado. ¿Y tú?	*He is **a little** tired, and you?*
Estoy **muy** nervioso hoy.	*I am **very** nervous today.*
Me gustan los refrescos cuando están **bien** fríos.	*I like soft drinks when they are **very** cold.*
¿Estás preocupado ahora?	*Are you worried now?*
Sí, estoy **algo** preocupado.	*Yes, I am **somewhat** worried.*

Un poco, muy, algo, and **bien** may be placed before an adjective of condition in order to enhance or mitigate the quality expressed by the adjective.

Práctica

F. Tráigame una… Cuando tú y tus compañeros llegan a la mesa en un restaurante, hay varias cosas sucias. Pídanle al mesero que traiga otras limpias según el modelo.

■ **Modelo:** cuchara

Mesero, esta cuchara está sucia. Tráigame una cuchara limpia, por favor.

1. tenedor
2. vaso
3. cuchillos
4. servilletas
5. platos
6. taza

Possible answers, Ex. G
1. ¿Cómo está Julia hoy? Está un poco preocupada. 2. ¿Cómo está tu padre hoy? Está muy contento.
3. ¿Cómo está la profesora hoy? Está bien ocupada. 4. ¿Cómo están Sara y Ester hoy? Están algo tristes.
5. ¿Cómo están Jaime y Nicolás hoy? Están un poco cansados. 6. ¿Cómo están ustedes hoy? Estamos muy preocupados(as).

Ex. H: Pairs

G. ¿Cómo está Tina hoy? Un(a) compañero(a) de clase te hace varias preguntas sobre cómo están varias personas que Uds. conocen. Contesta sus preguntas según el modelo.

■ **Modelo:**   Tina / aburrido
—¿*Cómo está Tina hoy?*
—*Está muy aburrida.*
          o
—*Está algo aburrida.*
          o
—*Está un poco aburrida.*
          o
—*Está bien aburrida.*

1. Julia / preocupado
2. tu padre / contento
3. la profesora / ocupado
4. Sara y Ester / triste
5. Jaime y Nicolás / cansado
6. Uds. / preocupado

H. Intercambio. Siempre se conoce mejor a una persona cuando sabemos sus sentimientos. Hazle preguntas a un(a) compañero(a) y luego comparte la información con el resto de la clase. Sigue el modelo.

■ **Modelo:**   cansado
¿*Cuándo estás cansado?*
Estoy cansado(a) cuando no duermo bien.

1. cansado(a)
2. preocupado(a)
3. triste
4. nervioso(a)
5. alegre
6. aburrido(a)
7. ocupado(a)
8. furioso(a)
9. contento(a)
10. avergonzado(a)

ENFOQUE ESTRUCTURAL   El progresivo

Contextualize presentation of this structure. Use a transparency depicting several people doing things. Describe what each person is doing using the present progressive.

In Spanish, when you want to show that an action is in progress at the moment you are speaking, you use the *present progressive*. In the examples below, you will notice that all include a form of the verb **estar** plus a form of another verb that ends in **-ndo.** This form of the verb that ends in **-ndo** is known as the *present participle.*

¿Qué **estás haciendo** ahora mismo?	*What **are you doing** right now?*
Estoy estudiando.	*I am studying.*
¿Qué **está haciendo** Catarina ahora?	*What **is** Catarina **doing** now?*
Está hablando por teléfono.	*She is talking on the phone.*
¿Qué **están haciendo** tus amigos en este momento?	*What **are** your friends **doing** at this moment?*
Están mirando un programa de TV.	*They are watching a TV program.*

To form the present participle of **-ar** verbs, drop the **-ar** and add **-ando.**

hablar	hablando	comprar	comprando
bailar	bailando	estudiar	estudiando
tocar	tocando	nadar	nadando

To form the present participle of **-er** and **-ir** verbs, drop the **-er** or **-ir** and add **-iendo.**

comer	comiendo	salir	saliendo
correr	corriendo	escribir	escribiendo

The present participles of the following verbs are irregular.

leer	**leyendo**	oír	**oyendo**
dormir	**durmiendo**	pedir	**pidiendo**
creer	**creyendo**	repetir	**repitiendo**
decir	**diciendo**	servir	**sirviendo**

Julia **está leyendo** una revista.	*Julia **is reading** a magazine.*
José **está durmiendo** ahora mismo.	*José **is sleeping** right now.*

Notice that in the above examples of the present progressive, **estar** agrees with the subject, while the present participle (the **-ndo** form of the verb) never changes.

Some expressions you can use with the present progressive to stress that the action is in progress while you are speaking are:

ahora	*now*
ahora mismo	*right now*
en este momento	*at this moment*

Práctica

I. ¿Qué está haciendo... ? Pregúntale a un(a) compañero(a) lo que está haciendo la persona indicada. Debe contestar con el verbo indicado. Sigue el modelo.

■ **Modelo:** Pablo / comer
—*¿Qué está haciendo Pablo ahora?*
—*Está comiendo.*

1. Esteban / beber leche
2. Rafael y Marta / mirar la TV
3. Patricio / escuchar la radio
4. Carmen y Alicia / hablar por teléfono
5. Guillermo y Ricardo / jugar al fútbol
6. Isabel / estudiar para un examen
7. Linda / leer una revista
8. Julián / dormir

Ex. I: Pairs

Answers, Ex. I
1. Esteban está bebiendo leche.
2. Rafael y Marta están mirando la TV.
3. Patricio está escuchando la radio.
4. Carmen y Alicia están hablando por teléfono. 5. Guillermo y Ricardo están jugando al fútbol. 6. Isabel está estudiando para un examen. 7. Linda está leyendo una revista. 8. Julián está durmiendo.

J. ¿Qué están haciendo en este momento? Di lo que están haciendo las personas en los dibujos a continuación.

1. Jaime	2. Julia	3. Marirosa y Juan	4. Alberto

5. Carmen y Cristina	6. Juanito	7. Laura	8. Mario

K. ¿Qué está haciendo... ? Indica lo que están haciendo las personas en el siguiente dibujo.

VAMOS A ESCUCHAR: EN UN RESTAURANTE

Play Textbook audio.

El Sr. y la Sra. Pérez cenan en el restaurante La Barraca cuyo *(whose)* menú aparece al principio de esta *etapa*.

ANTES DE ESCUCHAR

Basado en lo que has aprendido en esta *etapa*, ¿qué información esperas escuchar en cuanto a *(with regard to)*

1. el aperitivo?
2. el segundo plato?
3. el postre?

Antes de escuchar la conversación, repasa las preguntas que aparecen en la sección *Después de escuchar.*

DESPUÉS DE ESCUCHAR

L. Comprensión. Escucha la cinta y contesta las siguientes preguntas.

1. ¿Dónde pide la mesa el Sr. Pérez?
2. ¿Piden aperitivo? ¿Qué?
3. ¿Qué tipo de sopa pide la Sra. Pérez?
4. ¿Quién pide pescado?
5. ¿Qué piden de postre?
6. ¿Cómo va a pagar la cuenta el Sr. Pérez?

M. ¿Como lo dicen? Escucha la cinta otra vez para determinar lo siguiente:

1. ¿Cómo pide Sr. Pérez "a table for two"?
2. ¿Cómo pide la cuenta el Sr. Pérez?

Ex. L Pairs

Pair students for this activity. Ask them to listen to the tape once without taking any notes. Then have students discuss what they heard and try to answer the comprehension questions. Have students listen a second time, this time allowing them to take notes if they wish. Review comprehension questions and answers. Finally, have students listen a third time, this time trying to answer the *cómo lo dicen* questions.

Have students write down some of the expressions. Have them place a check mark next to the expression each time they hear it on the tape. Or have them write the following words on a piece of paper: **gambas, gazpacho, sopa, chuletas,** and **ensalada.** Then have them indicate with a check mark each time they hear the words.

Answers, Ex. L
1. cerca de la ventana 2. sí; unas gambas al ajillo 3. gazpacho 4. el Sr. Pérez 5. él, helado de fresa; ella, flan 6. con una tarjeta de crédito

Ex. M: Pairs

Answers, Ex. M
1. Quisiéramos una mesa para dos, por favor.
2. ¿Pudiera traernos la cuenta, por favor?

Comentarios

culturales *Xitomatl, mahiz, papa*

Xitomatl es la palabra náhuatl, lengua de los aztecas, para el tomate. Hoy día en México se usa la palabra *jitomate* en vez de *xitomatl,* pero en otras partes del mundo hispano se usa la palabra *tomate.* Se cree que esta fruta se cultiva en México y en partes de América Central desde hace más de 5.000 años. Los exploradores españoles fueron los que introdujeron esta fruta en Europa.

El maíz, conocido como *mahiz* en la lengua de los indios del Caribe, es un producto importantísimo que se originó en las Américas hace 5.000 años. En la época precolombina se cultivaba desde lo que hoy es Chile hasta el sur de Canadá.

En las altas montañas de los Andes, los indios no podían cultivar maíz a causa del frío. Sin embargo, cultivaban la patata, conocida como *papa* en quéchua. Esta lengua, hablada por los incas, se habla todavía hoy en los países andinos. Los indios de los Andes inventaron una manera peculiar de conservar los distintos tipos de papas que cultivaban: por medio del frío y del calor las deshidrataban y congelaban a la vez.

INTEGRACIÓN CULTURAL

1. ¿Cómo le llamaban los aztecas al tomate?
2. ¿Dónde se originó el maíz?
3. ¿Por qué no se cultivaba el maíz en los Andes?
4. ¿Cuáles son dos palabras para *potato* en español?

Tú dirás

N. En el restaurante. Vas a un restaurante con un amigo. Pide una mesa, discute el menú, pide algo para comer. Uno(a) de tus compañeros(as) va a hacer el papel de mesero(a). Consulta el menú de la página 378 para decidir lo que vas a pedir.

Ñ. Anoche nosotros cenamos en... Imagína que anoche cenaste con un(a) amigo(a) en el restaurante cuyo menú está en la página 378. Discute con un(a) amigo(a) lo que comiste y si te gustó o no.

PARA EMPEZAR: La Guía del ocio

La Guía del ocio: Guide to leisure-time activities

🔖 **Transparency 31:** La Guía del ocio

Preparación: As you get ready to begin this *etapa,* think about where you go to find information about what to do during your free time.

- Does your newspaper publish a special weekend supplement with information on various activities?
- Does your town have a special publication that is dedicated to this information? How often is it published?
- What type of information can you find in the publication? Movies? Concerts? Plays?
- How about restaurants?

CULTURE: The word *ocio* means *free time* in Spanish. The **Guía del ocio** is published weekly and contains a wealth of information regarding what to do in one's free time, including movies, plays, concerts, sporting events, restaurants. The text at the beginning of this *etapa* is taken directly from the Guía del ocio.

▶ *Guía del ocio*

¡A TODO MÉXICO! • ¡A TODO MÉXICO! San Bernardino, 4. Tel. 541 93 59. Plaza República del Ecuador, 4. Tel. 259 48 33. San Leonardo, 3. Tel. 247 54 39. Cocina mexicana. Especialidad: tamales, carnitas, mole poblano. Admite tarjetas. (3).

• AIRIÑOS DO MAR. ORENSE, 39. Tel. 556 00 52. Cocina gallega. Especialidad: pescados y mariscos. Cerr. dom. (3).

• ASADOR REAL. Dr. Fleming, 22 (esquina Panamá). Tel. 250 84 60. Esp. cordero asado. Cerr. fest. noche y dom. (3).

la baranda • LA BARANDA. Augusto Figueroa, 32. Tel. 522 55 99. De 13 a 16 y de 21 a 24 h. Vier. y sáb. hasta la 1 h. Ensaladas, crepes, pizzas y pastas. (2).

LA Barraca • LA BARRACA. Reina, 29. (Centro-Cibeles). Tel. 532 71 54. Especialidad: paellas, arroces y cocina española. (3).

• EL CACIQUE. C/ Padre Damián, 47. Tel. 259 10 16. Cocina Argentina. Especialidad: Carnes a la brasa. Panqueques y dulce de leche. (4).

• CASA FABAS. Plaza Herradores, 7. Tel. 541 11 03. Cocina casera. Especialidad: Fabada Asturiana. Callos. Cordero asado. Repostería casera. Cierra domingos noche y lunes todo el día. (2).

• CASA GALLEGA. Bordadores, 11 (frente a Iglesia San Ginés). Tel. 541 90 55. Cocina gallega. Esp.: mariscos, pescados y carnes. (3).

• CASA GADES. Conde Xiquena, Tel. 522 75 10. Cocina Italiana. Especialidad: pastas, pizzas y postres caseros. (3).

• CASA PEDRO. Nuestra Señora de Valverde, 119. Tel. 73402 01. Cocina castellana. Horno de leña. Esp.: cordero, cochinillo y perdices. Leche frita. (4).

• LOS CHAVALES. Plaza Valvanera, 4 (parque de San Juan Bautista). Tel. 415 79 86. Especialidad en mariscos. Cerrado domingos tarde. No admite tarjetas. (2).

• CHIKY. Restaurante-Pub. Mayor, 24 (Centro-Sol) y Cololeros, 3. Tel. 266 24 57 y 265 94 48. Especialidad: todos los días, paella y cocido madrileño. Hasta las 2 h. (2).

• DA NICOLA. Plaza de los Mostenses, 11 (junto a parking). Tel. 542 25 74. Cocina italiana y pizzas para llevar. Abierto todo el verano. (2).

• DE LA DIVA. Cochabamba, 13. (250 77 57). De lunes a viernes de 13 a 18 horas. Cocina casera. Especialidad: Almejas a la marinera con arroz blanco y cola de gambas. Pecho de ternera al horno. (3).

• DON EMILIANO. Plaza de los Herradores, 10. (541 13 72). Coc. mexicana, regionales. Esp.: carnes, aves, pescados, mariscos y cócteles tropicales. No admite tarjetas. (2).

• DONZOKO. Echegaray, 3 y 9 (Centro). (429 57 20 y 429 62 24). Cocina japonesa. Cerrado domingos. No admite tarjetas. (2).

• FIGÓN FAUSTINO. Palencia, 29. (253 39 77). Cocina segoviana. Cordero y cochinillo encargado. Sábados cerrado. Visa. (2).

• LA FLOR DE LA CANELA. General Orgaz, 21 (altura Orense, 39). (571 18 13). Cocina española-peruana. Especialidad: paellas y arroces. Abierto domingos y festivos mediodía. Paellas y platos de encargo. (2).

• PAPARAZZI. Sor Angela de la Cruz, 22 (Centro). (279 67 67). Cocina italiana. Esp.: pastas, frito mixto de gambas y calamares, pallarda. Tarjetas. (2).

• XOCHIMILCO. Piano-bar. Esquilache, 4 (Cuatro Caminos). (535 17 98). Cocina mexicana. Esp. desde "antojitos" a "chiles en nogada". Admite tarjetas. Cierra domingos noche. (3).

Guía de precios

En España la mayoría de los restaurantes abre, aproximadamente, de las 12:30 a las 16:00 h. y de las 20:00 a las 24:00 h. Los números entre paréntesis que aparecen al final del texto de cada restaurante indican el precio aproximado por persona: (1) menos de 1.000 pesetas; (2) de 1.000 a 2.000 pesetas; (3) de 2.000 a 3.000 pesetas; (4) de 3.000 a 4.000 pesetas y (5) más de 4.000 pesetas.

Ex. B:  Pairs

Práctica

A. Recomendaciones. Unos amigos de los Estados Unidos te están visitando en Madrid. Ellos te piden recomendaciones sobre dónde comer ciertos tipos de comida. Consulta la *Guía del ocio* en la página anterior para determinar los restaurantes que recomendarías a una persona que desea:

1. paella	5. Italian food	9. shrimp and squid
2. seafood	6. Argentine food	10. Mexican food
3. lamb	7. Japanese food	
4. pizza	8. Galician food	

Después de escoger los diez restaurantes, determina cuánto va a costarle a cada persona.

Repaso

B. ¿Qué piensas hacer esta tarde? Pregúntale a un(a) compañero(a) sobre sus planes para las fechas indicadas. Usa expresiones como: pensar, querer, ir a, tener ganas de.

■ **Modelo:** esta tarde
¿Qué tienes ganas de hacer esta tarde?
Tengo ganas de dormir, pero voy a estudiar.

1. mañana por la tarde
2. esta noche
3. el viernes por la noche
4. pasado mañana
5. el miércoles próximo
6. el fin de semana que viene

C. ¿Cómo estás cuando... ? Pregúntale a un(a) compañero(a) cómo está en cada una de las siguientes situaciones.

1. cuando tienes un examen
2. cuando no hay clase
3. cuando tienes que estudiar gramática
4. cuando llueve y no tienes paraguas
5. cuando sacas una "A" en un examen
6. cuando pierde un partido tu equipo de fútbol favorito
7. cuando recibes una buena noticia
8. cuando tienes un problema
9. cuando no tienes dinero
10. cuando no tienes nada que hacer

ENFOQUE ESTRUCTURAL — Pronombres de complemento directo e indirecto

Both direct object pronouns and indirect object pronouns were introduced before. (See Chapter 7 for direct object pronouns and Chapter 8 for indirect object pronouns.) Below you have a chart with all the forms for a quick review.

Pronombres de complemento directo

	Singular		Plural
me	*me*	**nos**	*us*
te	*you (familiar)*	**os**	*you (familiar)*
lo	*you (formal), him, it (m.)*	**los**	*you (formal), them (m.)*
la	*you (formal), her, it (f.)*	**las**	*you (formal), them (f.)*

Pronombres de complemento indirecto

me	*to me* or *for me*	**nos**	*to us* or *for us*
te	*to you* or *for you*	**os**	*to you* or *for you (familiar)*
le	*to* or *for you (formal), her, him*	**les**	*to* or *for you (formal), them*

Pronouns exist so that we don't have to repeat nouns each time we want to refer to them. Notice how unnatural the following conversation sounds without the use of pronouns:

Ana:	¿Quién te compró el vestido?
Julia:	Mi novio me compró el vestido.
Ana:	¿Cuándo te compró el vestido?
Julia:	Me compró el vestido ayer.

Now observe how much more natural it sounds when you use direct and indirect object (double object) pronouns:

Ana:	¿Quién te compró el vestido?
Julia:	Mi novio me lo compró.
Ana:	¿Cuándo te lo compró?
Julia:	Me lo compró ayer.

Because of the shared information that Ana and Julia have (both are referring to **el vestido**), they don't have to repeat the words **el vestido** each time they have to refer to the dress.

Position of direct and indirect object pronouns

When a direct and indirect object pronoun are used together, both are placed before the conjugated verb—with the indirect object pronoun always preceding the direct object pronoun.

You will recall from Chapter 8 that the indirect object pronouns for the third person singular and plural are **le** and **les**. These pronouns become **se** when used with the direct object pronouns **lo, la, los,** and **las.**

¿Quién **le** compró la camisa **a Jorge?**	*Who bought the shirt **for Jorge?***
Su novia **se la** compró.	*His girlfriend bought **it for him.***
¿Quién **les** trajo el libro **a tus hermanos?**	*Who brought the book **for your brothers?***
Mi esposo **se lo** trajo.	*My husband brought **it for them.***

IRM Master 48:
Pronombres de complemento directo e indirecto

You may bring in various clothing items to have students practice double object pronouns with the verb **comprar.** Use the questions in the examples or create similar ones to elicit the indirect object pronouns **me, te, nos** with the direct object pronouns (¿Quién te compró la blusa? Mi novio me la compró). To keep it simple, use only double object pronouns with the indirect object pronouns **me, te,** and **nos.**

Ask students to look over this section as homework the night before you present it in class. In class, present these structures as a drill exercise, incorporating restaurant vocabulary. Use several props from a table setting. Give the salt shaker to a student, then tell the class: **La sal, se la pasé a Ana... se la pasé.** Tell that student: **Ana, la sal, me la pasas por favor.** Do this several times, then use a new prop and new verb form; e.g., **Está pasándomela.** As students seem more comfortable with these structures, ask them to start describing what you are doing as you pass items.

Have students conduct a conversation in English, similar to the exchange between Ana and Julia. Point out that their language has a similar construction and make students aware of how they use these pronouns in their everyday speech.

Create questions to elicit the indirect object pronouns **le** and **les** with the direct object pronouns (¿Quién le compró la blusa? Su novio le compró la blusa.). Once the students learn how to use **le** and **les** with the complete direct object, lead them into converting these to **se** before **lo, la, los,** and **las.**

The following chart may help you remember this:

| le
les | + | lo
la
los
las | = | se | + | lo
la
los
las |

but

| me, te, nos, os never change before | lo
la
los
las |

Position of object pronouns with infinitives and present participles

Double object pronouns may either be attached to the end of an infinitive or present participle or they may go before the conjugated form of the verb that is being used with the infinitive or present participle.

| Carlos va a comprár**melo**.
o
Carlos **me lo** va a comprar. | *Carlos is going to buy **it for me**.* |

| Juan está comprándo**melo**.
o
Juan **me lo** está comprando. | *Juan is buying **it for me**.* |

¡OJO! Notice that when you attach both pronouns to the end of an infinitive, an accent mark is added to the vowel before **-r**. With present participles, an accent mark is added to the vowel before **-ndo** even if only one pronoun is added at the end.

Review some common infinitive constructions (**tener que, querer, pensar,** and **ir** + **a** + *inf.*), and show how pronouns will be attached to the infinitive. Point out the accent mark when the pronouns are attached.

Review the formation of the present participle along with its use with **estar** to form the present progressive and show how pronouns will be attached to the participle. Point out the accent mark when the pronouns are attached.

Práctica

D. ¿Quién te recomendó... ? Estás en un restaurante con unos amigos hablando de recomendaciones. Contesta las siguientes preguntas, empleando pronombres de complemento indirecto y directo según el modelo.

■ **Modelo:** ¿Quién te recomendó el flan? (mi novio[a])
Mi novio(a) me lo recomendó.

1. ¿Quién te recomendó las gambas? (mi hermana)
2. ¿Quién les recomendó la sopa de ajo? (la mesera)
3. ¿Quién te recomendó la ensalada mixta? (mi hermano)
4. ¿Quién les recomendó el pescado frito? (mi prima Berta)
5. ¿Quién te recomendó la ternera? (el mesero)

Answers, Ex. D
1. Mi hermana me las recomendó.
2. La mesera nos la recomendó.
3. Mi hermano me la recomendó.
4. Mi prima Berta nos lo recomendó.
5. El mesero me la recomendó. 6. Mi tío nos los recomendó. 7. Mi hermana me lo recomendó. 8. Mi amiga nos lo recomendó. 9. Mi esposo(a) me las recomendó. 10. Mi novio(a) nos lo recomendó.

6. ¿Quién les recomendó los calamares? (mi tío)
7. ¿Quién te recomendó el pollo al chilindrón? (mi hermana)
8. ¿Quién les recomendó el vino tinto? (mi amiga)
9. ¿Quién te recomendó las chuletas de cordero? (mi esposo[a])
10. ¿Quién les recomendó el restaurante? (mi novio[a])

E. ¿Quién va a servirte... ? Siguen hablando en un restaurante. Contesta las siguientes preguntas, empleando pronombres de complemento indirecto y directo según el modelo.

■ **Modelo:** ¿Quién va a servirte el flan? (el mesero)
    El mesero me lo va a servir. / El mesero va a servírmelo.

1. ¿Quién va a comprarles la comida? (mi hermana)
2. ¿Quién va a mostrarte los postres? (la mesera)
3. ¿Quién va a traerles la bebida? (el mesero)
4. ¿Quién va a servirte el aperitivo? (la mesera)
5. ¿Quién va a mostrarles la mesa? (el mesero)
6. ¿Quién va a traerte la cuenta? (la mesera)

Answers, Ex. E
1. Mi hermana nos la va a comprar (va a comprárnosla). 2. La mesera me los va a mostrar (va a mostrármelos). 3. El mesero nos la va a traer (va a traérnosla). 4. La mesera me lo va a servir (va a servírmelo). 5. El mesero nos la va a mostrar (va a mostrárnosla). 6. La mesera nos la va a traer (va a traérnosla).

ENFOQUE LÉXICO

Expresiones afirmativas y negativas

You have already learned that you can make Spanish sentences negative by simply placing **no** before the conjugated verb: **No voy a ir a la fiesta mañana.** Another way to express negation in Spanish is to use other negative words. See the following examples:

Nadie va a la fiesta, ¿no?	*Nobody is going to the party, right?*
Alberto **no** va y Mario **tampoco.**	*Alberto is not going and Mario is not going either.*
¿Quiere **alguien** ir conmigo al partido?	*Does someone want to go with me to the game?*
No quiere ir **nadie.**	*No one wants to go.*
Sabes tú **algo** de biología?	*Do you know anything about biology?*
No, no sé **nada** de biología.	*No, I don't know anything about biology.*
¿Hay **algún** estudiante aquí?	*Is there a student here?*
No, no hay **ningún** estudiante aquí.	*No, there is not a single student here.*
¿Va Alberto **o** Nico a la fiesta?	*Is either Alberto or Nico going to the party?*
No va **ni** Alberto **ni** Nico.	*Neither Alberto nor Nico is going.*

Contextualize presentation of vocabulary by telling students you are surveying the class's collective travel experience. Ask students: ¿Sabes tú algo de España? ¿Vas a ir algún día a España? etc. Ask several students, then write results on the board; e.g., Algunos estudiantes van a ir a España este verano or Ningún estudiante va a España este verano.

GRAMMAR NOTE:
Ningún and **ninguna** are normally used in the singular since they literally mean "not one." An exception would be a noun that is only used in the plural (e.g., **ganas**): **No tengo ningunas ganas de comer pizza.**

Here are some negative words in Spanish along with their affirmative counterparts:

nadie	*no one, nobody*	**alguien**	*someone, somebody*
		todo el mundo	*everyone*
ningún		**algún**	
ninguno	*none*	**alguno**	*a, an*
ninguna		**alguna**	
		algunos	*some*
		algunas	
nada	*nothing*	**algo**	*something*
tampoco	*neither, either*	**también**	*also*
nunca	*never*	**una vez**	*once*
		algún día	*some day*
		siempre	*always*
		cada día	*every day*
		todos los días	*every day*
ni... ni...	*neither ... nor*	**o... o...**	*either ... or*

Notice that the words **alguno** and **ninguno** become **algún** and **ningún** before a singular masculine noun.

Notice also that in Spanish it is possible to have a double negative construction like **No sé nada, No quiere ir nadie, No hay ningún estudiante aquí.**

In the examples below notice that **nadie, nunca,** and **tampoco** can be placed before the verb. If placed before the verb, no other negative word is necessary. If placed after the verb, the word **no** has to be used before the conjugated verb.

Nadie quiere ir al concierto	**No** quiere ir **nadie** al concierto.
Nunca voy al teatro	**No** voy al teatro **nunca.**
Tampoco voy al cine.	**No** voy al cine **tampoco.**

Answers, Ex. F
1. Alberto no va a pedir paella tampoco. 2. Nadie quiere comer calamares. 3. No quiero comer nada antes de salir de casa. 4. Su familia no come en un restaurante nunca. 5. Elena nunca pide la misma comida que su hermana. 6. Ningún estudiante va a comer pizza el viernes. 7. Ni Alberto ni Enrique va a ir al mercado. 8. Alicia no come ensaladas nunca.

Práctica

F. No, no y no. Expresa negativamente las siguientes ideas. No olvides utilizar la doble negación si es necesario. Sigue el modelo.

■ **Modelo:** Nilda va a ese restaurante todos los días.
    Nilda nunca va a ese restaurante.

1. Alberto va a pedir paella también.
2. Alguien quiere comer calamares.
3. Yo quiero comer algo antes de salir de casa.

4. Su familia come en un restaurante cada día.

5. Elena siempre pide la misma comida que su hermana.

6. Algunos estudiantes van a comer pizza el viernes.

7. Alberto o Enrique va a ir al mercado.

8. Alicia come ensaladas todos los días.

G. Otra vez no.
Vas a cenar con una persona que te hace varias preguntas sobre los restaurantes en tu ciudad. Contesta sus preguntas negativamente.

1. ¿Va tu amigo a cenar con nosotros también?

2. ¿Sirven algún plato típico en este restaurante?

3. ¿Hay algo interesante en el menú?

4. ¿Sirven paella en este restaurante también?

5. ¿Alguien te recomendó este restaurante?

H. ¿Alguien come allí?
Un(a) compañero(a) te hace varias preguntas sobre un restaurante muy malo que hay en tu pueblo. Tú le contestas negativamente.

1. ¿Alguien come en ese restaurante?

2. ¿Hay algo sabroso en el menú?

3. ¿Sirven alguna comida étnica?

4. ¿Te gusta algún plato de los que sirven allí?

5. ¿Sirven paella o sirven arroz con pollo allí?

6. Tu familia siempre come allí, ¿verdad?

Comentarios culturales

Xocoatl: Regalo de los dioses

La palabra *xocoatl* es la palabra que usaban los aztecas para el chocolate. Las leyendas entre los indígenas precolombinos nos dicen que el chocolate fue un regalo de los dioses. El emperador azteca, Moctezuma, era **aficionado** *(lover of)* al chocolate y se dice que tomaba cincuenta pequeñas tazas de chocolate cada día. Hernán Cortés, conquistador español, probó el chocolate por primera vez en la corte de Moctezuma. Moctezuma tenía la costumbre de dar unas cenas elegantes en las que se servía carne de **ciervo** *(deer)* y **pavo** *(turkey)* exquisitamente preparada junto con varios tipos de frutas exóticas. Después de la cena, se llevaba a cabo una ceremonia en la que les servían chocolate a los **huéspedes** *(guests)* — mezclado con **miel** *(honey)*, especias, vainilla — en unas pequeñas tazas de **oro** *(gold)*.

Cuando Cortés volvió a España, le llevó chocolate a Carlos V, el rey de España. La bebida fascinó a Carlos V y llegó a ser una bebida preferida entre los reyes y nobles. Hasta 1615 el chocolate fue un secreto de los españoles pero en ese año Ana de Austria, una princesa española, se casó con Luis XIII de Francia. Como regalo, Ana le llevó chocolate a su nuevo esposo. El chocolate llegó a ser muy popular en Francia y los franceses lo introdujeron al resto del mundo—pero los indígenas precolombinos fueron los primeros que probaron esta delicia.

INTEGRACIÓN CULTURAL

1. Según los indígenas, ¿de dónde vino el chocolate?
2. ¿Dónde probó Cortés el chocolate por primera vez?
3. ¿Cuánto chocolate bebía Moctezuma cada día?
4. ¿Quién era Ana de Austria?
5. ¿Cómo conocieron los franceses el chocolate?

VAMOS A ESCUCHAR: MI FAMILIA

Luis y Sonia están cenando en el restaurante La Barraca.

ANTES DE ESCUCHAR

Basado en lo que has aprendido en esta *etapa*, ¿qué información esperas escuchar en cuanto a *(with regard to)*

1. lo que van a pedir como segundo plato?
2. lo que van a pedir para beber?
3. lo que van a pedirle al mesero?

Antes de escuchar la conversación, repasa las preguntas que aparecen en la sección *Después de escuchar.*

DESPUÉS DE ESCUCHAR

I. Comprensión. Escucha la cinta y contesta las siguientes preguntas.

1. ¿Qué tipo de sopa pide Sonia?
2. ¿Qué pide Sonia para tomar?
3. ¿Pide Luis sopa?
4. ¿Qué va a tomar Luis?
5. ¿Por qué pide Luis otro tenedor?

J. ¿Como lo dicen? Escucha la cinta otra vez para determinar lo siguiente.

1. ¿Cómo pregunta Luis sobre la sopa?
2. ¿Qué dice Sonia de las gambas?

Answers, Ex. I
1. sopa de ajo 2. agua mineral
3. No, no quiere sopa. 4. vino tinto
5. porque el que tiene está sucio.

Answers, Ex. J
1. ¿Qué tal está la sopa?
2. ¡Están pero riquísimas!

Tú dirás ....

K. Anoche nosotros cenamos en... Escoge un restaurante de la lista que aparece en la página 389. Imagina que un(a) amigo(a) y tú cenaron allí anoche. Preparen entre los dos una breve presentación en la que expliquen qué comieron, cómo fue la comida y cuánto costó todo.

L. La guía local. Trae a clase el equivalente local de *La guía del ocio* y con un grupo de compañeros escriban una sección en español para los restaurantes que aparecen allí. Usen *La guía del ocio* de la página 389 como modelo.

K: Pairs

Ex. K Allow students 4–5 minutes to plan for this role play. Encourage them to make any notes necessary. Let them practice and then ask several pairs to perform for the class without their notes.

Ex. L: Group

TERCERA ETAPA

PARA EMPEZAR: *La comida Tex-Mex*

Preparación: As you get ready to begin this *etapa*, think about what you know about Mexican food. Think about Mexican food you have had in this country.

- What are the common fast-food restaurants that serve this type of food? What do they serve?
- Are there other types of Mexican food restaurants that you are familiar with?
- What is your favorite Mexican food?

Start discussion by asking students these questions in Spanish.

¿Cuál es tu plato mexicano favorito? ¿Los tacos? ¿Las enchiladas? ¿Los burritos? ¿Las chimichangas? ¿Los nachos con salsa picante? Los norteamericanos están acostumbrados a la comida mexicana, pero la comida mexicana que se come en los Estados Unidos—la comida Tex-Mex—no es como la comida que generalmente se prepara en México. La comida Tex-Mex que comemos en este país es una adaptación de las **recetas** que se usan en México.

recipes

Nachos, salsa, tostadas, tacos, enchiladas...Todos ejemplos de la rica comida Tex-Mex.

was born Today	Esta comida tiene una larga historia. En 1800, en Álamo, Texas, **nació** el famoso "chile con carne", plato oficial de la cocina tejana. **Hoy día** la mayoría de los supermercados de Estados Unidos tienen una sección especial dedicada a los productos que se usan para preparar la comida Tex-Mex.
has enjoyed since on the side tastes, preferences	La comida Tex-Mex **ha disfrutado** de una popularidad fenomenal en este país. Un caso interesante de esta comida son los nachos. En México no se conocen los nachos, **ya que,** es una comida que se inventó aquí en los Estados Unidos. Pero los nachos son tan populares que hasta en los partidos de béisbol se comen en vez de los "hot dogs". Otros platos de la cocina Tex-Mex son las fajitas, los burritos y los tacos. Estos platos se sirven siempre con una salsa **al lado.** La salsa puede ser picante o no picante, según los **gustos** de cada persona. En 1992, la salsa superó al "catsup" como el condimento más popular en los Estados Unidos.

Práctica

A. ¿Puedes decir... ? Contesta las siguientes preguntas según lo que comprendiste de la lectura.

1. ¿En qué se diferencia la comida Tex-Mex de la comida mexicana?
2. ¿Cuándo se inventó el "chile con carne"?
3. ¿Dónde se pueden comprar productos para preparar los platos Tex-Mex?
4. ¿Dónde se inventaron los nachos?
5. ¿Con qué se sirven los platos Tex-Mex?
6. ¿Cuál(es) es (son) tu(s) plato(s) favorito(s) de la cocina Tex-Mex?

B. La comida Tex-Mex. Tu amigo del Perú quiere saber más sobre ciertas comidas Tex-Mex. Describe cómo son las siguientes comidas. También comenta si te gustan o no.

1. nachos
2. tacos
3. salsa picante
4. burritos
5. chile con carne

Ex. B Pairs Expand into a pair writing activity. Ask students to write a short description of each of these foods. Let them spend 5–10 minutes writing and then give them another 3–4 minutes to edit their writing. When done share with the rest of the class.

Assign reading as homework. Ask students to read the article then write a summary of the most pertinent information. In class, ask several students to present their summaries, perhaps without notes for additional oral practice.

Comentarios
culturales
El chile

Los chiles son un ingrediente importante en la comida Tex-Mex. Hay más de 2.000 tipos de chiles. La palabra chile viene de la lengua náhuatl. Esta lengua todavía se habla en México y es la que hablaban los aztecas cuando llegaron los españoles en 1519. Muchas variedades de chiles se cultivaban en la América Latina en tiempos precolombinos. Los chiles se preparan de diferentes maneras, o sea, a veces se muelen (they are ground) para hacer salsas o se sirven enteros o cortados según la receta. Hay chiles rojos, verdes y amarillos. Algunos de los chiles más conocidos son el jalapeño, el serrano, el pequín, el chipotle y el ancho. Dicen que el habanero, cultivado en Yucatán, es probablemente el más picante de todos los chiles cultivados en la América Latina y tal vez en el mundo. Lo picante se mide en Unidades Scoville, en honor del científico que inventó la escala. Un jalapeño, por ejemplo, sólo mide entre 3.000 y 5.000 Unidades Scoville, mientras que un habanero puede medir hasta 500.000 Unidades Scoville.

Un hispano en Nuevo México cultiva sus plantas de chile.

INTEGRACIÓN CULTURAL

1. ¿Te gustan los chiles?
2. ¿Te gusta la comida picante o no muy picante?
3. ¿Cuáles son los nombres de algunos chiles?
4. ¿Cómo se llama el científico que inventó la escala para medir lo picante?

Answers, Integración
1. Answers will vary.
2. Answers will vary.
3. jalapeño, serrano, pequín, chipotle, ancho
4. Scoville

Repaso

C. Mil preguntas. Un amigo te está haciendo varias preguntas sobre tu visita a un restaurante. Contesta empleando pronombres de complemento indirecto y directo.

1. ¿Quién te recomendó el restaurante?
2. Tú no sabías dónde estaba el restaurante. ¿Quién te dio direcciones?
3. ¿Quién te mostró la mesa?
4. ¿Quién te trajo el menú?
5. ¿Quién te sirvió los aperitivos?
6. ¿Quién te mostró los postres?
7. ¿Quién te trajo la cuenta?
8. ¿Te aceptaron la tarjeta de crédito?

D. ¿Te gusta... ? Pregúntales a varios compañeros de clase si les gustan las siguientes comidas. Ellos contestarán según sus opiniones individuales.

■ **Modelo:** sopa de ajo

—¿Te gusta la sopa de ajo?
—Sí, me gusta la sopa de ajo.

o

—Sí, me encanta la sopa de ajo.

o

—No, no me gusta la sopa de ajo.

o

—No, detesto la sopa de ajo.

1. gambas	5. pescado frito	9. té
2. espárragos	6. ternera asada	10. helado
3. calamares	7. flan	11. vino tinto
4. chuletas de cordero	8. café	12. mariscos

ENFOQUE ESTRUCTURAL

Los mandatos con pronombres de complemento directo e indirecto

When a pronoun is used with an affirmative command, it is attached to the end of the command. If the command is negative, the pronoun must be placed before the command form. The same is true when two pronouns are used together.

¿Te compro el vestido?	*Should I buy you the dress?*
Sí, **cómpramelo.**	*Yes, buy it for me.*
No, no **me lo compres.**	*No, don't buy it for me.*
¿Le compro el sombrero a Marcos?	*Should I buy Marcos the hat?*
Sí, **cómpraselo.**	*Yes, buy it for him.*
No, no **se lo compres.**	*No, don't buy it for him.*

Notice that when you attach both pronouns to the end of an affirmative command, you put an accent mark on the fourth to the last syllable. Remember, the indirect object pronoun always comes before the direct object pronoun.

Práctica

E. ¿Te sirvo... ? Contesta las siguientes preguntas, empleando mandatos afirmativos informales según el modelo.

■ **Modelo:** ¿Te sirvo el gazpacho?
     Sí, sírvemelo.
     ¿Les sirvo el gazpacho?
     Sí, sírvenoslo.

1. ¿Te muestro el restaurante?
2. ¿Te compro un café?
3. ¿Te traigo el menú?
4. ¿Te muestro los postres?
5. ¿Te compro la comida?
6. ¿Te traigo otro tenedor?
7. ¿Les compro un helado?
8. ¿Les sirvo las ensaladas?
9. ¿Les traigo la cuenta?
10. ¿Les compro unas cervezas?

Ahora repite el ejercicio, empleando mandatos negativos informales según el modelo.

■ **Modelo:** ¿Te sirvo el gazpacho?
     No, no me lo sirvas.

Ahora repite el ejercicio otra vez, empleando mandatos afirmativos formales según el modelo.

■ **Modelo:** ¿Le sirvo el gazpacho?
     Sí, sírvamelo.

Ahora repite el ejercicio por última vez, empleando mandatos negativos formales según el modelo.

■ **Modelo:** ¿Le sirvo el gazpacho?
     No, no me lo sirva.

F. ¿Les sirvo... ? Juega el papel de mesero y hazles preguntas a tus compañeros de clase. Ellos deben contestar empleando mandatos formales y pronombres de complemento indirecto y directo. Sigan el modelo.

■ **Modelo:** les / traer / el menú
     ¿Les traigo el menú?
     Sí, tráiganoslo.
     o
     No, no nos lo traiga.

1. les / traer / la cuenta
2. les / mostrar / los postres
3. le / servir / el gazpacho
4. le / traer / otro tenedor
5. les / servir / la sopa
6. les / traer / las ensaladas
7. le / mostrar / la mesa
8. les / traer / otra silla

GRAMMAR NOTE:
You may want to review the commands with **Ud.** and **Uds.** in Chapter 3, and commands with **tú** in Chapter 6.

Answers, Ex. E
Mandatos afirmativos informales:

1. Sí, muéstramelo. 2. Sí, cómpramelo. 3. Sí, tráemelo. 4. Sí, muéstramelos. 5. Sí, cómpramela. 6. Sí, tráemelo. 7. Sí, cómpranoslo. 8. Sí, sírvenoslas. 9. Sí, tráenosla. 10. Sí, cómpranoslas.

Mandatos negativos informales:

1. No, no me lo muestres. 2. No, no me lo compres. 3. No, no me lo traigas. 4. No, no me los muestres. 5. No, no me la compres. 6. No, no, me lo traigas. 7. No, no nos lo compres. 8. No, no nos las sirvas. 9. No, no nos la traigas. 10. No, no nos las compres.

Mandatos afirmativos formales:

1. Sí, muéstremelo. 2. Sí, cómpremelo. 3. Sí, tráigamelo. 4. Sí, muéstremelos. 5. Sí, cómpremela. 6. Sí, tráigamelo. 7. Sí, cómprenoslo. 8. Sí, sírvanoslas. 9. Sí, tráiganosla. 10. Sí, cómprenoslas.

Mandatos negativos formales:

1. No, no me lo muestre. 2. No, no me lo compre. 3. No, no me lo traiga. 4. No, no me los muestre. 5. No, no me la compre. 6. No, no, me lo traiga. 7. No, no nos lo compre. 8. No, no nos las sirva. 9. No, no nos la traiga. 10. No, no nos las compre.

Answers, Ex. F
1. ¿Les traigo la cuenta? Sí, tráiganosla. o No, no nos la traiga. 2. ¿Les muestro los postres? Sí, muéstrenoslos. o No, no nos los muestre. 3. ¿Le sirvo el gazpacho? Sí, sírvamelo. o No, no me lo sirva. 4. ¿Le traigo otro tenedor? Sí, tráigamelo. o No, no me lo traiga. 5. ¿Les sirvo la sopa? Sí, sírvanosla. o No, no nos la sirva. 6. ¿Les traigo las ensaladas? Sí, tráiganoslas. o No, no nos las traiga. 7. ¿Le muestro la mesa? Sí, muéstremela. o No, no me la muestre. 8. ¿Les traigo otra silla? Sí, tráiganosla. o No, no nos la traiga.

ENFOQUE ESTRUCTURAL — Se impersonal

There are several ways in Spanish to express an action that is carried out
by an unmentioned person or persons. This is called an *impersonal*
action. In English several words can be used to refer to impersonal actions
that are performed by no one in particular: *one, you, they, people.* In
Spanish, one way to make these impersonal statements is to place **se**
before the third person form of the verb: **se come, se habla, se vende,**
etc.

Se habla español aquí.	***You (people, they, one)* speak(s)** *Spanish here.*
Se come bien en España.	***You (people, they, one)* eat(s)** *well in Spain.*

Práctica

G. Acciones impersonales. Cambien las siguientes oraciones según el
modelo.

Modelo: Vivimos bien en España.
Se vive bien en España.

1. Comen bien en ese restaurante.
2. Sirven una paella excelente en ese restaurante.
3. Siempre bailamos en las fiestas.
4. Estudian mucho en la universidad.
5. Viven bien en este país.
6. Bajan por esta escalera.
7. No compran fruta en la farmacia.
8. Antes de la sopa sirven el aperitivo.
9. Después del segundo plato, sirven el postre.
10. A veces comen la ensalada después del plato principal.

H. ¿Qué se hace? Hagan unos comentarios impersonales sobre las actividades
que la gente debe hacer o no hacer en las siguientes situaciones o lugares.

Modelo: la biblioteca
Se estudia en la biblioteca.
o
Se lee en la biblioteca.
o
No se habla en la biblioteca.

1. el restaurante
2. el fin de semana
3. un día típico
4. una fiesta de cumpleaños
5. la universidad
6. una tienda de ropa

VAMOS A ESCUCHAR: COMIDA TEX-MEX

Luis y Alberto deciden almorzar en un restaurante que sirve comida Tex-Mex.

ANTES DE ESCUCHAR

Basado en lo que has aprendido en esta *etapa*, ¿qué información esperas escuchar en cuanto a lo que van a pedir para

1. comer?
2. beber?

Antes de escuchar la conversación, repasa las preguntas que aparecen en la sección *Después de escuchar.*

DESPUÉS DE ESCUCHAR

I. Comprensión. Escucha la cinta y contesta las siguientes preguntas.

1. ¿Qué va a comer Alberto?
2. ¿Qué pide Luis para comer?
3. ¿Qué pide Luis para tomar?
4. ¿Por qué pide Luis salsa?
5. ¿Piden los dos postre?

J. ¿Cómo lo dicen? Escucha la conversación otra vez para determinar lo siguiente.

1. ¿Cómo dice Luis "a little salty"?
2. ¿Cómo dice Alberto "a little sweet"?

Answers, Ex. I
1. unos nachos 2. unas fajitas de pollo y un guacamole 3. un vaso de agua con mucho hielo 4. porque las fajitas no tienen sabor 5. Luis no pide postre, Alberto pide flan.

Answers, Ex. J
1. Está un poco salado.
2. Está algo dulce.

Tú dirás ....

K. En el restaurante. Prepara la siguiente escena con otros(as) compañeros(as) de clase:

• pidan una mesa
• hablen sobre la comida que van a pedir
• pidan la comida
• comenten el sabor de cada plato
• decidan quién va a pagar.

L. Una cena Tex-Mex. Con dos compañeros(as) de clase, organicen una comida Tex-Mex para un día especial (cumpleaños, 5 de mayo, 16 de septiembre). Decidan cuándo va a ser la comida, a quién van a invitar, qué van a comer. Y qué va a traer cada invitado.

Ex. K: Group

Ex. K Allow students 4–5 minutes before doing the role play to plan out what they are going to say. When doing the role play do not allow them to use notes.

Ex. L: Group

LECTURA: Como agua para chocolate—las cebollas y el nacimiento de Tita

Laura Esquivel (México, 1950–) es la autora de uno de los libros más vendidos, no sólo en su país sino en todo el mundo. Esta extraordinaria novela tiene el título completo de *Como agua para chocolate: Novela de entregas mensuales con recetas, amores y remedios caseros.* Es una obra sabrosa, romántica y dinámica, tanto por sus coloridas descripciones como por sus gráficas escenas de la tumultuosa vida de una familia mexicana a principios del siglo XX. La acción se desarrolla en Piedras Negras, lugar situado en la frontera con Texas.

La autora no sólo les enseña a sus lectores cómo se prepara la comida, sino que les abre el apetito para que sigan leyendo y leyendo sobre las aventuras tragicómicas de una serie de personajes inolvidables. La obra ha sido traducida a varias lenguas. La versión cinematográfica de la novela ha tenido un gran éxito internacional y con ella Laura Esquivel ha obtenido varios premios, entre otros, por el mejor guión, escrito por ella misma.

ANTES DE LEER

A. Lee el título de esta lectura. ¿Qué idea general te da del contenido del texto?

B. Ahora lee la breve introducción para saber algo del libro de donde viene la lectura y para contestar las siguientes preguntas.

1. ¿Qué tipo de libro es *Como agua para chocolate?*
2. ¿Cómo se llama la autora? ¿Dónde nació? ¿Cuándo?
3. ¿Qué ha ayudado a hacer esta obra famosa?

GUÍA PARA LA LECTURA

C. Lee el texto rápidamente para encontrar las palabras que tengan que ver con la comida y los ingredientes. Trabaja con otro(a) estudiante para hacer una lista. (Hay como doce ingredientes, especias o alimentos.)

D. Información general. El fragmento que vas a leer pertenece a la novela de Laura Esquivel, *Como agua para chocolate*. El texto constituye el principio del primer capítulo de la novela y por lo tanto una de las funciones que realiza es la de presentar a varios de los personajes, entre ellos, dos de los principales: Tita y Nacha.

1. **La narradora:**
   Es la persona que cuenta la historia y es diferente de la autora. Si lees las primeras frases de esta novela, verás que el texto lo narra una primera persona. ¿Cómo lo sabemos? Mira estos ejemplos:

   > "Les sugiero ponerse...": El verbo en primera persona y el pronombre nos indican que la persona que narra se dirige a los lectores (**les**) para darles un consejo.

   > "No sé si a ustedes les ha pasado, pero a mí la mera verdad sí.": La narradora de nuevo se dirige a los lectores (**ustedes**) y aporta un dato personal (**a mí sí** [me ha pasado]).

   > ¿Qué relación hay entre esta narradora y Tita, uno de los personajes principales? Lee la última frase del primer párrafo.

2. **Los personajes:**
   Tita: El fragmento narra el día de su nacimiento. Es la hija menor de esta familia y es el personaje principal.

   Nacha: La cocinera y la persona que cuida a Tita cuando es niña.

   Narradora: El miembro de la familia que escribe la historia. En este pasaje recuerda el día en que nació Tita.

   Hay por lo menos otro personaje que se menciona en este fragmento. Lee el texto por encima y busca los nombres propios de persona. ¿Sabes quién es?

E. Ideas principales. A continuación, y para que puedas anticipar mejor el contenido concreto de este texto, hay una lista de las ideas principales. Identifica el párrafo donde aparece cada una de ellas. Escribe la frase, o parte del texto donde se expresa esa idea.

1. los efectos que tiene el picar cebolla en Tita
2. el nacimiento de Tita en la cocina
3. después del nacimiento: el amor de Tita por la cocina
4. Nacha, la cocinera, se ocupa de (*takes care of*) Tita
5. Tita, la cocina y los horarios para comer
6. risas y lágrimas en la vida de Tita y Nacha
7. el mundo de Tita

For additional pre-reading work, encourage students to browse the Internet for information about Esquivel and her novel. They can make oral presentations to the class about the information they found.

Answers, Ex. D:
1. Fía es la tía abuela de la narradora.
2. Nacha, Mamá Elena.

Answer, Ex. E.
1. Párrafo 1, "evitar el molesto lagrimeo..." 2. Párrafo 2, "Tita arribó a este mundo prematuramente... ." 3. Párrafo 3, "Este inusitado nacimiento determinó el hecho de que Tita sintiera un inmenso amor por la cocina... " 4. Párrafo 4, "Nacha se ofreció a hacerse cargo de la alimentación de Tita... " 5. Párrafo 4, "Sus hábitos alimenticios estaban condicionados al horario de la cocina... " 6. Párrafo 5, "Algunas veces lloraba de balde... " 7. Párrafo 6, "Ese gigantesco mundo que... "

Suggestion, Lectura: For
additional comprehension and for
expansion into a writing activity, ask
students to work in pairs and compile
a list of Tita's characteristics,
including both those that the text
explicitly offers and those which are
suggested and which the students
can infer. Then have them jointly
compose a diary entry that Tita might
make in which she talks about herself
and describes herself. Allow students
time to edit what they compose
before sharing with the class. Where
students have inferred characteristics,
ask them which parts of the text
prompted their inferences.

COMO AGUA PARA CHOCOLATE —LAS CEBOLLAS Y EL NACIMIENTO DE TITA

Manera de hacerse

La cebolla tiene que estar finamente picada. Les sugiero ponerse un pequeño trozo de cebolla en la mollera con el fin de evitar el molesto lagrimeo que se produce cuando uno la está cortando. Lo malo de llorar cuando uno pica cebolla no es el simple hecho de llorar, sino que a veces uno empieza, como quien dice, se pica, y ya no puede parar. No sé si a ustedes les ha pasado pero a mi la mera verdad sí. Infinidad de veces. Mamá decía que era porque yo soy igual de sensible a la cebolla que Tita, mi tía abuela.

Dicen que Tita era tan sensible que desde que estaba en el vientre de mi bisabuela lloraba y lloraba cuando ésta picaba cebolla; su llanto era tan fuerte que Nacha, la cocinera de la casa, que era medio sorda, lo escuchaba sin esforzarse. Un día los sollozos fueron tan fuertes que provocaron que el parto se adelantara. Y sin que mi bisabuela pudiera decir ni pío, Tita arribó a este mundo prematuramente, sobre la mesa de la cocina, entre los olores de una sopa de fideos que se estaba cocinando, los del tomillo, el laurel, el cilantro, el de la leche hervida, el de los ajos y, por supuesto, el de la cebolla. Como se imaginarán, la consabida nalgada no fue necesaria pues Tita nació llorando de antemano, tal vez porque ella sabía que su oráculo determinaba que en esta vida le estaba negado el matrimonio. Contaba Nacha que Tita fue literalmente empujada a este mundo por un torrente impresionante de lágrimas que se desbordaron sobre la mesa y el piso de la cocina.

En la tarde, ya cuando el susto había pasado y el agua, gracias al efecto de los rayos del sol, se había evaporado, Nacha barrió el residuo de las lágrimas que había quedado sobre la loseta roja que cubría el piso. Con esta sal rellenó un costal de cinco kilos que utilizaron para cocinar por bastante tiempo. Este inusitado nacimiento determinó el hecho de que Tita sintiera un inmenso amor por la cocina y que la mayor parte de su vida la pasara en ella, prácticamente desde que nació, pues cuando contaba con dos días de edad, su padre, o sea mi bisabuelo, murió de un infarto. A Mamá Elena, de la impresión, se le fue la leche. Como en esos tiempos no había leche en polvo ni nada que se le pareciera, y no pudieron conseguir nodriza por ningún lado, se vieron en un verdadero lío para calmar el hambre de la niña. Nacha, que se las sabía de todas respecto a la cocina —y a muchas otras cosas que ahora no vienen al caso— se ofreció a hacerse cargo de la alimentación de Tita. Ella se consideraba la más capacitada para «formarle el estómago a la inocente criaturita», a pesar de que nunca se casó ni tuvo hijos. Ni siquiera sabía leer ni escribir, pero eso sí sobre cocina tenía tan profundos conocimientos como la que más. Mamá Elena aceptó con agrado la sugerencia pues bastante tenía ya con la tristeza y la enorme responsabilidad de manejar correctamente el rancho, para así poderle dar a sus hijos la alimentación y educación que se merecían, como para encima tener que preocuparse por nutrir debidamente a la recién nacida.

Por tanto, desde ese día, Tita se mudó a la cocina y entre atoles y tés creció de lo más sana y rozagante. Es de explicarse entonces el que se le haya desarrollado un sexto sentido en todo lo que a comida se refiere. Por ejemplo, sus hábitos alimenticios estaban condicionados al horario de la cocina: cuando en la mañana Tita olía que los frijoles ya estaban cocidos, o cuando a medio día sentía que el agua ya estaba lista para desplumar a las gallinas, o cuando en la tarde se horneaba el pan para la cena, ella sabía que había llegado la hora de pedir sus alimentos.

Algunas veces lloraba de balde, como cuando Nacha picaba cebolla, pero como las dos sabían la razón de esas lágrimas, no se tomaban en serio. Inclusive se convertían en motivo de diversión, a tal grado que durante su niñez Tita no diferenciaba bien las lágrimas de la risa de las del llanto. Para ella reír era una manera de llorar.

De igual forma confundía el gozo del vivir con el de comer. No era fácil para una persona que conoció la vida a través de la cocina entender el mundo exterior. Ese gigantesco mundo que empezaba de la puerta de la cocina hacia el interior de la casa, porque el que colindaba con la puerta trasera de la cocina y que daba al patio, a la huerta, a la hortaliza, sí le pertenecía por completo, lo dominaba. Todo lo contrario de sus hermanas, a quienes este mundo les atemorizaba y encontraban lleno de peligros incógnitos. Les parecían absurdos y arriesgados los juegos dentro de la cocina, sin embargo, un día Tita las convenció de que era un espectáculo asombroso el ver cómo bailaban las gotas de agua al caer sobre el comal bien caliente.

VÍDEO CULTURAL: *Ricos sabores*

A. Anticipación. Indica si los siguientes alimentos son dulces y si te gustan a ti.

	¿Es dulce?		¿Te gusta?	
	Sí	No	Sí	No
1. miel	___	___	___	___
2. carne	___	___	___	___
3. huevo	___	___	___	___
4. cacao	___	___	___	___
5. mazapán	___	___	___	___
6. camarón	___	___	___	___
7. arroz	___	___	___	___
8. pescado	___	___	___	___
9. frijol	___	___	___	___
10. naranja	___	___	___	___
11. maíz	___	___	___	___
12. chile	___	___	___	___

B. Preparación. Escoge la letra de la palabra que expresa una idea similar.

1. después   a. patata
2. lengua   b. clase
3. gozar   c. luego
4. papa   d. disfrutar
5. tipo   e. idioma

C. Participación. Mientras escuchas y miras el vídeo, apunta las comidas que se mencionan. ¿Cuáles son los colores y los tamaños que se mencionan?

Color   Tamaño (grande o pequeño)
1. _____   _____
2. _____   _____
3. _____   _____
4. _____   _____
5. _____   _____
6. _____   _____

D. Comprensión

1. Indique si las siguientes frases sobre la papa son verdaderas o falsas.
   a. Hay poca variedad de papas en los países andinos.
   b. Hay cientos de tipos de papa que se comen en los Andes.
   c. La papa es un tesoro del imperio azteca.
   d. Deshidratan la papa para preparar el chuño.

2. Completa cada frase sobre el maíz.
   a. El maíz fue cultivado hace _____ mil años.
   b. El maíz fue uno de los _____ fundamentales de las civilizaciones precolombinas.
   c. La _____ de maíz sigue siendo indispensable en la comida de muchos países de Latinoamérica.
   d. Las tortillas se comen con _____, carne y casi todo.

3. Completa cada frase sobre el chocolate con la respuesta correcta.
   a. Los mayas, los toltecas y los _____ cultivaron el cacao.
   b. El chocolate es una bebida de la civilización _____.
   c. Otro nombre para el chocolate es _____.
   d. El emperador Moctezuma bebía muchas tazas de chocolate cada día. ¿Cuántas? _____.

4. El plato típico de muchos países consiste en arroz y frijoles. ¿Cómo se llama este plato?
   a. en Costa Rica
   b. en Cuba

Ex. E: Pairs

E. Personalización. Discuta las siguientes preguntas con otro(a) estudiante.

1. ¿Qué frutas son cultividas en los Estados Unidos? ¿Cuáles eran originarías de los EE.UU? Nombre algunas comidas que fueran intercambiadas entre los colonizadores ingleses que vinieron a Norteamérica y los nativos americanos.

2. ¿Cuál es tu plato favorito? Explícales a tus compañeros de clase como prepararlo. Describe algunos platos típicos de los EE.UU a un(a) estudiante internacional.

ATAJO

Writing activities for this chapter are presented in the Activities Manual. For specific references to tasks supported by *Atajo*, please consult the Activities Manual.

Intercambio: *Para poner la mesa*

Con un(a) compañero(a), completen el siguiente crucigrama con diferentes objetos para poner la mesa.

Van a necesitar las siguientes expresiones:

Sirve para...
Se pone a la derecha/izquierda...

Recuerden: Cuando uno(a) de los dos no comprenda algo, deben usar expresiones como **No comprendo, ¿puedes repetir?**

Estudiante A

En el crucigrama que está a continuación tienes la parte horizontal pero faltan las respuestas para la parte vertical.

Tu compañero(a) va a describir, sin mencionar la palabra, los objetos para poner la mesa que aparecen en su crucigrama y tú tienes que escuchar atentamente y adivinar la palabra que está describiendo.

Tu compañero(a) va a empezar describiendo el número 1 vertical. Cuando descubras la respuesta, sigues tú describiendo el número 1 horizontal.

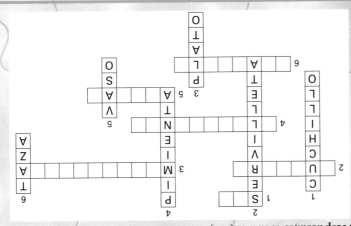

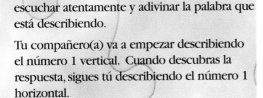

Tú vas a empezar describiendo el número 1 vertical. Cuando tu compañero(a) descubra la respuesta, le toca a él (ella) describir el número 1 horizontal.

vinar la palabra que está describiendo.

Tu compañero(a) va a describir, sin mencionar la palabra, los objetos para poner la mesa que aparecen en su crucigrama y tú tienes que escuchar atentamente y adivinar la palabra que está describiendo.

En el crucigrama que está a continuación tienes la parte vertical pero faltan las respuestas para la parte horizontal.

Estudiante B

Vocabulario

Para charlar

Para pedir una mesa en un restaurante
Requesting a table in a restaurant

Quisiera / *I would like* | una mesa para...
Quisiéramos / *We would like* | personas, por favor. / *a table for . . . people, please.*

Para pedir la comida   *Ordering food*
¿Qué quisiera pedir como aperitivo?   *What would you like as an appetizer?*
   sopa?   *soup?*
¿Qué quisieran pedir como segundo plato?   *What would you (pl.) like as an entree?*
   postre?   *a dessert?*

Como / *As*
aperitivo	*an appetizer*	
sopa	*soup*	quisiera...
segundo plato	*an entree*	*I would like . . .*
postre	*a dessert*	

Para indicar preferencias   *Indicating preferences*
Tengo ganas de comer...   *I feel like eating . . .*
Yo quisiera comer...   *I would like to eat . . .*
Me encanta la comida china (griega, italiana, francesa, etc.).   *I love Chinese (Greek, Italian, French) food*
Se come bien en este restaurante.   *One eats well in this restaurant.*

Para pedir la cuenta   *Requesting the bill*
La cuenta, por favor.   *The check, please.*
¿Podría traernos la cuenta, por favor?   *Could you bring us the check, please?*

Quisiera / *I would like* | la cuenta, por favor.
Quisiéramos / *We would like* | *the check, please.*

Expresiones para comentar sobre el sabor de la comida   *Expressions for commenting on the flavor of the food*
¿Qué tal está(n)...?   *How is (are) . . . ?*
Está muy rico(a).   *It's very good.*
Están muy ricos(as).   *They are very good.*
¡Está riquísimo(a)!   *It's delicious!*
¡Están riquísimos(as)!   *They're delicious!*
¡Qué rico(a) está...!   *. . . is great!*
¡Qué ricos(as) están!   *. . . are great!*

Está un poco (muy, algo, bien) picante.   *It's a little (very, somewhat, very) spicy.*
Está un poco (muy, algo, bien) dulce.   *It's a little (very, somewhat, very) sweet.*
Está un poco (muy, algo, bien) salado(a).   *It's a little (very, somewhat, very) salty.*
Está un poco (muy, algo, bien) sabroso(a).   *It's a little (very, somewhat, very) tasty.*
No tiene(n) sabor.   *It has no flavor.*

Temas y contextos

Expresiones para dar énfasis   *Expressions for giving emphasis*
algo   *somewhat*   muy   *very*
bien   *very*   un poco   *a little*

La mesa   *The table*
el aceite   *olive oil*
el azúcar   *sugar*
la cuchara   *spoon*
la cucharita   *teaspoon*
el cuchillo   *knife*
la mantequilla   *butter*
la pimienta   *pepper*
el platillo   *saucer*
el plato   *dish, plate*
el plato hondo   *bowl*
la sal   *salt*
la servilleta   *napkin*
la taza   *cup*
el tenedor   *fork*
el vaso   *glass*
el vinagre   *vinegar*

Expresiones afirmativas y negativas   *Affirmative and negative expressions*
algo   *something*
alguien   *someone, somebody*
algún/alguno/alguna/algunos/algunas   *a, an, some*
algún día   *someday*
cada día   *every day*
nada   *nothing*
nadie   *no one, nobody*
ni...ni   *neither . . . nor*
ningún/ninguno/ninguna   *none*
nunca   *never*
o...o   *either . . . or*
siempre   *always*

también   *also*
tampoco   *neither*
todos los días   *every day*
una vez   *once*

El menú   *The menu*
Aperitivos   *Appetizers*
  calamares fritos   *fried squid*
  chorizo   *sausage*
  espárragos a la parmesana   *asparagus with Parmesan cheese*
  gambas al ajillo   *shrimp in garlic*
  jamón serrano   *Spanish ham, similar to prosciutto*
  tortilla española   *Spanish omelette*

Segundo plato   *Entree*
  arroz   *rice*
  bistec   *steak*
  chuletas de cordero   *lamb chops*
  enchiladas   *soft corn tortillas filled with cheese, meat, or chicken*
  filete de ternera   *veal fillet*
  paella valenciana   *Spanish dish with rice, shellfish, and chicken*
  pescado frito   *fried fish*
  pollo al chilindrón   *Spanish dish with chicken in a spicy tomato sauce*
  tacos   *tacos, corn tortillas filled with meat and other things*

Ensaladas   *Salads*
  ensalada mixta   *mixed salad*
Postres   *Desserts*
  flan   *caramel custard*
  fruta   *fruit*
  helados variados   *varied ice creams*
  queso manchego   *cheese from La Mancha region in Spain*
Sopas   *Soups*
  gazpacho andaluz   *cold soup with tomatoes, garlic, onion*
  sopa de ajo   *garlic soup*
    del día   *soup of the day*
    de mariscos   *shellfish soup*
    de pescado   *fish soup*
Bebidas   *Drinks*
  agua mineral con gas   *mineral water with carbonation*
    sin gas   *without carbonation*
  café   *coffee*
  cerveza   *beer*
  chocolate   *chocolate*
  refrescos surtidos   *assorted soft drinks*
  sangría   *sangría, a wine and fruit drink*
  té   *tea*
  vino blanco   *white wine*
  vino tinto   *red wine*

Vocabulario general   General vocabulary

Verbos como **gustar**
   Verbs like **gustar**
apetecer   *to appeal*
caer bien/mal   *to like/not like (people)*
encantar   *to like very much*
faltar   *to need, lack*
importar   *to matter*
interesar   *to interest*
parear   *to seem*
preocupar   *to worry*
tocar   *to be one's turn*

Adjetivos   *Adjectives*
abierto(a)   *open*
aburrido(a)   *bored*
alegre   *happy*
avergonzado(a)   *ashamed; shy*
caliente   *hot*
cansado(a)   *tired*
cerrado(a)   *closed*
contento(a)   *happy*
enfermo(a)   *sick*
enojado(a)   *angry*
frío(a)   *cold*

furioso(a)   *furious*
limpio(a)   *clean*
lleno(a)   *full*
mojado(a)   *wet*
nervioso(a)   *nervous*
ocupado(a)   *busy*
preocupado(a)   *worried*
seco(a)   *dry*
sucio(a)   *dirty*
tranquilo(a)   *calm; quiet*
triste   *sad*
vacío(a)   *empty*

12 El transporte

Los taxis de Buenos Aires, Argentina.

DATOS ESTADÍSTICOS DE RENFE

Kilómetros recorridos (miles)	1994	1995	1996
Trenes de viajeros:			
• AVE	5.989	6.638	7.070
• Largo recorrido	37.170	37.768	37.121
• Regionales	26.356	26.922	27.585
• Cercanías	47.857	49.805	50.795
Suma trenes viajeros	**117.372**	**121.133**	**122.571**

Trenes de mercancías:			
• Cargas completas	24.130	27.545	25.411
• Contenedores	9.284	11.022	11.593
• Paquetería	3.353	1.373	27.585
Suma trenes mercancías	**36.767**	**39.940**	**37.004**

Índice de puntualidad (%)	1994	1995	1996
Trenes de viajeros:			
• AVE	99,6%	99,9	99,8
• Largo recorrido	91,5	93,6	94,0
• Regionales	91,6	94,8	94,8
• Cercanías	97,3	98,5	98,4

Trenes de mercancías:			
• Cargas	83,1%	90,3	91,7
• Combinado	83,5	90,7	91,2
• Paquetería	87,1	95,3	

Viajeros transportados: (millones)			
AVE y Talgo AVE	3,56	3,86	4,09
Largo recorrido	11,13	11,60	11,58
Regionales	21,05	21,39	22,32
Cercanías	315,79	328,65	339,89
Total viajeros	351,53	365,50	377,89

Source: RENFE

CHAPTER OBJECTIVES:

In this chapter you will learn to make arrangements in Spanish for traveling by train, plane, subway, bus, or car. You will see that in many instances making travel plans is similar to what you are familiar with, and in other cases, there are differences to keep in mind, such as the use of the metric system when measuring distances.

After completing this chapter you should be able to carry out the following tasks:

- ◎ **make travel arrangements**
- ◎ **ask and answer questions about schedules and distances**
- ◎ **read maps**
- ◎ **indicate plans for the future**
- ◎ **talk about things you have already done**
- ◎ **Vocabulary for:**
    - train and subway stations and airports
    - automobile and bus travel
    - travel agencies
- ◎ **Grammatical structures:**
    - prepositions of place
    - future tense and its special uses
    - subjunctive and indicative with **cuando** and **aunque**
    - "if" clause and indicative
    - present perfect tense
    - irregular participles
    - past perfect tense

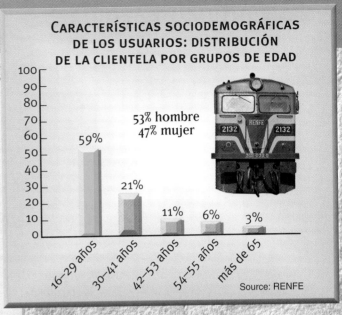

CARACTERÍSTICAS SOCIODEMOGRÁFICAS DE LOS USUARIOS: DISTRIBUCIÓN DE LA CLIENTELA POR GRUPOS DE EDAD

53% hombre
47% mujer

59% — 16–29 años
21% — 30–41 años
11% — 42–53 años
6% — 54–55 años
3% — más de 65

Source: RENFE

Aerolíneas de la Red

España
Air Europa	http://www.g-air-europa.es/
Iberia	http://www.Iberia.com/
Spanair	http://www.Spanair.com/

Argentina
| Aerolíneas Argentinas | http://www.Aerolineas.com.ar/ |
| Austral Líneas Aéreas | http://www.austral.com.ar/ |

América central
Lacsa (Costa Rica)	
Aviateca (Guatemala)	
Taca (El Salvador/Honduras)	http://flylatinamerica.com/
Copa (Panamá)	
Nica (Nicaragua)	

Colombia
| Intercontinental de aviación | http://www.insitenetwork.com/Inter/ |

Chile
| Lan Chile | http://www.LanChile.com/ |

Perú
| AeroPerú | http://www.AeroPeru.com/ |

México
| Mexicana | http://www.mexican.com/ |
| Taesa | http://www.wotw.com/wow/mexico/city/taesa.html |

MEXICANA

PARA EMPEZAR: Los trenes en España

Begin discussion of this new topic by asking students these questions in Spanish. Ask additional questions, such as: ¿Cuáles son algunas ventajas de viajar en tren? ¿Cuáles son las desventajas?

There are Internet sites in Spain that offer train schedules and even metro lines and schedules. For additional "whole language" practice, ask students to search the Web to get information about traveling by train to different parts of Spain, or even within different cities such as Barcelona and Madrid.

Preparación

- Have you ever traveled by train? Do you like it? Why or why not?
- If you have not traveled by train, would you like to? Why or why not?
- What kind of questions do you need to ask when you are making arrangements to travel by train?
- How do you usually make arrangements for traveling by train? By going to the station? Through a travel agent? Now read the ad for train travel in Spain.

RENFE

La Red Nacional de Ferrocarriles Españoles

España ahora toma el tren

En los últimos años en este país vimos muchas cosas nuevas. Escribimos páginas importantes de nuestra reciente historia en ellas. Estamos caminando hacia el futuro, a la **búsqueda** *(search)* de un mundo mejor. Ahora tomamos el tren y miramos hacia adelante, contemplamos con tranquilidad el panorama, **disfrutando** *(enjoying)* de nuestro viaje.

El tren a diario

El mundo no **para** *(stop)*. Todos los días pasan miles de cosas. Y para seguir su ritmo hay que saber estar ahí, sin perder el tren. Aceptando el **reto** *(challenge)* a cada instante. Sacando conclusiones del pasado. Mirando hacia el futuro. Sólo así podemos

llegar lejos. Sólo así podemos **estar al momento** *(to be up to date)*. Con un medio que es para todos los días. Que es para siempre. Como el tren.

Tome el tren y viva su propia historia

Mire hacia cualquiera de los cuatro **puntos cardinales** *(compass points)*. Cualquiera que sea el lugar que quiera visitar, seguro que está lleno de tradiciones, historias, gentes agradables. Seguro que el tren pasa muy cerca. Que forma ya parte del paisaje. **No lo dude** *(Don't doubt it)*, llegue hasta él. Con tranquilidad. Disfrutando de España. Dedicándose a lo que le guste. El tren **le deja las manos libres para acariciar** *(leaves your hands free to caress)* la vida. Para vivir su propia historia.

▶El horario de trenes

RENFE prepara horarios regionales que indican las salidas y llegadas de los trenes entre la mayoría de las ciudades principales de España.

Salidas — DEPARTURES

Tren / TRAIN	Destino / DESTINATION	Hora / TIME	Via / PLATFORM
AVE	Cordoba-Sevilla	14:00	
TALGO	Caceres-Lisboa	14:05	
REG	C.Real-Badajoz	14:20	
REG	Cuenca		14:22
EN TAQUILLAS. E			

Otros signos

- ○   Llegada.
- ■   Origen/destino del tren o rama.
- Ⓐ   Suplemento tren cualificado tipo A, B.
- Ⓖ   Precio global.
- Ⓢ   Suplementos internacionales.
- ¦   El tren no circula por ese tramo.
- ¦   El tren no para en ese tramo o estación.
- ①   Llamada remitiendo a pie de página.
- apd, apt   Apeadero, apartadero.
- cgd   Cargadero.
- 🚉   Estación fronteriza.
- Talgo P.   Talgo Pendular.
- Talgo C.   Talgo Camas.
- Reg.Exp.   Regional Exprés.
- Interurb.   Interurbano.
- Cercan.   Cercanías.
- ▬   INTERCITY.
- ▬   Eurocity. Tren europeo de calidad.

Composición de los trenes

- 1, 2   1ª y 2ª clase.
- ⊷   Coche-literas.
- ⇞   Coche-camas.
- ⇞   Cama Gran Clase.
- ·   Cama Ducha.
- ✕   Tren con servicio de restaurante.
- ▮   Tren con servicio de cafetería.
- ▼   Tren con servicio de bar.
- ⟐   Mini-bar.
- ▭   Tren con servicio de vídeo.
- ♪   Megafonía.
- ⤳   Coche guardería.
- ๐ิ   Coche Rail Club.
- ⇁   Autoexpreso
- ⇜   Motoexpreso

Horario

Tipo de tren		Interurb.	Diurno	Interurb.	Interurb.	Diurno	Reg.Exp.
Número circulación		36004	684	32042	36006	686	6008
Número ordenador			684			686	
Plazas sentadas		1-2	1-2	2	1-2	1-2	1-2
Plazas acostadas							
Prestaciones						▽	
Suplementos/P. Global		Ⓖ				Ⓖ	Ⓖ
Circulación y notas		Ⓐ					①
Origen		■	■	■	■	■	■
Madrid-Atocha		6 00	9 15	11 00	13 35	15 45	19 45
Aranjuez	○	6 41	9 51	11 42	14 11	16 21	20 21
Aranjuez		6 42	9 52	11 43	14 12	16 23	20 22
Ontígola (apd)							20 31
Ocaña		7 01		12 05	14 30		20 41
Noblejas (apd)				12 11	14 34		20 45
Villarrubia de Santiago		7 13		12 18	14 40		20 52
Santa Cruz de la Zarza		7 25		12 31	14 53		21 09
Tarancón		7 39	10 37	12 45	15 05	17 10	21 22
Huelves (apd)		7 48					
Paredes de Melo		7 53					
Vellisca (apd)		8 00					
Huete		8 11	11 04	13 20	15 32	17 38	21 50
Caracenilla (apd)							
Castillejo del Romeral (apd)							
Cuevas de Velasco		8 29		13 41	15 51		22 11
Villar del Saz de Navalón (apd)		8 34					
Chillarón		8 44		14 02	16 13		
Cuenca	○	8 52	11 43	14 11	16 22	18 23	22 35
Cuenca		■	11 45	14 16	■	18 30	■
La Melgosa (apd)							
Los Palancares							
Cañada del Hoyo (apd-cgd)				14 43			
Carboneras de Guadazaón			12 17	14 51		19 00	
Arguisuelas				15 05			
Yemeda-Cardenete				15 24			
Villora (apd)				15 33			
Enguídanos (apd)				15 44			
Camporrobles				16 03			
Cuevas de Utiel (apd)				16 14			
Utiel (apt-cgd)			13 20	16 24		20 00	
San Antonio de Requena (apd)				16 32			
Requena			13 30	16 40		20 10	
Rebollar (apt)							
Siete Aguas (apd)				17 06			
Venta Mina-Siete Aguas (apt)				17 10			
Buñol				17 24			
Chiva (apt)				17 31			
Cheste				17 37			
Loriquilla-Llano (apt-cgd)				17 48			
Aldaya				17 56			
Vara de Quart (apt-cgd)							
Valencia-Término	○		14 45	18 12		21 15	
Destino			■	■		■	

①   Rio Huecar.

Práctica

A. Sobre el anuncio de RENFE. Contesta las preguntas en español.

1. ¿Cuáles son las cinco palabras o frases que se repiten con más frecuencia en el anuncio en la página 414?
2. ¿Qué efecto tiene en el lector el uso de tantas frases y oraciones breves en el anuncio?
3. Este anuncio no tiene que ver sólo con el tren. ¿Qué más "vende" el anuncio?
4. ¿Qué sección del anuncio te gusta más? ¿Por qué?

B. Un horario. Contesta las siguientes preguntas sobre el horario de los trenes entre Madrid y Valencia en la página 415.

1. ¿Cuántos trenes diarios hay entre Madrid y Valencia?
2. ¿Cuántas horas toma el viaje entre Madrid y Valencia?
3. Si estás en Cuenca y quieres ir a Valencia, ¿cuántas horas toma el viaje? ¿Hay trenes directos?
4. ¿Hay un tren con servicio de restaurante entre Madrid y Valencia?
5. ¿Qué trenes van a Cuenca como destino final?

C. Más información. Varios de tus amigos quieren tomar el tren entre Madrid y Valencia pero necesitan más información. Consulta el horario en la página 415 para contestar sus preguntas. Sigue el modelo.

■ **Modelo:** Quiero llegar a Cuenca a las 12:00. ¿Qué tren debo tomar desde Madrid?
Es necesario tomar el tren de las 9:15.

1. Quiero llegar a Valencia esta noche a las 8:00 para cenar con la familia. ¿Qué tren debo tomar desde Madrid?
2. Voy a Valencia pero quiero desayunar con unos amigos a las ocho antes de salir. ¿Qué tren puedo tomar?
3. ¿Cuántas paradas *(stops)* hace el tren de las 6:00 entre Madrid y Cuenca?
4. Quiero llegar a Valencia antes de las 9:00 esta noche. ¿Qué tren debo tomar desde Madrid?

Answers, Ex. B
1. tres 2. cinco horas y media 3. de 3 a 4 horas; sí 4. no 5. los trenes números 36004, 36006 y 6008

To provide more cultural context, provide a detailed map of Spain so that students can point out the city pairs mentioned in these exercises. For additional work, before doing the activities have students search the Internet for a little information on each of these cities. Finding interesting events or opportunities in each city, they can then comment on why someone would be traveling between the two.

Answers, Ex. C
1. Es necesario tomar el tren de las 11:00. 2. Puedes tomar el tren de las 9:15 o el de las 11:00. 3. El tren hace 13 paradas entre Madrid y Cuenca. 4. Es necesario tomar el tren de las 11:00.

Contextualize presentation of vocabulary. Display on the overhead a Spanish train schedule. Then talk to them about a trip you would like to take. For example: **Este verano voy a estar en España por un mes. Primero voy a Madrid, pero de Madrid quisiera viajar a Sevilla en tren. Vamos a ver los horarios...** Ask questions throughout presentation to check comprehension.

ENFOQUE LÉXICO — Expresiones para viajar en tren

Quisiera una **plaza de segunda** **plaza de primera**	*I'd like a second class seat* *first class seat*
Quisiera **reservar una plaza** para Barcelona.	*I'd like to reserve a seat for Barcelona.*
Quisiera **una plaza en la sección de no fumar.**	*I'd like a seat in the no smoking section.*
Quisiera **un billete de ida y vuelta.**	*I'd like a round-trip ticket.*
¿A qué hora sale/llega el tren?	*What time does the train leave/arrive?*
¿De que **andén** sale?	*From which platform does it leave?*
¿Cuál es **el número del vagón?**	*What is the car number?*
¿El tren llegará **retrasado/adelantado /a tiempo?**	*Will the train arrive late/early/ on time?*

Práctica

D. En la taquilla.
Compra unos billetes para el tren, usando la información que sigue. Otro(a) estudiante puede ser el (la) empleado(a). Sigan el modelo.

Ex. D:  Pairs

Tell students to pretend that they are in Madrid. Display a map of Spain so students can see the distances between Madrid and the cities in this exercise. Look up the exchange rate for pesetas and encourage students to discuss what the price of the ticket might be. Incorporate asking for ticket prices into the activity.

■ **Modelo:** 4 / Sevilla / ida / segunda clase

Estudiante 1: *Quisiera reservar (Necesito) cuatro plazas para Sevilla, por favor.*

Estudiante 2: *¿De ida y vuelta?*
Estudiante 1: *No, de ida nada más.*
Estudiante 2: *¿Primera o segunda clase?*
Estudiante 1: *Segunda, por favor.*

1. 1 / San Sebastián / ida / primera clase
2. 2 / Bilbao / ida y vuelta / segunda clase
3. 3 / Granada / ida y vuelta / primera clase
4. 4 / Valencia / ida / segunda clase

E. Vamos a reservar nuestras plazas.
Usa la información que sigue para reservar unas plazas para viajar en tren. Trabaja con otro(a) estudiante que puede ser el (la) empleado(a). Sigan el modelo.

Ex. E:  Pairs

■ **Modelo:** 3 / salida (16 de septiembre, 14:25) / no fumar / vuelta (26 de septiembre, 9:00)

Estudiante 1: *Quisiera reservar tres plazas, por favor.*
Estudiante 2: *¿Cuándo quiere salir?*
Estudiante 1: *El 16 de septiembre. ¿Es posible reservar tres plazas en el tren de las 14:25?*
Estudiante 2: *Sí, ¡cómo no! ¿En la sección de fumar o no fumar?*
Estudiante 1: *No fumar.*
Estudiante 2: *Y la vuelta, ¿para cuándo?*
Estudiante 1: *La vuelta para el 26 de septiembre, a las nueve de la mañana, si es posible.*

F. Los detalles del viaje.
Vas a viajar con un(a) amigo(a) que organizó los detalles para ustedes. Cuando llegas a la estación, le haces preguntas sobre el viaje. Quieres saber la hora de la salida del tren, el número del andén, el número del vagón donde tienen plazas, si tienen mucho tiempo. El (Ella) te contesta según la información indicada.

Ex. F:  Pairs

■ **Modelo:** 10:50 / G /15 /10:30
—*¿A qué hora sale el tren?*
—*Sale a las 10:50.*
—*¿De qué andén sale?*
—*Del andén G.*
—*¿Cuál es el número del vagón?*
—*Quince.*
—*¿Cuánto tiempo nos queda?*
—*Nos queda veinte minutos.*

1. 9:44 / F / 18 / 9:25
2. 11:40 / I / 14 / 11:37
3. 15:51 / B / 12 / 15:50
4. 18:20 / C / 16 / 18:05

Comentarios

culturales *Los trenes en España*

Como España es un país relativamente pequeño, la gente viaja más en tren que en avión. La red nacional española de trenes es bastante **eficaz** *(efficient)*. Además, viajar en tren es mucho más barato que viajar en avión. Los españoles están **orgullosos** *(proud)* del desarrollo extenso del sistema ferroviario en los últimos diez años. Los trenes generalmente ofrecen buen servicio y son cómodos y bastante puntuales. El gobierno español, que administra el sistema de transporte conocido como RENFE, ha contribuido con más de 3.000 millones de pesetas para mejorar las **vías** *(rail routes)* y aumentar la velocidad de los trenes. En algunas líneas (Madrid—Barcelona—Valencia—Madrid) la velocidad **ha subido** *(has risen)* a 160 kms por hora. Desde 1992 existe un tren de alta velocidad, el AVE, entre Madrid y Sevilla que viaja a unos 300 kms por hora.

RENFE divide el calendario del año en tres períodos: **días blancos, días rojos** y **días azules.** Los mejores días para viajar son los días azules porque hay menos viajeros y el precio de los billetes es más barato por los descuentos que RENFE ofrece en esos días. Los precios son más caros en los días blancos (los fines de semana de ciertos meses) y especialmente en los días rojos (días festivos).

INTEGRACIÓN CULTURAL

1. ¿Cuál es el sistema de transporte más popular en España? ¿Por qué?
2. ¿Cómo son los trenes españoles generalmente?
3. ¿A cuántos kilómetros por hora viajan algunos trenes?
4. ¿Cuál es la velocidad equivalente en millas por hora?
5. ¿Cómo divide RENFE el calendario del año? ¿Por qué lo dividen así?

Expresiones de lugar

GRAMMAR NOTE:
Remember that you learned **cerca de** and **lejos de** in Chapter 3, page 101.

En julio pensamos ir **a** España.	*In July we plan to go **to** Spain.*
Vamos a comer gazpacho **en** Sevilla y mariscos **en** la costa.	*We are going to eat gazpacho **in** Seville and seafood **on** the coast.*
Vamos a salir **de** Nueva York.	*We are going to leave **from** New York.*
Vamos a viajar **por** todo el país.	*We are going to travel **through(out)** the entire country.*
Después vamos a salir **para** Francia.	*Then we are going to leave **for** France.*
¿Qué distancia hay **entre** Madrid y París?	*What's the distance **between** Madrid and Paris?*
Vamos a seguir **hasta** la frontera italiana.	*We are going to continue on **all the way to** the Italian border.*
Vamos a caminar **hacia** los Pirineos.	*We are going to walk **in the direction of** the Pyrenees.*
Segovia está **cerca de** Madrid.	*Segovia is **close to (near)** Madrid.*
Cádiz está **lejos de** Madrid.	*Cádiz is **far from** Madrid.*

All of the prepositions shown are often used to tell something about a location. These prepositions describe places in the following ways:

- as the location itself (**en**)
- as a starting point or place of origin (**de**)
- as a final destination (**a, hasta**)
- as movement toward a place (**hacia, para**)
- as a reference to the distance between it and another place (**entre**)
- as a reference to traveling through a place (**por**)
- as an indication of general proximity (**cerca de, lejos de**)

Práctica

G. Lugares, lugares. Según el contexto, indica cuál de las palabras entre paréntesis es la correcta.

Answers, Ex. G
1. para 2. en 3. a 4. de 5. lejos de
6. entre 7. a 8. entre 9. de

■ **Modelo:** Mis tíos ahora viven (de / en / hasta) México.
Mis tíos ahora viven en México.

1. Mañana el tren sale (entre / en / para) Andalucía a las 8:05.
2. ¿Quiénes quieren almorzar (hasta / entre / en) el Parque del Retiro?
3. Prefiero ir (en / a / entre) la Costa del Sol.
4. Aranjuez está a 25 kms (hacia / de / a) Madrid.
5. ¿Sólo son 25 kms? Entonces Aranjuez no está (cerca de / lejos de / para) Madrid.
6. Dicen que el tren hace seis paradas (en / por / entre) Madrid y Málaga.
7. Pienso llevar a mi sobrino (de / en / a) la playa este fin de semana.

8. El niño durmió en el tren (para / entre / a) Barcelona y Zaragoza.
9. El plan es salir (lejos de / de / hacia) la estación de Atocha porque tiene los trenes más rápidos.

H. Preguntas sobre un viaje.

Hazle las siguientes preguntas a un(a) compañero(a). Cuando hagas la pregunta, escoge la preposición que corresponde a la que aparece en inglés entre paréntesis. Después tu compañero(a) contestará la pregunta con **sí** o **no**, usando la misma preposición. Sigan el modelo.

Modelo: ¿Vas _____ la playa con tu familia este verano? *(to)*
Tú: *¿Vas a la playa con tu familia este verano?*
Él (Ella): *Sí, voy a la playa con mi familia.*
o
Él (Ella): *No, voy a la playa con mis amigos.*

1. ¿Van a estar Uds. _____ una ciudad? *(far from)*
2. ¿Cuándo piensas regresar _____ tu casa? *(to)*
3. En su viaje, ¿van a pasar _____ el pueblo donde viven tus abuelos? *(through)*
4. ¿Van a poder conducir _____ Francia en un coche tan viejo? *(all the way to)*
5. ¿Van _____ el norte el segundo día de su viaje? *(in the direction of)*
6. ¿Vas a comer _____ el famoso restaurante de mariscos que está _____ la costa? *(in/on)*

ENFOQUE ESTRUCTURAL — El futuro

So far, to talk about future time you have used either the present tense with a future reference (**Mañana visitamos a tus primos**), the immediate future with **ir a** + *infinitive* (**Vamos a ver una película esta noche**), or an expression that implies the future such as **quiero, pienso, espero** + *infinitive* (**Espero ir a Madrid este verano**).

Spanish also has a future tense that, like the future tense in English, expresses what will happen. Note the following examples:

¿Visitaremos el castillo mañana?	***Will we visit*** *the castle tomorrow?*
Sí, **llamaré por teléfono** para confirmarlo.	*Yes,* ***I'll call*** *to confirm it.*
¿Dónde **nos encontraremos**?	*Where* ***will we meet****?*
Te **esperaré** enfrente del banco.	***I'll wait*** *for you in front of the bank.*

In Spanish, however, this tense is not used in everyday conversation with as much frequency as the three alternatives you already know.

Verbos regulares

To form the future tense, simply add the endings **-é, -ás, -á, -emos, -éis, -án** to the infinitive form of the verb (whether it is an **-ar, -er,** or **-ir** verb).

llegar

yo	llegar**é**		nosotros(as)	llegar**emos**
tú	llegar**ás**		vosotros(as)	llegar**éis**
Ud.			Uds.	
él	llegar**á**		ellos	llegar**án**
ella			ellas	

ver

yo	ver**é**		nosotros(as)	ver**emos**
tú	ver**ás**		vosotros(as)	ver**éis**
Ud.			Uds.	
él	ver**á**		ellos	ver**án**
ella			ellas	

pedir

yo	pedir**é**		nosotros(as)	pedir**emos**
tú	pedir**ás**		vosotros(as)	pedir**éis**
Ud.			Uds.	
él	pedir**á**		ellos	pedir**án**
ella			ellas	

Verbos irregulares

Some of the verbs that you have learned don't use the infinitive to form the future tense. Because of this, they are considered "irregular." The endings that attach to this form, however, are the same as those you just learned **(-é, -ás, -á, -emos, -éis, -án).** Some commonly used irregular verbs in the future tense are:

decir, hacer, querer

yo	**diré**		nosotros(as)	**diremos**
tú	**dirás**		vosotros(as)	**diréis**
Ud.			Uds.	
él	**dirá**		ellos	**dirán**
ella			ellas	

hacer	**har-**	yo **haré**	**-ás, -á, -emos, -éis, -án**
querer	**querr-**	yo **querré**	

Note that in the following verbs the **-e** of the infinitive is dropped to form the new stem.

poder, saber

poder	**podr-**	yo **podré**	**-ás, -á, -emos, -éis, -án**
saber	**sabr-**	yo **sabré**	

Remember that **hay** *(there is, there are)* comes from the verb **haber**, which forms the future in the same way as **poder** and **saber**. Therefore, the future form of **hay** is **habrá** *(there will be)*.

In these nest verbs the **-er** or **-ir** infinitive ending is replaced by **-dr** before adding the future tense endings.

poner, salir, tener, venir		
poner	**pondr-**	yo **pondré**
salir	**saldr-**	yo **saldré**
tener	**tendr-**	yo **tendré**
venir	**vendr-**	yo **vendré**

-ás, -á, -emos, -éis, -án

Práctica

Answers, Ex. I
1. Juana irá al campo, tomarán, estarán 2. Iremos, podremos tomar, nadaremos, querremos aprender 3. Jorge y su primo irán, se quedarán, comerán 4. Iré, estaré, te escribiré 5. Estarás, cuidarás, recibirás

Assign as homework. In class put students in pairs and allow them 4–5 minutes to share their answers. Circulate to check for accuracy. When you call time, ask for questions.

Answers, Ex. J
1. Hoy no, pero mañana mi hermana podrá llevarlos al parque.
2. ...estudiaremos. 3. ...iré al cine con mi novio(a). 4. ...llamará... .
5. ...tomaré el tren... 6. ...saldremos temprano. 7. ...compraré las bebidas... 8. ...tendré tiempo libre.
9. ...Carlos vendrá a la casa.
10. ...habrá tiempo... .

Ex. K: Pairs

I. De vacaciones. Indica lo que harán las siguientes personas durante sus vacaciones. Cambia las oraciones al tiempo futuro según el modelo.

◼ **Modelo:**   Mario está en Madrid. Visita el Museo del Prado.
Después va a Toledo.
Mario estará en Madrid. Visitará el Museo del Prado.
Después irá a Toledo.

1. Juana va al campo con sus padres. Toman el sol. Están al aire libre.
2. Vamos a la playa. Podemos tomar el sol y nadar. Queremos aprender a usar la tabla-vela.
3. Jorge y su primo van a Sevilla. Se quedan en casa de sus abuelos. Comen mucho gazpacho.
4. Voy a Portugal. Estoy allí por tres días. Te escribo una tarjeta postal.
5. Estás en casa. Cuidas a tu hermano. Recibes cartas de tus amigos.

J. Hoy no, pero mañana sí. Indica que las siguientes personas harán mañana lo que no pueden hacer hoy. Sigue el modelo.

◼ **Modelo:**   ¿Puedes ir al banco hoy?
Hoy no, pero iré mañana.

1. ¿Tu hermana puede llevar a los niños al parque?
2. ¿Piensan estudiar ustedes?
3. ¿Vas al cine con tu novio(a)?
4. ¿Puede llamarnos Carmen por teléfono?
5. ¿Ud. quiere tomar el tren a Granada?
6. ¿Pueden salir ustedes temprano?
7. ¿Puedes comprar las bebidas en el supermercado?
8. ¿Tienes tiempo libre hoy?
9. ¿Carlos puede venir a la casa?
10. ¿Hay tiempo para ir a la playa?

K. ¿Qué harás? Usa los elementos indicados para hacerle preguntas a un(a) compañero(a), que después te contestará. Expresa el futuro empleando el tiempo futuro u otra estructura que conozcas. Sigue el modelo.

■ **Modelo:** hacer / después de la clase
—¿Qué harás tú después de la clase?
—Yo iré (voy, voy a ir, pienso ir, etc.) al centro.

1. hacer / después de esta clase
2. hacer / esta tarde después de volver a tu casa
3. hacer / esta noche
4. ver / en el cine la semana próxima
5. comprar / en la nueva tienda de ropa
6. comer / en el restaurante mexicano
7. recibir / como regalo de cumpleaños
8. aprender a hacer / el próximo verano
9. hacer / el año próximo
10. viajar / el mes que viene

Follow-up:

When finished, have students play fortune teller for their partner. Have each come up with a list of 5 things that the other will do in the future. Allow 3–4 minutes to create lists and then another 2–3 to share. Circulate to check for accuracy.

Possible answers, Ex. K
1. ¿Qué harás tú después de esta clase? Yo iré a casa. 2. ¿Qué harás tú esta tarde después de volver a tu casa? Estudiaré. 3. ¿Qué harás esta noche? Miraré la televisión. 4. ¿Qué verás en el cine la semana próxima? Veré una película muy buena. 5. ¿Qué comprarás en la nueva tienda de ropa? Compraré un suéter. 6. ¿Qué comerás en el restaurante mexicano? Comeré tacos de pollo. 7. ¿Qué recibirás como regalo de cumpleaños? Recibiré unos libros. 8. ¿Qué aprenderás a hacer el próximo verano? Aprenderé a nadar. 9. ¿Qué harás el año próximo? Estudiaré en España. 10. ¿Adónde viajarás el mes que viene? Viajaré a Washington.

Ask students to read over this section as homework the night before you present it in class. In class, contextualize this presentation by talking about your impending trip abroad. Tell students that you have a friend who goes to Spain frequently and has given you a lot of advice about your trip. For example: **Cuando él va a Madrid, siempre se aloja en el hotel Meliá. Pero este hotel es muy caro. Cuando yo vaya, voy a alojarme en un hotel más económico... Mi amigo dice que yo tengo que seguir sus consejos porque tiene mucha experiencia con los viajes a España. Sin embargo, aunque él tenga toda la experiencia posible, no me alojaré en un hotel tan caro...** As you use them, write contrasting phrases on the board and accentuate the subjunctive verb forms.

ENFOQUE ESTRUCTURAL

El subjuntivo y el indicativo con **cuando** y **aunque**

Notice the difference in meaning for each pair of sentences below.

Hablaremos con Mario **cuando llegue.**	*We'll talk with Mario **when he arrives.*** (It has not happened yet.)
Hablé con Mario **cuando llegó.**	*I spoke with Mario **when he arrived.*** (This is what happened that time)
Cuando vaya a México, comeré muchos tacos.	***When I go*** *to México, I'll eat lots of tacos.* (The next time I go, whenever that may be, I will do this.)
Siempre como muchos tacos **cuando voy** a México.	*I always eat lots of tacos **whenever I go** to Mexico.* (This happens on a regular basis.)
Aunque sea inteligente, Víctor no estudia.	***Even though he may be*** *intelligent, Victor doesn't study.*
Aunque es inteligente, Víctor no estudia.	***Even though he is*** *intelligent, Victor doesn't study.*
No podré ir, **aunque insistas.**	*I won't be able to go, **even though you may insist.***
No podré ir, **aunque insistes.**	*I won't be able to go, **even though you are insisting.***

Cuando is followed by a verb in the subjunctive when it refers to something that has not yet happened. **Cuando** is followed by a verb in the indicative when it refers to something that has already happened (past) or happens on a regular basis (present).

Aunque is followed by a verb in the subjunctive when it refers to an outcome that is seen as indefinite. **Aunque** is followed by a verb in the indicative when it refers to an established fact (past or present).

Práctica

L. ¡Qué viaje! Completa la información sobre unos amigos con la forma apropiada del verbo.

Cuando mi hermano ___ (ganar) la lotería la semana pasada, invitó a la familia a viajar a Brasil el verano que viene. Aunque nadie ___ (saber) portugués, no será ningún problema. Cuando se ___ (hablar) español como nosotros, es posible entender bastante bien a los brasileños cuando nos ___ (hablar) en portugués. Sin embargo, creo que cuando yo ___ (ganar) la lotería algún día, invitaré a todos a ir a España, porque cuando yo ___ (estar) en ese país siempre hablo español con todo el mundo allá.

M. Lo que hago y lo que haré. Trabajando con otro(a) estudiante, usen el primero verbo para indicar lo que hacen siempre o lo que van a hacer en el futuro, usando la forma apropiada del segundo verbo después de **cuando.** Sigan el modelo.

■ **Modelo:** ir / estar
Iré a España cuando estén mis tíos en Sevilla.
o
Siempre voy a España cuando están en Sevilla mis tíos.

1. visitar / poder
2. comer / tener hambre
3. ir / comprar
4. reservar plazas / costar
5. escribir postales / viajar
6. descansar / llegar

VAMOS A ESCUCHAR EN LA ESTACIÓN DE ATOCHA

Varios pasajeros van a la Estación de Atocha en Madrid. Enrique va a comprar billetes y reservar dos plazas. Carmen y Antonio Altabé comienzan sus vacaciones y quieren ir a Valencia.

ANTES DE ESCUCHAR

Basándote en lo que has aprendido en esta *etapa,* contesta las siguientes preguntas.

1. ¿Qué palabras de vocabulario crees que van a usar los pasajeros y el empleado?
2. ¿Qué preguntas esperas escuchar?

Ahora lee las preguntas en la sección *Después de escuchar* para ver cuáles coinciden con lo que has pensado. Escucha el diálogo y contesta las siguientes preguntas.

DESPUÉS DE ESCUCHAR

N. Comprensión. Escucha el diálogo y contesta las preguntas.
Enrique
1. ¿De qué tipo son los billetes que compra?
2. ¿De qué clase son los billetes?
3. ¿Adónde piensa viajar?
4. ¿A qué hora sale el tren que prefiere?
5. ¿Qué información importante le da el empleado?

Carmen y Antonio Altabé

6. ¿Adónde piensan viajar Carmen y Antonio?
7. ¿Cuál es el problema con el tren en que van a viajar?
8. ¿Qué quiere saber Carmen al final?
9. ¿Qué piensa hacer Antonio mientras esperan?

Ñ. ¿Cómo lo dicen?

1. ¿Cómo indica Enrique que "he would like to know something?"
2. ¿Cómo dice "would like to make a reservation?"
3. ¿Qué expresión usa el empleado para "wish Enrique a good trip"?
4. ¿Cómo pregunta Carmen "At what time does the train leave?"
5. ¿Cómo dice "reserved seats?"
6. ¿Cómo dice "train car?"

Tú dirás ....

O. Un itinerario. Trabaja con otro(a) estudiante. Están en Madrid y quieren visitar Burgos, una famosa ciudad conocida por su arquitectura gótica y arte medieval. Después de leer la información en el folleto, preparen un itinerario, basándose en lo siguiente.

1. what day you are going to leave
2. from which station in Madrid the train leaves
3. to what city you're going to take the train
4. what time the train leaves for this city
5. whether there is a stop along the way
6. what time you will arrive at your destination
7. where you will stay during the visit
8. what you plan to visit in the city
9. what day you will be leaving Madrid
10. what time you will be back in Madrid

Programa
Sábado

8.30 h. Salida en tren Ter de Madrid-Chamartin

11.23 h. Llegada a Lera. *Transbordo a autocar. Circuito a Lerma.

12.30 h. Covarrubias. Vista a la Colegiata. Tiempo libre para almorzar.

16.30 h. Salida en autocar para visitar Santo Domingo de Silos y La Yecla.

20.00 h. Llegada a Burgos. Traslado al hotel. Tiempo libre.

21.30 h. Saludo del Ayuntamiento en el antiguo onasterio de San Juan, vino y actuaciones folclóricas. Elicción de la madrina del Tren.

Domingo

8.00 h. Desayuno en el hotel.

8.30 h. Recogida en el hotel en autobús. Visita guiada a la Catedral, Monasterio de las huelgas, Monasterio de San Pedro de Cardeña (posibilidad de oír misa) y Cartuja.

14.00 h. Tiempo libre para almorzar.

16.30 h. Visita panorámica de la Ciudad. Traslado a la Estación.

17.45 h. Salida en tren Ter hacia Madrid.

21.30 h. Llegada a madrid Charmartin. Fin de viaje.

*NOTA: El tren TER continúa a Burgos, llegando a las 12.10 h. Los viajeros no interesados en la excursión pueden continuar a Burgos y hacer uso de sus habitaciones en el hotel elegido.

Burgos, cuna del Cid. Donde el románico y el gótico se entremezclan para formar una de las provincias má ricas en arte medieval. Lerma, Covarrubus, Silos y Burgos capital, donde el gótico culmina en una gran obra, la Catedral.

La catedral de Burgos

P. Cuando seas rico(a)... Tu compañero(a) es más optimista que tú. Por eso, él (ella) cree que va a tener mucho dinero algún día. Usa la información que sigue para hacerle preguntas sobre lo que él (ella) hará cuando sea rico(a). Usa los verbos en el tiempo futuro según el modelo.

■ **Modelo:** dónde / vivir
—*¿Dónde vivirás cuando seas rico(a)?*
—*Viviré en California (en Nueva York, en España, etc.) cuando sea rico(a).*

1. dónde / vivir
2. qué / (ropa) llevar
3. qué / comer
4. adónde / viajar
5. qué coche / comprar
6. cuánto dinero / tener
7. a quién / quiénes/dar dinero
8. qué / hacer con tu tiempo

SEGUNDA ETAPA

PARA EMPEZAR: *Un viaje por carretera*

Begin discussion by asking students these questions in Spanish.

Transparency 0-1: El mapa de carreteras

Preparación

- Have you traveled long distances by car or bus?
- What is one of the longest trips you've made?
- When you plan a long trip by car, what kinds of things do you usually need to know or keep in mind?
- Do you normally use road maps when you travel by car in the country where you live? What about when you take a road trip in a country you are visiting?

CULTURE: You will not find road maps in gas stations in Mexico. It's a good idea to obtain one before starting a road trip by going to an office of the Secretaría de Turismo or the Asociación Mexicana Automovilística (AMA).

VOCABULARY EXPANSION: In Mexico it is common to hear people refer to **billetes** as **boletos**.

Los autobuses

El autobús, o camión, como dicen los mexicanos, es un medio ideal para recorrer el interior del país. Distintas compañías, como Enlaces Terrestres Mexicanos, Flecha Amarilla, Ómnibus de México, entre otras, ofrecen recorridos completos entre las ciudades y los pueblos del país a un precio moderado. En los años más recientes se han ampliado las líneas con camiones nuevos con aire acondicionado, asientos cómodos y ventanas grandes. En algunas líneas, el pasajero puede disfrutar de televisor, un bar y algo de comer. Se recomienda que las reservaciones y la compra de billetes se hagan con un día de anticipación. Por lo general, es un sistema de camiones moderno y eficaz y los horarios se siguen puntualmente.

El mapa de carreteras

El Departamento de Turismo publica una serie de mapas detallados de cada región de México. Estudia el siguiente mapa. **Fíjate en** la capital del país y en otras ciudades y pueblos cerca de ella.

notice

Las señales de tráfico

Algunas de las señales *(signs)* que se ven por las calles y carreteras de los países de habla española son parecidas a las señales que se ven en los Estados Unidos. Otras señales son distintas.

No adelantar

No virar/girar

No hay paso

En obras / trabajo

Aduana

No estacionar

Práctica

A. Los autobuses. Basándote en la información sobre los autobuses en México, contesta las siguientes preguntas.

1. ¿Cuál es otra palabra que usan los mexicanos para referirse a un autobús?
2. ¿Cuáles son los nombres de algunas compañías de autobuses?
3. ¿Qué servicios se le ofrecen al pasajero?
4. ¿Qué se recomienda en cuanto a la reserva de billetes?

B. ¿Es largo el viaje de México a Cuernavaca? Oyes a dos jóvenes mexicanos hablar de un viaje que van a hacer en coche. Tú no conoces bien la geografía de México y quieres saber si el viaje será largo. Por eso les haces varias preguntas. Sigue el modelo.

■ **Modelo:** México—Cuernavaca (90 kms / 1 hora y $\frac{1}{2}$)
—*¿Es largo el viaje de la Ciudad de México a Cuernavaca?*
—*No, no muy largo. Cuernavaca está a noventa kms de México.*
—*¿Cuánto tarda el viaje de México a Cuernavaca en coche?*
—*Es una hora y media.*

1. México—Acapulco (418 kms / 6 horas)
2. México—Taxco (173 kms / 2 horas y $\frac{1}{2}$)
3. Guadalajara—México (580 kms / 7 horas)
4. Toluca—México (66 kms / 45 minutos)
5. Puebla—Veracruz (280 kms / 3 horas y $\frac{1}{2}$)
6. México—Puebla (125 kms / 1 hora y 45 minutos)

C. Las señales. Mira las señales en la página 427 y decide qué quieren decir. ¿Cómo se dice en español lo siguiente?

1. Do not enter
2. Customs
3. No parking
4. Do not pass
5. No turns
6. Construction zone

Comentarios

culturales *Kilómetros y millas*

$\mathcal{E}$l sistema métrico es el que se usa en los países de habla española. Para la persona que está acostumbrada a pensar en millas, en lugar de kilómetros, la siguiente fórmula puede resultar útil para calcular distancias. Para convertir kilómetros a millas se divide el número de kilómetros por ocho. Después se multiplica el resultado por cinco. Por ejemplo, 160 kilómetros dividido entre ocho son 20, que multiplicado por cinco da 100 millas.

INTEGRACIÓN CULTURAL

Ahora, usa las distancias indicadas para decidir a cuántas millas equivalen aproximadamente los kilómetros indicados.

a. México—Acapulco (418 kms) d. Toluca—México (66 kms)
b. México—Taxco (173 kms)   e. Puebla—Veracruz (280 kms)
c. Guadalajara—México (580 kms) f. México—Puebla (125 kms)

Answers, Integración
a. 261 mi. b. 106 mi. c. 365 mi.
d. 41 mi. e. 175 mi. f. 78 mi.

Repaso

D. Preguntas sobre un viaje. Hazle las siguientes preguntas a un(a) compañero(a). Cada vez que hagas una pregunta, llena el espacio con la preposición que corresponde a las palabras entre paréntesis. Después, tu compañero(a) contestará con **sí** o **no,** usando la misma preposición. Sigan el modelo.

Ex. D: Pairs

Allow students 5–7 minutes to complete this activity. Circulate around the classroom to check for accurate usage of prepositions.

■ **Modelo:**   ¿Irás ___ la playa con tu familia este verano? *(to)*
               Sí, iré a la playa con mi familia.
               o
               No, no iré a la playa con mi familia. Iré con mis amigos.

1. ¿Cuándo saldrán ustedes ___ la ciudad? *(from)*
2. ¿Cuándo volverás ___ tu casa? *(to)*
3. ¿En su viaje pasarán ___ el pueblo donde viven tus abuelos? *(through)*
4. ¿Podrán conducir ___ la playa en un coche tan viejo? *(all the way to)*
5. ¿Irán ___ el norte el segundo día de su viaje? *(in the direction of)*
6. ¿Comerás ___ un restaurante famoso? *(in)*

E. ¿Qué se hace… ?   Un(a) amigo(a) te pregunta qué se hace en varios sitios. Tú le contestas empleando el **se** impersonal. Sigue el modelo.

Ex. E: Pairs

Possible answers, Ex. E
1. ¿Qué se hace en la discoteca? Se baila en la discoteca. 2. ¿Qué se hace en el restaurante? Se come en el restaurante. 3. ¿Qué se hace en la clase de español? Se habla español en la clase de español. 4. ¿Qué se hace en la aduana? Se muestra el pasaporte en la aduana. 5. ¿Qué se hace en la tienda de ropa? Se compra ropa en la tienda de ropa. 6. ¿Qué se hace en la fiesta? Se baila en la fiesta. 7. ¿Qué se hace en el aeropuerto? Se toma un avión en el aeropuerto. 8. ¿Qué se hace en el tren? Se viaja en el tren.

■ **Modelo:**   el parque
               —*¿Qué se hace en el parque?*
               —*Se juega.*
               —*Se camina.*
               —*Se descansa.*

1. la discoteca
2. el restaurante
3. la clase de español
4. la aduana
5. la tienda de ropa
6. la fiesta
7. el aeropuerto
8. el tren

IRM Master 51: Usos especiales del futuro

ENFOQUE ESTRUCTURAL   Usos especiales del futuro

Present this structure in context by telling students about an eccentric old friend you have who is constantly telling you that you should prepare for your retirement as soon as possible. For example: **Tengo un amigo aquí en la universidad en el departamento de biología. No sé cuántos años tiene, pero tendrá unos setenta por lo menos. Bueno, como este amigo es tan viejo siempre me aconseja que me prepare para el futuro, para cuando me jubile...**

El futuro de probabilidad

The future tense is often used in Spanish to wonder about an action or a situation related to the present. Note the following examples.

¿Cuántos años **tendrá** ese actor?	*I wonder* how old that actor *is.*
¿Quién **será** esa persona?	*I wonder* who that person *is.*
	*(Who **can** that person **be?**)*

Using the future tense you can express probability or uncertainty with regard to an action or a situation in the present. In other words, when you make a comment that is really more of a guess or speculation, rather than actual knowledge, the future tense is used:

Tendrá unos treinta.	***He's probably (He must be)*** *about thirty.*

El futuro en oraciones condicionales

Look at the following examples and notice that when the verb in the main clause is in the present or future tense, the verb in the **si** clause will always be in the present tense. In this type of conditional clause the indicative is used after **si** because the speaker is assuming that something will take place.

Compraremos ese coche rojo **si tenemos** el dinero.	*We will buy that red car **if we have** the money.*
Estaré contento **si** me **escribes.**	*I will be happy **if you write** to me.*
Si pierdes ese reloj, será una lástima.	***If you lose** that watch, it will be a shame.*
Pasaré por ti **si** me **esperas.**	*I will stop by for you **if you wait** for me.*
Si Carlos **trabaja** mucho, aprenderá mucho.	***If** Carlos **works** hard he will learn a lot.*

Práctica

F. Me pregunto... Convierte las siguientes oraciones en preguntas que expresen una conjetura. Utiliza palabras interrogativas como: **dónde, cuándo, cómo, qué**... Sigue el modelo.

■ **Modelo:** El tren no sale a tiempo.
¿Cuándo saldrá el tren?

1. El tren llega más tarde.
2. No comemos en el restaurante de la estación.
3. No puedo pagar con un cheque de viajero.
4. No sirven el desayuno en el tren.
5. Hay muchos pasajeros alemanes.
6. Este tren no llega a tiempo.
7. El tren no para en Huelva.
8. Los ingleses no van a Málaga.
9. Mi padre no tiene las maletas.

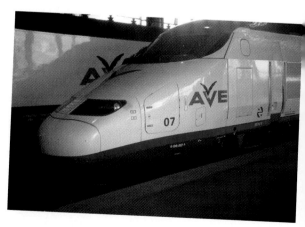

G. ¡No sé, José! José, el hijo de unos amigos españoles, viaja en el tren contigo. Sólo tiene ocho años y es muy persistente con las preguntas que hace. Como tú no sabes contestarlas de una manera exacta, expresa la probabilidad o la duda usando el mismo verbo que él usa pero cambiándolo al tiempo futuro. Sigue el modelo.

■ **Modelo:** —¿Qué hora es?
—*¡No sé, José! Serán las nueve.*

1. ¿Cómo se llama el conductor del tren?
2. ¿Qué sirven para comer en el tren?
3. ¿Qué tipo de música escucha esa chica en su "Walkman"?
4. ¿Qué tiene esa señora en su maleta?
5. ¿A qué hora llega ese señor a su casa?
6. ¿Cuántas personas hay en este tren?
7. ¿Qué pueblo es éste?
8. ¿Dónde estamos ahora?
9. ¿Quién es ese señor alto del sombrero negro?
10. ¿A cuántos kilómetros por hora vamos en este momento?

H. Suposiciones.
Trabaja con un(a) compañero(a) de clase. Completa las oraciones con la suposición que tú quieras hacer.

■ **Modelo:** Te podré ayudar si…
Te podré ayudar si me llamas.

1. Sabré el número del vuelo si…
2. Iré al aeropuerto contigo si…
3. Mi novia dice que podré usar su coche si…
4. Compraré los boletos para el viaje si…
5. El avión llegará temprano si…
6. Iremos a México el verano próximo si…
7. Estaré muy contento(a) si…
8. No tendremos dificultades en el viaje si...

I. Consecuencias.
Trabaja con un(a) compañero(a) de clase para completar las oraciones, indicando las consecuencias de la acción previa. Sigue el modelo.

■ **Modelo:** Si esperas media hora…
Si esperas media hora, iremos juntos a la terminal.

1. Si sales a tiempo…
2. Si el autobús sale tarde…
3. Si no llega el autobús pronto…
4. Si te gusta viajar…
5. Si cuesta demasiado dinero…
6. Si el hotel es bonito…
7. Si el pasaporte no está en la maleta…
8. Si hablas con el agente de viajes…
9. Si tus amigos no quieren viajar en autobús…
10. Si ustedes leen el horario…

Ex. G:  Pairs

Answers, Ex. G
1. ¡No sé, José! Se llamará… .
2. Servirán… . 3. Escuchará… .
4. Tendrá… . 5. Llegará… .
6. Habrá… . 7. Será… .
8. Estaremos… . 9. Será… .
10. Iremos… .

Ex. H:  Pairs

Possible answers, Ex. H
1. Sabré el número del vuelo si el agente me lo dice. 2. Iré al aeropuerto contigo si quieres. 3. Mi novia dice que podré usar su coche si tengo cuidado. 4. Compraré los boletos para el viaje si no cuestan mucho. 5. El avión llegará temprano si no para en Monterrey. 6. Iremos a México el verano próximo si tenemos dinero. 7. Estaré muy contento si me llamas. 8. No tendremos dificultades en el viaje si llevamos un mapa.

Ex. I: Pairs

Allow students 4–6 minutes per exercise to work together on the answers. Circulate around the class to check for accuracy. When done, comment on any particular problems that came up while doing the exercise.

IRM Master 52: El presente perfecto

ENFOQUE ESTRUCTURAL El presente perfecto

The present perfect tense is used to talk about an action that has happened already, either in the general past or quite recently in relation to the moment of speaking. The equivalent in English is to have done something. Sometimes it may be used to suggest that the effects of a past event carry over into the present: "I've always done it that way (and still do)." Note the following examples:

¿Han viajado últimamente?	***Have you traveled** lately?*
Hemos visitado España y Portugal.	***We've visited** Spain and Portugal.*
¿Ha salido el tren para Segovia?	***Has** the train **left** for Segovia?*
No, **no ha salido.**	*No, **it hasn't left**.*

This tense has two parts, exactly as in English: the first part is called a "helping" verb ("have" in English and **haber** in Spanish). The second part is a past participle. The past participle of an **-ar** verb is formed by substituting **-ado** for **-ar.** The ending for both **-er** and **-ir** verbs is **-ido.**

Note that this two-part verb is *not* split up in Spanish by a negative as it is in English.

Carlos **no ha llegado.**	*Carlos has **not** arrived.*

Notice also that this compound verb is not split up by the subject or subject pronoun when it is used in a question as it is in English.

¿Ha llegado el tren?	***Has** the train **arrived?***
Sí, sí **ha llegado.**	*Yes, **it has**.*

haber + participio pasado

		-ar	-er	-ir
yo	he			
tú	has			
Ud., él, ella	ha	bailado	comido	salido
nosotros(as)	hemos			
vosotros(as)	habéis			
Uds., ellos, ellas	han			

Here are more examples of past participles:

infinitivo	participio pasado	infinitivo	participio pasado
hablar	**hablado**	aprender	**aprendido**
dar	**dado**	comer	**comido**
estar	**estado**	comprender	**comprendido**
jugar	**jugado**	ir	**ido**
trabajar	**trabajado**	seguir	**seguido**
mandar	**mandado**	pedir	**pedido**

Participios irregulares

Here are some of the more common past participles that are exceptions to the general rule previously described:

infinitivo	participio pasado	infinitivo	participio pasado
abrir	**abierto**	hacer	**hecho**
cubrir	**cubierto**	poner	**puesto**
decir	**dicho**	resolver	**resuelto**
describir	**descrito**	romper	**roto**
descubrir	**descubierto**	ver	**visto**
escribir	**escrito**	volver	**vuelto**

Assign this as homework the night before you present the structure in class. In class allow students 3–4 minutes to compare their answers. Circulate to check for accuracy.

Práctica

J. ¿Qué ha pasado antes? Mario y Marta Mendoza han llegado a la terminal de autobuses. Explica lo que han hecho antes de su llegada.

■ **Modelo:** leer la guía turística sobre México
Han leído la guía turística sobre México.

1. ir a su agencia de viajes
2. discutir sus planes
3. pedir reservaciones de plazas en el autobús
4. llevar el gato a la casa de un amigo
5. descubrir un nuevo hotel
6. preparar las maletas
7. salir temprano de casa
8. tomar un taxi a la terminal
9. romper un vaso en el restaurante

Answers, Ex. J
1. Han ido a su agencia de viajes.
2. Han discutido sus planes. 3. Han pedido reservaciones de plazas en el autobús. 4. Han llevado el gato a la casa de un amigo. 5. Han descubierto un nuevo hotel. 6. Han preparado las maletas. 7. Han salido temprano de casa. 8. Han tomado un taxi a la terminal. 9. Han roto un vaso en el restaurante.

K. Todavía no, pero... *(Not yet, but . . .)*

Cuando un(a) amigo(a) te hace unas preguntas, dile que todavía no has podido hacer eso pero que has hecho otra cosa. Sigue el modelo.

■ **Modelo:** viajar en autobús
—¿Has viajado en autobús?
—No, todavía no he viajado en autobús, pero he viajado en tren.

1. comer gazpacho
2. ir al Ballet Folklórico de México
3. leer una novela de Carlos Fuentes
4. viajar en tren
5. estudiar portugués
6. vivir en Madrid
7. beber sangría
8. pasar un mes de vacaciones en México
9. subir a una pirámide azteca
10. bailar el flamenco
11. correr con los toros por las calles de Pamplona
12. oír la música de mariachis mexicanos

Ex. K: Pairs

Answers, Ex. K
1. ¿Has comido gazpacho? he comido... . 2. ¿Has ido al Ballet Folklórico de México? he ido... .
3. ¿Has leído una novela de Carlos Fuentes? he leído... . 4. ¿Has viajado en tren? he viajado... . 5. ¿Has estudiado portugués? no lo he estudiado... . 6. ¿Has vivido en Madrid? he vivido... . 7. ¿Has bebido sangría? no la he bebido, ... 8. ¿Has pasado un mes de vacaciones en México? he pasado... . 9. ¿Has subido una pirámide azteca? he subido... . 10. ¿Has bailado el flamenco? no lo he bailado, ...
11. ¿Has corrido con los toros por las calles de Pamplona? he corrido... .
12. ¿Has oído la música de mariachis mexicanos? he oído... .

L. Ya lo he hecho.
Un(a) amigo(a) te hace preguntas sobre un viaje que vas a hacer. Contéstale que ya has hecho todo lo necesario. Usa pronombres para abreviar *(abbreviate)* tus respuestas.

■ **Modelo:** ¿Ya viste los nuevos billetes que venden?
Sí, ya los he visto.

1. ¿Ya fuiste a la agencia de viajes?
2. ¿Ya hiciste todas las preparaciones?
3. ¿Ya les dijiste a tus padres que vas a ir a Guadalajara?
4. ¿Ya viste el horario de trenes?
5. ¿Ya pusiste tu maleta en el coche?
6. ¿Ya hiciste una llamada telefónica a Guadalajara?
7. ¿Ya escribiste la lista de regalos que vas a comprar?

VAMOS A ESCUCHAR: UN VIAJE EN COCHE

Patricia del Valle va de viaje en coche con sus dos hijos—Alonso, de 10 años y Claudia, de 7 años. Viven en la Ciudad de México. Van a pasar ocho días con la hermana de Patricia en Querétaro. Están en camino en la carretera número 57.

ANTES DE ESCUCHAR

Basándote en lo que has aprendido en esta *etapa*, contesta las siguientes preguntas.

1. ¿Cuáles son algunas de las preguntas que los niños siempre hacen cuando están de viaje en un coche?
2. ¿Qué tipos de comentarios generalmente les hacen los adultos a los niños?

Antes de escuchar el diálogo, lee las preguntas en la sección *Después de escuchar*.

DESPUÉS DE ESCUCHAR

M. Comprensión.
Ahora escucha el diálogo y contesta las siguientes preguntas.

1. ¿Cuánto toma el viaje de la Ciudad de México a Querétaro?
2. ¿Qué quieren los hijos que les compre su mamá?
3. ¿Por qué no quiere parar el coche la mamá?
4. ¿Qué le prometen los niños a su mamá?
5. ¿Por fin dónde decide parar el coche la madre?

N. ¿Cómo lo dicen?
1. ¿Cómo pregunta Alonso "How long will the trip take"?
2. ¿Qué frase usa la madre para indicar cuántas horas dura el viaje?
3. ¿Cómo dice la madre "Do you understand me"?

Tú dirás ....

Ñ. Vamos a descubrir los Estados Unidos. En un grupo de tres estudiantes, (1) hablen de algunos de los estados de los Estados Unidos que han visitado y mencionen algunas de la ciudades y lugares que han visto en estos viajes. Hagan preguntas sobre las impresiones generales que tienen de estos estados y los lugares. Después de hacer esto, (2) hablen de algunos estados que todavía no han visitado, indicando cuáles quieren visitar y por qué.

O. Unas postales... Cuando viajas, a veces no tienes tiempo para escribir cartas; es más fácil mandar postales. Imagina que estás de viaje en España o México. Escríbele una postal a un(a) amigo(a) en que le dices dónde estás y qué has hecho en los últimos tres días.

Ex. Ñ: Group of 3
The day before doing this exercise, encourage students to bring in photos of their trips to other states in the USA. They can use these to discuss some of the things they have done and some of the places they have visited. As a follow-up activity, students can circulate and find at least 2 other people who traveled to 2 of the same places to which they have traveled.

TERCERA ETAPA ◎

PARA EMPEZAR: *En avión*

Preparación

- **When was the last time you traveled by plane? Where did you fly?**
- **What's the longest plane trip you've ever taken?**
- **Name one of the biggest airports in the United States.**
- **What is the fastest way to get to the nearest airport where you live?**
  Now read the information that follows.

Begin discussion of this topic by asking students these questions in Spanish.

Este aeropuerto es uno de los más importantes del mundo. Por sus puertas pasan millones de viajeros cada año.

El Aeropuerto Internacional de México Benito Juárez

En general, muchos de los aviones que van de los Estados Unidos a México llegan al Aeropuerto Internacional de México Benito Juárez. El aeropuerto queda bastante lejos del centro de la Ciudad de México pero hay muchas maneras de hacer el viaje entre el aeropuerto y la ciudad—en la línea roja del metro a la Estación Pantitlán, en autobús o en taxi.

For further introduction to this *etapa*, have students look up flight schedules and prices to Mexico City from your city and then report back to the class. Students can obtain this information on the Internet or by calling airlines directly. Suggest that students who call the airline ask for assistance in Spanish.

En la Ciudad de México, los pilotos tienen que saber despegar y aterrizar sus aviones con mucho cuidado. Esto se debe a las grandes montañas que rodean la ciudad.

to share / van

La manera preferida de viajar al centro para mucha gente es en un *colectivo*. Cada persona paga un precio fijo para **compartir** el coche o la **camioneta** con otras personas que viajan en la misma dirección. El conductor vende los boletos antes de comenzar el viaje a las zonas en que está dividida la ciudad.

El Aeropuerto Internacional Benito Juárez es famoso por ser uno de los centros de tráfico aéreo más importantes del mundo. Casi todas las aerolíneas extranjeras llegan a este aeropuerto. En un año típico, pasan millones de viajeros por la ciudad, y muchos de ellos viajan en avión. Los pasajeros siempre tienen una vista espectacular de la capital de México.

since
sea level / surrounded
training / to take off
to land

skill

Como la Ciudad de México está a una altura de 2.240 m (más de 7.000 pies) sobre el **nivel del mar,** pero dentro de un gran valle **rodeado** de altos volcanes, los pilotos reciben un **entrenamiento** especial. Tienen que aprender a **despegar** y **aterrizar** los aviones dentro de un espacio bastante limitado. Para hacer esto sin problemas, tienen que saber subir o descender en grandes círculos con mucha **destreza** por las muchas montañas que rodean la ciudad. ¡Para algunos pasajeros es una experiencia inolvidable!

Práctica

A. Al llegar a la Ciudad de México...

1. ¿Cuáles son algunos de los medios de transporte para ir del aeropuerto al centro de la ciudad?
2. ¿Cuál es la manera más popular de viajar entre el aeropuerto y el centro?
3. ¿Cómo se decide quién viaja en un "colectivo"?
4. ¿Cómo describirías este aeropuerto en cuanto a su tráfico y el número de personas que lo usan?
5. ¿A qué altura está el Aeropuerto Internacional de México?
6. ¿Por qué es tan única la localización del aeropuerto?
7. ¿Qué tipo de entrenamiento especial reciben los pilotos que usan este aeropuerto?

ENFOQUE LÉXICO

Expresiones necesarias en un aeropuerto

pasar por la aduana	*to go through customs*
mostrar el pasaporte/visado	*to show a passport/visa*
la sala de reclamación de equipaje	*baggage claim*
facturar las maletas	*to check bags*
recoger las maletas	*to pick up bags*
¿Cuál es el número del vuelo?	*What's the flight number?*
¿Cuál es el número de la puerta (de llegada/salida)?	*What is the gate number (arrival/departure)?*

Práctica

B. La llegada al aeropuerto. Explícale a un(a) amigo(a) lo que tiene que hacer cuando llega al Aeropuerto Internacional Benito Juárez. Usa las expresiones que siguen pero en el orden correcto. Usa también las palabras **primero, luego, después,** y **finalmente.**

■ **Modelo:** *Primero, bajas del avión. Después, tú..., luego..., etc.*

Ex. B: Pairs

Ex. C: Pairs

ropuerto Internacional de la Ciudad de México

C. ¿Has perdido tu maleta? Trabaja con otro(a) estudiante que hará el papel de agente del aeropuerto. Explícale que has perdido una maleta y él (ella) te hará preguntas sobre la maleta (tamaño, color, contenido, identificación, etc.) y el vuelo (número, hora de llegada, puerta, etc.).

Repaso

D. Desde que llegué, he hecho lo siguiente. Trabaja con un(a) compañero(a) de clase para explicarle lo que has hecho desde tu llegada a la Ciudad de México hace dos semanas. Usa el presente del perfecto para contarle tus actividades.

E. En el año 2025. Imagina cómo será el mundo en el año 2025. Cambia los verbos en las siguientes oraciones al tiempo futuro. Después escoge cinco de las situaciones en la lista y comenta sobre ellas, también usando el tiempo futuro. Para cada situación de la lista, incluye por lo menos dos detalles más, inventados por ti para predecir el futuro.

1. Podemos pasar las vacaciones en la luna.
2. No tenemos armas nucleares.
3. Podemos manejar un automóvil en el aire.

4. Hacemos viajes interplanetarios.
5. No hay contaminación en el aire.
6. Los niños aprenden por lo menos cuatro lenguas en la escuela.
7. Sabemos curar el cáncer.
8. No se usa el dinero.
9. Venden la comida en forma de pastilla.
10. Vienen a la tierra habitantes de otros planetas.

ENFOQUE ESTRUCTURAL

El pluscuamperfecto

The past perfect tense is used to indicate that something had already happened before something else occurred. Just as in English, this tense needs another action in the past as a reference point, whether it is stated or not, in order to make sense. Note the following examples:

Carlos no fue porque ya **había visto** al agente de viajes.	*Carlos didn't go because he **had** already **seen** the travel agent.*
Mis padres **habían llegado** a Madrid cuando me llamaron.	*My parents **had arrived** in Madrid when they called me.*
El tren ya **había salido** cuando llegamos a la estación.	*The train **had** already **left** when we arrived at the station.*

haber + participio pasado

		-ar	-er	-ir
yo	**había**			
tú	**habías**			
Ud., él, ella	**había**	hablado	comido	salido
nosotros(as)	**habíamos**			
vosotros(as)	**habíais**			
Uds., ellos, ellas	**habían**			

Like the present perfect, the past perfect has two parts: the "helping" verb haber and the past participle. The only difference between the present perfect and past perfect tenses is in the form of haber, which is formed

Práctica

F. Ya lo había hecho cuando… Cambia las oraciones según el modelo para indicar que algo ya había pasado antes de otra cosa.

■ **Modelo:** El mesero sirvió las enchiladas y después yo llegué.
El mesero ya había servido las enchiladas cuando yo llegué.

1. El avión llegó y después yo llamé por teléfono.
2. El agente de viajes preparó el itinerario y después Mario compró los boletos.

IRM Master 54: El pluscuamperfecto

Contextualize the presentation of this structure by telling students about your good intentions and bad timing. Tell them about a good friend of yours for whom you wanted to do something nice. Every time you tried to buy him/her something or take him/her somewhere, this person had already bought it/done it. Display a transparency of two calendar pages for the same month; one is yours and the other is your friend's. Fill in your calendar with activities on certain days, e.g., **comprar rosas para Teresa, invitar a Teresa al concierto de Rubén Blades,** etc. Fill in your friend's calendar page with these same activities on earlier days. Tell class: **Primero pensé invitarla al concierto de Rubén Blades, pero cuando la llamé me dijo que ya había ido al concierto el día 15...** When using the past perfect, point to the relevant calendar days so that the students can visualize that the action occurred before another past action.

GRAMMAR NOTE:
Reminder:
You may want to review the irregular past participles presented on page 433. They are used in this tense as well as with the present perfect tense.

Answers, Ex. F
1. El avión ya había llegado cuando yo llamé por teléfono. 2. El agente de viajes ya había preparado el itinerario cuando Mario compró los boletos.

3. Vimos el horario y después fuimos a comer.

4. El empleado nos dijo algo sobre el vuelo y después oímos las noticias.

5. Pediste una mesa en la sección de no fumar y después nos llamó el mesero.

6. Mi papá hizo las reservaciones y después yo llegué.

7. En el restaurante comimos demasiado y después nos sirvieron el postre.

8. Yo salí para Veracruz y después me mandaste la tarjeta.

9. Le escribí cinco postales a mi novia y después ella llamó.

10. Ustedes se durmieron en el avión y después el piloto nos habló de las condiciones atmosféricas.

G. ¿Qué dijeron? Durante la cena, el teléfono suena y tú contestas. Varias personas en tu familia quieren saber quién es y qué ha dicho. Indica quién llamó, y usa el pluscuamperfecto *(past perfect tense)* al repetir lo que la persona que llamó te dijo. Cambia los verbos al pasado y los pronombres a las formas que corresponden a la situación. Sigue el modelo.

Modelo: José llama. Te dice que ha ido al cine y que ya ha visto la película que van a dar.
Llamó José. Me dijo que había ido al cine pero que ya había visto la película.

1. Francisco llama. Te dice que ha hablado con el agente de viajes y que no ha podido comprar los boletos para el avión.

2. Alicia llama. Te dice que ha ido al centro y que ya ha vuelto a su casa.

3. Tu tío Guillermo llama. Te dice que ha puesto un regalo para ti en su coche pero que todavía no ha tenido tiempo de ir a tu casa para dártelo.

4. Tu amigo Luis llama. Te dice que el profesor ha cambiado el día del examen.

5. Una persona que no conoces llama. Te dice que ha marcado este número tres veces y que ha tenido problemas con la línea.

6. Tu amiga Silvia llama. Te dice que ha recibido una invitación para la fiesta de Carlos y ya ha comprado un vestido nuevo.

7. El empleado de la biblioteca llama. Te dice que ha buscado el libro que necesitas pero que no lo ha encontrado.

8. La secretaria de tu papá llama. Te dice que ha recibido una llamada urgente y que ha estado preocupada.

H. Antes de cumplir dieciocho años... Averigua *(Find out)* tres o cuatro cosas interesantes o inolvidables *(unforgettable)* de la vida de tres de tus compañeros(as) de clase antes de los dieciocho años de edad.

Modelo: —¿Qué cosa(s) interesante(s) habías hecho antes de cumplir dieciocho años?
—Antes de cumplir dieciocho años, yo ya había...
o
—Cuando cumplí dieciocho años yo ya había...

Después escribe una lista de esta información para leérsela a la clase.

ENFOQUE LÉXICO

Antes de, después de + infinitivo

Antes del viaje, hablaré con mis padres por teléfono.	***Before*** *the trip, I'll speak to my parents on the phone.*
Antes de comprar los billetes, quiero ver el horario de trenes.	***Before*** *buying the tickets, I want to see the train schedule.*
Después de las vacaciones, no estaré cansado.	***After*** *vacation, I will not be tired.*
Después de visitar los museos, mis amigos sabrán mucho sobre España.	***After*** *visiting the museums, my friends will know a lot about Spain.*

Both the prepositional phrase **antes de** *(before)* and **después de** *(after)* may be used with a noun **(antes del viaje)** or an infinitive **(antes de comprar)**, **(después de las vacaciones)**, **(después de visitar)**.

Remember that when the masculine singular article **el** is used with **de**, it becomes **del**.

Práctica

I. ¿Cuándo? Sustituye las palabras en cursiva por las palabras entre paréntesis y haz los cambios necesarios.

1. Antes de *la salida del tren*, pensamos desayunar. (la llegada / el viaje / la parada / la llamada telefónica)
2. Después de *la visita al museo*, pasaré por tu casa. (la película / el desayuno / las vacaciones / el viaje)
3. Antes de *visitar a mi abuela*, llamaremos por teléfono. (ir al restaurante / organizar el viaje / ir a la estación / salir para Segovia)
4. Después de *hacer las reservaciones*, regresaremos al hotel. (consultar el horario / caminar por el parque / llamar por teléfono)

J. La partida. Los siguientes dibujos cuentan el viaje de dos jóvenes que se llaman Susan Haley y Charles Latowsky. Mira los dibujos y escribe seis frases que describan su viaje. Utiliza la preposición *antes de* en tres frases y *después de* en las otras tres frases.

Answers, Ex. I
1. antes de la llegada, antes del viaje, antes de la parada, antes de la llamada telefónica 2. después de la película, después del desayuno, después de las vacaciones, después del viaje 3. antes de ir al restaurante, antes de organizar el viaje, antes de ir a la estación, antes de salir para Segovia 4. después de consultar el horario, después de caminar por el parque, después de llamar por teléfono

Assign these exercises as homework. In class allow students a few minutes to compare their answers and ask any questions.

VAMOS A ESCUCHAR: ¿DÓNDE ESTÁ LA MALETA?

Durante un vuelo a Guadalajara, Judy Miller habla con el señor y la señora Castillo.

ANTES DE ESCUCHAR

Basándote en lo que has aprendido en esta *etapa*, contesta las siguientes preguntas.

1. ¿Cuando viajas en avión, ¿facturas tu maleta o la llevas en el avión contigo?
2. ¿Qué haces si no puedes encontrar tu maleta en la sala de reclamación de equipaje?

Ahora lee las preguntas en la sección *Después de escuchar*.

DESPUÉS DE ESCUCHAR

K. Comprensión. Escucha el diálogo y contesta las siguientes preguntas.

1. ¿Cuántas maletas tiene Judy?
2. ¿De qué color es la maleta que Judy no ha encontrado?
3. ¿Es grande o pequeña la maleta que busca Judy?
4. ¿Qué identificación lleva la maleta perdida?
5. ¿Dónde cree Judy que dejó la maleta?
6. ¿Qué lección dice Judy que aprendió?

L. ¿Cómo lo dicen?

1. ¿Cómo se dice en español "baggage room"?
2. ¿Cómo dice Judy que "the couple is very kind"?

Tú dirás ....

M. En una agencia de viajes. Trabaja con otro estudiante para hacer planes para un viaje en tren, autobús o avión. Uno de ustedes hace el papel del agente de viajes y el otro el del viajero. Hablen de (1) el destino, (2) el mejor medio de transporte para el viaje, (3) el horario, (4) el precio de los billetes y (5) cualquier otra información que necesiten (i.e., hoteles, puntos de interés turístico, etc.) Después de organizar el viaje, el viajero informará a la clase de sus planes.

N. Antes de cumplir dieciséis años. Averigua (*Find out*) tres o cuatro cosas interesantes o inolvidables de la vida de tres estudiantes en tu clase antes de los dieciséis años de edad. (Usen tales frases como: ¿Qué cosa(s) interesante(s) habías hecho antes de cumplir dieciséis años? Antes de cumplir dieciséis años, él/ella/yo ya había... Cuando cumplí/cumplió dieciséis años él/ella/yo ya había...)

Después escribe una lista de la información para leérsela a la clase.

LECTURA: *Un recorrido por la Ciudad de México en metro*

ANTES DE LEER

1. ¿Has viajado en metro alguna vez?
2. ¿Te gusta viajar en metro? ¿Por qué sí o por qué no?
3. Lee el título y mira la foto que acompaña el artículo. ¿Qué ideas generales dan sobre su contenido?

GUÍA PARA LA LECTURA

A. Haz lo siguiente para entender mejor la lectura.

1. Lee la breve introducción para confirmar tu impresión general. ¿Qué más sabes ahora?
2. Busca todos los números en los dos primeros párrafos. ¿Qué importancia tienen?
3. Lee la primera oración de cada párrafo y resume la información que da.
4. Haz una lista de los países mencionados en el artículo.
5. Haz una lista de los nombres de personas famosas en la historia mexicana.

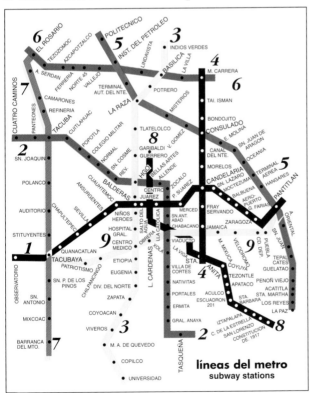

líneas del metro
subway stations

B. Contesta las siguientes preguntas sobre el artículo.

1. ¿Cuándo abrieron el metro mexicano por primera vez?
2. ¿Cuáles son las horas más populares para viajar en el metro?
3. En comparación con el uso de los metros de otros países, ¿qué lugar ocupa México en el mundo?
4. ¿Qué encontraron cuando los obreros hicieron las excavaciones?

Una estación del metro mexicano adornada con enormes esculturas de la época de las grandes civilizaciones indígenas.

Un recorrido por la Ciudad de Mexico en metro

El Sistema de Transporte Colectivo de la Ciudad de México es uno de los más extensos del mundo. Es una manera rápida y económica de viajar de un lado a otro en el Distrito Federal, la capital de la nación. La Ciudad de México es uno de los centros urbanos más grandes del mundo; tiene más de 20 millones de habitantes que disfrutan de un metro limpio y eficiente como éste.

El metro mexicano se inauguró en septiembre de 1969. Para poder servir bien al público, tiene nueve líneas de diferentes

tracks
average

colores, 105 estaciones, y 136 kms de **vías.** En ciertas partes el metro corre a una velocidad máxima de 90 kms por hora, aunque el **promedio** en general es 35 kms por hora. Durante los primeros años, el precio de un boleto era muy barato: un peso, nada más. En años recientes ha subido el precio de los boletos. Sin embargo, el metro todavía es una manera de viajar bastante económica y muy popular.

Todos los días, más de cinco millones de personas viajan en el metro. Al comparar los números de pasajeros que usan el metro mexicano con los de otros países, México ocupa el tercer lugar en el mundo, después de Moscú en Rusia y Tokio en el Japón. Durante las horas más populares—antes de las 10:00 de la mañana y después de las 4:00 de la tarde—el metro está completamente lleno. Obviamente, es mejor viajar durante el día a otras horas.

workers

Es interesante señalar que durante las excavaciones que hicieron para construir el sistema subterráneo, los **obreros,** arquitectos y arqueólogos encontraron muchas ruinas de las antiguas civilizaciones de la época anterior a la llegada de Colón. La Ciudad de México está construida sobre Tenochtitlán, la antigua capital de los aztecas. Por esta razón, al excavar, se descubrieron pequeños templos, como el que está en el centro de la Estación de Pino Suárez, y muchos artefactos de la época: artículos artísticos de piedras semipreciosas, pequeñas

clay / jewels

figuras de **barro** y **joyas** de oro y de plata. El gobierno mexicano mandó a hacer réplicas de muchos de estos objetos y ahora la gente que viaja en el metro puede verlos en las estaciones.

Cada una de las hermosas estaciones del metro tiene decoraciones artísticas y su propio símbolo. Algunas estaciones llevan el nombre de alguna

illustrious, famous

persona **ilustre** de la historia mexicana: el

Las estaciones del metro son grand y bellas.

emperador azteca Moctezuma; el héroe de la Independencia, José María Morelos; el General Ignacio Zaragoza; el Presidente Benito Juárez; y el revolucionario Emiliano Zapata, entre otros. También hay "módulos de información" en las estaciones donde el público puede conseguir mapas y asistencia general. Sin duda, hacer un **recorrido** por la Ciudad de México en el metro es una experiencia interesante. ¡Como el metro de México no hay dos!

trip, a run

VÍDEO CULTURAL: Pasajeros a bordo

Play Textbook audio.

Before having students carry out this activity, allow them 3–4 minutes to plan out their individual parts of the task. Tell them that they will not use any notes when doing the activity. Remind students to stay entirely in Spanish and to request confirmation if they do not understand their partners.

Answers, Ex. B
1. b 2. e 3. d 4. a 5. c

Answers, Ex. D
1. b 2. b 3. a
4. a 5. b 6. b
7. a 8. b 9. Red Nacional de Ferrocarriles Españoles

A. Anticipación. ¿Cuál es tu medio de transporte favorito? ¿Por qué? ¿Y el que menos le gusta? Pregunta a tus compañeros de clase qué tipo de transporte prefieren.

B. Preparación. Para cada elemento de la columna A encuentra su opuesto en la columna B.

1. lo más lento
2. lo moderno
3. acá
4. búsqueda
5. primero

a. encuentro
b. lo más rápido
c. último
d. allá
e. lo antiguo

C. Participación. Haz apuntes mientras miras el vídeo.

D. Comprensión. Escribe la respuesta correcta a estas preguntas sobre el metro.

1. El metro es un medio de transporte
   a. inconfortable.
   b. conveniente.
2. El metro es muy
   a. lento.
   b. rápido.
3. En la Ciudad de México unos _____ de personas diarias usan el metro a diario.
   a. cinco o seis millones
   b. quince o dieciséis millones
4. Viajar en metro en la Ciudad de México es como viajar por la rica _____ de esta ciudad.
   a. historia
   b. teoría
5. Cada estación del metro tiene su propio
   a. pasado.
   b. símbolo.
6. La estación del Zócalo se identifica con el símbolo nacional del águila y la
   a. llama.
   b. serpiente.
7. También en la estación del Zócalo se encuentra un templo
   a. azteca.
   b. inca.
8. En la estación de Bellas Artes, abundan réplicas de
   a. águilas gloriosas.
   b. arte precolombino.
9. ¿Qué significa RENFE, según el vídeo?

E. Personalización.

1. What modes of transportation were used by the Native Americans? Which do they continue to use today?
2. What do you think about the idea of creating high speed trains in the United States? Discuss the advantages and disadvantages of the train and the automobile.

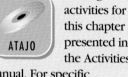

Writing activities for this chapter are presented in the Activities Manual. For specific references to tasks supported by Atajo, please consult the Activities Manual.

Intercambio: Un viaje a Sevilla

Estudiante A

Tienes que ir a Sevilla mañana y llamas a la agencia de viajes para hacer la reserva de billete.

1. Call the agency and say you need a plane ticket to Sevilla. You don't like to travel by train, and besides, since you are in a hurry, you need to get there as soon as possible.

Tell the agent the following:

2. You need to leave tomorrow morning.
3. You don't know when you are coming back. It will probably be the same day, but it's not certain.

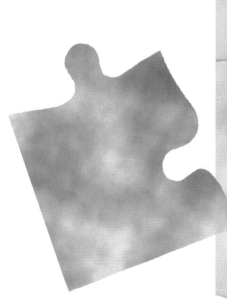

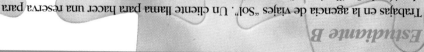

On pages 447 and 448 you have all the information you need about the AVE to convince the customer.

4. Tell the person what kind of ticket he or she needs to buy given the circumstances.
3. If the customer hesitates to take the train, explain all the good things about this new train service.
2. Suggest to the customer that he or she can take the train. There is a new high-speed train called AVE (Alta Velocidad) that gets to Sevilla in two and a half hours.
1. Explain that the plane Madrid-Sevilla is sold out.

el avión de Sevilla de mañana por la mañana.

Trabajas en la agencia de viajes "Sol". Un cliente llama para hacer una reserva para

Estudiante B

HORARIOS

MADRID Puerta de Atocha · CIUDAD REAL · PUERTOLLANO · CORDOBA · SEVILLA Santa Justa

TIPO DE TREN (*)	VALLE	LLANO	LLANO	LLANO	PUNTA	LLANO	LLANO	LLANO	LLANO	LLANO	LLANO	LLANO
NÚMERO DE TREN	9614	9616	9618	9622	9628	9630	9632	9634	9636	9638	9640	9642
OBSERVACIONES	(1)	(2)				(3)	(4)		(5)		(4)	(6)
MADRID Puerta de Atocha	7:00	8:00	9:00	11:00	14:00	15:00	16:00	17:00	18:00	19:00	20:00	21:00
CIUDAD REAL	7:49	-	-	-	-	-	-	-	-	-	-	21:49
PUERTOLLANO	8:05	-	-	-	-	-	-	-	-	-	-	22:05
CORDOBA	8:51	9:40	10:47	12:47	15:40	16:47	17:47	18:47	19:47	20:47	21:47	22:51
SEVILLA Santa Justa	9:40	10:25	11:35	13:35	16:25	17:35	18:35	19:35	20:35	21:35	22:35	23:40

SEVILLA Santa Justa · CORDOBA · PUERTOLLANO · CIUDAD REAL · MADRID Puerta de Atocha

TIPO DE TREN (*)	VALLE	LLANO	LLANO	LLANO	PUNTA	LLANO	LLANO	LLANO	LLANO	LLANO	LLANO	LLANO	LLANO
NÚMERO DE TREN	9615	9617	9619	9623	9629	9631	9633	9635	9637	9639	9641	9643	9645
OBSERVACIONES	(1)	(2)				(3)	(4)		(5)		(4)	(6)	(7)
SEVILLA Santa Justa	7:00	8:00	9:00	11:00	14:00	15:00	16:00	17:00	18:00	19:00	20:00	21:00	21:45
CORDOBA	7:44	8:44	9:44	11:44	14:44	15:44	16:44	17:44	18:44	19:44	20:44	21:44	22:29
PUERTOLLANO	8:26	-	10:26	-	-	-	-	-	-	-	-	22:26	-
CIUDAD REAL	8:42	-	10:42	-	-	-	-	-	-	-	-	22:42	-
MADRID Puerta de Atocha	9:40	10:25	11:40	13:35	16:25	17:35	18:35	19:35	20:35	21:35	22:35	23:40	00:10

(*) El tipo de tren hace referencia al precio aplicado al mismo a su denominación: valle, llano o punta. En cualquier caso, todos los servicios se prestan con trenes AVE.
OBSERVACIONES: **(1)** No circula los días 25/12 y 1/1. **(2)** No circula los domingos ni los días 12/10, 1/11, 9/11, 6/12 y 8/12. No circula el 24/12 al 8/1. **(3)** Circula los viernes y el día 23/12. No circula del 24/12 al 8/1.
(4) No circula los sábados ni los días 10/10, 11/10, 31/10, 7/11, 8/11 y 5/12. No circula del 24/12 al 8/1.
(5) Circula los viernes y domingos y los días 12/10, 1/11, 9/11, 8/12 y 23/12. No circula los días 10/10, 31/1, 0, 7/11 y 5/12. No circula el 24/12 al 8/1.
(6) No circula los días 24/12 y 31/12. **(7)** Circula los domingos, excepto los días 10/10, 31/10, 7/11 y 5/12.

PRECIOS(*)

Válidos a partir del 5·9·93

	TURISTA			PREFERENTE			CLUB		
	VALLE	LLANO	PUNTA	VALLE	LLANO	PUNTA	VALLE	LLANO	PUNTA
MADRID-SEVILLA	6.600	7.900	8.900	9.100	10.800	12.500	12.100	14.300	16.500
MADRID-CORDOBA	4.800	5.800	6.500	6.700	7.900	9.100	8.800	10.400	12.000
MADRID-PUERTOLLANO	3.000	3.500	4.000	4.100	4.800	5.600	5.400	6.400	7.400
MADRID-CIUDAD REAL	2.400	2.900	3.300	3.300	3.900	4.600	4.400	5.300	6.200
CIUDAD REAL-SEVILLA	4.200	5.000	5.600	5.800	6.900	7.900	7.700	9.000	10.300
CIUDAD REAL-CORDOBA	2.400	2.900	3.200	3.400	4.000	4.500	4.400	5.100	5.900
CIUDAD REAL-PUERTOLLANO	600	600	700	800	900	1.000	1.000	1.100	1.200
PUERTOLLANO-SEVILLA	3.600	4.400	4.900	5.000	6.000	6.900	6.700	7.900	9.100
PUERTOLLANO-CORDOBA	1.800	2.300	2.500	2.600	3.100	3.500	3.400	4.000	4.700
CORDOBA-SEVILLA	1.800	2.100	2.400	2.400	2.900	3.400	3.300	3.900	4.500

(*) Incluyen el IVA, el Seguro Obligatorio de Viajeros y la reserva de plaza.

TARIFAS

GENERAL	La especificada en el Cuadro de Precios.	*Sí admite cambio y anulación.*
IDA Y VUELTA	20% DESCUENTO sobre Tarifa General. Regreso dentro de los 60 días siguientes a la fecha del viaje de IDA, formalizando la VUELTA en taquilla. Necesariamente igual trayecto.	*Sí admite cambio y anulación.*
DIA (Ida y Vuelta)	30% DESCUENTO sobre Tarifa General. Necesario cerrar IDA y VUELTA y siempre para el mismo día y trayecto. Si no está seguro de la hora de su vuelta, acójase a IDA y VUELTA 20% descuento.	*No admite cambio ni anulación.*
BILLETE ABIERTO	6 meses de validez desde la emisión del billete. Reserva por teléfono hasta 1 hora antes de la salida del tren (91) 534 05 05 y (95) 454 03 03 Es imprescindible formalizar su viaje en taquilla antes de realizar el viaje, hasta 10 minutos antes de la salida del tren.	*Sí admite cambio sin coste alguno. Sí admite anulación.*
INFANTIL	40% DESCUENTO sobre Tarifa General. Niños de 4 a 11 años.	*Sí admite cambio y anulación*
DORADA	25% DESCUENTO sobre Tarifa General. Titular de Tarjeta Dorada.	*Sí admite cambio y anulación.*
GRUPOS	15% DESCUENTO sobre Tarifa General. Grupos de 10 a 25 personas. Los billetes deben adquirirse al menos, el día anterior a la fecha del viaje.	*No admite cambio y sí anulación total.*
GRANDES GRUPOS Y TRENES CHARTER	Grupos de más de 25 personas. Teléfonos consultas: (91) 527 80 37 - 527 31 60 extensiones 3485 y 3610 (95) 441 18 55	
INTERNACIONAL	Titulares de: EURAILPASS, EURODOMINO Y TARJETA TURISTICA	*Sí admite cambio y anulación.*

Reducción:	1ª Clase	2ª Clase
CLUB	60%	-
PREFERENTE	65%	-
TURISTA	85%	85%

Los billetes para trenes AVE Larga Distancia pueden adquirirse, hasta con 60 días de antelación a la fecha de viaje, en puntos de venta RENFE y en Agencias de viaje.

Para charlar

Expresiones para viajar en tren   *Expressions for train travel*

Quisiera plaza de segunda.   *second class seat*
    plaza de primera   *first class seat*
Quisiera reservar una plaza para Barcelona.
  I'd like to reserve a seat for Barcelona.
Quisiera una plaza en la sección de no fumar.
  I'd like a seat in the no smoking section.
Quisera un billete de ida y vuelta.
  I'd like a round-trip ticket.
¿A qué hora sale/llega el tren/autobús?
  What time does the train/bus leave/arrive?
¿De que andén sale?   *From which platform does it leave?*
¿Cuál es el número del vagón?   *What is the car number?*
¿El tren llegará retrasado/adelantado/a tiempo?
  Will the train arrive late/early/on time?

Expresiones necesarias en un aeropuerto   *Expressions needed in an airport*

el avión   *airplane*
¿Cuál es el número del vuelo?   *What's the flight number?*
¿Cuál es el número del vuelo   *What's the gate number*
  (de llegada/salida)?   *(for arrival/departure)?*
facturar las maletas   *to check bags*
mostrar el pasaporte/visado   *to show a passport/visa*
pasar por la aduana   *to go through customs*
reclamar el equipaje (perdido)   *to claim (lost) luggage*
recoger las maletas   *to pick up bags*
la sala de reclamación de equipaje   *baggage claim*

Para hablar del tiempo que se necesita para viajar en coche   *Talking about the time needed to travel by car*

¿Cuánto toma el viaje de... a... ?   *How long does the trip from . . . to . . . take?*
¿Cuánto tiempo se necesita para ir a...?   *How much time is needed to go to . . . ?*
¿En cuánto tiempo se hace el viaje de... a... (en coche)?   *How much time does the trip from . . . to . . . (by car) take?*
¿Son... horas de viaje de... a... (en coche)?   *Is it . . . hours from . . . to . . . (by car)?*
Se hace el viaje de... a... en... horas (en coche).   *The trip from . . . to . . . (by car) is made in . . . hours.*
¿Cuántas (as) millas/kilómetros son?   *How many miles/kilometers is it?*

Temas y contextos   *Themes and Contexts*

El coche   *The Car*
la carretera   *highway*
la llanta   *tire*
el mapa de carreteras   *highway map*
el neumático   *tire*
a visa   *visa*

Señales de tráfico   *Traffic Signs*
aduana   *customs*
en obras/trabajo   *under construction*
no adelantar   *no passing*
no estacionar   *no parking*
no hay paso   *do not enter*
no virar   *no u-turns*

Vocabulario general   GeneraI vocabulary

Verbos
aterrizar   *to land*
compartir   *to share*
despegar   *to take off*
fijarse en   *to notice*
haber   *to have (auxiliary verb)*
llegar   *to arrive*
pedir   *to ask for, request*

Sustantivos
el (la) acompañante   *traveling companion*
la ayuda   *help*
el boleto/billete   *ticket*
el calendario   *calendar*
la camioneta   *van, light truck*
el departamento de literas   *berth compartment*
el departamento de plazas
una plaza/un asiento   *a space, a seat*
sentadas   *seating compartment*
la destreza   *skill*
el entrenamiento   *training*
el horario   *schedule*
la red   *network*

Preposiciones
a   *to, at*
antes de   *before*
de   *of, from*
después de   *after*
en   *in*
entre   *between*
hacia   *toward*
hasta   *until*
lejos de   *far from*
para   *for, in order to*
por   *for, during*

13 El arte y la música

Santiago
Matamoros

Museo del Prado

Mariachi

CHAPTER OBJECTIVES:

In the final two chapters of *¡Tú dirás!*
you will learn about music, art, and literature
while continuing to develop your reading skills.

After completing this chapter, you should be
able to carry out the following tasks:

- ◉ **Understand texts and conversations about fine art, popular art, and music in the Spanish-speaking world**

- ◉ **Express wishes, desires, emotions and hopes**

- ◉ **Talk about the probable and the improbable**

- ◉ **Refer to possibilities and impossibilities**

- ◉ **Talk about fine art, popular art, and music**

The tools you will use to carry out
these tasks are:

- ◉ **Vocabulary for:**

    - fine art, popular art, and music

    - emotions, desires, and hopes

- ◉ **Grammatical structures:**

    - Review of the present subjunctive

    - Reflexive verbs in the subjunctive

    - More on subjunctive with emotion

    - Subjunctive with expressions of uncertainty

    - Subjunctive with indefinite or imaginary antecedents

Una mola

Músico
peruano

⊚ PARA EMPEZAR:
Siete artistas del siglo XX

Preparación: Upon beginning this *etapa,* answer the following questions.

- **Do you like art?**
- **Who are your favortite artists?**
- **What are the characteristics of their works? Are they realist? abstract?**

LECTURA: El muralismo mexicano

ANTES DE LEER

A veces los artistas crean murales enormes para que toda la gente (no solamente la elite que visita los museos de arte) los pueda ver y apreciar. Esta lectura trata el tema del muralismo mexicano, un movimiento artístico del siglo XX.

A. Contesta las siguientes preguntas.

1. ¿Hay algún mural en la universidad donde estudias?
2. ¿Cuál es el tema del mural?
3. ¿Qué sabes de arte público?
4. ¿Has visto algún mural en tu ciudad o pueblo?

B. Estudio de palabras.
Trata de adivinar el significado de las siguientes palabras que aparecen en la lectura sobre el muralismo mexicano. Encuentra las palabras en inglés en la lista de la derecha que corresponden a las palabras en español en la lista de la izquierda.

1. pilares	a. season, period of time
2. obtuvo	b. because of
3. prerrenacentista	c. rebirth
4. cuya	d. pre-Renaissance
5. en boga	e. whose
6. quedó	f. pillars
7. temporada	g. obtained
8. debido a	h. in vogue, in style
9. extranjera	i. remained
10. renacimiento	j. foreign

GUÍA PARA LA LECTURA

C. Lee rápidamente el texto que aparece en las páginas 452 y 453 y busca todas las fechas. Escríbelas en una hoja de papel, indicando lo que pasó en cada fecha.

D. Un bosquejo *(outline).* Completa el siguiente bosquejo que se basa en la lectura sobre el muralismo mexicano.

El muralismo mexicano

1. Diego Rivera
   a. _____ 1886
   b. Con otros artistas fundó un movimiento pictórico en 1921.
   c. _____ 1957

2. _____
   a. Nació en Chihuahua el 29 de diciembre de 1896.
   b. _____ 1971
   c. _____ 1974

3. _____
   a. _____ 1883
   b. _____ 1927
   c. Murió el 7 de septiembre de 1949.

E. ¿Qué sabes sobre el muralismo? Contesta las siguientes preguntas en español.

1. ¿Quiénes son los tres muralistas mexicanos más importantes?
2. ¿Quién fue el mayor? ¿Quién fue el menor?
3. ¿En qué orden murieron?
4. ¿Quién fue Giotto?
5. ¿Quién pintó algunos murales en Detroit?
6. ¿Quién pintó algunos murales en Dartmouth College?
7. ¿Qué influencia tuvo el Dr. Atl en los muralistas?
8. ¿Cuál de los muralistas empezó más controversias y fue encarcelado por sus ideas?

José Clemente Orozco, Zapatistas

Answers, Ex. D
1. a. Rivera nació en Guanajuato, estado de Guanajuato, el 8 de diciembre de 1886. c. Rivera murió en la Ciudad de México el 25 de noviembre de 1957. 2. David Alfaro Siqueiros b. Terminó su trabajo *La marcha de la humanidad* en 1971. c. Siqueiros murió en Cuernavaca el 6 de enero de 1974. 3. José Clemente Orozco a. Nació en Ciudad Guzmán el 23 de noviembre de 1883. b. Recibió el encargo de pintar un mural para Pomona College en California en 1927.

Answers, Ex. E
1. Los tres muralistas mexicanos más importantes son Diego Rivera, David Alfaro Siqueiros y José Clemente Orozco. 2. El mayor fue David Alfaro Siqueiros. El menor fue Diego Rivera. 3. José Clemente Orozco murió primero, Diego Rivera segundo y Siqueiros tercero. 4. Giotto fue un pintor italiano prerrenacentista que influyó a Rivera. 5. Rivera pintó algunos murales en Detroit. 6. Orozco pintó algunos murales en Dartmouth College. 7. El Dr. Atl animaba a los pintores a que dejaran las culturas extranjeras y cultivaran los temas de la tierra mexicana. 8. Siqueiros fue encarcelado por sus ideas y empezó más controversias.

Transparency P-1: José Clemente Orozco, *Zapatistas*

Note that Padre Hidalgo, shown in Orozco's mural is considered the father of Mexican independence. On September 16, 1810, he issued the famous **"grito de Dolores"** declaring Mexico independent from Spain. He was living in Dolores when independence was declared. You can also compare Mexico's declaration of independence from Spain with that of the 13 colonies from England.

Ask students what they think of art museums and who goes to them. Ask if they ever go. There is a feeling that art museums are for the elite of society and not really for the common man or woman. The Mexican muralists reacted to this by creating large murals in public places where everyone, rich and poor alike, could view and appreciate art.

F. El muralismo mexicano. Usa la información de la lectura para escribir un informe breve sobre uno de los muralistas mexicanos. Escoge una de las pinturas en las páginas 451–453 y descríbela brevemente para ilustrar tu informe. Prepárate para presentar tu informe en clase.

▶ El muralismo mexicano

constituted

⌐ **Transparency P-3:**
Diego Rivera, *Vendedor de flores,* 1935

move
scholarship

distance himself
in vogue

founded

exhibited / commission

El arte de Diego Rivera **constituyó** uno de los pilares sobre los que se basa el muralismo mexicano. Rivera nació en la ciudad de Guanajuato, el 8 de diciembre de 1886. Después del **traslado** a la capital mexicana cuando tenía diez años, obtuvo una **beca** del gobierno para asistir a la Academia de Bellas Artes. Más tarde pasó unos años en Europa donde investigó la técnica mural del pintor italiano prerrenacentista Giotto, cuya influencia le hizo **apartarse** del cubismo, un movimiento artístico que **estaba en boga** durante aquella época. En 1921 regresó a México y **fundó,** junto con David Alfaro Siqueiros y José Clemente

Diego Rivera, Vendedor de Flores, 1935

Orozco, un movimiento pictórico conocido como la escuela mexicana de pintura. Durante estos años pintó varios murales en México y con la expansión de su fama **expuso** algunas obras en Nueva York. Después de esta exhibición recibió el **encargo** de pintar grandes murales en el Instituto de Arte en Detroit y otro en Rockefeller Center. El tema principal de Rivera era la lucha de las clases populares indígenas. Su última obra, un mural épico sobre la historia de México, quedó incompleta cuando murió en la Ciudad de México el 25 de noviembre de 1957.

⌐ **Transparency P-2:**
David Alfaro Siqueiros,
Etnografía, 1931

to expand, widen

suffering

weapon

cry, shout

Otro pilar de este movimiento artístico fue David Alfaro Siqueiros, que nació en Chihuahua el 29 de diciembre de 1896. Después de iniciar sus estudios artísticos en la Ciudad de México, pasó una temporada en Europa con el objeto de **ampliar** su formación. Los temas de las obras de Siqueiros son el **sufrimiento** de la clase obrera, el conflicto entre el socialismo y el capitalismo y la decadencia de la clase media. El arte para Siqueiros era un **arma** que se podía utilizar para el progreso del pueblo y un **grito** que podía inspirar la rebelión entre la gente que sufría la injusti-

David Alfaro Siqueiros, Etnografia, *1931*

cia y la miseria. Durante su vida sufrió varios **encarcelamientos** y **destierros** debido a sus actividades políticas, pero esto no impidió que sus murales decoraran importantes edificios públicos en la capital mexicana. Uno de sus últimos trabajos, *Del porfirismo a la revolución,* ocupa una **superficie** de 4.500 metros cuadrados en el Museo de Historia Nacional. Otro, que mide 4.000 metros cuadrados y está en el Hotel de México, se llama *La marcha de la humanidad.* Fue terminado en 1971 después de cuatro años de exhaustivo trabajo. Siqueiros murió en Cuernavaca el 6 de enero de 1974.

El tercer pilar del muralismo mexicano fue José Clemente Orozco. Éste nació en Ciudad Guzmán, en el estado de Jalisco, el 23 de noviembre de 1883 y, a los siete años se trasladó, con su familia, a la capital. Allí, como estudiante en la Academia de San Carlos, pronto mostró su **genio** para el arte pictórico. Conoció al Dr. Atl, que **animaba** a sus compañeros **a que dejaran** las culturas extranjeras y cultivaran los temas de la tierra mexicana. Orozco pintó grupos de campesinos e imágenes de destrucción, sacrificio y renacimiento después de la Revolución de 1910. Su fama se extendió fuera de México y en 1927 recibió el encargo de pintar un mural para Pomona College en California. En 1932 fue profesor de pintura mural en Dartmouth College, donde hoy día podemos ver varios murales que pintó allí. Orozco murió el 7 de septiembre de 1949 en la Ciudad de México.

imprisonments / exiles

surface

genius
inspired / that they leave

Transparency:
José Clemente Orozco,

Mural por José Clemente Orozco, Guadalajara, México

LECTURA: *Frida Kahlo*

ANTES DE LEER

Ex. G:  Pairs

Pair students to do this exercise. Allow them 5–10 minutes to answer the questions and then call on different students to share their answers with the class.

G. Contesta las siguientes preguntas.

1. Mira el título de la lectura y la reproducción que aparece en la página 456. ¿Conoces a esta artista? ¿Qué sabes de ella?
2. ¿Qué animales aparecen en la pintura?
3. ¿Qué tipos de acontecimientos *(events)* extraordinarios asocias con la vida de un(a) artista?
4. ¿Crees que en general los artistas sufren de un modo especial? Explica tu respuesta.

H. Cognado, contexto o diccionario. Localiza las siguientes palabras en el texto en la página 455. Al tratar de adivinar su significado indica si la palabra es un cognado, si la adivinaste por medio del contexto o si tuviste que buscarala en el diccionario. Si tuviste que buscarla en un diccionario, indica la forma de la palabra que aparece en el diccionario y el significado que encontraste allí.

	cognado	contexto	diccionario	forma en el diccionario	significado
combina					
imaginería					
enamorarse					
casarse					
autorretratos					
disfrutara					
juguetona					
cariño					
afueras					
recuerdos					

Answers, Ex. J
4; 2; 1; 3; 5

Variation: Split the class into two sides. Ask that students on one side find the answers to the first 5 questions and that students on the other side answer the last 5 questions. Pair each student with one from the other side of the room and have students ask their partners to explain the answers to the questions they did not answer the night before. They should do this part orally without their notes. After students have shared their answers, ask them to compose a short paragraph on Frida Kahlo using the information obtained in this exercise.

GUÍA PARA LA LECTURA

I. Lee el texto rápidamente y busca todas las fechas. Escríbelas en una hoja de papel, indicando lo que pasó en cada fecha.

J. El orden cronológico... Organiza las siguientes oraciones sobre la vida de Frida Kahlo en orden cronológico. Busca las fechas en el texto para justificar tus respuestas.

1. Se casó con Diego Rivera.

2. Fue atropellada por un tranvía.

3. Pintó *Autorretrato con changuito.*

4. Nació.

5. Murió en la Ciudad de México.

K. Frida Kahlo. Contesta las siguientes preguntas en español.

1. ¿Cuándo nació Frida Kahlo?

2. ¿Qué elementos combina en su arte?

3. ¿Cuáles fueron sus dos accidentes?

4. ¿Qué sufrió en uno de sus accidentes?

5. ¿Qué diferencia de edad había entre Frida y Diego?

6. ¿Qué pintó Kahlo entre 1937 y 1945?

7. ¿Qué es un *ixcuincle?*

8. ¿Qué significado tiene el perrito en el *Autorretrato con changuito* de Kahlo?

9. ¿Cuántos años tenía cuando murió?

10. ¿Dónde está el Museo Frida Kahlo?

L. Una pintura de Frida Kahlo. Con un(a) compañero(a) describe la pintura de Frida Kahlo. Al terminar, compartan su descripción con la clase.

Answers, Ex. K
1. 1910 2. el pasado precolombino, la imaginería católica, las artes populares de México y la vanguardia europea 3. un tranvía y su esposo Diego Rivera 4. una fractura de columna, de la pelvis y de la pierna derecha 5. 24 años 6. varios autorretratos 7. un tipo de perro precolombino 8. Tal vez anuncia su muerte. 9. 44 años 10. Coyoacán

Transparency P-4:
Frida Kahlo, *Autorretrato con changuito y loro,* 1942

CULTURE:
The chihuahua is descended from the *ixcuincle,* a small hairless dog still bred in Mexico as an exotic pet.

Frida Kahlo, *Autorretrato con changuito y loro,* 1942

▶*Frida Kahlo*

Frida Kahlo nació el mismo año en que empezó la Revolución Mexicana: 1910. Más que ningún otro artista mexicano, en su obra ella combina el pasado precolombino, la imaginería católica del período colonial, las artes populares de México y la vanguardia europea. Con colores sumamente brillantes **deja constancia** de su dolor físico, su **muerte cercana** y su tempestuoso matrimonio con Diego Rivera.

she left evidence

approaching death

En 1951 Frida le dijo a una periodista, "He sufrido dos accidentes graves en mi vida. En uno, **un tranvía me atropelló** cuando yo tenía dieciséis años: fractura de columna, veinte años de inmovilidad... El otro accidente es Diego..." El primer accidente ocurrió el 17 de septiembre de 1925, cuando Frida era estudiante y se preparaba para **ingresar** en la escuela de medicina de la universidad. El autobús en que ella viajaba **chocó con** un tranvía. Se fracturó la columna en dos lugares, la pelvis en tres y además la pierna derecha.

El segundo accidente fue su matrimonio con el famoso muralista mexicano Diego Rivera. A los trece años, Frida vio a Rivera, gordo y feo, por primera vez. Se enamoró de él y les confesó a sus amigas que se iba a casar con él. Frida y Diego se casaron el 23 de agosto de 1929. Ella tenía diecinueve años y él, establecido como el pintor más importante de México, tenía cuarenta y tres.

Muchas de las pinturas de Frida son autorretratos. Entre 1937 y 1945 se autorretrató varias veces con **monos.** Aquí, podemos ver *Autorretrato con changuito y loro,* pintado en 1945. En otra obra, *Autorretrato con changuito,* además de un changuito incluye un tipo de perro precolombino, casi extinto en la actualidad, llamado *ixcuincle.* En tiempos precolombinos el *ixcuincle* **se sepultaba** con su **amo** para que el muerto disfrutara de su compañía juguetona y su cariño en la otra vida. En este autorretrato tal vez Kahlo esté usando el perrito para anunciar su muerte. En su *Autorretrato como tehuana,* 1943, lleva el vestido tradicional de una india tehuana y en la frente tiene un retrato de Diego.

Para principios de la década de los años cincuenta la salud de Frida se había dete-riorado mucho. El 13 de julio de 1954 murió en su casa en Coyoacán, en las afueras de la Ciudad de México, donde nació, vivió con Diego Rivera y pintó muchas de sus obras. La casa, que ahora es el Museo Frida Kahlo, contiene muchos recuerdos suyos y su colección de arte.

Margin glosses:
a streetcar hit me

to enroll in
ran into

monkeys

was buried with / master

ENFOQUE ESTRUCTURAL — **El subjuntivo: Un repaso**

In Chapters 6, 7, and 8 you learned that the subjunctive is used in sentences that have more than one clause when the subjects in the two clauses are different. You will recall that the two parts of the sentences are connected by the word **que.** Remember that for most verbs, the present subjunctive is formed by removing the **o** of the **yo** form of the present indicative tense and adding the following endings:

-ar verbs				
habl**ar**	→	habl**o**	→	habl**e** habl**emos**
				habl**es** habl**éis**
				habl**e** habl**en**

-er verbs

comer	→	como	→	coma	comamos
				comas	comáis
				coma	coman

-ir verbs

escribir	→	escribo	→	escriba	escribamos
				escribas	escribáis
				escriba	escriban

You can use this rule for forming the present subjunctive of the following verbs you have previously encountered in *Tú dirás* as well as of the new verbs provided.

-ar verbs

acampar	comprar	expresar	preguntar
ahorrar	contestar	ganar	presentar
alquilar	cuidar	gustar	prestar
andar	cultivar	hablar	regatear
anunciar	charlar	llamar	regresar
aprovechar	descansar	llevar	sudar
arreglar	desear	mandar	terminar
bailar	disfrutar de	mirar	tomar
bajar	doblar	nadar	trabajar
cambiar	escuchar	necesitar	trotar
caminar	esperar	odiar	viajar
cantar	estudiar	pasar	visitar
cenar	exagerar	planear	

-er verbs

aprender	correr	leer	ver
comer	creer	romper	
comprender	deber	vender	

We have introduced the subjunctive briefly in Chapters 6, 7, and 8 in order to give the students a feel for this mood. Research has shown that teachers make too much of the subjunctive (Tracy Terrell, "The subjunctive in Spanish interlanguage: Accuracy and comprehensibility.") In this article he points out that verbs in the present subjunctive comprise only about 3% of all the verbs a native speaker uses in daily conversation.

Students never really internalize all of the uses of the subjunctive, and even advanced undergraduates and graduate students still struggle with some of its subtleties. We recognize that this is an introductory text and want only to present the students with an overview of the subjunctive. In the Preface we noted that some structures are presented in *Tú dirás* for full control, others for partial control, and yet others for conceptual awareness. We feel the subjunctive falls into the latter category (conceptual awareness), for as students continue in their study of Spanish, they will undoubtedly see this mood over and over again. What we are focusing on in our presentation here is the syntactic pattern in which the subjunctive occurs, i.e., in the **que** clause. Terrell's study indicates that if the syntactic pattern is correct, the message is conveyed, and while the learner may not use the verb correctly in the subjunctive, native speakers don't perceive this error to be as serious as others they might make (e.g., noun–adjective agreement).

After our presentation, we feel students should fully control the syntactic pattern and some of the more common uses of the subjunctive, such as after the verb **querer** and some of the impersonal expressions. The other uses are presented in order to make the students aware of the concept of the subjunctive, and as they continue their study, we expect them to build upon this awareness and gain fuller control of this complex structure.

-ir verbs

asistir a	discutir	recibir
compartir	escribir	subir
describir	insistir en	vivir

Below are some common verbs that you have learned in *¡Tú dirás!* and that undergo certain spelling changes when conjugated in the present indicative and subjunctive.

verbs that change *e* to *ie*

entender →	entiendo →	entienda, entiendas, entienda, entendamos, entendáis, entiendan
pensar →	pienso →	piense, pienses, piense, pensemos, penséis, piensen
perder →	pierdo →	pierda, pierdas, pierda, perdamos, perdáis, pierdan
querer →	quiero →	quiera, quieras, quiera, queramos, queráis, quieran

The **e** changes to **ie** in all forms except **nosotros(as)** and **vosotros(as).**

verbs that change *o* to *ue*

encontrar →	encuentro →	encuentre, encuentres, encuentre, encontremos, encontréis, encuentren
poder →	puedo →	pueda, puedas, pueda, podamos, podáis, puedan
volver →	vuelvo →	vuelva, vuelvas, vuelva, volvamos, volváis, vuelvan

The **o** changes to **ue** in all forms except **nosotros(as)** and **vosotros(as).**

dormir →	duermo →	duerma, duermas, duerma, durmamos, durmáis, duerman

The **o** of **dormir** changes to **ue** in all forms except in the **nosotros(as)** and **vosotros(as)** forms, where the **o** changes to **u.**

verbs that change *e* to *i*

pedir	→	pido	→	pida, pidas, pida, pidamos, pidáis, pidan
repetir	→	repito	→	repita, repitas, repita, repitamos, repitáis, repitan
seguir	→	sigo	→	siga, sigas, siga, sigamos, sigáis, sigan

The **e** changes to **i** for these verbs in all forms, even **nosotros(as)** and **vosotros(as).**

Below are more verbs that undergo spelling changes when conjugated in the present indicative and subjunctive.

verbs with *g* in the stem

decir	→	digo	→	diga, digas, diga, digamos, digáis, digan
hacer	→	hago	→	haga, hagas, haga, hagamos, hagáis, hagan
oír	→	oigo	→	oiga, oigas, oiga, oigamos, oigáis, oigan
poner	→	pongo	→	ponga, pongas, ponga, pongamos, pongáis, pongan
tener	→	tengo	→	tenga, tengas, tenga, tengamos, tengáis, tengan
traer	→	traigo	→	traiga, traigas, traiga, traigamos, traigáis, traigan
salir	→	salgo	→	salga, salgas, salga, salgamos, salgáis, salgan
venir	→	vengo	→	venga, vengas, venga, vengamos, vengáis, vengan

verbs that change *z* to *c*

cruzar	→	cruzo	→	cruce, cruces, cruce, crucemos, crucéis, crucen
comenzar	→	comienzo	→	comience, comiences, comience, comencemos, comencéis, comiencen
empezar	→	empiezo	→	empiece, empieces, empiece, empecemos, empecéis, empiecen

The change from **z** to **c** before **e** or **i** is simply a spelling change dictated by the Real Academia Española in 1726 to avoid any combination of **z** + **e** or **z** + **i.** It was an artificial rule since a word spelled with a **c** + **e** or a **z** + **e** would be pronounced the same way by a speaker of peninsular Spanish or of the Spanish of the Americas. The rule was also applied to words Spanish borrowed from other languages and that were spelled with the "ze" or "zi" combination, e.g., **cero** *(zero),* **cebra** *(zebra),* **cénit** *(zenith),* **circón** *(zircon),* **cítara** *(zither).*

The change from **c** to **qu** is not artificial, however. It conserves the sound of /k/ when **-e** is added to the stem of the infinitive. Review with students the sounds of:

a	**café**
c + o	**comer**
u	**cubano**

and have them compare these sounds to:

e	**cena**
c + i	**cine**

On a transparency or the board you may want to write the word **practicar;** take off the **ar** and add the **-e** so you have "practice" and have students pronounce the word. Point out that changing the **c** to **qu** conserves the /k/ sound of the infinitive.

The change from **g** to **gu** is not artificial, either. It conserves the sound of /g/ when **-e** is added to the stem of the infinitive. Review with students the sounds of:

a	**gato**
g + o	**gordo**
u	**gustar**

and have them compare these sounds to:

e	**general**
g + i	**gimnasio**

Again you may want to write the word **pagar;** take off the **ar** and add the **-e** so you have "page" and have students pronounce the word. Point out that changing the **g** to **gu** conserves the /g/ sound of the infinitive.

verbs that change *c* to *qu*

buscar	→	busco	→	busque, busques, busque, busquemos, busquéis, busquen
practicar	→	practico	→	practique, practiques, practique, practiquemos, practiquéis, practiquen
tocar	→	toco	→	toque, toques, toque, toquemos, toquéis, toquen
tonificar	→	tonifico	→	tonifique, tonifiques, tonifique, tonifiquemos, tonifiquéis, tonifiquen
explicar		explico		explique, expliques, explique, expliquemos, expliquéis, explíquen

verbs that change *g* to *gu*

jugar	→	juego	→	juegue, juegues, juegue, juguemos, juguéis, jueguen
pagar	→	pago	→	pague, pagues, pague, paguemos, paguéis, paguen
llegar	→	llego	→	llegue, llegues, llegue, lleguemos, lleguéis, lleguen

Finally, the following verbs form the subjunctive in a way that is not based on the **yo** form of the present indicative tense:

dar	→	dé	→	des	dé	demos	deis	den
estar	→	esté	→	estés	esté	estemos	estéis	estén
haber	→	haya	→	hayas	haya	hayamos	hayáis	hayan
ir	→	vaya	→	vayas	vaya	vayamos	vayáis	vayan
saber	→	sepa	→	sepas	sepa	sepamos	sepáis	sepan
ser	→	sea	→	seas	sea	seamos	seáis	sean

El subjuntivo con expresiones de voluntad

You have already learned several expressions that take the subjunctive **(querer, es necesario).** All of these expressions convey a feeling (a transferring of will) that influences the action of the verb in the **que** clause. **(Quiero que tú estudies.)** Because of the effect that these verbs and expressions have on the verb in the **que** clause, this verb must be in the subjunctive. Here are other verbs and expressions that convey a similar effect and trigger the use of the subjunctive in the **que** clause that follows.

esperar	*to hope*	**prohibir**	*to forbid, to prohibit*
preferir (ie, i)	*to prefer*	**es importante**	*it is important*
mandar	*to order*	**es aconsejable**	*it is advisable*
insistir en	*to insist that*	**recomendar (ie)**	*to recommend*
sugerir (ie)	*to suggest*	**es aconsejable**	*to advise*

Práctica

M. Espero que...
Indica lo que esperas que hagan otras personas. Crea frases según el modelo.

■ **Modelo:** Uds. comen más.
Espero que Uds. coman más.

1. Tú ahorras dinero.
2. Pedro alquila un coche.
3. El mesero arregla la cuenta.
4. Juana baila el merengue.
5. Los profesores explican bien.
6. Tú caminas a la universidad.
7. Mi amigo cena con nosotros.
8. Mi esposo compra un coche nuevo.
9. Mi hermana mayor cuida a mi hermano.
10. Mi amigo charla menos.

N. Es aconsejable que...
Ahora expresa lo que es aconsejable que hagan tú y los otros miembros de tu familia.

■ **Modelo:** Mi hermano come mucho.
Es aconsejable que mi hermano coma mucho.

1. Mis padres disfrutan de sus vacaciones.
2. Nosotros escuchamos las instrucciones de mi padre.
3. Mi hermano no mira mucho la televisión.
4. Mi padre nada 30 minutos cada día.
5. Mi hermana regresa temprano a casa todos los días.
6. Tú terminas la tarea temprano esta noche.
7. Yo tomo seis vasos de agua cada día.
8. Mi padre viaja a Chicago cada mes.
9. Mi madre camina cinco millas cada lunes, miércoles y viernes.
10. Nosotros visitamos a nuestros abuelos en diciembre.

Ñ. No quiere...
Varias personas que tú conoces no quieren hacer nada. Pero tú sabes que es importante que ellos hagan las actividades indicadas. Sigue el modelo.

■ **Modelo:** Simón no quiere escuchar a la profesora.
Es importante que Simón escuche a la profesora.

1. Julia no quiere nadar hoy.
2. Julián no quiere estudiar francés.
3. Mi hermanito no quiere comer vegetales.
4. Nosotros no queremos regresar temprano.
5. Beatriz y Rosa no quieren arreglar su cuarto.
6. Tú no quieres cenar conmigo.
7. Magda no quiere ahorrar dinero para la universidad.
8. Mi hermano no quiere cuidar al niño esta noche.
9. Nosotros no queremos ver el programa de televisión en PBS.
10. Marcos y Laura no quieren correr todos los días.

ENFOQUE LÉXICO — Ojalá (que)

Ojalá (que) is an expression in Spanish that means *I hope (that)*. It is normally used as an exclamation and is followed by a verb in the subjunctive.

¿Vas al cine el viernes?	*Are you going to the movies on Friday?*
¡Ojalá (que) pueda ir!	**I hope** *I can go!*
¿Puedes llamarme por teléfono esta noche?	*Can you call me tonight?*
Tengo mucho que estudiar. **¡Ojalá (que)** tenga tiempo!	*I have a lot to study.* **I hope** *I have time!*

Comentarios culturales — Palabras árabes

*L*a expresión **ojalá que** es de origen árabe y significa *"may Allah grant that"* en inglés. Los musulmanes invadieron la Península Ibérica en 711 d. C. y permanecieron allí hasta que fueron expulsados en 1492. Durante este período, casi ocho siglos, muchas palabras árabes entraron a la lengua española. Los lingüistas han determinado que hay aproximadamente 4.000 palabras de origen árabe en el español moderno. Muchas de las palabras españolas que empiezan con **al-** son de origen árabe: **alcohol, álgebra, alcachofa, alfalfa, alberca, alcoba, algodón, almendra, almohada, almanaque, alfombra, albóndigas.** Algunas palabras que comienzan en **a-** también son de origen árabe: **aceite, aceituna, ajedrez, ajonjolí, arroz, azúcar, aduana, azulejo, azucena.** Otras palabras interesantes que son de origen árabe son: **jazmín, jarabe, naranja, cifras** y **cénit**. Algunas de estas palabras también han entrado a la lengua inglesa: *alcohol, algebra, almond, alfalfa, almanac, alcove, jasmine* y *zenith*.

INTEGRACIÓN CULTURAL

1. ¿Cuántos años duró la dominación musulmana de la Península Ibérica?
2. ¿Cuáles son algunas palabras relacionadas con la matemática que son de origen árabe?
3. ¿Te gusta jugar al ajedrez? ¿Sabías que los árabes inventaron este juego?

Práctica

O. ¿Con quién… ? Un(a) amigo(a) te pregunta lo que vas a hacer y tú le contestas con lo que esperas hacer empleando la expresión **ojalá que.**

▪ **Modelo:** comer mañana
—*¿Con quién vas a comer mañana?*
—*¡Ojalá que coma con Yara!*

1. estudiar
2. bailar
3. caminar a clase
4. cenar el viernes por la noche
5. mirar la televisión esta noche
6. escuchar tu disco compacto nuevo
7. viajar a España el próximo verano
8. asistir al concierto el próximo sábado

P. El profesor prefiere… Indica lo que el profesor de español quiere que hagan tú y tus compañeros de clase. Haz frases según el modelo.

▪ **Modelo:** Yo repito la respuesta.
El profesor prefiere que yo repita la respuesta.

1. Tú haces la tarea.
2. Ella trae su libro a clase.
3. Juan no duerme durante la clase.
4. Nosotros salimos después de la clase.
5. Sara encuentra su tarea.
6. Tú piensas antes de hablar.

Q. Es aconsejable… Dáles consejos a tus compañeros de clase. Empieza tus consejos con **Es aconsejable que…**

▪ **Modelo:** Tú repites la respuesta.
Es aconsejable que tú repitas la respuesta.

1. Él dice la verdad.
2. Ellos vienen a clase temprano.
3. Tú no pierdes tus libros.
4. Ella entiende las instrucciones del profesor.
5. Nosotros dormimos ocho horas cada noche.
6. Yo vuelvo a casa temprano hoy.

R. No quiere… Alguien indica que otra(s) persona(s) no quiere(n) hacer algo, pero tú insistes en que lo haga(n). Sigue el modelo.

▪ **Modelo:** Miguel no quiere ser más responsable.
Insisto en que Miguel sea más responsable.

1. Javier no quiere estar aquí mañana.
2. Lilia no quiere dar un paseo ahora.
3. Nosotros no queremos saber si hay un examen mañana.
4. Tú no quieres ir a la biblioteca.
5. Francisco y Ramón no quieren ser más responsables.
6. Uds. no quieren estar en la clase mañana.
7. Paula y Raúl no quieren ir a la escuela.

Possible answers, Ex. O
1. ¿Con quién vas a estudiar mañana? ¡Ojalá que estudie contigo! 2. ¿Con quién vas a bailar mañana? ¡Ojalá que baile con Juan! 3. ¿Con quién vas a caminar a la escuela? ¡Ojalá que camine a la clase con mi hermano! 4. ¿Con quién vas a cenar el viernes por la noche? ¡Ojalá que cene con mi familia! 5. ¿Con quién vas a mirar la televisión esta noche? ¡Ojalá que mire la televisión con mi novia! 6. ¿Con quién vas a escuchar tu disco compacto nuevo? ¡Ojalá que escuche mi disco compacto nuevo con mi vecina! 7. ¿Con quién vas a viajar a España el próximo verano? ¡Ojalá que viaje con Felipe! 8. ¿Con quién vas a asistir al concierto el próximo sábado? ¡Ojalá que asista al concierto con David!

Answers, Ex. P
1. El profesor prefiere que tú hagas la tarea. 2. …que ella traiga su libro a clase. 3. …que Juan no duerma durante la clase. 4. …que nosotros salgamos después de la clase. 5. …que Sara encuentre su tarea. 6. …que tú pienses antes de hablar.

Ex. P: Pairs
Have students do these exercises in pairs. Allow 3–5 minutes each and then select different students to share their answers. After various answers, try to personalize the sentences with direct questions. For example: **¿Recomiendas que todos los estudiantes hagan la tarea todos los días?**

Answers, Ex. Q
1. Es aconsejable que él diga la verdad. 2. …que ellos vengan a clase temprano. 3. …que tú no pierdas tus libros. 4. …que ella entienda las instrucciones del profesor. 5. …que nosotros durmamos ocho horas cada noche. 6. …que yo vuelva a casa temprano hoy.

Answers, Ex. R
1. Insisto en que Javier esté aquí mañana. 2. Insisto en que Lilia dé un paseo ahora. 3. Insisto en que nosotros sepamos si hay un examen mañana. 4. Insisto en que tú vayas a la biblioteca. 5. Insisto en que Francisco y Ramón sean más responsables. 6. Insisto en que Uds. estén en la clase mañana. 7. Insisto en que Paula y Raúl vayan a la escuela.

S. Es importante… Tú quieres expresar lo que es importante que hagan tú y tus compañeros. Haz frases según el modelo.

■ **Modelo:**   Yo saco la basura todos los días.
        Es importante que yo saque la basura todos los días.

1. Yo tonifico el cuerpo con ejercicio aeróbico.
2. Tú llegas temprano a clase.
3. Yo cruzo la calle con mi hermano.
4. Ellas tocan el piano en la fiesta.
5. Sara empieza a estudiar a las 7:30.
6. Tú practicas algún deporte.
7. Nosotros pagamos la cuenta.
8. Yo busco las llaves antes de salir de casa.

LECTURA: *Tres pintores españoles— Picasso, Miró, Dalí*

ANTES DE LEER

T. Contesta las siguientes preguntas.

1. ¿Qué sabes del arte del siglo XX?
2. ¿Quiénes son algunos de los pintores más importantes?
3. ¿Has visto alguna obra cubista? ¿Y alguna surrealista?
4. Lee el título del texto. ¿Reconoces algunos de los nombres?

U. Estudio de palabras. Trata de adivinar el significado de las siguientes palabras que aparecen en la lectura sobre los tres artistas españoles del siglo XX. Encuentra las palabras en inglés en la lista de la derecha que corresponden a las palabras en español en la lista de la izquierda.

1. tonalidades	a. suggest
2. predominio	b. tones
3. esporádicas	c. influenced
4. sugieren	d. predominance
5. búsqueda	e. aptitude
6. impulsado	f. eccentricities
7. se adhirió a	g. intermittent, sporadic
8. excentricidades	h. he joined
9. aptitud	i. political position
10. postura política	j. search

GUÍA PARA LA LECTURA

V. Mira el texto e identifica en qué época del siglo XX vivieron los tres pintores.

W. ¿Qué acontecimientos históricos relacionas con esos años?

X. ¿Picasso, Miró o Dalí? Indica si las siguientes oraciones se refieren a Picasso, Miró o Dalí.

1. Nació en Barcelona.
2. Nació en Málaga.
3. Murió en Barcelona.
4. Murió en Mallorca.
5. Fue surrealista.
6. Fue escultor.
7. Sus temas incluyen pájaros y estrellas.
8. Fue cubista.
9. Trabajó en dos películas.
10. Tiene una escultura en Chicago.

Y. Sobre los artistas. Contesta las siguientes preguntas en español.

1. ¿Cuál de los tres artistas era el mayor?
2. ¿Cuál de los tres artistas era el menor?
3. ¿En qué orden murieron?
4. ¿Quién fue Georges Braque?
5. ¿Qué es el cubismo?
6. ¿Qué trataba de demostrar Miró en su arte?
7. ¿Por qué se mudó Dalí a París?
8. ¿Quién fue Luis Buñuel?
9. ¿Cómo fue la vida de Dalí después de llegar a ser famoso internacionalmente?
10. ¿Por qué expulsaron los surrealistas a Dalí de su grupo?

Z. El arte español del siglo XX. Usa la información de la lectura para escribir un informe breve sobre uno de los artistas españoles del siglo XX. Escoge una de las pinturas en esta etapa y descríbela brevemente en tu informe.

▶ *Tres pintores españoles: Picasso, Miró, Dalí*

Picasso

Probablemente el artista español más universal es Pablo Picasso. Su obra dejó una profunda **huella** en la pintura moderna. Nació en Málaga el 15 de octubre de 1881. Su padre, pintor y profesional del dibujo, lo inició en el arte pictórico. Picasso demostró muy pronto una aptitud extraordinaria para la pintura y fue admitido, cuando sólo tenía 14 años, en la Escuela de Bellas Artes en Barcelona. Desde 1900 hizo varios viajes a Madrid y París, donde finalmente estableció su **taller.**

Entre 1900 y 1906 Picasso pasó por sus períodos azul y rosa. Estas dos épocas se llaman así por las tonalidades predominantes en las obras que pintó durante esos años. Después de esto, junto con Georges Braque, creó el estilo que hoy se conoce como el "cubismo". Este movimiento artístico se caracteriza por el uso o predominio de formas

mark, imprint

studio, workshop

Pablo Picasso, Retrato de Ambroise Vollard, *1910*

geométricas. Picasso es una de las figuras más representativas de este movimiento artístico. También hizo unas incursiones esporádicas en el **ámbito** de la escultura. Dos de estas obras son *La cabra* que está en el Museo de Arte Moderno en Nueva York y una escultura gigantesca de metal que se encuentra en la ciudad de Chicago. Picasso murió en la Riviera francesa el 8 de abril de 1973.

Miró

Joan Miró nació el 20 de abril de 1893 en Barcelona. Desde 1948 dividió su tiempo entre España y París. En esta época el pintor comenzó una serie de obras de intenso contenido poético cuyos símbolos estaban basados en el tema de la mujer, el pájaro y la **estrella.** En las obras de Miró podemos ver un juego de co-lores brillantes, contrastes fuertes y líneas que sólo su-gieren imágenes. Su abundante obra representa la búsqueda de un lenguaje artísti-co abstracto, con el que **intentaba plasmar** la natu-raleza tal como la **vería** un hombre primitivo o un niño. Su obra **desemboca** en un surre-alismo mágico, rico en color. Miró murió el 25 de diciembre de 1983 en Mallorca.

Joan Miró, Mujer y pájaro por la noche, *1945.*

Dalí

Salvador Dalí nació en Figueras el 11 de mayo de 1904. Pronto mostró habilidades para el dibujo, y su padre lo envió a Madrid a estudiar en la Escuela de Bellas Artes de San Fernando. En 1928, impulsado por el pintor Joan Miró, **se mudó** a París y se adhirió al movimiento surrealista. En estos años colaboró con Luis Buñuel en dos célebres películas—*Un chien andalou (Un perro andaluz)* y *L'âge d'or (La edad de oro)*—y pintó algunas de sus mejores obras: *La persistencia de la memoria* y *El descubrimiento de América.* Su exposición en 1933 lo **lanzó** a la fama interna-cional y, entonces, comenzó a llevar una vida llena de excent-ricidades. Esta actitud, consid-erada por algunos como una forma de comercializar sus obras, junto a su falta de postu-ra política, causaron su expul-sión del grupo surrealista. Murió en Barcelona el 23 de enero de 1989.

Tú dirás ....

AA. Un(a) profesor(a) exigente *(demanding).*

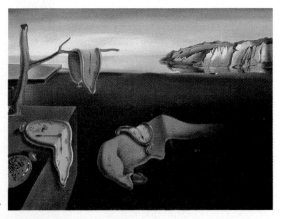

Salvador Dalí, La persistencia de la memoria, *1931*

Imagina que tu amigo(a) y tú tienen un(a) profesor(a) muy exigente este año.

Comentarios

culturales — *El museo del Prado*

INTERNET

http://tudiras.heinle.com

El Museo del Prado, localizado en Madrid, es uno de los museos de arte más importantes del mundo. El museo se abrió al público en 1819 en un edificio nuevo y se llamaba Museo de la Colección Real de Pintura. Tenía ese nombre porque, anteriormente, las pinturas pertenecían a la colección que muchos reyes españoles habían reunido durante varios siglos.

En el Prado hay actualmente más de 5.000 cuadros, pero en las salas del museo solamente se puede ver la mitad. El resto de los cuadros están guardados o están prestados a otros museos.

Museo del Prado

También forma parte del Museo del Prado un museo que se llama el Casón del Buen Retiro, en el que hay una colección histórica sobre arte español. Allí se pueden ver los cuadros de los pintores de la escuela Catalana, quienes prepararon el camino para el joven Pablo Picasso.

La colección de pintura española que tiene el Prado no tiene igual en el mundo. Se puede ver allí una muestra de las obras de los mejores pintores españoles, por ejemplo, Velázquez, Goya y El Greco.

El cuadro *Guernica,* de Picasso, volvió a España después de estar muchos años en el Museo de Arte Moderno de Nueva York. Inicialmente este cuadro se instaló en el Casón del Buen Retiro, pero desde 1992 está en el Museo Reina Sofía, un museo nuevo dedicado al arte español del siglo XX. Junto con el cuadro están también los dibujos que hizo Picasso mientras planeaba la realización de esa magnífica pintura.

INTEGRACIÓN CULTURAL

1. ¿Dónde está el Museo de Prado?
2. ¿Cuándo se inauguró el museo?
3. ¿Aproximadamente cuántos cuadros se exhiben allí?
4. ¿Cómo se llama el museo donde se encuentra el *Guernica*, el famoso cuadro de Picasso?

Answers, Integración
1. Madrid
2. 1819
3. 5.000
4. en el Museo Reina Sofía

Ex. AA: 👤👤 Pairs

Elaboren una lista con las cosas que el/la profesor(a) quiere que sus alumnos hagan y compártanla con el resto de la clase. Utilicen expresiones como **esperar que, mandar que, insistir en que, prohibir que, etc.** Comparen su lista con las de otros compañeros y deciden quién tiene el la profesor(a) más exigente de todos.

BB. ¿Qué es aconsejable que haga un(a) buen(a) estudiante?
Dos estudiantes que acaban de matricularse (*to enroll*) en la universidad vienen a pedirte consejo. Diles cuáles son las cosas que deben y no deben hacer para tener éxito (*to have success*) en sus clases. Al darles consejos, utiliza expresiones como **es aconsejable que, es importante que, espero que, recomendar que, sugerir que, etc.**

Ex. BB: 👤👤 Pairs

CC. La pintura. Vas a preparar una breve presentación sobre una obra de arte. Escoge una de las pinturas que aparecen en esta *etapa* u otra obra de uno de los artistas que presentan aquí. Empieza tu presentación con una breve descripción de la obra. Incluye también algunos de los detalles de la vida del artista. Puedes trabajar con un(a) compañero(a).

Ex. CC: 👤👤 Pairs

⊚ SEGUNDA ETAPA

⊚ *PARA EMPEZAR: El arte popular*

Preparación: Before beginning this *etapa,* answer the following questions.

- Have you ever been to a crafts fair or festival?
- What types of art do you find there that may be different from what you might find in an art museum? Glass work? Quilts? Ceramic work? Tapestries?

LECTURA: *Las molas de los indios cunas*

ANTES DE LEER

A. Mira las molas en la página 472. ¿Qué animales ves?

B. Estudio de palabras. Trata de adivinar el significado de las siguientes palabras que aparecen en la lectura sobre las molas de los indios cunas. Encuentra las palabras en inglés en la lista de la derecha que corresponden a las palabras en español en la lista de la izquierda.

1. habitadas
2. arena fina
3. coralinos
4. tribu
5. artesanía
6. sucumbieron
7. manera de ser
8. amable
9. pectorales
10. estandarte
11. superpuestas
12. tienen a la venta
13. cuidadosos
14. desnudez
15. semejantes

a. behavior, way of being
b. breastplates
c. banner; standard
d. placed on top of
e. have for sale
f. nudity
g. kind, amiable
h. careful, meticulous
i. similar
j. coral
k. fine sand
l. inhabited
m. gave into, succumbed
n. crafts
ñ. tribe

GUÍA PARA LA LECTURA

C. ¿Aparece o no aparece en la lectura? Lee la lectura sobre los indios cunas en la página 472 e indica si los siguientes lugares, nombres, temas, etc. se mencionan. Si se mencionan, indica en qué párrafo se encuentran, y a qué se refieren.

1. pájaros y flores
2. Nueva York y Boston
3. rasgos exóticos
4. Francisco Pizarro
5. Nicaragua
6. el siglo XX
7. gente desagradable
8. islas

D. Más sobre molas y los indios cunas. Contesta las siguientes preguntas en español.

1. ¿Cuántas de las islas panameñas están habitadas por los indios cunas?
2. ¿Cuándo pasó Colón por la costa de Panamá?
3. Haz una lista de las características de los indios cunas.
4. ¿Cuáles son algunos de los adornos que llevan las mujeres cunas?
5. ¿Dónde podemos comprar molas?
6. ¿Qué diseños caracterizan las molas?
7. ¿Cuál es el origen de la mola?
8. ¿Qué plantas y animales se encuentran frecuentemente en las molas?

E. Las molas. Usa la información de la lectura para escribir un informe breve sobre la evolución de las molas de los indios cunas. Prepárate para presentarlo en clase.

Answers, Ex. B
1. l 2. k 3. j 4. ñ 5. n 6. m 7. a
8. g 9. b 10. c 11. d 12. e 13. h
14. f 15. i
For additional language practice, ask students to try to explain in Spanish the meaning of each of these words. Have each student pick a word without saying which one and then explain it. See if the other students can guess which word is being explained.

Answers, Ex. C
1. Aparece en el párrafo 4. Se refiere a los motivos que aparecen en las molas. 2. Aparece en el párrafo 3. Se refiere a las ciudades donde se pueden comprar molas. 3. Aparece en el párrafo 2. Se refiere a los rasgos de las mujeres cunas. 4. No aparece, pero sí aparece el nombre de Cristóbal Colón en el párrafo 1. 5. No aparece, pero sí aparece Panamá, otro país de Centroamérica. 6. No aparece. 7. No aparece. 8. Aparece en el párrafo 1. Se refiere a las 300 islas en la costa oriental de Panamá de las cuales 50 están habitadas por los indios cunas.

Answers, Ex. D
1. Sólo 50 islas panameñas están habitadas por los indios cunas. 2. Colón pasó por la costa de Panamá en 1502. 3. Los indios cunas son atractivos en su físico y en su manera de ser. 4. Las mujeres cunas llevan narigueras, pectorales de oro, pendientes y blusas hechas con molas. 5. Podemos comprar molas en las tiendas de regalos de grandes ciudades como Nueva York, Boston, San Francisco, Tel Aviv y Tokio. 6. Diseños geométricos o de flora y fauna reales o de la mitología caracterizan las molas. 7. Las molas surgieron como sustituto de la pintura del cuerpo. 8. Se encuentran los pájaros y las flores frecuentemente en las molas.

Do this as a jigsaw activity where each student is responsible for answering half the questions. After students pair up and exchange answers, have them write a brief paragraph incorporating the information they learned.

Las molas de los indios cunas

eastern — Cerca de la costa **oriental** de Panamá hay más de 300 islas idílicas de las cuales 50 están habitadas por los indios cunas. En las otras sólo se ven playas desiertas de arena fina y agua transparente, donde los peces nadan por *reefs* — entre los **arrecifes** coralinos los indios cunas se relacionan con el mundo exterior desde que Cristóbal Colón navegó por la costa de Panamá en 1502, en su cuarto viaje. La cuestión es: ¿Cómo mantienen los cunas sus *one realizes, takes into account* — tradiciones, **si se tiene en cuenta** que prácticamente todas las tribus de indios americanos que tenían algo que los europeos deseaban (tierras, artesanías, etc.) sucumbieron ante las influencias extranjeras?

possess — Los cunas **poseen** todos estos atractivos. Las islas en las que viven son de una belleza extraordinaria. Los propios indios llaman la atención por su carácter acoge- *nose rings* — dor y por su natural hermosura. Las mujeres utilizan adornos como **narigueras,** *earrings* — pectorales de oro, inmensos **pendientes** y blusas hechas con molas, con el fin de

resaltar su atractivo. Estos adornos son un buen ejemplo de la artesanía que se produce en el mundo hispánico.

ambassadors — Si las mujeres son las **embajadoras** de los cunas ante el mundo, las molas son su estandarte. Las tiendas de regalos de grandes ciudades como Nueva York, Boston, San Francisco, Tel Aviv y Tokio tienen a la venta estos rectángulos de *fabrics* — vivos colores. Están hechos de **telas** superpuestas con incrustaciones que forman o bien diseños geométricos, o bien imágenes de flora y fauna reales o mitológicas.

appeared — Las molas son relativamente recientes, pues **surgieron** en la segunda mitad del siglo XIX como sustituto a la pintura del cuerpo. Tradicionalmente las mujeres se pintaban el cuerpo con dibujos complicados y cuidadosos, pero el cristianismo y el comercio no eran compatibles con la desnudez del torso. Para adaptarse a la *transferred, transposed* — situación, las mujeres **traspasaron** los colores y los dibujos del cuerpo a las telas con las que se hicieron blusas. De esta manera entraron en la "civilización moderna" llevando molas. Al andar por una aldea a cualquier hora del día se ve a las *sewing* — mujeres **coser,** moviendo las manos con gran rapidez. La variedad de molas es *surprising* — **sorprendente** y revela una diversidad impresionante de formas y temas. Entre los numerosos motivos de la flora y la fauna figuran los pájaros y las flores. Los dibujos abstractos son semejantes a las formas geométricas que solían verse en las primeras molas.

After reading about **molas** and the designs that characterize them, have students look at the molas here and on page 470 and tell what designs they see in them.

Repaso

F. Prefiero que tú… Tú le estás diciendo a un(a) amigo(a) lo que quieres que haga y no haga. Construye frases originales que empiecen con **Prefiero que tú…** Emplea los verbos que siguen. Sigue el modelo.

■ **Modelo:** estudiar
   Prefiero que tú estudies tres horas.
   o
   Prefiero que tú estudies en la biblioteca.
   o
   Prefiero que tú no estudies con María.

1. estudiar
2. cenar con
3. mirar… en la televisión
4. escuchar
5. asistir al concierto de
6. compartir el libro con

G. Insisto en que… Ahora, sigue diciéndole a un(a) amigo(a) lo que es necesario que haga. Construye frases originales que empiecen con **Insisto en…** y emplea los verbos que siguen.

1. llamar a… por teléfono
2. comprar
3. caminar a
4. regresar a… a las
5. leer
6. discutir el problema con

Possible answers, Ex. F
1. Prefiero que tú estudies el español.
2. Prefiero que tú cenes conmigo.
3. Prefiero que tú mires el partido de fútbol en la televisión. 4. Prefiero que tú me escuches. 5. Prefiero que tú asistas al concierto de rock.
6. Prefiero que tú compartas el libro con ella.

Possible answers, Ex. G
1. Insisto en que tú llames a tu mamá por teléfono. 2. Insisto en que tú compres un regalo para Juan.
3. Insisto en que tú camines a la sinagoga. 4. Insisto en que tú regreses a casa a las doce. 5. Insisto en que tú leas el libro de Cervantes.
6. Insisto en que tú discutas el problema con tu mejor amigo(a).

IRM Master 58: Verbos reflexivos en el subjuntivo

We have included all of the reflexive verbs that the students have had. Students should focus on the syntactic pattern that characterizes the use of the subjunctive as they review the reflexives.

ENFOQUE ESTRUCTURAL | Verbos reflexivos en el subjuntivo

Reflexive verbs form the subjunctive in the same way as nonreflexive verbs. The reflexive pronoun is in the same position in the subjunctive mood as in its other uses. Note the following examples:

Es necesario que yo **me levante** temprano.	*It is necessary for me **to get up** early.*
Mi esposo quiere que **nos acostemos** temprano.	*My husband wants (for) us **to go to bed** early.*

Here are some of the most common reflexive verbs you have already learned:

acostarse (ue)	**levantarse**
afeitarse	**llamarse**
bañarse	**maquillarse**
desayunarse	**peinarse**
dormirse (ue, u)	**ponerse**
ducharse	**quedarse**
encontrarse con (ue)	**quitarse**
lavarse	**sentarse (ie)**
lavarse los dientes	**vestirse (i)**

Answers, Ex. H
1. Quiere que yo me acueste a las 10:30 cada noche. 2. Quiere que mi hermano se levante a las 6:30 todos los días. 3. Quiere que nosotros nos duchemos antes de las 7:00.
4. Quiere que mi hermana no se maquille todos los días. 5. Quiere que mi hermano se afeite antes de ducharse. 6. Quiere que nosotros nos vistamos antes de bajar al comedor. 7. Quiere que mi hermanito se peine con más cuidado. 8. Quiere que nosotros nos desayunemos a las 7:30. 9. Quiere que nosotros nos lavemos los dientes después de comer. 10. Quiere que yo me ponga un suéter antes de salir de casa.

Práctica

Answers, Ex. I
1. No es posible que Pablo entienda bien la tarea. 2. Dudo que Mario vaya a la biblioteca todas las noches. 3. Es imposible que Isabelina se acueste a la 1:00 de la mañana. 4. Es improbable que Alejandro navegue en tabla de vela. 5. No creo que Susana sea más inteligente que su hermana. 6. Es improbable que Manuel pase sus exámenes sin estudiar. 7. No puede ser que Ramón tenga más paciencia que Alberto. 8. No es verdad que Alfredo pinte muy bien.

Answers, Ex. I
1. Primero es necesario que te bañes. Después es necesario que te acuestes. Finalmente es necesario que te duermas. 2. Primero es necesario que te levantes. Después es necesario que te desayunes. Finalmente es necesario que te laves los dientes. 3. Primero es necesario que te vistas. Después es necesario que te maquilles. Finalmente es necesario que te peines. 4. Primero es necesario que te quites la ropa. Después es necesario que te duches. Finalmente es necesario que te acuestes.

Possible answers, Ex. J
1. Es bueno que tú no fumes. 2. Es bueno que Julia lea mucho. 3. Es bueno que Isabel se acueste temprano. 4. Es bueno que nosotros nos levantemos a las 6:30. 5. Es bueno que ellos hagan ejercicios para tonificar el cuerpo. 6. Es bueno que nosotros hablemos español en clase.

H. Mi madre quiere que... Tú le estás contando a un(a) amigo(a) lo que tu madre quiere que hagan los miembros de tu familia cuando tú la visitas durante las vacaciones. Haz frases según el modelo.

■ **Modelo:** Nosotros nos desayunamos todos los días.
Mi mamá quiere que nosotros nos desayunemos todos los días.

1. Yo me acuesto a las 10:30 cada noche.
2. Mi hermano se levanta a las 6:30 todos los días.
3. Nosotros nos duchamos antes de las 7:00.
4. Mi hermana no se maquilla todos los días.
5. Mi hermano se afeita antes de ducharse.
6. Nosotros nos vestimos antes de bajar al comedor.
7. Mi hermanito se peina con más cuidado.
8. Nosotros nos desayunamos a las 7:30.
9. Nosotros nos lavamos los dientes después de comer.
10. Yo me pongo un suéter antes de salir de casa.

I. Es necesario... Ordena las siguientes actividades cronológicamente. Usa las expresiones primero, después y finalmente para establecer el orden. Sigue el modelo.

■ **Modelo:** desayunarse, lavarse los dientes, ducharse
Primero es necesario que te duches.
Después es necesario que te desayunes.
Finalmente es necesario que te laves los dientes.

1. acostarse, dormirse, bañarse
2. desayunarse, lavarse los dientes, levantarse
3. maquillarse, peinarse, vestirse
4. quitarse la ropa, acostarse, ducharse

J. ¿Es aconsejable o no? Di si es aconsejable o no lo que hacen tú y tus compañeros de clase. Sigue el modelo.

■ **Modelo:** Jaime estudia cinco horas todos los días.
Es aconsejable que Jaime estudie cinco horas todos los días.
o
No es aconsejable que Jaime estudie cinco horas todos los días.
Debe divertirse más.

1. Tú no fumas.
2. Julia lee mucho.
3. Isabel se acuesta temprano.
4. Nosotros nos levantamos a las 6:30.
5. Ellos hacen ejercicios para tonificar el cuerpo.
6. Nosotros hablamos español en clase.

Q IRM Master 60: El subjuntivo con expresiones de emoción

Use the examples to point out how these words and expressions affect what is going on in the subordinate clause, thus requiring the subjunctive.

ENFOQUE ESTRUCTURAL — Más sobre el subjuntivo con expresiones de emoción

As you have already seen on Chapters 7 and 8, when a verb or expression in the main clause expresses an emotion or some sort of reaction, the verb in the **que** clause must be in the sunjunctive.

To recapitulate, the following are expressions that you have already learned:

alegrarse de	*to be happy*	**sentir (ie, i) que**	*to regret*
¡Qué bueno que... !	*how great that*	**¡Qué malo que... !**	*how terrible that*
¡Qué lástima que... !	*what a pity that*	**¡Qué pena que... !**	*What a shame that*

Other expressions used in Spanish to convey emotion are:

estar contento(a) de que	*to be happy*	**temer que**	*to fear that*
¡Qué raro... !	*how strange*	**¡Qué maravilla... !**	*how wonderful*
¡Qué vergüenza	*what a shame*	**¡Qué interesante... !**	*how interesting*

Look at the following sentences:

Estoy contento de que puedas ir a la fiesta	***I am happy that*** *you can go to to the party*
¡Temo que no podamos asistir a la conferencia	***I fear that*** *we can't attend the lecture*
¡Qué raro que Juan no este aquí hoy!	***How strange that*** *Juan is not here today!*
Qué vergüenza que tú no estudies más!	***What a shame that*** *you don't study more*

Práctica

K. Me alegro de… Un(a) compañero(a) está contando lo que hacen algunos de tus compañeros de clase. Tú reaccionas con una frase que empieza con **Me alegro de…** Sigue el modelo.

■ **Modelo:** María / dormir ocho horas cada noche
María duerme ocho horas cada noche.
Me alegro de que María duerma ocho horas cada noche.

1. Juan / lavar los platos después de comer
2. Benito / dormir ocho horas cada noche
3. Sebastián / estudiar cuatro horas cada noche
4. Nora / hacer ejercicios cada tarde después de la escuela
5. Jaime / levantarse temprano los sábados
6. Susana / acostarse temprano antes de un examen

L. ¡Qué bueno! Haz frases según el modelo.

■ **Modelo:** Tú visitas a tu abuela con frecuencia.
¡Qué bueno que tú visites a tu abuela con frecuencia!

1. Lucas estudia solo.
2. Él no come mucho.
3. Susana llega a casa temprano.
4. Uds. hacen su tarea antes de mirar la televisión.
5. Tú vas a la biblioteca ahora.
6. Ellos terminan la lección.

Answers, Ex. K
1. Juan lava…, Me alegro de que Juan lave… 2. Benito duerme…, Me alegro de que Benito duerma… 3. Sebastián estudia…, Me alegro de que Sebastián estudie… 4. Nora hace ejercicios…, Me alegro de que Nora haga ejercicios… 5. Jaime se levanta…, Me alegro de que Jaime se levante… 6. Susana se acuesta…, Me alegro de que Susana se acueste…

Answers, Ex. L
1. ¡Qué bueno que Lucas estudie solo! 2. ¡Qué bueno que él no coma mucho! 3. ¡Qué bueno que Susana llegue a casa temprano! 4. ¡Qué bueno que Uds. hagan su tarea antes de mirar la televisión! 5. ¡Qué bueno que tú vayas a la biblioteca ahora! 6. ¡Qué bueno que ellos terminen la lección!

In *A History of Mexico* Henry Bamford
Parkes provides considerable
information on the **Virgen de
Guadalupe.** To begin with, the
Spanish religion, with its invocations
to the Virgin Mary, the patron saint
Santiago, and other countless saints
was virtually polytheistic. This
blended easily with the polytheism of
the indigenous peoples of Mexico
who, in becoming Christians, did not
cease to be polytheistic. Instead of
Huitzilopochtli (the Hummingbird
Wizard who represented the sun and
wrestled at night with the stars and
moon to bring in each new day) and
Tlaloc (the rain god), they now
worshiped the Virgin Mary and other
saints represented by wooden and
bejeweled images which had
miraculous powers and were able to
cure disease and control weather. Of
these religious objects the most
celebrated was the **Virgen de
Guadalupe.** According to legend, in
December of 1531, a mere ten years
after Cortés completed his conquest
of Mexico, a newly baptized
indigenous peasant, Juan Diego, was
crossing a hill (el Cerro de Tepeyac)
north of Mexico City when the Virgin
appeared and informed him that she
wished a church built in her honor on
the spot where she was standing.
Juan Diego informed the bishop, who
would not believe him. The Virgin
appeared to Juan Diego a second
time and ordered him to climb to the
top of the hill and pick roses he
would find there and to place them in
his cloak. He climbed the hill and
found—in a place where nature
produced only cactuses—a garden of
roses. He wrapped the roses in his
cloak and returned to the bishop.
When he opened the cloak, he found
a picture of the Virgin. News that the
Virgin had appeared to a member of
the conquered race caused the
greatest excitement among the
Indians—particularly when the Pope
said no other race in history had been
honored in such fashion. Thus, the
task of converting the indigenous
people was made considerably easier.

M. ¡Qué raro! Haz frases según el modelo.

■ **Modelo:** Juan no llega tarde.
¡Qué raro que Juan no llegue tarde!

1. Luis no está aquí.
2. Marisol no viene a clase.
3. Tú no vas con ellos.
4. Jaime y Esteban no conocen a Marilú.
5. Uds. no pueden asistir al concierto.
6. Ellas no tienen tarea esta noche.

LECTURA: Los santeros de Nuevo México

ANTES DE LEER

N. Contesta las siguientes preguntas.

1. La palabra **santero** es un derivado de la palabra **santo.** Si **panadero** significa
"la persona que hace pan", ¿qué crees que significa **santero?**
2. Mira el título y las imágenes que acompañan este texto. ¿Qué palabras reconoces en el título?
3. ¿Cómo se llaman?

Ñ. Cognado, contexto o diccionario. Localiza las siguientes palabras en
el texto. Al tratar de adivinar su significado indica si la palabra es un cognado, si la
adivinaste por medio del contexto o si tuviste que buscarla en el diccionario. Si
tuviste que buscarla en un diccionario, indica la forma de la palabra que aparece en
el diccionario y el significado que encontraste allí.

	cognado	contexto	diccionario	forma en el diccionario	significado
aisladas					
sumamente					
surgieron					
tallaban					
santos					
razones					
muestra					
especie					
han resucitado					
cruz					
cuadro					
recobró					

GUÍA PARA LA LECTURA

O. Cierto o falso. Di si las siguientes oraciones son verdaderas o falsas.
Si la oración es falsa, explica por qué.

1. Los nuevos mexicanos no eran muy religiosos.
2. La tradición de tallar santos se desarrolló *(developed)* solamente en Nuevo México.
3. En los años 50 casi murió esta tradición en Nuevo México.
4. Eulogio Ortega y su esposa viven en una aldea en las montañas de las Filipinas.
5. San Antonio es el santo más popular entre los franciscanos.
6. San Isidro también es un santo importante en España.

P. Nuevo México y sus santos. Contesta las siguientes preguntas en español.

1. ¿Por qué surgió la tradición de hacer retablos y bultos en Nuevo México?
2. ¿Cuál es la diferencia entre un bulto y un retablo?
3. ¿Cuáles son los dos tipos de bultos que encontramos en Nuevo México?
4. ¿Quién es Eulogio Ortega?
5. ¿Cómo ayuda la Sra. Gutiérrez de Ortega a su esposo?
6. ¿En qué sentido es San Antonio diferente de San Francisco?
7. ¿Por qué es importante Santiago?
8. ¿Qué milagro se asocia con San Rafael?

▶ Los santeros de Nuevo México y cómo identificar los santos más populares

Durante los siglos XVIII y XIX las **aldeas** en lo que hoy es el norte de Nuevo México y el sur de Colorado estaban bastante aisladas del resto del mundo hispano. Los habitantes hispanos en esta parte de la Nueva España, como en el resto del mundo hispano, eran sumamente religiosos. A causa del **aislamiento** y la falta de atención de la Ciudad de México, que era la capital de la Nueva España, surgieron aquí varias tradiciones religiosas que son un poco diferentes de las del resto del mundo hispano. En las iglesias no había objetos religiosos, así que la gente empezó a crear pinturas y esculturas de imágenes religiosas. A veces pintaban escenas religiosas en **trozos** de madera. También tallaban esculturas en madera de los santos más importantes. Las pinturas se conocen como "retablos" mientras que las esculturas se conocen como "bultos".

La tradición de tallar santos no sólo ocurrió en esta región, sino también en otras partes del mundo que colonizaron los españoles. Por ejemplo, en Puerto Rico y en las Islas Filipinas también esculpían santos por las mismas razones que en Nuevo México. Los bultos pueden ser de dos clases. Una clase se pinta con colores llamativos mientras que la otra clase no se pinta. Tenemos con estas imágenes religiosas una impresionante muestra de arte popular.

San Antonio de Padua

villages

isolation

pieces

Francisco de Coronado first explored what is now New Mexico in 1540–42. Juan de Oñate founded San Gabriel about 30 miles north of Santa Fe, the first colony in what later became New Mexico, in 1598. The first order of business for the early settlers was to build a chapel, and like all Catholic chapels, it had to be decorated with saints important to the community. Thus, these **santos** were carved from whatever materials were in the region. In New Mexico, aspen and cottonwood were commonly used because they are soft and easy to carve. Spanish has been spoken continuously in that part of the USA since 1598. Santa Fe, the oldest capital in the USA was founded in 1610. Compare Jamestown (1607) and Plymouth Rock (1620). The Southwest (New Mexico, Arizona, Texas, California, Nevada, Utah, and part of Colorado) was only annexed to the USA in 1848 through the Treaty of Guadalupe.

Two of the earliest disciples of Jesus were the brothers James **(Santiago)** and John. Their mother Salome was the sister of the Virgin Mary (thus the two brothers were Jesus' cousins). Both brothers were at the crucifixion.

In 44 AD, Santiago, having persisted in his energetic propagation of the faith, was beheaded, on order of King Herod, thus becoming the first of Jesus' followers to achieve martyrdom. Legend says Santiago's body was taken to Spain for burial around 44 AD. Legend also says that in 812 a hermit saw a star hovering over a field, and when he reported this to religious superiors, excavations brought the body of Santiago to light, uncorrupted by time. He often appeared in battles between Christians and Moors; in the legendary Battle of Clavijo in 844 he was seen by Spanish Christians riding on a white horse, swinging a great sword, killing Moors by the thousands. Hence, he gained the name by which he is known in Spain, **Santiago Matamoros.**

teachers

Upon retiring

monk

skull

vest

laborers

oxen

plow

Santiago became the patron saint of Spain and his burial place the most sacred spot in Spain, Santiago de Compostela. The shrine at Compostela became a great pilgrimage center, equal to Jerusalem and Rome. Pilgrims adopted the cockleshell, found on Galician beaches, as their badge. Santiago is often shown as a pilgrim, with a shell. For a more thorough discussion of Santiago and the Road to Santiago, see Michener's classic book, *Iberia*.

Hidalgo, which brought an end to the Mexican-American War. Before 1848, the area had been part of New Spain **(La Nueva España)** until 1821, when Mexico declared its independence from Spain. Thus, from 1521 to 1821 it was part of Spain and from 1821 to 1848 it was part of Mexico. San Isidro appears with the angel, the plow, and one or two oxen. The belief among the people is that when it is time to work the fields, San Isidro goes off to pray, and the angel appears and does the plowing for him.

En Nuevo México a mediados de este siglo casi murió esta tradición, pero recientemente ha ocurrido una especie de renacimiento. Algunas personas se han interesado en la historia y en las tradiciones hispanas y han resucitado esta forma de arte popular. Un buen ejemplo de esto es Eulogio Ortega y su esposa Zoraida Gutiérrez de Ortega que viven en Velarde, una aldea en las montañas del norte de Nuevo México. Ambos fueron **maestros** de escuela primaria por más de cuarenta años. **Al jubilarse,** el Sr. Ortega empezó a tallar santos en madera. Como él no ve los colores muy bien, después de tallar un santos la Sra. Gutiérrez de Ortega lo pinta. Juntos han contribuido al renacimiento de esta forma de arte popular en Nuevo México. Aparte del bulto de Santiago, las fotografías en la página 479 muestran algunos bultos que ha tallado el Sr. Ortega con una breve descripción para ayudarles a identificar algunos de los santos más populares en Nuevo México.

San Antonio de Padua

San Antonio es, después de San Francisco, el santo más popular para los franciscanos. Lleva un hábito azul de **monje** y nunca lleva barba. Frecuentemente lleva un libro y un niño.

San Francisco de Asís

El fundador de la Orden de los Franciscanos, lleva un hábito azul de monje y siempre lleva barba. Generalmente lleva una cruz en la mano derecha y una **calavera** en la otra.

San Isidro Labrador

Lleva un saco azul y pantalones negros, **chaleco** rojo y un sombrero. Debe ser así como se vestían los **labradores** en la época colonial en Nuevo México. Siempre aparece con uno o dos **bueyes** y un **arado** y a veces también aparece con un ángel. Es el santo patrón de Madrid y de los labradores de Nuevo México.

Santiago

Según las leyendas, Santiago, el santo patrón de España, aparecía durante las batallas entre moros y cristianos y ayudaba a los españoles a triunfar. En el Nuevo Mundo se dice que apareció varias veces en batallas entre españoles e indios. Una de estas apariciones ocurrió en Nuevo México en 1599 cuando Santiago ayudó a Juan de Oñate y a sus soldados españoles mientras luchaban contra los indios en el pueblo de Acoma.

Nuestra Señora de Guadalupe

Siempre se representa como aparece en el cuadro que está en la Basílica de Guadalupe en la Ciudad de México. Lleva un vestido rojo y un **manto** azul. A sus pies siempre hay un ángel y una **luna creciente**.

robe
crescent moon

Nuestra Señora de los Dolores

Es una figura que simboliza los dolores de la vida de la Virgen María y es una de las imágenes más populares en Nuevo México. Lleva una bata roja, un manto azul y una o más **espadas clavadas** en el pecho.

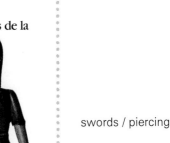

swords / piercing

San Rafael

Es el ángel que se le apareció a Tobías. San Rafael le dijo a Tobías que **cogiera** un pescado, lo **quemara**, y que le pusiera las **cenizas** en los ojos a su padre que era **ciego**. Según la leyenda, el padre de Tobías recobró la **vista** a causa de esto. San Rafael siempre se representa con un pescado.

he should catch
burn
ashes
blind

sight

Nuestra Señora de Guadalupe

San Rafael

Tú dirás ....

Q. Es necesario. Haz una lista de lo que es necesario que haga un(a) estudiante antes de ir a clase cada mañana. Compara tu lista con la de un(a) compañero(a) de clase. ¿En qué son semejantes *(alike)*? ¿En qué son diferentes? Decidan cuáles son las cinco actividades más importantes y compartan la información con la clase.

R. Las reacciones. Con un(a) compañero(a) haz una lista de algo que está ocurriendo en tu vida o en las noticias locales, nacionales o mundiales en estos días. Después reaccionen antes los acontecimientos *(events)*. Cuando terminen, comparen las reacciones de la clase.

■ **Modelo:** una fiesta el viernes
¡Qué lástima que María no vaya a la fiesta el viernes!

S. Las molas. Escoge una de las molas que aparece en esta *etapa* (o puedes traer una foto, tarjeta postal, etc. de otra mola) y descríbela. Incluye también algunos de los detalles sobre el origen de las molas y otra información que te parece importante de la lectura.

T. Los santos de Nuevo México. Usa la información en la lectura sobre los santos de Nuevo México y prepara una breve presentación oral sobre este tema. Usa un mapa de los Estados Unidos y México para ilustrar tu presentación.

Ex. Q: **Pair**
Remind students to discuss their lists only in Spanish and not to just show their partner their list. After discussing the activities, ask students to rank 5 activities from the most important down. Tell them that they must agree on the ranking so that if there is a disagreement one student has to convince the other to go along with him or her.

Ex. R:  **Pairs**

Have students prepare their descriptions for homework. In class have them share their work with partners. The partner will respond first to the content and then to the form of the writing. Allow 15–20 minutes for this peer editing. Allow students one more night to make any additional changes to their work.

Assign this as a homework assignment. In class allow 10–15 minutes to share presentations with a partner. When done have students group with 3 other students and present their work.

◎ PARA EMPEZAR: *La música en el mundo hispano*

Preparación: Upon beginning this *etapa,* think about what you know about music in the Spanish-speaking world and answer the following questions.

- In general, do you like music?
- What type of music do you prefer?
- Do you ever listen to or hear music in Spanish?
- Are you familiar with the music of a Spanish-speaking singer? Who?

Begin the discussion of this topic by asking the students these questions in Spanish.

LECTURA: *La historia de la bamba*

ANTES DE LEER

A. Contesta las siguientes preguntas.
1. Mira el título y la foto que acompaña este texto. ¿Conoces la canción "La bamba"?
2. ¿Sabes quién es Ritchie Valens?

B. Cognado, contexto o diccionario. Al tratar de adivinar el significado de las siguientes palabras, indica si la palabra es un cognado, si la adivinaste por medio del contexto o si tuviste que buscarla en el diccionario. Si tuviste que buscarla en un diccionario, indica la forma de la palabra que aparece en el diccionario y el significado que encontraste allí.

	cognado	contexto	diccionario	forma en el diccionario	significado
indudablemente					
procedentes					
occidental					
hispanohablante					
ritmo					
nocturnos					
arpa					
tropas extranjeras					
centenares					
híbrido					

GUÍA PARA LA LECTURA

C. ¿Aparece o no aparece en la lectura? Lee la lectura sobre la bamba e indica si se mencionan los siguientes temas. Si se mencionan, indica en qué párrafo se encuentran y a qué se refieren.

1. una ciudad en la costa sur de México
2. un autor
3. un explorador español
4. un lugar en África
5. un país europeo
6. un director de cine
7. un artista de cine
8. un país de la América del Sur

D. Para bailar la bamba se necesita… Contesta las siguientes preguntas en español.

1. ¿En qué parte de México se originó esta canción?
2. ¿Quién fue Ritchie Valens?
3. ¿Quién es Luis Valdez?
4. ¿Qué tipos de culturas han venido a esa parte de México?
5. ¿Cuál es una teoría sobre los orígenes de la canción?
6. ¿Cuándo apareció la canción por primera vez?

E. Evolución de "La bamba"… Usa la información en la lectura y escribe un informe breve sobre la evolución de la canción para presentarlo en clase. Usa un mapa del mundo para ayudarte a ilustrar tu presentación.

▶ *La historia de la bamba*

Se dice que esta canción, indudablemente una de las más populares de todos los tiempos, llegó al puerto de Veracruz con los **esclavos** procedentes de un lugar en África llamado Mbamba.

¿Es "La bamba" la canción más conocida del mundo occidental? Probablemente sí. Su **reconocimiento** es instantáneo. La canción **pertenecía** solamente a la América hispanohablante hasta finales de 1958, cuando Richard Valenzuela, cuyo nombre artístico fue Ritchie Valens, le dio a la melodía tradicional un alegre ritmo de *rock and roll*—como se ve en la película del mismo título que fue dirigida por Luis Valdez. Desde entonces se ha convertido en un elemento básico del repertorio de toda banda de barrio desde el este de Los Ángeles hasta el sur del Bronx. Treinta años después de que Valens introdujera la canción con su letra en español en la cultura americana, "La bamba" se ha convertido en un clásico en prácticamente todos los países desde Canadá hasta la Argentina.

La canción que ahora **resuena** en clubes nocturnos, fiestas y radios de todas partes tuvo sus orígenes en la costa sur de Veracruz, México, donde la música regional se caracteriza por el humor de sus letras y sus instrumentos de **cuerda:** guitarras de varios **tamaños,** un arpa pequeña, a menudo un **bajo de** pie y algunas veces un violín.

Desde que Hernán Cortés llegó a la costa del golfo en 1519, Veracruz ha **presenciado** la llegada de misioneros católicos, piratas caribeños, esclavos africanos y tropas extranjeras. El resultado ha sido la fusión de la tradición española con la vida africana, caribeña y nativa. La población de **sangres mezcladas** vino a ser llamada "mestiza". Sus canciones, junto con sus bailes y ritmos únicos, fueron conocidas como canciones al estilo "jarocho". De los centenares de melodías que evolucionaron de ese híbrido, la de "La bamba" es la más **duradera.**

---

slaves

recognition / belonged

resounds

string
sizes / a bass

witnessed

mixed blood

long lasting

---

century

"La bamba" vivirá para siempre, pero sus orígenes precisos son desconocidos. Entre las teorías existentes, una de las más interesantes es la de su posible origen africano. A principios del **siglo** XVII, los españoles llevaron esclavos a la costa del golfo de diferentes partes de África occidental incluyendo un lugar llamado Mbamba. Hacia el final de ese siglo, una canción llamada "La bamba" surgió en esa misma parte de Veracruz. *La bamba* era aparentemente una fusión del español y lenguas africanas.

You may want to bring in a recording of this song. Virtually all recording artists who sing in Spanish have recorded their own version. Los Lobos, a group from East Los Angeles, recorded the song for the soundtrack of the movie, *La Bamba*, about the life of Ritchie Valens.

Ritchie Valens

La letra de "La bamba"

Para bailar la bamba,
para bailar la bamba
se necesita una poca de gracia
pa' mí y pa' ti
ay arriba y arriba
ay arriba y arriba
por ti seré, por ti seré, por ti seré
Yo no soy marinero
yo no soy marinero, soy capitán
soy capitán, soy capitán,
Bamba, bamba
Bamba, bamba

Repaso

F. Yo quiero que tú… Imagina que tú tienes tres hijos y les dices lo que quieres que hagan. Emplea los siguientes verbos y expresiones: **levantarse, ducharse, peinarse, desayunarse, lavarse los dientes, ponerse el abrigo.**

G. Los quehaceres. Tú y tus compañeros tienen que arreglar la casa para una cena especial. Contesta las preguntas de tu amigo(a) empleando los verbos **esperar** o **preferir.** Sigue el modelo.

Ex. G:  Pairs

Answers, Ex. G
1. ¿Quién va a limpiar la cocina? Espero (Prefiero) que Marta la limpie. 2. ¿Quién va a hacer la cama? Espero (Prefiero) que Juan la haga. 3. ¿Quién va a poner la mesa? Espero (Prefiero) que Esteban la ponga. 4. ¿Quién va a hacer la ensalada? Espero (Prefiero) que Harry la haga. 5. ¿Quién va a preparar el postre? Espero (Prefiero) que Elisabeth lo prepare. 6. ¿Quién va a quitar la mesa? Espero (Prefiero) que Sara la quite.

■ **Modelo:**   sacar la basura / Juan
   —*¿Quién va a sacar la basura?*
   —*Espero que Juan la saque.*
        o
   —*Prefiero que Juan la saque.*

1. limpiar la cocina / Marta
2. hacer la cama / Juan
3. poner la mesa / Esteban
4. hacer la ensalada / Harry
5. preparar el postre / Elisabeth
6. quitar la mesa / Sara

H. ¡Qué vergüenza... ! Usa cada una de las expresiones en la página 475 para expresar una reacción a algo que está ocurriendo con uno(a) de tus compañeros(as).

■ **Modelo:** *¡Qué vergüenza que Juan no estudie más!*

Ex. H:  Pairs

ENFOQUE ESTRUCTURAL   El subjuntivo con expresiones de incertidumbre

As you learned earlier, the subjunctive is used in dependent clauses (after **que**) following expressions such as **querer que, es necesario que, es bueno que.** Spanish speakers also use the subjunctive in dependent clauses with expressions that indicate uncertainty or doubt about people, things, or events and also in dependent clauses after expressions that refer to something unknown or nonexistent.

In a question, **creer** and **no creer** may be used with the subjunctive to cast doubt on the action that follows. They can also be used with the indicative in a question that does not carry doubt.

In answer to any question, **creer** is used in the indicative because it expresses the idea of complete certainty. In other words, here it takes on the meaning of what the speaker *believes,* rather than just *thinks* or *wonders* about something.

An answer with **no creer** will usually be in the subjunctive if there is a good deal of doubt. The indicative (usually in the present or future tense) when there is no such doubt.

Dudo que Ramón **entienda** la situación política.	***I doubt** that Ramón **understands** the political situation.*
¿Es posible que el tren **llegue** a tiempo?	***Is it possible** that the train **will arrive** on time?*
No es probable que el tren **llegue** a tiempo.	***It's not likely** that the train **will arrive** on time.*
Puede ser que el avión **salga** tarde.	***It could be** that the plane **will leave** late.*
Es increíble que Marisol **tenga** esa actitud.	***It's incredible** that Marisol **has** that attitude.*
No creemos que Carmen lo **compre.**	***We don't think** Carmen **will buy** it.* (Doubt is implied.)
No creo que Carlos **tenga** tiempo.	***I don't think** Carlos **has/will have** time.* (I fully believe he won't.)

1. Whenever a verb or expression in the first half of a sentence (a) expresses doubt about a person, thing, or event, (b) places it within the realm of either possibility or impossibility, or (c) views it as unreal or unknown, the verb in the second half of the sentence is used in the subjunctive.

2. The following verbs and expressions convey doubt, uncertainty, and unreality and require the use of the subjunctive. So do expressions of possibility, impossibility, probability, and improbability, whether used with **no** or without it.

> **Dudo...**
>
> **Es dudoso...**
>
> **Puede ser...**
>
> **No estar seguro(a)...**
>
> **Es increíble...**
>
> **Es imaginable...**
>
> **No es verdad...**   **+   que**
>
> **No es cierto...**
>
> **(No) Es posible...**
>
> **(No) Es imposible...**
>
> **(No) Es probable...**
>
> **(No) Es improbable...**

Answers, Ex I.
1. No es posible que Pablo entienda bien a tarea. 2. Dudo que Mario vaya a la biblioteca todas las noches. 3. Es imposible que Isabelina se acueste a la 1:00 de la mañana. 4. Es improbable que Alejandro navegue en tabla de vela. 5. No creo que Susana sea más inteligente que su hermana. 6. Es improbable que Manuel pase sus exámenes sin estudiar. 7. No puede ser que Ramón tenga más paciencia que Alberto. 8. No es verdad que Alfredo pinte muy bien.

Ex. J: 👤👤 Pairs

Práctica

I. Lo dudo. Imagina que eres una persona que duda de todo. Usa las expresiones entre paréntesis y el subjuntivo para expresar tus dudas y tus incertidumbres sobre las actividades de tus amigos.

◼ **Modelo:**   Miguel es sincero. (dudo)
               Dudo que Miguel sea sincero.

1. Pablo entiende bien la tarea. (no es posible)
2. Mario va a la biblioteca todas las noches. (dudo)
3. Isabelina se acuesta siempre a la 1:00 de la mañana. (es imposible)
4. Alejandro navega en tabla de vela. (es improbable)
5. Susana es más inteligente que su hermana. (no creo)
6. Manuel pasa sus exámenes sin estudiar. (es improbable)
7. Ramón tiene más paciencia que Alberto. (no puede ser)
8. Alfredo pinta muy bien. (no es verdad)

J. ¿Es posible? ¿Es imposible? Escribe una serie de seis a ocho oraciones sobre tus actividades, tus proyectos, tus gustos, etc. Algunos comentarios pueden ser ciertos; otros pueden ser exageraciones. Después, comparte tus oraciones con la clase. Tus compañeros de clase van a reaccionar a lo que dices, usando las expresiones **es posible que, es imposible que, dudo que, es probable que, no creo que, es improbable que,** etc. Sigue los modelos.

◼ **Modelo:**   —Tengo diez perros y ocho gatos.
               —*No es posible que tengas diez perros y ocho gatos.*
               —Me caso la semana que viene.
               —*Dudo que te cases la semana que viene.*

El subjuntivo con antecedentes indefinidos o imaginarios

IRM Master 62: El subjuntivo con antecedentes indefinidos o imaginarios

Suggestion:
Begin by reviewing (1) the indicative to express certainty: **Hay alguien aquí que... Tengo un(a) amigo(a) que...** (2) the use of the subjunctive to talk about nonexistent people or things that are imagined: **No hay nadie aquí que..., Carlos quiere un coche que...**

An adjective clause is one that describes a preceding noun (antecedent). When the noun being described is known by the speaker, the indicative is used. Look at the following examples in which the indicative is used.

La bamba es una canción **que muchos conocen.**	La bamba *is a song **that many people know.***
La canción **que ahora suena** en muchos clubs tuvo su origen en la costa sur de Veracruz.	*The song that is heard today in many clubs originated from the south coast of Veracruz.*

However, when the noun described does not exist or is unknown by the speaker, the subjunctive is used in the adjective clause.

No conozco a nadie **que toque** la guitarra.	*I don't know anyone **who plays** guitar. (I know of no such person.)*
¿Hay alguien **que sepa** cantar *La bamba.*	*Is there anyone **who knows how** to sing La bamba? (There may not be such a person.)*

Remember that an indefinite article is used to mark an unknown person or thing, while the definite article is used with something that is already known. By noticing whether a definite article or an indefinite article is used, you will be better able to determine whether the speaker is talking about something imagined or not, and it will also help you choose between the indicative and the subjunctive when you are speaking. Look at the following pairs of sentences:

Quiero **un coche que corra** rápido.	*I want **a car that goes** fast (An unspecified car; it may not exist)*
Quiero **el coche que corre** rápido.	*I want **the car that goes** fast. (That car, right there)*
Busco **un hombre que sea** piloto.	*I am looking for **a man who is** a pilot. (He may not exist)*
Busco **al hombre que** es piloto.	*I am looking for **a man who is** a pilot. (I know this man; I just don't know where he is.)*

Notice that the personal **a** is not used before an indefinite article if the noun refers to someone unknown. Also notice that when **nadie** and **alguien** are used as direct objects, they are always preceded by a personal **a.**

The following are some more examples that illustrate the use of the subjunctive with unknown or imaginary antecedents:

Necesitamos **un empleado que hable** sueco.	*We need **an employee who speaks** Swedish.*
No conozco a **nadie que hable** sueco.	*I don't know **anyone who speaks** Swedish.*
¿Busca a **alguien que pueda** ayudarlo?	*Are you looking for **someone who can** help you?*
Buscamos **una casa que no cueste** mucho dinero.	*We are looking for **a house that doesn't cost** much.*

K. ¿Existe o no existe? Completa las siguientes oraciones con la forma apropiada de los verbos entre paréntesis. Decide si es necesario usar el subjuntivo o el indicativo.

1. Éste es el cuadro de Frida Kahlo que el museo no _____ (tener).
2. No hay ningún jugador aquí que _____ (jugar) al básquetbol como Michael Jordan.
3. ¿Hay alguien aquí que _____ (querer) boletos para el concierto de Cheryl Crow?
4. Buscamos una persona que _____ (cantar) bien en español y en inglés.
5. Ken Griffey, Jr. es el beisbolista que yo _____ (preferir).
6. Ustedes quieren una persona que _____ (escribir) más de cien palabras por minuto.
7. Edward James Olmos es un actor hispano que _____ (trabajar) en Hollywood.
8. ¿Hay un cuarto en el Hotel Tropicana que _____ (costar) un poco menos?
9. Buscamos el famoso teatro que _____ (presentar) El Ballet Folklórico de México.
10. Todos los estudiantes que _____ (leer) la novela *Don Quijote* el verano próximo, recibirán el premio de un viaje gratis a España.

L. ¿Qué buscas? Un(a) amigo(a) te menciona algo sobre su vida o su trabajo. Indica que entiendes la situación haciendo una pregunta con la información entre paréntesis. Sigue el modelo.

Modelo: Esta compañía no paga bien. (una compañía / pagar mejor)
—*Ah, entonces, ¿buscas una compañía que pague mejor?*

1. La película que dan en el cine Variedades es demasiado triste. (una película / ser cómica)
2. Mi amigo Francisco escribe a máquina muy mal. (una persona / escribir bien)
3. No me gusta ese cuadro porque tiene pocos colores. (un cuadro / tener muchos rojos y verdes)
4. Ese programa me parece demasiado politizado. (un programa / ser más objetivo)
5. Los discos compactos en esa tienda son muy caros. (unos discos compactos / costar menos)
6. Ese tren sale demasiado temprano el lunes. (un tren / salir el lunes por la tarde)
7. Mi jefe no entiende la situación. (una persona / entender lo que pasa)
8. Mi tía no sabe usar la nueva computadora. (una persona / saber cómo funciona)
9. El agente de viajes está muy ocupado. (un agente / ayudarte ahora)
10. Ese vuelo no llegará a tiempo para cenar. (un vuelo / llegar a las 5:00)

M. Idealmente... Piensa en "un(a) amigo(a) ideal" o "un viaje ideal" y prepara seis oraciones para conversar con uno(a) de tus compañeros(as) de clase. Menciona cinco o seis características de esta persona o cosa, usando verbos en el subjuntivo después de la frase **Un ___ ideal para mí es un ____ que...**, etc. Sigue el modelo.

Modelo: *Un amigo ideal para mí es un amigo que sea inteligente*, etc.

LECTURA: *Jon Secada*

ANTES DE LEER

N. Mira el título y las fotos que acompañan este texto y contesta las siguientes preguntas.

1. ¿Qué quiere decir el título de esta lectura?
2. ¿Conoces a este cantante? ¿Quién es?
3. ¿Sabes que canta en español también?
4. ¿Conoces alguna de sus canciones en español? ¿Cuál?
5. ¿Conoces alguna de sus canciones en inglés? ¿Cuál?

GUÍA PARA LA LECTURA

Ñ. Lee el texto rápidamente e indica si se mencionan los temas a continuación. Si se mencionan, indica en qué párrafo se encuentran y a qué se refieren.

1. el lugar de nacimiento de Secada
2. palabras en inglés
3. nombres de algunas ciudades
4. sus padres
5. algunos números
6. nombres de otros cantantes

O. ¿Qué sabes de Jon Secada? Contesta en español.

1. ¿Dónde nació Jon Secada?
2. ¿Dónde asistió a la universidad?
3. ¿Cómo se llama su álbum en español?
4. ¿Qué hizo por sus padres?
5. ¿Cuánto tiempo estuvo su *hit* "Just Another Day" entre la lista de las primeras 10 canciones más populares?
6. ¿Por qué ha tenido éxito en el mundo hispano?

▶ *Jon Secada, un éxito bilingüe: Irresistible en inglés y en español*

Estamos con Jon Secada, que acaba de volver a casa después de una sesión en la que hizo algunos ajustes a su nuevo álbum. El cantante nació en La Habana y se crió en Miami. Moreno y atractivo, no muy alto, quizás mide 5′10″ de estatura, lleva sus incondicionales "jeans", camiseta negra y botas de "cowboy" del mismo color. Para mantenerse en forma y verse bien, corre, hace ejercicio y juega al tenis. Pero más que su condición física le preocupa el estado de sus cuerdas vocales. "Si en la mañana puedo llegar a estas notas altas, sé que el resto del día marchará bien. Presiento que no voy a tener problemas en el estudio", nos dice Jon.

Secada no sólo es un cantante bien parecido, es un cerebro, un académico certificado. Tiene un diploma de maestría en música, específicamente en ejecución de jazz, obtenido con dedicación y esfuerzo en la Universidad de Miami. Su historia es una de verdadero éxito: trabajó durante seis años de universidad cantando por las noches con una banda llamada *The Company*. Todavía, hasta hace poco, iba a ayudarles a sus padres a hacer café cubano o a atender la caja registradora del restaurante de comida cubana que ellos tenían en Hialeah, un barrio de Miami. Con su gran éxito Jon ha conseguido que sus padres se retiren y les ha comprado un auto nuevo y una casa también nueva en su antiguo barrio.

Cuando le preguntamos qué siente al ser famoso, responde: "Es un sentimiento bueno. No me puedo quejar, especialmente por el éxito internacional. Eso es lo más emocionante—ver el disco en otros lugares y otros países." Su ascenso ha sido rápido. "Recuerdo cuando nos dijeron que 'Just Another Day' se estaba moviendo", dice refiriéndose a la escalada de su canción en las listas de popularidad. "Entonces me dije a mí mismo, 'bueno, lo único que quiero es que se coloque entre los primeros 40 lugares de popularidad.' Cuando se colocó entre ellos dije, 'sólo quiero

que llegue a los primeros 20.' Cuando estuvo entre los primeros 20, yo seguí cruzando los dedos: ¡Sería fantástico que llegara a los primeros 10!" Por supuesto todos sus deseos se cumplieron y el disco llegó a los 10 primeros puestos. Jon Secada todavía mueve la cabeza con incredulidad y se ve en la necesidad de contar con más detalle cómo fue su salto definitivo a la fama.

"Me acuerdo que regresaba de Toronto. Nos comunicaron que la canción estaba en el número 6. Ahí me di cuenta de que teníamos un verdadero *hit* y supe con certeza que la canción iba a quedarse dando vueltas por un tiempito. ¡Estuvo entre las primeras 10 durante 12 semanas!"

Desde entonces, Secada se ha mantenido en la cima. Y con un mérito doble porque ha conquistado el mercado inglés y el español, algo muy raro en el mundo de la música. Durante las Navidades de 1992 se vendieron más de un millón de copias de "Just Another Day" mientras que en América Latina y España se vendió la misma cantidad de "Otro día más sin verte", la versión en español del mismo álbum. Ni siquiera veteranos como Julio Iglesias han conseguido triunfar de una forma tan rápida en el mercado americano. Pero, Secada le lleva bastante ventaja: es cubanoamericano, su inglés es tan impecable como su español y ha vivido 21 años en los Estados Unidos. Tiempo suficiente para desarrollar su personalidad tipo "cool" cultivada, sin duda, en el circuito de jazz latino en Miami y por escuchar durante años a sus ídolos Stevie Wonder, Elton John, Billy Joel; además de ver mucha televisión en este país.

Encourage students to search the Internet for sound bytes and additional information about Latin and Spanish music.

Tú dirás ....

Q. Busco algo. Piensa en algo que deseas tener, por ejemplo, un apartamento o casa ideal. Haz una lista de las características. Entonces dile a un(a) compañero(a) lo que buscas.

■ **Modelo:** *Busco un apartamento que esté cerca de la universidad, que tenga piscina, que sea barato y que pueda compartir con mi mejor amigo(a).*

R. ¿Es posible? Piensa en cómo será tu vida en diez años. Haz una lista de cinco posibilidades y compara tu lista con la de un(a) compañero(a). Después, cuéntenle a la clase las posibilidades. Usa expresiones como **es posible, es probable, es imposible, dudo que...**

S. La música en el mundo hispano. Usa la información en las lecturas de esta *etapa* y prepara una breve presentación oral sobre este tema. Tal vez quieras traer música para acompañar tu presentación.

LECTURA: *Andrés Segovia, inventor de la guitarra*

ANTES DE LEER

A. Contesta las siguientes preguntas.

1. ¿Te gusta la música de guitarra?
2. ¿Conoces la música de algún guitarrista? ¿Eric Clapton? ¿Eddie van Halen? ¿Ottmar Liebert? ¿Carlos Santana? ¿Paco de Lucía? ¿John Williams?
3. ¿Tienes un guitarrista favorito?
4. Mira el título y la foto que acompañan este texto. ¿Conoces a este guitarrista?
5. ¿Qué crees que significa "inventor" en esta lectura?

B. Cognado, contexto o diccionario. Al tratar de adivinar el significado de las siguientes palabras, indica si la palabra es un cognado, si la adivinaste por medio del contexto o si tuviste que buscarla en el diccionario. Si tuviste que buscarla en un diccionario, indica la forma de la palabra que aparece en el diccionario y el significado que encontraste allí.

	cognado	contexto	diccionario	forma en el diccionario	significado
nombramiento					
internarse					
arritmia					
cardíaca					
capa					
lentes					
redondos					
maravillas					
entusiasmó					

GUÍA PARA LA LECTURA

C. ¿Aparece o no aparece en el texto?
Lee el texto rápidamente e indica si se mencionan los siguientes temas a continuación. Si se mencionan, indica en qué párrafo se encuentran y a qué se refieren.

1. la edad de Segovia cuando murió
2. nombres de algunos meses
3. nombres de instrumentos musicales además de la guitarra
4. nombres de ciudades españolas
5. algunas fechas
6. nombres de compositores famosos

D. ¿Qué sabes de Segovia?
Contesta en español.

1. ¿Dónde y cómo murió Segovia?
2. ¿Qué inspiró a Segovia a tocar la guitarra?
3. ¿Cuáles eran sus tres características típicas?
4. ¿Por qué se dice que Segovia es el inventor de la guitarra?
5. ¿Cuáles son algunos de los premios que recibió en España?
6. ¿Ganó premios en otros países? ¿Cuáles?

ANDRÉS SEGOVIA, "INVENTOR" DE LA GUITARRA

Andrés Segovia fue a la guitarra lo que Paganini fue al violín: un genio de la interpretación. A los 94 años, no tenía intenciones de morirse. Acababa de llegar de Nueva York donde, desde marzo, había dado una serie de clases que coincidieron con su nombramiento como doctor **honoris causa** en Artes Musicales de la Manhattan School of Music. En abril tuvo que internarse en una clínica por una arritmia cardíaca. Se recuperó y volvió a su hogar en Madrid. Se sentía bien. Estaba mirando la televisión con su esposa, Emilia Corral, y su hijo menor, Carlos Andrés, de 17 años cuando, de pronto, se sintió cansado y dejó de respirar.

"Mi pasión por la música pareció **estallar en llamaradas** cuando aún niño tuve la ocasión de escuchar el preludio de Francisco Tárraga, interpretado por Gabriel Ruiz de Almodóvar en Granada." Desde entonces Segovia no abandonó más su vocación de guitarrista. Desde los tres a los ocho años, en la localidad de Jaén en el sur de España, siguió clases de **solfeo** y violín y se había aficionado a la pintura, promovido económicamente por unos tíos, pues sus padres no tenían muchos recursos.

Comenzó tocando flamenco y melodías populares, pero pronto se **dio cuenta de que** con la guitarra se podían interpretar las composiciones más complejas. **Tuvo éxito** en toda España. En Madrid se hizo famoso por su capa negra, su pelo largo y unos lentes redondos de **marco grueso** que usaba en los recitales.

Segovia se transformó en un verdadero "inventor" de la guitarra como instrumento de concierto. En sus **giras** por todo el mundo demostró cómo se podía hacer maravillas con ella entre los brazos y con una **partitura** de Bach, Beethoven o Joaquín Rodrigo. Otros grandes compositores contemporáneos comenzaron a producir obras especialmente para él. Entusiasmó a miles cuando creó los cursos de Información e Interpretación de Música Española en Compostela, hasta donde comenzaron a llegar **becarios** de todos los continentes.

"La música es para mí el océano", decía, "y los instrumentos son las islas. La guitarra es un maravilloso instrumento, de una gran variedad de colores musicales y con una capacidad para la armonía superior al violín y al violonchelo. La guitarra es como una orquesta pequeña."

El gran guitarrista recibió centenares de premios. Entre ellos están las grandes cruces de Isabel la Católica y Alfonso X el Sabio; el premio "Una vida por la música", considerado el Nóbel de su género; el Premio Nacional (1981) y muchas medallas y discos de oro de diversos países. El Rey Juan Carlos le dio a Segovia el título nobiliario de Marqués de Salobrena en 1981 y dos años después fue recibido como miembro de honor de la Real Academia de Bellas Artes de Santa Isabel de Hungría en Sevilla, la Academia de Estocolmo (Suecia) y la de Santa Cecilia de Roma.

Andrés Segovia

VÍDEO CULTURAL: *Hecho a mano*

VÍDEO CULTURAL

A. Anticipación. ¿Cómo se dice en español?

1. wood   3. glass   5. wool   7. gold
2. steel   4. leather   6. clay   8. silver

B. Participación. El segmento que vas a mirar tiene muchos cognados que pueden ayudarte a entender el contenido. Mira las palabras siguientes y trata de usarlas en una frase completa.

alpaca	llama	apreciar	incorporar	estético
artesano(a)	método	colaborar	metal	variado
delicadeza	paciencia	aumentar	laminado	utilizar
figura	disciplinado			

C. Participación. Mientras miras el vídeo, indica los países en que se trabaja con los siguientes materiales.

	Bolivia	Costa Rica	España	México
1. oro	____	____	____	____
2. lana	____	____	____	____
3. acero	____	____	____	____
4. cerámica	____	____	____	____
5. vidrio	____	____	____	____
6. cuero	____	____	____	____
7. papel de colores	____	____	____	____

D. Comprensión. Contesta las preguntas.

1. ¿En qué ciudad de México hay una antigua fábrica donde los artesanos crean piezas de cerámica?
   a. México, D.F.   b. Guadalajara   c. Puebla

2. ¿Cómo se llama un famoso producto de cerámica de esta antigua fábrica?
   a. talavera   b. taller   c. talento

3. ¿Qué parte del cuerpo utiliza el artesano para hacer objetos de cerámica?
   a. las ranas   b. las mentiras   c. las manos

4. ¿Qué instrumentos usan los artesanos para hacer sus hermosos diseños?
   a. pincel y pintura   b. paciencia y talento   c. pieza y producción

5. ¿Adónde va *primero* el producto final después de salir del taller de cerámica?
   a. a la fábrica   b. a la tienda   c. al hogar

6. ¿Adónde va *luego* el producto final después de salir del taller de cerámica?
   a. a la fábrica   b. a la tienda   c. al hogar

7. Indica si las siguientes afirmaciones son verdaderas (V) o falsas (F).
   a. La piñata tiene una larga tradición desde la época de los aztecas.
   b. Se usan las piñatas en los cumpleaños y en el mes de diciembre.
   c. La artesana da forma a la piñata, usando goma y papel de diversos colores.

E. Personalización. Discuten las siguientes preguntas en grupos.

1. Which traditional arts and crafts most typify your hometown or state? Describe their origins.
2. What are your personal preferences in crafts from different parts of the world? Describe some of their characteristics and their uses.

Intercambio: *El arte y la música*

Con un(a) compañero(a), completa el siguiente crucigrama con la información sobre el arte y la música que has aprendido en este capítulo.

Antes de empezar, mira bien las palabras que aparecen en tu crucigrama. Si hay algo que no sabes, repasa el capítulo para encontrar la información necesaria. Elabora una definición para cada una de las palabras que tienes en tu parte de la actividad. Recuerden: Cuando uno de los dos no comprenda algo, deben usar expresiones como **No comprendo, ¿puedes repetir?**

Estudiante A

En el crucigrama que está a continuación tienes la parte horizontal pero faltan las respuestas para la parte vertical.

Tu compañero(a) va a darte definiciones y pistas *(hints)* para que descubras las palabras que aparecen en su crucigrama y tú tienes que escuchar atentamente y adivinar lo que está describiendo.

Tu compañero(a) va a empezar describiendo el número 1 vertical. Cuando descubras la respuesta, sigues tú describiendo el número 1 horizontal.

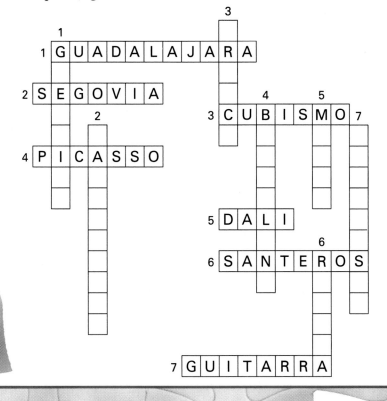

Estudiante B

En el crucigrama que está a continuación tienes la parte vertical pero faltan las respuestas para la parte horizontal.

Tu compañero(a) va a darte definiciones y pistas *(hints)* para que descubras las palabras que aparecen en su crucigrama y tú tienes que escuchar atentamente y adivinar lo que está describiendo.

Tú vas a empezar describiendo el número 1 vertical. Cuando tu compañero(a) descubra la respuesta, le toca a él (ella) describir el número 1 horizontal.

Ahora entre los dos, van a trabajar un poco más. Seleccionen tres palabras verticales y tres horizontales. Busquen toda la información que puedan sobre ellas y preparen tres preguntas de *verdad* o *falso.* Cuando todos los estudiantes hayan terminado, cada pareja hará sus preguntas al resto de la clase.

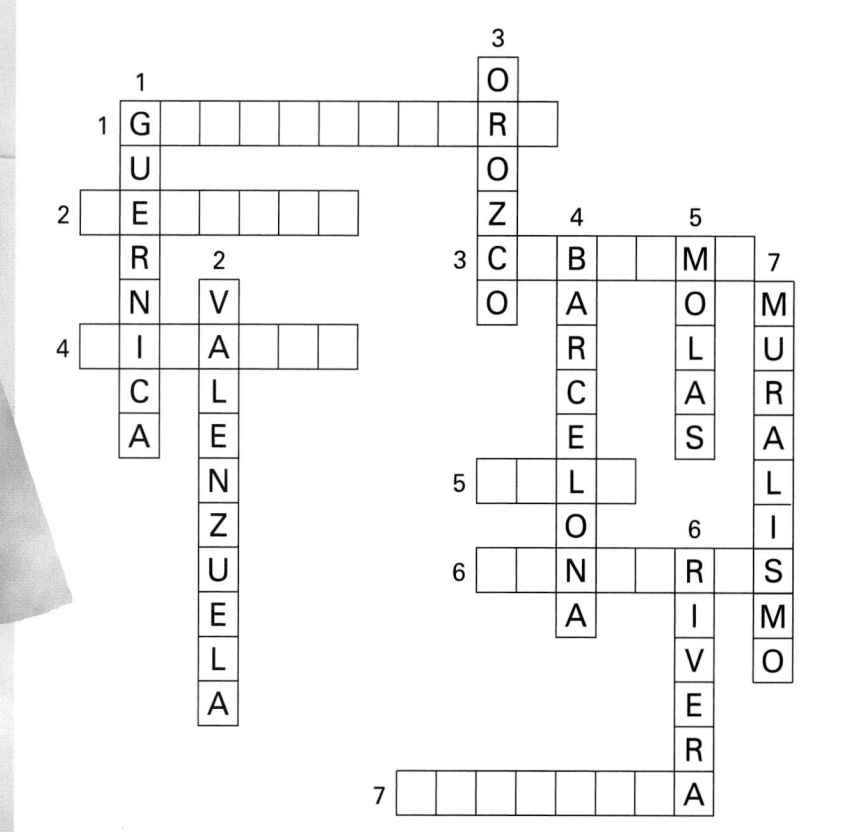

Vocabulario

Para charlar

Para expresar emociones y reacciones
Expressing emotions and reactions

Estoy contento(a) de que... *I'm happy that...*
Me alegro de que... *I'm happy that...*
Qué bueno que... *How great that...*
Qué lástima que... *What a pity that...*
Qué maravilla que... *How wonderful that...*
Qué pena que... *What a shame that...*
Qué raro que... *How strange that...*
Qué vergüenza que... *What a shame that...*
Siento que... *I regret that...*
Temo que... *I fear that...*

Para expresar voluntad o preferencias, deseos
Expressing need or preferences

Él (Ella) manda que... *He (She) orders that...*
Es aconsejable que... *It's advisable that...*
Es importante que... *It's important that...*
Es necesario que... *It's necessary that...*
Espero que... *I hope that...*
Insisto en que... *I insist that...*
Ojalá (que)... *I hope (that)...*
Prefiero que... *I prefer that...*
Prohibo que... *I prohibit...*
sugiero que... *I suggest that...*
recomiendo que... *I recommend that...*
aconsejo que... *I advise that...*
deseo que... *I wish that...*

Para expresar duda, incertidumbre e improbabilidad *Expressing doubt, uncertainty, and improbability*

Dudo que... *I doubt that...*
Es dudoso que... *It is doubtful that...*
Puede ser que... *It could be that...*
No estoy seguro(a)... *I'm not sure...*
No creo que... *I don't think that...*
Es increíble que... *It's incredible that...*
No es verdad que... *It's not true that...*
No es cierto que... *It's not true that...*
(No) Es posible que... *It is (not) possible that...*
(No) Es imposible que... *It is (not) impossible that...*
(No) Es probable que... *It is (not) likely that...*
(No) Es improbable que... *It is (not) unlikely that...*

Para hablar del arte *Talking about art*
Sustantivos
el (la) artista *artist*
el autorretrato *self-portrait*
el color *color*
el cubismo *cubism*
el dibujo *drawing*
el diseño *design*
la diversidad *diversity*
el espíritu *spirit*
la fabricación *manufacture, fabrication*
la fauna *fauna*
la flora *flora*
la forma *form, shape*
la imagen *image*
la imaginería *imagery*
la incrustación *incrustation*
el motivo *motive*
el mural *mural*
el muralismo *muralism*
la obra *work*
la pintura *painting*
el rectángulo *rectangle*
el surrealismo *surrealism*
el taller *studio, workshop*
la tela *cloth, fabric*
el tema *theme*
la tonalidad *tonality*

Adjetivos
abstracto *abstract*
complicado *complicated*
creador *creative*
cuidadoso *careful*
llamativo *flashy, showy*
mitológico *mythological*
real *real*
superpuesto *superimposed*

Verbos

coser *to sew*
dibujar *to draw*
exponer *to exhibit*
pintar *to paint*
tallar *to carve*

Adjetivos

alegre *happy*
conocido *known*
corajudo *hot-tempered*
rechazado *rejected*

Para hablar de la música *Talking about music*

el bajo *bass*
la canción *song*
la danza *dance*
el desengaño *deception*
el estilo *style*
la guitarra *guitar*
el instrumento de cuerda *stringed instrument*
el intérprete *singer*
la letra *lyrics*
la melancolía *melancholy*
la melodía *melody*
la onda *wave*
el piano *piano*
el rasgo *trait*
el ritmo *rhythm*
el repertorio *repertoire*
el violonchelo *violoncello*
el arpa *harp*
el baile *dance*

14 El mundo de las letras

■ **PRIMERA ETAPA**
El Premio Nobel de Literatura:
España y América Latina

■ **SEGUNDA ETAPA**
El realismo y el idealismo

■ **TERCERA ETAPA**
El realismo mágico

INTEGRACIÓN:
LECTURA: Casos
VÍDEO CULTURAL: La literatura es fuego
INTERCAMBIO: ¿Quién es?
ESCRITURA: Actividades en el manual

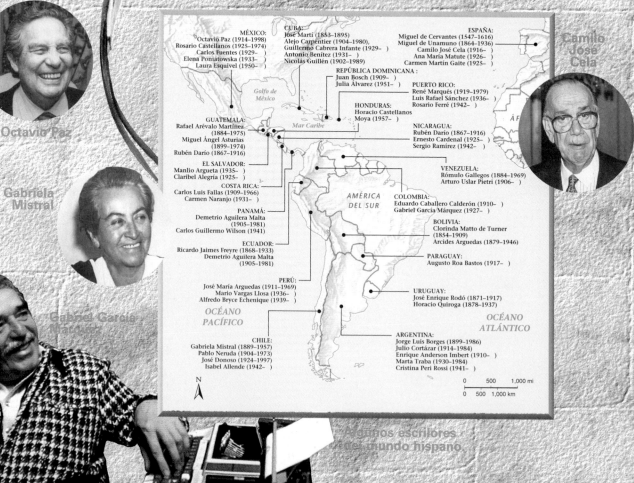

MÉXICO:
Octavio Paz (1914–1998)
Rosario Castellanos (1925–1974)
Carlos Fuentes (1929–)
Elena Poniatowska (1933–)
Laura Esquivel (1950–)

CUBA:
José Martí (1853–1895)
Alejo Carpentier (1904–1980),
Guillermo Cabrera Infante (1929–)
Antonio Benítez (1931–)
Nicolás Guillén (1902–1989)

REPÚBLICA DOMINICANA:
Juan Bosch (1909–)
Julia Álvarez (1951–)

HONDURAS:
Horacio Castellanos
Moya (1957–)

ESPAÑA:
Miguel de Cervantes (1547–1616)
Miguel de Unamuno (1864–1936)
Camilo José Cela (1916–)
Ana María Matute (1926–)
Carmen Martín Gaite (1925–)

PUERTO RICO:
René Marqués (1919–1979)
Luis Rafael Sánchez (1936–)
Rosario Ferré (1942–)

GUATEMALA:
Rafael Arévalo Martínez
(1884–1975)
Miguel Ángel Asturias
(1899–1974)
Rubén Darío (1867–1916)

EL SALVADOR:
Manlio Argueta (1935–)
Claribel Alegría (1925–)

COSTA RICA:
Carlos Luis Fallas (1909–1966)
Carmen Naranjo (1931–)

PANAMÁ:
Demetrio Aguilera Malta
(1905–1981)
Carlos Guillermo Wilson (1941)

ECUADOR:
Ricardo Jaimes Freyre (1868–1933)
Demetrio Aguilera Malta
(1905–1981)

PERÚ:
José María Arguedas (1911–1969)
Mario Vargas Llosa (1936–)
Alfredo Bryce Echenique (1939–)

NICARAGUA:
Rubén Darío (1867–1916)
Ernesto Cardenal (1925–)
Sergio Ramírez (1942–)

VENEZUELA:
Rómulo Gallegos (1884–1969)
Arturo Uslar Pietri (1906–)

COLOMBIA:
Eduardo Caballero Calderón (1910–)
Gabriel García Márquez (1927–)

BOLIVIA:
Clorinda Matto de Turner
(1854–1909)
Arcides Arguedas (1879–1946)

PARAGUAY:
Augusto Roa Bastos (1917–)

URUGUAY:
José Enrique Rodó (1871–1917)
Horacio Quiroga (1878–1937)

ARGENTINA:
Jorge Luis Borges (1899–1986)
Julio Cortázar (1914–1984)
Enrique Anderson Imbert (1910–)
Marta Traba (1930–1984)
Cristina Peri Rossi (1941–)

CHILE:
Gabriela Mistral (1889–1957)
Pablo Neruda (1904–1973)
José Donoso (1924–1997)
Isabel Allende (1942–)

Golfo de México
Mar Caribe
AMÉRICA DEL SUR
OCÉANO PACÍFICO
OCÉANO ATLÁNTICO
ÁF
N
0   500   1,000 mi
0   500   1,000 km

Octavio Paz

Gabriela Mistral

Gabriel García Márquez

Camilo José Cela

Algunos escritores del mundo hispano

Chapter Objectives:

In this chapter you will learn about different types of literature that are representative of several Spanish-speaking countries. By reading brief sample passages from legends, poems, short stories, and novels you will gain an understanding of how literary writing reflects oral tradition, makes creative use of language, involves representations of reality, and relies on the active use of the imagination.

After completing this chapter you will be able to carry out the following tasks:

- talk about the general characteristics of literary texts
- refer to what may or may not occur under certain conditions
- speculate and talk about conditions contrary to fact

The tools you will use to carry out these tasks are:

- **Vocabulary for:**
  - the form and content of legends, poems, short stories, and novels

- **Grammatical structures:**
  - adverbial conjunctions used with the subjunctive
  - the conditional tense and its special uses
  - the imperfect subjunctive and the conditional with "if" clauses
  - more on the subjunctive and the sequence of tenses

Se dice que la cola del quetzal tiene un poder mágico.

Molinos de viento. La Mancha, España.

⟟ PARA EMPEZAR: El Premio Nóbel de Literatura: España y América Latina

Begin the discussion of this topic by asking the students these questions in Spanish.

You might remind students that some of the Nobel Prize winners for Literature from the USA are:

Eugene O'Neill (1936)
Pearl Buck (1938)
William Faulkner (1949)
Ernest Hemingway (1954)
John Steinbeck (1962)
Saul Bellow (1976)
Joseph Brodsky (1987)
Toni Morrison (1993)

Preparación

- Do you know what the Nobel Prize for Literature is?
- Who are some of the people who have won this prize?
- Can you name two or three of the Nobel prize winners for the United States?
- What is the name of the African American woman who received the Nobel Prize in 1993?
- Do you know the name of a writer from Latin America or Spain who has won the prize?

playwright

Prereading:
Make use of this section with a series of questions and answers in Spanish that require the students to scan for information, focusing on one writer at a time. Some exercises are provided for you, but you might add questions of your own.

Desde que se empezó a dar el Premio Nóbel de Literatura a fines del siglo XIX a los mejores escritores del mundo, la Real Academia de Suecia les ha dado el prestigioso premio a diez escritores de países de habla española.

Los cinco ganadores de España son el **dramaturgo** José Echegaray (1904), el dramaturgo Jacinto Benavente (1922), el poeta Juan Ramón Jiménez (1956), el poeta Vicente Aleixandre (1977) y el novelista Camilo José Cela (1989).

Los escritores de América Latina que han ganado el premio son la poeta chilena Gabriela Mistral (1945), el novelista guatemalteco Miguel Ángel Asturias (1967), el poeta chileno Pablo Neruda (1971), el novelista/cuentista colombiano Gabriel García Márquez (1982) y el poeta/ensayista mexicano Octavio Paz (1990).

Los mini-retratos biográficos que siguen dan una idea de quiénes son algunos de estos distinguidos autores del mundo de las letras.

Gabriela Mistral (1889–1957)

País natal: Chile. Fue profesora, diplomática, periodista y poeta por excelencia. El hombre con quién iba a casarse murió trágicamente y este hecho tuvo gran influencia en su obra. En sus versos líricos expresó su visión de la vida como un "valle de lágrimas" donde todos sentimos gozo y dolor. Sus temas constantes son el amor por los niños, la naturaleza, la religión y la compasión por la gente que sufre. Llenos de emoción, sueños y musicalidad, sus mejores poemas están en las colecciones *Desolación, Ternura, Tala* y *Lagar.* Premio Nóbel: 1945.

Camilo José Cela (1916–   )

País natal: España. Ha sido soldado, torero, pintor, actor de cine y periodista, entre otras cosas. Más que nada, ha escrito novelas y ensayos que han tenido gran influencia en España después de la Guerra Civil (1936–1939). Al deformar la realidad en su obra, Cela trata de mostrar que la vida es fea y cruel para mucha gente. El autor cree que la culpa es de la sociedad y que la causa del crimen y la tragedia es la falta de responsabilidad social. La violencia es un grito de protesta en novelas como *La familia de Pascual Duarte* y *La colmena*. Premio Nóbel: 1989.

Prereading: You may wish to read two of these mini-portraits to the class while students follow along, thus using the texts for aural comprehension as well as reading exercises. You can also deal with this section through a series of questions and answers (in Spanish) that oblige students to scan for information, focusing on one writer at a time. Some exercises are provided, but you may add questions of your own.

Gabriel García Márquez (1927–   )

País natal: Colombia. Ha dicho que todo lo que ha escrito o ya lo sabía o ya lo había oído de sus abuelos antes de los ocho años. Trabajó como periodista por muchos años. Muchos de sus fabulosos cuentos y novelas tienen lugar en Macondo—un

pueblo ficticio, pero con todos los aspectos geográficos, históricos y sociopolíticos de su país y de América Latina. Sus personajes pueden ser considerados tragicómicos. La fantasía, el humor y la exageración son elementos típicos de sus novelas, *Cien años de soledad, El otoño del patriarca, El amor en los tiempos del cólera* y *El amor y otros demonios,* así como de algunos de sus cuentos. Premio Nóbel: 1982.

Octavio Paz (1914–1998)

País natal: México. Fue editor, diplomático, profesor universitario y poeta por excelencia. Luchó con las fuerzas republicanas durante la Guerra Civil española. Los temas esenciales de sus ensayos y poemas son la soledad, el tiempo, el amor, la comunicación y la naturaleza. Escribió sobre las actitudes y el carácter del mexicano pero con una preocupación por el destino de todos los seres humanos. Creía que se puede restablecer el diálogo entre la gente por medio de la poesía y el amor. Su obra ensayística incluye *El laberinto de la soledad* y *El arco y la lira*. Sus mejores poemas se encuentran en *Libertad bajo palabra* y *Ladera este*. Premio Nóbel: 1990.

Práctica

A. Significados. Adivina el significado de algunas de las palabras de los mini-retratos biográficos. Encuentra las palabras en inglés en la lista de la derecha que corresponden a las palabras en español en la lista de la izquierda.

1. periodista	a. stories
2. los sueños	b. guilt
3. la libertad	c. joy
4. ficticio	d. nature
5. la soledad	e. liberty
6. los cuentos	f. journalist
7. los personajes	g. destiny
8. los ensayos	h. fictitious
9. el destino	i. dreams
10. el gozo	j. characters
11. la culpa	k. solitude
12. la naturaleza	l. essays

B. Temas literarios. Para cada tema literario que sigue, nombra a la persona en los mini-retratos que tiene un interés especial en el tema.

1. la fantasía y la exageración
2. la poesía y el amor como medios de comunicación
3. la imposibilidad de vivir de una manera honesta
4. la violencia como manera de protestar
5. la vida alegre y triste de los perros de la ciudad
6. la vida como un valle de lágrimas

C. ¿Has comprendido? Contesta las siguientes preguntas sobre la información que aparece en los mini-retratos de los escritores.

1. ¿Quién les tiene un cariño especial a los niños?
2. ¿A quién le interesa escribir ensayos sobre los problemas ecológicos?
3. ¿Qué escritor cree que la falta de responsabilidad social causa el crimen?
4. ¿Quién escribe con humor sobre un pueblo que representa a América Latina?
5. ¿Cuál de los escritores incluye mucha información sobre la música en sus libros?
6. ¿Para quién son importantes las actitudes y el carácter de los mexicanos?

D. Un diálogo imaginario. Usando la información que se encuentra en los mini-retratos, escribe un diálogo en español entre dos de los ganadores del Premio Nóbel. Incluye en las preguntas y en los comentarios de la conversación información sobre su vida, su obra y sus actitudes y preferencias. (Trata de escribir de 16 a 20 oraciones en total.)

LECTURA: *Poemas de una ganadora del Premio Nóbel*

ANTES DE LEER

E. Mira las palabras glosadas para saber su significado antes de leer el poema. ¿Qué idea te dan sobre el contenido del poema?

F. ¿Qué significa el título? ¿Qué te viene a la mente cuando piensas en una nevada?

Estos versos son un ejemplo de la emoción que Gabriela Mistral (Chile, 1889–1957) sentía por la naturaleza. Varios de sus poemas revelan una espiritualidad que asocia la naturaleza con un poder divino. Los sentimientos religiosos de la poeta siempre incluyen el mundo físico de los objetos. Los versos de Mistral son buenos ejemplos del uso del lenguaje sencillo.

GUÍA PARA LA LECTURA

G. Rimas. ¿Cuáles son algunas de las palabras claves que contienen sonidos similares? Añade otras palabras que sigan las mismas rimas. Por ejemplo: **flor, Señor.**

H. El sentido *(sense)* del poema. Contesta las preguntas sobre el poema.

1. ¿Qué adjetivos usa Mistral en sus descripciones?
2. Según la poeta, ¿qué es posible que sea la nieve?
3. ¿Qué ejemplos hay de la humanización de la naturaleza?
4. ¿Qué emociones se expresan en el poema? ¿En qué versos?
5. ¿Por qué tenemos la impresión de que estamos incluídos en el poema?
6. ¿Cuál sería "el mensaje a los hombres" que se sugiere al final?

I. Resumen. Lee el poema otra vez y escribe un breve resumen de cinco a seis oraciones sobre lo que describe Mistral en este poema.

Mientras baja la nieve

Ha bajado la nieve, divina criatura,
    el valle a conocer,
Ha bajado la nieve, esposa de la **estrella**   star
    ¡Mirémosla caer!
¡Dulce! Llega sin ruido, como los suaves seres
    que **recelan** dañar.   they fear
Así baja la luna y así bajan los sueños.
    ¡Mirémosla bajar!
¡Pura! Mira tu valle como los está **bordando**   embroidering
    de su ligero **azahar.**   orange flower
Tiene unos dulces dedos tan leves y sutiles
    que **rozan** sin rozar.   they rub
¡Bella! ¿No te parece que sea el **don** magnífico   gift
    de un alto **Donador?**   Giftgiver
Detrás de las estrellas su ancho **peplo** de **seda**   a short skirt / silk
    desgaja sin **rumor.**   it breaks into pieces / noise
Déjala que en tu frente te **diluya** su pluma   dilute
    y te **prenda** su flor.   pin on
¡Quién sabe si no trae un mensaje a los hombres
    de parte del Señor!

Ex. I:  Group

Variation: Put students in groups of 3 and tell them that they will be writing a literary review of Mistral's poem. Have them answer the questions and then structure the answers into a brief written review of the poem. Allow 5–10 minutes to answer the questions (or assign as homework) and then allow 10–15 minutes to write and edit the review. Once done, have each group exchange their review with another group's. After allowing time for reading ask different groups to comment on how the review they just read differs or is similar to theirs.

Master 63: Más sobre el subjuntivo

Contextualize the presentation of this structure by telling students about your plans for this weekend. Tell them that the class discussions about the prize-winning authors has inspired you to do more reading. You are trying to make time in your schedule this weekend to be able to buy some books and do your reading. Tell them: **Voy a poder pasar todo el fin de semana leyendo libros con tal de que no me molesten mis compañeros de casa (hijos...). En caso de que me interrumpan yo les diré que estoy enfermo(a) y necesito descansar todo el fin de semana...** Use as many of the adverbial expressions as possible. Check for comprehension.

GRAMMAR NOTE:

Note: The first letter of each of these conjunctions in this order spells the word **ESCAPA,** which may help you remember them.

ENFOQUE ESTRUCTURAL — El subjuntivo y otras expresiones adverbiales

El subjuntivo después de ciertas conjunciones: *en caso de que, sin que, con tal de que, a menos que, para que, antes de que*

There are certain conjunctions in Spanish after which the subjunctive is always used because they usually relate one event to another by projecting them into the realm of the unknown or by linking them to an event that may or may not occur.

En caso de que salga temprano, te llamaré.	*In case I leave early, I'll call you.*
El perro no puede salir **sin que** lo **veamos.**	*The dog can't get out **without (our) seeing** him.*

The following conjunctions are always used with the subjunctive: **en caso de que, sin que, con tal de que, antes de que, para que, a menos que.**

Iré al cine **con tal de que** tú **pagues.**	*I'll go to the movies **as long as** you **pay.***
No pueden llamar **a menos que** les **des** tu número.	*They can't call **unless** you **give** them your number.*
Elsa habla español en casa **para que** sus hijos lo **aprendan.**	*Elsa speaks Spanish at home **so that** her children will **learn** it.*
¿Piensas comer **antes de que lleguemos?**	*Do you plan to eat **before** we **arrive?***

Práctica

J. Circunstancias. Elige uno de los verbos entre paréntesis para completar las frases siguientes.

1. Yo no pienso salir de viaje a menos que ustedes _____ (llegar, terminar, escribir, regresar, llamar).
2. Mi tía Alicia dice que está preparada en caso de que yo no _____ (volver, llamar, entender, ganar, correr).
3. El jefe siempre lleva el dinero al banco antes de que los empleados _____ (salir, ir, terminar, venir).
4. Mis padres hacen todo lo posible para que nosotros _____ (aprender, divertirse, estudiar, viajar, entender).
5. Ese empleado siempre se va temprano sin que el jefe lo _____ (permitir, ver, saber, llamar, parar).
6. Todos te ayudaremos con tal de que tú _____ (trabajar, pagar, venir, estar, volver).

K. Todo depende... Trabaja con un(a) compañero(a) de clase para completar las oraciones de una manera original, indicando que la situación depende de algo. Sigan el modelo.

■ **Modelo:**   El editor publica la revista para que la gente...
               El editor publica la revista para que la gente lea en español.

1. Dicen que la actriz siempre sale del teatro sin que el público...
2. ¿Quiénes pueden leer esa novela antes de que el profesor...?
3. No quiero comprar la novela a menos que yo...
4. ¿Qué piensas hacer en caso de que tu novio(a) no...?
5. Muchos actores de cine dicen que sólo trabajan para que el público...
6. El (La) novelista espera escribir otra obra con tal de que él (ella)...

LECTURA: *El agua lo trajo, el agua se lo llevó* *(leyenda maya)*

▶*Introducción: Las raíces de la literatura en América Latina*

La leyenda que sigue es un ejemplo de las leyendas de la civilización maya que floreció muchos siglos antes de la llegada de los españoles en lo que hoy es México y Centroamérica. Recientemente el traductor Domingo Dzul Poot, de Campeche, México, adaptó de la lengua maya al español varias de estas leyendas.

ANTES DE LEER

L. Verbos. Mira el texto de la leyenda rápidamente e identifica los verbos de la siguiente lista. Después, con otro(a) estudiante escribe una definición que explique su significado. Ahora, consulta un diccionario para ver las definiciones que allí aparecen, comparándolas con las que ustedes escribieron.

1. rezar   4. pastar   7. retrasarse
2. mezclar   5. darse prisa   8. ahogarse
3. ordeñar   6. cruzar

M. Ahora busca los nombres de personas que aparecen en el texto e indica quiénes son los que se llaman así.

GUÍA PARA LA LECTURA

N. El contenido. Lee el texto y contesta las siguientes preguntas.

1. ¿Qué tipo de trabajo hace Tata Bus?
2. ¿Qué tipo de persona es el vecino de Tata Bus? ¿Cómo lo sabemos?
3. ¿Quién es San Isidro?
4. ¿Qué le promete Tata Bus a San Isidro?
5. ¿Cuál es el milagro que hace San Isidro?
6. ¿Qué hace Tata Bus inmediatamente después del milagro?
7. ¿Para qué sirve el calabazo?
8. ¿Qué decidió hacer un día Tata Bus con la leche que le pidió una señora?
9. Después de esto, ¿qué pasó con las vacas?

Ñ. Interpretación

1. ¿Qué significan las palabras de Tata Bus "¡y qué más da! El agua me las trajo, el agua se las llevó!"?
2. Después de todo, ¿qué tipo de persona es Tata Bus?
3. ¿Cuál es una de las lecciones que enseña esta leyenda?
4. ¿Cuál sería otro título que podría tener esta leyenda?

▶ *El agua lo trajo, el agua se lo llevó (Leyenda maya)*

Tata Bus era un pobre campesino que vivía en un pequeño pueblo. Tata Bus rezaba a San Isidro, el santo patrón de los animales.

—¡Ay, San Isidro! Por favor, dame tan siquiera una vaca con su **becerro.** Te prometo que yo nunca venderé leche mezclada con agua como lo hace mi **vecino** al que llaman "**aguador**".

Un día San Isidro hizo un **milagro** y le concedió su deseo. Tata Bus comenzó a vender leche pura de su vaquita a tres personas.

Un día vino una señora y le suplicó:

—Tata Bus, véndeme siquiera medio **calabazo** de leche cada día.

Tata Bus dijo que iba a pensarlo. Si le ponía medio calabazo de agua a toda la leche que **ordeñaba,** seguramente no se notaría. De ese modo podría venderle a la señora lo que le pedía. Y así lo hizo. Con el dinero que ganó de la **venta** del medio calabazo diario de agua, compró dos vaquitas más. Todos los días las llevaba al campo a **pastar.**

Un día, mientras pastaba su **ganado,** cayó un torrencial **aguacero.** Tata Bus se dio prisa para llevar de nuevo sus vacas al pueblo. La vaca que le había dado San Isidro cruzó por una **hondonada** pero las dos que había comprado con el dinero de la venta del medio calabazo de agua se **retrasaron** y se **ahogaron** ahí. Entonces Tata Bus dijo:

—¡**Y qué más da!** ¡El agua me las trajo, el agua se las llevó!

Comentarios

culturales

El multiculturalismo hispanohablante

 Play Textbook audio.

Por lo general, los países hispanohablantes se formaron de la mezcla de diversas razas y culturas. Ésta es una de las complejas y fascinantes realidades que se reflejan en su cultura. En efecto, muchos escritores hispanohablantes siguen la tradición del gran maestro español Miguel de Cervantes que incorporó elementos españoles, árabes, africanos, orientales, europeos y mediterráneos en sus famosos libros de ficción.

A lo largo de los siglos, los escritores de lengua española, sean de España o de América Latina, tienen en común no sólo el poder expresivo de su idioma, sino también una visión totalizadora del mundo. En esta visión se incluye lo histórico y lo mítico, lo sublime y lo grotesco, lo bello y lo feo, lo real y lo irreal, lo serio y lo cómico.

INTEGRACIÓN CULTURAL

1. Por lo general, ¿cuál es un aspecto importante de la formación de las culturas hispanohablantes?
2. ¿Qué escritor español ha servido como maestro para muchos escritores a lo largo de los años?
3. ¿Qué tienen en común los escritores de España y de América Latina?
4. ¿Cómo se caracteriza la visión del mundo que tienen muchos escritores hispanohablantes?

Answers, Integración

1. La mezcla de diversas razas y culturas
2. Miguel de Cervantes
3. el idioma; una visión totalizadora del mundo
4. incluye lo histórico y lo mítico, lo sublime y lo grotesco, lo bello y lo feo, lo real y lo irreal, lo serio y lo cómico

Tú dirás

O. Factores de importancia. Trabaja con otro(a) estudiante para completar las siguientes frases de una forma lógica. Presten atención a las expresiones adverbiales para saber si deben usar el indicativo o el subjuntivo.

Ex. O: Pairs

■ **Modelo:** Pienso ir a la conferencia literaria a menos que...
   Pienso ir a la conferencia literaria a menos que tú no puedas ir.

1. El escritor va a la ceremonia para que...
2. Compraremos algunas de las novelas cuando...
3. Es importante saber algo del escritor antes de que...
4. Leeré esos cuentos con tal de que...
5. Hablaremos sobre el ganador del Premio Nóbel aunque estoy seguro(a) que...
6. El profesor siempre da ejemplos del texto en caso de que...
7. No quiero leer esa obra porque...
8. Siempre hay un examen después de la conferencia a menos que...

P. ¿Qué pasará? Habla con otro(a) estudiante sobre varias posibilidades para el futuro. Indiquen algunas cosas que pueden interferir con estos planes. Usen el tiempo futuro y las siguientes expresiones adverbiales prestando atención al subjuntivo de los verbos en la segunda cláusula: **en caso de que, sin que, con tal de que, antes de que, para que, a menos que.**

SEGUNDA ETAPA

PARA EMPEZAR: El realismo y el idealismo

Present this new topic to the students by developing a class discussion in Spanish based on these questions.

Suggestion: Discuss idealism and realism in general terms in English before focusing on the opening reading about how these characteristics are represented in Cervantes' characters. Ask students to point out the differences in meaning between the two terms and ask for examples to help clarify.

Preparación

- Have you heard of don Quijote de la Mancha? Sancho Panza? Miguel de Cervantes?
- What do the terms "realism" and "idealism" mean to you in general?

Comentarios culturales

La popularidad de El Quijote.

El ingenioso hidalgo don Quijote de la Mancha es una de las creaciones literarias más populares en la historia de la literatura. Después de la *Biblia* es una de las obras más publicadas y más traducidas del mundo. El vocabulario que usa Cervantes en esta obra es uno de los más extensos de la historia literaria. Como ejemplo, en comparación con las 6.000 palabras distintas que contiene la versión inglesa de la *Biblia* (King James), Cervantes usa unas 8.200 palabras distintas en *El Quijote.*

Los lectores de la famosa novela de Cervantes han hecho innumerables

Don Quijote y Sancho Panza pintados por Pablo Picasso

interpretaciones de ella a lo largo de los siglos. Sin embargo, la mayoría está de acuerdo en que los dos protagonistas, don Quijote y Sancho Panza, representan **valores** *(values)* espirituales que nos dan una **amplia** *(broad)* y rica visión de la naturaleza humana y del **destino** *(destiny, fate)* del ser humano en general. Don Quijote y Sancho son hijos de España pero, a la vez, son hombres universales y **eternos** *(eternal)*.

Don Quijote, el gran idealista, tiene una **fe ciega** *(blind faith)* en los valores del espíritu como la **bondad** *(kindness)*, la **honra** *(honor)*, la **valentía** *(courage)*, la **lealtad** *(loyalty)* y el amor a la justicia. Está convencido de que es todo un caballero que tiene la noble misión de reformar el mundo. Sale en busca de aventuras con la idea de hacer bien a todos para que triunfe la justicia. Por el contrario Sancho, el humilde realista, con su fuerte sentido práctico de las cosas, tiene mucho interés en las cosas materiales. Es un **labrador** *(farm-hand, peasant)* **sencillo** *(simple)* y **grosero** *(vulgar)* que siempre tiene hambre y sed. La razón por la que decide acompañar a don Quijote en sus aventuras es porque espera convertirse en un hombre rico y famoso cuando vuelva a su casa.

Miguel de Cervantes (1547–1616) cambinó el realismo y el idealismo, al escribir una de las obras más universales de la literatura: El ingenioso hidalgo don Quijote de la Mancha.

INTEGRACIÓN CULTURAL

Verdadero / Falso. Decide si las siguientes oraciones son verdaderas o falsas. Corrige las falsas de acuerdo con la información que acabas de leer.

1. Cervantes escribió una de las obras literarias más leídas del mundo.
2. En su novela clásica Cervantes presenta una visión universal de cómo sienten y cómo actúan los seres humanos en general.
3. Los críticos han hecho sólo dos o tres interpretaciones de esta obra.
4. Don Quijote cree que es posible mejorar las cosas.
5. Don Quijote tiene mucho interés en la comida y la bebida.
6. A Sancho le interesa la manera más directa y eficiente de hacer las cosas.
7. Sancho Panza casi siempre piensa en cómo puede ayudar a la gente.

Explain that the illustration is an example of the engraved illustrations that appeared in early editions of novels of chivalry dating back some five hundred years. The books were popular reading before and during Cervantes' time, and he chose to satirize them in his classic work. Ask students in English what a "knight in shining armor" is. Brainstorm together about the ideals and values associated with chivalry. Ask if students can identify any famous knights from myth, literature, or film (such as Ivanhoe, King Arthur and the Knights of the Round Table— including Lancelot, Sir Galahad, and Luke Skywalker from the Star Wars movie trilogy) and, of course, don Quijote from the Broadway musical *Man of La Mancha*.

LECTURA: *Don Quijote: Nuestro héroe*

ANTES DE LEER

A. Los caballeros andantes. Antes de leer el pasaje sobre don Quijote, piensa en lo que sabes de los caballeros andantes y contesta las siguientes preguntas.

1. ¿Cómo son los caballeros andantes? ¿Qué características asocias con ellos?
2. ¿Qué hacen los caballeros andantes por lo general?
3. ¿Puedes dar un ejemplo de un caballero andante? ¿Quién es?

Una de las páginas de una novela de caballerías que era muy popular en la época de Cervantes

Answers to Ex. B
aventurero, individualista, valiente, delgado, curioso, ambicioso

B. Así es. ¿Cuáles de las siguientes palabras asocias con don Quijote?

perezoso	gordo	curioso	cruel	bajo
joven	valiente	pobre	ambicioso	tonto
débil	delgado	antisocial	alegre	malo
aventurero	aburrido	fuerte	egoísta	
individualista	guapo	activo	paciente	

C. Para anticipar el contenido. Ahora lee las preguntas en la sección *Comprensión* para anticipar el contenido. Después lee el pasaje y contesta las preguntas.

GUÍA PARA LA LECTURA

Answer, Ex. D: 3

D. ¿Comprendiste? Escoge la frase que mejor describa el propósito del narrador del texto que acabas de leer.

1. dar una serie de opiniones personales sobre los viejos locos
2. narrar una secuencia de acontecimientos importantes en la historia española
3. describir el temperamento de un protagonista interesante
4. convencer a los lectores que vale la pena leer libros de caballerías

E. Comprensión.
Contesta en español las siguientes preguntas sobre la lectura.

1. ¿Quiénes vivían con el hidalgo en su casa?
2. ¿Cuántos años tenía don Quijote?
3. ¿Cómo era físicamente?
4. ¿Cómo pasaba don Quijote la mayoría de su tiempo?
5. ¿Cómo lo afectó esta actividad?
6. ¿Cuál era el tema de las disputas entre don Quijote, el cura y el barbero?
7. ¿Qué decidió hacer don Quijote por fin? ¿Por qué tomó esta decisión?
8. Después de limpiar las armas, ¿qué descubrió don Quijote que necesitaba?
9. ¿Cómo resolvió el protagonista su problema?

F. ¿Qué pasará con don Quijote?
Ahora que ya sabes algo sobre el carácter de don Quijote, escribe un párrafo de seis oraciones describiendo lo que tú crees que él hará al día siguiente. Usa el tiempo futuro en tu descripción.

▶Don Quijote por Miguel de Cervantes

Nuestro héroe

En un lugar de la Mancha, de cuyo nombre no quiero acordarme, no hace mucho tiempo que vivía un **hidalgo** de los de **lanza en astillero, adarga** antigua, **rocín** flaco y **galgo corredor.** Tenía en su casa un **ama** que pasaba de cuarenta años, y una sobrina que no llegaba a los veinte. La edad de nuestro hidalgo era de cincuenta años; era fuerte, delgado, muy activo y amigo de la **caza.** Los momentos en que no tenía nada que hacer (que eran la mayoría del año), se dedicaba a leer libros de caballerías con tanta afición y gusto que olvidó casi completamente el ejercicio de la caza, y aun la administración de su hacienda. Llegaron a tanto su curiosidad y locura en esto, que vendió muchas tierras para comprar libros de caballerías para leer, y así llevó a su casa muchos libros de esta clase.

Tuvo muchas disputas con el **cura** de su lugar, y con maestro Nicolás, el barbero del mismo pueblo, sobre cuál había sido mejor caballero, Palmerín de Inglaterra o Amadís de Gaula, y sobre otras cuestiones semejantes que trataban de los personajes y episodios de los libros de caballerías. Se aplicó tanto a su lectura que pasaba todo el tiempo, día y noche, leyendo. Se llenó la cabeza de todas aquellas locuras que leía en los libros, tanto de **encantamientos** como de disputas, batallas, duelos, heridas, amores, infortunios y absurdos imposibles. Tuvieron tal efecto sobre su imaginación que le parecían verdad todas aquellas invenciones que leía, y para él no había otra historia más cierta en el mundo.

Como ya había perdido **su juicio,** le pareció necesario, para aumentar su gloria y para servir a su nación, hacerse **caballero andante,** e irse por todo el mundo con sus armas y caballo a buscar aventuras. Pensaba dedicarse a hacer todo lo que había leído que los caballeros andantes hacían, destruyendo todo tipo de deshonor y poniéndose en circunstancias y peligros, donde, terminándolos, obtendría eterna gloria y fama. Lo primero que hizo fue limpiar unas **armas** que habían sido de sus **bisabuelos.** Las limpió y las reparó lo mejor que pudo, pero vio que tenían una gran falta, y era que no tenían **celada;** más con su habilidad hizo una celada de

Answers, Ex. E
1. Un ama de casa y una sobrina vivían con el hidalgo. 2. Don Quijote tenía 50 años. 3. Era fuerte y delgado. 4. Pasaba la mayoría de su tiempo leyendo. 5. Olvidó el ejercicio de la caza y la administración de su hacienda y vendió tierras para comprar libros. 6. Disputaban sobre cuál había sido el mejor caballero, Palmerín de Inglaterra o Amadís de Gaula. 7. Decidió hacerse caballero andante para aumentar su gloria y para servir a su nación. 8. Descubrió que necesitaba una celada. 9. Hizo una celada de cartón.

Ex. F: Pairs

Do this as a pair activity where students spend 5–10 minutes writing the paragraph and then another 3–4 minutes editing their paragraph. When done, have the pairs share their texts with others.

nobleman / lance / shield
racinghound / housekeeper

hunting

priest

magic spells

sanity
knight-errant

weapons
great-grandparents
visor

cardboard / sword

Ex. G:  Pairs

Ex. H: Pairs

cartón. Para probar si era fuerte, sacó su **espada** y le dio dos golpes con los que deshizo en un momento la que había hecho en una semana. Volvió a hacerla de nuevo y quedó tan satisfecho de ella, que sin probar su firmeza la consideró finísima celada.

Repaso ·······························

G. Planes inseguros. Trabaja con otro(a) estudiante para completar la siguiente información con tu propio comentario. Presta atención al uso de los verbos en el subjuntivo.

1. Pensamos ir a escuchar el discurso del novelista a menos que...
2. Debemos terminar de leer la novela para que...
3. Siempre voy a las librerías en caso de que...
4. Te ayudaré con tu ensayo crítico con tal de que...
5. Ese escritor dice que siempre escribe sin que...
6. Es una buena idea leer toda la obra antes de que...
7. Iremos a ver la película en que se basa la novela a menos que...

H. Una persona ideal. Discute con un(a) compañero(a) las características que definirían a un(a) compañero(a) de apartamento ideal. Comiencen sus comentarios con "un(a) compañero(a) ideal para mí es un hombre/una mujer que…" Recuerda que los verbos que uses deben estar en el subjuntivo porque estas personas todavía son parte de tu imaginación.

ENFOQUE ESTRUCTURAL — El condicional

El condicional

The conditional tense in Spanish is equivalent to the English structure *would* + verb. It simply expresses what would happen if the conditions were right.

¿Viajarías conmigo?	*Would you travel with me?*
Sí, **me gustaría** viajar contigo.	*Yes, I would like to travel with you.*
¿No **irían** tus primos con ellos?	*Wouldn't your cousins go with them?*
¿Venderías tu bicicleta?	*Would you sell your bicycle?*
Pedro dijo que **llegaría** a las 6:00.	*Pedro said he would arrive at 6:00.*

Another way to think about the conditional is that it is related to the past the way the future is to the present. That is, the conditional refers to the *future* of an action in the *past*:

Dicen que **volverán** temprano.	*They say they will return early.*
Dijeron que **volverían** temprano.	*They said they would return early.*

The conditional tense is very similar to the future tense. It is formed by adding the endings **-ía, -ías, -ía, -íamos, -íais,** and **-ían** to the infinitive, whether it be an **-ar, -er,** or **-ir** verb.

llegar

yo	llegaría		nosotros	llegaríamos
tú	llegarías		vosotros	llegaríais
Ud.			Uds.	
él	} llegaría		ellos	} llegarían
ella			ellas	

ver

yo	vería		nosotros	veríamos
tú	verías		vosotros	veríais
Ud.			Uds.	
él	} vería		ellos	} verían
ella			ellas	

pedir

yo	pediría		nosotros	pediríamos
tú	pedirías		vosotros	pediríais
Ud.			Uds.	
él	} pediría		ellos	} pedirían
ella			ellas	

The conditional *is not* used in Spanish to refer to something that "used to be" the way *would* can be used in English: "When we were kids, we would always go to the movies on Saturdays." (As you have learned, the imperfect tense is used in Spanish to talk about habitual actions in the past.)

As you have learned already, some verbs use a different stem to form the future tense. They use these same stems to form the conditional tense. The endings, however, are the same as for regular verbs (**-ía, -ías, -ía, -íamos, -ías, -ían**). The most common verbs that do not use the infinitive as the stem to form either the future or the conditional tense are:

decir	**dir-**	yo **diría**	
haber	**habr-**	yo **habría**	
hacer	**har-**	yo **haría**	
poder	**podr-**	yo **podría**	
poner	**pondr-**	yo **pondría**	
querer	**querr-**	yo **querría**	} tú **dirías**, etc.
saber	**sabr-**	yo **sabría**	
salir	**saldr-**	yo **saldría**	
tener	**tendr-**	yo **tendría**	
venir	**vendr-**	yo **vendría**	

Suggestion: Write some sentences on the board that contain other examples of the conditional used for wondering about something, e.g., **¿Cuánto costaría...? ¿Dónde estaría...?** Ask students to contribute examples as well.

IRM Master 65: Usos especiales del condicional

Usos especiales del condicional

Just as the future tense may be used in Spanish to wonder about an action or a situation related to the present, so the conditional tense is used to make a guess about something in the past.

¿Cuántos años **tendría** ese escritor?	*I wonder how old that writer was?* (How old could that writer have been?)
Tendría unos setenta años.	*He was probably* about seventy years old.
¿Quién sería esa persona?	*I wonder who* that person was? (Who could that person have been?)

Another common use of the conditional tense is to express politeness in a statement or soften a request, much as the phrases *I would like to . . .* or *Would you mind . . .* do in English.

¿Te gustaría ir conmigo?	*Would you like* to go with me?
¿Tendría Ud. tiempo para ayudarme?	*Would you have* time to help me?

Práctica

Answers, Ex. I
1. Me dijeron que les darían un premio a los tres mejores escritores. 2. Ramón dijo que le gustaría leer los poemas de Neruda. 3. ¿Dijeron Uds. que no irían a la ceremonia? 4. Mi amigo dijo que no leería esa novela. 5. ¿Dijiste que no escribirías la composición? 6. Los críticos dijeron que la gente no entendería la novela. 7. El editor dijo que publicaría otra revista en español. 8. ¿Ustedes dijeron que no sería difícil encontrar a esa autora? 9. Carlos y Marta dijeron que verían a muchos escritores en la fiesta. 10. Yo dije que algún día Carlos Fuentes, de México, ganaría el Premio Nóbel.

I. ¿Qué dijeron que harían? Cambia el primer verbo al pretérito y el segundo al condicional para hacer una referencia al pasado.

■ **Modelo:** Dice que escribirá una novela.
Dijo que escribiría una novela.

1. Me dicen que les darán un premio a los tres mejores escritores.
2. Ramón dice que le gusta leer los poemas de Neruda.
3. ¿Dicen ustedes que no irán a la ceremonia?
4. Mi amigo dice que no leerá esa novela.
5. ¿Dices que no escribirás la composición?
6. Los críticos dicen que la gente no entenderá la novela.
7. El editor dice que publicará otra revista en español.
8. ¿Ustedes dicen que no será difícil encontrar a esa autora?
9. Carlos y Marta dicen que verán a muchos escritores en la fiesta.
10. Yo digo que algún día Carlos Fuentes, de México, ganará el Premio Nóbel.

J. ¿Quién sabe por qué? Contesta las siguientes preguntas, expresando incertidumbre o conjetura *(conjecture)* sobre el pasado. Usa la información entre paréntesis en tu respuesta. Sigue el modelo.

■ **Modelo:** ¿Por qué no aceptó ese autor el premio literario? (estar/muy enojado) *Estaría muy enojado.*

1. ¿Cuántos años tenía el escritor cuando murió? (tener / ochenta años)
2. ¿Quiénes vinieron para hablar de la novela? (venir / los que la leyeron)
3. ¿Sabes quién llamó por teléfono durante la ceremonia? (ser / el presidente)
4. ¿Qué dijo el maestro de ceremonias? (decir / lo que siempre dice)
5. ¿Por qué no caminaron todos por el parque después de la reunión? (hacer / mucho frío)

6. ¿Cómo regresaron los escritores al hotel a la medianoche? (tomar / un taxi)

7. ¿Cuánto costó ese libro tan viejo de Cervantes? (costar / unos 300 dólares)

8. ¿Cómo pagó el comité por el premio si no tenía fondos? (pagar / con contribuciones de los socios)

9. ¿Por qué puso la escritora el libro en su maleta? (poner / para no dejarlo en el cuarto del hotel)

10. ¿A qué hora llegaron los jueces anoche? (ser / las 3:00 de la mañana)

K. La cortesía es importante. Cambia las oraciones a una forma más cortés *(courteous)*. Sigue el modelo.

■ **Modelo:** ¿Puedes ayudarme con el coche?
¿Podrías ayudarme con el coche?

1. ¿Puedo usar tu raqueta esta tarde?
2. ¿Tiene usted tiempo para ir conmigo?
3. Ella no debe hablar de esa manera.
4. Prefiero ver otra película.
5. ¿Me puede decir usted qué hora es?
6. ¿Les gusta a tus padres viajar en tren?
7. No es ninguna molestia.
8. ¿Me da usted la oporunidad de trabajar aquí este verano?
9. Es posible hablar con el jefe mañana.
10. Puedes hablarme de tu problema.

IRM Master 66: El imperfecto del subjuntivo

ENFOQUE ESTRUCTURAL — El imperfecto del subjuntivo

You have already learned that the subjunctive mood is always used in situations involving (a) transfer of will, (b) emotional reactions, and (c) the uncertain or unreal ("the twilight zone"). Another matter related to the use of the subjunctive involves the sequence of tenses in two-part sentences with a verb in each part.

1. If the present tense verb in the main clause of a sentence calls for the use of the subjunctive in the **que** clause, the verb in the **que** clause will be in the present subjunctive.

2. If the preterite or imperfect tense verb in the main clause calls for the use of the subjunctive in the **que** clause, the verb in the **que** clause will be in the imperfect (past) subjunctive.

This is an automatic sequencing that does not always translate word-for-word into English.

Pablo **quiere** que yo lo **ayude.**	*Pablo **wants** me to **help** him.*
Pablo **quería** que yo lo **ayudara.**	*Pablo **wanted** me to **help** him.*
El médico **recomienda** que **comamos** pescado.	*The doctor **recommends** that we **eat** fish.*
El médico **recomendó** que **comiéramos** pescado.	*The doctor **recommended** that we **eat** fish.*

| Mi abuela siempre **pide** que mi mamá le **sirva** sopa de pollo. | *My grandmother always **asks** that my mother **serve** chicken soup to her.* |
| Mi abuela siempre **pedía** que mi mamá le **sirviera** sopa de pollo. | *My grandmother always **used to ask** that my mother **serve** chicken soup to her.* |

It is easy to form the past subjunctive of all verbs (**-ar, -er,** and **-ir**) when you already know the **ustedes** form of the preterite. Simply remove the **-on** ending and add the past subjunctive endings **-a, -as, -a, -amos, -ais, -an.** Notice that the **nosotros** form of the past subjunctive has a written accent on the third syllable from the end (**llamáramos, pudiéramos, pidiéramos**).

llamar

Pretérito: llamaron, llamar-

yo	llamar**a**	nosotros(as)	llamár**amos**
tú	llamar**as**	vosotros(as)	llamar**ais**
Ud.		Uds.	
él }	llamar**a**	ellos }	llamar**an**
ella		ellas	

poder

Pretérito: pudieron, pudier-

yo	pudier**a**	nosotros(as)	pudiér**amos**
tú	pudier**as**	vosotros(as)	pudier**ais**
Ud.		Uds.	
él }	pudier**a**	ellos }	pudier**an**
ella		ellas	

pedir

Pretérito: pidieron, pidier-

yo	pidier**a**	nosotros(as)	pidiér**amos**
tú	pidier**as**	vosotros(as)	pidier**ais**
Ud.		Uds.	
él }	pidier**a**	ellos }	pidier**an**
ella		ellas	

Práctica

L. Las cosas de la niñez *(childhood).* Trabaja con un(a) compañero(a) de clase para hablar de su niñez completando las siguientes oraciones. Presten atención al imperfecto del subjuntivo. Sigan el modelo.

■ **Modelo:** mis padres siempre pedían que yo...

Cuando era pequeño(a), mis padres siempre pedían que yo me acostara temprano.

1. mis padres no permitían que yo...
2. no era posible que...
3. me molestaba mucho que mi hermano(a)...
4. era probable que yo...
5. un día me pareció muy extraño que...
6. yo siempre dudaba que...
7. mi hermano(a) nunca quería que yo...
8. yo sentía mucho que no...
9. mi papá me pidió una vez que yo...
10. me parecía increíble que mis padres...

M. El (La) profesor(a) pidió que...

Explícale a un(a) compañero(a) que no pudo ir a la clase de literatura ayer lo que el (la) profesor(a) pidió que ustedes hicieran la tarea. Usen los verbos de la columna A con la forma apropiada del imperfecto del subjuntivo. Escojan palabras de la columna B para completar la información. Sigan el modelo.

■ **Modelo:** Ayer el (la) profesor(a) pidió que nosotros... (hacer)

Ayer la profesora pidió que nosotros hiciéramos la tarea.

A	**B**
hacer	la novela
leer	la composición
estudiar	un poema
empezar	el cuento
escribir	el tema central
corregir	el cuarto capítulo
discutir	350 palabras
terminar	la tarea
analizar	cinco páginas
aprender	diez versos

N. Le recomendé que...

Trabaja con un(a) compañero(a). Escriban de seis a ocho recomendaciones que le han hecho recientemente a un(a) estudiante de intercambio de Colombia que les pidió consejos para su visita de seis meses a los Estados Unidos. Usen **Le recomendé que...** con cada sugerencia. Traten de incluir en su lista de seis a ocho verbos en el imperfecto del subjuntivo. Después le pueden leer la lista a la clase.

ENFOQUE ESTRUCTURAL

El imperfecto del subjuntivo y el condicional en oraciones con *si*

The conjunction **si,** meaning *if,* is used to set up a situation contrary to fact. The statement that immediately follows **si** indicates that you are talking about something hypothetical (that doesn't exist or is unlikely to happen).

The statement that follows si also indicates that you are imagining what might possibly happen under certain

Possible answers, Ex. L
1. Cuando era pequeño(a), mis padres no permitían que yo saliera por la noche. 2. ...no era posible que viajara solo(a). 3. ...me molestaba mucho que mi hermano(a) se burlara de mí. 4. ...era probable que yo causara problemas en casa. 5. ...un día me pareció muy extraño que mi perro no volviera a casa. 6. ...yo siempre dudaba que existiera Papá Noel. 7. ...mi hermano(a) nunca quería que yo recibiera regalos. 8. ...yo sentía mucho que no tuviera una bicicleta. 9. ...mi papá me pidió una vez que yo sacara la basura. 10. ...me parecía increíble que mis padres no me dieran una bicicleta.

Ex. M: Pairs

Answers, Ex. M
...hiciéramos... ...leyéramos...
...estudiáramos... ...empezáramos...
...escribiéramos... ...corrigiéramos...
...discutiéramos... ...termináramos...
...analizáramos... ...aprendiéramos...

Ex. N: Pairs

◯ **IRM Master 67:** El imperfecto del subjuntivo y el condicional en oraciones con *si*

Suggestion: Write on the board: **Si tengo bastante dinero, iré a Europa.** Ask students: **¿Tengo bastante dinero? No estoy seguro(a). Puede que sí, puede que no.** Then write: **Si tuviera bastante dinero, iría a Europa.** Ask: **¿Tengo bastante dinero? No. Entonces, no es posible que yo vaya a Europa.** Summarize tense patterns on the board.

---

conditions. You can always tell that the projection is into "the twilight zone" from the use of the conditional tense. The conditional tense sets up what would happen if the hypothetical situation were to occur.

Whenever the conditional tense appears in the main clause, any verb used after **si** in the dependent clause will always be in the imperfect (past) subjunctive form.

Compraríamos ese coche rojo **si tuviéramos** más dinero.	*We would buy that red car **if we had** more money.*
Estaría contento **si me escribieras.**	*I would be happy **if you wrote** to me.*
Si perdieras ese reloj, sería una lástima.	***If you were to lose** that watch, it would be a shame.*
Pasaría por ti **si me esperaras.**	*I would stop by for you **if you were to wait for me**.*

Notice that there are several ways in English to translate a contrary-to-fact clause like **Si aceptaras la invitación**... All of the following are used: *If you were to accept the invitation . . . , If you accepted the invitation . . . ,* and *If you would accept the invitation . . . .*

Práctica

Ñ. No va a pasar... pero si pasara... Indica lo que podría pasar bajo ciertas circunstancias, usando el imperfecto del subjuntivo en la cláusula con *si* y el tiempo condicional en la otra cláusula. Sigue el modelo.

Modelo: No tengo dinero, pero si lo _____ (tener), yo _____ (comprar) ese coche.
*No tengo dinero, pero si lo **tuviera**, yo **compraría** ese coche.*

1. No van a invitarlo, pero si ellos lo _____ (invitar), Ramón _____ (ir) a México.
2. No puedo salir a las 3:00, pero si yo _____ (poder), ustedes _____ (ir) conmigo.
3. No podemos terminar la composición, pero si la profesora nos _____ (dar) más tiempo, nosotros la _____ (terminar).
4. No tengo dinero, pero si _____ (ganar) más, yo no _____ (tener) problemas.
5. Ese hotel es muy caro. Si ustedes _____ (ir) a otro, ustedes _____ (pagar) menos.
6. No sabemos quién va a la fiesta, pero si Cristina y Raquel _____ (estar), todo el mundo _____ (estar) contento.
7. Mi tío Pepe dice que no le gusta el arte abstracto, pero si alguien le _____ (vender) un cuadro famoso, él lo _____ (comprar) para su oficina.

O. Imagínate... Completa las oraciones según tus propias opiniones.

Modelo: Yo estaría muy triste si...
Yo estaría muy triste si tuviera que asistir a otra universidad.

1. Yo te llamaría por teléfono a las 2:00 de la mañana si...
2. Creo que el (la) profesor(a) te invitaría a la cena si...
3. Mis compañeros de clase estarían muy contentos si...
4. Me gustaría leer la novela *Don Quijote* si...
5. ¿Trabajarías diez horas por día si...?

P. En una isla desierta. Hazle seis u ocho preguntas a un(a) compañero(a) acerca de lo que haría si estuviera unos meses en una isla desierta. Usa los verbos en el condicional. Sigue el modelo.

■ **Modelo:** ¿Cuánto tiempo podrías pasar en la isla?
Podría pasar dos meses (cuatro meses, un año, etc).

Ex. P: Pairs

LECTURA: *Don Quijote—Los molinos de viento*

ANTES DE LEER

En La Mancha, la región donde don Quijote tuvo muchas de sus aventuras, hay muchos molinos de viento. En un episodio de la famosa novela de Cervantes, el héroe ataca un molino con su lanza, creyendo que es en realidad un enorme gigante. ¿Qué dice don Quijote de los molinos? ¿Qué diría Sancho que son?

Q. Estudio de palabras. Piensa en dos sinónimos para las palabras que aparecen en la lista. Usa un diccionario cuando sea necesario.

1. enorme
2. una batalla
3. precipitarse
4. la furia
5. el asno
6. un encantador
7. la derrota
8. la enemistad

GUÍA PARA LA LECTURA

R. La locura *(madness)* de don Quijote. Don Quijote percibía la realidad de una forma muy especial. Lee el primer diálogo del texto. ¿Qué ve don Quijote? ¿Qué piensa hacer con ellos?

S. Sancho Panza, el realista. Vuelve a leer el primer diálogo. ¿Cómo responde Sancho al comentario de su amo?

T. Y entonces... Completa las siguientes frases de acuerdo con lo que se narra en la lectura.

1. Don Quijote y Sancho iban caminando por el campo cuando de pronto descubrieron allí...
2. Don Quijote pensaba hacer batalla, diciéndole a Sancho que lo que veían eran...
3. Al oír esto, Sancho respondió que...
4. Sin prestar atención a su escudero, don Quijote picó con la espuela a Rocinante y...
5. En ese momento un viento fuerte...

Assign as homework. In class the next day put students in groups of 3 or 4 and have each take turns at choosing a word (without explicitly stating which one) and offering its synonyms. The others try to guess which word it is and offer feedback on whether the student has used correct synonyms.

Answers, Ex. T
1. ...treinta o cuarenta molinos de viento que había en aquel campo.
2. ...enormes gigantes. 3. ...parecían ser gigantes pero que eran molinos de viento. 4. ...fue a atacar los molinos. 5. ...se levantó y las aspas comenzaron a moverse.
6. ...descubrió que no podía moverse. 7. ...el encantador Frestón había cambiado los gigantes en molinos.

6. Sancho corrió para ayudar a don Quijote pero cuando llegó...

7. La explicación de esta aventura que ofreció don Quijote fue que...

U. Comprensión. Contesta en español las preguntas sobre la lectura.

1. ¿Cuántos molinos de viento había en el campo?
2. ¿Qué creía don Quijote que eran los molinos?
3. ¿Qué dijo don Quijote que haría con los molinos?
4. ¿Cómo reaccionó Sancho cuando oyó lo que don Quijote pensaba?
5. A pesar de los gritos de Sancho, ¿qué hizo don Quijote?
6. ¿Qué pasó cuando el viento empezó a mover las aspas del molino?
7. ¿Cómo explicó don Quijote lo que había pasado?
8. ¿Crees tú que es mejor ser como don Quijote o como Sancho Panza? ¿Por qué?

V. Entrevistas con don Quijote y Sancho Panza. Trabajando con un(a) compañero(a), preparen seis preguntas sobre el incidente de los molinos para don Quijote y seis para Sancho. Después un(a) estudiante hará el papel de don Quijote para contestar las preguntas que le hace el (la) entrevistador(a), y el otro hará el papel de Sancho para contestar las preguntas que le tocan a este personaje.

▶ Los molinos de viento

Don Quijote y Sancho iban caminando por el Campo de Montiel cuando de pronto descubrieron treinta o cuarenta **molinos de viento** que había en aquel campo. Cuando don Quijote los vio, dijo a su **escudero:** —La fortuna **está guiando** nuestras cosas mejor de lo que podemos desear; porque ves allí, amigo Sancho Panza, treinta o pocos más enormes **gigantes,** con quienes pienso hacer batalla y quitarles a todos la vida.

—¿Qué gigantes? —dijo Sancho Panza.

Molinos de viento, La Mancha, España

—Aquéllos que allí ves, —respondió su **amo**—, de los brazos largos, que los tienen algunos de casi dos **leguas.**

master
leagues (a measured length)

—Mire **vuestra merced,** —respondió Sancho—, que aquéllos que allí parecen ser gigantes son molinos de viento, y lo que en ellos parecen brazos son las **aspas,** que, cuando el viento las mueve, hacen andar la piedra del molino.

Your Grace
blades (of windmill)

—Bien parece, —respondió don Quijote—, que **no estás versado** en las aventuras: ellos son gigantes; y si tienes miedo, quítate de ahí porque voy a entrar con ellos en feroz batalla.

you're not well-informed

Y diciendo esto, **picó con la espuela** a su caballo Rocinante, sin prestar atención a los gritos que su escudero Sancho le daba, diciéndole que, sin duda alguna, eran molinos de viento, y no gigantes, aquéllos que iba a atacar. Pero él estaba tan convencido de que eran gigantes, que no oía los gritos de su escudero Sancho, ni se dio cuenta, aunque estaba muy cerca, de lo que eran; al contrario, iba diciendo en voz alta: —¡**No huyáis, cobardes** y viles criaturas, porque un solo caballero es el que os ataca!

he dug in his spurs

Don't flee / cowards

Se levantó en este momento un poco de viento, y las grandes aspas comenzaron a moverse. Cuando vio esto, don Quijote dijo: —Pues aunque mováis todos los brazos juntos, me lo pagaréis.

Y diciendo esto, después de dedicarse de todo corazón a su señora Dulcinea, pidiéndole su ayuda en tan peligroso momento, **se precipitó** a todo el galope de Rocinante, y atacó con la lanza al primer molino que estaba delante. El viento movió el molino con tanta furia, que hizo pedazos la lanza, llevándose detrás de sí al caballo y al caballero, que **fueron rodando** por el campo. Fue a ayudarle Sancho Panza a todo el correr de su **asno,** y cuando llegó, descubrió que no podía moverse.

he hurled himself

went rolling
donkey

—¡**Válgame Dios!** —dijo Sancho—, ¿por qué no miró bien vuestra merced lo que hacía. ¿No le dije que eran molinos de viento y no gigantes?

Good heavens!

—**Calla,** amigo Sancho, —respondió don Quijote—; que las cosas de la guerra más que otras están sujetas a continua transformación. Por eso yo pienso que un **encantador** llamado Frestón ha cambiado estos gigantes en molinos para quitarme la gloria de su derrota; tal es la **enemistad** que me tiene; pero al fin, al fin, poco podrán hacer sus **malas artes** contra la bondad de mi espada.

Be quiet
magician

ill-will
evil arts

—Así es, —respondió Sancho Panza; y ayudándole a levantarse, volvió a subir sobre Rocinante. Y hablando de la pasada aventura, siguieron el camino.

Tu dirás ······································

W. ¿Qué le pasaría a don Quijote hoy? Trabaja con otro(a) estudiante para hacer una descripción de una visita imaginaria de don Quijote a tu pueblo o ciudad. Usen los verbos en el tiempo condicional. Incluyan detalles sobre cómo sería la visita, cómo sería don Quijote, lo que haría él y cómo reaccionaría él a la gente y la gente a él. Comenten específicamente sobre lo que haría en cierta situación y lo que pensaría sobre algún objeto de la época moderna. (Si es necesario, repasen las lecturas de este capítulo sobre esta fascinante figura literaria.)

X. En ese caso... Indica lo que tú o las personas mencionadas harían en las circunstancias indicadas. Sigue el modelo.

Assign as homework. The next day in class pair students to share their descriptions. Have them incorporate information from both descriptions into one that they will jointly compose in class. Allow students 15–20 minutes to compose and edit their descriptions. Then have them share their descriptions with other pairs. When done, ask students to comment on the differences between different students' descriptions.

Ex. W: Pairs

Have students work in pairs to complete this activity. Circulate around room to check for accuracy. When done, ask different students to volunteer their answers for the class.

Possible answers, Ex. X
1. Yo saldría corriendo. 2. Compartiría su paraguas conmigo. 3. Tomaría aspirinas. 4. Me pediría dinero. 5. La ayudaría. 6. Llamarían un taxi. 7. Comprarían más comida. 8. aceptaría con mucho gusto. 9. Buscaría ayuda. 10. Se enojarían conmigo.

■ **Modelo:** Ves un coche parado en la carretera con una llanta desinflada *(flat tire)*. ¿Qué harías?
   Ayudaría a la persona a cambiar la llanta.

1. Estás en un restaurante cuando alguien grita, "¡Fuego en la cocina!" ¿Qué harías?
2. Tu amigo y tú caminan por la calle cuando empieza a llover. Tú no tienes paraguas, pero él sí. ¿Qué haría tu amigo?
3. Tienes un dolor de cabeza. ¿Qué harías?
4. Tu hermano quiere comprar una bicicleta pero le falta dinero. ¿Qué haría él?
5. Tú ves a una niña de tres años que no sabe nadar. Se cae en la piscina. ¿Qué harías?
6. Tus amigos quieren ir a una fiesta pero nadie tiene coche. ¿Qué harían?
7. Tus padres no están preparados para una visita. Reciben una llamada telefónica de unos parientes que dicen que van a pasar a visitarlos a las 6:00 de la tarde. ¿Qué harían tus padres?
8. Una escritora recibe las noticias de que ha ganado un premio literario. ¿Qué haría ella?
9. En un autobús tú ves que un muchacho está enojado y que golpea a otro muchacho. ¿Qué harías?
10. Tus compañeros están cansados y tú estás tocando música rock muy alto. ¿Qué pasaría?

⊚ TERCERA ETAPA

⊚ *PARA EMPEZAR: El realismo mágico*

Present this new topic to the students by developing a class discussion in Spanish based on these questions.

Preparación

- **Have you heard the term "magical realism"?**
- **Even if you have not, what do you think "magical realism" means as opposed to just "realism"?**
- **Can you think of some examples of the way "unreal" things actually form part of a large reality?**

renew
storytelling

Gabriel García Márquez (Colombia, 1928–) Entre los escritores hispanoamericanos de nuestra época que incluyen en su obra muchos aspectos variables de la realidad está Gabriel García Márquez. Algunos críticos lo han comparado con Miguel de Cervantes. Aunque los separan casi cuatro siglos, los dos han sabido **renovar** el arte de **contar** —y lo han hecho con un gran sentido del humor. Además, los dos consideran lo real y lo **sobrenatural** como parte del mismo mundo de la realidad. *Cien años de soledad* y *El ingenioso hidalgo don Quijote de la Mancha* son excelentes ejemplos de cómo representar la realidad en sus varias dimensiones a lo largo de una narración llena de claridad, crítica social e incidentes cómicos.

Gabriel García Márquez ha dicho en varias ocasiones que no le ha pasado nada interesante en la vida desde que murió su abuelo cuando era niño en Aracataca, Colombia. Insiste que desde ese entonces todo lo que ha escrito hasta ahora o ya lo sabía o ya lo había oído antes de cumplir los ocho años. Durante esos años vivió con sus abuelos, que le contaban cuentos todos los días, y según él, tuvo una niñez "fabulosa".

Gabriel García Márquez

Comentarios

culturales   *El realismo mágico*

*L*a originalidad y el uso de la imaginación le han dado fama a la literatura hispanoamericana contemporánea en todas partes del mundo. La popularidad de esta literatura, en especial la de la novela, **tiene mucho que ver con** *(has a lot to do with)* "el realismo **mágico** *(magical)*" que existe independientemente de una explicación racional. Para un escritor mágicorrealista, este tipo de escritura sería una distorsión de la realidad si la presentara sólo desde un punto de vista lógico o intelectual. Sin embargo, lo que intenta expresar es la emoción de la realidad sin eliminar su dimensión misteriosa o "mágica".

Uno de los objetivos del realismo mágico es hacer una combinación de lo real y de lo mágico para representar una nueva dimensión. Un **hecho** *(fact)* en sí es real y podría tener una explicación lógica, pero lo que interesa más es que tenga una explicación **mítica** *(mythical)*. Esta explicación está basada en las **creencias** *(beliefs)* populares, en las leyendas y en los sueños colectivos de la gente. Por ejemplo, si una mujer **se ahoga** *(drowns)* en un **pozo** *(well)*, la explicación, según el realismo mágico, sería que era el pozo el que la necesitaba porque quería transformarla en una serpiente. Como dijo Miguel Ángel Asturias, los escritores que incluyen el realismo mágico en sus obras "viven con sus personajes en un mundo en que no hay fronteras entre lo real y lo fantástico, en que un hecho cualquiera—cuando lo **cuentan** *(they tell a story)*—**se vuelve** *(becomes)* parte de un algo **extraterreno** *(from another world)*. Lo que es hijo de la fantasía **cobra** *(takes on)* realidad en la mentalidad de las gentes".[1]

[1]From "Quince preguntas a M. A. Asturias," "Revolución." 17 de agosto, 1959, p. 23.

INTEGRACIÓN CULTURAL

Decide cuál de las cuatro posibilidades explica *mejor* las siguientes frases o nombres que aparecen en la lectura.

1. el realismo mágico
   a. explicaciones racionales
   b. hechos históricos
   c. la dimensión misteriosa
   d. injusticias sociales

2. Miguel Ángel Asturias
   a. romántico
   b. realista
   c. mágicorrealista
   d. existencialista

3. creencias populares
   a. personajes interesantes
   b. leyendas y mitos
   c. las facetas de la sociedad
   d. el chocolate y el hielo

LECTURA: *Cien años de soledad*

ANTES DE LEER

A. Lee las preguntas del ejercicio *Comprensión* para tener una idea general del contenido de la lectura. Después, contesta las siguientes preguntas.

1. Piensa en un bloque de hielo. ¿Con qué lo puedes comparar?
2. En general, ¿cómo reaccionan las personas ante lo desconocido?
3. ¿Qué significa la palabra "soledad"?
4. Busca los nombres del padre y sus dos hijos en el pasaje. ¿Cómo se llaman?

GUÍA PARA LA LECTURA

B. Una técnica favorita. A García Márquez le gusta usar adjetivos descriptivos dramáticos para exagerar las cosas. ¿Cuáles de las siguientes frases de la lectura son ejemplos de la exageración? ¿Cómo dirías algo parecido en inglés?

1. piedras blancas y enormes como huevos prehistóricos
2. la feria de los gitanos
3. la portentosa novedad
4. un anillo de cobre en la nariz
5. infinitas agujas internas
6. una explicación inmediata
7. el diamante más grande del mundo
8. se le hinchaba el corazón de temor
9. la prodigiosa experiencia
10. el pequeño José Arcadio
11. el gran invento de nuestro tiempo

C. ¿Qué pasó? Pon las siguientes acciones en orden cronológico según la lectura.

1. El padre dijo que era un diamante.
2. Un gigante de torso peludo abrió un cofre de pirata.
3. Uno de los niños también puso la mano sobre el hielo.
4. El gigante dijo que era hielo.
5. Dentro del cofre había un bloque transparente.
6. Un día un hombre llevó a sus hijos a la feria de los gitanos.
7. El padre curioso puso la mano sobre el bloque.
8. Los tres entraron en una carpa.

D. Comprensión. Contesta en español las siguientes preguntas.

1. ¿Cómo era Macondo cuando el coronel Aureliano Buendía y su hermano eran niños?
2. ¿Adónde querían el pequeño Aureliano y su hermano que los llevara su padre cuando estaban en la feria?
3. Cuando los tres entraron en la carpa, ¿qué vieron primero? Describe lo que vieron.
4. ¿Qué había dentro del cofre?
5. ¿Qué explicación dio el padre de lo que vio en el cofre?
6. ¿Cómo reaccionó el padre cuando tocó el objeto que estaba en el cofre?
7. ¿Qué dijo Aureliano después de tocar el objeto?
8. ¿Te gustó esta lectura? ¿Por qué sí o por qué no?

Cien años de soledad por Gabriel García Márquez

El bloque de hielo

Muchos años después, frente al **pelotón de fusilamiento,** el coronel Aureliano Buendía recordaría aquella tarde remota en que su padre lo llevó a conocer el hielo. Macondo era entonces una **aldea** de veinte casas de **barro** y caña construidas a la **orilla** de un río de aguas cristalinas que corrían por unas piedras **pulidas,** blancas y enormes como huevos prehistóricos. El mundo era tan reciente que muchas cosas no tenían nombre, y para mencionarlas se tenían que **señalar** con el dedo.

El día que fueron a la **feria** de los **gitanos,** su padre los llevaba a él y a su hermano de cada mano para no perderlos en el tumulto. Habían insistido en ir a conocer la **portentosa novedad** de los **sabios** de Egipto, anunciada a la entrada de una **carpa** que, según decían, había sido del rey Salomón. Tanto insistieron los niños, que José Arcadio Buendía pagó los treinta **reales,** y los llevó hasta el centro de la carpa, donde había un gigante de torso **peludo** y cabeza **rapada,** con un anillo de cobre en la nariz, cuidando un **cofre** de pirata. Cuando el gigante lo abrió, el cofre dejó escapar un **aliento** glacial. Dentro sólo había un bloque transparente, con **infinitas agujas internas** en las cuales se **despedazaba** en estrellas de colores la claridad del **crepúsculo.** Preocupado, porque sabía que los niños esperaban una explicación inmediata, José Arcadio Buendía **murmuró:**

—Es el diamante más grande del mundo.

—No —corrigió el gitano—. Es hielo.

firing squad

little village / hamlet / clay
edge / polished

to point

fair / gypsies

extraordinary novelty / wise men,
sages / tent
unit of money
hairy / shaved / ring
large trunk or chest / rush of air,
breath / countless internal
needles / was breaking up
twilight
murmured

José Arcadio Buendía, sin entender, extendió la mano hacia el bloque, pero el gigante se la quitó: —Cinco reales más para tocarlo —dijo. José Arcadio Buendía los pagó, y entonces puso la mano sobre el hielo, y la dejó puesta por varios minutos, mientras el corazón se le **hinchaba** de temor y de alegría al contacto del misterioso objeto. Sin saber qué decir, pagó otros diez reales por los hijos; así ellos podrían vivir también la **prodigiosa** experiencia. El pequeño José Arcadio se negó a tocarlo. Aureliano, en cambio, dio un paso hacia adelante, puso la mano y la retiró inmediatamente. —¡Está **hirviendo**! —exclamó con miedo. Pero su padre no le prestó atención. **Asombrado** por la evidencia del **prodigio,** pagó otros cinco reales, y con la mano puesta en el bloque, como si estuviera expresando un testimonio sobre el texto **sagrado**, exclamó:

—Éste es el gran **invento** de nuestro tiempo.

was swelling up

marvelous

boiling
Amazed / wonderous object

sacred

invention

Repaso

E. Casi todo era posible en Macondo. Para cada espacio en blanco, da la forma apropiada del imperfecto del subjuntivo del verbo entre paréntesis.

1. Era posible que un bloque de hielo _____ (ser) un enorme diamante.

2. Era posible que una persona _____ (vivir) más de cien años.

3. No era imposible que un ángel _____ (visitar) a una pareja pobre del pueblo.

4. Era posible que los muertos _____ (hablar) con los vivos.

5. Era posible que una niña _____ (transformarse) en una araña por desobedecer a sus padres.

6. No era imposible que una bella mujer _____ (elevarse) al cielo.

7. Era posible que _____ (llover) más de cuatro años sin parar.

8. Era posible que un hombre no _____ (dormir) por el ruido de las estrellas.

F. ¿Qué consejo darías? El ama de casa de don Quijote te habla de los problemas que tiene con don Quijote y Sancho Panza. Usa la información entre paréntesis para indicar lo que harías tú **en tal caso** *(in such a case)*.

■ **Modelo:** Me canso de recoger los libros de caballerías que don Quijote lleva a la casa. (ponerlos en la biblioteca de la casa)
Yo los pondría en la biblioteca de la casa.

1. Nunca tenemos dinero porque don Quijote lo usa para comprar libros. (pedirle a don Quijote cierta cantidad de dinero cada semana)

2. Me molestan las disputas que don Quijote tiene en la casa con el cura y el barbero. (salir de la casa cuando las tienen)

3. Don Quijote pasa el día y la noche leyendo y no quiere comer cuando es hora. (dejar la comida a su lado en la biblioteca)

4. A Sancho le gusta demasiado el vino. (abrir sólo una botella cuando visita a don Quijote)

5. La sobrina de don Quijote dice que su tío está un poco loco. (decir lo mismo dadas las circunstancias)

6. Necesito unos días de descanso pero no quiero dejar solo a don Quijote. (pedirle ayuda a la sobrina)

7. Don Quijote va a limpiar todas las armas viejas en la sala. (ayudarle a llevar las armas al establo)

8. Sancho siempre pierde dinero en la taberna del pueblo. (no preocuparse y aceptar que es su dinero)
9. Don Quijote tiene la barba demasiado larga. (hacer una cita para él con el barbero)
10. Me pongo nerviosa cuando don Quijote dice que va a viajar con Sancho. (aceptar que don Quijote no va a cambiar)

IRM Master 68: Más sobre el subjuntivo y la secuencia de los tiempos verbales

ENFOQUE ESTRUCTURAL

Más sobre el subjuntivo y la secuencia de los tiempos verbales

When the future tense or the present perfect (have done something) in the main clause require the use of the subjunctive in the que clause, the verb in that dependent que clause will be in the present subjunctive. Note that in both instances, the present subjunctive refers to future action.

En este caso, el director **pedirá** que los escritores **acepten** su idea.	*In this case, the director **will ask** that the writers **accept** his idea.*
En este caso, el director **ha pedido** que los escritores **acepten** su idea.	*In this case, the director **has asked** that the writers **accept** his idea.*

When the conditional tense or the past perfect tense (had done something) in the main clause requires the use of the subjunctive in the **que** clause, the verb in that dependent **que** clause will be in the imperfect subjunctive.

En este caso, el director **pediría** que los escritores **aceptaran** su idea.	*In this case, the director **would ask** that the writers **accept** his idea.*
En este caso, el director **había pedido** que los escritores **aceptaran** su idea.	*In this case, the director **had asked** that the writers **accept** his idea.*

This is an automatic sequencing in Spanish that does not always translate word-for-word into English.

Práctica

G. ¿Qué más? Completa las oraciones siguientes con la información que quieras añadir. Presta atención a la secuencia de los tiempos verbales y al uso del subjuntivo.

■ **Modelo:** No será posible que...
No será posible que nosotros salgamos temprano hoy.

1. No será necesario que...
2. La profesora había pedido que...
3. Nosotros sentiríamos mucho que...
4. Mis padres insistirían en que...

Possible Answers, Ex. G
1. No será necesario que vayamos a la librería mañana. 2. La profesora había pedido que nosotros escribiéramos una composición. 3. Nosotros sentiríamos mucho que no tuviéramos una fiesta este fin de semana. 4. Mis padres insistirían en que yo comprara gasolina para el coche. 5. El presidente del club había querido que cambiáramos la fecha de la reunión. 6. Para mejorar la situación, yo sugeriría que mandaran una carta. 7. La profesora explicará el poema para que todos lo entiendan bien. 8. Mis amigos y yo vamos a pedir que nos dejen salir temprano el viernes. 9. Será mejor que todos los estudiantes terminen su tarea esta tarde. 10. Me alegraría mucho de que nevara el lunes próximo.

5. El presidente del club había querido que...
6. Para mejorar la situación, yo sugeriría que...
7. La profesora explicará el poema para que...
8. Mis amigos y yo vamos a pedir que...
9. Será mejor que todos los estudiantes...
10. Me alegraría mucho de que...

H. Sólo un sueño. Cambia el verbo entre paréntesis a la forma apropiada del imperfecto del subjuntivo para completar la historia que sigue.

Un niño salió de la casa silenciosamente para que nadie lo _____ (oír). Se había llevado el dinero de un cajón de la cocina y no quería que sus padres lo _____ (descubrir). Tenía miedo, por supuesto, porque sabía que era posible que sus padres _____ (despertarse) y lo _____ (buscar). Fuera de la casa, empezó a correr. Esperaba que el tren todavía _____ (estar) en la estación y que no lo _____ (dejar). Si esto _____ (pasar), tendría que esconderse en algún lugar hasta la llegada de otro tren. A pesar del pánico que sentía, decidió no volver a casa. En ese momento, el niño se despertó y se dio cuenta de que todo sólo había sido un sueño. Se alegró mucho de que _____ (estar) todavía en su cama en su propio cuarto. Decidió ir a despertar a sus padres para contarles su sueño.

LECTURA: *La casa de los espíritus por Isabel Allende*

Isabel Allende (Chile, 1942–) es una de las novelistas que siempre aparece en la lista de los mejores escritores contemporáneos de habla española. Ha publicado cinco novelas, *La casa de los espíritus* (1982), *De amor y de sombra* (1984), *Eva Luna* (1987), *Afrodita: cuentos, recetas y otros afodísialos* (1997). *El plan infinito* (1991), *Paula* (1994) y una colección de cuentos, *Los cuentos de Eva Luna* (1989). Su primera obra, de donde viene la selección que sigue, se considera la mejor que ha escrito hasta ahora. En esta novela presenta la vida de varias generaciones de una familia chilena por medio del prisma del realismo mágico. Sus fuertes personajes femeninos son inolvidables como mujeres de carne y hueso, como espíritus y como símbolos de la reforma general que la sociedad necesita si la vida va a mejorar para todos.

ANTES DE LEER

I. Imagínate a un animal doméstico que crece y crece y crece. Contesta las siguientes preguntas.
1. ¿Qué pasaría si un perro, por ejemplo, llegara a ser de repente *(suddenly)* del tamaño de un caballo?
2. ¿Cómo reaccionaría la gente?

3. ¿Qué crees que harían?

4. ¿Qué harías tú si tu perro, o tu gato, se convirtiera en un animal gigantesco?

J. Anticipación. ¿Qué crees que va a pasar con Clara y su perro?

GUÍA PARA LA LECTURA

K. ¿Cómo es Barrabás? Prepara una lista de las características de este perro extraordinario, tomando en cuenta las siguientes categorías: **su apariencia física, su temperamento, sus hábitos** y **gustos.**

L. Comprensión. Contesta en español las siguientes preguntas sobre la lectura.

1. Cuando llegó el perrito a la casa, ¿cómo lo trató la niña Clara?

2. ¿Qué pensaba su padre Severo del animal?

3. ¿Qué dijo Clara que haría en caso de que Barrabás no pudiera quedarse con ella?

4. ¿Qué descubrieron cuando bañaron al perro?

5. ¿Qué quería la Nana hacer con la cola?

6. ¿Cómo reaccionó Clara a esta idea?

7. ¿Cómo era su cola?

8. ¿Por qué estaba preocupada Nívea, la madre de Clara?

9. ¿Cómo era el temperamento del perro?

10. ¿Dónde dormía Barrabás?

11. ¿Qué hacía el perro a la hora de la comida cuando no lo encerraban?

12. ¿Te gustaría tener un perro como Barrabás? ¿Por qué sí o por qué no?

M. Un diálogo entre Clara y su padre. Trabajando con un(a) compañero(a) de clase, imagínense una conversación entre Clara y su padre. ¿Cómo sería un intercambio entre ellos con Barrabás como el centro del conflicto? Escriban juntos un diálogo de unas diez a doce líneas, preparándose para después presentarlo en la clase.

▶*La casa de los espíritus:*

La niña Clara y su perro Barrabás

La niña Clara **se hizo cargo del** perrito enfermo. Lo sacó de la canasta, lo abrazó a su pecho y con el cuidado de misionera le dio agua en el **hocico hinchado** y **reseco.** Clara **se convirtió** en una madre para el animal, dudoso privilegio que nadie quería disputarle. Un par de días más tarde, su padre Severo se fijó en la criatura que su hija llevaba en los brazos.

—¿Qué es eso? —preguntó.

—Barrabás —dijo Clara.

—Déselo al jardinero, para que lo lleve de esta casa. Puede contagiarnos con alguna enfermedad —ordenó Severo.

—Es mío papá. Si me lo quita, le prometo que dejaré de **respirar** y me moriré.

Se quedó en la casa. Al poco tiempo corría por todas partes **devorándose** las cortinas, las alfombras y las patas de los muebles. Se recuperó de su enfermedad con gran rapidez y empezó a **crecer.** Cuando lo bañaron por primera vez, se descubrió que era negro, de cabeza cuadrada, patas muy largas y pelo corto. La Nana quería cortarle la cola, diciendo que así parecería perro fino, pero Clara se enojó tanto que

Answers, Ex. L
1. Clara lo trató con cariño. 2. Severo pensaba que el perro era contagioso. 3. Clara dijo que dejaría de respirar y moriría. 4. Descubrieron que era negro, de cabeza cuadrada, patas muy largas y pelo corto. 5. La Nana quería cortarle la cola. 6. Clara se enojó muchísimo. 7. Su cola era muy larga. 8. La madre de Clara dudaba que fuera perro. 9. El perro no daba muestras de ninguna ferocidad. 10. Barrabás dormía en la cama de Clara, o al lado de la cama. 11. El perro entraba al comedor y daba una vuelta a la mesa, tomando sus bocadillos preferidos de los platos. 12. Answers will vary.

Ex. M:  Pairs

took charge of the
muzzle / swollen
dried out / became

to breathe

devouring

to grow

	tuvo un ataque de asma y nadie volvió a mencionar la idea. Barrabás se quedó con
length	la cola entera. Con el tiempo ésta llegó a tener el **largo** de un palo de golf y sus
swept	movimientos descontrolables **barrían** las porcelanas de las mesas y rompían las
	lámparas.

<table>
<tr><td>breed</td><td>Era de raza desconocida. No tenía nada en común con los perros que andaban por la calle y mucho menos con los de pura raza de algunas familias aristocráticas. El veterinario no supo decir cuál era su origen, y Clara supuso que era de la China, porque había llegado en el equipaje de su tío que había visitado ese lejano país.</td></tr>
<tr><td>sheep / colt</td><td>Tenía una ilimitada capacidad de crecimiento. A los seis meses era del tamaño de una oveja y al año tenía las proporciones de un potrillo. La familia estaba desesperada y se preguntaba hasta qué tamaño crecería.</td></tr>
</table>

hooves
crocodile / sharp
bite

—Dudo que sea realmente un perro—decía Nívea. Cuando observaba sus **pezuñas** de **cocodrilo** y sus dientes **afilados,** sentía en su corazón de madre que la bestia podía quitarle la cabeza a un adulto de una **mordida** y con mayor razón a cualquiera de sus niños.

covered up

leaned against / growl
panther
lock him up
delicately
snacks

Pero Barrabás no daba muestras de ninguna ferocidad. Por lo contrario, jugaba como un gatito. Dormía en los brazos de Clara, dentro de su cama, con la cabeza en la almohada de plumas y **tapado** hasta el cuello porque le daba frío, pero después cuando ya no cabía en la cama, se acostaba en el suelo a su lado, con su hocico de caballo **apoyado** en la mano de la niña. Nunca lo oyeron ladrar ni **gruñir.** Era negro y silencioso como una **pantera,** le gustaban el jamón y los dulces de fruta y cada vez que alguien visitaba la casa y olvidaban **encerrarlo,** entraba tranquilamente al comedor y daba una vuelta a la mesa, tomando **con delicadeza** sus **bocadillos** preferidos de los platos. Nadie hacía nada para impedírselo.

Tú dirás ....

Ex. N: Pairs

N. ¿Qué recomendarías? Trabajando con un(a) compañero(a) dile lo que tú recomendarías que hiciera una persona interesada en ser un novelista famoso. Haz seis recomendaciones. Después escucha lo que él (ella) recomendaría.

Ex. Ñ: Pairs

Ñ. Un mundo legendario. Imagína con un(a) amigo(a) que los dos hicieron un viaje a un mundo legendario donde era posible que ocurriera cualquier cosa. Describan algunas cosas que hicieron o que pasaron durante ese viaje, usando las formas correctas del imperfecto del subjuntivo después de tales frases como **"En este mundo legendario que visitamos... era posible que..., un rey quería que..., nuestros poderes extraordinarios permitieron que..."**

■ **Modelo:** *En el mundo legendario que visitamos era posible que voláramos de un lugar a otro, que habláramos lenguas que no conocíamos, que tuviéramos la forma de cualquier animal, que nadáramos al fondo del mar, etc.*

◎ INTEGRACIÓN

LECTURA: *Casos*

ANTES DE LEER

A. Cuentos cortos. Fíjate en la breve extensión de estos pasajes. ¿Crees que es posible contar un cuento en tan pocas palabras?

B. Títulos. Lee los títulos de cada "caso" y trata de adivinar de qué se trata sin leer lo que sigue.

GUÍA PARA LA LECTURA

C. Categorías. Trabajando con un(a) compañero(a) de clase, escribe en una hoja de papel una lista de las palabras que se usan en los casos de acuerdo con las categorías a continuación: **las personas, las partes del cuerpo, los objetos, los nombres.**

D. ¿Comprensión? Contesta en español las siguientes preguntas sobre los casos que leíste en la página 530.

1. ¿Cuáles son dos o tres características que todos los casos tienen en común?
2. ¿En qué caso hay una metamorfosis, o un cambio de forma?
3. ¿En qué casos aparecen seres que no son humanos?
4. ¿Cuál de los casos te parece más realista? ¿Por qué?
5. ¿En qué caso es más evidente el uso del realismo mágico? ¿Por qué?
6. ¿Cuál de los casos te parece más cómico? ¿Por qué?
7. ¿Cuál es el caso más extraño? ¿Por qué?
8. Hay tres casos en que se usa el subjuntivo. ¿Cuáles son? ¿Por qué se usa el subjuntivo en estos casos?

E. Títulos creativos. Lee otra vez los casos y con un(a) compañero(a) escriban un nuevo título, igual de breve o más largo, para cada caso. Piensen en su contenido y usen la imaginación.

Casos
por Enrique Anderson Imbert

Enrique Anderson Imbert (Argentina, 1910–   ) ha escrito cuentos fantásticos y lo que él llama "casos", una especie de micro-texto que contiene la esencia mínima de un relato. Un caso se podría definir como una cápsula narrativa que contiene principio, mitad y fin, y que cuenta algo imaginativo e irónico.

Prereading:
Point out that a narration can be very brief as long as it tells some kind of story. These little narrative "capsules" are clever examples. Ask some of the students to read the stories aloud before doing the exercises.

Ex. C:

Pairs

Possible answers, Ex. D
1. Los casos son breves, imaginativos y narran algo. 2. Hay una metamorfosis en "Las dulces memorias" y "Cortesía de Dios". 3. En "Las dulces memorias" y "Cortesía de Dios" aparecen seres que no son humanos. 4. Answers will vary. 5. Answers will vary. 6. Answers will vary. 7. Answers will vary. 8. El primer uso del subjuntivo es, "¿...para que la gente se ría de mí?". El subjuntivo es necesario porque la frase contiene "para que". El segundo uso es, "El viejo Manuel le pidió al Ángel que lo hiciera niño". El verbo "pedir" en este sentido requiere el subjuntivo en la oración secundaria. El tercer uso es, "¿Y si dejara la pierna izquierda aquí?". Se usa el subjuntivo porque es una oración con "si".

Ex. E:  **Pairs**

Alas

wings

you fly

Yo practicaba entonces la medicina, en Humahuaca. Una tarde me trajeron un niño con la cabeza herida: se había caído por el precipicio de un cerro. Cuando, para examinarlo, le quité el poncho, vi dos **alas.** Las miré: estaban sanas. Cuando el niño pudo hablar le pregunté:

—¿Por qué no **volaste,** mi hijo, cuando empezaste a caer?

—¿Volar? —me dijo—. ¿Volar, para que la gente se ría de mí?

Las dulces memorias

El viejo Manuel le pidió al Ángel que lo hiciera niño. ¡Eran tan dulces sus memorias de la niñez!

El Ángel lo hizo niño.

Ahora Manuelito no tiene memorias.

El hombre-mosca

houseflies / ceiling

He climbed
He would run through

Muchas veces Leonidas había visto **moscas** caminando por el **techo.** Pero la cosa ocurrió el miércoles 17, a las cinco de la tarde. Vio esa mosca y descubrió su vocación. Leonidas lo abandonó todo. **Trepó** por las paredes y ya no habló más. **Recorría** toda la casa, por el techo. Para comer, bajaba y andaba sobre las rodillas y manos.

Cortesía de Dios

corner

hidden
change my shape
hallway
sunken
snout

Hoy yo estaba descansando, en mi **rincón** oscuro,
cuando oí pasos que se acercaban. ¡Otro que descubría
dónde estaba **escondido** y venía a adorarme! ¿En qué
tendría que **metamorfosearme** esta vez? Miré hacia
el **pasillo** y vi a la pobre criatura. Era peludo,
caminaba en dos pies, en sus ojos **hundidos** había
miedo, esperanza, amor y su **hocico** parecía sonreír.
Entonces, por cortesía, me levanté, adopté la forma
de un gran chimpancé y fui a conocerlo.

El príncipe

tolling of bells / cannon shots
noise

Cuando nació el príncipe hicieron una gran fiesta nacional.
Bailes, fuegos artificiales, **revuelos de campanas, disparos de cañón...**
Con tanto **ruido** el recién nacido murió.

La pierna dormida

to drag / which is attached to it

sheets

Esa mañana, cuando se despertó, Félix se miró las piernas, abiertas sobre la cama, y, ya listo para levantarse, se dijo: —¿Y si dejara la pierna izquierda aquí?— Meditó un instante. —No, imposible; si pongo la derecha en el suelo, estoy seguro que va a **arrastrar** la izquierda, **que lleva pegada.** ¡Ea! Hagamos la prueba.— Y todo salió bien. Se fue al baño, saltando en un solo pie, mientras la pierna izquierda siguió dormida sobre las **sábanas.**

VÍDEO CULTURAL: *La literatura es fuego*

VÍDEO CULTURAL

A. Anticipación. ¿Cómo se dice en español?

1. essay
2. will
3. pregnant
4. reporter
5. wet
6. to transfer
7. jealousy
8. to cry

B. Participación. El segmento que vas a mirar tiene muchos cognados que pueden ayudarte a entender el contenido. Mira las palabras siguientes y trata de usarlas en una frase completa.

censura	prosa	boicotear
inconformismo	biográfico	denunciar
rebelión	inmortal	estimular
sensación	testimonial	reprochar
término	agitar	respetar

C. Participación. En parejas lean la siguiente información sobre tres escritores importantes del mundo hispánico. Luego, respondan a las preguntas a continuación.

    a. Elena Poniatowska es de México; es mexicana.
    b. Marjorie Agosín es de Chile; es chilena.
    c. Antonio Benítez-Rojo es de Cuba; es cubano.

1. Según el escritor peruano Mario Vargas Llosa, ¿cuál es la definición de la literatura?
2. Elena Poniatowska y Marjorie Agosín creen que la literatura es una forma de denuncia. Según Agosín, ¿qué otra función sirve el escribir?
3. Antonio Benítez-Rojo habla del juego interior que siente al empezar a escribir. ¿Cómo describe esa sensación?
4. ¿Qué posibilidad les ofrece la literatura al autor y al lector, según Benítez-Rojo?

D. Comprensión. ¿Con cuál(es) de los siguientes autores asocia Ud. las siguientes ideas?

    a. Agosín
    b. Benítez-Rojo
    c. Poniatowska
    d. Mario Vargas Llosa

1. La literatura es un arte.
2. Hay que respetar mucho a las palabras.
3. Lo que más le gusta es leer un libro.
4. Es una autora chilena.
5. Escribir es un arma de fuego que perdura.
6. La literatura es una forma de denunciar.
7. Piensa que la poesía es un obsequio.
8. Es un escritor cubano.
9. La literatura representa la posibilidad de visitar otros mundos.
10. Uno de sus libros más conocidos es *La noche de Tlatelolco*.
11. Es novelista mexicana.

Answers, Ex. D
2,4 = Agosín (a)
1, 7,8,9 = Benítez-Rojo (b)
3,10,11 = Poniatowska
5,6 = Mario Vargas Llosa (d)

E. Personalización. Discutan en parejas las siguientes afirmaciones.

1. Recite a favorite poem to a classmate. Discuss its meaning and origin.
2. What kinds of literature do you enjoy reading? Explain. What prose or poetry have you read in its original language? Describe the experience.

▶ *Intercambio: ¿Quién es?*

Estudiante A

Selecciona uno de los escritores de la lista que tienes a continuación. Tu compañero(a) tiene que decubrir quién es. Para ello va a hacer preguntas a las que tú sólo puedes contestar SÍ o NO. Cuando él (ella) adivine el nombre del escritor, es tu turno para empezar a preguntar.

Camilo José Cela

Isabel Allende

Octavio Paz

Estudiante B

Tu compañero(a) va a pensar en un escritor y tú tienes que adivinar quién es. Para ello vas a hacer preguntas a las que sólo puede contestar SÍ o NO. Cuando adivines el nombre del escritor que ha seleccionado, es tu turno para seleccionar uno de los escritores de la lista que tienes a continuación. Tu compañero(a) tiene que descubrir quién es.

Miguel de Cervantes

Gabriela Mistral

Gabriel García Márquez

Vocabulario

Para charlar

Para hablar del mundo de las letras *Talking about the literary world*

el (la) autor(a) *author*
el (la) cuentista *storyteller*
el cuento *story*
el (la) dramaturgo(a) *playwright*
el (la) ensayista *essayist*
el ensayo *essay*
el (la) escritor(a) *writer*
la leyenda *legend*
la literatura *literature*
la novela *novel*
el (la) novelista *novelist*
la obra *work*
el (la) periodista *journalist*
el periódico *newspaper*
los personajes *characters*
la pieza teatral *play*
el poema *poem*
el (la) poeta *poet*
el premio *prize*
la revista *magazine*
el teatro *theater*
el tema *theme*

Para expresar resultados imaginarios o dependientes de acciones previas *Expressing imaginary results or those dependent on previous actions*

Antes de que... *Before . . .*
En caso de que... *In case . . .*
A menos que... *Unless . . .*
Para que... *So that . . .*
Sin que... *Without . . .*

Para hablar de condiciones irreales y hacer hipótesis *Talking about unreal conditions and making hypotheses*

Si tuviera tiempo, iría... *If I had time, I would go . . .*

Para expresar suposiciones *Expressing suppositions*

Si tengo tiempo, iré... *If I have time, I will go . . .*

Temas y contextos

Para hablar más del arte y la literatura *Talking more about art and literature*

Sustantivos
las corrientes (artísticas) *(artistic) trends*
la creación *creation*
el (la) crítico(a) *critic*
la historia (literaria) *(literary) story*
el idealismo *idealism*
las novelas de caballerías *novels of chivalry*
el realismo *realism*
la sátira *satire*

Verbos
añadir *to add*
desarrollar(se) *to develop*
negar *to deny*
publicar *to publish*
reflejar *to reflect*
representar *to represent*
traducir *to translate*
trazar *to trace*

Adjetivos
amplio(a) *broad, wide*
eterno(a) *eternal*
fiel *faithful*
grosero(a) *vulgar*
idealista *idealistic*
profundo(a) *deep*
realista *realistic*
sencillo(a) *simple*
trágico(a) *tragic*
universal *universal*

Otras palabras y expresiones
de carne y hueso *of flesh and blood*

Vocabulario general General vocabulary

Sustantivos

el amor *love*
una araña *spider*
el barro *mud*
los bisabuelos *great-grandparents*
el caballero *knight, gentleman*
las campanas *bells*
las creencias *beliefs*
el crepúsculo *twilight*
la dama *lady*
el destino *destination, destiny*
la dignidad *dignity*
la fantasía *fantasy*
la fe *faith*
la fe ciega *blind faith*
la feria *fair*
la fusión *fusion*
la honra *honor*
la imaginación *imagination*
la incertidumbre *uncertainty*
la irrealidad *unreality*
la justicia *justice*
el labrador *farmhand*
la lealtad *loyalty*
las leyes *laws*
la mezcla *mixture*
los mitos *myths*
una mordida *bite*
una mosca *fly*
la nobleza *nobility*
una oveja *sheep*
una pantera *panther*
la patria *patriotism*
los poderes *powers*
el premio *prize*
el punto de vista *point of view*
la realidad *reality*
un rincón *corner*
el ruido *noise*
la soledad *solitude*
la valentía *courage*
los valores *values*

Verbos

aparecer *to appear*
caber *to fit*
crecer *to grow*
desaparecer *to disappear*
encerrar *to enclose*
ganar *to earn*
incluir *to include*
ladrar *to bark*
murmurar *to murmur*
perder *to lose*
recorrer *to run through*
renovar *to renew*
respirar *to breathe*
señalar *to point*
soñar *to dream*
volver(se) *to return*

Adjetivos

extraterreno(a) *from another world*
hinchado(a) *swollen*
literario(a) *literary*
mágico(a) *magic*
misterioso(a) *mysterious*
mítico(a) *mythical*
reseco(a) *dried out*
sobrenatural *supernatural*

Otras expresiones

contar un cuento (una historia, un sueño, etc.) *to tell a story (a tale, a dream, etc.)*
convertirse en *to become*
de golpe *suddenly*
hacerse cargo de *to take charge of*
llamar la atención *to call attention*
tener que ver *to have to do with*

Capítulo preliminar xvi

Para empezar: ¡Hola! ¿Qué tal?

Antonio: Buenos días, Raúl.
Raul: Buenos días, Antonio. ¿Cómo estás?
Antonio: Muy bien, gracias. ¿Y tú?
Raul: Más o menos.
Laura: ¡Hola, Anita! ¿Qué tal?
Anita: Muy bien, Laura. Y tú?
Laura: Bien, gracias. Anita, te presentó a Juan. Juan, Anita.
Juan: ¡Hola!
Anita: Mucho gusto.
Patricia: ¡Hola! ¿Cómo te llamas?
Gabriel: Me llamo Gabriel. Y tú?
Patricia: Mi nombre es Patricia. Mucho gusto, Gabriel.
Gabriel: Igualmente, Patricia.

Capítulo uno 12

PRIMERA ETAPA

Para empezar: Te invito a un café

Señorita: Pst, camarero.
Camarero: Sí señorita, ¿qué desea tomar?
Señorita: Una limonada, por favor.
Camarero: ¿Y usted?
Muchacho: Un batido de fresa, por favor.
Camarero: Aquí tienen. Una limonada y un batido de fresa.
Muchacho: Muchas gracias.
Camarero: De nada.
Rafael y Pablo están en un restaurante en México.
Mesero: Buenos días, señores. ¿Qué van a pedir?
Rafael: Yo quisiera comer un taco de pollo con frijoles.
Pablo: Para mí, una enchilada de carne con arroz.
Mesero: ¿Y para tomar?
Rafael: Un vaso de agua con limón.
Mesero: Y para Ud., señor?
Pablo: Una limonada, muy fría, por favor.
Mesero: Muy bien.
Sara y Carlos, dos turistas españoles, están de visita en México.
Sara: Mm... ¡Qué comida más rica! ¿Qué es?
Señora: Son enchiladas con salsa.
Carlos: ¡Ay!... ¡Qué picante! No me gusta. Es muy picante para mí.
Señora: Aquí hay otra enchilada que no es picante.
Carlos: Mm... ¡Sí! Ésta me gusta. ¡Riquísima!
Sara: Carlos, el flan es delicioso también.
Carlos: Sí. ¡Qué bueno!

Sara: Me gusta mucho la comida mexicana. Es muy diferente de la comida española.

Vamos a escuchar: En un café

Clara: ¡Pst, camarero!
Camarero: ¿Qué desean tomar?
Ana: Una limonada.
Clara: Yo quisiera un café.
Camarero: ¿Y usted?
Francisco: Quisiera comer algo. Un sándwich de jamón y queso.
Ana: ¡Ah! Y yo, un pastel con el café.
Camarero: Bien, entonces, una limonada, un café, un pastel y un sandwich de jamón y queso.
Francisco: Y una botella de agua mineral.
Camarero: Está bien, ahora mismo.

SEGUNDA ETAPA

Vamos a escuchar: En un bar de tapas

Un camarero: ¡Una de calamares!
Otro camarero: ¡Unas aceitunas!
Otro camarero: Hola, buenos. ¿Qué van a tomar?
Beatriz:: Mmm... tortilla de patata y una cerveza. ¿Y tú, Linda?
Linda: Yo quiero unos calamares y para beber, mmm..., cerveza también.
Camarero: ¿Algo más?
Cristina: ¡Hola, Beatriz! ¡Hola, Linda!
Linda y Beatriz: ¡Hola, Cristina!
Cristina: Yo voy a tomar un vino tinto y pan con chorizo.
Camarero: Está bien.

TERCERA ETAPA

Vamos a escuchar: En una cantina mexicana

Camarero: Buenos días, ¿qué van a pedir?
Carolina: Para mí, unos tacos de pollo y frijoles.
Verónica: Yo quisiera unas enchiladas de queso con salsa de chile.
Camarero: ¿Y para tomar?
Carolina: Yo, una cerveza.
Camarero: Y Ud., ¿cerveza también?
Verónica: No, no me gusta la cerveza. Una limonada bien fría.
Camarero: Muy bien, un momento.
(The waiter brings the food.)
Pepe: ¡Carolina!
Carolina: ¡Pepe!
Pepe: ¡Hola, Carolina! ¿Qué tal estás?
Carolina: Muy bien, ¿y tú?
Pepe: Mm... ¡Qué comida más rica! ¿Qué es?
Carolina: Enchiladas con salsa de chile.
Pepe: ¡Qué picante! Está riquísima. Mmm...

Carolina: Perdona, Pepe. Ésta es Verónica, una amiga de Costa Rica.
Pepe: ¡Hola, Verónica! ¿Qué tal?
Verónica: Oye, tú no eres de aquí. ¿De dónde eres?
Pepe: De Salamanca.
Verónica: ¡Español! ¿Qué haces aquí?
Pepe: Soy estudiante.

Capítulo dos 48

PRIMERA ETAPA

Para empezar: ¿De quién es?

A woman's voice:
Hola, vivo en una casa. Allí hay un estéreo. Para ir al centro voy en coche. ¿Cómo vas tú al centro?
A man's voice:
Yo vivo en un apartamento. Allí hay un vídeo. Para ir al centro voy en autobús. ¿Cómo vas tú al centro?
A woman's voice:
Hola, vivo en una residencia estudiantil. Allí hay un televisor. Para ir al centro voy a pie.

¿Cómo vas tú al centro?

Vamos a escuchar: Aquí vivo. En mi cuarto tengo...

Hola, me llamo Miguel. Vivo en una casa con mi familia. En mi cuarto tengo un estéreo, un escritorio, una silla, una cama y una máquina de escribir. Para ir a clase voy en bicicleta. Llevo una mochila con mi cuaderno, mi calculadora y mis libros.

Buenos días, me llamo Isabel. Vivo en un apartamento cerca de la universidad con otros estudiantes. En mi cuarto tengo pósters, una cómoda, una computadora, un televisor. No tengo estantes y hay muchos libros en mi escritorio. Para ir a clase voy en coche.

SEGUNDA ETAPA

Para empezar: ¿Qué te gusta?

José: No me gusta la música.
Ana: Me gusta la música.
Mía: Me gustan los animales.
Lucía: No me gustan los animales.
Juan: Me gustan los deportes.
Olga: No me gustan los deportes.
Lucas: Me gusta la naturaleza.
María: No me gusta la naturaleza.
Jaime: No me gusta el arte.
Julia: Me gusta el arte.
Esteban: Me gustan las lenguas.
Paulo: No me gustan las lenguas.
Enrique: No me gustan las ciencias... no me gusta la química.
Laura: Me gustan las ciencias... me gusta la química.
Marta: No me gusta la biología.

Anita:	Me gusta la biología.
Lourdes:	Me gustan las películas.
Juan:	¿Qué películas te gustan más—las cómicas, las de horror, las de aventura o las de ciencia ficción?
Lourdes:	Me gustan más las películas de horror.
Marta:	Me gusta mucho la música.
Pablo:	¿Qué te gusta más—la música rock, el jazz o la música clásica?
Marta:	Me gusta más las música rock.
Susana:	Me gusta el arte.
Paco:	¿Qué te gusta más—la pintura o la escultura?
Susana:	Me gusta más la escultura.
Ángela:	Me gustan los animales.
Raúl:	¿Qué animales te gustan más—los perros, los gatos o los pájaros?
Ángela:	Me gustan más los pájaros.
Miguel:	Me gustan los deportes.
Alán:	¿Qué te gusta más—el fútbol, el fútbol americano, el básquetbol, el béisbol o el vólibol?
Miguel:	Me gusta más el béisbol.

Vamos a escuchar: ¿Qué te gusta?

Miguel:	Isabel, ¿te gusta el cine?
Isabel:	Sí.
Miguel:	¿Qué películas te gustan más? ¡Las películas de horror, de aventuras, de ciencia ficción?
Isabel:	Umm..., me gustan las películas de horror, pero las de ciencia ficción son mis favoritas. No me gustan las películas de aventuras. ¿Te gusta el cine?
Miguel:	No mucho. Me gustan más los deportes.
Isabel:	Ah, sí. ¿Qué deportes te gustan más?
Miguel:	Me gustan todos los deportes, pero mis favoritos son el fútbol americano y el básquetbol.

TERCERA ETAPA
Para empezar: Ésta es mi familia

Buenos días. Me llamo Tomás Torres Galindo. Tomás es mi nombre de pila y Torres es mi apellido. Tengo una familia pequeña. Hay cuatro personas en mi familia. Mi padre se llama Esteban y mi madre se llama Carmela. Mis padres están divorciados. No tengo hermanos pero tengo una hermana. Ella se llama Sofía. Ella es alta, delgada, morena y bonita. Tiene el pelo largo y rizado y los ojos verdes. Vivimos en una casa en Springfield, Massachusetts, con mi madre, mi abuela Luisa y mi abuelo Fernando. Mi padre vive en Cabo Rojo, Puerto Rico. Los padres de mi padre también viven allí.

Hola, me llamo Juan Mejía Castillo. Vivo con mi padre y madre en San Antonio, Texas. Tengo una hermana. Se llama Elena. Es rubia, tiene los ojos azules y el pelo corto. Es diverti-

da y simpática y tiene muchos amigos. Vive con su marido, Rafael, en Atlanta, Georgia. No tienen hijos. Cerca de nosotros vive mi tía Teresa, hermana de mi madre, y mi tío Felipe, su esposo. Mis abuelos maternos, es decir los padres de mi madre, también viven en San Antonio. No tengo abuelos paternos.

Vamos a escuchar: Mi familia

Hola, me llamo Miguel García. Tengo una familia muy grande—dos hermanos y tres hermanas. Mis abuelos también viven con nosotros. Mi padre se llama Luis y mi madre se llama Sara. Mi madre es periodista y mi padre es ingeniero. Mis hermanos no trabajan. Son estudiantes en la universidad.

Hola, me llamo Isabel Vásquez. Tengo una familia pequeña. Vivo con mi mamá y mi hermanito, Jose. Mis padres están divorciados. Mi madre es profesora de matemáticas y mi padre es contador. Vive en otra ciudad con su esposa. Mis abuelos tienen restaurante donde trabajo de camarera los fines de semana.

Capítulo tres   88

PRIMERA ETAPA
Vamos a escuchar: ¿Adónde van?

Gloria:	Oye, Marilú. Tengo que ir al centro para hacer unas compras. ¿Quieres ir?
Marilú:	Bueno, prefiero ir al cine, pero, sí, vamos pues.
Gloria:	¡Bien! Podemos almorzar tambien si quieres, en el nuevo restaurante italiano.
Marilú:	Buena idea. Tengo hambre. ¿Adónde vamos primero?
Gloria:	Bueno, primero vamos a la librería porque tengo que comprar un libro de historia. Luego a la farmacia y después al correo.
Marilú:	¡Un momento, un momento, Gloria! Tienes mucho que hacer. Creo que voy a descansar mientras vas a comprar. ¿Por qué no vamos al restaurante a las 3:00?
Gloria:	¡Ay, no! Mira, mejor vamos al restaurante primero y después vamos de compras. ¿Prefieres comer primero?
Marilú:	Bueno, ya que insistes. Sí, tengo ganas de comer ahora.
Gloria:	Vamos, entonces. Yo te voy a comprar la ensalada de pasta que tanto te gusta.
Marilú:	¡Ay qué rico! ¡Vamos!

SEGUNDA ETAPA
Vamos a escuchar: ¿Dónde está la biblioteca?

Señora:	Perdón, señor. No soy de aquí. ¿Dónde está la biblioteca?
Señor:	Está cerca del banco central. ¿Sabe

dónde está el banco?

Señora:	Creo que está cerca de la oficina de correos.
Señor:	Exacto. La biblioteca está en la esquina de la calle donde están el correo y el banco.
Señora:	Muchas gracias.
Señor:	No hay de qué.

TERCERA ETAPA
Vamos a escuchar: ¿Dónde está la Calle González Obregón?

Señor:	Perdone, señorita. ¿Dónde está la Calle González Obregón? Quiero ir a la Secretaría de Educación Pública.
Señorita:	¿La Calle González Obregón? Cómo no. Está cerca de aquí.
Señor:	¿En qué calle estamos ahora?
Señorita:	Estamos en la Calle Madero. Siga recto hasta llegar a la plaza de la Constitución. Después doble a la izquierda y siga cuatro cuadras y ahí está la Calle González Obregón. Doble allí a la derecha y al final de la cuadra está la Secretaría de Educación Pública.
Señor:	Muchas gracias, señorita.
Señorita:	No hay de qué.

Capítulo cuatro   120

PRIMERA ETAPA
Para empezar: ¿Vas al centro?

-¿Vas al centro esta tarde?
-Sí, voy a ver a unos amigos. Tenemos una cita a las 2:00.
-¿Vas en autobús?
-No, voy a tomar el metro.
-¿Tienes ganas de ir al cine esta noche?
-Sí, qué buen idea. ¿Tomamos el metro?
-No, vamos en autobús.
-Tengo que ir al centro hoy para ir de compras. ¿Quieres ir conmigo?
-Sí, yo también tengo que comprar unas cosas. ¿Vamos a pie?
-No, vamos en el coche de mi hermana.
-Tengo que ir al centro para hacer un mandado. Debo ir al correo.
-Voy contigo. Tengo que hacer un mandado.
-Perfecto. Vamos juntos y después damos un paseo.

Vamos a escuchar: ¿Quieres ir conmigo?

Juan:	Hola, Laura. ¿Qué tal?
Laura:	Muy bien, Juan. ¿Y tú?
Juan:	Bastante bien, gracias. ¿Qué haces?
Laura:	Tengo que ir al centro.
Juan:	¿Para qué vas?
Laura:	Tengo que hacer un mandado para mi padre. ¿Quieres ir conmigo?
Juan:	¡Cómo no! Yo también tengo que ir al centro. Quiero comprar un disco compacto nuevo.

Laura:	Vamos entonces. Primero hacemos el mandado y después pasamos por la tienda de discos.
Juan:	¡Perfecto! ¿Cómo quieres ir? ¿A pie?
Laura:	¡No, qué va! No tenemos todo el día. Vamos en metro.

SEGUNDA ETAPA

Para empezar: Vamos a tomar el subte

Elena y su prima Clara van a tomar el subte para ir al Museo de Arte Moderno. La casa de Elena está cerca de la estación de metro. Las dos jóvenes miran el mapa del subte que está a la entrada de la estación.

Elena:	Bueno. Estamos aquí, en la estación San Juan.
Clara:	¿Dónde está el museo?
Elena:	Está cerca de la Estación Callao. Allí.
Clara:	Entonces, ¿qué hacemos?
Elena:	Es fácil. Tomamos la línea C en dirección de Retiro.
Clara:	¿Tenemos que cambiar de tren?
Elena:	Sí, tenemos que cambiar de trenes. Cambiamos en 9 de julio. Allí tomamos la línea B en dirección de Federico Lacroz.
Clara:	Y bajamos en Callao, ¿verdad?
Elena:	Exacto, allí en Callao bajamos.

Vamos a escuchar: ¿Vamos al centro?

Carmen:	Hola, Ramón.
Ramón:	Hola, Carmen. ¿Qué quieres hacer?
Carmen:	¿Por qué no vamos al centro?
Ramón:	¿Para qué?
Carmen:	Quiero comprar un libro para mi clase de literatura.
Ramón:	Yo también quiero ir al centro. Tengo ganas de ver una película.
Carmen:	¿Por qué no pasamos por la Librería Acosta primero? Después podemos ir al cine.
Ramón:	Buena idea. ¿Cómo vamos? ¿En autobús?
Carmen:	No, no. Nos queda más cerca si vamos en metro. Tomamos la línea A en Loria que está aquí al lado. Cambiamos en Avenida de Mayo y bajamos en San Martín. La librería está muy cerca y también hay muchos teatros donde podemos ver la película que quieres. ¿Qué crees?
Ramón:	¡Vamos!

TERCERA ETAPA:

Para empezar: ¿Tomamos un taxi?

Linda y Julia van a almorzar en La Cabana, un restaurante en Buenos Aires. Piensan tomar un taxi.

Linda:	¡Taxi! ¡Taxi!
Chofer:	¿Adónde van?

Ellas suben al taxi.

Linda:	Al Restaurante La Cabana en la Calle Entre Ríos por favor. ¿Cuánto tarda en llegar?
Chofer:	Diez minutos... quince como máximo.

Llegan al restaurante. Julia baja del taxi y Linda va a pagar:

Linda:	¿Cuánto es, señor?
Chofer:	Ocho pesos.
Linda:	Tome, veinte pesos.
Chofer:	Aquí tiene Ud. el cambio, doce pesos.

Linda le da dos pesos de propina al chofer:

Linda:	Y esto es para Ud.
Chofer:	Muchas gracias. Hasta luego.

Vamos a escuchar: Vamos a cenar

Pedro:	Tengo mucha hambre. ¿Por qué no vamos a cenar?
Lydia:	Vamos. Conozco un restaurante donde sirven un bistec riquísimo y no es muy caro.
Pedro:	¿Cómo vamos? ¿En el subte o en taxi?
Lydia:	Vamos en taxi. Llegamos muy rápido.
Pedro:	¡Taxi, taxi! ¿Está libre?
Taxista:	Sí, sí, ¡cómo no! ¿Adónde van?
Lydia:	Queremos ir al restaurante La Estancia. Es un restaurante que está en la Calle Lavalle, 941.
Pedro:	¿Cuánto tarda en llegar?
Taxista:	Unos quince minutos, más o menos. Depende en el tráfico.

Llegan al restaurante.

Lydia:	¿Cuánto es?
Taxista:	Doce pesos.
Lydia:	Aquí tiene.
Taxista:	Tome su cambio—ocho pesos. Muchísimas gracias.
Lydia:	A Ud., señor. Hasta luego.

Capítulo cinco 154

PRIMERA ETAPA

Vamos a escuchar: El viaje de Elena

[Sound effects: Phone ringing-person picks it up]

Rafael:	Hola, Elena. Te habla Rafael. ¿Cómo estás?
Elena:	Hola, Rafael. Estoy bien, gracias. ¿Y tú?
Rafael:	Muy bien. Te llamé anoche pero no te encontré en casa. ¿Qué tal el viaje a Los Ángeles?
Elena:	Bastante bién. Volé desde Los Ángeles a Nueva York y no llegué a San Juan hasta esta mañana.
Rafael:	¡Qué viaje más largo! ¿Qué hiciste todas esas horas en el avión?

Elena:	Bueno, la pasé bastante bien, fíjate. Escuché música, vi una película, jugué naipes, leí varias, hablé con una señora muy interesante de Bolivia, tomé muchos refrescos, y luego al final del viaje pasó algo realmente extraordinario. Es algo que prefiero decirte esta noche.
Rafael:	¿Cómo? ¿Qué pasó? ¿Me lo dices esta noche? Pues bién. ¿Quieres cenar esta noche y me dices lo que pasó?
Elena:	Cómo no. ¿Por qué no vamos al Restaurante Las Brisas? Prefiero hablar de esto contigo ahí.
Rafael:	Bueno, ya me dejaste en suspenso pero paso por ti a las 7:30 y me cuentas todos los detalles de lo que pasó.
Elena:	Claro que sí. Nos vemos a las 7:30. Hasta luego.
Rafael:	Adiós. Hasta luego.

[Sound effect: Phone hanging up]

SEGUNDA ETAPA

Para empezar: ¿Adónde fuiste?

Es el lunes por la mañana, antes de clase. Carlos y su amiga Cristina hablan de adónde fueron ellos y algunos de sus amigos el sábado por la tarde.

Carlos:	Hola, Cristina, ¿cómo estás?
Cristina:	Bién, y tú, qué tal?
Carlos:	Muy, muy bien. ¿Qué hiciste el sábado pasado? ¿Fuiste al cine?
Cristina:	No, no. No, fui al cine. Roberto y yo fuimos al concierto. ¿Y tú?
Carlos:	Yo fui a la biblioteca.
Cristina:	¿Fuiste con tu novia?
Carlos:	No, ella fue al gimnasio.
Cristina:	Y tu hermano, ¿qué hizo? ¿Fue al gimnasio, también?
Carlos:	No, mi hermano y su novia fueron al partido de fútbol.

Vamos a escuchar: ¿Adónde fuiste de vacaciones?

Olga:	Hola, Juan. ¿Qué tal las vacaciones? ¿Adónde fuiste?
Juan:	Hola, Olga. ¿Cómo estás? Bien, bien. Fui con la familia a Puerto Plata en Santo Domingo por una semana.
Olga:	¿Ah, sí? ¡Puerto Plata! Pues, mi familia y yo fuimos hace dos años. ¿Te gustó?
Juan:	¡Pues, claro que sí! ¡Me gustó mucho! La pasamos muy bien allí.
Olga:	Pues, ¿qué hicieron?
Juan:	Bueno, nos quedamos en el Hotel Presidente y fuimos a la playa todos los días. Nadamos por la mañana y por la tarde mis hermanos y yo practicamos windsurf.

Olga:	¿Windsurf? ¿Fue difícil hacer windsurf?
Juan:	Pues, no fue tan difícil, fíjate, especialmente si sabes esquiar como yo. Un hombre en la playa me enseñó a hacer windsurf.
Olga:	¡Ah, qué bien!
Juan:	Al principio, fue un poco difícil pero aprendí a hacerlo bastante bien en una tarde.
Olga:	¿Y tus hermanos? ¿Ellos aprendieron también?
Juan:	Mi hermano mayo, Raul, también aprendió, pero a Pablo, que no nada muy bien, no le gustó.
Olga:	Pues, Juan, yo quiero hacer windsurf algún día.
Juan:	¡Cómo no! Yo creo que puedes hacerlo fácilmente porque también esquias mucho. Y yo te ayudo si quieres.
Olga:	Muy bien. ¡Buen idea! Algún día hacemos windsurf juntos, entonces. Bueno, Juan, hasta pronto. Adiós.
Juan:	Adiós, Olga.

TERCERA ETAPA

Para empezar: ¿Qué deportes practicaste el año pasado?

Esteban:	¡Hola! ¿Cómo estás?
Alberto:	Bien, gracias, ¿y tú?
Esteban:	Pues, estoy un poco cansado hoy porque jugué al fútbol ayer.
Alberto:	¿Estás en algún equipo?
Esteban:	Sí, estoy en el equipo de nuestra escuela.
Alberto:	¿Vas a practicar?
Esteban:	Sí, tengo que practicar los lunes, martes, miércoles y jueves.
Alberto:	¿Cuándo son los partidos?
Esteban:	Los partidos son los viernes por la noche. Y tú, ¿estás en algún equipo?
Alberto:	No. Me gusta mucho jugar al baloncesto, pero no estoy en un equipo. Sólo juego para hacer ejercicio.

Vamos a escuchar: Un partido importante

Sonia:	Hola, Mari, ¿qué tal?
Mari:	Muy bien, Sonia. ¿Y tú?
Sonia:	Más o menos. Estoy cansada.
Mari:	¿Qué pasó? ¿Fuiste a una fiesta anoche?
Sonia:	No, no. Nada de eso. Es que estoy en el equipo de baloncesto de la universidad y ayer practicamos por tres horas.
Mari:	¿Tres horas? ¿Por qué practicaron tanto?
Sonia:	Porque tenemos un partido muy importante el viernes y tenemos que ganar.

Mari:	¡Ah! ¿Contra quién juegan?
Sonia:	Es el equipo de la Universidad Nacional. Nos ganaron el año pasado. Pero este año nuestro equipo tiene mejores jugadores.
Mari:	¡Qué bueno! Oye, Sonia, ¿a qué hora juegan el viernes? Quisiera ir a ver el partido.
Sonia:	¡Cómo no! Mira, jugamos a las 2:00. ¿Quieres este boleto?
Mari:	¿De véras? ¡Qué amable eres! Muchas gracias.
Sonia:	De nada, Mari. Bueno, hasta luego.
Mari:	Hasta luego. ¡Y buena suerte!

Capítulo seis 196

PRIMERA ETAPA

Para empezar: En el centro comercial

Narrador: En una tienda de discos

Anoche, Beatriz y Mónica fueron a un concierto en el Centro Cultural de la Universidad Católica de Lima a escuchar a Patricia Saravia, una cantante peruana. A las dos les gustó mucho la música de Patricia y por eso hoy van a comprar uno de sus discos, "De Inga y de Mandinga".

Beatriz:	Mira, aquí están los discos compactos de Patricia. ¡Qué pena! No tengo suficiente dinero para comprarlos todos.
Mónica:	¿Cuáles quieres comprar?
Beatriz:	Bueno, sólo tengo dinero para uno, así que voy a comprar el último, "De Inga y de Mandinga".
Mónica:	¿Quieres ir a mirar las cintas? Normalmente son más baratas.
Beatriz:	¿Dónde están?
Mónica:	Allí, al lado de los vídeos.
Beatriz:	Bien, vamos.

Narrador: En una tienda de deportes

Elsa y Norma viven en La Paz. A las dos les gusta jugar al tenis y lo hacen con frecuencia. Hoy las dos amigas van a una tienda de deportes que está en Shopping Norte, uno de los centros comerciales de la ciudad. Elsa necesita comprar una raqueta nueva.

Dependiente:	Sí, señoritas, ¿qué necesitan?
Elsa:	Quisiera saber cuánto cuesta la raqueta del escaparate.
Dependiente:	¡Ah! Buen ojo. Es una raqueta muy buena y cuesta 300 bolivianos.
Elsa:	¿Cómo? ¿No está en oferta?
Dependiente:	No, lo siento. La oferta terminó ayer.
Elsa:	¡Qué pena! Bueno. Y las pelotas de tenis, ¿qué precio tienen?

Dependiente:	Mmm... nueve bolivianos la lata.
Elsa:	Bueno, voy a llevar tres.
Dependiente:	Aquí tiene. ¿Algo más?
Elsa:	Sí. Quiero ver unos zapatos de tenis también, por favor.
Dependiente:	Sí, ahora mismo. ¿Qué número tiene?
Elsa:	El 36.

[The clerk looks through a few boxes and finds a pair of shoes.]

Dependiente:	A ver éstos.

[Elsa tries the shoes on.]

Elsa:	Sí, éstos están bien. Son muy cómodos. ¿Cuánto cuestan?
Dependiente:	260.
Elsa:	Perfecto. Entonces, ¿cuánto cuesta todo?
Dependiente:	A ver, tres latas de pelotas, 27, más las zapatillas, 260, total, 287. ¿Cómo va a pagar?
Elsa:	Con tarjeta. Aquí tiene.

Narrador: En la tienda Moda Joven, en el centro comercial en Quito. Hoy sábado Mercedes y Sara van de compras al centro comercial en Quito, Ecuador. Necesitan comprar un regalo para el cumpleaños de Rosa. A las dos les gusta mirar escaparates.

Mercedes:	Aquí tienen ropa bonita.
Sara:	¡Mira esta falda azul! ¡Qué linda!
Mercedes:	A Rosa le va a gustar ese color. Con este cinturón negro queda muy bien. Creo que le va a gustar.
Sara:	Sí, tienes razón. Perfecto. Ahora quiero ver un vestido para mí.
Mercedes:	Aquí en frente hay una boutique muy elegante.
Sara:	Mmmm... entonces, seguro que es cara.
Mercedes:	No sé. ¿Vamos a ver el escaparate?
Sara:	Sí, ¿por qué no?

Vamos a escuchar: En el centro comercial

Conversación 1

Dependienta:	Hola, buenas tardes. ¿En qué puedo servirle?
Cliente:	Hola. Me hace falta una raqueta de tenis. Ya tengo una, pero está muy vieja. Además creo que pesa demasiado.
Dependienta:	Bueno. Le puedo mostrar unas que acaban de llegar. Llegaron ayer por la tarde y ya vendimos tres.
Cliente:	Bueno, está bien. Pero me

imagino que si acaban de llegar, todavía no estarán de oferta.

Dependienta: No, no, claro, no están de oferta, pero no son muy caras.

Cliente: Vale, a ver cómo son.

Conversación 2

Dependiente: Hola, buenas.

Cliente: Hola, estoy buscando un vestido para mi novia. ¿Puedo ver ése?

Dependiente: ¿Cuál? ¿Este verde?

Cliente: Sí, el verde. Muéstreme ése, por favor. ¿Cuánto cuesta?

Dependiente: Mil ochocientos.

Cliente: ¡Mil ochocientos! No, es carísimo. Lo compro por mil.

Dependiente: No, lo siento, no se lo puedo dejar en mil. Si quiere algo más barato ahí tenemos unos vestidos que están de oferta.

Conversación 3

Cliente 1: Oye, mira, tienen una selección fabulosa de rock.

Cliente 2: Sí, es cierto. Mi hermano estuvo aquí la semana pasada y pasó más de una hora.

Cliente 1: ¿Compró algún disco?

Cliente 2: No, creo que al final compró dos cintas y un disco compacto. Los compactos están bastante baratos aquí.

Cliente 1: Es verdad. Mira éstos de aquí. Creo que voy a comprar uno para mí y otro para mi novia.

SEGUNDA ETAPA 211
Para empezar: ¿Cuánto cuesta?

Narrador: En el mercado
Ayer domingo fue día de feria en Chinchero, un pueblo cerca de Cuzco. La señora Fernández, como siempre que hay feria, caminó al mercado para hacer las compras de frutas y verduras. En el mercado de Chincheros siempre encuentra productos frescos, baratos y de excelente calidad.

¿Qué se puede comprar?
Las verduras:

cebollas	champiñones
espárragos	guisantes
lechuga	maíz
papas	pepinos
tomates	zanahorias

Las frutas:

aguacates	bananas
fresas	limones
mangos	manzanas
melocotones	melón
naranjas	peras
uvas	

Narrador: En el supermercado

Una vez por semana Ricardo hace las compras para su casa en el supermercado. Hoy Rosa también tiene que ir al supermercado para comprar alimentos para su familia y los dos amigos van juntos. Primero, van a la sección de productos lácteos porque Ricardo tiene que comprar mantequilla, leche, yogur, crema y queso. Después van a la sección de conservas porque necesitan tres latas de sopa y una lata de atún, una botella de aceite y un paquete de galletas.

Luego pasan por la sección de productos congelados porque Rosa tiene que comprar pescado, una pizza, un pollo y también ¡helado de chocolate! A Rosa le encanta el helado.

Para terminar, compran pastas, harina, azúcar, sal, pimienta, arroz y mayonesa. El carrito de Rosa está muy lleno.

Vamos a escuchar: De compras en el mercado

Sr. Estévez: Hola, buenos días.

Dependienta: Hola, ¿cómo está?

Sr. Estévez: Bien, muy bien. Oiga, quiero preparar un guacamole para esta noche. ¿Tiene aguacates?

Dependienta: No, señor, se acabaron ya. Lo siento.

Sr. Estévez: Bueno, en fin, no importa. A ver, entonces, medio kilo de papas y dos cebollas.

Dependienta: Cómo no. Aquí tiene. ¿Algo más?

Sr. Estévez: Sí, mm..., estos mangos se ven muy bien. ¿Cuánto cuestan?

Dependienta: Esos dos le cuestan 150. Están bien dulces.

Sr. Estévez: Está bien. Me los llevo. Ah, y también quiero una lechuga.

Dependienta: ¿Ésta? ¿Le parece bien ésta?

Sr. Estévez: Sí, ésa está bien. Y unos tomates.

Dependienta: ¿Cuántos?

Sr. Estévez: Un kilo.

Dependienta: ¿Necesita algo más?

Sr. Estévez: No, eso es todo. ¿Cuánto es?

Dependienta: Son 534 en total.

Sr. Estévez: Aquí tiene.

TERCERA ETAPA 223
Para empezar: ¿Qué compraste?

Teresa: ¿Aló?

Patricia: ¿Está Teresa?

Teresa: Sí, soy yo. ¿Quién es?

Patricia: ¿Teresa? Hola, soy Patricia. ¿Qué tal?

Teresa: Hola, Patricia. Oye, te llamé ayer pero no te encontré en casa.

Patricia: Ya estuve fuera toda la tarde.

Teresa: ¿Qué hiciste?

Patricia: Pues fui con mi prima Clara al centro comercial. Pasamos la tarde mirando escaparates y también compramos algunas cosas.

Teresa: ¡Ah!

Patricia: Sí, la semana pasada Clara leyó en el periódico un anuncio sobre ofertas especiales para este fin de semana y decidimos ir a ver. Al llegar al centro comercial fuimos lo primero de todo a la tienda de discos. Allí oímos el último disco compacto de Rubén Blades y también vimos algunos vídeos.

Teresa: ¿Compraron algo?

Patricia: Bueno vimos muchas cosas pero al final lo único que compramos fue un par de cintas vírgenes para grabar en casa.

Teresa: ¿Vieron algo más?

Patricia: Sí, después de ver los discos, yo me fui a ver los escaparates de las tiendas de ropa. Vi unos vestidos increíbles pero sólo compré una camiseta para mí y otra para Jorge.

Teresa: ¿Y Clara?

Patricia: Creo que vio unas zapatillas de tenis en oferta y decidió comprarlas. Después fuimos juntas a la papelería. Allí Clara compró una tarjeta de cumpleaños para un amigo y unos sobres. Yo compré papel para la computadora.

Teresa: ¿Oye? ¿Qué vas a hacer esta tarde?

Patricia: No sé, creo que me voy a quedar en casa a descansar. Estoy muerta.

Teresa: Bueno, es que Martín llamó hace un rato para invitarnos a una fiesta en su apartamento.

Patricia: ¿A qué hora?

Teresa: A partir de las ocho. ¿Te apetece ir?

Patricia: Sí, sí, ¿nos vemos a las 7:30 en tu casa?

Teresa: Bien, entonces hasta las 7:30. Hasta luego.

Patricia: Adiós.

Vamos a escuchar: El regalo para Alberto

Laura: ¿Dígame?

Silvia: ¿Laura?

Laura: Sí, soy yo, ¿quién es?

Silvia: Laura, soy yo. Oye, tienes que ayudarme.

Laura: ¿Qué pasa?

Silvia:	Laura, necesito dinero.
Laura:	¿Cómo? ¿Que necesitas dinero?
Silvia:	Sí, mira, te explico. El sábado es el cumpleaños de Alberto y ayer fui al centro comercial a comprarle algo. Pues bien, no pude resistir la tentación, me gasté todo el dinero en ropa para mí. Me compré un vestido, un par de blusas y un disco de Patricia Saravia.
Laura:	Estás loca, Silvia. Está claro que no puedes ir de compras sola, y menos cuando están de oferta en las tiendas.
Silvia:	Mira, Laura, necesito dinero para comprarle algo a Alberto.
Laura:	¿Cuánto necesitas?
Silvia:	2.000.
Laura:	¿Qué piensas comprarle?
Silvia:	No sé, creo que una camisa. Vi una ayer que no es muy cara.
Laura:	¿Cuánto cuesta?
Silvia:	300.
Laura:	Silvia, hay algo que no comprendo. Si la camisa cuesta 300, ¿para qué quieres 2.000?
Silvia:	Es que también vi unos zapatos por 1.200, un precio increíble, ¿no crees?
Laura:	Lo siento, Silvia, olvídate de los zapatos. Mira te dejo 300 para el regalo de Alberto, pero nada más, ¿está claro?
Silvia:	Está bien, Laura. Gracias.

Capítulo siete   240

PRIMERA ETAPA
Vamos a escuchar: Conversaciones sobre el tiempo

Diálogo 1

Narrador: La familia Valenzuela está de vacaciones en Portillo, Chile, pero hace mal tiempo y los hijos no están contentos.

Marcelo:	¡Qué aburrido estoy! Hace mucho frío aquí. Está nublado. ¡Y hay tormenta ahora!
Susana:	¡Sí! En Acapulco problemente hace buen tiempo con mucho sol.
Papá:	¿Por qué están de mal humor? Por lo menos ayer esquiamos un poco.
Mamá:	Y todos comemos bien aquí, ¿no?
Susana:	Es verdad. Pasamos todo el día en el cuarto del hotel.
Papá:	Pero por lo menos estamos de vacaciones en familia y eso es bueno.

Diálogo 2

Narrador: Mañana es sábado. Patricia y sus amigos hablan de sus planes para el fin de semana, pero sus planes

dependen del tiempo que va a hacer.

Patricia:	¿Quieren ir a la playa mañana?
Margo:	No sé. ¿Qué tiempo va hacer?
Elena:	Escuché el pronóstico en la TV. ¡Mañana por la mañana va a llover a cántaros!
Margo:	Entonces yo prefiero ir al centro.
Patricia:	¿Y mañana por la tarde va a llover también?
Elena:	No, va a hacer buen tiempo. Va a hacer mucho calor.
Patricia:	¡Qué bien! Podemos ir a la playa por la tarde entonces. Margo, ¿quieres ir con nosotras?
Margo:	Sí, si ustedes van al centro conmigo por la mañana.
Elena:	De acuerdo. Vamos al centro por la mañana y a la playa por la tarde.

SEGUNDA ETAPA
Vamos a escuchar: ¡Qué feo es este auto!

Felipe ahorró su dinero y por fin compró un coche. Sus amigos inspeccionan el coche, pero sus reacciones no son muy positivas.

Claudia:	¡Qué feo es este coche! No me gusta nada. ¡Qué horror!
Felipe:	¡Cómo que feo! Miren... no es caro, es muy práctico.
Pablo:	¿Estás seguro de que funciona, Felipe?
Felipe:	¡Claro que sí, oigan! ¡Es pequeño, es económico y funciona muy bien y por lo menos tengo un coche! ¿Quieren dar una vuelta?
Claudia:	Bueno, yo sí. ¿Pero un coche violeta? Es un poco extraño, ¿no?

TERCERA ETAPA
Vamos a escuchar: Descripciones de personas

Diálogo 1

Roberto va a visitar su hermana Silvia el próximo fin de semana. Su amigo Raúl quiere saber cómo es Silvia y Roberto la describe.

Raúl:	¿Qué hace tu hermana, Roberto?
Roberto:	Es doctora en Chicago.
Raúl:	¿Cuántos años tiene?
Roberto:	Es mi hermana mayor. Tiene veintinueve años.
Raúl:	¿Cómo es?
Roberto:	Es muy independiente y seria. Le gustan los deportes y es atlética también. Por lo general, parece una persona muy feliz.
Raúl:	¿Es muy trabajadora?
Roberto:	Claro que sí. Pero es muy simpática y, a veces, es muy generosa con su tiempo y con su dinero.
Raúl:	Me gustaría mucho conocer a tu hermana. Parece perfecta.
Roberto:	¡Cuidado! ¡Es casada y tiene hijos!

Diálogo 2

Cecilia va visitar a Manuel, su hermano mayor, el próximo fin de semana. Ahora, ella le describe a su amiga Claudia cómo es su hermano.

Cecilia:	Mi hermano Manuel es muy simpático.
Claudia:	¿Qué hace?
Cecilia:	Está en la universidad. Va a ser ingeniero.
Claudia:	¿Cómo es?
Cecilia:	Es muy alto y guapo. Tiene el pelo castaño, los ojos verdes y una nariz pequeña.
Claudia:	¿Tiene bigote? Adoro a los hombres con bigote.
Cecilia:	No, pero tiene barba.
Claudia:	Me gustaría mucho conocer a Manuel. ¡Parece sensacional!
Cecilia:	¡Lo siento! ¡Tiene una novia muy celosa!

Capítulo ocho   278

PRIMERA ETAPA
Vamos a escuchar: El accidente de Felipe

Narrador: Carlos habla por teléfono con su amigo Felipe.

Carlos:	Hola, ¿Felipe? ¿Qué te pasa? No fuiste a la escuela hoy.
Felipe:	No, tuve en pequeño accidente.
Carlos:	¿Un accidente? ¿Te lastimaste?
Felipe:	Sí, me rompí la pierna.
Carlos:	¡Te rompiste la pierna! ¡No me digas! ¿Cómo te pasó?
Felipe:	Mira, es que soy verdaderamente torpe. Yo iba en mi bicicleta con Catarina. Hablábamos mucho. Nos reíamos. Nos divertíamos. No prestábamos atención. De repente un perro grande cruzó la calle en frente de nosotros. Y los dos nos caímos.
Carlos:	¿Y Catarina? ¿Se lastimó ella también?
Felipe:	Ella se torció un tobillo y se cortó el brazó. Pero no fue muy grave.

SEGUNDA ETAPA
Vamos a escuchar: En la farmacia

Farmacéutica:	Buenos días, señor. ¿En qué puedo servirle?
Cliente [sounding sick]:	Es que no me siento muy bien. Toso sin parar y me duele la garganta.
Farmacéutica:	¿Tiene usted fiebre?
Cliente:	Sí, un poco, pero necesito algo para la tos.
Farmacéutica:	Este jarabe es muy bueno.
Cliente:	¿Tiene algo para el dolor de garganta?
Farmacéutica:	¡Claro que sí! Le recomiendo estas pastillas.

Cliente:	Muchas gracias. ¿Puede darme unas aspirinas también?
Farmacéutica:	Sí, sí. Parece que usted tiene la gripe. Descanse y beba mucha agua y jugo de naranja.

TERCERA ETAPA
Vamos a escuchar: Comer bien

Héctor:	¿Cuánto mides, Felipe?
Felipe:	Mido exactamente un metro setenta y ocho.
Héctor:	¿Y cuánto pesas?
Felipe:	Setenta y dos kilos.
Héctor:	¿Y cómo guardas la línea?
Felipe:	Pues hago gimnasia todos los días y como bien.
Héctor:	¿Comes dulces y galletas?
Felipe:	A veces, pero por lo general prefiero evitarlos y comer bien. En casa preparamos unas comidas estupendas.
Héctor:	¿Qué preparan?
Felipe:	Bueno, pues comidas balanceadas. No comemos ni mucha carne ni muchos postres. Comemos vegetales y frutas todos los días.

Capítulo nueve   314

PRIMERA ETAPA
Vamos a escuchar: ¡Bienvenido a casa!

Sra. Álvarez:	¿Eres Patrick?
Patrick:	Sí, ¿Sra. Álvarez?
Sra. Álvarez:	Sí, hola, Patrick. ¿Qué tal?
Patrick:	Un poco cansado.
Sra. Álvarez:	Bueno, no te preocupes. En seguida llegamos a casa y si quieres puedes dormir una siesta.

Narrador: Llegan a la casa de los Sres. Álvarez, tocan el timbre y abre Pedro.

Pedro:	Hola, Patrick. ¿Qué tal el viaje? Debes estar cansado.
Patrick:	Sí, un poco porque no dormí mucho en el avión.
Pedro:	¿A qué hora saliste de Nueva York?
Patrick:	Llegué al Aeropuerto Kennedy a las 4:00 pero el avión no salió hasta las 6:00.
Sr. Álvarez:	Ven, Patrick. Vamos a llevar tus maletas a tu habitación.
Sra. Álvarez:	Aquí está tu habitación.
Patrick:	Muchas gracias, señora. Oh, es muy bonita.
Sra. Álvarez:	Sí, es muy cómoda. Tienes una cama grande, un sillón, este escritorio con su lámpara y ahí esos estantes para tus libros.
Patrick:	¿Dónde pongo mi ropa?

Sra. Álvarez:	Mira, ahí tienes un armario para colgar tus cosas. En esta cómoda con cajones puedes guardar lo que quieras.
Patrick:	Ah, ¿dónde está el baño?
Sra. Álvarez:	Está en el corredor a la derecha. Allí hay toallas y jabón. Allí puedes dejar tu ropa sucia. Lavo la ropa todos los sábados.
Patrick:	Muchas gracias, señora. Es Ud. muy amable.

SEGUNDA ETAPA
Vamos a escuchar: ¿Tienen habitación reservada?

Linda:	Buenas tardes.
Empleado:	Buenas tardes. ¿En qué puedo servirles?
Linda:	Tenemos una habitación reservada para esta noche.
Empleado:	Sí, a ver, un momento. ¿A nombre de quién?
Linda:	Klein, Linda Klein. Llamé la semana pasada para hacer la reserva.
Empleado:	Sí, espere. Klein, Klein, aquí está. Una habitación doble, ¿verdad?
Linda:	Sí, así es. Y, ¿cuánto cuesta?
Empleado:	El precio de la habitación es 6.000 colones por noche.
Linda:	Y, ¿está incluido el desayuno?
Empleado:	No, el desayuno es aparte. Si quieren, pueden pagar 650 colones más y desayunar en el hotel.
Linda:	Kelly, ¿qué piensas? ¿Desayunamos aquí?
Kelly:	Sí, ¿por qué no?
Empleado:	Bueno, aquí tienen la llave. La habitación es el número 38 y está en el tercer piso.
Kelly:	Gracias.
Empleado:	No hay de qué.

Narrador: Linda y Kelly suben hasta el tercer piso y entran en la habitación.

Linda:	Esta habitación es simple, pero no está mal.
Kelly:	Sí, mira, las camas son muy cómodas.
Kelly:	¡Uf! Estoy muerta. ¿Por qué no dormimos una siesta antes de salir?
Linda:	Sí, buena idea, Kelly.

TERCERA ETAPA
Vamos a escuchar: Buscamos un apartamento

Patrick:	¡Mira! Encontré un apartamento con dos dormitorios y está amueblado.
Richard:	¿Dónde está?

Patrick:	Muy cerca de la universidad.
Richard:	Eso está bien. Pero si está amueblado, debe ser muy caro.
Patrick:	Bueno, sí, un poco. El alquiler es 70.500 colones al mes.
Richard:	¡Espera un momento! ¡Es carísimo! No podemos pagar eso.
Patrick:	Bueno, está bien. Vamos a buscar otro más barato.
Richard:	Mira éste. Tiene dos dormitorios, comedor, baño y cocina y cuesta sólo 40.000 colones.
Patrick:	Sí, pero está vacío y además está en un barrio muy lejos de la universidad. ¿De dónde vamos a sacar los muebles?
Richard:	No sé. Podemos preguntarles a otros estudiantes. Sé que Cristina y Berta compraron un montón de cosas muy baratas en el mercado en Liberia.
Patrick:	Mira este otro. Está en Paseo Colón. Tiene dos dormitorios, está amueblado y cuesta sólo 60.000 colones.
Richard:	¿De verdad? ¡Es exactamente lo que necesitamos! ¿Por qué no llamamos a la agencia para ir a verlo mañana mismo?
Patrick:	¡Pura vida! ¡Llamas tú!
Richard:	Bien, dame el número.

Capítulo diez   346

PRIMERO ETAPA
Vamos a escuchar: Viernes por la mañana en casa de la familia de Cristina Gallegos

Sra. Gallegos:	¡Vamos, hijas! ¡Dense prisa! ¡Qué cosa, siempre igual! ¡Ya es hora de irse! Se les va a hacer tarde para llegar a clase.
María:	Mamá, no me grites a mí, yo no tengo la culpa. Es Belén. Se levanta a las 7:15 y se va al baño. Tarda media hora en ducharse, después se seca el pelo, y luego no sé qué más hace. Y a mí no me queda tiempo para nada, me ducho, me peino y ya.
Belén:	No es verdad, mamá. María se despierta antes de la 7:00, pero se levanta muy tarde. Se queda en la cama hasta las 7:45. Después, por fin, se levanta y se viste, pero ya es casi la hora de salir. Por eso nunca tiene tiempo para nada.
María:	¡Cómo exageras! Bueno, es igual, ya son las 8:00, vámonos. Adiós, mamá,

adiós, Cristina. No vemos
esta tarde.

Belén: Adiós, mamá.
Sra. Gallegos: Belén, ¿y el desayuno? ¿No
vas a desayunar? Pero,
¿cómo te vas a ir sin
comer?

SEGUNDA ETAPA
*Vamos a escuchar: El encuentro de Esteban y
Patricia después del viaje por Centro América*

Esteban: ¡Eh! ¡Patricia!
Patricia: ¿Esteban? ¡Hombre, qué sorpresa! ¿Qué clases tienes este año?
No te he visto en ninguna clase.
Esteban: Bueno, pues, todavía no lo sé.
No he tenido tiempo de decidir.
Acabo de llegar de vacaciones y
aún estoy un poco perdido.
Patricia: ¿Acabas de llegar? Increíble, o
sea que has aprovechado hasta
el último minuto. No está mal.
Esteban: Todavía no me creo que ya esté
aquí y que ya hayan empezado
las clases. Me fui a finales de
julio, y volví ayer.
Patricia: No sabía que hubieras pasado
todo el verano fuera. ¿Adónde
fuiste?
Esteban: Pues, mira, estuve con cuatro
amigos de viaje por Centro
América. La primera semana
estuvimos en El Salvador. Fue
una semana estupenda e hicimos un montón de cosas.
Después fuimos a Honduras y
nos quedamos allí otra semana.
¡Es un país increíble! Luego...
Patricia: Oye, ¡qué suerte! Me está dando
mucha envidia.
Esteban: Bueno, y no se acaba ahí.
Patricia: Oye, lo siento, ya me lo contarás
otro día, ahora tengo que ir a
clase a todo correr porque si no
voy a llegar tarde.
Esteban: Bien, pues a ver si nos vemos un
día de esta semana para ir a
tomar un café o para comer, ¿te
parece?
Patricia: Está bien, te llamo mañana.
Esteban: Sí, llámame. Adiós.

TERCERA ETAPA 363
*Vamos a escuchar: ¿Qué hacemos mañana
por la noche?*

Mónica: Oye, Enrique, tengo muchas
ganas de ir a bailar. ¿Qué te
parece si mañana por la noche
vamos a una discoteca?
Enrique: ¿A una discoteca? Pues no sé. Ya
sabes que a mí ir a bailar no me
gusta mucho.
Mónica: Mira, aquí en la guía hay información sobre una discoteca que se

llama Stratos. Dice que es el lugar
nocturno más popular en Managua.
Enrique: ¿Qué música ponen?
Mónica: La descripción de la guía dice que la
música es variada, rock, música afro-
caribeña, salsa, merengue. Como
ves, un poco de todo. Parece que el
ambiente es buenísimo y que va
mucha gente joven.
Enrique: Bueno, está bien. Veo que tienes
muchas ganas de ir allí.
Mónica: Entonces, ¿quieres ir?
Enrique: Sí, un día es un día. Pero, ¿qué te
parece si antes de ir a bailar
vamos a comer algo en un sitio
tranquilo?
Mónica: Está bien. ¿Adónde quieres ir?
Enrique: A ver, déjame ver la guía. Mira,
¿qué te parece si vamos a La
Fonda? Está en el centro y sirven
comida nicaragüense: gallo pinto,
carne asado, plátano verde con
queso frito...
Mónica: Mmm... parece muy sabroso. ¿Es
caro?
Enrique: No, creo que no. La guía no tiene
los precios, pero no parece un
sitio caro.
Mónica: Bueno, está bien.

Capítulo once 376
PRIMERA ETAPA
Vamos a escuchar: En un restaurante

Camarero: Buenas noches.
Sr. Pérez: Buenas noches, señor.
Quisiéramos una mesa para
dos, por favor.
Camarero: Muy bien. Tengo una mesa aquí
y otra allí cerca de la ventana.
¿Dónde prefieren sentarse?
Sr. Pérez: Cerca de la ventana, por favor.
Camarero: Vengan conmigo, por favor.
Aquí tienen los menús. ¿Quieren
pedir un aperitivo?
Sr. Pérez: Sí, como aperitivo, ¿por qué no
pedimos unas gambas al ajillo?
Sra. Pérez: Está bien.
Sr. Pérez: Por favor, quisiéramos unas
gambas al ajillo.

*(El camarero se va y en unos minutos
vuelve con el aperitivo.)*
Camarero: Aquí tienen. ¿Qué van a pedir?
¿Desean una sopa?
Sra. Pérez: Sí, yo quisiera el gazpacho.
Sr. Pérez: Y para mí una sopa de ajo.
Camarero: ¿Qué van a pedir como segundo
plato?
Sra. Pérez: Para mí las chuletas de cordero.
Sr. Pérez: Y para mí el pescado frito.
Camarero: ¿Quisieran una ensalada?
Sr. Pérez: Sí, sí. Una ensalada mixta para dos,
por favor.

*(Después de que los Pérez comieron los
segundo platos, vuelve el camarero
otra vez.)*

Camarero: ¿Qué quieren pedir como
postre?
Sra. Pérez: Yo, un flan.
Sr. Pérez: Y para mí un helado de fresa,
gracias.
Camarero: ¿Café también?
Sr. Pérez: Sí, por favor.
Camarero: ¿Desean algo más?
Sr. Pérez: No, no gracias. ¿Pudiera traer-
nos la cuenta, por favor?

*(Después de un rato, vuelve el
camarero otra vez.)*
Camarero: Sí, como no.
Sr. Pérez: ¿Aceptan tarjetas de crédito?
Camarero: ¡Claro que sí!

SEGUNDA ETAPA
Vamos a escuchar: ¡Qué rico está!

Luis: ¿Qué vas a pedir?
Sonia: No tengo mucha hambre. Voy a pedir
una sopa de ajo y unas gambas al
ajillo. ¿Y tú?
Luis: No sé. A ver... no quiero sopa. Voy a
pedir la ensalada mixta y las chuletas
de cordero y voy a tomar vino tinto.
¿Y tú?
Sonia: Tengo mucha sed. Voy a pedir agua
mineral.
Luis: Camarero, este tenedor está sucio.
Tráigame otro, por favor. Y a la
señorita le falta la servilleta.

*(Más tarde el camarero les trae la
comida.)*
Luis: ¿Qué tal está la sopa?
Sonia: Está muy rica. ¿Y la ensalada?
Luis: También está rica.
Sonia: ¿Y las chuletas?
Luis: Están riquísimas. ¿Y las gambas?
Sonia: ¡Están pero riquísimas! En este
restaurante se sirve una comida muy
buena.
Luis: Sí, estoy de acuerdo. Se come muy
bien.

TERCERA ETAPA
Vamos a escuchar: Comida Tex-Mex

Luis: ¡Hola, Alberto! ¿En qué andas?
Alberto: Nada pues. Voy aquí al restau-
rante éste para comer unos
nachos. ¿Me acompañas?
Luis: ¡Cómo no! Estoy que me muero
de hambre.
Alberto: Ándale pues. Vamos.
Camarero: ¿Qué van a pedir?
Alberto: Para mí unos nachos y una
cerveza bien fría, por favor.
Camarero: ¿Y para Ud.?
Luis: Para mí unas fajitas de pollo, un
guacamole y un vaso de agua
con mucho hielo, por favor.

(Más tarde el camarero les trae la comida.)

Camarero:	Aquí tienen, señores.
Alberto:	Oye, Luis, ¿qué tal están las fajitas?
Luis:	No sé. No tienen sabor. Voy a pedir una salsa picante. Camarero, ¿me trae una salsita picante, por favor?
Camarero:	Sí, señor. ¡Cómo no!
Alberto:	Y ahora, ¿qué tal están?
Luis:	Ahora sí que están pero riquísimas. ¿Y qué tal los nachos?
Alberto:	Están muy sabrosos. ¿Y el guacamole?
Luis:	Está un poco salado, pero me gusta.

(Después de un rato vuelve el camarero.)

Camarero:	Señores, ¿quieren algo de postre?
Luis:	Para mí no. Comí muchísimo.
Alberto:	Para mí un flan, por favor.
Luis:	¿Qué tal el flan?
Alberto:	Está algo dulce, pero me gustan las comidas dulces.

Capítulo doce   412

PRIMERA ETAPA
Vamos a escuchar: En la Estación de Atocha

Empleado:	Buenas tardes, señor. ¿En qué puedo servirle?
Enrique:	Buenas tardes. Pensamos ir a Barcelona y quisiera saber si hay algún tren que salga temprano por la mañana.
Empleado:	Sí, cómo no. Aquí tiene el horario. Uno sale a las 6:45 y otro a las 8:00.
Enrique:	Ah, muy bien. Prefiero el tren de las 6:45. Quisiera reservar dos plazas—de ida y vuelta, por favor.
Empleado:	Cómo no. ¿En primera o en segunda clase, señor?
Enrique:	En primera.
Empleado:	¿Y para qué día?
Enrique:	Para el miércoles, por favor. Y queremos volver a Madrid el martes de la semana que viene. Son días azules, ¿no?
Empleado:	Sí, señor. Aquí tiene sus billetes.
Enrique:	Muy bien. Y aquí tiene el dinero. ¡Muchas gracias!
Empleado:	De nada, señor. ¡Buen viaje!

(Inmediatamente después llegan Carmen y Antonio a la ventanilla de billetes.)

Empleado:	Buenas tardes. ¿En qué puedo servirles?
Carmen:	Buenas tardes, señor. ¿A qué hora sale el próximo tren para Valencia, por favor?
Empleado:	Según el horario, a las 15:00.
Antonio:	Ya compramos los billetes. ¿Podría decirnos si el tren saldrá a tiempo?
Empleado:	Es posible, pero en este momento el tren para Valencia está un poco retrasado.
Antonio:	Ah, entonces, tenemos tiempo para comer algo. ¿De qué andén sale el tren?
Empleado:	Vayan ustedes al andén C.
Carmen:	Gracias. ¿Y cómo se llega al andén C?
Empleado:	Por esa puerta cerca del quiosco. Los andenes A y B no quedan lejos de allí.
Carmen:	¿Y cuál es el número de vagón, por favor?
Empleado:	Tienen asientos reservados en el número 10.
Carmen:	Bien, muchas gracias, señor.
Empleado:	De nada. Les deseo un buen viaje.
Antonio:	Gracias. Adiós.

SEGUNDA ETAPA
Vamos a escuchar: Un viaje en coche

Alonso:	Mamá, tengo sed. ¿Podemos parar y comprar un refresco?
Claudia:	Yo también, mami. Tengo mucha, mucha, mucha, pero mucha sed. ¿Podemos parar?
Patricia:	¡Pero, hijitos! ¿Cómo es posible? Sólo hemos estado en el coche una hora. ¿No bebieron nada en casa?
Alonso:	Sí, sí, pero ahora tenemos sed. Es que hace calor en el coche y no hemos bebido nada desde que salimos. ¿Cuándo vamos a llegar? ¿Cuánto toma el viaje de México a Querétaro?
Patricia:	Son como cuatro horas a Querétaro, pero serán más si paramos cada media hora. ¿No pueden esperar una hora más?
Claudia:	No, mamita. Y te prometo que si paramos esta vez y me compras un refresco, que ya no tenemos que parar otra vez hasta llegar a casa de Tía Cuca.
Alonso:	Así es, mamá. Paramos ahora y después ya no te molestamos.
Patricia:	Ese cuento lo he oído antes. Pero, bueno, ¿qué le vamos a hacer? Si ven una tienda de refrescos, les compro uno. ¿De acuerdo?
Alonso:	¡Sí, sí! ¡Qué buena eres, mamá!
Claudia:	¡Sí, eres la mejor mamá del mundo! Yo quiero un refresco bien grande. ¡Grandotote!
Alonso:	Y yo quiero dos. ¡Bien fríos!
Patricia:	¡Ay, qué niños éstos!
Claudia:	¿Mamita?
Patricia:	Sí, mi hijita. Dime...
Claudia:	¿Sabes otra cosa, mamá?
Patricia:	A ver, dime, hijita. ¿Qué cosa?
Claudia:	¡Pues... ahora tengo que ir al baño también!
Patricia:	¡No me digas! Pues ya lo sabía. Miren, ahí hay una gasolinera más adelante. Vamos a parar y los dos van al baño. ¿Me entienden? Creo que no son cuatro horas a Querétaro, como he dicho. ¡Serán ocho!

TERCERA ETAPA
Vamos a escuchar: ¿Dónde está la maleta?

Sr. Castillo:	Pues ha sido un gusto conocerla, Judy.
Judy:	Gracias, igualmente. Y gracias por toda la información que me han dado. Me siento mucho mejor.
Sra. Castillo:	Me alegro. ¿Por qué no vamos con Judy a la sala de equipaje, Raúl?
Sr. Castillo:	Buena idea. Tenemos que pasar por ahí también.
Judy:	Muchas gracias. Son ustedes muy amables.

(Unos momentos después... en la sala de reclamación de equipaje)

Sra. Castillo:	¿Qué pasó Judy? ¿No ha encontrado sus maletas?
Judy:	Aquí tengo una, pero no he visto la otra.
Sr. Castillo:	¿De qué color es la maleta?
Judy:	Es amarilla.
Sra. Castillo:	¿Y de qué tamaño es?
Judy:	Pues, no muy grande. Es más pequeña que ésta.
Sra. Castillo:	Pues, ahora la vamos a encontrar. No se preocupe.
Judy:	¡Ah! ¿Saben? Creo que la dejé en el avión. ¡Qué tonta soy!
Sr. Castillo:	¡Ah! ¡Menos mal! Hablaré con el agente. Alguien podrá ir a buscarla en el avión, entonces.
Sra. Castillo:	Sí, y no se preocupe. Es que ha estado un poco nerviosa.
Judy:	Sí, es verdad. Y muchas gracias a ustedes. He aprendido una lección importante. Es mejor llevar una maleta grande que dos pequeñas.
Sra. Castillo:	Bueno, Raúl, habla con el agente y luego vamos a ver si encontramos las nuestras. Son verdes, ¡pero creo que he visto cien maletas verdes aquí!

APPENDIX A   Regular Verbs

Simple Tenses

hablar *(to speak)*

PRESENT INDICATIVE	IMPERFECT	PRETERITE	FUTURE	CONDITIONAL	PRESENT SUBJUNCTIVE	PAST SUBJUNCTIVE	COMMANDS
hablo	hablaba	hablé	hablaré	hablaría	hable	hablara	
hablas	hablabas	hablaste	hablarás	hablarías	hables	hablaras	habla (no hables)
habla	hablaba	habló	hablará	hablaría	hable	hablara	hable
hablamos	hablábamos	hablamos	hablaremos	hablaríamos	hablemos	habláramos	hablemos
habláis	hablabais	hablasteis	hablaréis	hablaríais	habléis	hablarais	hablad (no habléis)
hablan	hablaban	hablaron	hablarán	hablarían	hablen	hablaran	hablen

aprender *(to learn)*

PRESENT INDICATIVE	IMPERFECT	PRETERITE	FUTURE	CONDITIONAL	PRESENT SUBJUNCTIVE	PAST SUBJUNCTIVE	COMMANDS
aprendo	aprendía	aprendí	aprenderé	aprendería	aprenda	aprendiera	
aprendes	aprendías	aprendiste	aprenderás	aprenderías	aprendas	aprendieras	aprende (no aprendas)
aprende	aprendía	aprendió	aprenderá	aprendería	aprenda	aprendiera	aprenda
aprendemos	aprendíamos	aprendimos	aprenderemos	aprenderíamos	aprendamos	aprendiéramos	aprendamos
aprendéis	aprendíais	aprendisteis	aprenderéis	aprenderíais	aprendáis	aprendierais	aprended (no aprendáis)
aprenden	aprendían	aprendieron	aprenderán	aprenderían	aprendan	aprendieran	aprendan

vivir *(to live)*

PRESENT INDICATIVE	IMPERFECT	PRETERITE	FUTURE	CONDITIONAL	PRESENT SUBJUNCTIVE	PAST SUBJUNCTIVE	COMMANDS
vivo	vivía	viví	viviré	viviría	viva	viviera	
vives	vivías	viviste	vivirás	vivirías	vivas	vivieras	vive (no vivas)
vive	vivía	vivió	vivirá	viviría	viva	viviera	viva
vivimos	vivíamos	vivimos	viviremos	viviríamos	vivamos	viviéramos	vivimos
vivís	vivíais	vivisteis	viviréis	viviríais	viváis	vivierais	vivid (no viváis)
viven	vivían	vivieron	vivirán	vivirían	vivan	vivieran	vivan

Compound Tenses

Present progressive

estoy	estamos			
estás	estáis	hablando	aprendiendo	viviendo
está	están			

Present perfect indicative

he	hemos			
has	habéis	hablado	aprendido	vivido
ha	han			

Past perfect indicative

había	habíamos			
habías	habíais	hablado	aprendido	vivido
había	habían			

APPENDIX B   Stem-changing Verbs

INFINITIVE PRESENT PARTICIPLE PAST PARTICIPLE	PRESENT INDICATIVE	PAST IMPERFECT	PRETERITE	FUTURE	CONDITIONAL	PRESENT SUBJUNCTIVE	PAST SUBJUNCTIVE	COMMANDS
pensar *to think* e → ie pensando pensado	**pienso** **piensas** **piensa** pensamos pensáis **piensan**	pensaba pensabas pensaba pensábamos pensabais pensaban	pensé pensaste pensó pensamos pensasteis pensaron	pensaré pensarás pensará pensaremos pensaréis pensarán	pensaría pensarías pensaría pensaríamos pensaríais pensarían	**piense** **pienses** **piense** pensemos penséis **piensen**	pensara pensaras pensara pensáramos pensarais pensaran	**piensa (no pienses)** **piense** **pensemos** **pensad (no penséis)** **piensen**
acostarse *to go to bed* o → ue acostándose acostado	me **acuesto** te **acuestas** se **acuesta** nos acostamos os acostáis se **acuestan**	me acostaba te acostabas se acostaba nos acostábamos os acostabais se acostaban	me acosté te acostaste se acostó nos acostamos os acostasteis se acostaron	me acostaré te acostarás se acostará nos acostaremos os acostaréis se acostarán	me acostaría te acostarías se acostaría nos acostaríamos os acostaríais se acostarían	me **acueste** te **acuestes** se **acueste** nos acostemos os acostéis se **acuesten**	me acostara te acostaras se acostara nos acostáramos os acostarais se acostaran	**acuéstate (no te acuestes)** **acuéstese** **acostémonos** acostados **(no os acostéis)** **acuéstense**
sentir *to feel* e → ie, i sintiendo sentido	**siento** **sientes** **siente** sentimos sentís **sienten**	sentía sentías sentía sentíamos sentíais sentían	sentí sentiste **sintió** sentimos sentisteis **sintieron**	sentiré sentirás sentirá sentiremos sentiréis sentirán	sentiría sentirías sentiría sentiríamos sentiríais sentirían	**sienta** **sientas** **sienta** **sintamos** **sintáis** **sientan**	**sintiera** **sintieras** **sintiera** **sintiéramos** **sintierais** **sintieran**	**siente (no sientas)** **sienta** **sintamos** sentid **(no sintáis)** **sientan**
pedir *to ask* e → i, i pidiendo pedido	**pido** **pides** **pide** pedimos pedís **piden**	pedía pedías pedía pedíamos pedíais pedían	pedí pediste **pidió** pedimos pedisteis **pidieron**	pediré pedirás pedirá pediremos pediréis pedirán	pediría pedirías pediría pediríamos pediríais pedirían	**pida** **pidas** **pida** **pidamos** **pidáis** **pidan**	pidiera pidieras pidiera pidiéramos pidierais pidieran	**pide (no pidas)** **pida** **pidamos** pedid **(no pidáis)** **pidan**
dormir *to sleep* o → ue, u durmiendo dormido	**duermo** **duermes** **duerme** dormimos dormís **duermen**	dormía dormías dormía dormíamos dormíais dormían	dormí dormiste **durmió** dormimos dormisteis **durmieron**	dormiré dormirás dormirá dormiremos dormiréis dormirán	dormiría dormirías dormiría dormiríamos dormiríais dormirían	**duerma** **duermas** **duerma** **durmamos** **durmáis** **duerman**	**durmiera** **durmieras** **durmiera** **durmiéramos** **durmierais** **durmieran**	**duerme (no duermas)** **duerma** **durmamos** dormid **(no durmáis)** **duerman**

INFINITIVE PRESENT PARTICIPLE PAST PARTICIPLE	PRESENT INDICATIVE	PAST IMPERFECT	PRETERITE	FUTURE	CONDITIONAL	PRESENT SUBJUNCTIVE	PAST SUBJUNCTIVE	COMMANDS
comenzar (e → ie) *to begin* **z → c before e** comenzando comenzado	comienzo comienzas comienza comenzamos comenzáis comienzan	comenzaba comenzabas comenzaba comenzábamos comenzabais comenzaban	**comencé** comenzaste comenzó comenzamos comenzasteis comenzaron	comenzaré comenzarás comenzará comenzaremos comenzaréis comenzarán	comenzaría comenzarías comenzaría comenzaríamos comenzaríais comenzarían	**comience** **comiences** **comience** **comencemos** **comencéis** **comiencen**	comenzara comenzaras comenzara comenzáramos comenzarais comenzaran	comienza (**no comiences**) **comience** **comencemos** comenzad (**no comencéis**) **comiencen**
conocer *to know* **c → zc before a, o** conociendo conocido	**conozco** conoces conoce conocemos conocéis conocen	conocía conocías conocía conocíamos conocíais conocían	conocí conociste conoció conocimos conocisteis conocieron	conoceré conocerás conocerá conoceremos conoceréis conocerán	conocería conocerías conocería conoceríamos conoceríais conocerían	**conozca** **conozcas** **conozca** **conozcamos** conozcáis **conozcan**	conociera conocieras conociera conociéramos conocierais conocieran	conoce (**no conozcas**) **conozca** **conozcamos** conoced (**no conozcáis**) **conozcan**
pagar *to pay* **g → gu before e** pagando pagado	pago pagas paga pagamos pagáis pagan	pagaba pagabas pagaba pagábamos pagabais pagaban	**pagué** pagaste pagó pagamos pagasteis pagaron	pagaré pagarás pagará pagaremos pagaréis pagarán	pagaría pagarías pagaría pagaríamos pagaríais pagarían	**pague** **pagues** **pague** **paguemos** **paguéis** **paguen**	pagara pagaras pagara pagáramos pagarais pagaran	paga (**no pagues**) **pague** **paguemos** pagad (**no paguéis**) **paguen**
seguir (e → i, i) *to follow* **g → gu before a, o** siguiendo seguido	**sigo** sigues sigue seguimos seguís siguen	seguía seguías seguía seguíamos seguíais seguían	seguí seguiste siguió seguimos seguisteis siguieron	seguiré seguirás seguirá seguiremos seguiréis seguirán	seguiría seguirías seguiría seguiríamos seguiríais seguirían	**siga** **sigas** **siga** **sigamos** **sigáis** **sigan**	siguiera siguieras siguiera siguiéramos siguierais siguieran	sigue (**no sigas**) **siga** **sigamos** seguid (**no sigáis**) **sigan**
tocar *to play* **c → qu before e** tocando tocado	toco tocas toca tocamos tocáis tocan	tocaba tocabas tocaba tacábamos tocabais tocaban	**toqué** tocaste tocó tocamos tocasteis tocaron	tocaré tocarás tocará tocaremos tocaréis tocarán	tocaría tocarías tocaría tocaríamos tocaríais tocarían	**toque** **toques** **toque** **toquemos** **toquéis** **toquen**	tocara tocaras tocara tocáramos tocarais tocaran	toca (**no toques**) **toque** **toquemos** tocad (**no toquéis**) **toquen**

APPENDIX D Irregular Verbs *Verbs with irregular *yo*-forms in the present indicative

INFINITIVE PRESENT PARTICIPLE PAST PARTICIPLE	PRESENT INDICATIVE	PAST IMPERFECT	PRETERITE	FUTURE	CONDITIONAL	PRESENT SUBJUNCTIVE	PAST SUBJUNCTIVE	COMMANDS
andar *to walk* andando andado	ando andas anda andamos andáis andan	andaba andabas andaba andábamos andabais andaban	**anduve** **anduviste** **anduvo** **anduvimos** **anduvisteis** **anduvieron**	andaré andarás andará andaremos andaréis andarán	andaría andarías andaría andaríamos andaríais andarían	ande andes ande andemos andéis anden	**anduviera** **anduvieras** **anduviera** **anduviéramos** **anduvierais** **anduvieran**	anda (no andes) ande andemos andad (no andéis) anden
*dar *to give* dando dado	**doy** das da damos dais dan	daba dabas daba dábamos dabais daban	**di** **diste** **dio** **dimos** **disteis** **dieron**	daré darás dará daremos daréis darán	daría darías daría daríamos daríais darían	**dé** **des** **dé** **demos** **deis** **den**	diera dieras diera diéramos dierais dieran	da **(no des)** **dé** **demos** dad **(no deis)** den
*decir (e → i, i) *to say; tell* **diciendo** **dicho**	digo **dices** **dice** decimos decís **dicen**	decía decías decía decíamos decíais decían	**dije** **dijiste** **dijo** **dijimos** **dijisteis** **dijeron**	**diré** **dirás** **dirá** **diremos** **diréis** **dirán**	**diría** **dirías** **diría** **diríamos** **diríais** **dirían**	**diga** **digas** **diga** **digamos** **digáis** **digan**	**dijera** **dijeras** **dijera** **dijéramos** **dijerais** **dijeran**	**di (no digas)** **diga** **digamos** **decid (no digáis)** **digan**
*estar *to be* estando estado	**estoy** **estás** **está** estamos estáis **están**	estaba estabas estaba estábamos estabais estaban	**estuve** **estuviste** **estuvo** **estuvimos** **estuvisteis** **estuvieron**	estaré estarás estará estaremos estaréis estarán	estaría estarías estaría estaríamos estaríais estarían	**esté** **estés** **esté** **estemos** **estéis** **estén**	estuviera estuvieras estuviera estuviéramos estuvierais estuvieran	**está (no estés)** **esté** **estemos** **estad (no estéis)** **estén**
haber *to have* habiendo habido	**he** **has** **ha [hay]** **hemos** **habéis** han	había habías había habíamos habíais habían	**hube** **hubiste** **hubo** **hubimos** **hubisteis** **hubieron**	**habré** **habrás** **habrá** **habremos** **habréis** **habrán**	**habría** **habrías** **habría** **habríamos** **habríais** **habrían**	**haya** **hayas** **haya** **hayamos** **hayáis** **hayan**	hubiera hubieras hubiera hubiéramos hubierais hubieran	he (no hayas) haya hayamos habed **(no hayáis)** hayan
*hacer *to make, do* haciendo **hecho**	**hago** haces hace hacemos hacéis hacen	hacía hacías hacía hacíamos hacíais hacían	**hice** **hiciste** **hizo** **hicimos** **hicisteis** **hicieron**	**haré** **harás** **hará** **haremos** **haréis** **harán**	**haría** **harías** **haría** **haríamos** **haríais** **harían**	**haga** **hagas** **haga** **hagamos** **hagáis** **hagan**	**hiciera** **hicieras** **hiciera** **haciéramos** **hicierais** **hicieran**	**haz (no hagas)** **haga** **hagamos** **haced (no hagáis)** **hagan**

INFINITIVE PRESENT PARTICIPLE PAST PARTICIPLE	PRESENT INDICATIVE	PAST IMPERFECT	PRETERITE	FUTURE	CONDITIONAL	PRESENT SUBJUNCTIVE	PAST SUBJUNCTIVE	COMMANDS
ir *to go* yendo ido	voy vas va vamos vais van	iba ibas iba íbamos ibais iban	fui fuiste fue fuimos fuisteis fueron	iré irás irá iremos iréis irán	iría irías iría iríamos iríais irían	vaya vayas vaya vayamos vayáis vayan	fuera fueras fuera fuéramos fuerais fueran	ve (no vayas) vaya vamos (no vayamos) id (no vayáis) vayan
*oír *to hear* oyendo oído	oigo oyes oye oímos oís oyen	oía oías oía oíamos oíais oían	oí oíste oyó oímos oísteis oyeron	oiré oirás oirá oiremos oiréis oirán	oiría oirías oiría oiríamos oiríais oirían	oiga oigas oiga oigamos oigáis oigan	oyera oyeras oyera oyéramos oyerais oyeran	oye (no oigas) oiga oigamos oíd (no oigáis) oigan
poder (o → ue) *can, to be able* pudiendo podido	puedo puedes puede podemos podéis pueden	podía podías podía podíamos podíais podían	pude pudiste pudo pudimos pudisteis pudieron	podré podrás podrá podremos podréis podrán	podría podrías podría podríamos podríais podrían	pueda puedas pueda podamos podáis puedan	pudiera pudieras pudiera pudiéramos pudierais pudieran	puede (no puedas) pueda podamos poded (no podáis) puedan
*poner *to place, put* poniendo puesto	pongo pones pone ponemos ponéis ponen	ponía ponías ponía poníamos poníais ponían	puse pusiste puso pusimos pusisteis pusieron	pondré pondrás pondrá pondremos pondréis pondrán	pondría pondrías pondría pondríamos pondríais pondrían	ponga pongas ponga pongamos pongáis pongan	pusiera pusieras pusiera pusiéramos pusierais pusieran	pon (no pongas) ponga pongamos poned (no pongáis) pongan
querer (e → ie) *to like* queriendo querido	quiero quieres quiere queremos queréis quieren	quería querías quería queríamos queríais querían	quise quisiste quiso quisimos quisisteis quisieron	querré querrás querrá querremos querréis querrán	querría querrías querría querríamos querríais querrían	quiera quieras quiera queramos queráis quieran	quisiera quisieras quisiera quisiéramos quisierais quisieran	quiere (no quieras) quiera queramos quered (no queráis) quieran
*saber *to know* sabiendo sabido	sé sabes sabe sabemos sabéis saben	sabía sabías sabía sabíamos sabíais sabían	supe supiste supo supimos supisteis supieron	sabré sabrás sabrá sabremos sabréis sabrán	sabría sabrías sabría sabríamos sabríais sabrían	sepa sepas sepa sepamos sepáis sepan	supiera supieras supiera supiéramos supierais<P> supieran	sabe (no sepas) sepa sepamos sabed (no sepáis) sepan

INFINITIVE / PRESENT PARTICIPLE / PAST PARTICIPLE	PRESENT INDICATIVE	PAST IMPERFECT	PRETERITE	FUTURE	CONDITIONAL	PRESENT SUBJUNCTIVE	PAST SUBJUNCTIVE	COMMANDS
*salir *to go out* saliendo salido	salgo sales sale salimos salís salen	salía salías salía salíamos salíais salían	salí saliste salió salimos salisteis salieron	saldré saldrás saldrá saldremos saldréis saldrán	saldría saldrías saldría saldríamos saldríais saldrían	salga salgas salga salgamos salgáis salgan	saliera salieras saliera saliéramos salierais salieran	sal (no salgas) salga salgamos salid (no salgáis) salgan
ser *to be* siendo sido	soy eres es somos sois son	era eras era éramos erais eran	fui fuiste fue fuimos fuisteis fueron	seré serás será seremos seréis serán	sería serías sería seríamos seríais serían	sea seas sea seamos seáis sean	fuera fueras fuera fuéramos fuerais fueran	sé (no seas) sea seamos sed (no seáis) sean
*tener (e → ie) *to have* teniendo tenido	tengo tienes tiene tenemos tenéis tienen	tenía tenías tenía teníamos teníais tenían	tuve uviste tuvo tuvimos tuvisteis tuvieron	tendré tendrás tendrá tendremos tendréis tendrán	tendría tendrías tendría tendríamos tendríais tendrían	tenga tengas tenga tengamos tengáis tengan	tuviera tuvieras tuviera tuviéramos tuvierais tuvieran	ten (no tengas) tenga tengamos tened (no tengáis) tengan
traer *to bring* trayendo traído	traigo traes trae traemos traéis traen	traía traías traía traíamos traíais traían	traje trajiste trajo trajimos trajisteis trajeron	traeré traerás traerá traeremos traeréis traerán	traería traerías traería traeríamos traeríais traerían	traiga traigas traiga traigamos traigáis traigan	trajera trajeras trajera trajéramos trajerais trajeran	trae (no traigas) traiga traigamos traed (no traigáis) traigan
*venir (e → ie, i) *to come* viniendo venido	vengo vienes viene venimos venís vienen	venía venías venía veníamos veníais venían	vine viniste vino vinimos vinisteis vinieron	vendré vendrás vendrá vendremos vendréis vendrán	vendría vendrías vendría vendríamos vendríais vendrían	venga vengas venga vengamos vengáis vengan	viniera vinieras viniera viniéramos vinierais vinieran	ven (no vengas) venga vengamos venid (no vengáis) vengan
ver *to see* viendo visto	veo ves ve vemos veis ven	veía veías veía veíamos veíais veían	vi viste vio vimos visteis vieron	veré verás verá veremos veréis verán	vería verías vería veríamos veríais verían	vea veas vea veamos veáis vean	viera vieras viera viéramos vierais vieran	ve (no veas) vea veamos ved (no veáis) vean

SPANISH–ENGLISH GLOSSARY

Gender of nouns is indicated except for masculine nouns ending in –o and feminine nouns ending in –a. Masculine forms of adjectives are given; feminine forms are given when irregular. Verbs appear in the infinitive form. The number(s) following the entries refer to the chapter(s) in which the word or phrase first appears. The following abbreviations are used in this glossary:

adj.	adjective	*prep.*	preposition
m.	masculine	*CP*	Capítulo preliminar
adv.	adverb	*pron.*	pronoun
pl.	plural	*n.*	noun
f.	feminine		

A

a *prep.* to, at *CP*
  a la derecha to the right 3
  a la izquierda to the left 3
  a mano by hand 10
  a menos que unless 14
  a menudo often 3
  a partir from 6
  a pie on foot 1
  a tiempo on time 9
  a veces sometimes 1
  a ver let's see 6
abanico de techo ceiling fan 9
abogado lawyer 2
abrigo coat 6
abril April 5
abstracto *adj.* abstract 13
abuela grandmother 2
abuelo grandfather 2
aburrido *adj.* boring 2
acariciar to caress 12
accidente *m.* accident 8
acción *f.* action 5
aceite *m.* oil 4
aceituna olive 1
acero steel 13
acompañante *m.* (*f.*) companion 12
aconsejable *adj.* advisable 6
acontecimiento event 4
acostarse to go to bed 8
activo *adj.* active 7
actor *m.* actor 1
actriz *f.* actress 1
actualidad *f.* present time 6
adelantado *adj.* ahead of schedule, early 12
adelantar to advance 12
además *adv.* besides 1
adicional *adj.* additional 8
adiós good-bye
adjetivo adjective 1
admitir to admit 8
adónde to where 3
adorar to adore 7
aduana customs 12
adverbio adverb 1
aeróbico *adj.* aerobic 8
aeropuerto airport 3
afeitarse to shave 8
afiche *m.* poster 2
aficionado fan 11

afilado *adj.* sharp 14
agilidad *f.* agility 5
agosto August 5
agua *f.* water 1
aguacate *m.* avocado 1
aguaprieta *f.* dark water 8
aguja needle 14
ahogar to drown 14
ahora *adv.* now 11
ahora mismo *adv.* right now 3
ahorrar to save 7
aire acondicionado *adj.* air conditioned 9
ajedrez *m.* chess 13
ajo garlic 11
al to the 1
  al final de at the end of 3
  al fondo at the end 9
  al lado de next to 3
  al menos at least 9
ala *f.* wing 14
alberca swimming pool 13
albergue *m.* lodge 9
alcachofa artichoke 13
alcanzar to reach 8
alcoba bedroom 13
aldea village 13
alegrarse to become glad, happy 7
alegre *adj.* happy 2
alemán *m.* (**alemana** *f.*) German 1
alergia allergy 8
alfabetización *f.* literacy
alfombra rug 2
algo something, anything 1; somewhat 11
algodón *m.* cotton 4
alguien someone 11
algún some, any 2
algún día some day 10
alguno(a,os,as) some, any 8
aliento breath 14
alimento food 6
allá there 6
almendra almond 13
almidón *m.* starch 8
almohada pillow 2
almuerzo lunch 1
aló hello 6
alpinismo mountain climbing 5
alquilar to rent 5
alquiler *m.* rent 2
alrededor *adv.* around 7
alto *adj.* tall 2

alumno student 2
ama de casa housekeeper 14
amable *adj.* friendly 9
amargo *adj.* bitter 8
amarillo *adj.* yellow 6
ambicioso *adj.* ambitious 7
ámbito medium 13
amigo(a) friend 4
amo master 13
amor *m.* love 14
ampliar to expand, widen 13
amplio *adj.* broad, wide 14
amueblado *adj.* furnished 9
añadir to add 7
anaranjado *adj.* orange 6
andaluz *adj.* from Andalucía 11
andar to walk 5
andén *m.* platform 12
anfitrión host 9
anfitriona hostess 9
animal *m.* animal 2
  animal doméstico *m.* pet 2
animar to inspire, animate 13
año year 3
anoche last night 5
anteayer the day before yesterday 5
antes de *prep.* before 12
antibiótico antibiotic 8
anticipación f. anticipation 1
antihistamínico antihistamine 8
antipático *adj.* disagreeable *CP*
antojito food, dish, whim 1
anual *adj.* annual 8
anunciar to announce 3
anuncio ad 9
aparentemente *adv.* apparently 8
apartamento apartment 2
apartarse to distance oneself 13
apellido last name 2
aperitivo appetizer 11
apetecer to appeal 11
apocopado *adj.* shortened 4
apoyado *adj.* leaning against 14
aprender to learn 1
aquel(la) *adj.* that 6
aquél(la) *pron.* that one 6
aquellos(as) *adj.* those 6
aquéllos(as) *pron.* those 6
aquí here 1
arado plow 13
araña spider 14

árbol *m.* tree 7
arder to burn 8
arena sand 9
argentino Argentine 1
arma weapon **13**
armadura suit of armor 8
armario cupboard, wardrobe 2
aro hoop, ring 8
arpa *m.* arpa 13
arquitecto architect 2
arquitectura architecture 2
arrasar to devastate 10
arrastrar to drag 14
arrecife *m.* reef 13
arreglar to fix 9
arroyuelo little stream 9
arroz *m.* rice 1
arte *m.* art 2
artesanía craft 5
artículo article 1
artista *m.* (*f.*) artist 13
ascensor m. elevator 9
asentamiento settlement 10
asistir a to attend 2
asombrado adj. amazed 14
aspirina aspirin 8
aterrizar to land 12
atlético *adj.* athletic 7
atropellar to hit, run over 13
aunque even though, although 12
australiano Australian 1
autobús *m.* bus 2
autónomo *adj.* autonomous 1
autor *m.* (**autora** *f.*) author 1
autorretrato self-portrait 13
avenida avenue 3
aventura adventure 2
avergonzado *adj.* ashamed, shy 11
avión *m.* airplane
ayer yesterday 5
ayuda help 12
ayudar to help 13
azahar *m.* orange flower 14
azúcar *m.* sugar 4
azul *adj.* blue
azulejo tile 4

B

bailar to dance 1
baile *m.* dance CP
bajar to get off 4
bajo *adj.* short 2; *prep.* under 5
bajo bass 13
balanceado *adj.* balanced 8
baloncesto *m.* basketball 5
banana banana 1
banca seat 4
banco bank 2
banderillas tapas 1
baño bathroom 2
bar *m.* bar 1
barato *adj.* cheap 4
barba beard 7
barrer to sweep 14

barro clay 12
básquetbol *m.* basketball 2
batido milkshake 1
bebé *m.* (*f.*) baby 8
beber to drink 1
bebida drink 1
beca scholarship 13
becario *adj.* scholarship 13
béisbol m. baseball 2
bendecir to bless 9
benéfico *adj.* charitable, beneficent 2
biblioteca library 3
bicicleta bicycle 2
bien *adv.* well
bigote *m.* mustache 7
bilingüe *adj.* bilingual 4
billete *m.* ticket 12
billetera wallet 2
biología biology 2
bisabuela great-grandmother 14
bisabuelo great-grandfather 14
bistec *m.* steak 6
blanco *adj.* white 1
blusa blouse 6
boca mouth 8
bocadillo sandwich, snack CP
boletín *m.* bulletin 7
boleto ticket 12
bolígrafo ballpoint pen 2
boliviano Bolivian
bolsa handbag 6
bondad f. kindness 14
bonito *adj.* pretty 2
bordado *adj.* embroidered 10
bordar to embroider 14
borrador *m.* eraser 2
bosque *m.* forest 4
    bosque de palmeras palm grove
bota boot 6
botella bottle 1
brazo arm 8
bronceado *adj.* tan 7
buceo diving 5
buen ojo good eye 6
bueno *adj.* good CP
¿bueno? hello? 6
buey *m.* ox 9
buscar to look for 5
búsqueda search 12

C

caballería chivalry 14
caballero andante knight errant 14
caballero knight, gentleman 14
caber to fit 14
cabeza head 8
cacahuete *m.* peanut 1
cacao cocoa 11
cada each 6
caerse to fall 8
café *m.* coffee 1
cafetería coffee house 2
cafetín *m.* small café 5
caimán *m.* alligator 8

caja de seguridad safe, security deposit
    box 9
cajero cashier 1
cajón *m.* drawer 2
calamares fritos *m.* fried squid
calavera skull 13
calcetines *m. pl.* socks 6
calcio calcium 8
calculadora calculator 2
calcular to calculate 2
calendario calendar 12
caliente *adj.* hot 11
callar to quiet 14
calle *f.* street 3
calor *m.* heat 7
caloría calorie 8
cama bed CP
cámara camera 2
camarero waiter 1
camarón shrimp 11
cambiar to change 4
cambio change 4
    cambio de moneda money exchange 9
camboyano adj Cambodian 1
caminar to walk CP
camioneta van, light truck 12
camisa shirt 6
camiseta t-shirt 6
campana bell 14
campaña campaign 5
cana gray hair
caña cane CP beer on tap 1
canadiense Canadian
cancha court 9
canción *f.* song 13
cansado *adj.* tired 3
cansarse to get tired 8
cantante *m.* (*f.*) singer 1
cantar to sing 1
cántaro bucket 5
cantidad *f.* quantity 6
cantina bar, tavern 1
capital *f.* capital 5
capítulo chapter
cara face 8
carácter *m.* personality 7
carcel *f.* prison
cariño affection 13
carne *f.* meat 1
carnicería butcher shop 3
caro *adj.* expensive 6
carpa tent 14
carrito cart 6
carta letter 1
cartel *m.* poster 2
cartera wallet 2
cartón *m.* cardboard 14
casa house 2
casado *adj.* married 2
casarse to get married 13
casi almost 5
castaño *adj.* hazel 7
castellano Castillian 1
catalán (language) *m.* Catalan 1
catálogo catalogue 6

catarro cold 8
catedral *f.* cathedral 3
católico Catholic
catorce fourteen 2
cauce *m.* river bed 9
caucho rubber 4
causa causa 8
caza hunt14
cebolla onion 1
celada helmet 14
celebrar to celebrate 3
cena dinner 1
cenar to eat dinner 5
ceniza ash 13
centro downtown 2
   centro comercial shopping center 6
cepillarse to brush 8
cerca near 3
cercano *adj.* approaching, nearby 13
cereal *m.* cereal 4
cero zero 2
cerrado *adj.* closed 11
cerrar to close 12
cerro hill 10
cerveza beer 1
cesta basket 6
chaleco vest 13
champiñón *m.* mushroom 6
chao bye
chaqueta jacket 6
charlar to chat CP
cheque *m.* check 6
Chile Chile 1
chile *m.* pepper 1
chileno Chilean 1
chino Chinese 1
chocar con to run, crash into 13
chocolate *m.* chocolate 1
chorizo sausage 1
chuleta chop 11
churro Spanish fried pastry 1
ciclismo cycling 5
ciego adj. blind 13
cien one hundred 2
ciencia science 2
   ciencia ficción science fiction 2
ciento one hundred 4
ciervo deer 11
cigüeña stork CP
cilantro cilantro 1
cinco five 2
cincuenta fifty 2
cine *m.* movie theatre 3
cinta tape 2
   cinta virgen blank tape 6
cinturón *m.* belt 6
cita date, appointment 4
ciudad *f.* city 2
ciudadano citizen 9
ciudananía citizenship 5
civilización *f.* civilization 10
claro que sí of course 4
clase *f.* class 1
clásico *adj.* classical 1

clavado *adj.* piercing, pierced 13
cliente *m.* (*f.*) customer 6
clima *m.* climate 7
cobarde *m.*(*f.*) coward 14
coche *m.* car 2
cocina kitchen 9
cocinar to cook 9
cocinero cook 1
coco coconut 8
cocodrilo crocodile 14
código code 2
codo elbow 6
cofre *m.* large trunk, chest 14
coger to catch, get 13
colegio school 3
colombiano Colombian 1
color *m.* color 6
comedor *m.* dining room 9
comentar to comment 1
comentario commentary 1
comenzar to begin 4
comer to eat CP
cómico funny 2
comida food 1
como de costumbre as usual 10
cómo how
como máximo at most 4
cómoda dresser 2
cómodo *adj.* comfortable 2
compañero de clase classmate 2
compañía company 2
comparación *f.* comparison 6
compartir to share 1
completo *adj.* complete 7
complicado *adj.* complicated 7
comprar to buy 5
comprender to understand 1
comprensión *f.* understanding 1
compromiso commitment 4
computadora computer 2
comunidad *f.* community 1
con delicadeza delicately 14
con *prep.* with 1
   con retraso late 9
concurso contest 3
condominio condominium 2
conducir to drive 6
confortable *adj.* comfortable 9
congelado *adj.* frozen 6
conmigo with me 4
conocer to meet 4 to know 7
conocido *adj.* known 13
consecuencia consequence 12
conseguir to obtain, to get 4
constancia evidence 13
constantemente *adv.* constantly 8
constituir to constitute 13
consultorio office 8
contador(a) *m.* accountant 2
contar to tell 14
contento *adj.* content 3
contestar to answer
contexto context 1
conversación *f.* conversation 3

convertirse en to become 14
corajudo *adj.* hot-tempered 13
corazón *m.* heart 5
cordillera mountain range 4
coreano Korean 1
correo mail 3
correr to run 1
corriente *adj.* current 7
corriente *f.* trend 14
cortarse to cut 8
corto *adj.* short 2
cosa thing 4
coser to sow 13
costar to cost 6
costarricense *m.* (*f.*) Costa Rican 1
costumbre *f.* habit, custom 4
creación *f.* creation 14
creador(a) *adj.* creative 13
crecer to grow 14
creciente crescent 13
creencia belief 14
creer to believe 6
crema cream 6
crepúsculo twilight 14
crítico critic 14
croissant *m.* croissant 1
cruel *adj.* cruel 2
cuaderno notebook CP
cuadrado *adj.* square 4
cuadro painting 2
cuál which 2
cuándo when 1
cuánto how much 2
cuarenta forty 2
cuatro room 2; four 2; forth, quarter 9
cuatrocientos four hundred 4
cubano Cuban 1
cubismo cubism 13
cuchara spoon 11
cucharita teaspoon 11
cuchillo knife 11
cuello neck 8
cuenta bill, check 11
cuentista *m.* (*f.*) storyteller 14
cuento story 14
cuerda string, cord 13
cuero leather 4
cuerpo body 8
cuidado care 7
cuidadoso *adj.* careful 13
cultura culture 1
cultural *adj.* cultural 1
cumpleaños birthday 5
cumplir to turn 5
cura priest14
curioso *adj.* curious 5
curso course 9

D

dama lady 14
danza dance 13

dar to give CP
    dar un paseo to take a walk, a ride 4
    dar una vuelta to turn over 7
darse cuenta de to realize 13
de *prep.* from, of
    de acuerdo in agreement, agreed 3
    de carne y hueso of flesh and blood 14
    de costumbre usually, customarily 8
    de golpe *adv.* suddenly 14
    de qué color es… what color is
    de repente *adv.* suddenly 8
    de vez en cuando once in a while 3
débil *adj.* weak 7
debo (deber) I should 4
decidir to decide 6
décimo tenth 9
decir to say 1
dedo finger 8
    dedo del pie toe 8
definido *adj.* definite 1
del of the 3
delante de in front of 3
delgado *adj.* thin 2
delicioso *adj.* delicious
demasiado too (much) 5
dentista *m. (f.)* dentist
depender de to depend on 5
dependiente salesperson 6
deporte *m.* sport 2
derecho right 1
derrotar to defeat 10
desafío challenge 12
desaparecer to disappear 14
desarrollado *adj.* developed 10
desarrollar to develop 8
desarrollar(se) to develop 14
desayunarse to eat breakfast 8
desayuno breakfast CP
descamisado *adj.* shirtless 4
descansar to rest 3
descripción *f.* description 7
desde luego of course 13
desear to desire, to want 1
desembocar to meet, join with 13
desengaño deception 13
desfile *m.* parade 3
desgajar to break into pieces 14
deshonesto *adj.* dishonest 7
deslumbrar to dazzle 13
despedazar to break into pieces 14
despedida saying good-bye CP
despegar to take off 12
despejado *adj.* clear 7
despertarse to wake up 8
después *adv.* afterwards, later 1
    después de *prep.* after 12
destacado *adj.* outstanding 4
destierro exile 13
destino destination 14
destreza skill 12
detrás de behind 3
día *m.* day
diario *adj.* daily 10
dibujar to draw 13

dibujo drawing 13
diciembre December 5
diecinueve nineteen 2
dieciocho eighteen 2
dieciséis sixteen 2
diecisiete seventeen 2
diente *m.* tooth 8
diez ten 2
difícil *adj.* difficult
dificultad *f.* difficulty 8
¿diga? (decir) hello? 6
    ¿dígame? hello? 6
digestión *f.* digestion 8
dignidad *f.* dignity 14
diluir to dilute 14
dinámico adj. energetic 2
dinero money 1
dirección *f.* direction 4
    direcciones *f. pl.* directions 3
director(a) director 8
disco record 5
    disco compacto compact disk 2
discoteca discotheque 3
discreto *adj.* discreet 7
diseño design 13
disfrutar to enjoy 5
distancia distance 12
diversidad *f.* diversity 13
diversión *f.* pastime, amusement 5
divertido *adj.* fun, amusing 2
divertirse to have fun 8
divorciado *adj.* divorced 2
doble *adj.* double 1
doce twelve 2
docena dozen 6
doler to hurt 8
dolor de cabeza *m.* headache 8
domingo Sunday 4
dominicano Dominican 1
don gift 14
donador giftgiver 14
dónde where 1
dondequiera wherever 5
dormir to sleep 4
    dormirse to fall asleep 8
dormitorio bedroom, dormitory 2
dos two 2
doscientos two hundred 4
dramaturgo playwright 14
ducha shower 9
ducharse to take a shower 8
duda doubt 8
dudar to doubt 12
dudoso *adj.* doubtful 13
dulce *adj.* sweet 1
duradero *adj.* log lasting 13
durante *prep.* during CP
duro *adj.* hard 9

E

echar una siesta to take a nap 5
eclipse *m.* eclipse 10
económico *adj.* economical 7

ecuatoriano Ecuadoran 1
edad *f.* age 3
efectivo cash 6
egipcio Egyptian 1
egoísta *adj.* selfish 2
ejercicio exercise 5
el the
él *pron.* he
electrodoméstico appliance 6
elegante *adj.* elegant 7
elegir to elect 4
ella *pron.* she 1
ellos(as) *pron.* they 1
elote *m.* corn 6
embajada embassy 4
embajador(a) ambassador 13
empezar to begin 4
empleado employee 9
en *prep.* in, at 1
    en boga in vogue 13
    en caso de in case 14
    en forma in shape 8
enamorarse to fall in love 13
encantado delighted CP
encantador(a) magician 14
encantamiento magic spells 14
encantar to like very much, to love 11
encarcelamiento imprisonment 13
encargo commission 13
encerrar to enclose 14
enchilada soft corn tortilla filled with cheese,
    meat, or chicken 1
escribir to write 1
encontrar to find 6
encontrarse to meet 3
enemistad *f.* ill will 14
energía energy 8
enérgico *adj.* energetic 7
enero January 5
énfasis *m.* emphasis 11
enfermero nurse 2
enfermo *adj.* sick 3
enfoque *m.* focus
enlazado *adj.* woven together 4
enojado *adj.* angry 3
enorme *adj.* enormous 7
ensalada salad 11
ensayista *m. (f.)* essayist 14
ensayo essay 14
entero *adj.* entire, whole 10
entonces *adv.* then 3
entrar to enter 5
entre *prep.* between 3
entreabierto *adj.* half open 8
entrenamiento training 12
epidemia epidemic 8
equipaje *m.* baggage 5
equipo team 5
esbozo sketch, outline 14
escaleras *f. pl.* stairs 2
escalofrío chill 8
escaparate *m.* shop window 6
esclavo slave 13
escoltar to escort 8

escondido adj. hidden 14
escribir to write 5
escritor(a) writer 1
escritorio desk 2
escritura writing 4
escuchar to listen 1
escudero shield bearer 14
escuela school 3
escuela secundaria high school 3
escultura sculpture 2
ese(a) adj. that 6
ése(a) pron. that one 6
esencial adj. essential 8
esos(as) adj. those 6
ésos(as) pron. those 6
espada sword 13
espalda back 8
español m. Spanish (language)1
espárragos m. pl. asparagus 6
especial adj. special 4
espectacular adj. spectacular 7
esperanza hope 4
esperar to hope 4
espíritu m. spirit 13
esposa wife 2
esposo husband 2
esquí acuático m. water skiing 5
esquí m. skiing 5
esquina corner 3
establecer to establish 6
estación f. station 3 season 5
estacionamiento parking lot 3
estacionar to park 12
estadio stadium 3
estadounidense adj. American, from the
    United States 1
estallar to explode 13
estante m. bookshelf 2
estar to be CP
    estar al momento to be up to date 12
    estar de buen humor to be in a good
    mood 5
    estar de mal humor to be in a bad
    mood 5
este(a) adj. this 1
éste(a) pron. this one 6
estéreo stereo 2
estilo style 7
esto pron. this 1
estómago stomach 2
estornudar to sneeze 8
estos(as) adj. these
éstos(as) pron. these 6
estrella star 5
estudiante m. (f.) student 2
estudiantil adj. student 2
estudiar to study 1
etapa stage 1
eterno adj. eternal 14
euskera m. Euskarian, Basque (language) 1
exactamente adv. exactly 8
excursión f. excursion 9
exponer to exhibit 13
expresar to express 1

expresión f. expression 2
extra-académico adj. extra-curricular 9
extranjero adj. foreign 13
extraño adj. strange 7
extraterreno adj.from another world 14

F

fabricación f. fabrication 13
fácil adj. easy
facilitar to facilitate 8
facturar to check 12
falda skirt 6
faltar to need, lack 11
fama fame 10
familia family 2
famoso adj. famous 4
fantasía fantasy 14
farmacéutico(a) pharmacist 8
farmacia pharmacy CP
fauna fauna 13
favor m. favor 1
favorito adj. favorite 6
fe f. faith 14
febrero February 5
fecha date 5
felicitaciones f.pl. congratulations 14
feliz adj. happy
femenino adj. feminine 1
feo adj. ugly 2
feria fair 1
feroz adj. ferocious 7
fibra fiber 8
fiebre f. fever 8
fiel adj. loyal 14
fiesta party, holiday 3
fijarse en to notice 12
filete m. fillet 11
filipino adj. Philippine 1
fin de semana m. weekend 1
finalmente adv. finally 10
físico adj. physical 7
flan m. caramel custard 1
flauta fried taco 1
flora flora 13
florería flower shop 3
folklórico adj. folkloric 3
folleto brochure 5
forma form 13
formal adj. formal CP
formar to form 8
formidable adj. formidable 7
francés(francesa) French 1
frecuencia frequency 8
frecuentemente adv. frequently 4
frente f. forehead 8
    frente a across from 3
fresa strawberry 1
fresco adj. fresh 6
frijol m. bean 1
frío cold 1
frito adj. fried 1
frívolo adj. frivolous 2
frontera border 8

fruta fruit 6
fuego fire 3
    fuegos artificiales fireworks 3
fuerte adj. strong 7
fuerza strength 5
fumador(a) smoking 4
fumar to smoke 4
funcionar to function 7
fundar to found 13
furioso adj. furious 6
fusión f.fusion 14
fútbol m. soccer 2
    fútbol americano m. football 2
futuro future 4

G

gallego Galician (language) 1
galleta biscuit, cookie 6
galón m. gallon 6
gamba shrimp 5
ganadero stock farmer 6
ganado cattle 4
ganar to win 1 to earn 14
garaje m. garage 2
garganta throat 8
gastar to spend 6
gato cat 2
gaveta drawer 2
gazpacho cold soup with tomatoes, garlic,
    onion 11
general adj. general 2
genio genius 13
gente f. people 1
gigante m.(f.) giant 7
gimnasia gymnastics 8
gimnasio gymnasium 5
gira tour 13
giro turn CP
gitano gypsy 14
golf m. golf 5
gongo gong 8
gordo adj. fat 2
gorguera throat piece 8
gota drop 8
gozar to enjoy 11
grabar to record 6
gracias thank you
gramo gram 6
gran adj. great 7
granadina grenadine 1
grande adj. big 2
granjero farmer 6
grasa fat 8
griego Greek 11
gripe f. flu 8
gris adj. gray 6
grito cry, shout 13
grosero adj. vulgar 14
grueso adj. thick 13
gruñir to growl 14
guapo adj. handsome 2
guaraní m. Guaraní (language) 4
guardar la línea to watch one's weight 8

guatemalteco *adj.* Guatemalan 1
guayaba guava (a fruit) 6
guerra war *CP*
guiar to guide 14
guisante *m.* pea 6
guitarra guitar
gustar to like 1
gusto taste, pleasure *CP*

H

haber to have (auxiliary verb) 12
  había there was, there were 9
  hubo there was, there were 9
habitación *f.* room. 9
habitante *m.* inhabitant 4
habitual *adj.* habitual 8
hablar to speak
hacer to do 1
  hace mal tiempo it's bad weather 7
  hacer las maletas to pack 5
  hacer un viaje to take a trip 5
  hacerse cargo de to take charge of 14
hacia *prep.* toward 12
hamaca hammock 10
hambre *f.* hunger *CP*
hamburguesa hamburger 1
harina flour 6
hasta *prep.* until *CP*
hay (haber) there is, there are
hecho fact 14
helado ice cream *CP*
hermana sister 2
hermanastra stepsister 2
hermanastro stepbrother 2
hermano brother 2
hermoso *adj.* beautiful 4
hervir to boil 10
hidalgo nobleman 154
hielo ice 7
hierba herb 5
hierro iron 8
hija daughter 2
hijo son 2
hilo thread
hinchado *adj.* swollen 14
hindú *adj.* Indian 1
hipótesis f. hypothesis 14
hispano *adj.* hispanic 3
historia history 2 story 14
histórico adj. historic 7
hocico muzzle 14
hockey *m.* Hockey 5
hogar *m.* home 5
hoja piece 6
hola hello
hombre *m.* man 1
hombro shoulder 8
hondo *adj.* deep 8
hondonada ravine 14
hondureño adj. Honduran 1
honesto *adj.* honest 2
hongo mushroom 1
honra honor 14
hora hour, time 3

horario schedule 4
horno oven 2
horóscopo horoscope 7
horror *m.* horror 2
hospital *m.* hospital 2
hotel *m.* hotel *CP*
hoy today 4
  hoy día nowadays 11
huella mark, imprint 13
hueso bone 8
huésped *m.* (f.) guest 11
huir to flee 14
humo smoke
hundido *adj.* sunken 14

I

ida y vuelta round-trip 4
idealismo idealism 14
idealista *adj.* idealistic 7
idioma *m.* language4
iglesia church 3
igualdad *f.* equality 6
igualmente *adv.* likewise
imagen *f.* image 13
imaginación *f.* imagination
imaginar to imagine
imaginativo *adj.* imaginative 2
imaginería imagery 13
impaciente *adj.* impatient 7
imperio empire 6
impermeable raincoat 6
importante *adj.* important
imposible *adj.* impossible 4
impuesto tax 5
incertidumbre *f.* uncertainty 14
incluido *adj.* included 9
incluir to include 14
increíble *adj.* incredible 9
incrustación *f.* incrustation 13
independencia independence 3
independiente *adj.* independent 7
indicación *f.* indication 8
índice *m.* index 4
indio Indian 1
indiscreto *adj.* indiscreet 2
infantil *adj.* infantile 7
infección *f.* infection 8
infinito *adj.* infinite 14
informal *adj.* informal
ingeniero engineer 2
ingenuo *adj.* naive 2
inglés *m.* English (language) 1
ingresar to enroll 13
injertar to insert 13
insistir to insist 13
instrumento de cuerda stringed
    instrument 13
integración *f.* integration 1
intelectual *adj.* intellectual 7
inteligente *adj.* intelligent 2
intensidad *f.* intensity 9
intentar to intent 13
intercambio exchange 1
interesante *adj.* interesting 2

internacional *adj.* international 2
interno *adj.* internal 14
intérprete *m.* (*f.*)singer 13
inútil *adj.* useless
invento invention 14
invierno winter 5
invitación *f.* invitation 10
ir to go *CP*
  ir de camping to go caomping 5
  ir de pesca to go fishing 5
  irse to go, go away 8
iraní *adj.* Iranian 1
iraquí *adj.* Iraqi 1
irreal *adj.* unreal 14
irrealidad *f.* unreality 14
isla island 5
israelí *adj.*Israeli 1
italiano *adj.* Italian 1

J

jai-alai *m.* jai-alai 5
jamón *m.* ham
  jamón serrano Spanish ham, similar to
  prosciutto 11
japonés *m.* Japanese (language) 1
jarabe *m.* syrup 8
jardín *m.* garden 9
jornada journey 9
joven *adj.* young 2
joya jewel 12
jubilado *adj.* retired 2
jueves Thursday 4
jugador(a) player 5
jugar to play 4
jugo juice 1
juguetón (juguetona) *adj.* playful 13
juicio sanity 14
julio July 5
junio June 5
juntos *adv.* together 6
justicia justice 14

K

keniata *adj.* Kenyan 1
kilo kilogram 6
kilómetro kilometer 4

L

la the 1
labrador(a) laborer 13
labrar to work 9
lácteo *adj.* dairy 6
ladrar to bark 14
lágrima tear 8
lámpara lamp 2
lana wool 13
lanzar to launch 13   (to launch)
laosiano *adj.* Laotian 1
lápiz *m.* pencil 2
largo *adj.* long 2; length 14
las the 1
lástima pity 13
lastimarse to hurt 8

látigo whip 8
lavandería laundry 9
lavar to wash 1
   lavar en seco to dry clean 9
lavarse to wash 8
leal *adj.* loyal 7
lealtad *f.* loyalty 14
leche *f.* milk CP
lechuga lettuce 6
lectura reading 1
leer to read 1
legua league (unit of distance) 14
lejos far 3
   lejos de *prep.* far from 12
lengua language, tongue 2
letra lyrics 13
levantar la voz to raise one's voice 13
levantar to lift 5
levantarse to get up 8
léxico *adj.* lexical
ley *f.* law 14
libra pound 6
librería bookstore 3
libro book CP
ligero *adj.* light 7
límite *m.* limit 4
limón *m.* lemon CP
limonada lemonade
limpio *adj.* clean 11
lípido lipid 8
liquidación *f.* sale 6
listo *adj.*ready 3
litera berth 12
literario *adj.* literary 14
literatura literature 14
litro liter 6
llamada call 10
llamar la atención to call attention 14
   llamarse to call oneself
llamarada flame 13
llamativo *adj.* flashy, showy 13
llanto weeping 8
llanura plain 4
llave *f.* key 2
llegada arrival 12
llegar to arrive 3
lleno *adj.* full 6
llevar to take, carry 2
llover to rain 5
lloviznar to drizzle 7
lograr to succeed, to accomplish 4
los the 1
luego *adv.* Then, later
lugar *m.* place 5
luna moon 7
lunes Monday CP

M

madera wood 4
madrastra stepmother 2
madre *f.* mother 2
madrugada dawn 8
maestro teacher 13

mágico *adj.* magic 14
maíz *m.* corn 6
mala arte evil art 14
maleta suitcase 7
malo *adj.* bad 2
mañana morning, tomorrow 3
mandado order 4
mandar to order, to send 5
mango mango 6
mano *f.* hand 8
manta robe 13
mantenerse to maintain 8
mantequilla butter CP
manzana apple 6
maquillarse to put on make-up 8
máquina de escribir typewriter 2
mar *m.* sea 7
maravilla wonder 13
marcar to mark, to dial CP
marco frame 13
mariposa butterfly 9
marisco shellfish 11
marrón *adj.* brown 6
martes Tuesday 4
mártir *m.* (f.) martyr
marzo March 5
más *adv.* more CP
matemáticas *f. pl.* mathematics 2
materia subject 2
máximo maximum 4
mayo May 5
mayonesa mayonaise 6
mayor older 6
mayoría majority 4
mazapán *m.* marzipan 11
medianoche *f.* midnight 3
medias *f. pl.* stockings 6
médico doctor 2
medida measurement 4
medio *adj.* half 3
   medio kilo a half kilogram 6
mediodía *m.* midday
medios *m. pl* means 2
medir to measure 8
mejor better 3
mejorar to improve 8
melancolía melancholy 13
melocotón *m.* peach 6
melodía melody 13
melón *m.* melon 6
menor *adj.* younger 2
menos less 6
   menos…que less…than 6
menú *m.* menu 1
mercado market 3
   mercado al aire libre outdoor market 6
merienda snack 1
mermelada jelly, marmelade 1
mes *m.* month4
mesa table 11
mesero waiter 1
mestizaje *m.* mixture 4
metamorfosearse to change one's
   shape 14

metro metro (subway) 4
mexicano *adj.* Mexican 1
mezclado *adj.* mixed 13
mi *adj.* my CP
microbio microbe 8
miel *f.* honey 11
mientras while 4
miércoles Wednesday 4
mil thousand 4
milla mile 5
millón million 4
mineral *adj.* mineral 1
minuto minute 5
mirar to look at, watch 1
misa mass 3
misterioso *adj.* mysterious 14
mitad *f.* half 12
mítico *adj.* mythical 14
mito myth 14
mitológico *adj.* mythological 13
mixto *adj.* mixed 11
mochila knapsack 2
moda fashion 6
modelo model 2
moderno *adj.* modern 6
modos *m. pl.* means 4
mojado *adj.* wet 11
molino de viento windmill 14
momento moment 6
moneda coin 4
monje *m.* monk 13
mono monkey 8
montaña mountain 2
montar to ride 5
   montar en bicicleta to ride a bicycle 5
morado *adj.* purple 6
mordida bite 14
moreno *adj.* dark-haired, brunet 2
morirse to die 8
mosca fly 14
mostrar to show 10
motivo motive 13
motocicleta motorcycle 2
movimiento movement 8
mozo waiter 1
mucho *adv.* much CP
   muchísimo *adv.* very much 1
mudarse to move 13
mueble *m.* furniture 6
muerte *f.* death 13
muerto *adj.* dead 6
muestrario example 13
mujer *f.* woman 2
mundo world 4
muñeca wrist 8
mural *m.* mural 13
muralismo muralism 13
murmurar to murmur 14
muscular *adj.* muscular 8
músculo muscle 8
museo museum 2
música music 1
muslo thigh 8
muy *adv.* very CP

N

nacer to be born 5
nacimiento birth 12
nacionalidad *f.* nationality
nada nothing 5
nadar to swim 5
nadie nobody 11
naranja orange CP
nariguera nose ring 13
nariz *f.* nose 7
natación *f.* swimming 5
natural *adj.* natural
naturaleza nature 2
neblina fog 7
necesitar to need 1
negar to deny 14
negocio business 2
negrero slavedriver 8
negro *adj.* black 6
nervio nerve 8
nervioso *adj.* nervous 11
nevar to snow 7
nevera refrigerator 2
ni…ni neither…nor 11
nicaragüense *adj.* Nicaraguan 1
niebla fog 7
nieta granddaughter 7
nieto grandson 7
nieve *f.* snow 7
nigeriano Nigerian 1
ningún none, not one 11
ninguno(a) none, not one 11
nivel *m.* level 5
   nivel del mar *m.* sea level 12
nobleza nobility 14
noche *f.* night CP
nocturno *adj.* nocturnal, night 8
nombre *m.* name CP
normalmente *adv.* normally 1
norteamericano *adj.* North American
novecientos nine hundred 4
novedad *f.* novelty 14
novela novel 7
novelista *m.* (*f.*) novelist 14
noveno ninth 9
noventa ninety 2
novia girlfriend, fiancée 7
noviembre November 5
novio boyfriend, fiancé 7
nube *f.* cloud 7
nublado *adj.* cloudy 7
nuestro *adj.* our 1
nueve nine 2
nuevo *adj.* new 4
número number 4 size 6
nunca *adv.* never 3

O

o or CP
   obra work, piece 7
obra teatral play 7
obrero worker 12

---

ochenta eighty 2
ocho eight 2
ochocientos eight hundred 4
octavo eighth 9
octubre October 5
ocupado *adj.* occupied 11
ocupar to occupy 4
oferta sale 6
oficial *adj.* official 9
oficina de correos post office 3
oficina office 2
ofrecer to offer 6
oír to hear 6
ojalá I hope 13
ojo eye 7
oler to smell 1
once eleven 2
onda wave 4
opinión *f.* opinion 7
oportunidad *f.* opportunity 3
optimista *adj.* optimistic 2
órden *f.* order 6
ordenador computer 2
oreja ear 8
oriental *adj.* oriental, eastern 13
origen *m.* origin 1
orilla edge 14
oro gold 11
otoño fall 5
otro *adj.* Other, another 1
oveja sheep 14

P

paciente *adj.* patient 2
padrastro stepfather 2
padre *m.* father 2
paella valenciana Spanish dish with rice, shellfish, and chicken 11
pagar to pay 4
país *m.* country 4
pájaro bird 2
palabra word 2
pálido *adj.* pale 7
palmera palm 4
pan *m.* bread 6
panadería bakery 3
panameño Panamanian 1
pantalla screen 2
pantalones *m. pl.* trousers 6
pantera panther 14
papa potato 1
papel *m.* role 4; paper 6
papelería paper store 6
paquete *m.* package 6
para *prep.* for, in order to
   para que so that 14
paraguayo *adj.* Paraguayan 1
paraje *m.* area, stop, spot 10
parar to stop 12
parecer to seem, appear 7
pareja couple 12
parmesana parmesan 11
parque *m.* park 1

---

parte *f.* part 8
participación *f.* participation
particular *adj.* particular 7
partido game, match 2
partitura score (musical) 13
pasado past 5
pasaporte *m.* passport 12
pasar to spend, to pass 6
   pasar tiempo to spend time 5
pasatiempo pastime 5
paseo ride, walk 4
pasillo hallway 14
pasta pasta 6
pastel *m.* pie CP
pastilla pill 8
patata potato 1
patinar to skate 5
   patinar en ruedas to roller skate 5
patio patio 7
patria homeland 14
pavimentado *adj.* paved 10
pavo turkey 11
pecho chest 8
pedazo piece 6
pediatra *m.* (*f.*) pediatrician 8
pedir to order, to ask for 1
pedregoso *adj.* rocky 9
pegado *adj.* attached 14
peinarse to comb 8
película movie, film 2
pelirrojo *adj.* redheaded 2
pelo hair
pelota ball 6
pelotón de fusilamiento *m.* firing squad 14
peludo *adj.* hairy 14
peña rock CP
pena sorrow CP
pendiente *m.* earring 13
pensar to think 4
peor worse 6
pepino cucumber 6
peplo short skirt 14
pequeño *adj.* small 2
pera pear 6
perder to lose 5
perezoso *adj.* lazy 2
perfecto *adj.* perfect 7
periódico newspaper 3
periodista *m.* (*f.*) journalist 1
período period (of time) 7
perro dog 2
persona person 2
personaje *m.* character 14
personal *adj.* personal 1
personalización *f.* personalization 1
persuasión *f.* persuasion 6
pertenecer to pertain, belong 13
peruano *adj.* Peruvian 1
pesado *adj.* heavy 7
pesar to weigh CP
pesas *f. pl.* weights 5
pesca fishing 5
pescado fish 1
pescaíto fish 1

---

peseta peseta, a monetary unit 2
pesimista *adj.* pessimistic 2
peso peso (a monetary unit) *CP*, weight 8
pezuña hoof 14
piano piano 8
picante *adj.* spicy 1
picar con la espuela to dig in one's spurs 14
pie *m.* foot 2
piel *f.* fur, skin 4
pierna leg 8
pieza teatral play 14
pilar *m.* pillar 13
pimienta pepper 6
pincho tapa 1
pintar to paint 13
pintor *m.* painter 7
pintura painting 2
piscina swimming pool 5
piso floor 9
pizarra chalkboard 2
plan *m* plan 4 floor plan 9
plancha iron 9
planta plant 2
plástico *adj.* plastic 4
platillo saucer 11
plato plate, dish 1
plato hondo bowl 11
   playa beach 5
plaza de primera first class seat 12
plaza de segunda second class seat 12
plaza de toros bullring 3
plaza seat 12
plaza square, plaza 3
pluma fountain pen 2
plural plural 1
población *f.* population 5
poco a little 1
poder to be able to 4 power 14
poema *m.* poem 14
poesía poetry 3
poeta *m.* (*f.*) poet 14
policía police (department) 3
político *adj.* political 1
pollo al chilindrón Spanish dish with chicken in a tomato sauce 11
pollo chicken 1
poner to put 9
ponerse to get, become, put on 8
   ponerse en forma to get in shape 8
popular *adj.* popular 3
por by, through, along, for 1
   por eso therefore 6
   por lo menos at least 7
por qué why 2
por supuesto of course 3
portafolio briefcase 2
portátil *adj.* portable 9
portentoso *adj.* extraordinary 14
portugués *adj.* Portuguese 7
poseer to possess 13
posesión *f.* possession 2
posibilidad *f.* possibility 5
positivo *adj.* positive 7
póster *m.* poster 2

postre *m.* dessert 11
potrillo colt 14
práctica practice 1
practicar to practice 1
práctico *adj.* practical 7
precio price 6
precipitarse to hurl oneself 14
preferencia preference 5
preferir to prefer 3
pregunta question 1
preguntar to ask 2
preliminar *adj.* preliminary
premio prize 3
prender to pin on 14
preocupado *adj.* worried, preoccupied 8
preparación *f.* preparation 1
presenciar to witness 13
presentación *f.* presentation, introduction *CP*
presentar to present; to introduce *CP*, to present 8
presidente *m.* president 2
prima cousin 2
primavera spring 5
primer first 9
primero first 1
primo cousin 2
principal *adj.* principal 4
privado *adj.* private 2
probable *adj.* probable 13
probar to try 1
prodigioso *adj.* marvelous 14
producto product 4
profesión *f.* profession *CP*
profesor(a) *m.* professor 2
profundo *adj.* deep 14
programa *m.* program 7
   programa de intercambio *m.* exchange program 9
prohibir to prohibit 13
promedio average 12
pronombre *m.* pronoun 1
pronóstico forecast 7
propina tip 4
propio *adj.* own 4
proteína protein 8
próximo *adj.* next 4
publicar to publish 14
pueblo town 3
puertorriqueño *adj.* Puerto Rican
pues *adv.* then, well
pulido *adj.* polished 14
pulmón *m.* lung 8
punto point 8
   punto de vista point of view 14

Q

que *pron.* who, that
qué what 2
   qué bueno que how great that 7
   qué lástima que too bad that 7
   qué más da who cares 14
   qué pena que what a pity that 7
   qué pena what a pity

   qué te pasa? What's the matter with you? 8
quedarse to stay, remain 8
quemar to burn 13
querer to want, to love
queso cheese
queso manchego cheese from La Mancha region 11
quién who 1
química chemistry 2
quince fifteen 2
quinientos five hundred 4
quinto fifth 9
quiosco kiosk 3
quisiera (querer) I would like *CP*
quisiéramos (querer) we would like 9

R

ración *f.* ration 1
radio *m.* radio (the set), *f.* radio (the network) 3
rapado *adj.* shaved 14
raqueta racquet 6
rara vez *adv.* rarely 3
rasgo trait 13
rato while, short time 6
ratón *m.* mouse 2
raza breed, 14
razonable *adj.* reasonable 5
reacción *f.* reaction 7
real *m.* real, a unit of money 14
real *adj.* real 13
realidad *f.* reality 14
realismo realism 14
realista *adj.* realistic 2
rebaja reduction, sale 6
rebanada slice 1
recelar to fear 14
recepción *f.* reception desk 9
receta prescription 8
rechazado *adj.* rejected 13
recibir to receive 1
recoger to pick up 12
reconocimiento recognition 13
recorrer to run through 14
recorrido journey, trip 12
rectángulo rectangle 13
recuerdo memory 13
recuperar to recuperate 8
red *f.* network 12
reflejar to reflect 14
refresco refreshment
regalar to give 12
regalo gift 3
regresar to return 4
regular *adj.* okay, regular 7; to regulate 8
regularidad *f.* regularity 8
relucir to shine 9
remedio remedy 8
renovar to renew 8
repaso review 1
repertorio repertoire 13
repetir to repeat 8

representar to represent 14
repujado *adj.* shining 8
resbaloso *adj.* slippery 7
reseco *adj.* dried out 14
reserva reservation 9
reservación *f.* reservation 9
residencia residence, dormitory 2
resonar to resound 13
respirar to breathe 8
respiratorio *adj.* respiratory 8
responder to respond CP
responsible *adj.* responsible 7
respuesta answer CP
restaurante *m.* restaurant CP
resultado result 8
retrasado *adj.* behind schedule, late 12
retrasarse to fall behind 14
reunir to meet, gather 6
revista magazine 1
revuelo tolling 14
Reyes Magos *m. pl.* Three Kings 3
rico *adj.* delicious 1
rincón *m.* corner 14
riquísimo *adj.* delicious 1
risa laughter 13
ritmo cardíaco heart rate 8
ritmo rhythm 13
rizado *adj.* curly 2
rodeado *adj.* surrounded 12
rodilla knee 8
rojo *adj.* red 6
romántico *adj.* romantic 7
romperse to break 8
ropa clothing 6
ropero closet 2
rosa *adj.* pink 6
rosado *adj.* pink 6
rozar to rub 14
rubio *adj.* blond 2
ruido noise 14
rumor *m.* noise 14
ruso Russian 1
rutina routine 10

S

sábado Saturday 4
sábana sheet 14
saber to know CP
sabio wise man 14
sabroso *adj.* delicious, tasty 11
sacapuntas *m.* pencil sharpener 2
sacar to take out something, to obtain 5
sagrado *adj.* sacred 14
sal *f.* salt 6
sala de estar living room 9
sala de reclamación de equipaje baggage claim 12
salado *adj.* salty 11
salida exit 9, departure 12
salir to leave, to go out, depart CP
salsa sauce CP
salud *f.* health 8
saludar to greet CP

saludo greeting CP
salvadoreño *adj.* Salvadoran 1
samoano *adj.* Samoan 1
sandalias sandals 6
sándwich *m.* sandwich CP
sangre *f.* blood 13
sangría wine and fruit drink 1
sátira satire 14
secadora de pelo hair dryer 9
sección *f.* section 12
seco *adj.* dry 11
secretario secretary 2
seda silk 14
seguir to follow 4
segundo plato entrée 11
segundo second 1
seguro *adj.* sure 6
seis six 2
seiscientos six hundred 4
selva jungle 8
semana week 4
semanalmente *adv.* weekly 9
semilla seed 4
señal de marcar *f.* dial tone 12
señal *f.* signal, sign 8
señalar to point 14
sencillo *adj.* simple 9
señor *m.* Mr., sir CP
señora Mrs., ma'am CP
señorita Miss CP
sensacional *adj.* sensational 7
sentarse to sit down 8
sentir to feel 4 to feel sorry 7
  sentirse to feel 8
septiembre September 5
séptimo seventh 9
sepultarse to be buried 13
ser to be 1
serio *adj.* serious 2
servicio despertador wake-up service 9
servilleta napkin 11
servir to serve 4
sesenta sixty 2
setecientos seven hundred 4
setenta seventy 2
sexto sixth 9
si if 1
siempre *adv.* always 1
siesta nap 5
siete seven 2
siglo century 4
silla chair 2
sillón *m.* armchair 2
simpático *adj.* nice 2
simple *adj.* simple 7
sin que without 14
sincero *adj.* sincere 2
singular *adj.* singular 1
sino but, rather 13
sintético *adj.* synthetic 4
síntoma *m.* symptom 8
sitio place 4
sobre *m.* envelope 6 CP
sobre *prep.* over, on 1

sobrenatural *adj.* supernatural 14
sobrina niece 4
sobrino nephew 4
soda soda 1
sofisticar to sophisticate 1
sol *m.* sun 5
soledad *f.* solitude 14
solfeo musical notation (sol-fa) 13
sombra shadow 8
soñar to dream 14
sonreír to smile 8
sopa soup 1
sorprendente *adj.* surprising 13
soya soy 4
su *adj.* his, her, your, their, its 2
subir to go up, climb rise 9
substraer to subtract 7
subte subway 4
sucio *adj.* dry 11
sudar to sweat 8
suéter *m.* sweater 6
suficiente enough
sufrimiento suffering 13
sugerir to suggest 8
sujeto subject 2
super *adj.* super 6
superficie *f.* surface 7
superpuesto *adj.* superimposed 13
suposición *f.* supposition 12
surafricano *adj.* South African 1
surfing *m.* surfing 5
surgir to appear, surge 13
surrealismo surrealism 13
surtido *adj.* assorted 11
sustantivo noun 1

T

tabaco tabacco 4
taco tortilla filled with meat, chicken or cheese 1
tailandés (tailandesa) *adj.* Thai 1
tal *adj.* such CP
talla size 6
tallar to carve 13
taller *m.* studio, workshop 13
tamaño size 5
también also 1
tambor *m.* drum 8
tampoco either, neither 1
tan... como as . . . as 6
tanto... como as much . . . s 6
tapa small dish that is served with wine or beer 1
tapado *adj.* covered up 14
tapeo the serving of small dishes with wine and beer 1
tardar to take 4
tarde *f.* afternoon, *adv.* late CP
tarea homework 7
tarjeta card 6
  tarjeta de crédito credit card 9
  tarjeta de cumpleaños birthday card 6
  tarjeta postal post card 3

taxi *m.* taxi 4
taza cup 11
té *m.* tea 1
teatral *adj.* theatrical
teatro theater 3
techo roof, ceiling 2
teclado keyboard 2
tejido woven, knitted 10
tela cloth 6
telefónico *adj.* telephone 3
teléfono directo direct phone 9
televisión *f.* television 1
televisor *m.* television set 2
tema *m.* theme 1
temer to fear 13
temperatura temperature 7
temporada season 13
temprano *adv.* early 8
tenedor *m.* fork 11
tener to have 1
   tener calor to be hot 3
   tener dolor de…to have a …ache 8
   tener en cuenta to take into account 13
   tener éxito to be successful 13
   tener frío to be cold 3
   tener ganas de to feel like 3
   tener hambre to be hungry 3
   tener que to have to 3
   tener que ver to have to do with 14
   tener sed to be thirsty 3
   tener sueño to be sleepy 3
   tener… años to be . . . years old 3
tenis *m.* tennis 2
tenista *m. (f.)* tennis player 1
tercer third 9
tercero third 1
terminal *f.* terminal 3
terminar to finish 5
ternera veal 11
terraza terrace, porch 7
terremoto earthquake 5
tía aunt 2
tiempo time 5; weather 7
tienda store 3
tímido *adj.* timid, shy 7
tina tub 9
tinto *adj.* red (wine) 1
tío uncle 2
típico *adj.* typical 1
tipo type 11
tobillo ankle 8
tocar to play an instrument, to touch 1 to be one's turn 11
todavía still 5
todo all 1
todos los días every day 8
tomar to take 1
   tomar el sol to sunbathe 5
tomate *m.* tomato ...
tonalidad *f.* tonality 13
tonificarse to tone up 8
tono tone 8
tonto *adj.* foolish, silly 2
torcerse to sprain, twist 8

tormenta storm 7
torta cake 1
tortilla cornmeal pancake, Spanish omelette *CP*
tos *f.* cough 8
toser to cough 8
tostado *adj.* toasted 1
trabajador *adj.* hard-working 7
trabajar to work 1
traducir to translate 14
traer to bring 6
trágico *adj.* tragic 14
tranquilo *adj.* calm, quiet 7
transporte *m.* transportation 2
trasladar to move 13
traspasar to transfer, transpose 13
tratar de to try to 8
   tratarse de to be about 6
trazar to trace 14
trece thirteen 2
treinta thirty 2
tren *m.* train 3
trepar to climb 14
tres three 2
trescientos three hundred 4
trigo wheat 4
triste *adj.* sad 3
tronar to thunder 7
trozo piece 13
tu *adj.* your
tú *pron.* you
tumba tomb 6
TV por cable cable TV 9

U

último *adj.* last 10
un(a) a 1
un poco *adv.* a little 11
una vez once 6
unas some 1
universal *adj.* universal 14
universidad *f.* university 2
uno one *CP*
unos some 1
uruguayo *adj.* Uruguayan 1
usted (Ud.) *pron.* you (formal) *CP*
ustedes (Uds.) *pron.* you (formal pl.) *CP*
usualmente *adv.* usually 4
útil *adj.* useful 9
uva grape 6

V

vaca cow 9
vacaciones *f. pl.* vacation 5
vacío *adj.* vacant, empty 9
valentía courage 14
válgame Dios good heavens 14
valiente *adj.* brave 2
valor value 14
vaqueros *m. pl.* bluejeans 6
variado *adj.* varied 7
variedad *f.* variety 1

vasija pot 6
vaso glass 1
veces *f. pl.* times 8
vecino neighbor 7
vegetal *m.* vegetable 4
veinte twenty 2
veinticinco twenty-five 2
veinticuatro twenty-four 2
veintidós twenty-two
veintinueve twenty-nine 2
veintiocho twenty-eight 2
veintiséis twenty-six 2
veintisiete twenty-seven 2
veintitrés twenty-three 2
veintiuno twenty-one 2
vela sailing 5; sail 8
velear to sail 5
vendedor(a) salesman 6
vender to sell 1
venezolano *adj.* Venezuelan 1
venir to come 4
ventaja advantage 5
ventana window 9
ventilador *m.* fan 9
ver to see *CP*
verano summer5
verdad *f.* truth, *adj.* true *CP*
verdaderamente *adv.* truly 8
verde *adj.* green 1
verdura vegetable 6
vergüenza shame 13
versado informed 14
vestido dress 6
vestirse to get dressed 8
vez *f.* time 1
vía track 12
viajar to travel 1
viaje *m.* trip 9
viajero(a) traveller
vida life 2
vídeo *m.* video 1
videocasete *m.* VCR 2
videocasetera VCR 2
vidriera stained glass 10
vidrio glass 13
viejo *adj.* old 2
viento wind 7
viernes Friday 4
vietnamita *adj.* Vietnamese 1
vinagre *m.* vinegar 11
vino wine 1
violeta *adj.* violet 6
violín *m.* violin 2
violonchelo violoncello 13
virar to turn 12
visado visa 12
visión *f.* vision 8
visitante *adj.* visiting 9
visitar to visit 5
vista sight 13
vitamina vitamin 8
vivienda housing 2
vivir to live 1
vivo *adj.* alive 5

vocabulario vocabulary 1
volar to fly 14
volcán *m.* volcano 9
vólibol *m.* volleyball 2
volver(se) to return, become *CP*
vos *pron.* you
vosotros *pron.* you (pl. informal) 1
vuelo flight 12
vuestra merced your grace 14
vuestro(a) *adj.* your 2

W

windsurf *m.* windsurfing 5

Y

y and
yerba herb 4
yo *pron.* I 1
yogur *m.* yogurt 6

Z

zanahoria carrot 6
zapatería shoe store 6
zapato shoe 4
   zapato de tacón high-heeled shoe 6
   zapato de tenis tennis shoe 6
zona area, zone 6
zumo juice 1

ENGLISH-SPANISH GLOSSARY

Gender of nouns is indicated except for masculine nouns ending in **–o** and feminine nouns ending in **–a**. Masculine forms of adjectives are given; feminine forms are given when irregular. Verbs appear in the infinitive form. The number(s) following the entries refer to the chapter(s) in which the word or phrase first appears.

adj.   adjective
f.   feminine
m.   masculine
n.   noun
pl.   plural

A

abstract abstracto 13
(to) accept aceptar 8
accident accidente *m.* 8
accountant contador(a) *m.* 2
active activo 7
(to) add añadir 14
additional adicional 8
(to) admit admitir 8
(to) adore adorar 7
advantage ventaja 9
advisable aconsejable 13
after después 1
afternoon tarde *f.* 4
afterwards luego 6
agreeable simpático 7
air conditioned aire acondicionado *m.* 9
airport aeropuerto 3
al least al menos 9
allergy alergia 8
also también 1
although aunque 14
always siempre 1
ambitious ambicioso 7
American estadounidense *m.(f.)* 1
angry enojado 3
ankle tobillo 8
(to) announce anunciar 3
annual anual 8
another otro(a,os,as) 4
antibiotic antibiótico 8
antihistamine antihistamínico 8
apartment apartamento 2
apparently aparentemente 8
(to) appeal apetecer 11
(to) appear parecer 7; aparecer 14
appetizer aperitivo 11
apple manzana 6
April abril 5
architecture arquitectura 2
Argentina Argentina 1
Argentinian argentino 1
arm brazo 8
armchair sillón *m.* 2
(to) arrange arreglar 9
(to) arrive llegar 3
art arte *m.* 2
artist artista *m(f.)* 13
ashamed avergonzado 11
(to) ask for pedir 4; preguntar 6

asparagus esparragos *m. pl.* 6
aspirin aspirina 8
at least por lo menos 5
athletic atlético 7
(to) attend asistir a 5
August agosto 5
aunt tía 2
Australia Australia 1
Australian australino 1
author autor(a) 14
avenue avenida 3
avocado aguacate *m.* 6

B

baby bebé *m.(f.)* 8
back espalda 8
bad malo 2
baggage equipaje *m.* 12
bag maleta 12
bakery panadería 3
balanced balanceado 8
ball pelota 6
banana banana 1
bank banco 3
(to) bark ladrar 14
baseball béisbol *m.* 2
basketball básquetbol *m.* 2 baloncesto 5
bass bajo 13
bathroom baño 9
(to) be ser 1; estar 3
    (to) be able to poder 4
    (to) be in a bad mood estar de mal humor 7
    (to) be in a good mood estar de buen humor 7
    (to) be one's turn tocar 11
bean frijol *m.* 1
beard barba 7
beautiful hermoso 4
(to) become convertirse en 14
bed cama 2
bedroom dormitorio 9
beer cerveza 1
before antes de 12
(to) begin comenzar, empezar 4
belief creencia 14
bell campana 14
belt cinturón *m.* 6
berth litera 12
besides además 6
better mejor 6
between entre 12
bicycle bicicleta 2
bill cuenta 11
biology biología 2
bird pájaro 2

birth nacimiento 12
birthday cumpleaños 6
biscuit galleta 6
bite mordida 14
black negro 6
blind ciego 14
blond rubio 2
blouse blusa 6
blue azul 6
body cuerpo 8
Bolivia Bolivia 1
Bolivian boliviano 1
bone hueso 8
book libro 2
bookshelf estante 2
bookstore librería 3
boot bota 6
border frontera 8
boring aburrido 2
bottle botella 1
bowl plato hondo 11
boy(girl)friend novio(a) 7
brave valiente 2
bread pan *m.* 1
(to) break romperse 8
breakfast desayuno 1
breathe respirar 14
briefcase portafolio 2
(to) bring traer 6
broad amplio 14
brochure folleto 9
brother hermano 2
brown marrón 6
brunet(te) moreno(a) 2
(to) brush cepillarse 8
bus autobús *m.* 2
bus terminal terminal de autobuses *f.* 3
businessman(woman) hombre *m.*(mujer *f.*) de negocios
busy ocupado 11
butter mantequilla 1
(to) buy comprar 5

C

cable TV TV por cable *f.* 9
café café *m.* 1
calcium calcio 8
calculator calculadora 2
calendar calendario 12
calm tranquilo 11
calorie caloría 8
camera cámara 2
Canada Canadá 1
Canadian canadiense *m.(f.)* 1
car coche *m.* 2; (train) vagón *m.* 12
card tarjeta 6

careful cuidadoso 13
carpet alfombra 2
carrot zanahoria 6
(to) carry llevar 2
(to) carve tallar 13
cash efectivo 6
cat gato 2
cathedral catedral *f.* 3
cause causa 8
(to) celebrate celebrar 3
cereal cereal *m.* 8
chair silla 2
(to) change cambiar 4
change cambio 4
character personaje *m.(f.)* 14
cheap barato 4
(to) check (bags) facturar 12
check cheque *m.* 6; cuenta 11
cheese queso 1
chemistry química 2
chest pecho 8
chicken pollo 6
Chile Chile 1
Chilean chileno 1
China China 1
Chinese chino 1
chocolate chocolate *m.* 1
chop chuleta 11
church iglesia 3
citizen ciudadano 9
city ciudad *f.* 2
claim reclamación *f.* 12
class clase *f.* 1
classic(al) clásico 7
clean limpio 11
clear despejado 7
(to) climb subir 9
closed cerrado 11
closet ropero 2
cloth tela 13
clothing ropa 6
cloudy nublado 7
coat abrigo 6
coffee café *m.* 1
cold catarro 8; frío 7
Colombia Colombia 1
Colombian colombiano 1
color color *m.* 13
colt potrillo 14
(to) comb one's hair peinarse 8
(to) come venir 4
comfortable cómodo, confortable 9
commitment compromiso 4
companion acompañante 12
complicated complicado 13
computer computadora, ordenador m. 2
congratulations felicitaciones *f.pl.* 14
constantly constantemente 8
contest concurso 3
conversation conversación *f.* 3
(to) cook cocinar 9
cookie galleta 6
cool fresco 6
corn maíz *m.* 6

corner rincón *m.* 14
Costa Rica Costa Rica 1
Costa Rican costarricense 1
cough tos *f.* 8
(to) cough toser 8
couple pareja 12
courage valentía 14
course curso 9
court (tennis, basketball, etc.) cancha 9
cousin primo(a) 2
creation creación *f.* 14
creative creador(a) 13
critic crítico 14
croissant medialuna 1
cruel cruel 2
Cuba Cuba 1
Cuban cubano 1
cubism cubismo 13
cucumber pepino 6
cup taza 11
customer cliente *m.(f.)* 6
customs aduana 12
(to) cut cortarse 8
cycling ciclismo 5

D

dairy lácteo 8
(to) dance bailar 1
dance baile *m.*, danza 13
date fecha 5
daughter hija 2
day día *m.* 5
　day before yesterday anteayer 10
December diciembre 5
deception desengaño 13
deep profundo 14
delicious delicioso 1
delighted encantado CP
dentist dentista *m.(f.)* 2
(to) deny negar 14
(to) depend on depender de 5
design diseño 13
desk escritorio 2
dessert postre *m.* 11
destination destino 14
destiny destino 14
(to) develop desarrollar 8
difficulty dificultad *f.* 8
digestion digestión *f.* 8
dignity dignidad *f.* 14
dining room comedor *m.* 9
direction dirección *f.* 4
dirty sucio 11
disagreeable antipático 2
(to) disappear desaparecer 14
discotheque discoteca 3
discreet discreto 7
dish plato 11
diversity diversidad *f.* 13
diving buceo 5
(to) do hacer 5
　(to) do aerobics hacer ejercicios
　　aeróbicos 8

doctor médico 2
dog perro 2
Dominican dominicano 1
Dominican Republic República Dominicana 1
dormitory residencia estudiantil 2
doubt duda 8
doubtful dudoso 13
downtown centro 4
(to) draw dibujar 13
drawing dibujo 13
(to) dream soñar 14
dress vestido 6
dresser cómoda 2
(to) drink tomar 1
(to) drive conducir 6
(to) drizzle lloviznar 7
dry seco 11
　dry cleaning lavado a seco 9
during por 12
dynamic dinámico 2

E

each cada 6
ear oreja 8
(to) earn ganar 1
(to) eat comer 1
　(to) eat breakfast desayunarse 8
　(to) eat dinner cenar 5
economical económico 7
Ecuador Ecuador 1
Ecuadoran ecuatoriano 1
Egypt Egipto 1
Egyptian egipcio 1
eight hundred ochocientos 4
eighth octavo 9
El Salvador El Salvador 1
elbow codo 8
elegant elegante 7
elevator ascensor *m.* 9
employee empleado 9
empty vacío 9
(to) enclose encerrar 14
energetic enérgico, dinámico 7
energy energía 8
engineer ingeniero 2
England Inglaterra 1
English inglés (inglesa) 1
enough suficiente 6
entrée segundo plato 11
envelope sobre *m.* 6
epidemic epidemia 8
eraser borrador *m.* 2
errand mandado 4
essay ensayo 14
essayist ensayista *m.(f.)* 14
eternal eterno 14
exactly exactamente 8
exchange intercambio (of money)
　cambio 9
excursion excursión *f.* 9
(to) exhibit exponer 13
exit salida 9
expensive caro 6

extra-curricular extra-académico 9
eye ojo 7

F

fabric tela 13
fabrication fabricación *f.* 13
face cara 8
(to) facilitate facilitar 8
fact hecho 14
fair feria 3
faith fe *f.* 14
faithful fiel 14
(to) fall caerse 8
   (to) fall asleep dormirse 8
fall otoño 5
family familia 2
famous famoso 4
fantasy fantasía 14
far from lejos de 12
farmhand labrador 14
fat gordo (adj.) 2 grasa (n.) 8
father padre *m.* 2
fauna fauna 13
favorite favorito 6
February febrero 5
(to) feel sentir 4
fever fiebre *f.* 8
fiancé(e) novio(a) 7
fiber fibra 8
fifth quinto 9
finger dedo 8
fireworks fuegos artificiales 3
first primer(o) 9
fish pescado 6
(to) fit caber 14
five hundred quinientos 4
(to) fix arreglar 9
flashy llamativo 13
flesh and blood de carne y hueso 14
flight vuelo 12
floor piso 9
   floor plan plan *m.* 9
flora flora 13
flour harina 6
flu gripe *f.* 8
fly mosca 14
fog niebla, neblina 7
(to) follow seguir 4
food comida 1
foolish tonto 2
football fútbol americano *m.* 2
for para CP; por 12
forecast pronóstico 7
forehead frente 8
fork tenedor 11
form forma 13
(to) form formar 8
formal formal 7
formidable formidable 7
four hundred cuatrocientos 4
fourth cuarto 9
France Francia 1
French francés *m.* 1

frequently frecuentemente 4; con frecuencia 8
fried frito 11
friend amigo(a) 4
friendly amable 9
frivolous frívolo 2
from de 1
fruit fruta 8
full lleno 6
fun divertido 2
(to) function funcionar 7
funny cómico 7
furious furioso 11
furnished amueblado 9
fusion fusión *f.* 14

G

game partido 5
garage garaje *m.* 9
garden jardín *m.* 9
generous generoso 7
gentleman caballero 14
German alemán (alemana) 1
Germany Alemania 1
(to) get dressed vestirse 8
(to) get up levantarse 8
(to) give regalar 12
glass vaso 1
(to) go ir 1
   (to) go for a walk dar un paseo 4
   (to) go shopping ir de compras 4
   (to) go through pasar 12
   (to) go to bed acostarse 8
   (to) go up subir 9
golf golf *m.* 5
good bueno 1
   good morning buenos días CP
   good afternoon buenas tardes CP
   good evening buenas noches CP
   good-bye adiós, chau CP
grandfather(mother) abuelo(a) 2
grandson(daughter) nieto(a) 7
grape uva 6
great-grandparents bisabuelos 14
Greek griego 11
green verde 6
grenadine granadina 1
(to) grow crecer 14
Guatemala Guatemala 1
Guatemalan guatemalteco 1
guitar guitarra 13

H

hair dryer secadora de pelo 9
hair pelo 8
half mitad *f.* 12
ham jamón *m.* 1
hamburger hamburguesa 1
hand mano *f.* 8
handbag bolsa 6
handsome guapo 2
happy alegre 2; contento 3

hard-working trabajador(a) 7
harp arpa *m.* 13
(to) have tener 1
   (to) have (auxiliary verb) haber 12
   (to) have a good time divertirse 8
he él 1
head cabeza 8
health salud *f.* 8
heart corazón *m.* 8
   heart rate ritmo cardíaco 8
heavy pesado 7
hello hola CP
help ayuda 12
her su (adj.) 2
here aquí 1
his su 2
Hispanic hispano 3
historical histórico 7
history historia 2
hockey hockey *m.* 5
homeland patria 14
Honduran hondureño 1
Honduras Honduras 1
honest honesto 2
honor honra 1
(to) hope esperar 4
horoscope horóscopo 7
hospital hospital *m.* 3
host(ess) anfitrión (anfitriona) 9
hotel hotel *m.* 3
hot-tempered corajudo 13
hour hora *f.* 5
house casa 2
how cómo 1
(to) hurt lastimarse 8
husband esposo 2

I

I yo 1
ice cream helado 6
ice hielo 7
idealism idealismo 14
idealistic idealista 7
if si 4
image imagen *f.* 13
imagery imaginería 13
imaginative imaginativo 2
impatient impaciente 7
improbable improbable 13
(to) improve mejorar 8
in en 1
(to) include incluir 14
included incluido 9
incredible increíble 9
incrustation incrustación *f.* 13
independent independiente 7
India India 1
Indian indio, hindú 1
indication indicación *f.* 8
indiscreet indiscreto 2
infantile infantil 7
infection infección *f.* 8
intellectual intelectual 7

intelligent inteligente 2
(to) introduce presentar 8
iron hierro 8
Italian italiano 1
Italy Italia 1

J

jacket chaqueta 6
January enero 5
Japan Japón 1
Japanese japonés (japonesa) 1
jelly mermelada 1
journalist periodista m.(f.) 2
journey jornada 9
July julio 5
June junio 5
justice justicia 14

K

Kenya Kenya 1
Kenyan keniata 1
key llave f. 2
keyboard teclado 2
kilogram kilo 6
kiosk quiosco 3
kitchen cocina 9
knapsack mochila 2
knee rodilla 8
knife cuchillo 11
knight caballero 14
(to) know (a fact) saber 5; (a person, place) conocer 7
known conocido 13

L

(to) lack faltar 11
lady dama 14
lamb cordero 11
(to) land aterrizar 12
language lengua 2
large grande 2
last night anoche 5
laundry lavandería 9
law ley f. 14
lawyer abogado(a) 2
lazy perezoso 7
leather cuero 6
(to) leave salir 5
leg pierna 8
lemon limón m. 1
lemonade limonada 1
lettuce lechuga 6
level nivel m. 12
library biblioteca 3
(to) lift weights levantar pesas 5
light ligero 7
(to) like gustar 1
     (to) like very much encantar 11
likewise igualmente CP
lipid lípido 8
(to) listen to escuchar 1
literary literario 14

literature literatura 14
living room sala de estar 9
lodge albergue 9
(to) look for buscar 5
(to) lose perder 5
love amor m. 14
(to) love querer 3; encantar 11
loyalty lealtad f. 14
lung pulmón m. 8
lyrics letra 13

M

magazine revista 14
magic mágico 14
(to) make hacer 4
mango mango 6
March marzo 5
market mercado 3
mass misa 3
mathematics matemáticas 2
May mayo 5
mayonaise mayonesa 6
meat carne f. 1
(to) meet encontrarse 3
melancholy melancolía 13
melody melodía 13
Mexican mexicano 1
Mexico México 1
microbe microbio 8
mile milla 5
milk leche f. 1
million millón 4
mineral mineral 8
minute minuto 5
Miss señorita 1
mixture mezcla 14
modern moderno 6
moment momento 6
money dinero 1
month mes m. 4
more más 1
morning mañana 4
mother madre f. 2
motive motivo 13
motorcycle motocicleta 2
mountain montaña 7
     mountain climbing alpinismo 5
mouse ratón m. 2
mouth boca 8
Mr. señor 1
Mrs. señora 1
much mucho 1
mud barro 14
mural mural m. 13
muralism muralismo 13
(to) murmur murmurar 14
muscle músculo 8
museum museo 3
mushroom champiñón m. 6
music música 1
mustache bigote m. 7
my mi,mis
mysterious misterioso 14

myth mito 14
mythical mítico 14
mythological mitológico 14

N

naïve ingenuo 2
name nombre m. 2
napkin servilleta 11
nationality nacionalidad f. 1
nature naturaleza 2
neck cuello 8
need necesitar 1
neighbor vecino(a) 7
neither tampoco 1
nerve nervio 8
nervous nervioso 11
network red f. 12
never nunca 3
new nuevo 4
newspaper periódico 9
next próximo 4
Nicaragua Nicaragua 1
Nicaraguan nicaragüese m.(f.) 1
nice simpático 2
Nigeria Nigeria 1
Nigerian nigeriano 1
night noche f. 4
     night vision visión nocturna 8
nine hundred novecientos 4
ninth noveno 9
no one nadie 11
nobility nobleza 14
nobody nadie 11
noise ruido 14
normally normalmente 8
North American norteamericano 1
nose nariz f. 7
notebook cuaderno 2
nothing nada 5
(to) notice fijarse en 12
novel novela 14
novelist novelista m.(f.)14
November noviembre 5
now ahora 3
number número 12
nurse enfermero(a) 2

O

(to) obtain obtener 5
October octubre 5
of de 1
     of course claro que sí 4
(to) offer ofrecer 6
often a menudo 3
oil aeite m. 6
old viejo 2
older mayor 6
olive aceituna 1
once una vez 6
one hundred cien 4
onion cebolla 6
open abierto 11

optimistic optimista 7
orange naranja 1
(to) order pedir 1
our nuestro(a,os,as) 2
outline esbozo 14

P

paint pintar 13
painter pintor(a) 7
painting cuadro, pintura 2
pair pareja 12
pale pálido 7
Panama Panamá 1
Panamanian panameño 1
panther pantera 14
paper papel *m.* 6
parade desfile *m.* 3
Paraguay Paraguay 1
Paraguayan paraguayo 1
park parque *m.* 3
parking lot estacionamiento 3
(to) pass pasar 6
passport pasaporte *m.* 12
pasta pasta 6
patient paciente 7
(to) pay pagar 4
pea guisante *m.* 6
peach melocotón *m.* 6
peanut cacahuete *m.* 1
pear pera 6
pen bolígrafo 2
pencil lápiz *m.* 2
people personas
pepper pimienta 6
period (of time) período 7
personality carácter *m.* 7
Peru Perú 1
Peruvian peruano 1
pessimistic pesimista 7
pet animal doméstico *m.* 2
pharmacy farmacia 3
piano piano 13
pill pastilla 8
pillow almohada 2
pink rosa, rosado 6
pity lástima 13
plant planta 2
plate plato 11
play (an instrument) tocar 1; (a game, sport) jugar 4
play pieza teatral 14
playwright dramaturgo(a) 14
plaza plaza 3
poem poema *m.* 14
point punto 8
    point of view punto de vista 14
(to) point señalar 14
police station estación de policía *f.* 3
poorly mal 1
porch terraza 9
portable portátil 9
positive positivo 7
post office oficina de correos 3

poster póster *m.* 2
potato patata 1; papa 6
power poder *m.* 14
practical práctico 7
(to) practice practicar 1
(to) prefer preferir 3
preoccupied preocupado 8
(to) present presentar 8
pretty bonito 2
price precio 6
prize premio 3
probable probable 13
professor profesor(a) 2
program programa *m.* 9
(to) prohibit prohibir 13
protein proteína 8
(to) publish publicar 14
Puerto Rican puertorriqueño 1
Puerto Rico Puerto Rico 1
purple morado 6
(to) put on (clothes) ponerse; (make-up) maquillarse 8
(to) put poner 9

Q

quiet tranquilo 11

R

racquet raqueta 6
raincoat impermeable *m.* 6
rarely rara vez 3
reaction reacción *f.* 7
ready listo 3
real real 13
realism realismo 14
realistic realista 7
reality realidad *f.* 14
record disco 6
rectangle rectángulo 13
(to) recuperate recuperar 8
red tinto (wine) 1; rojo 6
redheaded pelirrojo 2
(to) reflect reflejar 14
regular regular 7
regularly con regularidad 8
rejected rechazado 13
(to) remain quedarse 8
remedy remedio 8
(to) renew renovar 8
rent alquiler *m.* 9
(to) repeat repetir 8
repertoire repertorio 13
(to) represent representar 14
reservation reserva, reservación *f.* 9
responsible responsible 7
(to) rest descansar 3
restaurant restaurante *m.* 1
result resultado 8
(to) return volver 5
rhythm ritmo 13
rice arroz *m.* 1
(to) rise subir 9

romantic romántico 7
room cuarto 2; habitación *f.* 9
roommate compañero(a) de cuarto 2
round-trip ticket billete de ida y vuelta *m.* 12
rug alfombra 2
(to) run through recorrer 14
Russia Rusia 1
Russian ruso 1

S

sad triste 3
safe caja de seguridad 9
sailing vela 5
salesman(woman) vendedor(a) 6
salesperson dependiente *m.(f.)* 6
salt sal *f.* 6
Salvadoran salvadoreño 1
sandal sandalia 6
sandwich sándwich, bocadillo 1
satire sátira 14
sauce salsa 11
saucer platillo 11
sausage chorizo 1
(to) save ahorrar 7
(to) say decir 4
schedule horario 4
school colegio 3
science ciencia 2
screen pantalla 2
sculpture escultura 2
sea mar *m.* 7
seat plaza 12
second segundo 9
secretary secretario(a) 2
(to) see ver 4
selfish egoísta 2
self-portrait autorretrato 13
sensational sensacional 7
September septiembre 5
serious serio 2
(to) serve servir 4
seven hundred setecientos 4
seventh séptimo 9
(to) sew coser 13
(to) shave afeitarse 8
she ella 1
sheep oveja 14
shoe zapato 6
short bajo 2
shoulder hombro 8
(to) show mostrar 12
shower ducha 9
showy llamativo 13
shrimp gamba 11
shy avergonzado 11
sick enfermo 3
sign señal *f.* 8
silly tonto 2
simple simple 9; sencillo 14
(to) sing cantar 1
singer intérprete *m.(f.)* 13
sir señor 1
sister hermana 2

(to) sit down sentarse 8
six hundred seiscientos 4
sixth sexto 9
sketch esbozo 14
skill destreza 12
skirt falda 6
sleep dormir 8
slippery resbaloso 7
(to) smile sonreír 8
snack merienda 1
(to) sneeze estornudar 8
snow nieve *f.* 7
soccer fútbol *m.* 2
socks calcetines *m. pl.* 6
soda soda 1
solitude soledad *f.* 14
somebody alguien 11
someday algún día 10
someone alguien 11
something algo 1
sometimes a veces 1
son hijo 2
song canción *f.* 13
soup sopa 11
South Africa Suráfrica 1
South African surafricano 1
Spain España 1
Spanish español (española) 1
(to) speak hablar 1
special especial 4
(to) spend time pasar tiempo 5
spicy picante 1
spider araña 14
spirit espíritu *m.* 13
spoon cuchara 11
sport deporte *m.* 2
(to) sprain torcerse 8
spring primavera 5
squid calamar *m.* 1
stadium estadio 3
star estrella 5
starch almidón *m.* 8
(to) stay quedarse 8
steak bistec *m.* 6
stereo estéreo 2
stockings medias *f. pl.* 6
stomach estómago 8
store tienda 3
storm tormenta 7
story cuento, historia 14
storyteller cuentista *m.(f.)* 14
strange extraño 7
strawberry fresa 1
street calle *f.* 3
stringed instrument instrumento de cuerda 13
strong fuerte 7
student alumno, estudiante 2
studio taller *m.* 13
(to) study estudiar 1
style estilo 6
subway metro 4
suddenly de repente 8 de golpe 14
sugar azúcar *m.* 6

(to) suggest sugerir 8
summer verano 5
sun sol *m.* 7
super super 6
superimposed superpuesto 13
supernatural supernatural 14
sure seguro 6
surfing surfing *m.* 5
surrealism surrealismo 13
(to) sweat sudar 8
sweater suéter *m.* 6
(to) swim nadar 8
swimming natación *f.* 5
    swimming pool piscina 9
swollen hinchado 14
syrup jarabe *m.* 8

T

table mesa 11
taco taco 1
(to) take a nap echar, tomar, dormir una siesta 5
(to) take a shower ducharse 8
(to) take a trip hacer un viaje 5
(to) take llevar 2
(to) take off despegar 12
(to) take out (something) sacar 5; obtain sacar 5
(to) take tomar 1
tall alto 2
tan bronceado 7
tape cinta 2
taxi taxi *m.* 4
tea té *m.* 1
teaspoon cucharita 11
telephone teléfono 9
television (set) televisor *m.* 2
(to) tell decir 4
temperature temperatura 7
tennis tenis *m.* 6
tenth décimo 9
terrace terraza 9
that ese(a), aquel(la) 6
that one ése(a), aquél(la) 6
theater teatro 3
theatrical teatral 7
theme tema *m.* 13
then entonces 3; luego 6
there allí 6
these estos(as), éstos(as) 6
they ellos, ellas 1
thigh muslo 8
thin delgado 2
thing cosa 4
(to) think pensar 4
third tercer(o) 9
this este(a) 6
    this one éste(a) 6
thousand mil 4
three hundred trescientos 4
throat garganta 8
(to) thunder tronar 7
ticket boleto 12
timid tímido 7

tip propina 4
tired cansado 3
toast pan tostado *m.* 1
today hoy 4
toe dedo del pie 8
together juntos 6
tomato tomate *m.* 6
tomorrow mañana 4
tonality tonalidad *f.* 13
(to) tone up tonificarse 8
too (much) demasiado 5
tooth diente *m.*
(to) touch tocar 1
toward hacia 12
(to) trace trazar 14
tragic trágico 14
train tren *m.* 12
training entrenamiento 12
trait rasgo 13
(to) translate traducir 14
(to) travel viajar 1
trend corriente *f.* 14
trousers pantalones 6
true verdad, cierto 13
truly verdaderamente 8
try tratar de 8
t-shirt camiseta 6
twilight crepúsculo 14
two hundred doscientos 4

U

ugly feo 2
uncertainty incertidumbre *f.* 14
uncle tío 2
United States Estados Unidos 1
universal universal 14
university universidad *f.* 2
unless a menos que 14
unlimited sin límite 4
unreality irrealidad *f.* 14
until hasta 6
Uruguay Uruguay 1
Uruguayan uruguayo 1
useful útil 9
usually usualmente 4

V

vacant vacío 9
value valor 14
van camioneta 12
varied variado 7
veal ternera 11
vegetable verdura 6; vegetal *m.* 8
Venezuela Venezuela 1
Venezuelan venezolano 1
very muy 1
video vídeo *m.* 2
vinegar vinagre *m.* 11
violoncello violonchelo 13
virus virus *m.* 3
visa visado 12
(to) visit visitar 5
vitamin vitamina 8

volcano volcán *m.* 9
volleyball vólibol *m.* 2
vulgar grosero 14

W

waiter camarero
waitress camarera 1
  (to) walk andar, caminar 5
(to) wake up despertarse 8
wallet cartera 2
(to) want desear 1; querer 3
(to) wash lavarse 8; lavar 9
(to) watch mirar 1
(to) watch one's weight guardar la línea 8
water agua *f.* 1
waterskiing esquí acuático *m.* 5
wave onda 13
we nosotros(as) 1
weak débil 7

weather tiempo 7
week semana 4
weekend fin de semana *m.* 5
well bien 1
wet mojado 11
what qué 2
when cuando 14
where dónde 1
which cuál 6
white blanco 1
who quién 1
whole entero 10
why por qué 2
wide amplio 14
wife esposa 2
wind viento 7
window ventana 9
wine vino 1
winter invierno 5
with con 9

without sin 9
work obra 13
(to) work trabajar 1
workshop taller *m.* 13
worried preocupado 8
worse peor 6
wrist muñeca 8
(to) write escribir 5
writer escritor(a) 14

Y

year año 4
yellow amarillo 6
yogurt yogur *m.* 6
you tú (*fam.*), usted, ustedes, vosotros(as) 1
young joven 2
younger menor 6
your su, tu, vuestro(a,os,as) 2

INDEX

TEXT CREDITS

Chapter 2: p. 68B-1 map from Weber, The Spanish Frontier in America (1992); **Chapter 5:** pp. 194A–194B "República Dominicana: Guía Práctica" from Grandes Escapadas, verano 1997, Iberojet; **Chapter 7:** pp. 246, 284–285 travel information, reprinted from Turavia Clubs' Guías de Viaje-…poca; Chapter 8: p. 303D–303E "Balada de los dod abuelos," by Nicolás Guillén reprinted from Editorial Letras Cubanas; **Chapter 9:** p. 313B from Centro Linguístico Conversa, San José, Costa Rica; pp. 344B–344C "Las pintorescas carretas de Sarchí" reprinted from Américas, a bimonthly magazine published by the General Secretariat of the Organization of American States in English and Spanish; **Chapter 11:** pp. 415C–415E from Como agua para chocolate by Laura Esquivel. Copyright (c) 1989 by Laura Esquivel. Used by permission of Doubleday, a division of Bantam Doubleday Dell Publishing Group, Inc. **Chapter 12:** pp. 422, 423, 434A reprinted from RENFE brochure, Madrid; **Chapter 13:** pp. 468–470 "Frida Kahlo" reprinted from Américas, a bimonthly magazine published by the General Secretariat of the Organization of American States in English and Spanish; pp. 483, 484 "Las molas de los indios cunas" and pp. 491–493 "Los santeros de Nuevo México..." reprinted from Américas, a bimonthly magazine published by the General Secretariat of the Organization of American States in English and Spanish; **Chapter 14:** pp. 519–520 "Mientras baja la nieve" by Gabriela Mistral (permission pending at time of publication); p. 527 excerpts from Leyendas Mayas by Domingo Dzul Poot reprinted from Editorial Patria; p. 551 excerpts from Cien años de soledad by G. García Márquez reprinted from Editorial Sudamericana; pp. 557, 559 excerpt adapted from La casa de los espíritus by Isabel Allende; pp. 561–562 six short pieces adapted from "Casos" by Enrique Anderson Imbert

PHOTO CREDITS

Cover Quetzal by Tom Boyden

Capítulo preliminar Robert Frerck/Odyssey/Chicago **xvi, 1, 5, 6**; Roberto Bunge/DDB Stock Photo **xvi**; Ulrike Welsch **xvi**;
Capítulo 1 Francisco Po/DDB Stock Photo **12**; Miguel Raurich/DDB Stock Photo **12**; Robert Frerck/Odyssey/Chicago **14, 18, 24**; Walter Swarthout/The Stock Market **12**; Heinle & Heinle Publishers **14, 15, 16, 25, 26, 31, 38, 42**; PhotoDisc **15**; David Simson/Stock Boston **20**; Robert Fried/Stock Boston **32**;
Capítulo 2 Robin J. Dunitz/DDB Stock Photo **81**; Anthony Neste/Gamma Liaison **48**; Market/Gamma Liaison **48**; PhotoDisc **51**; Suzanne Murphy-Larrond/DDB Stock Photo **72**; Robert Frerck/Odyssey/Chicago **72**; Heinle & Heinle Publishers **58, 83, 84**; Rob Lewine/The Stock Market **48**;
Capítulo 3 Robert Frerck/Odyssey/Chicago **88, 94, 99, 107, 110, 115**; Cameramann/Image Works **88**; C. R. Sharp/DDB Stock Photo **101**;
Capítulo 4 Roberto Bunge/DDB Stock Photo **120, 126**; Robert Frerck/Odyssey/Chicago **126**; Alpamayo/DDB Stock Photo **126**; Rapael Wollman/Gamma-Liaison **149**;
Capítulo 5 Suzanne Murphy-Larronde/DDB Stock **160, 191**; Robert Frerck/Odyssey/Chicago **160, 176**; Antonio Ribeiro/Gamma **183, 184**; Saitz Art/Gamma **154**; National Baseball Library, Cooperstown, NY **154, 190**;
Capítulo 6 Robert Frerck/Odyssey/Chicago **196**; Virginia Ferrero/DDB Stock Photo **233**;
Capítulo 7 Robert Frerck/Odyssey/Chicago **240, 264**; David Ryan/DDB Stock Photo **240**; Chris R. Sharp/DDB Stock Photo **245**; Heinle & Heinle Publishers **261, 276, 278**; R. Bunge/Photoworks **240**; Tony Stone Images/Erica Lansner **272**; Tony Stone Images/Ralph H. Wetmore II **273**;
Capítulo 8 Craig Duncan/DDB Stock Photo **278**; Byron Augustin/DDB Stock Photo **285**; Robert Frerck/Odyssey/Chicago **306**; Heinle & Heinle Publishers **278, 290**;
Capítulo 9 Ulrike Welsch **314, 316**; John Mitchell/DDB Stock Photo **314, 321**; Robert Fried/Stock Boston **337, 341**; Inga Spence/DDB Stock Photo **314, 341**; Heinle & Heinle **324**;
Capítulo 10 Paul Howell/Gamma Liaison **346**; Robert Frerck/Odyssey/Chicago **348**; OAS **368**; Dave Bartruff/Stock Boston **346**; PhotoDisc **372**;
Capítulo 11 Robert Frerck/Odyssey/Chicago **376, 377, 388, 396, 399**; Inga Spence/DDB Stock Photo **388**; D. Donne Bryant/DDB Stock Photo **395**; Zigy Kaluzny/Gamma Liaison **404**;
Capítulo 12 Robert Frerck/Odyssey/Chicago **412, 413, 436**; Daniel Aubrey/Odyssey/Chicago **430**; J.P. Courau/DDB Stock Photo **426, 438**; Daemmrich/The Image Works **434**; Heinle & Heinle Publishers **414, 437, 444**;
Capítulo 13 José Clemente Orozco, *Zapatistas*, 1931. Oil on canvas. Collection, The Museum of Modern Art, New York, Mrs. Simon Guggenheim Fund **453**; Diego Rivera, Vendedor de flores, 1935. Oil and tempera on masonite. San Francisco Museum of Modern Art, Albert M. Bender collection, gift of Albert M. Bender in memory of Caroline Walter **454**; David Alfaro Siqueiros, *Etnografía* (1939) Enamel on composition board. Collection, The Museum of Modern Art, New York, Abby Aldrich Rockefeller Fund **454**; COMSTOCK Mural de José Clemente Orozco: Guadalajara, Mexico **455**; Frida Kahlo, *Autorretrato con changuito y loro*, 1942. Oil on board. Collection, IBM Corporation, Armonk, New York **457**; Art Resource, Pablo Picasso, *Portrait d'Ambroise Vollard* Museo Pushkin Moscow **467**; ARS, N.Y./ADAGP Joan Miró, *Mujer y pajaro por la noche*, 1945. Oil on canvas. Albright-Knox Gallery, Buffalo, New York, gift of Seymour H. Knox **468**; ARS, N.Y./Demart Pro Arte Salvador Dalí. *La persistencia de la memoria*, 1931. Oil on canvas. Collection, The Museum of Modern Art, New York, given anonymously **468**; Heinle & Heinle Publishers **469, 472**; John Gutiérrez **477, 478, 479**; AP/Wide World Photos **482**; (top) Bill Wisser/Gamma Liaison **488**; (bottom) John Neubauer **489**; The Bettmann Archive **492**
Capítulo 14 Heinle & Heinle Publishers **498, 499**; Carlos Angel/Gamma **498;** Art Resource **509**; Paul Steel/The Stock Market **520**; UPI/Bettmann **528**

América del Sur

GUATEMALA
HONDURAS
DOR
NICARAGUA
COSTA RICA
PANAMÁ

MAR CARIBE

Barranquilla
Cartagena
Maracaibo
Caracas
Port of Spain
TRINIDAD Y TOBAGO
R. Orinoco
VENEZUELA
Medellín
Georgetown
Manizales
GUYANA
Paramaribo
Bogotá
SURINAM
Cayenne
Cali
GUAYANA
COLOMBIA
FRANCESA

OCÉANO ATLÁNTICO

ECUADOR

Quito
R. Amazonas
Belem
Quayaquil
Manaus
ECUADOR
Iquitos
PERÚ
R. Madeira
Recife
Cajamarca
BRASIL
Machu Picchu
Lima
Salvador
Ayacucho
Cuzco
Brasilia
BOLIVIA
L. Titicaca
Arequipa
La Paz
Belo Horizonte
Arica
Sucre
Iquique
Potosí
São Paulo
Rio de Janeiro

OCÉANO PACÍFICO

Antofagasta
PARAGUAY
Santos
Salta
Asunción
CHILE
Tucumán
R. Paraná
Porto Alegre
Córdoba
R. Uruguay
Valparaíso
Mendoza
URUGUAY
Rosario
Santiago
Buenos Aires
Montevideo
Concepción
La Plata
Río de la Plata
ARGENTINA

TRÓPICO DE CAPRICORNIO

Bahía Blanca

Puerto Montt

CORDILLERA DE LOS ANDES

ISLAS MALVINAS

Punta Arenas
TIERRA DEL FUEGO
Cabo de Hornos
Estrecho de Magallanes

| 0 | 200 | 400 | 600 | 800 millas |
| 0 | 200 | 400 | 600 | 800 kilómetros |